Barbarian Tides

THE MIDDLE AGES SERIES

Ruth Mazo Karras, Series Editor
Edward Peters, Founding Editor

A complete list of books in the series is available from the publisher.

Barbarian Tides

The Migration Age and the Later Roman Empire

Walter Goffart

PENN

University of Pennsylvania Press
Philadelphia

10   9   8   7   6   5   4   3   2

Published by
University of Pennsylvania Press
Philadelphia, Pennsylvania 19104-4112

Library of Congress Cataloging-in-Publication Data

Goffart, Walter A.
   Barbarian tides : the migration age and the later Roman Empire / Walter Goffart.
      p. cm. — (The Middle Ages series)
   Includes bibliographical references and index.
   ISBN-13: 978-0-8122-3939-3
   ISBN-10: 0-8122-3939-3 (cloth : alk. paper)
      1. Migrations of nations.   2. Europe—History—392–814.   3. Rome—History—Germanic
Invasions, 3rd–6th centuries.   I. Title.   II. Series.
D135.G65   2006
937'.09—dc22   2005046713

To Eva Sophia Baldi Goffart

Contents

Preface

Twenty-five years ago I published *Barbarians and Romans* A.D. *418–584: The Techniques of Accommodation. Barbarian Tides* is a sequel, a rethought, revised, much expanded, and wholly rewritten version of the earlier book. It is a comprehensive, though certainly not an exhaustive introduction to the activities of northern barbarians in late antiquity, activities often called "the barbarian invasions." Quite a lot has happened to this field in twenty-five years. *Barbarians and Romans* pointed hesitantly in a footnote toward future discussions, observing that the continuity of "peoples" seemed to be a matter of current concern and that the idea of an enduring core of tribal tradition was arousing controversy. There has been much discussion since then of "peoples" and "cores of tradition" under the general heading of "ethnicity," and the claim has been widely made that ethnicity was very important in late antiquity. From another angle, late Roman studies have experienced an impressive increase in the attention paid to the cultures of the eastern provinces and to all manner of religious phenomena. By comparison, the intrusion of barbarians has receded to the margins of interest.

My central concern in the present book is not to talk about past ethnicities or "ethnogenesis theory" but to liberate barbarian history from the German nationalism that has suffused it ever since the sixteenth century and, in whatever disguises, continues to do so today. As long ago as 1972, I expressed a wish that someone should write a history of the Migration Age detached from German nationalism. The studies presented here attempt to fill this vacuum or at least illustrate some ways of doing so.

History is my subject, not nationalism. Passion of some sort motivates most scholars including me. Nationalism unashamedly affected a vast source collection that medievalists rightly extol and prize, namely, the Monumenta Germaniae historica, "the historical monuments of Germany." The motto its founders adopted at the start of their enterprise in 1819 was "*Sacer amor patriae dat animum*: A holy love of the fatherland inspires [us]"; and there is little doubt that, without the patriotism of its collaborators, the Monumenta enterprise would have fallen short of its prodigious (and continuing) achievements. Love of country is not on trial here; no apologies or retractions are called for. What is wanted is only a willingness to surmount entrenched tradition and come a little closer to understanding the activities of non-Romans in late antiquity. I take issue with misapprehensions of barbarian history, in particular the anachronistic belief, ubiquitous outside as well as inside Germany, that the Migration Age is a "Germanic" subject, in which "barbarians" are synonymous with "Germanic peoples." Strange as it may seem to hear it said, there were no Germanic peoples in late antiquity. The illusion that there were can be outgrown. The barbarian invasions are a deeply interesting slice of the European past; they concern a multiplicity of peoples with names of their own; and they can be approached in other than nationalistic ways. This book, like its predecessor, tries to move the subject in that direction.

Three institutions at Yale have welcomed me and kept me active: the Department of History, Berkeley College, and the Elizabethan Club. I am very grateful to them as well as to the Yale libraries and librarians that have served me extraordinarily well. The Rockefeller Foundation Study Center at Bellagio allowed me to benefit from its tranquility for an unforgettable month. Parts of this book have been delivered as lectures over the past five years at Chicago, Yale, Bellagio, Harvard, Kalamazoo, and Champaign-Urbana; the audiences that bore with these trial runs have my sympathy and gratitude. A slightly different form of Chapter 4 has appeared in *Speculum* 80 (2005): 379-98. I am indebted to Patrick Périn for advancing my archaeological education and to Josh Chafetz for help on a legal point. I take special pleasure in thanking Andrew Gillett, Michael Kulikowski, and Alexander C. Murray for looking at drafts of this book and offering their candid advice; readers will see how much I owe to their writings. My wife, Roberta Frank, always my most valued critic, has reconciled the demands of her stellar career with sustaining me through another book. My thanks are scant recompense for her care.

Introduction

A funny thing happened to the later Roman Empire on its way to the twenty-first century: it ran into a wave of "ethnicity" and "ethnogenesis."[1] A leading historian informs us, for example, that "from the late fourth century onwards, ethnicity began to return to the power struggles within the Roman world."[2] This was not something one used to be told. The dominant handbook of late antiquity in the 1960s was a massive work by A. H. M. Jones; it is doubtful that the term "ethnicity" ever darkens its pages and certain that "ethnogenesis" does not.[3] The standbys that accompanied college teaching at midcentury, such as Ferdinand Lot's *The End of the Ancient World and the Beginning of the Middle Ages*, spoke of Goths, Vandals, Franks, and other peoples, but ethnicity, let alone ethnogenesis, was not their concern. Henri Pirenne's famous *Mohammed and Charlemagne*, whose interest in barbarians is greater than sometimes suspected, disregarded ethnicity. J. M. Wallace-Hadrill's *The Barbarian West* did not have a pronounced ethnic flavor.[4] The turn toward ethnicity is striking. Did earlier historians miss something important? Where has this new preoccupation come from and should we follow in its tracks?

Herwig Wolfram's *Geschichte der Goten*, first published in 1979 and translated into English in 1988 as *History of the Goths*, presents itself as an example of "historical ethnography." The book was central to bringing ethnicity and ethnogenesis to the forefront of discussions. In focusing on the Goths, Wolfram, a historian by training, did not choose a neglected subject.[5] The Goths were much written about in connection with the other Migration Age peoples and the last centuries of the Roman Empire. Readers of English can learn about the Goths in J. B. Bury's *The Invasions of Europe by the Barbarians* (1928) or in the translation by Edward James (1975) of Lucien Musset's *Les Invasions*, volume 1, *Les vagues germaniques* (1965).[6] Everyone dealing professionally with this subject can hardly avoid relying on Ludwig Schmidt's very full and dependable *Geschichte der deutschen Stämme bis zum Ausgang der Völkerwanderung* (1938, 1941). The same ground has been ambitiously retraced by Émilienne Demougeot in the two-volume *La formation de l'Europe et les invasions barbares* (1969–79).[7] Accounts of the "Germanic peoples" in late antiquity on a people-by-people basis are plentiful; some nineteenth-century works of this kind, such as those by E. von Wietersheim and Felix Dahn, are still worthy of consultation.[8] What is new in Wolfram's "historical ethnography" is the author's unprecedented interest in the Gothicness of Goths and how they got that way, and the credit accorded to a problematic sixth-century narrative that he believes embodies authentic tribal history. Readers are invited to subscribe to a sheaf of findings (argued in dense separate studies), many of them based on names interpreted by etymological and other philological reasoning—"the hidden meaning of names, genealogy, and myth"—findings that make the Goths look more exotic than before.[9]

"Ethnogenesis" has been variously defined.[10] As presented in America, the concept allegedly redresses a great wrong inflicted by Romans and Greeks upon the peoples dwelling north of the Roman Empire: "The Germanic tribe, more than any other Germanic institution, has been the victim of an uncritical acceptance of Greco-Roman ideas concerning tribes inherited from both the Romans' own early traditions of tribal origins and from Greek ethnography. . . . [T]hroughout the tribal history of the Germanic peoples, these groups were more processes than stable structures, and ethnogenesis, or tribal transformation, was constant."[11] The contention is not only that the Romans were deeply mistaken in portraying tribes as fixed entities but that everyone else, too, through the ages, has been taken in by this illusion: "Until recently, our ideas about the 'Germans' were shaped by the Romans. The very term 'German' was Roman. And it was the Romans who were so sure that the Germanic tribes were 'ethnic groups' (*gentes*), that they insisted on thinking of these (in fact ever-changing) tribes as biological entities."[12]

These challenges to past errors suggest that students of the Migration Age should take a profound interest in tribes and tribe formations, that this subject is acutely important to understanding the role of the barbarians in late antiquity. Whether or not "ethnicity" returned to the Roman Empire in the fourth century is open to discussion, but there is no doubt—so it is alleged—that ethnicity should have a high priority in today's classroom. We are urged to reorient the focus of attention from wherever it was in the books of, for example, J. B. Bury, Ludwig Schmidt, or Lucien Musset and move instead toward a subject one used to pay little attention to, namely, the "Germanic tribe."[13] It seems to proponents of "ethnogenesis" that false views of "ethnic identity" should be discarded and replaced by right ones.[14]

This change of focus might be timely and desirable if it did not absorb all the energy of those concerned with the northern barbarians in the age of Rome's fall. Much else needs to be set right in narratives of the Migration Age. The concept of ethnogenesis does little to remedy other issues. A historian quoted a moment ago complained that "our ideas about the 'Germans' were shaped by the Romans." The alternative is not problem-free. The leading spokesmen for the early "Germans" are the modern ones, who since the sixteenth century have discerned their ancestors in the northern barbarians, have expressed their fascination by intensively studying them, and have pushed their antiquity further and further into prehistory. The Greco-Roman sources about "the Germans" can be personally checked by anyone knowing Greek and Latin and having access to a good library.[15] It is a much more arduous and delicate task to deal with the mass of discordant and tangled modern German research and speculation into "Germanic" antiquities—a turbulent flood of erudition and conjecture. There is no guarantee that our knowledge of the "early Germans" will be enriched and improved by no longer being shaped only by classical sources but by a body of commentators that includes superb, standard-setting scholars along with cranks, maniacs, and superpatriots. The main problem (at least as it looks from North America) is to tame the still-raging wave of the "science of Germanic antiquity" (*germanische Altertumskunde*) as it impinges on the late Roman period.

We know and have known for a long time that late Rome dealt actively with, among others, Goths, Vandals, Herules, Sueves, Saxons, Gepids, as well as Sarmatians, Alans, Huns, Avars, Picts, Carpi, and Isaurians. This multiplicity of barbarians, from various families of peoples, has not been recently discovered or recently forgotten. Successive generations of readers of the sources have been well aware that the Roman Empire was in contact with multiple foreigners, and not with a collectivity of barbarians acting in unison. Nevertheless, much of what is written about barbarians in late antiquity runs counter to this elementary awareness: never mind the multiplicity of peoples met in the sources; the Migration Age was the crowning moment of the German national saga and even its heroic age.

When multiplicity is subordinated to a unifying concept, the scenario that results can be simple and straightforward. That is how the northern barbarians of late antiquity are largely dealt with. A grand narrative of their history is wholly familiar today and widely accepted. It might, for purposes of illustration, be summarized as follows:

The centuries-long expansion of the Germanic peoples, mainly occasioned by population increase and migration in search of more and better land, resulted in continual hammering at the gates of the Roman Empire, in sharply mounting pressure on its frontiers, and eventually in the great Germanic invasions carried out by wave upon wave of Germanic peoples, before whom the Empire succumbed (at least in the West), leaving the future in the hands of Germanic kingdoms and opening it to Germanic culture. So the Germanic world overcame the Roman world that it had long opposed and inaugurated a new era.

As implemented by individual authors, this account has been tweaked in this direction or that, and has been intermittently contested in whole or in part, but it still stands, majestic and undimmed, at the dawn of European history. It is the opposite of what I maintain in this book.

The feature of the précis above needing immediate emphasis is the sixfold occurrence of "Germanic." This word (with its cognates) is customary and commonplace in accounts of the Migration Age; by general consent, the barbarian migrations (or invasions) were Germanic. As much is confirmed by the titles of well-known books.[16] The Germanness of the migrations has serious implications; it determines that the described course of events took place in a very distinctive way. The main actors, it tells us, were not peoples disconnected from one another with multiple names and multiple circumstances; instead, the Migration Age was inhabited by a coherent, interrelated, and populous group engaging in collective endeavors of expansion, population increase, migration, hammering frontiers, applying mounting pressure, and setting off great invasions, waves of movement, and kingdom foundations. There was, it seems, a Germanic "world" embodying an ancient Germanic civilization expressed by more than only a linguistic classification. The northern barbarians of late antiquity were Germans and rightly rank as progenitors of the Germans of today. So the story runs.

The overarching theme of my book is that late antiquity needs much less "Germanic" ethnicity than it has had from almost the first moments when it was studied. My main concern, especially in the first four chapters and the last, is to dislodge the barbarians of late antiquity from the "Germanic" setting in which they have commonly lived. I would be content if "German" and its derivatives were banished from all but linguistic discourse on this subject.

"German" is a familiar and honorable collective term; its application to the northern barbarians is consecrated by almost immemorial usage. It seems churlish to contest the place of this term in the Migration Age. Yet the operative fact is that Germany and its denizens are not an immutable feature of the world's landscape; like all countries, the land and its inhabitant have had a complex and often changing past. The Germany of today is the outcome of multiple vicissitudes all the way back to the Carolingian dynasty, ca. A.D. 800, in whose era the Germany (*Deutschland*) that we know had its most remote beginnings.[17] Since the sixteenth century, the belief that ancient or primitive Germans existed in prehistory and in parallel to the Roman Empire has been a fixed point in European historical writing (and in many other disciplines). Nourished by Latin works—notably the *Germania* of Tacitus, the Gothic history of Jordanes, and the Lombard history of Paul the Deacon—German humanists, such as the justly celebrated Beatus Rhenanus (1485–1547), concluded that the Goths, Vandals,

Franks, and other "barbarians" were the ancestors of the modern Germans, and that the lives and exploits of these forefathers should rightfully be claimed as the history of an "ancient" Germany, the progenitor of the Germany of modern times.[18]

This patriotic identification has continued undimmed down to the present. Despite its antiquity and its endorsement by admirable scholars too numerous to mention, the linear projection of modern Germany out of an ancient one is a mistake, no longer in keeping with the way we do history. "German" was basically a Roman word, used by authors in the early Empire as a shorthand term for many of the northern barbarians. "Germany" was the name of the provinces created by the Empire on the left bank of the Rhine after failing to conquer the right bank. The use of "German" waned sharply in late antiquity, when, for example, it was mainly reserved by Roman authors as an alternative to "Franks" and never applied to Goths or the other peoples living in their vicinity at the eastern end of the Danube. The peoples surveyed by Tacitus or those of the Migration Age were fragmented; they did not call themselves Germans but bore particular names, and they did not live in a territory they called "Germany." Many of them, and for a time the most prominent, originated in what to us is Eastern Europe. At best, they spoke dialects that our linguists call "Germanic," but even that common bond was (as far as we may tell) unknown to themselves until the eighth century. To evoke Germans and Germany before the Middle Ages is, very simply, an anachronism—an injection of the future into the past.

"German" and "Germanic" are entrenched in writings about the Migration Age barbarians. No single person or group is responsible for this situation, with which Europeans of all stripes have been comfortable for centuries. Anyone practiced in writing about these subjects is well aware of how naturally it comes to the pen to invoke "German" as the opposite of "Roman," and in archaeology to qualify non-Roman graves and artifacts as "Germanic." The adjective "German," an umbrella term for many of the diverse northern barbarians of the late Roman period, is the key to such unifying compounds as "the Germanic world," "Germanic migrations," "Germanic peoples," "Germanic style," "Germanic law," "Germanic grave goods": wherever it turns up it simplifies and unifies, and presides over collective actions that did not take place.[19] If it is agreed that the Germanization of late antiquity is an anachronism and has been a mistake in method, then—if we wish to arrive at a more accurate understanding of the past—a serious effort needs to be made to mend our ways. "German" will not go away by itself; it has to be stubbornly shown the door.

Among the peoples whom we call "Germanic"—but who, themselves, were alien to such terminology—the Frisians, Thuringians, Alamanni, Saxons,

Bavarians, Burgundians, and Franks were all "present" in late antiquity, and they very definitely had medieval futures; the Franks have even been considered the founders of both the French kingdom and the German empire to come.[20] We encounter these peoples in largely Latin sources. For example, the word "Thuringian" first occurs in a fifth-century veterinary treatise in connection with a breed of horses, and Bavaria mysteriously pops up out of nowhere in the sixth century.[21] However well-established these "ethnicities" would be in the Middle Ages, their ethnic pasts have left no trace. Our feeble means of inquiry cannot determine that they had definable ancient ethnic identities to project into the making of medieval England, France, Germany, or Europe. It is true that by serious learned efforts, utilizing scholarly methods practiced since the sixteenth century, we are able to remedy our profound ignorance to some extent. We can, for example, trace the Franks back to the third century in Latin sources; but we also know that the Franks of the sixth century, though very much in the ascendant at the time, could not conjure up an "ethnic" past extending further back than three generations.[22] Where does our responsibility lie in evoking these peoples in late antiquity? Should we loudly trumpet the ethnic traits we have been able to dredge up by philological and archaeological methods, or should we take the silence of the contemporary evidence seriously and avoid evoking ethnic consciousnesses that are wholly undocumented? The northern barbarians were more concerned to fit into the Roman sphere than to cling to and affirm their past; they adopted the religion of the Empire; they adapted to the imperial framework of law, government, and warfare; they sought and acquired positions defending and governing Roman provinces.[23] Their encounter with the Roman world, which needed them, is a much fuller and better documented story than their efforts, such as they may have been, to maintain or achieve continuity with their origins.

The main goal of this book is to reform thinking and writing about the barbarians in late antiquity by driving out the anachronistic terms "German" and "Germanic" and the baggage that goes with them and by giving full weight, instead, to the multiplicity of foreigners faced by the Roman Empire and to the advantage this gave Rome in maintaining its ascendancy. The book is composed of seven stand-alone chapters, not needing to be read in consecutive order; they are framed by this Introduction and a Conclusion. Four chapters address historiographical subjects. The second, longer part of the book consists of three chapters each focusing on sets of events that, to my mind, are crucial to the history of the barbarians in late antiquity.

The historiographical chapters are meant to discredit what appear to be mainstays of a "Germanic" interpretation of the barbarians in late antiquity. One way to condense their contents for purposes of introduction is to indicate the dialogue they involve between a "Germanic" contention and a reasoned alternative:

1. (Contention) The barbarian invasions are the culmination of a collective movement, namely, the many centuries of Germanic migration. (Alternative) There was a multiplicity of barbarians. Those who moved did so from positions of rest, having lived near the Roman borders for so long as to lose any memory of living elsewhere. They moved at the prompting of distinct leaders, for definite reasons, and, in general, over short distances.

2. (Contention) The expansion of the Germanic peoples exerted a mounting southward pressure that, in time, overcame the world of Rome. (Alternative) The northern barbarians were multiple and fragmented; the pressures weighing on the Empire did not have a united source and often came from within. Rome's neighbors in late antiquity wanted admission to the Empire and, increasingly, Rome wanted them as solutions to its internal problems.

3. (Contention) A many-centuried Germanic civilization lies behind and prepared medieval and modern Germany. (Alternative) "Ancient Germany" wholly lacked unity or a center. The myth of its existence as a collective phenomenon stems from two creative moments: Justinian's Constantinople and sixteenth-century Germany.

4. (Contention) An authentic oral tradition attests to the ancient migration of the Goths and other Germans out of Scandinavia. It is a major prop of Germanic continuity. (Alternative) The tale of emigration from Scandinavia is not a Gothic oral tradition. It was devised in Constantinople on the basis of classical sources by someone claiming to be a Goth at a time when the last Gothic resistance in Italy was being stamped out.

These contentions and alternatives schematize what is set out discursively in the corresponding chapters. Chapter 1 focuses on the concept of a "Migration Age," already used in my title and this Introduction and widely familiar to anyone concerned with the centuries of transition from Rome to the Middle Ages. The chapter indicates the three ways the concept is currently understood and argues for preferring its narrowest meaning. Chapter 2 sets out from the belief that the Roman Empire was overcome by "the Germans," a view widely championed since World War II. The chapter traces one very reputable historian's version of this argument step by step and undertakes to show that it cannot be sustained when subjected to critical scrutiny. Chapter 3 addresses the long-standing and current belief that an "ancient" Germany existed before the medieval and modern Germany we know, and it discusses the two sources that mainly explain why we have unduly accepted this origin myth. Chapter 4 shows that the sixth-century report locating Goths, Vandals, and other peoples at the ends of the earth, which is often mistaken for a Germano-ethnic "oral tradition," was instead crafted in Constantinople in the age of Justinian so as to distance and demonize barbarians who had been inside Roman territory for very long. Each of the four chapters tells a separate story but circles about the same center.

Historiographic discussions run the risk of being mere preaching unless complemented by a sustained effort to grapple with specific events and circumstances. The subjects that I offer are some of the encounters of Romans with their neighbors in late antiquity. They underscore both the diversity of the barbarian phenomenon and the mechanisms by which barbarians joined the late Roman world or were destroyed in the attempt.

Chapter 5 takes up one of the most conspicuous incidents of the Migration Age and offers a case study of what is meant by "migration" in late antiquity. The invasion across the Rhine by the Alans, Vandals, and Sueves in the first years of the 400s illustrates the problems historians grapple with when they try to understand events and circumstances that they have too little information to be certain about. Much is clouded but not everything. It is important to distinguish highly probable findings from those that are bound to remain in doubt. It is also important to show that "migration" accompanied what was going on and was not an independent force.

Whereas Chapter 5 concerns movement, Chapter 6 discusses barbarians at rest. The calm and lawful settlement of Burgundians and Goths in Roman Gaul and Italy is probably the best-documented case of peaceful accommodation of Romans with barbarians. I wrote about it in *Barbarians and Romans* (1980), and I reconsider it from the ground up in Chapter 6—the centerpiece of this book. Besides taking into account the many reviews and objections that my book of 1980 occasioned, I present a detailed reappraisal of the evidence and of the disputed question of whether tax law had a central part in the process. The weaknesses of the earlier book are repaired. I start from a demonstration that the practice of military *hospitalitas* (billeting), taken since 1844 to be crucial to barbarian settlement, was totally irrelevant to it. With *hospitalitas* or without, hardly anything could have been more important to the integration of foreigners in the Roman provinces than the peaceful means by which they obtained a place among settled owners of lucrative property.

Chapter 7 has three independent parts. Each part illustrates how the experiences of barbarians in late antiquity may be and should be narrated without anachronistic injection of "Germans." Part one is concerned with the late Roman circumstances that made the Empire more appreciative of barbarian "New Men" and facilitated the incorporation of foreigners into the ruling "families" of late Rome. Part two offers case studies of individual peoples, called by their own names, that illustrate their participation—in one case, virtual nonparticipation—in the affairs of the time. People-by-people accounts are commonplace in writings about the barbarians; the seven offered here attempt to mark out a new, chronologically shorter, and less speculative model for such discussions. Part three turns the spotlight on one particularly well-favored Gothic people and documents its sad inability to transmute ethnicity into a viable polity. The linking theme of the chapter is that persons and dynasties, not ethnicity, were what mattered in the relations of barbarians and Romans in late antiquity.

The Conclusion points out that the early Middle Ages did without civilian gentleman-landowners—the social category embodying the acme of well-being and privilege in the Roman Empire. Once past the sixth century there was no more room for "honorable leisure (*otium cum dignitate*)." The new age had only two privileged constituents, clergy and soldiers, persons entitled to economic support for exercising their professions. I suggest that this was the outcome, as much in the East as in the West, of a gradual and irreversible simplification of Roman economy and society, a process in which the northern barbarians played what proved to be an essential part. On the military side of things (the costliest of imperial expenditures), the barbarians were, and since the third century had continually been, the low-cost option, the alternative to outlays that the Empire was less and less able to afford. Side by side with Christianization, "barbarization" transformed society.

*   *   *

This book is based on written sources. My point of departure in dealing with many of its topics has been the conviction that certain texts—such as the Hydatius chronicle and Visigothic laws about barbarian settlement—contain information that other historians have not observed, and that these details cast new light on ostensibly well-known events. Some scholars develop their narratives by bringing together items gathered from a wide array of evidence and assembling them eclectically on the premise, at times justified, that the pieces fit together. It is an approach that gives historians considerable latitude for letting their opinions prevail, rather than allowing the sources to have the upper hand in the dialogue. Although I am not innocent of eclecticism, my preferred course is to focus on individual texts and make as much of them as I can. I try to achieve clarity by keeping the means austere.

Archaeology stands out as a type of documentation not utilized here. This has been a deliberate choice, based partly on a lack of training and partly on respect for the difficulties involved in informed handling of archaeological sources. Experience shows that, however concrete material remains may seem, they are sometimes as firm as a quicksand bog. Patrick Geary expresses confidence in what archaeology can prove: "Since linguistic data does not exist from the earliest period of 'Germanic' civilization, it is safer to talk from an archaeological perspective. According to this, Germanic society originated with Iron Age peoples who arose in the northern parts of central Europe . . . from the sixth century B.C. The earliest phases of this society [are] known as 'Jastorfkultur.' "[24] Alas, it may not in fact be "safer" to talk from this perspective. The Jastorf culture does form part of the archaeological landscape, as the north German counterpart of La Tène culture. Its legitimacy does little, however, to help with German origins: "Archaeologists now tend to dissociate themselves from an equation of the Jastorf culture with Germanic as an ethnological and linguistic entity." "The Jastorf-Kultur forms a culture-group but cannot be equated with the linguistically defined Germans, since the two spheres (*Bereiche*) [of culture and language] are not comparable (*unvergleichbar*). . . . There cannot be an archeological definition of Germans."[25] Geary unwittingly tapped into an old and optimistic wave of archaeology, not yet stilled, in which artifacts and history, culture and ethnicity, were confidently believed to combine into firm results enlarging the written record. Much of the archaeological grounding of the Migration Age was and, in several quarters, still is arrived at in just this way, with grave goods not only tagging ethnic groups but also charting their extensions over territory. That confidence in ethnic identifications lingers in some quarters; respected scholars have not yet shaken themselves loose from these practices that continue to haunt the interpretation of archaeological remains, especially as they relate to the Goths.[26] But critical approaches are beginning to take hold and to prevail.

As this happens, the "findings" of archaeology are more likely (at first) to shrink than to expand. I cite a few cases. Literary and legal texts assure us that there was a Visigothic kingdom and associated settlement in southwestern Gaul, but material signs of a Visigothic presence have yet to be unearthed.[27] The archaeology of Burgundians in southeastern Gaul, once abundant, is another melancholy story of withdrawal: the remains of Burgundians can no longer be distinguished from those of the other inhabitants of the land.[28] It was once thought that, in Spain, the presence of Visigoths had been firmly detected in a definable area, a set of graves on the central plateau; books exist with maps shading the area of these graves and identifying it with Visigothic settlement. Confidence in this identification has now been effaced; the Visigoths of Spain have joined those of Gaul in being nearly invisible outside written records.[29] In northern Gaul, graves ordered in rows accompanied by weapons as burial goods were taken as clear evidence of "Germanic" expansion and settlement (1950). Some fifty years later, the pendulum has swung; the foreign origin of these burials is no longer an established fact: a change in circumstances among the resident Gallo-Romans has been argued to be more probable.[30] Since the days when Gustaf Kossinna (1858–1931) confidently identified archaeological cultures with ethnic groups, material remains mixed with linguistics, anthropology, and other disciplines have claimed a place in the historical record, even charting migrations and dating settlements. Kossinna's influence, however qualified and attenuated, persists. It will take a long time before critical methods completely dominate Migration Age archaeology.

There is up-to-date archaeology. Bryan Ward-Perkins gave historians of late antiquity much to think about in *From Classical Antiquity to the Middle Ages.*[31] Michael Kulikowski's *Late Roman Spain and Its Cities* is a recent and admirable example of how present-day archaeology, critically appraised and imaginatively deployed, can augment and rectify the evidence of literary sources. Kulikowski's book, with its skilled analysis of the latest Spanish archaeology, has radical implications for our understanding of the Migration Age.[32]

The rollbacks induced by the critical turn in archaeology are not wholly negative in their results. Peter Wells has recently said: "There is no archaeological evidence for large-scale abandonment of the frontier regions before, during, or after the Roman conquests, nor is there indication of any mass immigration from outside. . . . [T]he genetic evidence for population movement in Europe supports the archaeological indications that there were no large-scale movements into the region at this time."[33] If I understand these lines correctly, Wells tells us that, however dramatically the Migration Age is inscribed in chronicles, narratives, laws, and art, it does not make itself visible on the ground; the exuberant language of waves, tides, and floods of barbarians, which holds so prominent a place in popular and even scholarly writing on the Migration Age, is not corroborated by material remains. Instead, Wells appears to bear out a justly admired comment by Susan Reynolds about the limited part played by movements of people in the Migration Age.[34] This does not mean that our notions of the Migration Age have to be revised from the ground up, only that we should cease thinking, if we ever did, that the age was about the movement of large masses of aliens to and fro over the provinces of the Roman Empire and their replacement of the sitting population. On this point, the texts and the new archaeology of frontier lands appear to agree.

Archaeology has its own methods and problems; its relations to history are delicate and continually subject to revision. It is also very dependent on texts, both in posing questions to be investigated and in interpreting unearthed results. Archaeologists have long been warned against "mixed argumentation"—a blending of disciplines that have not all been individually analyzed by wholly up-to-date criteria. "Mixed" in such cases often means muddled and circular. I have taken the warning to heart and made an effort to avoid argumentation of this kind.

Chapter 1

A Clarification: The Three Meanings of "Migration Age"

Not long ago my mail brought news of four DVDs called "The Wandering Tribes of Europe." The individual disk titles are a little history in themselves: (1) "From the Mists of the North, the Germanic Tribes"; (2) "Furor Teutonicus, Pax Romana"; (3) "Storm over Europe: The Huns Are Coming"; (4) "The End of Rome, the Birth of Europe." The "wandering tribes" package is obtainable from Films for the Humanities, in Princeton, for $640.[1] This effort at lucrative popular education is probably no worse than others, but one feature struck me as being specially mischievous, namely, the collective reference to "wandering tribes." The peoples to the north and east of the Roman frontier were no more "wandering" than the Celts or Greeks or Thracians. They were agrarian villagers like the other sedentaries mentioned, and like them, and us, they moved every now and then. Whoever decided to speak of "wandering tribes" badly misunderstood the meaning of "migration" in reference to the peoples usually called "Germanic."

The term "Migration Age" is the English counterpart of the German "*Völkerwanderung*" or Latin "*migratio gentium*," both meaning "migration of peoples." In whatever language, "Migration Age" is a concept in everyday academic use, similar, as such, to "the Crusades" or "the Hundred Years War." It involves selecting a set of events out of a long period and connecting them up into an explanatory whole, as though to say: here, in a nutshell, is what was going on. Such concepts are useful in the classroom or in ordering narrative; we cannot do without them. But they inject anachronism into the events. In 1095, Pope Urban was unaware of setting the Crusades in motion and, in 1337, no one anticipated that the war between France and England would last a hundred years. The vocabulary of late antiquity did not include "barbarian invasions" or "*migratio gentium*" as everyday concepts. For us, the phrase "barbarian invasions" has the virtue of being earthbound: if armed foreign forces transgress their neighbors' borders, they may be factually described as "barbarian invaders." There is a difference when the neutral term "migration" enters the picture. "Migration Age" or "*Völkerwanderung*" are more artistic constructions; they associate a certain set of events with timeless anthropological, sociological, historical, and biblical processes of human movement.

It is often said that, whereas modern German uses the neutral "*Völkerwanderung*," the Romance languages refer to pointed "invasions barbares." The actual practices of authors do not bear out this ostensibly plausible contrast; the polarity of "migration" vs. "invasion" is not reflected in any systematic or consistent way in the historical literature of whatever languages.[2] French and Italian authors frequently refer to "migrations," and Germans do not guard themselves against occasionally adverting to "invasions." Context tends to determine which of the two words is invoked. No ethnic or political fault line has been methodically demonstrated to exist, or (I believe) can be.

As used by scholars today, the term "Migration Age" has three meanings, comprising at least three different complexes of historical phenomena. Its primary or core meaning is identical to its blunter counterpart "the Barbarian Invasions." It might be described as follows:

In the mid-fourth century, various peoples were parked, perhaps enduringly, on the Roman frontier. They ranged from the Saxons in northwest Europe to the Quadi and Vandals on the middle Danube to the Goths on the lower Danube. Two centuries later, these foreigners had moved to new positions in a process of conquest, settlement, and kingdom foundation—in German, *Eroberung, Landnahme*, and *Reichsgründung*. Saxons had established themselves in Britain, Franks and Burgundians in Gaul, Goths in southwestern Gaul and Spain, Sueves in Lusitania, and Lombards in Italy. The Western Roman Empire was gone and the outlines of modern Western Europe had become faintly discernible. Movement in these cases began near the imperial border and ended, after relatively limited displacements, in settlement somewhere within the former frontiers of the Empire or (in quite a few cases) in annihilation.

"Migration Age" in this first sense was already described in 1515 in a brief summary by the humanist Konrad Peutinger. Since then, it has been restated in prose, as well as drawn on maps, hundreds of times.[3] The course of events from the 370s to 568 forms the solid underpinning of what is meant by "Migration Age." Its distinguishing feature, rarely observed, is that it starts from a position of tranquility or rest. The northern frontier of the Roman Empire, from Scotland to the Danube mouths, is unlikely to have ever been quiet along its whole course. But the premise of having *Wanderung* begin in the 370s is that, prior to this, in the decades after the emperor Diocletian and his partners brought the imperial frontiers under control in the early fourth century, an equilibrium had prevailed; no one was going anywhere. This equilibrium was ended by the onrush of Huns.[4]

Users of the term "Migration Age" have found it hard to limit it narrowly. Even contemporaries raised the question of where their alien neighbors came from, and the later one advances down the centuries, the more elaborate the answers become. As a result, the core meaning is often supplemented by an expansion.

The extended, looser, and peripheral concept of "Migration Age"/*Völkerwanderung* includes the core meaning as its chronological end point but stretches backward more or less broadly into time and space. It comes in at least two major varieties—Asian and Germanic.

Its more mysterious form—the Asian version—reaches across Eurasia and identifies the familiar Huns with the Hsiung-nu bordering northern China. One much abbreviated account runs as follows (the quotation comes from a recent historical atlas):

The Centuries which saw the crisis and fall of the Roman Empire in the West coincided with a period of great upheaval in the heart of Asia: for reasons still largely unknown, huge populations began moving from Central Asia towards the West, pushing before them the peoples they found settled on their routes. The groups which took part in these large-scale migrations can generally be identified with the Mongolian peoples of Hsiung-nu and Juan-Juan, well known in the West as the Huns and the Avars. It was these peoples, and the populations that they absorbed en route, that descended upon the Roman Empire and demolished its already tottering structure.[5]

An obvious goal of this version is to explain how the Huns came to burst into European space in the 370s. The sweep of the Asian version recommends it to world or universal historians, and its visual possibilities appeal to compilers of historical atlases. On the other hand, its vast Eurasian and multiempire setting makes the core sense of "Migration Age" dwindle to an incidental detail. The upshot is that this version seldom intrudes into works concerned with the European barbarians or late Roman antiquity.[6]

The alternate extended version—the Germanic expansion—is much more widely represented than its Asian cousin. This expansion fills in the pre-fourth-century past, real or legendary, of the peoples participating in the core migration, and sometimes even of the peoples deemed archaeologically to have preceded them. In its restrained (and oldest) form, the Germanic expansion starts with the emigration from our Denmark of the Cimbri and Teutons in the second century B.C. and strives to trace movements by central European peoples from that time to the fourth century A.D. Not long ago, a distinguished historian of Rome described a form of it as follows: "The so-called *Völkerwanderung* was no abrupt event set loose only by the attack of the Huns. Rather, it is the turbulent last stage of a Germanic expansion that is visible ever since early in the first millennium B.C. Proceeding from south Scandinavian/north German space, the Germans expanded in all directions."[7] The privileged geographical setting in this case is not China or Central Asia but Scandinavia, out of which the Goths, Vandals, Burgundians, Gepids, Herules, Lombards, and others are thought to have "originally" emigrated. Time is at least as important as space to the Germanic expansion. Some scholars uncover Germans as early as the Bronze Age if not earlier still. In this inflated perspective, the pluri-millennial development comprising the expanded *Völkerwanderung* witnesses many vicissitudes and attains only its climax in the Migration Age of late antiquity.[8]

In brief, the commonplace period name "Migration Age" presupposes three distinct schemes—narrow (core), Asian, and Germanic. All three call for additional comments.

The narrow or core Migration Age retains traces of its martial origins as the defanged counterpart of "barbarian invasions." Eighteenth-century historians inside and outside Germany conceived of the end of the Western Roman Empire as a conquest and settlement by Germanic peoples. "Migration" was already used in this context in the sixteenth century, as we saw Konrad Peutinger doing in 1515; it is not a recent refinement. The famous eighteenth-century Göttingen historian Johann Christoff Gatterer and his contemporary, the great French cartographer Bourguignon d'Anville, envisaged the end of the Western Roman Empire as a conquest and settlement by Germanic peoples. Their views were presumably typical of what was believed in their time. The vocabulary of conquest, settlement, and kingdom foundation—*Eroberung, Landnahme*, and *Reichsgründung*—betrays its descent from this basically bellicose scenario of conquest by outsiders.[9] What allowed and still allows the neutral notion of "migration" to be substituted for "invasions" is the irruption of the Huns in the 370s. Their unexpected attack on the Goths shattered the relative stability of the frontiers, set the northern peoples in motion, and precipitated the multiple events resulting by 568 in the fall of the Western Empire and the panorama of *Reichsgründungen* outlined above. The Goths did not "invade" the Empire in 376: they "migrated" into it under Hunnic pressure and, some years later, continued to "migrate" under the leadership of Alaric.

A comprehensive and well-argued rejuvenation of the core Migration Age was offered a few years ago by Peter Heather in an article centering on the Huns rather than the "Germanic peoples."[10] Insisting that the end of the Western Roman Empire had nothing to do with internal problems but came from outside, Heather outlined three steps by which the Huns brought about its fall.[11] His story is basically identical to the normal scheme of the core Migration Age except in its causative focus. In the traditional version, though the Huns set migrations in motion, the active agents continue to be "Germanic peoples" led by such heroes as Alaric, Geiseric, Theodoric, and Clovis.

Since the nineteenth century (and even before), the explanatory waters have been muddied by an awakened sensitivity to conditions inside the Roman Empire. The agent of change in relations between barbarians and Romans has seemed increasingly, in the opinion of some observers, to come from the imperial rather than the northern side of the border. A measured appreciation of the peaceful contacts of "Germans" with Romans forces us to qualify the one-sided vision of "conquests" and "land seizures" resulting from "barbarian invasions." The incomparable Theodor Mommsen observed, "The last phase of the Roman state is remarkable for its barbarization and especially its Germanization."[12] Roman armies were filled with barbarian recruits and Roman headquarters with barbarian officers; whole peoples fought for Rome as treaty allies or "federates." Franks and Goths were the shock troops in Roman civil wars. Franks, Vandals, and others married into the Roman aristocracy and even the imperial family. The new religion of the Empire was promptly adopted by the foreigners. Land grants to barbarians in southern Gaul and Italy were made pursuant to law and not by seizure.[13] To judge from legal, institutional, and religious structures, "barbarian" kingdoms are better termed "sub-Roman." From the angle of "progressive fusion," even the tempered appeal to "migration" may well be inappropriate and one-sided.[14] Immigrant Goths, Franks, Lombards, and others were few in number, and a Roman and Catholic population continued preponderant in Spain, Gaul, and Italy. There was a compelling logic in Heather's turning his sights entirely on the Asiatic Huns and making them, rather than migrating "Germans," the dominant agents of political rupture. The "northern barbarians" may have become too tainted by compromises with the Roman world to be held responsible any longer for its fall. The expression "Migration Age" is still on everyone's lips but, owing to an enhanced sense of Roman survivals in the West, it has lost the simple, straightforward meaning it used to have in the days when *Völkerwanderung* was the polite way of saying "barbarian invasions."

The narrow sense of "Migration Age," though basic, rarely exists uncontaminated to some degree by one or the other expanded definition.

About the Asian version there is little to say since it seldom communicates with the two others. Although very ambitious and far-ranging in its own appearances, it has had virtually no impact on accounts of early medieval Europe. The Asian version was born in the mid-eighteenth century in the work of a pioneering Sinologist, Joseph de Guignes, who observed the similarity between the names Hun and Hsiung-nu and connected them to each other (1756). The visual potential of his theory was grasped at once by the distinguished cartographer Nicolas Bellin, who designed a map to complement de Guignes's work (1759).[15] De Guignes's link between Chinese events and the Hunnic irruption into Europe attracted the attention of later historians. The connection greatly impressed Gibbon and influenced Gatterer's 1775 "maps for the history of the

Völkerwanderung."[16] Opinion was less favorable in the next century. De Guignes's argument was carefully retraced by Thomas Hodgkin, who, at the same time, recognized the frail, merely verbal connection between the two peoples' names, and emphasized the three-century period "of quiescence and of obscurity" that separates the fading of the Hsiung-nu and the first stirrings of the Huns. He concluded that "the hypothesis though looked upon with much less favour than it received a century ago, does not seem to be yet absolutely disproved."[17] Sustained by this wisp of a doubt, the theory has withstood refutation and even gathered strength, so that some form of it or other is regularly encountered in recent atlases of world history, and more rarely in world histories.[18] However that may be, almost all historians who deal with the Migration Age as a story of basically northern peoples obstinately refuse to be drawn into Central Asian wastes. Like the contemporary observer Ammianus Marcellinus, they are content to have the Huns break into Europe for their own reasons without needing to be pushed from farther east.[19]

The Germanic expansion of "Migration Age" is wholly in the mainstream of teaching and research. Almost every account or map of the core migration is amplified by a backward extension of some sort into geographical distance or the more remote past. For example, authors focusing on the Vandals or Lombards often hasten to remark "The Vandals came from Scandinavia," or "The Lombards moved from the lower Elbe"; the same distancing formula is applied to many other peoples. This extension often involves tales of origins. In Roman times, the peoples to the northeast of the Empire were identified wholesale with the Scythians who had once lived in that part of the world and were prominent in the writings of Herodotus and his descendants. The church father Ambrose of Milan consulted the Bible and derived the Goths from Gog, son of Japhet, son of Noah; this was a complementary rather than limiting identification. Isidore of Seville drew the Goths from the Scythians in one work, the Getae (Dacians) in another, and the biblical Magog in a third.[20] In the days of Justinian, the historian Procopius specified that the Vandals had migrated westward from the Maeotian swamp (our Sea of Azov) and his Latin-writing contemporary, Jordanes, alleged that, long before the Trojan war, the Goths and Gepids had moved to the Continent from the island of Scandinavia. The Franks acquired Trojan origins in the seventh century and the Saxons Macedonian ones in the tenth.[21] This medieval game of origins was tame by comparison with that of the patriot-prehistorians of the twentieth century, who did not hesitate to trace the "original" Germans backward to the Stone Age.[22] The erudite foundations for distant origins are rarely checked by current users. The information about such origins that comes to us in textbooks and college lectures is normally at second hand, derived from modern authorities, such as Musset's *Germanic Invasions*, Demougeot's *Formation de l'Europe*, or Herwig Wolfram's *History of the Goths*.

"Migration Age" in its Germanic expanded guise has been mainly an account of "the Germans" from the wandering of the Cimbri and Teutons into Roman space in 114 B.C.—the stuff of what, in Germany, is called "early Germanic history (*germanische Frühgeschichte*)," the long epoch that allegedly led up to the climactic migrations of late antiquity. As early as 1531, the levelheaded humanist Beatus Rhenanus firmly set the base line: the Cimbri and Teutons were not Celts, as the authoritative Orosius claimed (A.D. 417), but very definitely Germans.[23] With this solid starting point before the Incarnation, modern scholars confidently traced the early Germans in Greek and Latin sources through their struggles with the Romans, victory over Varus's three legions, contest with Marcus Aurelius, formation into larger confederacies, and emergence as neighbors of Rome in the fourth century.

Although this story has often been told and retold, "early Germanic history" does not fit everyone's expectations of what history should be. It is not a history of "Germans" but, necessarily, of fragmented peoples, such as Goths, Franks, Herules, Gepids, and Marcomanni—none of them conscious of forming a German collectivity. Narratives sometimes spill over to include non-Germanic peoples as well, such as the Sarmatians, with their particular names and destinies. Once past the age of Ariovistus, Arminius, and Maroboduus (first centuries B.C. and A.D.) and until late antiquity, it is a history almost wholly lacking personalities and human motivations or crises. No doubt there were leaders, but the Greek and Latin informants do not report their names and exploits. Impersonal forces—flood, famine, drought, overpopulation—or external agencies, such as the assumed pressure of one people upon another, do much of the work that, in normal history, is assigned to human beings and political circumstances. Migration, another disembodied force, is invoked whenever it seems to fit.

Scholars do what they can to compensate for their lack of information; they may even do too much. Donald Kelley points out, "What Tacitus [who more than anyone else made "early Germanic history" possible] inspired posthumously was not *historia* . . . but rather *eruditio*—not narrative history but the more profound and perhaps mystical search for the founding fathers (*Vorfahrer, vorfordern*) and the difficult and myth-ridden questions of national spirit and origins."[24] Kelley's comment holds true not only for the early scholars whom he had in mind, but at least as much for their descendants, as witness notoriously the linguist turned prehistorian Gustaf Kossinna (†1931), who trumpeted "German (*deutsche*) prehistory" as an "outstanding national science" and implemented a regressive "method of pursuing the frontiers of Germanic territory archaeologically from early historical (*frühgeschichtlicher*) time backwards as far as possible."[25] The two centuries of the core Migration Age are normal history, worked over by disciplined historians; the expanded Germanic version has ill-defined boundaries and, because so much rides on origins in a patriotic context, lends itself readily to abuses of many kinds. Non-Germans may be tempted to believe that the terrain of history would be enriched if the expanded Germanic form of "Migration Age"—that is, in effect, the whole of *germanische Frühgeschichte*—were totally dispensed with or at the very least shed its pretension to being a multicentury build up to the migrations of late antiquity.

For those immersed in "early Germanic history," it still matters much that medieval Germany—the progenitor of the Germany we know—should proceed from its own "Germanic antiquity," that the "quintessential" Germans extracted from Tacitus's *Germania* should live on in spirit, if not biologically, in their Migration Age and current descendants.[26] The scholarly incarnation today of this desire to connect past and present is the so-called "ethnogenesis theory," fathered by Reinhard Wenskus and promoted by the Institute for Austrian Historical Research in Vienna. In its focus on identity and the maintenance of identity and "ethnic consciousness" by "kernels of tradition" over enormous spans of time, "ethnogenesis theory" is a subtle device for demonstrating to the Germans of today that they are firmly linked to their ancient ancestors. The denial of disruption and longing for continuity that motivate this theory should be enough reason to cast ethnogenesis aside as yet another symptom of a tenacious nostalgia.[27]

The prehistoric Germans never existed under that name; they are an illusion of misguided scholars. The nonexistence of ancient Germans is perhaps the most important thing one can say about the barbarians of late antiquity. There were Chauci, Hermunduri, Marcomanni, and dozens more; but there were no peoples who called or recognized themselves as Germans. Even the Romans, who have the best claim to being the inventors of this blanket term, were circumspect and, in late antiquity, reticent in using it. The "Germanic world" is a damaging modern invention and usage that badly needs to be abandoned.

The same nonexistence goes for "migrating peoples," the ostensible actors in the Migration Age. "Migration" was not inherent in any of the peoples of late antiquity, not even the nomadic Alans, Huns, and Avars from the Asiatic steppes. Every now and then, for different reasons and with particular objectives, individuals and collectivities engaged in voluntary or involuntary changes of place. It is absurd to believe that the Huns attacked the Alans and then the Goths simply because migration pushed them in their direction, or that the same abstract impetus occasioned the later extension of Hunnic rule into the Carpathian basin and Attila's luckless invasion of Gaul. No metaphysical power of migration thrust the Huns westward; they had their reasons even if we have no idea what they were. "Migration" is apprehended after the fact and needs to be limited to this retrospective role.

The notion of "migrating peoples" is sustained, not by the events of late antiquity, but by the incessant evocation on the part of modern historians of the chronologically and geographically distant homelands from which the Goths, Vandals, Herules, and other are supposed to have "migrated"[28]—the practice that I typify by the casual, throwaway line found almost everywhere: "The Vandals [or Herules or Burgundians] came from Scandinavia." In fact, the Vandals were firmly rooted in the Danube valley since at least the second century A.D. It was from there, nearby, that they invaded Gaul in the early 400s; they were totally unaware of having lived anywhere else. But that is not the way our books treat them. This conjuring up of migrants from distant parts is the international equivalent of the tale of Germanic expansion traced long backward in space and time. In this perspective, widely adopted in the historical literature of many lands, the peoples are qualified as "migrating" because they started to travel long, long ago and far, far away, and never stopped shoving themselves forward until they were destroyed or settled inside the Roman world. One of the mysteries of historical research and writing today is why this scenario of *longue durée* migration is still cultivated in spite of the overwhelming evidence illustrating a different course of events before and during late antiquity. Migration was a means and a result, not a determinant; the barbarians of late antiquity were not "migrants," let alone "wanderers."

The core Migration Age starts near A.D. 370 from a position of rest and equilibrium. The Roman frontiers were much assailed and broken through in the third century, but the Empire overcame these disruptions, retreated here and there, and restored a position of stability or at least balance. The peoples living to the north of these borders were not newcomers. Some had been settled there for as many as four centuries, others for less but all for long enough to consider themselves well rooted. They were long past the point of having "come" from somewhere and were definitely not "going" anywhere. The core Migration Age starts from this moment of stability. Two centuries after the Huns had shattered this equilibrium political control in the West had changed hands; we are faced with a transformed geography. That two-century period of change, and not a diffuse and largely hypothetical and undocumented millennial expansion of Germans-who-did-not-know-themselves, is the object worthy of study.

Like "the Crusades" and the "Hundred Years War," the "Migration Age" or *Völkerwanderung* is here to stay. Established historical concepts are combated in vain. However deserving they are of criticism, they are too solidly implanted to be cleared away. But they can be defined and qualified. That is what has been attempted here.[29]

Chapter 2

A Recipe on Trial: "The Germans Overthrow the Roman Empire"

In the continuing debate over the fall of the Roman Empire, the view that the Empire was destroyed by external forces has always had eloquent and influential supporters. Even before the imperial period of Rome began, the Greek historian Polybius raised the specter that its downfall might come from an unforeseeable force outside itself. The Latin poets—at the height of Roman expansionism—probed imaginatively beyond the edges of Roman power, especially to the north, and envisaged multiple threats from the poor, unconquered, wild peoples in that quarter, coursing between the outer Ocean and the civilized world. As the first century B.C. drew to a close, the historian Sallust observed that "down to our time Romans have been convinced that, even though the rest of the world bowed to their power, they fought with the Gauls not for glory but for their very lives." The capture of Rome by the Gauls in 387 B.C. was an unforgettable date in Roman history—a continual reminder of the limits of military power and the dangers of northern barbarians.[1]

Were these apprehensions about the north well founded? A stellar gallery of ancient historians since World War II—André Piganiol, Arnaldo Momigliano, Moses Finley, A. H. M. Jones, to list only the most eminent—has espoused the formerly eclipsed thesis that external forces destroyed the Empire at least in the West. The thesis gained special force from the drastic undermining by Jones of the opposite theory that Rome rotted from within. In the final sentence of his great synthesis, he concluded, "The internal weaknesses of the empire cannot have been a major factor in its decline." A recent, extreme example of the ascendancy of external causation is the argument by an English historian that the Huns alone brought down the imperial edifice in three steps.[2]

A more moderate view, in circulation at least among scholars for hundreds of years, holds that the responsibility for the end of Rome at least in the West rested with "the northern barbarians," or more succinctly with "the Germans." This argument has been carefully expounded and personally endorsed by Alexander Demandt in a book exhaustively surveying "the judgment of posterity" on the fall of Rome. "[I]f the role of the Germans were taken away," Demandt concludes, "hardly anyone can be seen who, in their place, would have brought about the dissolution of the Empire."[3]

The argument that "the Germans," even disguised as "the northern peoples," overthrew the Roman Empire is deeply flawed. I propose to test it step by step taking as my point of departure Demandt's learned exposition of this theme. Demandt, a widely published and respected ancient historian at the Free University of Berlin, is singled out here as a particularly estimable and up-to-date advocate, a worthy representative of all those who share this opinion. He is also more sensitive than most historians of Rome to aspects of this argument emphasized in Germany. My translation of Demandt's full argument is supplied as Appendix 1; only this version does justice to his case. Taking care not to distort Demandt's meaning, I have condensed and paraphrased his pages into six points and use this condensation as the basis for a step-by-step response. The implied voice in my abridgment of Demandt's reasoning is the author's.

Rome and the Germans as Military Rivals

1. Demandt: The Roman Empire and the Germans Were Military Rivals since the Second Century B.C. and German Dynamism Eventually Triumphed

There is an old, convincing argument—already used by Panvinius (1558), Krause (1789), Mommsen (1893), Baynes (1943), and Jones (1964)—that external pressure is crucial to understanding the late Roman situation. Owing to the disadvantageously long river frontiers of the Roman Empire, the attack of the northern peoples on the European provinces could not ultimately be resisted.

(It has been proposed that special conditions in the East and the West predisposed each part to its distinct fate. These contrasts "do not work.")[4]

Why could the Romans not keep the Germans at bay as they had since the time of Cimbri and Teutons? Does the inferiority of Rome after A.D. 376 not prove its inner collapse? Of course! It would be foolish to dispute it. Nevertheless, the collapse was hastened, or even brought about, by the mounting pressure of Germans since the Marcomannic War (A.D. 166–80).

1. Response

The premise of Demandt's account is a one-to-one confrontation of Rome and a collectivity of northern peoples called "Germans" or "the Germanic world." Another way to describe this northern force is to maintain that multiple "Germanic" peoples were cemented by migration. This unified, collective phenomenon is called in German *Völkerwanderung*, here rendered in English as "the

Migration Age." The concept of migration as a unifying factor nudges causation away from multiple, fragmented peoples and toward a single "force."[5] The name "German" is not obligatory as focal point, although Demandt explicitly endorses it. The same role can be played by Goths alone (Herwig Wolfram) or by Huns and a shorter time frame (Peter Heather). The simplest, most guarded but nevertheless collective formula is "barbarian (or external) pressure," the premise being that a unified barbariandom faced a unified Roman civilization. Famous recent historians of antiquity, such as Momigliano and Finley, agree that barbarian "pressure" brought Rome low in the West.[6] This manner of thinking is ubiquitous; it is more reflexive than reasoned.

The premise of a one-to-one confrontation, however expressed, is false; the unity of Rome's northern neighbors is a verbal fiction.[7] A Germanic collectivity exists in linguistics but never existed anywhere else. The neighbors of Rome included not only "Germans" but also sturdily non-German Britons, Irish, Picts, Dacians, and Sarmatians. They existed in small, fragmented groups and had no mechanism for united action either in their early encounters with Rome or in late antiquity. Demandt and uncounted others in many countries evoke an "early Germanic world" that had no existence anywhere until it took form in the minds of scholars in sixteenth-century Europe and was thoughtlessly espoused by everyone else. Without a "Germanic" or "migratory" cement, the northern barbarians may be envisaged only as splinters with no collective ability to exert deliberate "pressure."[8] The Empire was disturbed by the uncoordinated activities of its multiethnic neighbors; its freedom of action was seriously limited by the need to defend its frontiers. But this instability was the cost of being an empire, that is, of itself exerting outward pressure of many kinds on the people whom it had not yet conquered but reserved the right to subjugate in the future.

No one disputes that the Roman Empire faced multiple, fragmented small peoples of varied cultures on its northern limits. When these neighbors are lumped together and formed into a conceptual unit, the terms of Rome's dealings with them are fundamentally distorted. The great fear of northern peoples expressed by Roman poets and writers was based on historical reminiscences of disasters at the hands of the Gauls and the Cimbri and Teutons. It is unlikely to have reflected the reasoned thinking of Rome's military high command.[9] When Roman expansionism came into violent contact with the northern peoples, the results included momentary coalitions of defenders and, often enough, hard fighting in which the Romans risked defeat. Their military superiority was limited; Romans did not pit firearms against clubs and spears. Nevertheless, the outcome was never in doubt. The "martial spirit" of the northerners was no match for the disciplined military force of Rome.

The Germans Continually Gained Strength

2. Demandt: The Changing Ratio of Force between the Germanic World and the Empire

Even A. H. M. Jones, let alone other ancient historians in our times, are blind or one-eyed to changes among the Germans. Developments in *barbaricum* contradict the belief that conditions there remained essentially the same from Ariovistus to Alaric. The so-called *Völkerwanderung* was no abrupt event set loose only by the attack of the Huns (ca. A.D. 370). Rather, it is the turbulent last stage of a Germanic expansion that is visible ever since early in the first millennium B.C.[10]

> a. Dynamic German expansion since the first millennium B.C. was occasioned by love of warfare, an ideal of freedom in preference to prosperity, and a society ruled by the "warrior ideal." This ideal when set alongside a Roman world more and more averse to warfare allowed a few Germans to dominate Roman majorities.
> b. Another reason: population increase. Besides what Roman-age authors say on this subject (such as Scandza as the womb of nations), Germanic population increase can be established archaeologically; "social conditions and a certain biological strength of the people" [*sic*] are among the explanations for it.
> c. "For Romans, war against the Germans meant at best a maintenance of things as they were; for the Germans war against Romans promised improvement of their own circumstances. Men's conduct normally depends less on conditions than on expectations."
> d. The civilizing process of Rome upon the Germans increased their offensive power. By employment as mercenaries and by trade the Germans since Caesar learned from the Romans and were turned into more dangerous enemies.
> e. The Germans eventually entered into large war-alliances against Rome. Arminius and Maroboduus (in the first century A.D.) showed the way. The political landscape changed in the third century, when the West Germanic small tribes formed the tribe-associations of Franks, Alamanni, and Saxons.
> f. In sum, the Romans considered it very desirable to have an adversary who kept their army at the highest level of training and preparedness. The Germans played this part, but in time the sparring partner proved harder than the champion.

2. Response

What Demandt recapitulates under these several analytical headings is the story of the "dynamic inner development of the Germans," the grand narrative of *germanische Frühgeschichte* from the beginning of encounters with Rome, or even before, down to late antiquity. This "inner development" is not an established, verifiable fact of ancient history; it is the aggregate of five or six discrete groups of facts, widely separate in time and space, joined together by emphatic affirmations that they combine into a coherent and progressive tale—the rise of "the Germans." It is a familiar story because found in whole or in part in a small library of books published in and out of Germany for several centuries whose theme—the "early Germans"—is still far from being repudiated.[11] One early twentieth-century scholar (Gustaf Kossinna, †1931) won praise for having added two thousand years to the past of the "early Germans." The more normal procedure has involved weaving the observations of Greek and Roman authors about central Europe with the evidence of archaeology, onomastics, philology, and whatever else and, with blithe disregard of discontinuities and incompatibilities, connecting up the dots in a scenario of vigorous growth.[12]

The existence of a Germanic civilization was especially read out of Tacitus's *Germania*, a Roman ethnographic work (written in A.D. 98) little known in the Roman Empire but rediscovered in fifteenth-century Europe and popularized thereafter. The ideal of freedom, the love of warfare, the unrestricted natality, the comparative poverty, and other features propounded by Tacitus have hardened into certainties, not necessarily false but perhaps not so true as to bear the edifices of inference built over them. None of Demandt's building blocks is uncontestable. Some of them may be knocked over by means of his own, later considerations (no. 4).[13] To the advocates of the story of the "early Germans," it is essential that it should appear dynamic, that is, should embody change—the change that Demandt reproaches certain historians of Rome for disregarding. Change is supplied in a variety of ways: first a pattern of migrations from north to south (buttressed by doubtfully scientific archaeology), then the idyll of early Germanic civilization read out of Tacitus's *Germania*, followed by a period of equilibrium; the march forward resumes with the Marcomannic War under Marcus Aurelius, prolonged in the third century by the formation of aggregations of tribes under the names of Franks, Alamanni, and Goths, and invasions by these collectivities. The result of these changes should be that "the Germans" on the eve of late Rome were much more formidable than they had been in the days of Augustus. But, as will presently be seen, no one, Demandt included, is able to claim that they were. Rome's northern neighbors had changed—archaeology bears this out—but not in such ways as to alter the balance of force facing the Empire.[14]

The "dynamic" tale of "Germanic early history (*Frühgeschichte*)" has been told again and again inside and outside Germany.[15] It is a composite wholly dependent on scholars' fitting together bits of Greco-Roman evidence and deciding that they form a meaningful pattern of Germanic expansion. The dynamism does not emerge from the evidence but is imprinted upon it from outside, by modern historians' judgments repeated again and again since the sixteenth century. The northern barbarians, splintered as usual and blind to their duty to overcome their divisions, were wholly unaware that they were "going" anywhere. Nowhere among the northerners may one find any hint of remembered "Germanic" glory in fighting Rome—either in the days of Augustus or of Marcus Aurelius or at any other time. Such exploits were lost to the descendants of their protagonists until, in our Renaissance, humanist collectors in Germany and elsewhere deciphered the traces in classical sources and built them into edifices of patriotic pride.

a. "The Dynamism of a Society Ruled by the 'Warrior Ideal' "

We know that Roman expansionism in the last days of the Roman Republic and in the early Empire came up against peoples in central Europe by no means willing to submit at the first sign of aggression.[16] The Britons and Pannonians, without being expansionist (or Germanic), put up determined resistance to Roman conquest; the natives of northern Italy and Spain were even more obstinate in combating the legions. There was nothing about "Germanic" resistance that cannot be paralleled on other Roman fields of conquest.[17] The imperial government stopped short of its ideal frontier against the peoples of the north, but that decision (*pace* Tacitus) had more to do with a prudent cost/benefit analysis than with the bravery, large numbers, and special warrior ideal of its opponents. Rome, a highly organized state with a sophisticated military tradition, did not need something so ephemeral as a "warrior ideal" to put effective armies in the field. The "fall" of the West Roman Empire is not now (perhaps not ever) envisaged as a military defeat by brave barbarians of enervated troops that had lost the will to fight.[18]

In 429 and 439, a comparatively small force of Vandals seized and imposed its will on a North Africa full of well-populated towns. The ostensible weakness of the Roman Empire in this and comparable instances stemmed from its practicing a deliberate division of labor that had civilians stick to their occupations and left fighting to official armies. Once the armed forces in North Africa failed to repel the invaders, there was no militia or national guard trained and equipped to form a second line of defense. The Vandals could take charge. Something on the Roman side may have been at fault in allowing this result, but it was not a lack of martial spirit. Organization not spirit was expected to keep North Africa in the Roman Empire. The Vandals themselves fell prey to the obvious advantages of the Roman division of labor; when Belisarius arrived in 533 with the East Roman forces entrusted to him by the emperor Justinian, not enough remained of the Vandal "martial spirit" to prevent an amazingly rapid conquest.[19]

b. "Population Increase"

It is easier to allege population increase among the northern barbarians than to substantiate it. Some standard of proof is needed to offset literary tradition. Demandt, in another book, thrusts forward natality as the explanation for the fourteen-year Marcommanic War: "[The war] illuminates the altered ratio of force [of Rome] vis-à-vis the Germans. The latter's periodic population surpluses had already led to the migrations of the Cimbri and Teutons and to the state formation of Ariovistus and Maroboduus. As long as the *limes* set a barrier to the further advances of the northern peoples, the land-seeking Germans fell back on the lands north of the Black Sea and the lower Danube."[20] Demandt (in the full text of his discourse) sets enormous store by the argument from increasing numbers. He has many predecessors. The already mentioned Gustaf Kossinna, almost the creator of the *Völkerwanderung* in its modern supposedly "scientific" guise, always took surplus population as the cause for emigration.[21] Greek historians and ethnographers such as Herodotus featured population increase as the all-purpose mainspring. The same cliché prospers in the twentieth century A.D. No one, Demandt included, has a definite idea of why and in what circumstances any of these movements took place. Instead, he links them with the ancient explanation of "excess population." Yet he is aware that many allegedly "land-seeking Germans" resided in the vastness of Ukraine, one of the world's bread baskets. If really land hungry, they might have satisfied their needs right where they were.

It was axiomatic in Greek science that a northern climate favored natality; and the literary image of a threat to the north encouraged writers to enlarge the numbers of northern peoples.[22] The idea that "the Germans" were particularly prolific has no quantitative basis. There is a wide gulf between the archaeological observation that certain cemeteries expanded and a collective conclusion of population growth for all northerners. Demandt later points out that the northerners constantly warred with each other and existed in want and privation (no. 4). *Barbaricum* in late antiquity was not boiling over with vast numbers of hungry barbarians in need of space for their minimum needs. The circumstances of late antiquity are complex, but whatever else they illustrate they do not suggest an overflowing abundance of barbarian souls.

*c. "Germans Could Hope for Improvement While Romans
Were Left with Only the Status Quo"*

The idea that the "Germans" had more to hope for from triumphing over Romans than the other way around is psychological speculation with no concrete basis. Perhaps its main flaw is the presupposition that the two parties were at war, continually testing their will to win—a return to the conception of a late antique competition between "the Germans" and Rome. On what fields of battle were "the Germans" to exemplify their superior morale? Barbarians spent fewer man-hours fighting against the Empire than on its behalf or that of contenders for the emperorship. The occasions when a psychological disparity between "German" and Roman troops might have come into play were few and far between. Rome did not lose the battle of Adrianople (378) for lack of fighting spirit.

d. "Contact with Rome Increased the Offensive Power of the Germans"

One might imagine that, in three or four centuries of frequent contacts across the frontiers, with much recruitment into the Roman army and many veterans returning to *barbaricum*, there would have been a steady learning process resulting in growing offensive power of barbarian armies. Did this in fact take place? Demandt does what he can to document a progressive improvement of barbarian fighting equipment and skills over the long term. That is not the same as demonstrating that such changes took place.[23] Hopping across the three or four imperial centuries from one hot conflict between the barbarians and Rome to the next, one finds no evidence of noticeable improvement of barbarian military capabilities. Were the northern enemies faced by Marcus Aurelius better trained and equipped than those fought by Tiberius? Did Alaric lead more competent forces than Arminius? No one can tell precisely; but, clearly, there were no flagrant disparities, no obvious improvements assuring us that the Goths of late antiquity were more formidable foes than the Cherusci who crushed Varus. The reverse would have been surprising. Armies reflect the societies that create them; the introduction of Roman weapons and drill among barbarian warriors could have only ephemeral effects unless sustained by radical sociopolitical transformations. These did not take place.[24]

e. "The Emergence of Large War-Alliances against Rome in the Third Century"

Accounts of "the dynamic growth of the Germans" invariably emphasize what is called a profound constitutional change in the third century among the peoples bordering Rome, called by Demandt a transformation of "the political landscape" that (he claims) greatly increased the offensive power against Rome of the peoples beyond the borders. The evidence for this change tends to be little else than the emergence, on the western borders, of the names of "Franks," "Ala-manni," and "Saxons," and on the lower Danube, of the Goths.[25]

The appearance of these names goes hand in hand with large scale attacks on the Empire that were gradually repelled. But these events were not one-sided. Simultaneously, the Empire was experiencing extreme internal turmoil and a succession of civil wars. The frontier breakthroughs can be attributed to opportunism on the part of the frontier barbarians rather than to constitutional change. The denuding of frontier defenses by troops withdrawn to fight civil wars offered outsiders opportunities for plunder that were not to be missed.[26]

If the political landscape had really been changed one would expect to discern lasting effects, but none is visible. The leadership of these peoples was not transformed; no leagues were created with a greater capacity for common action than before; if there were constitutional changes, they led nowhere, least of all to the fifth-century barbarian kingdoms. From the little we can tell, the Franks, Alamanni, and Saxons of the fourth-century West were as fragmented and free of collective leadership as the peoples of the early Empire. The Saxon conquest of Britain from the 450s onward resulted eventually in an assortment of seven kingdoms, and the Saxons who stayed behind on the Continent are noteworthy (in the eighth century) for lacking even a king.[27] As for the Goths, their major attacks on the Empire went hand in hand with large scale recruitment of Goths for service with the imperial army.[28] There seems to have been change in relations across the frontier—a greater reliance by Rome on foreign manpower—rather than in internal organization among the "Germanic" barbarians.

The demands of a discourse of "dynamic expansion" (as practiced by Demandt and many others) make it essential that "the Germans" should be somehow transformed before entering the late antique "act" of their history, the act in which, according to a scenario already firmly in place among eighteenth-century historians, they conquered the Empire and settled on its lands (*Eroberung, Landnahme, Reichsgründungen*).[29] Dramaturgy, however, can only go so far. The barbarians of late antiquity did not cease to be fragmented peoples. They did not enter into more than momentary "large war-alliances against Rome." The course of events was quite different.

f. "Romans Valued Having a Sparring Partner, But He Eventually Surpassed the Champion."

If any of Rome's adversaries forced it to keep its military skills honed, it was the Parthians and Persians on its eastern frontier, the only power whose armed forces were armed, organized, and led at a level comparably sophisticated to that of the Empire. Logistics, field engineering, siege warfare, and endurance were the signs of a highly developed army. These were not likely to be fully tested or needed in fighting enemies whose main tactic was an all-out charge. Long practice in chasing small bands of barbarian robbers is likely to have turned the Roman army into a gendarmerie overinclined to model itself on its militarily contemptible opponents. Demandt's argument might be turned right around, making the northerners a reason for the deterioration of Roman military technique. Where "sparring partners" are concerned, Alaric was a poor successor to Hannibal.

The Germans Go on the Offensive

3. Demandt: The Germans Go on the Offensive

Germanic attacks were the essential cause for the inner difficulties of the late Roman Empire. War on many fronts prepared the dissolution of the Roman state, and these crises were never wholly overcome. The beginning came with the first real double emperorship, by Marcus Aurelius and Lucius Verus, as the Danube and the Euphrates frontiers were simultaneously threatened. Many crises later, the Diocletian-Constantinian reforms brought some calm. An apparatus of formerly unnecessary officials collected taxes.

3. Response

Demandt overstates the case when he maintains that "Germanic" attacks were the "essential" reason for Rome's troubles in and after the third century. The qualifier "essential" implies that other features of the third century—the emergence of a rejuvenated and much more dangerous Sasanian Persia on the eastern frontiers and Rome's own radical instability in its emperorship and continual civil wars—were unimportant by comparison with "Germanic" attacks. Demandt cannot be more certain of this than any other historian of imperial Rome. One might argue, on the contrary, that only the denuding of frontiers for civil wars was "essentially" responsible for barbarian inroads.[30] As for wars on several fronts—allegedly initiated when the Danube barbarians attacked the Empire while it was at war with Parthia—Rome had, in fact, successfully fought quite a few such wars in the era of its great conquests.[31]

Demandt makes these excessive claims because of the fragility of his position. He is forced to pretend that "the Germans" were a single entity when they were multiple and to ascribe to them a single mind that "takes the offensive" and rolls gloriously into late antiquity. Yes, there were Marcoman invasions and, in the third century, Gothic, Frankish, Alamannic, and other ones. But who is to say that these are dots to be connected up into a panorama of deliberate aggression? There was no coherent barbarian plan or desire to subvert, let alone conquer the Roman Empire. A strategically successful step by Rome amid these crises was to relinquish its most exposed northern outposts—the province of Dacia and the *agri decumati*—but no one can claim that, when the Goths and Alamanni invaded the Empire, their goal was to bring about these retreats.[32] The largely undocumented third century is likely to remain something of a historical mystery. It does not help to populate it with collective "Germans" taking the offensive.

German Distress Intensifies Pressure on Rome

4. Demandt: The Mounting Distress of the Germans Intensified Their Pressure on Rome

Conditions "on the Germanic side" were not good. The Germanic tribes were normally at war with one another. Privation made the denizens of *barbaricum* aggressive. Hunger for land and booty attracted the Germans to the Empire. Rome had to yield to the external pressure.

4. Response

Whereas in no. 3 Demandt has the glorious "Germans" go on the offensive against Rome, in no. 4 they suddenly are miserably poor and at each other's throats (Demandt switches again in no. 5).[33] Perhaps "martial spirit" had an underside after all; we are finally offered a glimpse of the possibly enervating internal life of the northerners (not that this is less speculative than a different scenario would be). Demandt seems to acknowledge what any thoughtful observer of the early fourth century sees when considering the northern barbarians, namely, that they had gained little if anything since the first century and were not poised for great advances. I commented on this issue elsewhere:

[The] final step [of the allegedly grandiose expansion of "the Germans"] turns out to be remarkably modest: those involved in it were a mere handful of people, each group numbering at the most in the low tens of thousands, and many of them—not all—were accommodated within the Roman provinces without dispossessing or overturning indigenous society. In other words, the barbarians whom we actually find coming to grips with the Roman Empire in the fourth to sixth centuries, and leading the earliest successor kingdoms of the West, are remarkably deficient in numbers, cohesion, assertiveness, and skills—altogether a disappointment when juxtaposed with the long and massive migrations that are thought to characterize their past.[34]

Rather than dwell on the comparative changelessness of life in *barbaricum*, Demandt turns the liabilities of the foreigners into an argument for greater offensive power: the miseries of "the Germans" made them more aggressive and formidable. Faced with the pressure of these wretched hungry peoples, Rome had to yield. Really? Empires are not known to bend in the face of the wretchedness of the weak. On the contrary, northerners were so far in Rome's control that large numbers of them were continually recruited into the Roman army and, where necessary, settled as laborers on provincial soil.

Frontier defense continued in late antiquity to be an everyday concern for the Empire. The barbarian "problem" was not about to disappear, but it was manageable and compatible with treating *barbaricum* as a reservoir of manpower. Just as Diocletian and his collaborators had stabilized the emperorship and the border with Persia, so they reduced the recent turbulence of the northern frontiers to manageable proportions.[35] The talk of an expanding "Germania" taking the offensive is empty rhetoric. When the emperor Julian was advised that he might, if he saw fit, fight the "deceitful and treacherous" Goths, he replied that "he was looking for a better enemy; that for the Goths the Galatian [that is, Cappadocian] traders were enough, by whom they were offered for sale everywhere without distinction of rank." These ostensibly formidable neighbors could be counted on to be in a state of constant inner war, to feed their captives into the slave trade, and to pay in this way for a constant stream of imports from the Empire.[36]

Demandt counterbalances the weakness of the northerners, which he has himself pointed out, by evoking that of the Romans. He implies (in no. 1) that, after Adrianople, self-interested "Germans" took collective advantage of Roman "inferiority." Seemingly, such leaders as Alaric, Geiseric, Euric, and Theoderic sought to promote "Germanic" interests at the expense of a hapless Empire. We are again offered the fatally flawed premise of a "German" idea to which all barbarian leaders in Roman service were presumably attached and preferred to loyalty to their paymaster. A famous saying attributed to the Goth Athaulf is that he had first thought of turning Romania into a Gothia, but had finally realized that the only possible course open to him was to use Gothic strength to make a greater Rome.[37] The comments of Julian and Athaulf are irreconcilable with the thrust of Demandt's discourse. Their affirmations of Gothic helplessness in the face of Rome are an insuperable obstacle to Demandt's (widely shared) scenario of a dynamic growth of the "early Germans."

The Two Options Open to the Roman Empire

5. Demandt: The Outcome

Two courses for the dissolution of the unity of the Roman state are conceivable: either the amputation of provinces surrendered to foreigners, as outlined by

Ennodius of Pavia to Theoderic the Ostrogoth; or intensified admission of barbarians into the Empire. Since the fourth century barbarian soldiers had been the buttresses of the Empire. The more Roman troops perished fighting civil and foreign enemies, the greater efforts were needed to replenish the ranks from additional barbarians. It was axiomatic that domestic recruitment was not an option.

Because the Germans were eager to fit into the Roman system, they could have grown more into the Empire than they did. "If a successful large scale settlement of land-hungry groups on the waste fields of Greece, Italy, and Africa had succeeded, the collision harmful for the Empire might have been avoided at the time when it took place [that is, put off until a later date]."[38]

5. Response

Demandt finally shakes off his German bias. He recognizes that the barbarians were eager to fit into the Roman system and that intensified admission of foreigners into the Empire was a sensible course of action. But he then turns around and becomes a partisan of non-negotiable Roman conditions: land-hungry barbarians needed to be "successfully" settled in waste parts of the Empire. The shadow of a well-guarded stockade looms before us—anything else and the barbarians would soon be out of control. Although Demandt has written eloquently elsewhere about the incorporation of foreigners into the imperial élite, nothing of the sort is envisaged here; "success" is restricted to the import of submissive laborers and cannon fodder. And yet, Demandt is well aware that Rome, from its beginnings, had been a melting pot of peoples and prided itself on this role. He also knows that, in late antiquity, barbarians and Romans mingled in the upper layers of society: Theodosius I married Stilicho to his favorite niece; Arcadius's wife had a Frankish father; Geiseric married his heir to a daughter of Valentinian III. All this is forgotten. At the end of the argument, Demandt's barbarians have turned into Arnold Toynbee's menacing "external proletariat," and his sympathies have switched from the north to Rome.[39]

A Failed Defense and Aborted Recovery

6. Demandt: Contours of the Dark Age Ahead

The dissolution of the Empire therefore illustrates not only a failed defense, but equally a failed incorporation of the Germans.[40] The Romans ultimately lost what they had, but the Germans did not gain what they sought. They proved unable to carry forward the Roman culture that seemed worthy of enthusiasm and did not learn how to retain for themselves the land they had conquered. With the exception of the Frankish kingdom the Germanic states on imperial soil vanished.

6. Response

Demandt, still garbed as an ancient historian, offers a somber glimpse into the "dark" Western future. Convinced that barbarians or foreigners or "Germans" were unworthy of Roman civilization, Demandt cannot accept any other outcome than total victory for either party. If the Romans did not succeed in keeping the foreigners underfoot, then the certainty was that the wild Franks, Burgundians, and Saxons spoiled and ravaged what Rome had created. The West under its non-Roman kings illustrates how the barbarians were incapable of retaining the fine things they coveted. The only Rome, shining and admirable, that survived into the Middle Ages was that of Constantinople.

The position taken by Demandt illustrates an attachment to the boundaries laid down by traditional historical periodization. An excellent ancient historian runs the risk of approaching the earliest centuries of the Middle Ages in the crudely negative terms inculcated into schoolboys of his generation. Demandt's point of view is at best out of date. The future of the medieval West was anything but dark. In addition to the Frankish kingdom that he recognizes, the Saxons in England, the Lombards and the popes in Italy, the Bavarians on the Danube, and the Goths in Spain all carried forward noteworthy parts of the Roman heritage. Even the idea of a universal empire went into abeyance in the West for only 250 years.

Conclusion: A Less than Compelling Explanation

Demandt's argument assembles the efforts of many scholars and molds miscellaneous facts about the *frühgeschichtliche* "Germanic" peoples into a dynamic but ultimately miscarried tale of emergence. He summarizes "the turbulent last stage of a Germanic expansion that is visible ever since early in the first millennium B.C." The individual fragments of this story are not contested here. Tacitus's *Germania* is an excellent ethnography in the ancient manner, complete with lessons of virtue and vice for its Roman readers. The invasions of the Cimbri and Teutons, the struggles of Ariovistus, Arminius, and Maroboduus with the Romans, the gradual settling down of the German *limes*, the Marcomannic War, and even the appearance of single-named Franks, Alamanni, and Saxons in the third century: all have respectable factual bases. The issue is what these and many other fragments add up to. Should they be pinned together into a story line moving in a definite direction? Were the northerners engaged in a deliberate rivalry with their Roman neighbors? Supposing the northern barbarians were a block, were they in a more favorable position vis-à-vis the Empire in the fourth century than they had been in the first? The facts of barbarian activity between Augustus and Theodosius are not, in general, in dispute: what makes the difference is how one fills the empty chronological and geographical space between the facts and how the discontinuities are papered over with warm rhetoric.

Demandt, rolling with a powerful, centuries-old tide of German scholarly interpretation of the evidence—an interpretation widely and often uncritically espoused outside Germany—answers in the affirmative. The argument is not compelling. The fragments on which it is based continue to be fragments that no amount of scholarship and patriotism can link together into a decisive whole. There was no unity among the northerners; they exerted no mounting pressure. The Roman Empire may well have found its existence harder in the fourth century than it had in the first, but the culprit was not a greater force exerted by northern neighbors, since they were no more numerous, no better organized, no more fearsomely armed, and no more hostile than they had been. Leave the Goths to the Cappadocian slave dealers, Julian said—this after he had personally spent years in cat-and-mouse games with Franks and Alamanni on the Rhine. The Persians were worthy of Julian's steel, not the northerners.

It can never be said often enough that the vision of polarity—a coherent north pressing downward along the long river frontiers with the Empire—is a historian's mirage, having only enough substance to nourish an illusion. One way to counteract the image is to remember that the Roman north faced an abundance of non-Germans: unconquered Irish and Britons to the west of Roman Britain, Picts beyond Hadrian's Wall, Sarmatians coursing through the Hungarian steppes, Dacians and Carpi on the lower Danube. Rome's foreign relations in late antiquity were with Huns, Alans, and Avars as well as with Goths, Alamanni, and Herules. This ethnic diversity sets sharp limits on Demandt's contention that only "the Germans" had the ability to dissolve the Empire. Contemporaries had a very different (and more limited) sense of who Germans were than we do. It took until the Carolingian period for a few remarkable intellectuals to recognize that Franks and Goths were linguistic kin.[41] In late Roman times Irish and Picts, Suebic Quadi and Sarmatians, Carpi and Goths could combine intermittently against the Empire, just as they could engage in the sport of warring among themselves. The strains affecting the Empire came as much from its own desire for peace and security for its borders as from the turbulence of its neighbors. External security for the Empire presupposed internal restraint and discipline; it was critically undermined by civil wars between competitors for the imperial throne. Church fathers plucked out of the Hebrew Bible the image of a vat in the north disgorging its masses onto the tremulous weaklings to the south. The notion of external pressure is not a recent invention. Then as now the vat is fuller of emotion than of ferocious enemies.

Demandt's argument twice hinges on changing sides and contradicting previous positions. He starts as a *laudator Germanorum*, brandishing the millennial expansion of the Germanic peoples and their development into a formidable force eventually taking the offensive against the mighty Empire—the traditional discourse of *germanische Frühgeschichte*. But when his account reaches late antiquity he recognizes the weakness of Rome's neighbors and recoups the argument by claiming that poverty enhanced their aggressiveness. The possibility that poverty might turn them instead into dependents of Rome, or of the Huns, is not allowed to intrude.[42] Finally, he abandons "the Germans" altogether and turns into a stern schoolmaster, propounding the view that the barbarians were only fit to be laborers and cannon fodder; Rome's trouble came from letting the immigrants get out of line. Many of them were eliminated, and the survivors spoiled everything, initiating a dark age. Demandt's end point is startlingly remote from the Germanic triumphalism of his beginning.

The injection of a few historical incidents may sharpen the course of the argument. Five years before Odoacer dislodged the last Western emperor, the Eastern emperor Leo rid himself by murder of his overmighty Alanic generalissimo Aspar (471). This purge cleared the way for Leo's son-in-law Zeno, a lately baptized barbarian from Isauria (in Asia Minor), to become his successor. Although Leo's purge is considered symbolic of the Byzantine desire to keep aliens in their place, the symbol is shadowed by its consequence: Leo, in effect, opened the way to the emperorship to a personage, Zeno, arguably more barbarous than the murdered Alan.[43] After Zeno's death, his successor Anastasius in turn purged the Isaurians in a six-year campaign and liberated the government from their grasp. Constantinople shed its barbarian taint and, with the advent of Justinian (527), eventually imposed its domination even over some of the "occupiers" of the West.[44] The ideology of exclusion espoused by Demandt reflects the hostile spirit of sixth-century Byzantium. Barbarians were useful enough in their place. Justinian's armies were full of foreign recruits. Even some of his generals were non-Romans. What was intolerable was that the Empire should harbor independent foreign kings ruling over formerly Roman provincials. Constantinople preferred to have its Balkan provinces continually trodden under foot by invaders rather than see them occupied by autonomous alien residents who might have kept them safe. Byzantine policy toward its backyard in the centuries to come normally preferred a wasteland to independent residents.

Demandt's insistence that barbarians should be suitably stockaded is a view widely shared by his fellow ancient historians. So Justinian's conception of a narrowly Roman empire triumphs, relegating the Goths and Franks to a "barbarian" West, populated not by picked foreigners once thought worthy of marriage into the imperial family but by repugnant aliens (like the Vandals and the Goths) insistently affirmed to be from the Maeotian swamp or Scandinavia— unimaginably distant and savage lands.

That Constantinopolitan outlook was real in its time (we can document it); but nothing compels us to make it our own. Western lands under Gothic or Frankish or even English kings, and underpinned by a Latin church, were as credible offshoots of late Rome as was the East Rome of Byzantium; they were as pure or impure in their Romanity as the city of Constantine. Demandt's decision after a start as *laudator Germanorum* to end with a Byzantine perspective is not one that every reasonable person is compelled to share.

He did not attain this outlook by espousing an all-Roman aversion to "barbarians"; there was no such aversion. He himself has written eloquently about Rome as a melting pot, agreeable to sharing power without awkward questions about ancestry, a Rome confident that the right sort of foreigners was worth having and well aware that its own history was one of continual absorption of (originally) foreign persons and ideas. The military aristocracy of the late Roman Empire, to whose detection Demandt has enormously contributed, was well designed to absorb barbarian military leaders (and followers) and to harness them to the defense of imperial values.[45] It is a mystery, in view of Demandt's other writings, how he manages to forget himself when speaking about the ultimate effects of foreigners in late antiquity.

Chapter 3

An Entrenched Myth of Origins:
The Germans before Germany

Ernst Stein was a major twentieth-century historian of late antiquity. Austrian by birth and education, he obtained a personal chair of ancient history at the University of Berlin in 1927 and was visiting Belgium in 1933 when Hitler became chancellor of Germany. Stein, a Jew, responded decisively to the advent of Hitler. Immediately resigning his German ties, he stayed in Belgium and after various hardships died in Switzerland in 1945.[1]

This historian totally without illusions about the Germany of his day needs to be kept in mind when considering the received wisdom about Germans before Germany. Stein had been reared in the days of Wilhelm II and Franz Josef; he had no reservations about the existence of a coherent primitive Germanic civilization prior to our Middle Ages. Though he stopped writing in German as a protest against Nazism, his excellent *Histoire du Bas-Empire* affirms that the northern barbarians had imported Germanic culture into the western Roman provinces they occupied.[2] If Germanic continuity out of the distant past was an unqualified certainty to a man of Stein's learning and political decisiveness, it is hardly surprising that many scholars of today in Europe and the United States still cherish the existence of a "Germanic world" long antedating medieval and modern Germany.

Stein's widely shared misconception needs to be actively challenged. A common opinion about the late Roman Empire is that it experienced a one-to-one confrontation with a barbarian or northern or "Germanic" world, and that the foreigners won. An American medievalist proposed in 1988 that "the Germanic world was perhaps the greatest . . . creation of Roman political and military genius."[3] In other words, we should admire Rome for spawning the monster by which it was destroyed. Exaggerations of this sort are encouraged by the deeply entrenched myth of a prehistoric and early Germany (*germanische Vor- und Frühgeschichte*), foreshadowing the one we know. The subject I am discussing is not what happened to the Roman Empire in late antiquity, and who or what was responsible for its fate.[4] What matters is whether its purported antagonist—the alleged entity called "the Germanic world"—existed and, no less important, how we happen to believe that it did.

Rome Faced a Fragmented "Outside"

The Roman Empire of the fourth century has left us a document that opens by listing "all the [imperial] provinces," diocese by diocese, then complements them with a catalogue of "the barbarian peoples who have multiplied under the emperors."[5] The catalogue aligns fifty peoples bordering the Empire, running— to select fourteen names out of the fifty—from Irish and Picts in the far west; Franks, Alamanni, and Juthungi on the Rhine; Quadi and Vandals on the middle Danube; Sarmatians, Carpi, and Goths on the lower Danube; Armenians and Palmyrenes in the east; then back west again to Moors in Mauretania and Cantabrians in the Pyrenees. The message of this Verona List is of a highly organized Roman state looking outward to a dust cloud of fragmented peoples of varying ethnicities normally unable to unite with each other. This image of fragmentation belongs not just to the fourth century but to all the "barbarian" frontiers as they existed in the imperial period, with the possible exception of Parthia and Sasanian Persia in the east. Some of the peoples named in the list are known *to us* as Germans, though it is certain that they did not use this name among themselves. Quite a few others, such as the Irish, the Sarmatians, the Carpi, the Armenians, and the Moors were not German by any standard. Today's historians sometimes speak of the Empire as having had a "German problem" or something comparably concentrated to worry about. No contemporary (after Tacitus) uses such words. The most paranoid Roman author of late antiquity evokes only "wild nations" hiding behind natural obstacles and assailing every frontier.[6] There is a great difference between this vision of incoherence or, at least, multiplicity and the belief that Rome faced, let alone created, a "Germanic world."

Real German History and Its Fictional Anticipation

There is no doubt that today's Germany has a long and captivating history, but it starts only in the Christian Middle Ages. "In the decades around 800 scholars close to the Carolingian court begin to grapple with the nature of the Germanic vernaculars. . . . Smaragdus of St. Mihiel was struck by the similarities of Gothic and Frankish personal names, and, like a good ethnologist, Smaragdus made the linguistic affinity the basis for a thesis of a historical link between the two peoples. . . . The idea of a common Germanic linguistic heritage was evidently discussed by Hrabanus [Maurus], Freculph [of Lisieux], Walahfrid [Strabo] and others at court, and led to the idea that the Germanic-speaking peoples had a shared history."[7] The Carolingian period was fruitful in the creation of a German consciousness. It is then that we first encounter the word *thiudiscus*, out of which eventually came the term *Deutschen* for medieval and modern Germans and *Deutschland* for Germany.[8] Many of the peoples who lived toward A.D. 850 in what we think of as German space may have been Slavs or something else; the past that many others identified with was Saxon or Frankish or Bavarian rather than German. However that may be, Charlemagne's grandson Louis "the German" was originally provided with the duchy of Bavaria, and the widening of this land after his father's death foreshadows the German territory of the Ottos and other medieval emperors. The complicated process by which a Germany came into being was under way. There was a monarchy around which the peoples of the east Frankish kingdom might rally and, before very long, that same monarchy assumed the vacant imperial crown.[9]

The Germans of today have a more-than-millennial history; in the competition among nations for venerable antiquity, they cannot complain of being shortchanged. But many modern authors in and out of Germany have not been content with so shallow a past. Some considered it essential—much as their medieval ancestors had—to supply their land with an older pedigree. Extravagance in the search for ancient roots was by no means limited to medieval and early modern players of this game.[10] In and around 1910, the philologist and prehistorian Gustaf Kossinna (†1931), by the application of a "regressive method," happily extended the origins of the "ancient Germans" from the second century B.C. backward into the Bronze Age (the second millennium B.C.) and even to the Paleolithic. Jumping nimbly from one discipline to the next—linguistics, archaeology, physical anthropology, and more—Kossinna mapped the changing boundaries of the Germanic homeland and reconstructed in bold, decisive strokes a "first" Germanic migration of peoples (*Völkerwanderung*) that extended all over Europe.[11] In a different place and age, Kossinna's crude racism and extreme interpretations might have earned him the label of a crank; in Wilhelmine Germany he won a chair of prehistory at the University of Berlin (1900). His ideas about the early Germans, which have long circulated apart from his name, have been only superficially purged from the writings of today.[12] Although Kossinna and the prehistoric "Germany" that he helped to create deserve to be better known and pilloried, the concept of an ancient Germanic civilization that he elaborated was far from being his invention. It was already deeply entrenched when he appeared on the scene. He gave archaeological grounding to widely espoused ideas.[13] If Europe has had a supreme invented tradition, that of the Germans before Germany is it—so much so that most people who speak about it do not realize that they are dealing with fiction.

This tale of anticipation—Germans before Germany—which has seemed monumentally solid in recent centuries and certainly formed a block when Ernst Stein appealed to it, has a complicated past whose intricacies have been studied by many scholars inside and outside Germany. Some, like Paul Joachim-sen, have striven to see how the "true" story about Germanic antiquity detached itself from medieval and Renaissance legends. Others without concern for his-toricity have focused on the legends themselves as not lacking in interest and charm.[14] Others still have drawn our attention to lasting illusions: "[Jacob] Grimm [ca. 1830] and those who followed him [regarded] Germanic antiquity as a common civilization of those who spoke the Germanic languages, and a civilization to which they clung tenaciously through the centuries."[15] Scholars who (as in a case noted below) sentimentalized about good fairies laying the gift of Tacitus's *Germania* in the cradle of German history were hardly free of a per-sonal desire to detect and confirm definable ancient roots.

Some medieval legends offer avenues of reflection preferable to those pro-posed by modern scholarship. Vernacular chroniclers in twelfth- and thirteenth-century Germany held that the early Germans whom Julius Caesar had defeated joined and helped him to seize the supreme power that his successors conveyed to Charlemagne. A tale of this sort, with its vision of Germans developing via a detour through Rome, would have had scant appeal in Wilhelmine Germany (1888–1918); but, as a metaphor for the course of events between the first and sixth centuries, it stands closer to historical truth than Kossinna's *Urgermanen* in the Bronze Age.[16] The tale shows that medieval Germans agreed with their de-scendants in wishing to have a pre-Christian past. This version rubbed shoulders with many competing medieval notions of early Germans. It, along with many of its competitors, has since been wiped from the slate in preference for ostensibly scientific substitutes.

Origin Stories and Tacitus's *Germania*

Only two of the multiple traditions once in circulation have weathered the gauntlet of scholarly criticism and continue down to the present to imprint on all and sundry a belief in a "Germanic world." They are, first, Tacitus's brief ethnographic treatise *Germania*, little noticed in antiquity but rediscovered in fifteenth-century Europe with spectacular results; and, second, origin stories common to medieval historiography from before the Carolingian age and rolling on unhindered in historical literature down to our time. The convergence and mingling of these elements, later enriched by a philological concept of the Germanic languages, produced the firm doctrine that Ernst Stein learned in school and never doubted.[17] This doctrine grounded in early sources continues to be presented to us in all simplicity and sincerity as though it were indeed our window into a true past.

A century ago, John Bagnell Bury was named Regius Professor of Modern History at the University of Cambridge, where "modern" history was understood to begin at the fall of Rome. Bury was already famed for a superb edition of Gibbon's *Decline and Fall of the Roman Empire* as well as for several histories of his own of late Rome and Byzantium; he opened his Cambridge teaching with lectures about the barbarians in the late Roman world (1903). These lectures, continually improved, appeared posthumously under the title *The Invasions of Europe by the Barbarians* and have long been a standard work on this subject.[18] Bury's introductory chapter on "The Germans and their Wanderings" rests foursquare on Tacitus's *Germania* as regards the Germans and on Jordanes's *Gothic History* as regards their travels. At the other extremity of the twentieth century, a widely circulated collection of translated sources for the history of the European Middle Ages opens with a section called "The Barbarian World," in which are aligned Tacitus's *Germania*, the *Gothic History* of Jordanes, and the surviving fragment of an Old High German heroic poem called *Hildebrandslied*.[19] These items, possibly excepting the third, are representative of an almost unshakable tradition in presentations of "Europe" on the eve of the Middle Ages. Students being introduced to the barbarian past are not diverted by the dust cloud of fifty foreign neighbors of the Empire that would greet them in the Verona List; they are presented instead with a single "barbarian world" alternative to the Roman Empire.

To students only just encountering this subject, as well as to instructors specializing in other medieval (and even later) periods, Tacitus and Jordanes have a look of inevitability, as the voices of unvarnished historical truth. The two authors have precisely defined roles. The first seats the early Germans firmly in readers' consciousness, giving them a collective identity and equipping them with the continuity of established institutions and customs. The somewhat uncouth Jordanes, who knows "Germans" only in a narrow sense and rarely mentions them, is the apostle of origins and "migration," establishing beyond question that the "foreigners" were truly alien to Rome and wandered south from far distant lands. Tacitus considered the Germans aboriginal, since so unappealing a land could not attract immigrants, but Jordanes, more amply informed, conjures up an island of "Scandza" (Scandinavia) in the northern Ocean from which his Goths and their companion peoples set forth on their long travels.[20] Although Tacitus and Jordanes are usually set before readers in the chronological order of their birthdays, they are better understood historiographically if Jordanes is placed in the lead, since his influence, unlike Tacitus's, was exercised from the earliest centuries of the Middle Ages.

Emigrations from Exotic Homelands

In the A.D. 600s the by then long-established Frankish kingdom acquired a pedigree that reached back to the Trojan War, the seedbed of Greek and Roman history. According to the anonymous historian whom we call Fredegar, the earliest Franks were, like the descendants of Aeneas, refugees from the fall of Troy. Fredegar also relates the remote beginnings of the Burgundians and the Lombards. He even reports a second Frankish origin tale, more precisely a royal genealogy, involving a sea monster.[21] Some 250 years earlier, Ambrose of Milan at a moment of crisis on the lower Danube frontier had recalled the Old Testament prophecies portending "a seething pot pouring forth the families of the kingdoms of the north" upon hapless Jerusalem: "Thus saith the Lord, Behold, a people cometh from the north country and a great nation shall be raised from the sides of the earth" (Jeremiah 6:22). Generalized references such as these to the Old Testament were superseded by precise details from the time of Justinian (A.D. 518–65) onward through the Middle Ages. Allusions to vaguely northern peoples were gradually replaced by individual tales documenting how Goths, Burgundians, Lombards, and Saxons got the better of the mighty Roman Empire. Among today's historians this panorama of barbarian migration and conquest devised in the Middle Ages is by no means outdated. The stately library of modern works on this theme, begun in the sixteenth century, has now been rounded out by Walter Pohl's *Die Völkerwanderung: Eroberung und Integration*, a work wholly in the mainstream of current scholarship.[22]

From the sixth century onward, authors shaped and reshaped the historical consciousness of Christian Europe. Jordanes, sitting in the capital of the East Roman Empire after 551, wrote an account of the Goths in which he claimed that, eons ago, even before the Trojan War, they had migrated southward from Scandinavia. The northernness of the Goths had been established by Ambrose (†397) and their descent from frigid climates had been confirmed by the poet Claudian († ca. 404).[23] Jordanes supplied a precise identification: the Goths were led by King Berig out of the island of Scandza which lay at the extremity of the world and was a veritable womb of nations. On Jordanes's say-so, other foreign peoples, such as the Vandals and Gepids, could be traced to distant homes on the shores of the Baltic.[24] The game of ethnic origins, initially handled with vague biblical generalities about the north, had an intensive workout in the two centuries between Justinian and Charlemagne. Jordanes's Scandzan identification was launched in Constantinople, where other authors were busy, too, rewriting and fudging the origins of Rome so as to elevate the status of the New Rome over the Old. From the Goths the same remote origin was carried over to the tales of Lombard and Burgundian beginnings.[25] These various initiatives rarely referred to Germans; no one claimed to be relating the prehistory of a single ethnic group. Taken collectively, the narratives of how one people after the other traveled from far away and settled into Roman territory could add up to what the humanists Konrad Peutinger and Beatus Rhenanus in the sixteenth century recognized as "*conmigrationes*" and what today Walter Pohl still relates in the same terms, namely, accounts of a collective "migration of peoples" or *Völkerwanderung*.[26] To us moderns, these are not just any old migrants: they are portrayed as emphatically "Germanic," even though none of the participants was aware that such might be the case.

Historians in the Middle Ages had little incentive to purify the stories they received. Isidore of Seville (†636), though the greatest scholar of his age, had never heard of a Gothic connection to Scandinavia. He did not mind presenting the Goths (among whom he had been born and lived) as having three origins— Scythians, Getae, and Magog, son of Japhet.[27] Since any sort of certainty was elusive, what mattered was that the story told should be adapted to the needs of the author's clients or audience. In this way, for example, Widukind of Corvey in the tenth century imagined that (unlike the Franks descended from Troy) the Saxons were Macedonian soldiers stranded in the wars of Alexander the Great.[28] Stabs at criticism, minor as they were, sometimes had the effect of propagating Byzantine fictions. Frechulf of Lisieux, a distinguished historian in the Carolingian age, was not wholly satisfied by the established theory that the Franks started as refugees from the Trojan War. Others believe, he said, that they were from Scandinavia like the Goths and the other *nationes Theotistae*.[29]

Frechulf's precocious attempt to impose reason on diversity easily leads to modern misconceptions that there was a medieval "debate (*Auseinandersetzung*)" among competing traditions and that a particular side "won":

In the Middle Ages there arose a debate of [on the one hand] the tribal traditions brought by the Germanic tribes from their homes with [on the other hand] old Roman and biblical traditions that related to the Roman Troy story, reports of ancient geographers and ethnographers about Getae and Scythians and about fabulous peoples such as the Amazons, and finally the ethnographic information of the Old Testament.

This debate led to the most peculiar combinations of diverse traditions, but the autonomous (*eigenständig*) Germanic tradition succeeded in winning out. Knowledge of homeland and migration route was not lost. The derivation of the Goths, Burgundians, and Langobards from Scandinavia is maintained in Jordanes, Fredegar, the *Passio Sigismundi regis*, the *Origo Langobardorum*, and Paul the Deacon.[30]

Erich Zöllner, the author of these lines, argues in a circle, helped along by his fantasy of "good" Germanic memories encountering "old Roman and biblical traditions." This allows him to segregate the tales brought by barbarians from "their homes," which he regards as being authentic, that is to say, those origins that he by a wholly modern choice decides embody "the autonomous (*eigenständig*) Germanic tradition."[31] Medieval authors were as unsystematic as Isidore. Jordanes, prized by moderns for evoking Scandinavia, does not limit himself to that; he has the Goths also descend from the Scythians, the Parthians, the Amazons, and the Getae—the more the merrier. There was no debate between Germanic and Mediterranean traditions because the ostensible debaters neither were able to distinguish which was which nor cared to do so.[32]

As well illustrated by Frank Borchardt's *German Antiquity in Renaissance Myth* (1971), the national or tribal origins articulated at the close of the Middle Ages were wonderfully disorganized and copious. Where they seemed incomplete, the imagination of Annius of Viterbo and Johannes Trithemius rounded them out by invention. In 1557, the Viennese Wolfgang Lazius published a voluminous, illustrated treatise "About certain migrations of peoples," showing how nations had trekked from far and near to take their places in the scraggly dominions of the Habsburg rulers of the Holy Roman Empire. Lazius was a Renaissance humanist, but his image of a Migration Age culminating in the Habsburg lands of his day was wholly in keeping with the uncritical spirit of medieval historical writing.[33]

Few modern accounts of barbarians in late antiquity avoid being fixated on distant origins; Pohl's is no exception. Goths or Vandals or Franks cannot be mentioned simply as peoples who lived on the edge of the Roman world in A.D. 150 or 250. "Here, too, [as with other peoples] the first question that has to be asked concerns the homeland and origins of [the Goths] who had such a decisive influence on important phases of the Great Migrations."[34] The unshakable premise is that misty "homelands" have priority over the lands where the Goths resided for at least two centuries before they moved west. As prelude to the Lombard invasion of Italy in 568, another author invokes "the people of the 'Longbeards' coming from the Elbe." The Lombards, though reliably attested in the lower Elbe ca. A.D. 98, are recorded near the Danube in the later second century and were well ensconced in the Danube valley by 489 and until they invaded Italy.[35] What possible relevance does the Elbe still have to Lombards in

568? What compulsion is there to probe "points of origin" that are usually un-knowable? *Cui bono?* These questions are unasked. Any respectable book about the barbarians and Rome treats us, people by people, with multiple speculations about origins, on the premise that where erudition has made so much smoke there must be fire.[36] A whole library of nineteenth- and twentieth-century schol-arship can be evoked to show that a "Germanic antiquity" existed in parallel to its Greco-Roman counterpart. Émilienne Demougeot explains what lies behind her volumes on "the formation of Europe and the barbarian invasions": "To [the knowledge] of Roman Europe there correspond the first syntheses of K. Mül-lenhoff, F. Kauffmann, and A. Meitzen down to the *Vorgeschichte der deutschen Stämme* published under the direction of H. Reinerth [Gustav Kossinna's chief disciple], taken up or condensed by various *Germanische Stammeskunde,* and all the way to the *Geschichte der deutschen Stämme* of L. Schmidt, general studies that are further enriched by the monographs devoted to the different peoples."[37] Sheer speculations elaborated with scholarly fervor appear to become weighty— better founded than the discarded alternatives. On the basis of labored erudi-tion, an earlier existence is almost always evoked, from which the relevant peoples departed in order to cluster eventually around the Roman imperial frontier.[38] Behind a mask of erudition and critical rigor, modern historians of the barbarians associate themselves with tales that seem true for having been passed from mouth to mouth for about fifteen hundred years. They are worthy heirs to the inventive medieval narrators of distant origins who set the Migra-tion Age in motion.

The Good Fairy's Baptismal Gift

The myth of the Germans before Germany has a second component, much later in making its appearance. Unlike the exuberant medieval chapter, this con-stituent specifically concerns Germany. Its point of departure was the rediscov-ery of Tacitus's *Germania* in the late fifteenth century. The dissemination of this treatise on the eve of the Reformation had revolutionary effects on the collec-tive consciousness of Germans: it was "the Magna Carta of their national self-confidence."[39] Around Tacitus's *Germania* an early German history arose, carried forward without pause down to the present. Germanic devotion to the martial virtues, their unrestricted birthrate, and their love of liberty were among the moral traits conveyed out of the Germanic forests into medieval Europe. Taci-tus, who recognized the multiplicity of the peoples of "Germania," gave them a semblance of unity by describing their collective "institutions" and mores, selected primarily to be as different as possible from those of the "civilized" world. Recently written books retracing Tacitus's footsteps, with ostensible improvements, are widely found in bookstores and libraries.[40]

When Tacitus's brief ethnography called *Germania* appeared in A.D. 98, it may or may not have had an audience; but Tacitus's little book had long been forgotten when the Goth Alaric and the Vandal Geiseric broke into the city of Rome (A.D. 410, 455), and it did not enjoy a revival. There is no reason for us, any more than there was for fourth-century Romans, to believe that anything that Tacitus wrote about first-century Germans had any relevance to peoples or problems in late antiquity. The *Germania*, after its initial appearance, surfaced fleetingly in the sixth century and again in the ninth, never creating any turbulence.[41] Tacitus's ethnography finally won popularity almost a millennium and a half after its composition. A twentieth-century commentator, somewhat carried away, referred to it as being the baptismal gift that "a good fairy of our people laid in the cradle of our fatherland's history."[42] However that may be, the unearthed *Germania* gave birth to the modern discipline of "Germanic antiquity," called *germanische* (or *deutsche*) *Altertumskunde*.

Tacitus designed the *Germania* to be informative about the peoples whom Roman armies faced across the Rhine. The work lost urgency when the hot spots of frontier defense moved eastward to the Danube and Dacia; and it was not found relevant later still when "German" (that is, Frankish) generals and troops had major roles in late Roman warfare. When the *Germania* was consulted on the sixth century, the subject focused on was merely amber.[43] In early modern Europe, however, Tacitus's ethnography won the attention it had formerly been denied because there now was a Germany, the "German nation" that had come into existence since the Carolingians, which Tacitus could now equip with a heaven-sent ancient dignity and pedigree. The *Germania* became a magnet around which humanists assembled and organized the information that ancient Latin and Greek authors supplied in abundance, but mainly in scraps, not only about Germans under that name but also about the various peoples that starred in the medieval origin legends. To those displeased with the Germany of the present, Tacitus offered an alternative Germany of the distant past. In an erudite tradition already ending its first century, the great Antwerp atlas maker Abraham Ortelius published a work in 1596 called "Image of the Golden Age, or Life of the Ancient Germans" (*Aurei saeculi imago, sive Germanorum veterum vita*). Another geographer, Philipp Clüver, spent years at Oxford compiling his *Germania antiqua*. This massive work, published in 1616 to the astonishment of the learned world, earned Clüver a research professorship at Leiden University.[44] These were chapters in the obsessive scholarship applied to ancient

Germany, an industry that has never flagged. Antiquities, archaeology, onomastics, philology—you name it: they all contributed to the elaboration of *deutsche Altertumskunde*, the still honored "science" of German antiquity.[45]

German *Altertumskunde* Today

Tacitus definitely wrote the *Germania*, and Jordanes just as definitely composed an account of the Goths. The sources that scholars have mined with mounting skill and refinement since the fifteenth century have factual content. Kossinna's cavemen as *Urgermanen* may be a bad joke played (however sincerely) on scholarship, but the Cimbri and Teutons, who were claimed as Germanic, did descend upon southern Gaul and northern Italy in the second century B.C., wreaking havoc before being totally destroyed.[46] The Cheruscan Arminius really did lead a rebellion that resulted in a great Roman defeat and the destruction of three legions that Augustus could ill afford. A coalition of Marcomanni and other peoples did fight for more than a decade against the emperor Marcus Aurelius. The Goths and Herules, Alamanni and Franks, all had moments of spectacular success against Rome in the third century.[47] The abundant, scattered evidence for the existence and activity of the peoples along the northern borders of the Roman Empire and farther inland is not discredited by the existence of a basically fictional collective history of Germans before Germany. What this collective history does imply is that the methods and presuppositions applied to forging this evidence into a consecutive whole have been better suited to producing fantasies of migration and of a coherent early Germany than to describing dispassionately the fragmented multiple neighbors faced by Rome.

The collapse of the Third German Reich in 1945 did not ruin *deutsche Altertumskunde* but dealt it a blow. The strictly German dimension has made some commentators uncomfortable, and the migrations of whole tribes across centuries and maps have been severely criticized.[48] More limited positions, however, are still very firmly anchored. As argued by Reinhard Wenskus, Herwig Wolfram, and their adherents, certain "Germanic" peoples maintained chains of tradition descending from a distant past, some reaching as far back indeed as Jordanes's Scandinavia or Paul the Deacon's equally remote geographical point of departure.[49] These "nuclei of tradition" (*Traditionskerne*), cherished and nursed by ancient families—which, among other things, perpetuated tribal names—allowed barbarian tribes to form and re-form by giving a focus to multicultural recruits and inspiring them to associate and identify themselves with the *Traditionskerne* that the leading families fostered.[50] The "tribe formations" of the early Middle Ages (so it is claimed) were the culmination of chains of tribe formations in the earlier "Germanic" past; Goths and Lombards linked the Scandinavian ancestors of the distant past with the Germans of today. Wolfram is listened to with approval in all countries that care about this subject. Another Vienna historian, Erich Zöllner, quoted a few paragraphs ago, has evoked "sources written altogether in the Germanic spirit even though [they are] in Latin and, at least partly, by authors of Romance origin." How this otherwise undocumented "Germanic spirit" is to be detected in Latin writings is left wholly unexplained; we are supposed to "know."[51] To hear Wolfram and others, Latin accounts of Goths, Franks, or Lombards should be regarded not as works of medieval historical literature, but as tribal histories faithfully safeguarding ethnic memories of religious intensity. Provided this channel is allowed to exist, large quantities of substantive "Germanic" content can be sent scuttling along it to the medieval world. To Wolfram, mere names and words divulge whole episodes of lost history in surprising and improbable detail.[52] It has been ever so in the optimistic erudition of *deutsche Altertumskunde*, in which, to take a salient example, the island of Bornholm in the Baltic has only to bear this name in order to prove that the Burgundian people originated from there or at least pulled in for a little rest.[53]

The myth of the Germans before Germany is hard to suppress because, owing to its great age and genesis in the sources themselves, it is solidly entrenched in the European mind. Even its younger component, the rediscovered *Germania*, has been assiduously publicized for more than five hundred years. The decisive steps in the creation of this myth were taken in sixth-century Constantinople and sixteenth-century Germany. From these remote (and therefore venerable) starting points almost irresistible beliefs descended upon the European historical consciousness—one tradition of peoples from far away pouring over the Roman Empire and taking away its lands, another tradition of Germans growing in strength, wisdom, and individuality beyond the imperial borders as the pre-Christian northern peoples whose virtues and customs built a new civilization in the formerly Roman provinces.

I began with Ernst Stein so as to show that a historian with impeccable credentials subscribed to the existence of Germans before Germany—that this myth was nonpartisan and all-European, and only tenuously connected to the terrifying ideologies of the mid-twentieth century. Herwig Wolfram begins many of his writings by complaining of being misunderstood and persecuted for writing about the Goths. These torments are imaginary. Wolfram has gardenered many honors; he is very widely read and translated; the Goths, among other interests, have buoyed up his eminent career. Adherents of his have claimed that their teachings have been smeared by association with Nazism.[54] Nothing could be further from the truth. There are much more serious reasons than belated denazification for trying to come to terms with this entrenched myth of origins. The faith in Germanic continuity has prevailed for many centuries, damaging everything it has touched: Germans and other Europeans need to be assured that they can dispense with a link to the *Germanen*, that there is such a thing as historical change, and that the transgressions of national pasts can indeed be outgrown.

The Byzantine Trap

As already mentioned, medieval Germany possessed a vernacular legend that the Germans were first subdued by Caesar then, by helping him, became heirs to the Roman Empire. As though to reproach this ancient tale, Hermann Aubin wrote (1943): "A great intellectual impetus was needed to roll away the enormous burden of biblical-classical convention in historical conceptualization and to find an independent point of departure for German history outside the *orbis universus*. Yet German historical research set about this liberation from [the time of] Beatus Rhenanus and Wimpfeling onward and has achieved it."[55] It needs to be asked whether this discovery of a launching pad outside the *orbis universus*—that is, Germans before Germany—was really a triumph of modern German historical conceptualization. Aubin's statement invites the question whether what he calls "liberation" was not rather an entanglement in someone else's historical deception. The sixth-century Goths and their fellow "barbarians" had been long-settled neighbors of the Empire and then fellow residents and sometimes rulers of imperial soil. When and under whose auspices did they lose their familiar cast and take on a truly alien appearance complete with remote launching pads? Aubin hails the sixteenth-century humanists who detached the Germanic peoples from Gog and Magog and Trojans and Scythians and set them upon their *emigrationes* and *conmigrationes*, preferably out of the distant north. But it needs to be asked who, besides Tacitus, gave the humanists the wherewithal for doing so and to what end? Aubin proceeded on the premise that an authentic spring of pure Germanic water had been tapped. He and the other devotees of *deutsche Altertumskunde* may simply have fallen into the trap laid by Byzantine historians in the sixth century when the latter provided their long-time "barbarian" neighbors, fellow residents, and helpers with remote nests to originate from and, as one might hope, to return to.

The multiple "northern" peoples who bordered the Roman Empire toward the middle of the fourth century were at rest. Sedentary and agrarian, they had been living there for a long time—some of them for a very long time indeed. With no apparent desire to move, their aggressive impulses were held in equilibrium by the Roman armies, and they engaged in lively exchanges across the borders. When a crisis came unexpectedly upon the Goths out of the east in the 370s, the Empire was where many of them rushed for protection. Nowhere do we detect a vibrant desire for independence, let alone an impulse to state forma- tion.[56] Even the new religion of the Empire had begun its penetration across the frontier, alienating its converts from their "native" traditions and inviting adher- ence to a Mediterranean myth. A notable intake of bodies into the Empire as sol- diers and laborers was well under way and had every appearance of continuing; the Roman provinces had room for immigrants, and not just as peasants and cannon fodder. The first name-giving Roman consul of Frankish birth took his one-year term of office in 362; it was the highest (subimperial) dignity to which a Roman could aspire, and it reflected the enormous place of Franks and Ala- manni as officers and troops in the Roman armies of the Western provinces.[57] It was certain in the fourth century that persons from beyond the established bor- ders could count on having Roman futures if they shaped up—as they clearly did—in the scramble for imperial dignities and honors. Here were New Men taking their places, as waves of provincial *novi homines* had before, in shoulder- ing the burdens of universal empire.

Our maps for history show Western Europe in 500 as postimperial, carved up into foreign successor kingdoms, called *germanische Reichsgründungen* by modern German authors. Reality was less straightforward and clear cut. As late as the advent of the emperor Justinian in 527, and for at least another decade, there was an uninterruptedly functioning Roman government in Italy and an equally continuous pope in Rome able to thwart the religious policies of East- ern emperors.[58] The Roman Empire was not a monolith; the double empire brought into being by Theodosius I in 395 continued to have meaning in the West even when its form had become diffuse. Among other signs of intimacy between Romans and their foreign associates, a Vandal married into the im- perial family, a Hun aspired to be an imperial brother-in-law, and a Gothic woman served as lady-in-waiting to a Roman empress in Constantinople.[59] The kings ruling in North Africa, Italy, the Rhone Valley, Aquitaine, and Spain had not seized their lands by force alone. Sustained by Roman sanction for their es- tablishment, the kings were by no means unable, with suitable lay and clerical helpers, to govern the Roman lands and people subjected to their rule. The arts of peace continued to be cultivated and the frontiers to be defended.

These facts did not fit into a Justinianic outlook. With the advent of Justin- ian's uncle, Justin I, in 518 a completely new clique took control of the palace at Constantinople.[60] In the perspective of Justinian's New Rome, various unprece- dented and politically convenient truths began to circulate. The Western Em- pire, it seems, had fallen into the hands of "Gothic" kings in 476; Odoacer, it seems, was a fur-clad king of Goths or even of Torkilingi (an otherwise wholly unknown but clearly alien people); the Vandals, it seems, had come from the remote Sea of Azov and were squatting lawlessly on Roman land; the Goths, it seems, had migrated from remote Scandinavia and had no right to Italy or Spain.[61] Western kings who ruled over Roman populations and churches, espoused Roman laws and institutions, and had no inkling of distant exotic pasts, ranked in Byzantium solely as repulsive aliens. The only Roman legitimacy was in the East. Whatever lay in the West could not be Roman; the last emperor had been toppled in 476 and his dominions had been seized by greedy aliens, who had taken advantage of his error in inviting their help.[62] This Constantinopolitan interpretation of recent history wiped the Roman name from the Western provinces except in lands won back for the emperor.

From the Renaissance to the present, the Justinianic interpretation of late antiquity—not recognized to be a partisan distortion—has proved extraordinarily appealing to students of late Roman and "early German" history. The great rolling tide of medieval tradition affirming exotic "tribal" beginnings swept modern observers along, the more so when the ancient Germany of Tacitus supplied a focus for turning a scattered story into the simple, compelling scenario of a one-to-one confrontation of "Germans" against Rome. In modern conceptions of late antiquity, the Germans before Germany express the impossibility of anything but a hostile contest between the Roman Empire and its foreign neighbors. Germans and Romans had for centuries, so it seemed, been in a fight to the death, and the Germans won. So conceived, the Germans before Germany are the instrument that wipes the Roman name from the Western provinces, installs crude and unruly barbarian kingdoms in its place, and begins a Dark Age in the West.

The idea of "barbarians" originating from precise remote places, such as the Sea of Azov or Scandinavia, far beyond the limits of the Roman world, dates from the age of Justinian; it went hand in hand with the discovery that the Western Empire of Rome ended in A.D. 476. These fictions suited the opinion makers of Justinian's time, justifying and glorifying the deeds of the regime. It was appropriate, in the Justinianic perspective, not to dwell on the long residence of Goths, Vandals, and others inside the Roman world or the continuity of a Western Roman government under the auspices of Gothic delegates. The fall of the West to aliens from afar, "facts" fashioned by sixth-century authors, proved only too agreeable to modern Germans seeking ancient roots far outside the *orbis universus*, as well as to generations of ancient historians wishing to have a definite date and firm circumstances for the end of the Roman Empire. Byzantine falsehoods went unrecognized as partisan manifestos and turned into historical truths; modern errors gained strength from being uncritically anchored in sources of venerable age.

I think we can wrestle free of this historiographic muddle. There was no Germanic world before the Carolingian age; late antiquity did not experience a one-to-one confrontation of barbarism against civilization. The myth of Germans before Germany makes a great difference to the way in which the early Middle Ages are envisaged. By dispensing with it, we should be able to outgrow talk of a Dark Age and, in its place, resurrect an early medieval West that was hardly less Roman in its existence than the overbearing New Rome at Byzantium.

Jordanes's Getica *and the Disputed Authenticity of Gothic Origins from Scandinavia*

The noted Prussian historian Heinrich von Sybel said, "A nation that does not keep a living connection with its origins is close to withering, as certainly so as a branch that has been cut from its roots. We are still today what we were yesterday."[1] This is a harmless remark—one historian's statement among many others affirming the civic relevance of his subject. It might be paraphrased as "History is important. A country that does not cultivate its history is like a branch torn from its trunk." What has importance when such a saying is invoked is the content poured by users into the neutral outlines. Is it enough for us Americans to maintain a living connection with the Revolution and George Washington, or do we need to go back to the first European immigrants, or to the homelands from which the Europeans came, or more remotely still to the past of native Americans? Should we understand ourselves to be still what the Hopewell people once were? A lighthearted answer might be, All the above and much more; you cannot have too much history. But, in some contexts (and Sybel's looks like one of them), history is deeply serious. To touch certain parts of it with the scalpel of criticism seems comparable to tearing out the heart of a nation. In the 1690s Gabriel Daniel was forced to retract the opening volume of his *Histoire de France* because he dismissed the historicity of the Merovingian ancestor Pharamond. So patriotism, faith in the good old story, triumphed over the temerity of the critic.[2] Cherished tales of origins die hard.

A Privileged Origin?

The report that the earliest Goths departed from Scandinavia for the Continent at some undetermined moment in the distant past still commands an impressive body of believers. The most recent translator of Jordanes's Gothic history into

French prizes the link to Scandinavia as "all the more precious information in that it is traced to the oral tradition of the Goths."[3] Experts in Germanic literature, who instantly discount reports of Trojan or Scythian or Noachic origins as being fabulous, solemnly assent: emigration from Scandinavia is an authentic "tribal memory," the one kernel of historicity to be plucked from an unholy stew of misconceptions and fabrications.[4] And that emigration from the far north holds not only for the Goths but for quite a few other peoples including the Burgundians and the Vandals. The Middle Ages mixed together all sorts of origin legends, but amid "the most peculiar combinations of diverse traditions, . . . the autonomous (*eigenständig*) Germanic tradition succeeded in winning out. Knowledge of homeland and migration route was not lost."[5] It is as though medieval Germans had such critical sensitivity, or obstinate patriotism, that in spite of being assailed by competing origin legends of learned origin, they clung fast to the old, true one reaching back to the frozen homelands.

This characterization of medieval Germans cannot be accurate. The amiably messy origin stories found in medieval and Renaissance writings by no means attest to the "success" of an autonomous Germanic tradition in "winning out." This alleged success required the discernment and acumen of modern scholars, who are indeed trained (as earlier scholars were not) to detect a difference between the descent of Goths from Scandinavia and their descent from the Scythians or Magog, grandson of Noah. Even here, there is a decisive condition: the source of the Scandinavian version has to be preferable for serious, historical reasons to the obviously literary alternatives. This, too, cannot be taken for granted.

"*Origo Gothica*, the Particular Origin of the Goths"

The story that the Goths (and others) departed from Scandinavia in the hoary mists of time—long before the Trojan War—survives originally in only one mid-sixth-century document, the *Gothic History*, or *Getica*, of Jordanes.[6] In the words of Peter Heather, "The core of any argument in favor of [a] link between the Goths and Scandinavia remains, therefore, the *Getica*'s account of Berig's migration." A later author, Arne Søby Christensen, states, "It is still only through an analysis of the text in the *Getica* that we can hope to verify or refute Jordanes's claim that the Goths once emigrated from *Scandza*—2,030 years before their kingdom met its downfall in 540."[7]

The position is not quite so simple as that. To some present-day scholars, Jordanes barely exists. The onus of the case rests, rather, on an *Origo Gothica*, "the particular origin of the Goths," nursed in the bosom of the Amals, the family of Theoderic the Ostrogoth in early sixth-century Italy. This is what we hear from Herwig Wolfram, whose writings and teaching in Vienna have dominated Gothic history since the 1970s: "Cassiodorus attests that Theoderic interested himself very much in the North, be it in the Scandinavian Gauti or the Baltic Aisti. . . . This must have been a particular Amal tradition and not a general Gothic one. I believe that this knowledge of the *Origo Gothica* was the knowledge of the royal family, whose tradition Theoderic forcefully monopolized."[8] Cassiodorus, the authority Wolfram refers to, was a minister of Theoderic's and the author, at the king's behest, of a twelve-book history of the Goths.[9]

Describing this work, Cassiodorus says of himself (in the third person), "Originem Gothicam historiam fecit esse Romanam." These six words can be and have been translated in several ways; I suggest, "He turned the descent [or 'past'] of the Goths into Roman-style history."[10] Wolfram, with these words in mind, but not my translation, proceeds rather differently in the introduction to his major *Geschichte der Goten*: "A historical ethnography of the Goths [by which Wolfram means his own work] turns Cassiodorus's historical structure upside down and seeks to allow the *Origo Gothica*, the particular origin of the Goths, to reemerge from the *Historia Romana*, the general goal of each tribe history[11] (*Eine historische Ethnographie der Goten stellt Cassiodors berühmtes Geschichtsgebäude auf den Kopf und sucht, aus der Historia Romana, dem allgemeinen Ziel jeder Stammesgeschichte, die Origo Gothica, die partikulare Herkunft der Goten, wieder erstehen zu lassen*).["12] Wolfram also refers to "the *Origo Gothica*, the work of Cassiodorus in the version of Jordanes."[13] Out of the three possibilities mentioned, the only one that concretely exists is Jordanes's history. Cassiodorus's history is completely lost, whereas the "*Origo Gothica*" is an extra—something that cannot be "lost" since only Wolfram's lavish repetitions of the name give it the semblance of life. It results from Wolfram's decision that Cassiodorus's "Originem Gothicam" does not mean something like "the Gothic past" (as most readers have understood), but rather should be interpreted as the *title* of a distinct "text" that may reemerge by a process of turning "Cassiodorus's [lost] historical structure upside down." Wolfram has consistently treated his interpretation of "Originem Gothicam" as the title of a real entity to be self-evidently legitimate. Nowhere in his many works (as far as I know) has he argued for the appropriateness or scholarly legitimacy of conjuring up this tertium quid.[14] Jordanes is mentioned ten times in Wolfram's *History of the Goths* (three times in the German second edition) as compared with thirty-one for *Origo Gothica* (thirty-two index entries in the German third edition).

In this nonargumentative way, by a play of definitions, Wolfram has built up layers of protection against the claim that Scandinavian origins might hinge on something so paltry as a single surviving (East Roman) narrative. There is little to be done with his presentation except to unveil what lies behind this intensively affirmed and doubly nonexistent *Origo Gothica*, which also materializes in the writings of Walter Pohl and Volker Bierbrauer.[15]

Is Jordanes a Pale Shadow?

Even when the nonexistent *Origo Gothica* is left out of account, we are still left with "the work of Cassiodorus, in the version of Jordanes." Jordanes may be alone to survive, but many scholars (especially in the past) have not regarded him as standing on his own feet. They have considered him to be a pale shadow behind a text that owes almost everything to Cassiodorus.[16] Wolfram refers to the latter's work as a "berühmtes Geschichtsgebäude" without mentioning that this "famous construction" has vanished, leaving behind only hints of its former being. Wolfram in fact regards Cassiodorus's Gothic history as existing, but "in the version of Jordanes." So Jordanes's *Getica*, instead of being the cornerstone supporting the edifice by the fact of existing at all, becomes an incidental detail—a window to the Cassiodoran narrative that lies behind him. There is an extensive modern literature on the question of how Jordanes's work relates to Cassiodorus's history, but Wolfram takes minimal account of the opinions of other scholars. His main interest in Cassiodorus is to "turn over" his history and let the *Origo Gothica* reemerge. Since that is the goal, a free hand is needed. Wolfram's introduction appropriately invokes this freedom as "die Selbstbehauptung des Historikers."[17]

Wolfram's prominence in Gothic and early medieval studies makes it essential that his method for dealing with narratives of Gothic history should be set out and given a hearing. Having now done so, I return to "the core" of the problem of origins from Scandinavia, but not simply to Jordanes's account in the *Getica*, although it is the sole survivor. Fuller consideration must be given to the question whether what we read is Jordanes or his more illustrious source.

Thanks to recent scholars, especially those writing in English, the problem of this relationship has made notable advances. The question was long overhung by a brilliantly argued and influential theory by Arnaldo Momigliano that inflated the role of Cassiodorus to extremes and even posited a second, enlarged edition of his Gothic history. That theory has been assailed from several different quarters, with all due respect for the greatness of its author, and may be regarded as having been unanimously swept from the scene. Its details need not be retraced.[18] When both Momigliano's theory and Wolfram's peculiar system are set aside, a large degree of agreement prevails on the question of Jordanes's dependence on a principal source:

1. Jordanes is not a westerner with first-hand knowledge of the Goths of Italy. His roots are in the Balkans (East Roman territory). He worked in Constantinople more than ten years after the downfall in 540 of the Gothic kingdom in Italy. He asks not to be considered a Gothic sympathizer, and he unequivocally applauds Belisarius's conquest of Gothic Italy on behalf of the emperor Justinian.[19]
2. Jordanes describes the origin of his Gothic narrative: a friend asked him to abridge in his own words and condense into a single *libellus* the twelve books (*volumina*) of Cassiodorus's "On the descent and deeds of the Getae from long ago down to the present, descending by generations and kings (*de origine actusque [sic] Getarum ab olim et usque nunc per generationes regesque descendentem*)." This project was undertaken when Jordanes was already engaged in composing a history of the world and of Rome.[20]
3. Cassiodorus exiled himself to Constantinople from Italy after 540, taking with him (among other baggage) his Gothic history, which had been completed no later than 533. Its twelve *volumina* were in the charge of Cassiodorus's Constantinopolitan *dispensator* when Jordanes was allowed to consult them.[21]
4. Jordanes does not promise to be a self-effacing condenser of his model. He says he has had only three days' access to Cassiodorus's grandiose twelve books. He wants readers to know his personal part in the enterprise. He has consulted additional Greek and Latin works and has added words of his own at the beginning, the end, and also the middle. Though he disclaims reproducing Cassiodorus's precise words (*verba*), he has grasped his "argument and factual information (*sensus et res actas*)" and conveys them.[22]

Detaching Cassiodorus and Jordanes from Each Other

Those four points summarize information on which everyone agrees; Jordanes's own words spell out his identity and procedures. The problem and the possibility of controversy begin when we try to determine more precisely how much of Jordanes's *Getica* abridges Cassiodorus and how much is his own. For example, do the words he added "at the beginning" include the story of Gothic origins in Scandinavia? In the case of another early medieval author, Gregory of Tours, when we try to judge how its seventh-century condensation by Fredegar compares with the original, we simply pull Gregory's full *Historiae* from the shelf, set it alongside Fredegar, systematically compare the two texts, and emerge with a factual answer.[23] This verification is impossible for Cassiodorus and Jordanes, since all we have is the abridgment. What can be done in a case like this?

The answer is, Not very much that satisfies everyone. Cassiodorus was a copious writer and many pages that he composed survive, including a twelve-book letter collection (the *Variae epistolae*), a treatise "On the soul," a commentary on the Psalms, and an "Introduction to Divine and Human Readings."[24] These works, which are not all in the same style, allow his authorial persona to be to some extent penetrated. Someone armed with a grasp of Cassiodorus's vocabulary and styles may approach the *Getica* and attempt to demarcate its Cassiodoran content. There is as much art as science in this procedure, and only profound training in Latin language and composition allows it to be attempted. Three persons have tried their hand systematically at this difficult exercise—Carl Schirren, Rolf Hachmann (a prehistorian by profession), and Johann Weißensteiner (a student of Herwig Wolfram's).[25] They have mainly demonstrated what everyone assumes from the start, namely, that Jordanes made much use of his main source.

An additional problem needs urgently to be taken into account, namely, the parts of Cassiodorus's history that Jordanes left out. Although the Cassiodoran presence may be detected in the *Getica*, his absence may be guessed at only in the vaguest way, such as that he must surely have said much more about Theoderic than Jordanes does.[26] If the *Histories* of Gregory of Tours were known only from its abridgers and *the oldest surviving manuscripts*, we would infer that the work was in six books rather than ten and that the author was mainly concerned with kings and royal business rather than with ecclesiastical affairs.[27] In the case of Jordanes, what fell to the cutting room floor remains an impenetrable mystery. He does not even give us an inkling of how Cassiodorus's twelve-book structure relates to his own 316 paragraphs, sixty chapters, and three parts. To equate Cassiodorus's history with the abridgment that Jordanes has left us, or to call it "Cassiodorus in the version of Jordanes," is therefore unjustified and too sweeping. Certainly Cassiodorus was Jordanes's principal source, but what Jordanes conveys is his own work, even if it is a compilation of scissors-and-paste borrowings. It is not an image of Cassiodorus's twelve-book history. That image, regrettably, is lost for all time. Jordanes himself contributed to its loss.

Scandinavian Origins as a *Lectio Difficilior*

We have returned to our point of departure, namely, Heather's and Christensen's affirmations that Gothic emigration from Scandinavia hinges entirely on "an analysis of the text in the *Getica.*" Even apart from the textual issues just explored, the modus operandi proposed by Heather and Christensen is not unanimously agreed upon. The most notable current defenders of the historicity of this migration story—Reinhard Wenskus and Walter Pohl—avoid textual analysis and insist rather on the broader outlines of Jordanes's message.[28] Their arguments are much alike and hinge on the information that Jordanes conveys.

Wenskus's mode of argument is somewhat reminiscent of Anselm of Canterbury's ontological (that is, self-sufficient) argument for the existence of God: "In the search for reasons why a sixth-century chronicler might feel motivated to assert, contrary to factual history, that his people (*Stamm*) originated from Scandinavia, one is forced to conclude that there simply were none. On the contrary it was considerably more obvious for a historian of this age to devise a connection to the famous peoples of antiquity, as many examples show. Jordanes's claim is wholly atypical for his time and therefore proceeds with a high degree of certainty from traditions that have a high degree of probability [that is, are very likely to be historically true]."[29] Wenskus proposes what in text editing is called a *lectio difficilior*, a correct reading recommended by its inherent improbability by comparison with the alternatives. But has he really attained this goal? Jordanes was not an obscure and naive "sixth-century chronicler" but a Constantinopolitan writer of history in a city boasting several other historians, notably the Greek Procopius, whose account of Justinian's *Wars* first appeared very near the time when Jordanes's two histories were published.[30] Jordanes's reference to "Scandza," our Scandinavia, is not "contrary to factual history"; rather, it was implied by established facts. Jordanes was the first to mention this "island" in connection with the Goths, but long before him the Goths had been associated with "the North" (the Old Testament as interpreted by Ambrose of Milan) and even with "the snowy regions beneath the icy constellation of the Bear" (the Latin poet Claudian). Nothing more startling takes place in Jordanes than the giving of a name out of classical geography to the "snowy region" out of which the Goths emerged. Besides not being a startling innovation, the identification is wholly in keeping with the practice of classical authors to dot those i's formerly left undotted. As a mere extension of already known information, Jordanes's Scandza can be just as classical as the rest of what he says.[31]

Walter Pohl also insists on a *lectio difficilior*. The report of migration from the far North has historicity, according to him, because Scandza is a misfit: "[My] second observation is the construction of the origin story in Jordanes. . . . The grandiose Scythian, Getic, and Dacian past that was blended into the literary mould of the Getica on the basis of Justinus, Orosius, and other works offers quite a smooth and well-constructed, if totally fictitious, origin story of the Goths. . . . The Scandinavian origin story does not fit in, comes in disorderly little bits and pieces, and subverts the orderly narrative based on the written sources. It contains material and names not attested in any other written text."[32] Pohl informs us that, besides Scandza, Jordanes provides the Goths with plural pasts—all of them traditional (and classical) except for his own addition of the Amazons (whom legend made offshoots of the Scythians anyway), who are identified as "Gothic women."[33] Scandinavia caps the edifice, or does it? According to Pohl it does not; on the contrary, it deforms what is otherwise "smooth and well constructed." Pohl continues: Scandinavia is included, awkward as it is, only because demanded by the (Gothic) audience, which has to be told what was in its oral tradition. The rest is an "orderly narrative based on the written sources" whereas the Scandinavian story is made up of "disorderly little bits and pieces" and comes from a different source of information.

Pohl has lately made much of the idea that audience response forced Cassiodorus and other early historians to report ethnic memories, sometimes against their better judgment. Where the Gothic narrative is concerned, Pohl has even gone so far as to evoke a sort of council of Gothic "elders (*maiores*)" informing Cassiodorus about ethnic tradition and keeping him true to it: "If we leave out everything . . . about the construed Scythian and Getic past of the Goths, we are left with some passages about Gothic origins from Scandinavia and with Amal genealogies. This may provide valuable clues to what Cassiodorus had not found in his books but heard from the elders of the Goths. . . . [New paragraph] Cassiodorus had to 'learn from his reading what the hoary recollections of our elders scarcely preserved.' But his constructions were not pure fantasy either, they had to take into account what these elders believed."[34] This council of elders is a figment of Pohl's imagination, an interpretation that creeps into the argument without even being pointed out and defended.

In Cassiodorus's letter describing his history, *maiores* occurs twice within seven lines of each other; one instance is implicitly "Gothic," the other "Roman." Only the second one is modified by an adjective of pertinence (I emphasize the words at issue).

Tetendit se etiam in antiquam prosapiem nostram, lectione discens quod vix *maiorum* notitia cana retinebat.

[He extended his labours even to the ancient cradle of our house, learning from his reading what the hoary recollections of *old men* scarcely preserved.][35]

Perpendite, quantum vos in nostra laude dilexerit, qui vestri principis nationem docuit ab antiquitate mirabilem, ut, sicut fuistis a *maioribus* vestris semper nobiles aestimati, ita vobis antiqua regum progenies inperaret.

[Think how much he loved you in praising me, when he showed the nation of your prince to be a wonder from ancient days. In consequence, as you have ever been thought noble because of your *ancestors*, so you are ruled by an ancient line of kings.][36]

Maiores is not a strong or concrete word. Nowhere does it denote a committee of elders entering into a dialogue with Cassiodorus. In both cases Cassiodorus simply invokes vague "old men" or "ancestors."

Pohl does not himself analyze the *Getica* and attempt to demonstrate the nonfit of the Scandinavian material. Apparently, Scandinavia is incongruous. According to Heather, however, it not only fits but can be attributed to an identified oral informant:

> Evidence for the Goths' Scandinavian origins has been found in two elements of the *Getica*'s text: the story of Berig . . . , of course, but also the names of some Scandinavian tribes that are mentioned just before it. . . . The extensive knowledge of Scandinavian ethnography demonstrated in this second passage has been taken as proof that Gothic oral history retained clear memories of the tribe's first home. . . .
>
> In the sixth century, however, there existed close links between the Baltic world and Ostrogothic Italy, where Jordanes' main source—the *Gothic History* of Cassiodorus—was composed. Cassiodorus sent letters, in Theoderic's name, to the Aestii who lived on the southern shore of the Baltic, and an exiled Scandinavian king—Rodulf of the Rani— sought refuge at the Ostrogothic court. He is mentioned in the *Getica* just after its long list of Scandinavian tribal names, and it seems a fair guess that he, rather than Gothic memories of their first homeland, was the ultimate source for most of the *Getica*'s Scandinavian ethnography.[37]

Italy had links with Scandinavia in the sixth century (and in the fifth), but I hesitate to believe that they were "close."[38] I do not share Heather's confidence that Cassiodorus interviewed the refugee king Rodulf to learn the details of Scandinavian ethnography. I am not even satisfied that the Scandinavian part of the *Getica* definitely derives from Cassiodorus rather than Jordanes. What is certain, however, is that the arguments of Wenskus and Pohl for a *lectio difficilior* do not compel assent.

The Literary Coherence of Scandinavian Origins

Pohl does less than justice to the literary coherence of the Scandinavian story. Jordanes traces a very clear path through twenty-five consecutive paragraphs, forming a geographical prologue (comparable to Procopius's opening of the *Vandal Wars*)[39] into a purposive quest among nearby islands for the remote Gothic homeland. Far from intimating that he proceeds on the basis of oral evidence, he never allows us to forget written documentation. I summarize:

The innumerable writers who have described the earth have also located islands large and small, not in the impassable Ocean, but in the clearly known nearer borders, along which islands are inhabited, such as Taprobane [Ceylon] in the East. The ocean in the west also has islands, such as the Orkneys and, at its farthest bounds, Thule. The same ocean contains Scandza, where the Goths come from [Jordanes injects a brief personal nod toward the patron of his history]. Britain is another island with its own geo- and ethnography. The geo- and ethnography of Scandza are distinct. Long ago, the Goths migrated from Scandza to Europe [under the leadership of King Berig] and, after about five generations, moved on to Scythia. The silly legends current in "our city [*urbs*]"— Constantinople [a Jordanes marker]—that have the Goths come from Britain are false because contradicted by authoritative books.[40]

By addressing his patron, Castalius, and mentioning his own city, Jordanes twice calls attention to himself. He refers to generalized books but also explicitly names Orosius, innumerable geographers, Virgil, Livy, Strabo, Tacitus, Dio (Chrysostom), Ptolemy (twice), ancient Gothic songs, Pomponius Mela, "Ablavius," ancient writers, and Josephus.[41] Except for the brief reference to "ancient songs"—an ethnographic cliché—we are in a heavily literate setting.[42] And so we should be, for neither Cassiodorus nor Jordanes could possibly have found "Scandia" as a leaf-shaped island in the northern ocean except in literate geography. Because all peoples do not spontaneously give the same names to geographical features, it takes a weird conception of any Gothic oral tradition to imagine that it would have supplied Jordanes or his source with *Scandinavia* in the same garb as Ptolemy, Pliny, and Pomponius Mela and would have added to it, besides, circumstantial recollections of the Goths' one-time neighbors when they emigrated 2,030 years ago.[43] Writings available to sixth-century authors are not so fully known to us that, if no written source can be identified, the information is attributable by default to oral tradition.

Christensen, the latest writer on this subject, concludes:

The decisive, innovative element in Cassiodorus's work was that he had the Goths originate on an island in the far north. He had found out about this island by reading works by Ptolemy and by listening to reports from people who had come to Ravenna from those regions. . . . Cassiodorus knew, both from Ptolemy and from his contemporary informants, that this island was home to a people whose name was strongly reminiscent of the name of the Goths. They were called Gauts, however, and had nothing at all to do with the Goths. . . . Isidore of Seville's failure to mention the Gothic origins in *Scandza* provides the final proof that Cassiodorus had himself invented that part of the story.

Had it been part of a living Gothic tradition in their *carmina prisca*, Isidore would have been familiar with the story.[44]

Christensen's conviction that Cassiodorus rather than Jordanes was the responsible party is conjectural. The "people who had come to Ravenna from those regions" are a pure speculation. Even Cassiodorus's belief that the addition of Scandinavia was very important cannot be taken for granted. The one certainty we can have is that the Goths as Berig's followers emerging from the frozen north were even more alien to the civilized world than they were in the guise of Scythians, Getae, or Britons. Someone may have wished this original remoteness of the Goths from civilization to be affirmed. For the rest, a careful sifting of the evidence, by Heather as well as Christensen, does not confirm the belief that descent from Scandinavia was a lively memory among the Goths or the Amal family.

Does Scandza Matter?

One needs to turn back to the words of Sybel and ponder how the downgrading of Scandinavian origins from history to legend—in agreement with earlier scholars[45]—affects the relations of present to past. "We are now what we once were": whatever it was that "we" have been, it can no longer include being companions of King Berig setting out from Scandinavia to the European mainland. Wenskus, whose "ontological" argument for Scandzan authenticity has been heard, should be listened to again explaining the importance of the ideological contribution of the Germanic *gentes*:

> Nothing better illustrates the significance of political ideas in the historical process than the destruction of the Roman Empire. This statement might seem exaggerated if it were not that the territory of an empire that considered itself universal, and had a conscious sense of state and civilization, was split apart by the naked force of timid barbarian armies and converted for all the future into a system of competing successor states. Until recently, this outcome seemed self-explanatory. Now, it has become exceedingly problematic.
>
> There was no historical necessity decreeing that the conquering Germanic peoples (*Stämme*), driven by an urge to power and wealth and ostensibly without a political conception of their own, should become creators of states [of their own] (*Reichsbildern*). Let us compare conditions in the universal empire at the other end of the ancient world. . . . [There, in China,] the aliens were very quickly absorbed and no longer appeared to be types with an original stamp.
>
> Why didn't the western world manage to make the majority of [its] invading barbarians the bearers of the Roman sense of state and culture? Because the barbarians

from the north were blinded by the glare of Rome, it should have been easy to keep them [true] to the Roman idea of empire. . . . Something more happened [in the fall of the Roman Empire] than simply the seizing of a portion of Roman soil. Simultaneously, a new political consciousness invaded the territory of ancient history—[a consciousness] that contrasted with the political thought of late antiquity. . . .

The *"Gentilismus"* [ethnic consciousness] of the conquering peoples was a politically stronger conception (*Denkform*) than the Roman imperial consciousness of the provincials.[46]

Out of the Germanic forests or the far north, the *Stämme* brought a particularist principle to the Roman Europe, and the rest has been history—an end to "the Roman sense of state and culture," and instead "a system of competing successor states." Wenskus believed he could show how these particularistic "kernels of tradition" descending from the distant Germanic past triggered successive political crystallizations and carried into the Middle Ages, overturning the Roman sense of state in doing so. The crown jewel of his theory was Gothic origin out of Scandinavia, proof positive of the uninterrupted centuries of the "gentile" polity-creating memory.[47]

In the eighteenth century, when an "ancient" and a "modern" period still accounted for all historical time,[48] the Germanic peoples were envisaged as having poured over the Roman Empire at the end of antiquity and having begun modern times by foreshadowing the contemporary European states—Saxons in England, Goths in Spain, Sueves in Portugal, Franks in France, Lombards in Italy. That rather old-fashioned image seems to have been in Wenskus's head. But had "imperial consciousness" faded away quite so easily as he suggested? The Catholic church was much heard of in the Middle Ages; Latin was the common medium of administration and higher culture for longer than sometimes seems believable; even the "Roman Empire" was re-created in the West only 250 years after its (temporary) demise and existed until 1806. None of these institutions was wholly equivalent to the Roman Empire of the past. What they assured was that particularism in Europe never existed alone, unchallenged, and unaided.[49] It is too simple to imagine that one system simply gave way to another or that "kernels" of particularistic "gentile" tradition did not exist at least side by side with a massive hoard of memory from the Greco-Romano-Christian past.

Jordanes's Compilation Is All We Have

My pages have shown how important it is to decide whether the reference to Scandza belongs to a disembodied *Origo Gothica*, to a lost Cassiodoran *Gothic History*, or to a surviving *De origine actibusque Getarum* by Jordanes. My most central conclusion probably is that only the surviving *Getica* can be taken into account. Jordanes so thoroughly snipped away at Cassiodorus, retaining only the parts he wanted, that what we are left with is like a ransom note composed of words and letters cut out of printed matter: the scissors wielder shaped the message. Cassiodorus was a Romano-Italian, a loyal subject of King Theoderic and his descendants, and a deservedly trusted official of the Ostrogothic kings; he composed his Gothic history before 533, perhaps at a moment when Theoderic's successor needed bolstering, but certainly in days when the Gothic regime still had a future.[50] The person through whose scissors the Gothic history passed was a very different creature. Jordanes was a Catholic (and anti-Arian) descended from Goths long settled in the East Roman Empire. Far from having any western or Italian connections, he worked in Constantinople, the repeatedly mentioned "royal city [*urbs regia*]" whose plague of 542 Jordanes recalls experiencing nine years before he wrote.[51] The *Getica* closes in such a way as to suggest that nothing had happened to the Goths after the fall of the Italian kingdom in 540 except the marriage (in the Eastern Empire) of Theoderic's granddaughter, Matasuintha, to the Roman general Germanus and the birth of a posthumous son. What matters here is not the appended joyful events of 550–51 but the downfall of 540. Although the regime Theoderic had founded ended in that year, there *was* strenuous Gothic resistance for many years afterward, but it has no place in Jordanes's Gothic narrative.[52] The only political fact for readers of the *Getica* is the end of the Amal kingdom, first announced by Jordanes as early as paragraph 81—a perspective that would have been totally alien to Cassiodorus's account of 533, indeed wholly subversive of its confidence in a Gothic future.

When did this anti-Arian, East Roman Goth condense Cassiodorus's history? There is a standard practice in the dating of medieval histories—especially chronicles—to set the date of composition at or just after the last (datable) event mentioned in its pages. This method often produces acceptable results, but it needs to be applied with circumspection when the accounts to be dated are by historians known to be careful craftsmen. To work, the method must presuppose an accidental element, such as the author's death—something implying that the account is unretouched, unpolished, left incomplete.[53] In the case of carefully crafted endings like those of Gregory of Tours's *Histories* or Bede's *Historia ecclesiastica*, what is offered to us is not an ending date worthy of trust— since it is not accidental—but the moment at which the author chose for his own reasons to draw the line. We can be certain he could not finish before the terminal date, but we have no firm ground (unless other facts are available) for determining when, afterward, he wrote and finished writing.[54]

Users and editors have lacked rigor in applying this dating method to the *Getica* and its companion piece, the *Historia Romana*. In modern writings, these two works are dated to ca. 550 or 551, as though to suggest that Jordanes stopped writing in this or the other year. Note that the last person claiming to be a king of Goths in Italy was defeated and killed in October 552, four months after the same fate befell his longer-lived and more illustrious royal predecessor Totila (June or July 552). The expedition that brought about these decisive results set out from Constantinople in April 551.[55] We are not dealing with casual years but with a complex of events in which mere months matter. Where the *Getica* is concerned, one indication of the ending date occurs in paragraph 314—that is, on the final page. That terminus is March 551. For slightly different reasons, precisely the same limit applies to the *Romana*.[56] The crucial fact, however, is that the same event of March 551 is signaled much earlier in the *Getica*, namely, in paragraph 81; that occurrence is no interpolation. Three-quarters of the *Getica* had to be written *after* March 551; and, although the first quarter could have been written before March 551, it, too, might perfectly well have been written later. If this evidence is coolly analyzed, the sensible conclusion should be that no concessions at all should be made to the early dating that Jordanes so deliberately wishes to impress on his readers. On the contrary, the whole of Jordanes's *Getica* was compiled after March 551, that is, in the months during which, under the leadership of Narses, every last bit of Gothic resistance was being stamped out, and Italy was being turned into a Constantinopolitan dependency.

Jordanes and the End of Gothic Italy

Jordanes's compilation of the *Getica* was part of the campaign concurrently taking place in Italy, namely, the elimination of Gothic rule in the peninsula and even (it was hoped) in Spain; Justinian had reached the point of utterly "hating . . . the Gothic name" and being determined to apply the force needed "to drive it out absolutely from the Roman domain."[57] Cassiodorus was in Justinian's capital with the now pathetic twelve-book history in which he had sought to show that the Goths were worthy rulers of the Western Empire. The existence of this work was widely known.[58] Circumstances had changed: the Amal kingdom had ended in 540, and now—after too long a delay—the lawless Gothic rebellion was well on the way to being stamped out. What was to be done with Cassiodorus's anachronistic Gothic history? The obvious answer was expurgation, and that was Jordanes's commission, the challenging but doable task of bringing Cassiodorus's history into harmony with what Justinian had done to the Gothic kingdom. The expurgation could be carried out with scissors and paste and perhaps a few additional readings.[59]

As Sybel tells us, history is important; but so is the historical criticism that scrapes away nonexistent slices of the past. Great efforts have gone into the defense of Gothic origins from Scandinavia. This has been a matter of urgent concern to well-intentioned persons, a way of affirming continuity and identity with a precious part of the supposed past. But Jordanes, Goth though he claimed to be, was not a spokesman for that past. He was, on the contrary, one of the obedient agents of Justinian's campaign of destruction. For the true end of the Goths was the affirmation that they (and their barbarian cousins) belonged outside, not within, the world of Rome in which they had lived and striven to exist enduringly for close to two centuries. That is the message of exclusion that Constantinople would propagate, via Jordanes and others, including Procopius, so that it might be more secure—even in a barbarous present—in claiming for itself alone the great heritage of imperial and Christian Rome.[60]

Would the Real Jordanes Please Stand Up?

It may help clarity if, in conclusion, the teachings about Jordanes and the *Getica* spelled out or implied in these pages are enumerated:

1. The *Getica* was written in Justinian's Constantinople at some time after March 551. The date cannot be more closely approximated but may well fall several years after the terminal mark. Indications of date in both of Jordanes's histories were crafted to mask the real (later) moment of composition.

2. The *Getica* celebrates the destruction of the Goths in the West by Belisarius and Justinian. It is best regarded as a record of Gothic history meant for an audience content with this ending or incapable of affecting it. The *Getica* is not designed to advocate a cause, least of all to champion Gothic-Roman reconciliation or a political outcome different from the one that was taking or had taken place.[61] It also is not intended to be a storehouse of authentic Gothic antiquities or to fill a Gothic audience with pride in its past; such roles are inconsistent with its origins.

3. The author Jordanes may be who he claims to be in *Getica* 265 and 315. Verification is impossible. On the internal evidence of Jordanes's writings, we would, except for this claim, consider him to be a Latin educated Constantinopolitan (Thracian or Illyrian). His assertion of Gothic descent gives an appearance of sincerity to his work and masks its destructiveness; it is therefore suspect.[62]

4. Jordanes approached Cassiodorus's twelve-book Gothic history as an expurgator, that is to say, a hostile appropriator, bent on eliminating any suggestion that, for example, Theoderic was the rightful ruler of Italy and that his descendants deserved to be its enduring monarchs. The least of Jordanes's concerns was to convey an exact and faithful abridgment of Cassiodorus's history.

5. Neither the *Getica* nor its Cassiodoran source was the prototype of a class or genre of *origines* of nonclassical *gentes*. The histories of Gregory of Tours, Isidore of Seville, and Bede—which would belong to the genre if it existed—were composed later than the *Getica* and all originated independently of its (and Cassiodorus's) influence.[63]

6. The *Getica* was often echoed in medieval historical writings. The earliest trace of its effect is the motif of Scandinavian origins first found in connection with the Lombards and later with other peoples, including the Franks.[64] Its evocation of Scandinavia as the womb of nations has had broad appeal down to modern times. First published by Konrad Peutinger in company with Paul the Deacon's *Historia Langobardorum* (1515), in the decades when the rediscovered *Germania* of Tacitus was thrilling German humanists, the *Getica* played a major part in the genesis of the concept of a *Völkerwanderung* and of the "science of German antiquity." The task of identifying and neutralizing its malign effect on modern accounts of the Migration Age leaves us much to do.

From Historiography to History

The four historiographic chapters that now end have been centrally concerned with what has been believed about barbarians and their "Germanness." Their goal has been to clear away misconceptions that distort the field of observation. The historical chapters that follow address, in their several ways, the scanty and perplexing source material of late antiquity.

Each of them is long and freestanding. Chapter 5 considers the most famous invasion but one of the Migration Age, explores its intricacies, and offers it as a case study of the phenomenon of barbarian "migration." Chapter 6 focuses on the main theme of my 1980 book *Barbarians and Romans*, namely, the settlement of Goths and Burgundians in Gaul and Italy, and reappraises its details in the light of twenty-five years of experience and reflection. Chapter 7, whose title emphasizes that the barbarians of late antiquity were not "Germans" or "Germanic," is in three parts and, though the parts complement each other and circle about the same phenomenon, they may be read as independent essays. Its second part supplies models of how one might speak of and display individual peoples of the Migration Age. The Conclusion (Chapter 8) returns to the historiographic mode. It underscores Gibbon's saying that his multivolume book had "described the triumph of barbarism and religion" and suggests that this, in a positive sense, is a helpful synopsis of what late antiquity was about.

Chapter 5

The Great Rhine Crossing, A.D. 400–420, a Case of Barbarian Migration

Unter Honorio brechen vollends die Dämme, so die Gräntzen decken sollten: und daher enstehet die so berufene grosse Wanderung der Völker. Die West-Gothen gehen nach Italien, und Alarich erobert. Der Rhein kan nicht länger die Teutschen Nachbarn von Gallien abhalten; die Vandalen und Sueven stifften eigne Reiche in Spanien; und die ersten gehen endlich nach Africa.

—J. J. Mascov, Geschichte der Teutschen bis zur Anfang
   der Fränkische Monarchie *(Leipzig, 1726)*

This was one of the greatest events in the period of the Germanic wanderings, and it brought a larger and more sudden change in the western provinces than any other single barbarian movement.

—J. B. Bury, The Invasions of Europe by the Barbarians,
   ed. F. J. C. Hearnshaw (London, 1928)

Les conséquences du passage du Rhin par ces hordes seront infiniment plus graves, plus durables, que le passage du Danube par les Goths, trente ans auparavant. À dire vrai, c'est cet événement dont les suites vont désorganiser, anémier, finalement tuer l'Empire d'Occident.

—Ferdinand Lot, Les invasions germaniques *(Paris, 1935)*[1]

Breakthrough across the Rhine: Synopsis

The invasion of Gaul in 406 by the Alans, Vandals, and Sueves is a famous event of late Roman history, a critical step in the penetration of aliens into the Roman Empire and the passage of the Western provinces from imperial to non-Roman control. When the fall of Rome was a widely respectable concept, the invasion of 406 was considered decisive in bringing it about. The focus has since tended to shift to the entry of the Goths in 376, but the special importance of the Alans, Vandals, and Sueves to the West is unquestioned.[2] The event of 406 involves several different peoples and lacks visible leadership; it contrasts with barbarian movements focused on single peoples and high-profile personalities, such as Alaric, Geiseric, and Attila. In the common schema of a "migration of peoples" or *Völkerwanderung*, the invasion of 406 was—for those participating in it—the forward thrust leading to a triumphant or tragic outcome. The incident is a concrete case allowing the Migration Age scenario to be more closely examined. In whichever ways interpretive preferences may fall, the invasion of 406 merits attention.

A summary of the subject may help to understand the discussion to follow. The peoples associated in the invasion, largely mid-Danubian in origin, trekked up the Danube, cut northwest to the upper Main, then concentrated at a point on the Rhine not far from Mainz. The time of the crossing, normally given as 406, has now been convincingly revised to New Year's Eve 405.[3] Earlier in the same year, Italy had been broken into by a large number of Goths under a king named Radagaisus. On the eve of 406 the Alans, Vandals, and Sueves invaded Gaul. Virtually unopposed at first, they eventually encountered Roman defenders, notably the forces brought to the Continent by a usurper out of Britain, who bested them in battle but could not pursue. Given the opportunity to recover, the associated peoples acquired a reputation for plunder and devastation especially in southwest Gaul. Another denuded frontier, this time in the Pyrenees, beckoned them farther south. In the autumn of 409, they entered Spain, ravaged it fiercely for two years, then divided it among themselves. The sharing out of the peninsula was the high point of their fortunes. They experienced rapid setbacks when the Roman government enlisted a Gothic army against them. At least half the Rhine crossers were obliterated, but two of the four peoples endured. The Asding Vandals with the Alan survivors entrenched themselves in the southern province of Baetica, and the Sueves held fast in northwest Spain. With the attainment of an equilibrium in 420, the invasion that set out from the middle Danube may be treated as a closed chapter in late Roman history. Some years later, Geiseric led the Vandals out of Baetica to North Africa but, for all practical purposes (as will be shown), that is a new and different story.

The Danubians who engaged in the Rhine crossing had long been in close contact with the Roman Empire. Many still lived where they had before Roman power established itself as their neighbor in the first century. It is hard to tell whether the guise they had at the beginning of the fifth century differed very much from the one they had assumed long before. The westward expedition they undertook into the Empire ended that condition and spawned new possibilities. The future that came to pass, or that they chose, made them isolated swimmers in a sea of Roman provincials. In that form or another, the invasion broke continuity and initiated accelerated change for the Romans and their attackers alike.

The aspects of the Alan, Vandal, and Sueve expedition considered here are its start until the invasion of the Empire; then, after a tumultuous (and ill-documented) passage through Gaul, their entrance into Spain and the course of their doings there down to 420. The start of the campaign in the early 400s raises questions of leadership and composition. Did the Huns set the various peoples in motion? Is there an alternative to Hunnish prodding? What relation is there between the expedition that reached Spain and the one that left the Danube valley? Later phases also raise special questions. Did the Hun-like Alans have a specially prominent part in the expedition? What was involved in the invaders' four-way division of Spain in 411? What was the high point of their success? Why is 420 a suitable end for what began in 405? What effect did the departure of Sueves and Vandals have on the Danubian lands they abandoned? These and other issues will be examined.

In the last part of the chapter, the case of the Alans, Vandals, and Sueves is discussed as a test of what is meant by speaking of "Migration Age" history. The events of the years 405–20 have an important part in that universally acknowledged phenomenon of late antiquity called the "migration of peoples" or *Völkerwanderung*. In the extended form adopted by many scholars, the *Völkerwanderung* sometimes reaches back through more than a millennium and involves every expansion of the "Germanic" peoples down to and including the disruptions of late antiquity. In its short form, preferred here (see Chapter 1), the Migration Age got under way in the 370s when the Huns attacked the Goths and sent them hurtling into the Roman Empire; it continued with varied additional movements, including the one interesting us, until the Lombards seized much of Italy (568). The Vandals are one of the star participants in the Migration Age, and the invasion of 405–6 is one of its climactic moments.[4] Period names such as *Völkerwanderung* or its English equivalent are solidly rooted in modern historical writing. The invasion of the Alans, Vandals, and Sueves permits a closer examination of what one very conspicuous phenomenon of migration was all about.

A Second Round of Disruption by the Huns?

Hunnic responsibility for setting the Rhine crossers in motion seems to have already been a moth-eaten "truth" when Gibbon endorsed it long ago, and that received wisdom, though not unanimously accepted, continues to hold the field. Peter Heather highlights the Rhine crossing among the three fateful, Hun-hatched crises that, he argues, were the stepping stones to the fall of the Roman West, a fall that, according to him, was exclusively the work of outsiders.[5] In the footsteps of many other historians, Heather expresses certainty that Hunnic pressure jolted the Alans, Vandals, and Sueves into flight from the Danube and invasion across the Rhine. In the 370s the Huns attacked the south Russian Goths; a generation later—so it is argued—they launched a second offensive, affecting the next layer of barbarian peoples to the west. E. A. Thompson summed up his conception of the events: "In the first years of the new century [the Huns] seem to have undertaken a tremendous drive through central Europe toward the West. . . . Scenes similar to those of 376 were witnessed again. . . . These movements, it is agreed, were caused by a westward expansion of the Huns."[6] Heather champions the analogy between the 370s and the early 400s: "There is no reason to suppose that the model Ammianus gives us for the movements of 376 does not apply here too."[7]

Despite the chorus of modern assent, direct evidence does not suggest that history repeated itself. Heather concedes the lack of proof and dispenses with an inappropriate text cited by Thompson. Hunnic pressure is established, in his view, by circumstantial considerations. He argues convincingly that, down to (and no doubt including) 395, most Huns stayed well to the east. It was from the eastern end of the Black Sea that they carried out a large, well-attested raid via the Caucasus into Asia Minor. Their westward movement took place in the next twenty-five years: "By the 420s, however, [the mass of the Huns was] definitely occupying middle Danubian regions west of the Carpathians."[8] It cannot be coincidental—so Heather maintains—that the Huns' arrival west of the Carpathians was preceded "by a huge convulsion among the tribal groups of the region," namely, the hordes of Radagaisus, the Rhine crossing by four peoples, and the (quickly defeated) Balkan invasion of 408 by the Hun Uldin.[9] Anticipating Heather's outlook, Émilienne Demougeot vividly evoked how the Huns pushed the Danubian tribes westward: "The [Suevic] Quadi and the Vandals [were] expelled from Moravia, Upper Silesia, and Galicia by the van of the Huns leaving Ukraine, who had crossed the Carpathian passes leading to the watershed of the Tisza well before other Hunnic bands, such as [Uldin]'s, were able to proceed up the Danube."[10] Demougeot's idea of Hunnic pressure is only an imaginative reconstruction, and the need for a full twenty-five years is left unexplained. If the Vandals and Sueves cleared out on their own initiative in 405, ten or five years would have been available for Hunnic immigration—a period no less plausible for this movement than Demougeot's quarter century.

According to the authors just cited, the extension of Huns west of the Carpathians down to the 420s is unimaginable without causing turbulence among the sitting population, driving it away, and clearing space for the newcomers and their satellites. An alternative is conceivable, however, namely, that peoples and leaders from different areas went south to Italy with Radagaisus or west to the Rhine for reasons of their own, leaving a political void, a void filled by the Huns without tumult and fighting. There was ample time between 405 and the years when the Hunnic presence in the Danubian steppe begins to be attested for them to extend their hold over vacated territories with a minimum of violence.

Contemporary informants do not encourage the idea that the Huns cleared fully occupied trans-Carpathian space by armed force. In the 370s the victims in south Russia loudly publicized the attacks upon them: Ammianus Marcelinus gives us a vivid account, and others, such as Ambrose of Milan and Orosius, follow suit. The advent of the Huns as a wholly new and particularly horrible phenomenon is, through the Goths, a notorious fact of late Roman history. A generation later, the publicity had changed. No one noticed that the hideous pony-riders had resumed their evil ways. Observers do not claim to see Hunnic attacks driving off long-implanted peoples; silence is total: "Nothing in our authorities indicates that behind Radagaisus stood another barbarian leader whose people were pushed by still another one, and so on."[11] If a contemporary or near-contemporary witness had denounced or applauded attacks by the Huns, it would be easier to believe that they were again terrifying settled peoples and putting them to flight.

Heather maintains that the Huns, besides expelling sedentaries, were themselves in the grip of an ineluctable fate: in all the immigrants (into Roman territory) from the 370s to 410 who "were attempting to escape the insecurity generated by the Huns," we contemplate "two phases of the same crisis, both prompted by the westward progression of the Huns in stages, from the outer fringes to the very heart of Europe."[12] The grandiose, synoptic viewpoint of a modern writer has no necessary connection with the real life of fourth- or fifth-century Huns, who, more probably, were as shortsighted as normal humans. When they and the Alans triumphed over the Goths of Ermanaric (ca. 370), they had no reason to imagine that they were in the grips of a "westward progression" leading them to the Loire in less than a century, or to the middle Danube by the 420s. In the 370s they had become masters of an enormous territory and a vast population; they presumably were sated. Heather's belief that the "Hunnic crisis" was fated to have a second phase lacks inherent logic. No unseen power commanded, "Go farther West, O Hun."

Huns on their ponies, ever mounted, are thought to have moved incessantly. Did they? As has rightly been pointed out, their initial attack—the one so loudly reported by Ammianus and others—achieved its goal far from the borders of the Roman Empire.[13] For decades afterward, the Huns stood in place, showing no signs of moving anywhere. Did they push beyond the Carpathians in the early fifth century from a desire to expand and dominate, or did they simply fill in after the lands in question emptied out? If the latter, their three or more decades in south Russia should be taken more seriously. The Huns may not have been a fighting machine poised to slice across Europe. Those who stopped in Russia seem to have been more anchored and less ambitious than their descendants who crossed the Carpathians, the ones whom Attila eventually ruled. Hunnic history need not have unfolded in a uniform and homogeneous fashion.[14]

Causes for Radagaisus's Invasion: The Huns, Goading by Constantinople, or the Leader's Initiative

The Rhine crossing of the Alans, Vandals, and Sueves, regardless of how set in motion, occurred a few months after a comparably massive attack into Italy. The Roman generalissimo Stilicho was on the verge of enlisting Alaric, a Gothic leader long in contact with the Roman military authorities, as a helper in a dispute with Constantinople (405). Just then, the Gothic king Radagaisus, previously unknown, led a multitude of Goths and others southwestward across the Danube, no one knows definitely from where.[15]

Radagaisus and most of his followers are widely accepted, on feeble grounds, to have been Greutungs or eastern Goths (often called Ostrogoths).[16] "Goth" was the generic term that Romans used for the peoples occupying southern Russia and the lower Danube valley. The swarm that headed for Italy in hostile array seems to have been composed of odds and ends of peoples who had stayed or been left behind in "Gothia" after the Goths made their authorized crossing into the Empire (376), and after the Tervingian king Athanaric had taken refuge in Constantinople (380). It is little wonder that Radagaisus's followers, whoever they were, are reported to us as "Goths." A subverted and disorganized Gothia had stewed for years. There were ample internal reasons for all concerned to choose flight toward lands that were reputed to be more secure and prosperous.[17]

The fears aroused in Italy by Radagaisus's attack are documented by hyperbolic estimates of numbers, reaching as high as four hundred thousand. He was said to have vowed to gorge his gods with Roman blood.[18] The invading army, whatever its size, could not be kept from breaking into Italy. Stilicho disposed the Roman defenders he had as best he could and, as reinforcements, engaged two available foreign legions, the Goths of Sarus and the already mentioned Huns of Uldin.[19] Radagaisus and his innumerable followers proved to be an inept mob rather than an effective fighting force; the expedition was tumultuous from the start. Stilicho's reinforced army encircled the invaders at Fiesole near Florence and, without a battle, overcame them by starvation. The attack that began in 405 ended in April 406.

Geography and date make it nearly certain that, if Huns were responsible for starting a stampede, they would have incited both Radagaisus's invasion of Italy and the Rhine expedition of the mid-Danubians. The push would have been the same even if the fugitives broke out in different directions.[20] The flaw (as said before) is that only the movements themselves are attested, and they might have had varied causes. There is no discernible trace of Huns taking a hand. The overt panic in the face of Hunnic attacks that definitely occurred in the 370s cannot be duplicated in the 400s. We are forced to consider the possibility that Radagaisus and the Alans and Vandals had their own reasons for setting out.

The arresting feature of Radagaisus's attack is its tempestuousness and pell-mell composition—an obscure king assembles every bewildered soul left in Gothia, a territory that had lost its prominent leaders to emigration. Even without Hunnic encouragement, an energetic chief in this chaotic land might have swept together many thousands of desperate men and led them toward Italy, hoping to earn, by troublemaking, the consideration that earlier Goths had won from the Empire. The frenzied formation of the expedition seems borne out by its instant, pitiful disaster. The invasion need not have been foredoomed. A force of great size and rumored ferocity might have somehow shaken the West Roman leadership into concessions. For a decade, using somewhat different assets, Alaric had been exacting largesse from the Roman government. Radagaisus may have had a calculated purpose though there is no evidence that he did.[21]

Another possibility comes to mind in view of Stilicho's plan to cooperate with Alaric against East Rome: might Constantinople have set Radagaisus in motion? During the very hard-fought usurpation of Magnentius (350–53), the emperor Constantius II incited the Rhine tribes to invade Gaul so as to immobilize the challenger. The "diverters," who did much damage, were still being chased out of Gaul long after Magnentius was suppressed.[22] A generation later, the Goths on the lower Danube were contacted by the usurper Maximus and urged to deflect Theodosius I from his campaign to the West. Conversely, Theodosius stirred up the Alamanni against Maximus. Later still, Stilicho was slandered with the claim that he summoned invaders into Gaul—the mid-Danubians we are concerned with—as a lever to force his ambitions upon the West Roman court.[23] The use of foreigners in internal Roman disputes was an ingrained practice. Throwing a diversion in Stilicho's way, such as Radagaisus's horde, would have helped Constantinople in 405; it promised to stop Stilicho in his tracks and in fact did so.

There is no proof of East Roman incitement any more than of Hunnic harassment. Radagaisus has to be allowed a choice of reasons for leading his mob to

Italy: personal initiative inspired by the recent success of Alaric in wringing concessions from the Empire; Constantinopolitan encouragement to thwart Stilicho; or goading by the Huns eager to go west. No explanation is better documented than the others. Huns are not the certain cause. And if not even Radagaisus's tragic adventure may be firmly laid at the Huns' door, the invasion of the Alans, Vandals, and Sueves is less likely than ever to have been incited by them.

The Invaders of Gaul Listed by Hydatius and Jerome

My subject is the other expedition of 405. Drawing its participants together on their stamping grounds is no easy task.

Christian Courtois, a major historian of the Vandals, refers to the throng crossing the Rhine as composed of "disparate peoples, brought together by the accident of a temporary coalition"; Otto Seeck evokes participants from different sectors gathered almost fortuitously at the Rhine.[24] According to the Hispano-Roman chronicler Hydatius, writing about a half century after the events, the coalition that entered Spain in 409 included four named peoples: Sueves, Asding Vandals, Siling Vandals, and Alans. His description of their partition of Spain provides a clear indication of the relative strength of the peoples in presence: Alans in the lead, next the Siling Vandals, finally the Sueves and Asding Vandals as the weakest contingents. Sueves are difficult to define because the name is generic—ancient, widespread, and applied to peoples with primary names of their own. The two kinds of Vandals were separate peoples in spite of the linking name and formed distinct groups in the expedition. The Alans, a steppe people, had been cattle-rearing nomads in their homelands. They were akin to the Sarmatians and are even more elusive, ethnically, than the Sueves.

Almost all the peoples who crossed the Rhine on this occasion did not accidentally coalesce; they had been associated long before. Speaking of the reign of Marcus Aurelius (A.D. 161–80), the historian Eutropius refers to "the Marcomannic War . . . which [the Marcomanni] unleashed together with the Quadi, Vandals, Sarmatians, Sueves, and all barbariandom."[25] The Marcomanni and Quadi, with names of their own, were no less Suevic than the peoples called Sueves pure and simple. The Vandals were not Suevic themselves, though they had been neighbors of Suevic peoples for more than two centuries and were probably impregnated with Suevic culture. They had shared in the ancient, disastrous war of Marcus's time and were typical mid-Danubians. The Alans, absent from Eutropius's sentence, are foreshadowed in his account by the nomad Sarmatians. The Sarmatian group called Iazyges had been attracted to this region by the emperor Tiberius (†37).[26] Common descent from Iranian stock did not make Sarmatians and Alans interchangeable entities. Texts tend to keep the names distinct, and it was only since the 370s that small numbers of Alans had begun to be seen in the Danube valley. But to the Sueves and Vandals who had long been in contact with Sarmatians and their steppe culture, Alans cannot have looked like total strangers.[27]

Despite this shared mid-Danubian past, the army that crossed into Gaul cannot be easily traced to four clearly defined stamping grounds. Hydatius names four invaders of Spain, and the order in which he lists them, Alans in the lead, seems to be one of relative importance (the contemporary Orosius has them in the same order). The same four remain in sight from 409, when we have Hydatius's guidance.[28] St. Jerome, a geographically more remote but contemporary observer, writing from Bethlehem in 409, supplies a longer and less tidy list of the attackers of Gaul: "Quadi, Vandals, Sarmatians, Alans, Gepids, Herules, Saxons, Burgundians, Alamanni and—pity the Empire—even Pannonians-turned-enemies."[29] Enumerations of alien names—a parade of foreigners, such as this one—had been a literary device deployed by Latin authors for a very long time.[30] Jerome's first four peoples are close to those of Hydatius provided "Quadi" substitutes for Sueves (which Quadi were), the two kinds of Vandals are bundled into one, and Sarmatians are linked with Alans. These adjustments, not guaranteed correct, at least do not disfigure Jerome's text. Orosius prepares us for the presence of additional peoples, in his case unnamed: "and many others with [the Alans, Sueves, and Vandals]."[31] Nevertheless, Jerome's list is not trouble free. Gepids and Herules, both of them "easterners"—from farther down the Danube—with settlements not very distant from the Vandals, are possible at least in modest numbers, though their participation lacks any kind of verification. Also acceptable are Pannonians—that is, renegade Roman provincials—on the assumption that the ruin of their province at the hands of barbarians had driven them to a lawless life and to joining the expedition.[32]

To this point the names on Jerome's list, though some are shaky, are better kept than discarded. The same does not hold for the Saxons, Burgundians, and Alamanni. All three, unlike the others, were fixed near the western border of the Empire. On past (and future) behavior, they were occasional attackers of Gaul and would have been known as such to Jerome. The Burgundians even entered Gaul in 411 on behalf of the Roman usurper Jovinus and acquired a kingdom on the left bank of the Rhine.[33] Nevertheless, the names in Jerome's letter look like padding, needed for a long list. There is no other sign of a connection between these "attackers of Gaul" and the mid-Danubians. Saxons, Burgundians, and

Alamanni organized their own enterprises without taking part in the crossing of December 31, 405.[34]

Sueves and Vandals before the Rhine Expedition

Hydatius's evidence about the invaders is tidy; Jerome's needs editing, but is somewhat usable. Neither specifies where our attackers came from. A persistent question in modern literature on barbarians concerns the "original home" of such-and-such a people. None of the fifth-century sources was interested in this question because the answer was self-evident: not only did the invaders not come from far away, they had actually been living along the Roman frontier from time immemorial, as written records such as the Verona List bear out.[35]

To illustrate what lay behind the invasion of Gaul, Christian Courtois provided an eye-catching map extending from the Black Sea up the Danube to the Rhine. Its dominant feature looks like a railroad trunk line with intermittent spurs; the trunk mainly follows the course of the Danube. The map starts in Wallachia, where Courtois supposed the (*Rox*)alani to have been and to have set the ball rolling. Running upriver, the train picks up successive participants—Asding Vandals from Hungary, Quadi (for Sueves) from Slovakia, and Siling Vandals from the upper Main—all the way to a marshaling yard opposite Mainz.[36] Courtois's map transmutes confusion into visual logic until one realizes that more guesses enter into it than ascertained facts. Only the Asding Vandals can be traced in reliable sources from (what we call) the Hungarian Lowlands to southern Spain. Otherwise, our information about points of departure is much blurrier than Hydatius's (and Courtois's) four well-ordered peoples.

From 411 and long after, western Spain would contain a kingdom of the Sueves. Not even the embryo of such a kingdom existed in *barbaricum* awaiting transfer to Roman soil. The middle Danube was full of Sueves. Tacitus observed (A.D. 98), "They possess the greater part of Germany and are, besides, divided into separate tribes with individual names, although they are called Suebi generically."[37] The Marcomanni and Quadi had been Sueves in good standing in the last decades B.C., when Rome had earnestly fought the Germans, and they lived on in the fourth century. Related but distinctive Sueves, usually synonymous with the Alamanni of southwest Germany—the Roman poets Ausonius and Claudian call them *Suebi*—are known in the middle and modern ages as "Swabians." Gregory of Tours and Otto Seeck believed that the Sueves who went to Spain were Alamanni. Other scholars demur. Swabians lived too far west to be linked with the invaders of 405.[38] The Sueves who reached Spain are more likely, because of their association with Vandals, to be from the middle Danube than from Alamannia.

Among other traces of "Danube Sueves," Eutropius's account of the Marcomannic War establishes that the generic name held its own alongside ancient, particular appellations for Sueves, such as "Quadi."[39] The fourth-century Marcomanni were in decline and soon ceased to be heard from; their worsening circumstances may have encouraged volunteers to join a distant adventure.[40] The Quadi were strong in the fourth century, trained and equipped like their Sarmatian steppe neighbors. The emperor Valentinian I was fighting them when, at a parlay with their envoys, their lame excuses made him so angry that he had a seizure and died.[41]

No single people, great or small, imposed its label on the Suevic component of the Rhine expedition. The comprehensive name would have been in keeping with the miscellaneity of the emigrants. The names borne by northern peoples normally were multiple and particular when they were long settled, and condensed to a general or homogeneous name when they transferred to foreign parts. Tervingi, Greutungi, Taifali, and the like north of the Roman frontier turn up as Goths on Roman soil; the various invaders of Britain became homogeneous Saxons; the multiple denominations of Danubian Sueves turn into Sueves alone in Spain.

The course of events in Spain down to 420 suggests that the Sueves formed the weakest contingent of the expedition. Many Sueves stayed put and continue to be attested in the Danube valley into the sixth century; even a Suevic king is attested in the later 460s.[42] But the two Suevic peoples with proud ancient names are not mentioned among the stragglers. We cannot be sure that the westward expedition was joined in force by the Marcomanni and Quadi but, after the expedition departed, their names vanish from the lands they had lived in for much longer than anyone could remember.

Alone of the Rhine crossers, the Vandals would have an illustrious but not very long future. They passed from Spain to North Africa under inspired leadership (429), reorganized their kingship, were feared, became militant Arian Christians, married into the Roman imperial family, and gained notoriety from varied accomplishments, especially by sea, such as the sack of Rome of 455, only to be crushed and wiped off the map by Justinian's general Belisarius in 534.[43]

Modern authors often assume that the Vandals led the expedition to the Rhine from its beginnings. Late Roman chroniclers not strictly contemporary to the events anticipated this point of view, impressed by the Vandals' recent renown: "In 406 the Vandals of King Gunderic crossed the Rhine and devastated all Gaul in a cruel molestation. They were accompanied by the Alans, a tribe matched [to them] in practices and savagery." The author of this entry, an anonymous continuator of Prosper of Aquitaine, wrote about the invasion of Gaul at a time when the Vandal seizure of Africa still startled and so attributed the initial thrust to the Vandals only.[44] Procopius followed suit a century later. His direct or indirect guide was Olympiodorus of Thebes, whose placement of the Vandals at the head of the invasion was influenced, like Prosper's, by the impact of Geiseric's sensational seizure of Carthage in 439.[45]

In 405 and immediately after, the Vandals inspired much less awe than after their conquest of Roman Africa. Their fighting forces were repelled from one offensive by no more than threats and then experienced two major defeats unredeemed by victories. A taint of cowardice clung to them, probably as an earned rather than a malicious reputation.[46] Other than being numerous and surviving grave adversities, Vandals did nothing remarkable until, in Spain, the Asdings had their backs to the wall and rose to the challenge. That will concern us later.

The peoples called Asding and Siling Vandals—none others are known in the fifth century—turn up briefly and sparsely in second-century Roman sources. Earlier authorities, notably Pliny and Tacitus, knew of a widespread "Vandil" people, including most of those whom philologists call East Germans. "Vandil," the collective term embracing them, was similar to "Sueve" and went together with particular tribal names. The fragmentary nature of these early accounts makes it difficult to speak of the Vandils with assurance or even to regard them as antecedents of the fifth-century Vandals.[47]

Procopius and Jordanes both wrote in the 550s, after the suppression of the Vandal kingdom in Africa, and were well aware of its fame; they were Byzantines of the age of Justinian. They had never heard of a Siling people or of generic Vandils; nevertheless, they spoke glibly about the Vandal past. Procopius fills in the distant origins that had not interested the fifth-century observers. He has the Vandals originate at the Maeotian swamp (our Sea of Azov) and emigrate directly to Gaul and Spain because their numbers had outgrown their lands. Procopius's contemporary, Jordanes, also mentions the Vandals in remote antiquity but in a different quarter. He has the Goths defeat the Vandals not far from the Baltic in remote centuries B.C. (a shadow of this triumph falls across the legend of Lombard beginnings).[48] Modern authors often turn these sixth-century inventions into facts. Jordanes is widely identified as the stand-in for the estimable (but not necessarily better informed) Cassiodorus; and Procopius, undoubtedly a great historian, is taken seriously even when his information about the Vandals and other aliens is error-laden. The accreditation of these fancies can distort the Vandal past more radically than Pliny's Vandils. Thanks in part to Procopius, modern maps of the barbarian invasions portray the

Vandals as second only to the Visigoths in the length of their "migration."[49] Comparably imaginative, and widely accepted, is Jordanes's account of a fourth-century Gothic victory over Vandals that resulted in Constantine's settling the losers in Roman territory. Recent historians divide roughly fifty-fifty on whether to take Jordanes's word about this defeat and Pannonian settlement.[50]

As a final element to muddy the waters, there are the Vandals of modern philology and archaeology. These are conjured up by stamping the Vandal name on a cultural province defined by material remains. Since World War II the same province has been cleared of Vandals and awarded to non-"Germans."[51] Generous helpings of erudition have made this patriotic modern concoction wholly acceptable to scholars, such as Courtois. It dominates the literature, evoking a past in which Vandals departed from prehistoric Scandinavia and populated Silesia before setting out for Spain and Africa. That migratory scenario is now on trial: "It is still a very dubious project to try to connect the historically known Vandals with the archeological ones."[52] Stalking the Vandals is like picking one's way through a quaking bog. Credible information is less responsible than the history of scholarship, ancient as well as modern, for bringing them into being.

These speculations are irrelevant to our subject. The Asding Vandals, with a documented past reaching back to Marcus Aurelius (A.D. 170s)—enough for all practical purposes—are the stable component of the Rhine crossing of 405. They lived for centuries in the Tisza valley (where their story touches on the archaeological Vandals), came to the Rhine in a large armed force (perhaps with their families as well), and after a time plundering Gaul made their way to Spain.[53] The Asdings are the Vandals who crossed to Africa and enjoyed a century of renown and prosperity.[54] The peoples who accompanied them from the Danube valley to Spain are more sporadically attested.

The Siling variety of Vandals is perplexing in everything except its destruction by the Goths of King Wallia in 418. The tale of the archaeological Vandals, on which the Silings depend very much, associates them with Silesia, where the Alexandrian geographer Ptolemy recorded them in his map of *Magna Germania*. The name "Siling" is apparently discernible in "Silesia" itself, and other Silesian toponyms were affected, it seems, by these residents. If the Silings lived where archaeologists say they did, their territory in late antiquity has yielded many rich "princely" graves. The wealth of the district is attributed to a flourishing trade from the Roman Empire into inner Germany.[55]

Courtois took it for granted that Silings were the Vandals referred to by Eutropius as participants in the Marcommanic War, but did not explain this choice. The one verified military exploit by Silings took place in the later third century. In company with Burgundians, their troops engaged the emperor Probus near a river, were bested by a stratagem and defeated. Forced to enlist in Roman service, they proved valuable in Britain. Courtois and others inferred that the Silings made a lasting settlement near the Burgundians, that is, on the upper Main, and joined the expedition to Gaul from there. On Courtois's "railroad" map, the Siling spur, running through central Germany far north of the Danube and connecting with the trunk line, is the last addition to the expedition before the Rhine was reached. This guess gracefully merges the Silings with the Rhine crossing, but falls of itself. An isolated incident of A.D. 278 should not be inflated into a major, enduring colony of Silings far to the west of their normal habitat, a colony of which no trace exists.[56]

The Silings probably formed the second largest component of the 405 expedition; the share of Spain awarded to them in 411 implies as much. Our ignorance about them is vast. Where in relation to the Asdings had they lived? How were they drawn into the expedition? Where did they join their three fellow invaders? The sources we have, admittedly scant, record no trace whatever of mutual support or friendship between the two Vandal branches.[57] Silings and Asdings did not have a constitutional union; Vandal brotherhood or comradeship cannot have been a motive. If the Silings lived where they are thought to have—an aspect of their surmised archaeological identity—they would have been virtually masked from disturbance to the east, and more remote from the Danube than from other routes. The Silings are a mystery, typical of the mists we grope through in trying to learn about most northern neighbors of the Roman Empire.[58]

The Danubian Sueves and Vandals impress by their adhesion to the ground. Their relation to the surmised migration of peoples (*Völkerwanderung*) in whose grip, allegedly, the "Germanic" peoples had long been is extremely shaky. The Marcomanni and Quadi had been middle Danubians before there had been a Roman frontier—an awe-inspiring span. The Vandals, despite their modern reputation as travelers, had been rooted in the Danube valley for more than two centuries. Lacking a memory of ancient migration, they were veteran sedentaries, who, for all anyone needs to care, had always been where they were. No one attributed a distant past to them until Justinian's contemporary, Procopius, did so. (By the time Procopius's work was published the attribution was posthumous, since the last surviving Vandals had been stamped out in Africa about twenty years before.) While other barbarians transgressed the Roman borders repeatedly during the third century, the Vandals had remained quiet, in a zone of tranquility of great value to the Empire.[59] Inertia so weighed on the mid-Danubian peoples who headed for the Rhine that they look like poor prospects for emigration.

Their going in 405 is certain, but when did they decide to head for the Rhine? Historically their axis of attack had been southward, not west. Besides, there had been little fighting on the middle Danube since the 370s. In the years concerning us, the first trace of military action occurs in 401–2; Vandals invaded Raëtia and were turned back by the Roman generalissimo Stilicho. After decades of quiescence, mid-Danubians took the war path as the 400s began. Their long-range plans are less clear.

The normal answer to the question why they moved is Hunnish pressure. External agency simplifies the problem. Without Huns, reasons for emigration are more difficult to formulate. One scholar with a wide outlook suggests that all Danubians wished to enter the Empire in the same way that a massive collection of Goths had in A.D. 376. They had expected to be admitted on the same favorable terms until an unforeseen contingency thwarted their wishes: the Goths revolted, won the battle of Adrianople, and set the Romans resolutely against admitting additional immigrants.[60] Exclusion did not efface the Danubians' desire to move inside the Roman frontiers. If normal life north of the river depended on exchanges with the Empire, the ravaging of neighboring provinces, notably Pannonia, was likely to damage the Vandals, Quadi, and other long-time residents of *barbaricum* no less than Roman provincials.[61] The Empire that supplied them with the prestige goods that their leaders had come to rely upon was receding from the old frontiers and withdrawing to its core Mediterranean lands. If a Hunnic role is discounted two influences on the mid-Danubians acquire importance: a serious deterioration in the conditions of life along the Danube owing to disruptions of trade and gift exchanges with the Empire; and the sense that Rome, dependent on alien troops and receptive to alien labor, was less restrictive to immigration than in the past. The mass admission of Goths had changed the outlook for life north of the Roman border. Once the door to the Empire was opened wide (even if shut again), life in *barbaricum* was profoundly devalued.

Vandals in Roman Raëtia

As the fifth century began, the poet Claudian, personal propagandist for the Roman generalissimo Stilicho, reported a barbarian incursion into Raëtia. His poem, referring to 401, is our first indication that "the natives were restless" on the middle Danube. When the Goth Alaric invaded Italy with his people through its low eastern heights, Stilicho could not concentrate his mobile forces to block his advance. His army was absent, forced to "fight another war." The mid-Danubians, whom Claudian does not name at first, had treaties with the Empire, mainly, one supposes, *foedera* of nonaggression. Encouraged by Alaric's march on Italy, they made light of their pledges and poured over the fields of Noricum and the woods of eastern Raëtia (Vindilicia). The routes through these provinces led to the same destination as Alaric—northern Italy. The possibility that the mid-Danubians would join the Goths was a mortal danger to the Roman defenders. Clear-sightedly, Stilicho fought them first.[62] Alamanni were better placed to attack Raëtia than the Sueves and Vandals who concern us, but the reference to Noricum, the Roman equivalent of Austria, moves the invasion far enough east to confirm the identity of the aggressors.

The Roman guards, detached from Stilicho's field army and deployed in forward defense of Italy, proved adequate to blunt the Danubians' advance.[63] Stilicho eventually freed himself from competing concerns and braved the Alps to take personal charge of his troops. Claudian shows him warning the barbarian intruders not to meddle in the war with Alaric: in Rome's struggle with Hannibal, Philip V of Macedon had dared to intervene and regretted it (215–205 B.C.). This threat ostensibly averted further hostilities and allowed Stilicho to enroll moderate numbers of the attacking barbarians as troops for the war in Italy. Claudian's poem then launches into a (figurative) parade of Roman detachments from Britain and Gaul proceeding to Italy, led by the successful defenders of Raëtia. The latter were covered with Vandal spoils—the sole passage giving an ethnic name to the attackers, in adjectival form at that.[64]

Claudian grudges information, even names; modern authors have been more daring. Émilienne Demougeot, in an early book, added Alans to the mentioned Vandals; later, she left Alans out and specified Quadi, Siling Vandals, and reluctant Marcomanni. Alan Cameron omitted Claudian's reference to Vandals and emphasized Alans: those recruited by Stilicho, he imagined, included the regiment of Saul, soon famed at the battle against Alaric at Pollentia. An editor of Claudian, Theodor Birt, anticipated these imports of surmised Alans. Courtois simply took it for granted that Raëtia was attacked by the coming invaders of Gaul: repelled from the route to Italy, they turned toward the Rhine.[65] The pause between 402 and 405 implies a languidly slow turn.

Courtois read Claudian more prudently than the others. For Stilicho to be alarmed and to dread a link with Alaric, the attackers of Raëtia had to be a large force, similar to the one that crossed the Rhine a few years later, but only similar. The Romans earned "Vandal spoils" by winning minor successes that Claudian merely implies. Neither side sought a full trial of strength. The invaders were wise to abstain if, as Claudian vaguely suggests, the defenders of Raëtia were reinforced by Roman units in transit from Britain and the Rhine to Italy. Stilicho had nothing to gain from dissipating his precious troops on another enemy than Alaric. The axis of attack by the mid-Danubians in 401 did not threaten Gaul. Noricum and Raëtia led to Italy and were on an almost direct line of advance from the stamping grounds of the Sueves and Vandals. The Rhine was far off in a different direction.

An entry in the *Gallic Chronicle of 452* forces us to consider whether the repulsed attackers of Raëtia were a part of Radagaisus's army (405–6). The chronicle claims that the latter had three divisions, each with its own leader. If Radagaisus alone was destroyed at Fiesole, then two of the divisions claimed by the Gallic chronicle are unaccounted for.[66] Modern conjectures have associated the Rhine crossers with Radagaisus. In one version, Vandals and Alans came up against Roman troops in Raëtia in 401, regrouped when driven back, and joined Radagaisus as one of his three divisions in Italy; then, "repelled by Stilicho in the spring of 406, they flowed back north and tried at the end of the year to cross the Rhine."[67] These twists and turns, leading nowhere, are too high a price to pay to make sense of the isolated Gallic chronicler. The report of three divisions, even if containing specks of truth, is too compressed and lacking a context to be more than a diversion.[68]

The Roman high command believed that the Vandals who attacked Raëtia in 401 wished to break through to Italy and join forces with Alaric. Its fears suggest a large force, one composed of more than Vandals; but no Alans are visible. The invaders of Raëtia, lacking élan, were cowed by threats more than force. Ineffectuality may have been typical Vandal behavior of the day. Still, Stilicho recruited volunteers for service against Alaric; he needed troops. Somewhat reduced from the force that had set out, the Vandals and their (unnamed) associates retreated north of the Danube, the way home.

This withdrawal to *barbaricum* need not have snuffed out the mid-Danubians' aspiration to penetrate Roman space. Warriors presumably from several peoples had worked themselves up to join in a distant, dangerous, potentially lucrative expedition. They had sampled realistic military life; promises had been made. Unexpended energy was left over from the aborted attack. The capacity for another push was there.

Alans before the Rhine Expedition

One people led the invasion of 405 across the Rhine, namely, the Alans. Early in the invasion, Alans turned about and rescued the Asding Vandals from annihilation by an army of Franks. When the associated invaders divided Spain among themselves, the Alans obtained two provinces, leaving their three partners with the remaining two. Hydatius explicitly affirms that the Alans "lorded it" over the Vandals and Sueves.[69] Alan preeminence in the expedition was a reality for more than a decade, but it did not last: Goths fighting for Rome brought the Alans to battle in 418, killed their King Addax, and massacred his people. The survivors fled to the Asding Vandals and exchanged their independence for Vandal protection. The Alan name was added to the Asding royal title, *rex Vandalorum et Alanorum,* a dual kingdom attested after the crossing to Africa. The downfall of 418 does not cancel the Alans' initial leadership. From the start of the expedition until the Gothic attack, they were foremost among the invaders.[70]

The Alans were prodigious. Famed fighters, they were steppe nomads like the Sarmatians and Huns and, although many were culturally Gothicized in the fifth and sixth century, their ancestry was Iranian. The Romans had known the Alans for a long time; so had Chinese observers. A prominent second-century Roman general serving on the eastern frontier wrote a treatise on how imperial forces should meet Alans in battle. Their grazing range in the fourth century was to the east of the Goths in south Russia. The Huns' first onslaught in the 370s was against them.[71] In the next decades, Alan detachments fought at the battle of Adrianople, in the army of the West Roman emperor Gratian, in a co-alition with Goths and Huns ravaging Pannonia, and under Theodosius I against the usurper Maximus. Their tastes in allies were catholic. During half the fifth century, a family of Alans in Roman service supplied Constantinople with its military strong men, the Eastern equivalents of the Aetiuses and Ricimers of the West. The emperors Marcian (450) and Leo I (456) owed their elevations to the purple to these Alan dignitaries, to whose personal staff they had belonged.[72] Meanwhile, bands of Alans accepted settlement here and there in Gaul. The corps headed by Sangiban had a central part in Aetius's defense against Attila (451). Another force, given to plunder, was fought by the emperor Majorian and quelled in Italy by the patrician Ricimer, who killed its king Beorg (457–64).[73] These incidents did not end the Alan story. Their old stamping grounds— steppelands between the Volga and Don rivers and the Caucasus—were not lost to them. Alans endured for centuries in the Caucasus. An obtrusive Byzantine empress in the eleventh century was Mary of Alania, and the Alanic language survives today among the Caucasian Ossetes.[74]

In one view of their adventures, the Alans were blown apart by the Huns and seen again only in particles that never coalesced into a larger entity. There might be truth to this view if the nomad Alans had been cohesive before the Huns attacked them. Ammianus notes, on the contrary, that the various Alan peoples were scattered over vast steppes. Their unity was cultural, not political.[75]

The Huns fought fiercely against the Alans in the 370s not to disrupt their nonexistent union but to gain their support in a larger campaign. In Ammianus's account, the Huns overpowered the Don Alans, who bordered the Gothic kingdom of Ermanaric, and they "join[ed] the [surviving Alans] to themselves in treaties of alliance" so as to carry out the conquest of Ermanaric's dominion. Ambrose abbreviates the circumstances, "The Huns threw themselves upon the

Alans, the Alans upon the Goths."[76] The Don Alans did not suffer irreparable damage at Hunnic hands. Thanks to their erstwhile attackers, they gained a spectrum of opportunities for martial enterprises and enrichment inside and outside the Roman borders. These opportunities were not scorned.

After their initial defeat by the Huns, Alans often fought in company with partners, notably Huns and Goths, and as recruits for Rome. Much is heard of them in these capacities in the later fourth century, as suggested above. One Alan force delayed the West Roman emperor Gratian on his way to assist Valens before Adrianople, and another, allegedly, was the cause of Gratian's downfall (383): "Slighting the army, [Gratian] coaxed a small corps of Alans into his service by a vast amount of gold and preferred it to veteran Roman soldiers. To such a degree was he taken with the company and almost the friendship of the barbarians that he sometimes journeyed in [barbarian] attire. Thus he aroused the hatred of the soldiers against himself."[77] Gratian's corps of Alans had the opportunity to visit Gaul—a remote land for recent arrivals at the lower Danube. The contingent of Alans and Huns engaged by Gratian's half brother Valentinian II to fight some Alamanni also gained familiarity with the distant West.[78] These exploits of the 370s and 380s took place long before the cross-Rhine invasion. At the time, Alan units were valued components of the West Roman army.

If, as seen above, the Sueves and two types of Vandals of the 405 invasion are hard to trace to a point of departure, the Alans are even harder. Courtois decided that they should be identified with the Rox*alani*—more normally called Rox*olani*—a Sarmatian tribe resident for many centuries in Wallachia. His interesting "trunk line" sets out from Wallachia with these quasi Alans. Wenskus advocated a similar but more nebulous idea. Both proposals, though made in earnest, lack support.[79] The majority view, recently demolished by Heather, was that the Alans in question originated from a coalition of Goths, Huns, and Alans that (so it was believed) fought at Adrianople, then extended their depredations into Illyricum, and were finally induced by the emperor Gratian in 380 to accept a settlement as *foederati* in Roman Pannonia. Heather's refutation of this influential and long-lasting theory is impressive, but has disturbing implications.[80] When the Alan *foederati* in Pannonia are blown away, and Courtois's and Wenskus's theories are rejected, the slate of scholarly opinion is wiped clean. No explanation is left for the Alans of 405.

There is another possibility, admittedly delicate and contestable. A passage of Orosius, lacking any firm interpretation, reports that, just about the time that concerns us, a mixed force of Alans and Huns in Roman service experienced a violent falling out and broke apart. The Alan member of this divorce can be proposed as the catalyst of the Rhine crossing. The expedition of 405 would have come about when the frustrated attackers of Raëtia joined forces with the Alans who (according to Orosius) had split from their Hunnic partners. Almost all of this is conjecture. Orosius allows us to see Alans breaking loose from Huns; we have to speculate that they went to the Danube valley and came upon the failed southward expedition of Vandals.

Orosius relates, in an early fifth-century context, that two groups of paired barbarians fell out with one another: two cavalry regiments (*cunei*) of Goths, and, next, a unit of Alans and Huns, "waste one another in various massacres"; they engaged in "frequent tearings apart" for reasons unknown to him.[81] No circumstances are stated, but the entire passage fits best into a progressive chronology. Orosius deplores the ill-use of the Empire by Rufinus and Stilicho after Theodosius's death (395). Four incidents are cited to document their misrule: Alaric is repeatedly pinned down but never destroyed; the battle of Pollentia is fought disgracefully on Easter Sunday under a pagan general; (item three is our passage) regiments of barbarian troops fall out and tear each other apart; finally, Radagaisus and his Goths invade Roman space.[82] Orosius evidently believed that the repeated escapes of Alaric's army and the circumstances of Pollentia were shameful. Also shameful in the logic of his argument were the fallings out among barbarian units; their losses were damaging to West Rome because the soldiers at each other's throats were, or had been till then, in imperial service, like the Alans recruited by Gratian and Valentinian II.[83] Assuming Orosius narrated chronogically, a date between 402 (Pollentia) and 405 (Radagaisus) is implied for these Alans to separate themselves with much bloodshed from their Hunnish associates.

The Hun-Alan unit that had fought in Raëtia for Valentinian II could not be meant by Orosius. Twenty years had passed, with Roman civil wars in the interval; Valentinian's force of steppe cavalry, if not paid off long before, had probably been expended or discharged by 395.[84] No matter. The recruitment of one or more Hun-Alan units into western service before 400 is wholly plausible and would not have had to be recorded. Alans of unknown origin distinguished themselves on the Roman side of the 402 campaign against Alaric.[85] Soon after that, according to Orosius, a mixed force of Alans and Huns tore apart along ethnic lines.

One outcome can be imagined for the Hun-Alan divorce—but only imagined; there is no evidence. Toward 403, veteran Alans familiar with the Western imperial army, and acquainted with western geography as well, were somewhere, out of work. In need of exercise and gainful employment, they conceivably withdrew toward the nearest steppeland. This Alan force comes to mind in connection with the imminent Rhine crossing. But not in a single step. Part of a regiment of cavalry, diminished by casualties, could not be the preeminent column of the 405 invasion. The Alans-divorced-from-Huns needed reinforcements.

Alans Join Mid-Danubians

Alans were one part of the expedition of 405; the returnees from Raëtia were the other. The merger of these elements is the condition for the Rhine crossing. The normal neighborhood of the Vandals and Sueves was the Danube and points south, not the Rhine. The attackers of 405 were real foreigners to the Rhine and to Gaul, only a little less so than the peoples gathered for Attila's offensive in 451. Of the parties in presence, the Alans are more likely to have turned the assembled forces in that direction. Their service with the West Roman army, the familiarity some may have had with the Rhine frontier, their need for lucrative employment; all draw the dynamic role toward them.

Nomadic horsemen proved skilled in late antiquity in giving leadership to agrarian tribes. The best publicized example involves the Asiatic, pony-riding Avars in the late sixth century inciting the Slavs in the Balkans and even in Central Europe; their successes were impressive. The Antes, a Slavic people, are said to owe their name to long association with Alans, conceivably their drill masters.[86] After the Huns moved into the Danubian steppes, they are found in company with client peoples whom they deployed as auxiliaries in their fifth-century raids into East and West Roman territory.[87] As the Huns and Avars excelled in marshaling helpers, so the Alans may have brought talents of leadership and enterprise to the Vandals and others whom they came upon in the middle Danube.

From the start of the Rhine expedition down to 418 in Spain, Alans were the dominant partners in the expedition. Hardly anyone believes that a reinforced battalion of Don Alans was forced or drifted westward to south Russia and up the Danube prior to 405. Orosius, however, testifies that one "free" Alan contingent formerly mixed with Huns in the Roman army was at large in the west, ca. 403. When the Vandals and associates retreated ingloriously from Raëtia, neither victorious nor defeated, they may have been greeted by Alans eager for enterprise.

This Alan company had to increase its numbers. The Danubian steppes used to be and may still have been dense with Sarmatians. In spite of a fourth century full of disasters and losses, some Sarmatians were left (as Jerome attests) and could be attracted to the banners of their Alan cousins.[88] To the east, in south Russia and on the Don, many Alans were at large; they had often been recruited by Goths, Huns, and Romans during the past decades. The Orosian group presumably sent out a call for fellow tribesmen to join them in a major enterprise, and the call was answered. These recruits, experienced cavalry, could concentrate in large numbers in little time.

When the Alans, Vandals, and Sueves reached the Rhine an Alan named Goar defected to the Romans. Alans formerly in Roman military service, besides having valuable intelligence, were also likely to have retained contacts in the Roman army. Goar, if from this group, is likely to have simply been bribed into defection. Alternatively, he may have been exasperated that rougher-hewn Alans were, by their numbers, acquiring supremacy in the swelling Alan formation, so that a king, Respendial, high-born but (conjecturally) from the eastern steppes, overshadowed the nucleus of Alans who had fought for Rome.[89] Commentators assume that Goar took with him a large part of the attacking force, but the outcome does not confirm this opinion. Whether estranged or merely bribed, Goar made little difference to the invasion by changing sides. He left for a prosperous future in Roman Gaul.[90] The Alans carried on under Respendial and continued to be highly effective.

My narrative has reached the Rhine. Many doubts remain about who went and how they got there. Which particular people assumed the generic name "Sueves"? Where had the Siling Vandals resided and what decided them to pack up and leave ancestral homes? From where did a mass of Alans flow toward a rendezvous with the mid-Danubians? In view of how ancient the Suevic peopling of this region was, what circumstances induced many inhabitants to set out once and for all? No definite answers are available.

One general point deserves to be made all the same. Between 401 and 411, four distinct groups of barbarians—different from Alaric's Goths—invaded Roman territory, all apparently on one-way journeys, in large-scale efforts to transpose themselves onto imperial soil and not just plunder and return home. These were the expeditions of the Vandals into Raëtia intending (in the view of Roman observers) to link up in Italy with Alaric; the expedition in 405 of Radagaisus and his large mixed horde into Italy; the invasion of the Alans, Vandals, and Sueves into Gaul on New Year's Eve 405 (a continuation in a different direction of what had been begun in 401); and the support of the Burgundians and Goar's Alans for the Roman usurper Jovinus in 411 whose outcome was the settlement of Burgundians on the left bank of the Rhine. The first two were abortive, as we know, but no less serious for that reason; the third allowed itself to be drawn farther into Roman territory than its leaders could have anticipated; and the fourth resulted in a principality in the north of Roman Gaul that lasted for more than two decades. What the four expeditions have in common is the ostensible abandonment by the participants of age-old homes for uncertain futures on Roman soil, a measure of despair in the condition of *barbaricum*, and the at least faint expectation that better things, enduring ones, were attainable by attacking the Roman Empire. It is hard to believe that these movements, though in three cases independent of each other, were not founded on similar hopes. The adventures of the Goths inside the Empire since 376 had not offered a spectacle of unqualified success; but it disclosed barbarians being taken more seriously and positively by Roman governments than they had ever been before. It is hard to believe that the wholesale desertion of *barbaricum* in these opening years of the fifth century was not shaped by the common perception, however indistinct, that warriors could improve their condition by forcing their existence on the attention of the Empire, demanding to be dealt with, and exacting a part in the imperial enterprise. This possibility of a common impulse inspired by the Gothic example is a conjecture that deserves to be advanced and entertained.[91]

Action at the Rhine

Gaul, one of the largest and richest regions of the Roman Empire, was practically undefended. Claudian reports a brief trip by Stilicho to the Rhine in 396, another to Raëtia in 401 (mentioned a few pages ago). Stilicho took steps to stiffen the Rhine and upper Danube frontiers while removing the veterans guarding them.[92] The available forces of Britain, Gaul, and the upper Rhine were withdrawn to northern Italy to face the Goths. The barbarians along the Rhine—Franks and Alamanni—responded positively to Stilicho, swore loyalty, and gave hostages. Claudian dwells lovingly on their unforced submission: fabled Roman generals had had to fight for years for what Stilicho won in as many days. The Rhine border, virtually denuded of Roman troops, was entrusted to deferential neighbors: "The garrison was removed and the Rhine was left to be defended by only one thing—the threat [of punishment]."[93]

Claudian, though a panegyrist, did not overstate the relative security of the Rhine: the Franks and Alamanni, long the main dangers to the frontier, stayed loyal. If a great migration of "Germanic" peoples was in progress, the Rhine peoples did not opt in. The mid-Danubians were more restless. Quadi, Vandals, and the like had normally been too distant to alarm anyone concerned with the Rhine. The same continued to be true near 401; the mid-Danubian strike force longing for war headed south, toward Italy and Alaric, giving no sign that the far west was its goal.

Then the Alans turned up, schooled by Roman service. It was they, presumably, who were aware of the opportunity offered by a Rhine stripped of defenders. The Roman side, alerted by the Raëtian clashes, could not have been totally surprised by the massing of troops at the Rhine in 405. They knew that undefeated, battle-ready troops were at large, and that their erstwhile Alan comrades-in-arms now stood on the hostile side. The token defenders of the Rhine had reason to be on guard, for all the good it did them: the nearest reinforcements were in Britain.[94]

These circumstances complement the unique fragment of historical narrative about the Rhine crossing—a lucky accident of text transmission: "Meanwhile Respendial, king of the Alans, turned his forces away from the Rhine. [He had several reasons.] Goar had passed over to the Romans; [what's more] the [Asding] Vandals were doing badly in war with the Franks. King Godegisel had been killed; almost 20,000 of their fighters had been killed. All the Vandals would have been wiped out if the main Alan force had not promptly relieved them."[95] This surviving quotation from a lost history is an abrupt ray of light. The Romans won an Alan leader to their side. Meanwhile, the Franks, true to their commitments to Stilicho, won a signal triumph over the Asdings. But despite their effectiveness in resisting the invaders, the Franks lacked the strength to turn them back. Respendial and his Alans shrugged off Goar's defection and rode to the rescue. The Frankish defeat of the Asdings led into a pursuit in which the surviving Vandals risked being exterminated. Respendial's Alans intervened and exacted a heavy toll from the Franks. The breakthrough into Gaul, which Orosius says involved "many peoples besides [the leading ones]," ran its course.[96]

The fragment of Frigeridus implies that the Vandals did not lead the invasion. The Asdings were defeated, the Silings and Sueves invisible. Respendial and his Alans were in the forefront of the action.

From Crossing the Rhine to Crossing the Pyrenees

What comes next is perhaps the most tangled segment of late Roman history. The crossing of the Rhine was anything but an isolated event. Stilicho and Alaric were planning a march on Constantinople; a Roman usurper, contesting Honorius's throne, arose in Britain and quickly won control of the entire Gallic prefecture; the Eastern emperor Arcadius died leaving a child as successor—an occasion for the West to intervene; Stilicho went from one plan to the next until overthrown in a coup d'état; Alaric took his Goths into Italy and marched about in search of an arrangement with the Roman authorities; Theodosian loyalists in Spain set an uprising in motion; Alaric carried out his famed seizure of Rome; North Africa was lost to a usurper and regained. These and other assertive disturbances pushed the Alan, Vandal, and Sueve invaders into the margins of historical interest.[97]

Defeated by the jumble of these events, contemporary authors proved incapable of untangling the knots and extracting linear narratives out of occurrences that called for topical treatment or parallel lines rather than a simultaneous advance in chronological order. The nearest to a contemporary observer, Orosius, writes too compactly to be helpful. Olympiodorus of Thebes, the most trustworthy historian of these years, comparatively near in time but known only from fragments, professed that he was merely supplying materials for history rather than a finished product. He felt forced by the subject matter to resort to multiple flashbacks in the midst of a topical organization. He focuses on Alaric and his doings down to the fall of Rome in 410, and only then switches back several years and pays attention to the usurper from Britain. The testimony of Olympiodorus survives in extracts made by Photius and, earlier, by the church historian Sozomen and the epitomator Zosimus.[98] The latter two had programs of their own; they copied Olympiodorus selectively and thought nothing of obscuring the source's design. Olympiodorus himself is not beyond blame as a reporter. Desperate battles or years of barbarian plundering in Gaul are given short shrift by comparison with close-ups of spectacular individual fates. The gallant death of general Gerontius, preventively killing his wife and a faithful retainer before botching his suicide, is only one of three or four such incidents eclipsing the anything-but-humdrum course of events.[99]

Guided by sources that are themselves disconnected and confused, generations of modern historians have found it impossible to synthesize the main witnesses without doing violence to parts of their testimony.[100] Where the Alans, Vandals, and Sueves are concerned, the main problem is lack of interest: there is almost no information about their time in Gaul. The Rhine crossing took place on December 31, 405. The clock starts to tick on the first day of 406. The interval to be accounted for lasts somewhat more than three and a half years, since Hydatius dates the crossing of the barbarians into Spain to September or October 409. How did the Alans, Vandals, and Sueves occupy themselves in this period?

As 406 began, the Asdings were depleted by their defeat at Frankish hands and weakened by the accession of a new king; the Alans were endangered by Goar's defection to the Romans. Neither loss was crippling. The four peoples were at large in a northern Gaul largely bereft of organized defense. They allegedly massacred a churchful of Christians in Mainz. Several other cities saw them and suffered at their hands. The Roman forces of Gaul and Aquitaine, whose best elements had been withdrawn to Italy in 402 and (as far as we know) never returned, were incapable of mounting any effective counterstroke. The invaders' ravaging of the north reached far west to the land of the Morini, a jumping-off point to Britain.[101]

The British diocese, cut off from the emperor in distant Italy, was threatened with having an enemy across its lines of communication. It was perhaps experiencing attacks by its perennial raiders, the Irish to the west, Picts from the north, and Saxons to the east. Desperate for leadership, the Roman army raised a certain Marcus to the emperorship and unseated him almost at once. Next came a certain Gratian, who in four months disappointed the hopes initially vested in him. Within his short reign the year changed from 406 to 407. The last of these British-made emperors, Constantine III, proved more enduring. Almost at once, he moved as much of the army of Britain as he could across the Channel to northern Gaul and rallied to himself the Roman forces of Gaul and Aquitaine, over which he appointed new generals. Even Spain accepted his officials. Constantine's dissident emperorship rapidly extended to the whole of the vast Gallic prefecture.[102]

Zosimus, an East Roman historian and one of the two users of Olympiodorus, situates at this point a major battle between the combined Roman forces led by Constantine and a large barbarian army that had come *over the Alps*. I am not the first to set aside this reference to the Alps as a mistake and to identify the barbarians with the pillaging Alans, Vandals, and Sueves from over the Rhine. For Constantine III to bring these four enemies to battle must have been a feat in itself. His forces prevailed, killing large numbers of the invaders (but not their leaders) and routing the survivors. Zosimus insists that, if a proper pursuit had been organized, the victory would have been decisive. But there was no pursuit; the invaders could regain their breath and rebuild their forces.[103]

Constantine had reason to disengage. Stilicho in Italy had enlisted the help of the Goth Sarus, recent victor over the hordes of Radagaisus, and sent him against the usurper. Constantine had to concentrate his troops to meet this challenge. Later still he had to reckon with the army Stilicho was mustering in Italy for a full-scale attack. Meanwhile, according to Orosius, Constantine was "tricked again and again by the unreliable treaties of the barbarians."[104]

Except for Orosius's account of treaties and a dramatic letter of Jerome, the exploits of the Alans, Vandals, and Sueves hardly ever impinge on the career of Constantine III during these months. His activities in Gaul and Spain, paralleling Alaric's no less absorbing activities in Italy, occupy historians to the exclusion of all other concerns. The balance of 407 saw the Goth Sarus single-handedly eliminating Constantine's two chief generals but then being chased from Gaul by the new generals appointed in their place. Withdrawing from Valence (where Sarus had briefly besieged him), Constantine established his capital at Arles.[105] Other problems were on his mind than pillaging in the Gallic countryside.

In 408 (during which the Eastern emperor Arcadius died in May and

Stilicho was the victim of a coup d'état in August), Spain was Constantine's main preoccupation. Relatives of Theodosius I—that is, of the legitimate imperial family, including the reigning Honorius—revolted against Constantine and had to be fought. The usurper gave his senior son Constans the title of Caesar (heir apparent), and sent him to Spain in the company of the British-born general Gerontius, famed for strict discipline. A difficult campaign defeated the Theodosian relatives and delivered them into Constans's hands. Constans was recalled to Arles for consultation with his father. The two Theodosian rebels were summarily executed en route. The year was still 408.[106]

The campaign against the Theodosian relatives had disturbed the military organization of Spain but left unchanged the rule that Pyrenean passes were defended by native Spanish militia. Either Constans or Gerontius dismissed the Spanish defenders of the passes and replaced them with the *Honoriaci*—units of Roman regulars recruited from among the Rhine peoples—whom Constantine had sent in 408 to reinforce his son's army. These were the (unreliable) defenders of the gates to Spain when the Alans, Vandals, and Sueves eventually headed in this direction.

What had happened to the Rhine crossers in the two years since they had been cowed but not crushed or turned back by the early efforts of Constantine? Tradition claims that they cut a swath of destruction across Gaul, with special attention to the south. The evidence for such a course of events is thin.[107] Arguing from the letter of Jerome and Orosius's reference to violated treaties, Kulikowski emphasizes that Jerome associates the Rhine crossers firmly with the northern provinces of Germania I and Belgica I and II, then more shakily with the far south, and little in between. He concludes that the invaders were bottled up in the north between 406 and 409 and concentrated their destructiveness there. Early in 409, Constantine's general, Gerontius, rebelled in Spain, opposed his erstwhile patron with a usurper of his own, Maximus, and called for barbarian help.[108] This call (it is conjectured) went to the Alans, Vandals, and Sueves, still in the north; it galvanized them into a new offensive that, first, took them quickly south and next, against the wishes of their sponsor, sent them hurtling into Spain, sweeping aside the unreliable defenders. Orosius explains, "[the *Honoriaci*] were entrusted with the care of the mountains mentioned above and their passes. There, [they] . . . , after betraying their watch over the Pyrenees and leaving the passes open, let into the Spanish provinces all the nations which were wandering over the Gauls and they themselves joined them."

Kulikowski's scenario has the merit of strictly interpreting the little information we have, but it leaves nagging problems; the sources are too fragmentary to permit confident reconstructions of the events. The year 409 is associated with a famous report that Britain and Armorica (northwest Gaul) threw off

Roman government; did the departure of the barbarians set off this revolt?[109] Besides, if the Alans, Vandals, and Sueves were latecomers to the riches of southern Gaul and only just beginning a course of pillage, why would they have turned away from these treasures almost at once and crossed into Spain? The storm over southern Gaul between the Rhine crossers' arrival from the north and their departure would have lasted an implausibly short time.[110] However loosely documented, the idea that the Alans, Vandals, and Sueves were at large in western Gaul over a period of years, taking advantage of Constantine III's distractions, rebuilding their strength, and gradually depleting the easy pickings of Gaul, helps to provide a reason for them to head onward into Spain.[111] One might imagine that the Alans, Vandals, and Sueves were scattered, widely engaging in pillage, but that the appeal of Gerontius, and smell of a fresh opportunity, drew them together again. With renewed force, the formerly defeated invaders of Gaul became invaders of confused and defenseless Spain.[112]

Before the Alans, Vandals, and Sueves leave Gaul a word should be said about their victims. Had the invasion been a shattering experience for the Gallo-Romans? There are two contemporary witnesses. One of them, already encountered, is Jerome writing from Bethlehem to a widow in Rome, counseling her against remarriage in view of the horrors currently being experienced. Jerome is very somber, and not necessarily badly informed, but a rather distant witness all the same. The other is Paulinus of Béziers, who refers clearly enough to ravaging Sarmatians, incendiary Vandals, and speedy plundering Alans but, in the more notable part of his discourse, evokes careful proprietors who quickly set to work repairing the damage and picking up their former lives, complete with their inveterate sins. "To judge from this poem," Pierre Courcelle comments, ". . . Gallo-Roman life, momentarily troubled, had not disappeared from all cities as a result of the Alans and Vandals. . . . [T]his first barbarian flood, always on the move, stayed only three years."[113] Also impressive is the indifference of posterity. The spirit of 417, reflected in Orosius and Rutilius Namatianus, was one of reconstruction: a storm had passed; better times were ahead. Salvian, somewhat later, is somber about many things, but not about the sufferings meted out by this invasion. Sidonius Apollinaris, born ca. 430, had not (as far as one may tell) been reared on tales of the horrors of 406–9. As for the historian Gregory of Tours (†594), he knows of an invasion but switches almost instantly to a garbled incident involving Sueves and Vandals whose setting had to have been Spain. His focus in any case is not barbarian plunder but persecution of Catholics by Arians.[114] The sounds coming from modern commentators, according to whom the invasion of 406 changed everything, are not wholly in keeping with those of contemporary observers.

The Sharing Out of Spain

The Spanish segment of the invasion is estimably documented by the *Chronicle* of Hydatius, bishop of Chavès in northwest Spain. Hydatius's work, a continuation of the world chronicle of Eusebius-Jerome, is almost a running account of Spanish affairs.[115] His description of the invasion is somberly colored and deeply felt.

Hydatius's chronicle has many gaps; its continuity is more apparent than real. A sentence or two for one year, even if carefully crafted, says little. Hydatius leaves out more happenings than he includes; to realize this one has only to compare his pared-down account of the invasion of Spain to the more circumstantial one of Orosius.[116] Composed about a half century after the events, Hydatius's narrative surpasses the shreds we have had to cope with thus far, but even with his help we are sparsely informed and have to bear in mind how little we know.

Hydatius gives the following sketch of the invasion of Spain down to the year when the barbarians adopted peaceful ways:

The Alans and Vandals and Sueves entered [the diocese of Spain] in [409].

[410] The barbarians who had entered [the diocese of Spain] plundered with lethal force.

Plague played its part in the devastation.

[Summary: long, colorful, emotional description of the plundering of Spain. Peoples or places are not named.][117]

In [411], having ruined the provinces of Spain by the ravages of these blows, the barbarians decided by God's mercy to make peace (*ad pacem ineundam . . . conversi*). They divided the territories of the provinces among themselves by an apportionment for [permanent] residence (*sorte ad inhabitandum sibi provinciarum dividunt regiones*). The Vandals and Sueves appropriated Gallaecia—a district at the edge of the western ocean. The Alans obtained Lusitania and Carthaginensis, and the Vandals surnamed Siling drew Baetica. The Spaniards of the cities and boroughs who had survived the barbarians' blows submitted to service in the provinces of the [new] masters. (*Gallaeciam Vandali occupant et Suevi sitam in extremitate oceani maris occidua: Alani Lusitaniam et Carthaginiensem provincias et Vandali cognomine Silingi Baeticam sortiuntur. Hispani per civitates et castella residui a plagis barbarorum per provincias dominantium se subiciunt servituti.*)[118]

Two issues have dominated discussions of the settlement of 411: did the distribution of territories take place "by lot," on the assumption that this is the correct rendering of *sorte*? And, did the four peoples become Roman *foederati* and obtain their lands by grace of the Roman government? The second question (as will be seen) involves the testimony of Orosius as well as Hydatius.

The drawing of lots has been strangely prominent in view of its improbability. Since there were four peoples and four provinces, drawing lots might have worked well to determine which province went to which people, but only if an equal division had taken place. The distribution in fact was not in a proportion of 1:1, but of 2:1:0.5:0.5. The Alans acquired two whole provinces (the entire center of the peninsula) and the Siling Vandals one (the much-developed south), while the Asding Vandals and the Sueves shared one province between them, in the remote, mountainous, and rainy northwest.

Helped by Mommsen's emendation of *sitam* to *sita*, which has no manuscript support, commentators have imagined that Hydatius meant to distinguish the two settlements in Gallaecia; the Sueves were at "the extremities." Hydatius's intention, however, was only to add a few words about the remote location of Gallaecia itself (it was his part of Spain): the Asdings and Sueves were settled as partners in a territory situated at the extremity of the ocean.

E. A. Thompson approached the uneven distribution of provinces among the four in a spirit of "I believe because it's absurd (*credo quia absurdum*)": the division was so irrational that only a drawing of lots could have brought it about.[119] Other commentators, less alert than Thompson, referred simply to a division by lot, as though *sors* allowed no alternative. But it does; the context matters.

The fourth-century panegyricist Pacatus was amazed that barbarians in Roman service *excubias sorte agere*. He did not mean that guard duty was done "by lot," but that the troops obediently "stand guard in turn." When Attila's sons divided the peoples subject to him among themselves, they did so *aequa sorte*, in equal shares, not by lot. When Jordanes shows Theoderic the Ostrogoth's father and uncle meeting, *missa sorte*, to decide that one would take his people West and the other his East, the destination of each one was determined by the practical circumstance of their respective strength vis-à-vis the Romans, not by a roll of the dice. Jordanes tells us the reasoning of the parties.[120]

Sors has a spectrum of meanings. Where property and its distribution are concerned, the word has as little to do with drawing lots as does our own word "(house-, wood-, city-) lot." No user of "lot (or allotment or allocation)" today, or long ago, presupposes that an appeal to chance or luck is being made. Although "lot" is associated in meaning to "fate" or "destiny," a deed referring to "a house on a lot 75 feet by 37" involves no gamble. The best indication that, in Hydatius, no drawing of lots took place among the four peoples is that an amicable and peaceful distribution resulted in markedly unequal shares, the two smallest being one-quarter the size of the largest. The well recorded meaning of *sors* as "apportionment, allocation, division, part" is surely the sense applicable here.[121] Without appealing to chance, the four peoples agreed among themselves about each share.

Orosius confirms the circumstances: "[The peoples coursing through Gaul broke into Spain;] after harsh spoliations of property and persons, which even they now regret, they held an apportionment, made a division, and, to the present [that is, ca. 417], remain in possession (*post graves rerum atque hominum vastationes, de quibus ipsos quoque modo paenitet, habita sorte et distributa usque ad nunc possessione consistunt*)."[122] *Habita sorte* anticipates Hydatius and (for readers wishing to primitivize) conjures up fur-clad warrior chiefs gravely drawing lots. This modern fascination with presumably barbaric games of chance is nourished by careless interpretations of *sors*. The harmony of Orosius and Hydatius records a calculated division of resources, not an appeal to Lady Luck.[123]

Hydatius leaves the Roman government out of the partition of the Spanish provinces. He comes closest to it when referring to "peace." Even there, the word characterizes only the mood of the invaders. God's mercy prompted them to change their ways and put down roots; the stimulus was divine, not imperial. Hydatius's *ad inhabitandum* qualifies the barbarians' mode of settlement. Prosper of Aquitaine uses the same phrase when describing the imperial arrangements with the Goths in southern Gaul (*ad inhabitandum*, 418) and with the Vandals in Africa (*ad habitandum*, 435). A technical sense seems involved, slippery though such senses are in late Latin. *Habitatio* is a dwelling as distinct from *hospitium*, a place of temporary sojourn. The meaning of *habitare* implied by the context is permanence of residence. Both Hydatius and Prosper point to lasting possession—only that, and not any specific form of ownership.[124]

The division Hydatius outlines affected provinces, large public districts. We are not told about carving up and awarding farms, vineyards, ranches, groves, or any other individual property. Nothing is said about how the provinces would produce revenue for the resident foreigners, except that the surviving provincials resigned themselves to pursue their accustomed duties for (wrongful) new masters. The Alans and their companions had been coursing as robbers over Spain, pausing or bivouacking wherever opportunity beckoned; now, they stopped and took enduring possession of the territories they allotted to each other. The manner in which the immigrants, as individuals or families, became proprietors, if they did, is not defined. There is no reason why, having convincingly seated their power, they could not proceed by requisition from the hapless residents and keep themselves well supplied in this despotic way.

The four groups in presence had been keeping company for quite a few years. The irregular shares of the division look as though they reflected the ratio of force and optimism among the partakers.[125] The Asding Vandals, with Gunderic as king since the Rhine crossing, had been hard-hit by their defeat at the hands of the Franks. Too few in numbers to take charge of a full province, they joined the other weak group, the Sueves, now or soon provided with a king, in sharing the least pleasing, but most remote and presumably "safest" part of the peninsula. Danubians may not have minded a rainy climate; they may even have welcomed cool temperatures.¹²⁶ The Siling Vandals were mighty and confident enough to take over Baetica, a rich prize. The Alans, numerous, self-assured, and bold, obtained Lusitania and with it Merida, the capital of the imperial diocese of Spain. Awarded Carthaginensis as well as Lusitania, an enormous two-province package, they took charge of lands with coastlines on the Atlantic and Mediterranean as well as an interior connecting them—a vast plateau with extensive grazing for a nomad people whose fearsomeness and mobility on horseback were well suited, it may have been hoped, to be responsible for an immense territory.¹²⁷

The Invaders and the Roman Government

Orosius and Procopius are responsible for the belief that the emperor had an active role in the Spanish settlement.¹²⁸ Procopius, as befits a late witness, is aware of only the Vandal branch that later seized Africa, to which he assigns preeminence in the events. The king he places over the Vandals in Spain is the one who was killed in battle with the Franks. Correct information even about simple facts in the past was out of his reach. Concerning the settlement in Spain, he states, "[The emperor] Honorius made an agreement with Godigisclus that [the Vandals] should settle there on condition that it should not be to the detriment of the country"; he then summarizes an alleged law of Honorius, providing that the period of Vandal occupation would be deducted from anyone's thirty-year prescription—a law affecting Roman landowners exclusively. With typically Procopian concern for the propertied, this law showed how "the detriment of the country" was averted.¹²⁹ That is all Procopius relates about the settlement. According to him, Honorius had no one else to deal with except (the deceased) Godegisel. Customary reverence for Procopius has lent credit to this report.

Orosius, a contemporary better situated than Procopius to know what he was talking about, intimates that the invaders eventually had dealings with the Roman government. He begins by referring to new participants in Spanish affairs, namely, the Goths:

[Wallia, king of the Goths,] risked his own safety for the sake of Roman security; he would fight against the other peoples occupying Spain and would vanquish on the Romans' behalf, although the other kings, namely those of the Alans, Vandals, and Sueves, would agree with us on the same conditions, declaring to the emperor Honorius, "While you have peace with everyone and receive everyone's hostages, we will fight one another, slay one another, and vanquish on your behalf. It will be an immortal benefit for your Empire if both sides perish." Who would believe this if the facts did not bear it out? Frequent trustworthy messengers now inform us that wars of peoples take place daily in Spain, and slaughters rage among the barbarians on every side.[130]

The Goths, headed by Alaric until his death in southern Italy, had been led out of Italy and into southern Gaul by Athaulf in 412 and had now passed into Tarraconensis, the one Spanish province untouched by the Alans, Vandals, and Sueves. Wallia was Athaulf's successor. Orosius gives us to understand that, whereas a definite agreement was concluded by the Romans with Wallia, the other barbarians made overtures to the imperial government, offering mutual peace guaranteed by hostages in return for a free hand to fight each other to extinction.[131] There is no sign that these proposals were accepted.

Should the non-Goths mentioned by Orosius be understood to have turned into imperial *foederati*? Bury believed that the Asdings and Sueves had succeeded "in obtaining the recognition of Honorius as federates"; Courcelle (in the wake of Ludwig Schmidt) has them become federates before dividing Spain; like him, Wenskus dispenses with Orosius and claims that, from 411, the Alans were quartered as federates; Demougeot, Stein, and others take Orosius to mean that the barbarian kings were applying to Honorius to become federates; Liebeschuetz proposes that the rebellious general Gerontius and his puppet emperor, Maximus, were responsible for the entire settlement. Other assorted opinions might be collected; based only on surmises, they cancel each other out. E. A. Thompson was right to dissent firmly. The territorial division of Spain involved no undertaking by the imperial government: there is no hint of any in the most reliable source, Hydatius. And even when, in Orosius's imaginative discourse, the kings offered mutual slaughter for the benefit of the Empire, they did not ask to do so as "treaty-partners" (*foederati*) or allies of the Empire.[132]

The conclusion that the imperial government stood aside is imposed by our informants. At provincial and municipal levels, Hispano-Romans may have cooperated in carrying out the conquerors' wishes. We can speculate about that; no contemporary tells us.[133]

The Spanish settlement lasted only a few years; how fast and fully it unraveled would have been hard to foresee. The ostensibly enduring arrangements of 411 came undone as soon as the West Roman government turned on the invaders. Its first concern since 407 had been to suppress domestic enemies, notably the usurper Constantine III. When he and other domestic rivals were eliminated and a measure of internal security achieved, Honorius's new strong man, Constantius, gave foreigners his full attention.[134] Hydatius tells the story:

[416] Wallia, [Athaulf's] successor as king [of the Goths], quickly made peace with the patrician Constantius and took the field against the Alans and Siling Vandals settled in Lusitania and Baetica.

Fredbalus, king of the [Siling] Vandal people, was captured by a trick, without any conflict, and sent to the emperor Honorius.

[417] Wallia, king of the Goths, carried out great slaughters of barbarians in the Spains for the sake of the Roman state.

[418] All the Siling Vandals in Baetica were exterminated by King Wallia. The Alans, who used to lord it (*potentabantur*) over the Vandals and Sueves, were massacred by the Goths to a drastic extent: their king Addax was killed, and the few survivors, dispensing with any royal office, submitted to the protection of Gunderic, king of the Vandals settled in Gallaecia.

The Goths were asked by Constantius to break off the combats they were waging and to return to Gaul.[135]

The Goths were brutally quick and effective in their role of policemen for Rome. The larger part of the recent ravagers of Gaul and Spain was stamped out in three campaigns. The Alans and Silings had not faced qualified foes for close to ten years and may have lost their battleworthiness. The Goths of Wallia so effectively pruned and trimmed the invaders of Spain that, down to our days, the Silings are a mere name and the preeminence of the Alans until 418 is rarely remembered.

The Silings and Alans were overwhelmed, and the Goths who had destroyed them were called away to Gaul. From this point, Hydatius takes up the story of how the changed balance of force in the peninsula affected the surviving occupiers:

[418] The few [Alan] survivors, dispensing with any royal office, submitted to the protection of Gunderic, king of the Vandals settled in Gallaecia.

[419] A conflict broke out between King Gunderic of the [Asding] Vandals and King Hermeric of the Sueves. The Vandals blockaded the Sueves in the Nerbasian Mountains.

[420] Owing to the intervention of Asterius, [Roman] count of Spain, the [Asding] Vandals broke off their siege of the Sueves. The *vicarius* Maurocellus killed a number of them at Braga while they were withdrawing. Abandoning Gallaecia, they passed over to Baetica.[136]

There were both Sueves and Asding Vandals in Gallaecia, but the Alans fleeing from massacre by the Goths took refuge only with the Vandals of King Gunderic. The Alans whom Gunderic welcomed were beaten troops and destitute refugees, but they nevertheless increased the Asdings' fighting strength and strained their limited resources. For both reasons, the equilibrium between Asdings and Sueves broke down. The reinforced Asdings needed more than they had and resolved to get it at the expense of their neighbors. The Sueves withdrew to the Nerbasian Mountains (which no one has been able to relate to modern geography); they put themselves out of reach and blunted the Vandal offensive.[137]

Then the chief Roman military commander—the count—intervened, not to protect the Sueves so much as to exploit the Asdings' plight.[138] Roman officials may have been stirred to assertiveness by the example of Gothic ferocity. The Vandals chose not to be victims. Alerted by the crushing of the Silings and Alans, they had taken initiatives against the Sueves and shown boldness. They now adopted the radical course of abandoning their assets in Gallaecia, clearing out, and transferring themselves to the former Siling share, Baetica, which Rome had evidently not repossessed. As the Asdings precipitately cleared out of Braga, probably the main city of their settlement, the chief of the Roman diocese (*vicarius*) turned up in an irregular military role and took advantage of the Asdings' preoccupation with flight to have his people do a little killing. Military experts recommended leaving the enemy an escape route and, as the distracted fugitives used it, mowing them down.[139] The augmented Asdings sustained some punishment, made good their escape, and imposed their control over Baetica.

Equilibrium returned in 420. The Alans and Silings, "muscle" of the expedition, had been destroyed. The Sueves had a foothold in Gallaecia and dug in. For more than forty years they would be the main but inglorious barbarians of Spain (both Hydatius and Jordanes deplored them). They lived on until deprived of their independence in 585 by the great Visigothic king Leovigild.[140] The other surviving people, the Asding Vandals, reinforced by Alan refugees, settled into Baetica and succeeded in defending themselves when challenged, notably in 422. Less than a decade later, an opportunity arose for them to abandon Spain and cross to North Africa. Their success does not need retelling. Under Gunderic's half brother Geiseric, who inaugurated his reign in Baetica (428), the Vandals began a new kingdom in Africa, prospered, and carried on until attacked by the forces of Justinian in 533–34 and stamped out.[141]

There is another way to describe the situation from 420 on. The Sueves and Vandals, having survived the test of initial endurance, were reborn as lasting components of the late Roman world. The Sueves carried on as a local military power and, soon, as the chronic obstacle to Hispanic tranquility. The Vandals turned into a formidable military force and a long-standing threat to Mediterranean security—a preoccupation of Roman governments for the next fifty years and even later. The past of both, either as mid-Danubians or as invaders, was over. They had acquired new identities.

In the Homelands

The end of our chain of events is not in Carthage, let alone at the Rhine, whose defenses are sometimes said, but wrongly, to have been swept away by the Alan and Vandal crossing. The fate of the Rhine frontier depended on whether or not its neighbors wished it to last. As early as 407, its defense had been restored. The invaders of 405 had been from relatively far away—a foretaste of Attila—breaking through an open door, but not caring whether it stayed open or was again shut. The proper finale for the invasion of 405 is at the middle Danube, where it began.

There, a number of long-settled peoples, not above raiding or other hostile activities, but basically sedentary and constructively engaged with their environment, had decided in 401 to uproot themselves and take seriously to the warpath toward Italy. The possible rewards of making themselves useful to Alaric and his Goths drew them on, but this prospect needed to be sustained by a basically gloomy outlook about their future if they continued to observe their treaties of nonaggression with Rome and stayed in place. That the Vandals were unprepared for a radical change of course is shown by the ease with which Stilicho's mobile forces turned them back near their point of departure. But they were not about to retreat to their old homes. However abortively, they had cut themselves off from their seats and were on the way to somewhere even if where was not yet clear. That was the situation when the Alans came upon them and offered participation in an invasion of undefended Gaul. Fifteen years after that expedition and the results we have seen, what apparent effect had the Rhine crossing had on the lands whose ancestral residents had joined the expedition?

Procopius, secretary to the conqueror of the Vandals in the 530s, tells of an embassy by stay-behind Vandals to their relatives in Africa, a story that many modern commentators treat as though it were historical.[142] Procopius does not specify where the ambassadors came from or under which Vandal king of North Africa they came (he never associates the Vandals with the Danube valley); these details seemed superfluous.[143] The envoys asked the African Vandals to renounce whatever rights they had to the common homeland (wherever it may have been!). The emigrants, much enriched, were ready to agree to this request until a wise elder reminded them of the precariousness of good fortune. They should retain their rights in case their luck changed and they needed a refuge to return to. The story is appealing. It shares its theme with two other passages in which Procopius evokes barbarians leaving the Empire and going back to live among their own kind.[144] In a more realistic vein he made it plain that, some time after the embassy, the Vandals who sent it ceased to exist. This apparition of emissaries from left-behind tribesmen is almost unique in a late Roman source. The circumstances are dubious enough, and expressed with so little authenticating detail, that their historicity is scarcely acceptable.[145] Outside this story, there is no trace of Vandal stragglers at their point of departure.

Were the armies that approached Mainz late in 405 composed of columns encumbered with women and children or of lean attack battalions? One might imagine that, for effectiveness, the Rhine crossing was carried out by picked fighting men. There is no way to tell.[146] Later, when the four peoples divided Spain and took up permanent residence, they would have needed dependents to serve them, but not necessarily families brought from home; accumulated captives might have done as well. The course of events from 405 to 411 neither supports nor disproves a movement from the middle Danube of entire populations accompanying their warriors. The one certainty is that we never find them there again.

How this emptying out and replacement came about completely eludes us. The next creditable information about ethnic conditions in the middle Danube is so far in the future—the early sixth century—that there is no way to measure the immediate effect of the emigration of 405. One emissary from the Roman Empire came to the Hungarian steppes on diplomatic business in 412 and another to seek mercenaries in 425. By then, clearly, Huns were present in numbers but not unified in leadership. How this immigration came about is completely undocumented: "No period in the political history of the Huns is darker than the 410's and 420's."[147] The claims by modern historians of great sweeps and vast billiard-ball movements of Huns and other peoples westward, which we examined earlier, should fit into the years before 412, but these vivid words are empty conjectures.

Ernst Stein clearly sums up the situation: "Towards 420, in a way we do not know more closely, there took shape in the center of eastern Europe a very extensive but rather loosely organized Empire in which the Huns who had penetrated into the Hungarian plain during the preceding decades were joined to the numerous mainly 'Germanic' tribes they had subjected."[148] The time scale might as well be a period of years as "decades," and some at least of the "subjects" of the Huns may have been volunteers rather than reluctant vassals. With these reservations, Stein aptly conveys our ignorance of what went on.

The Alans, Vandals, and Sueves left, and the next thing we know—about seven years later—is that there was a significant Hunnic presence in the area, widely defined. The two facts have no discernible relation to each other; we leave at one point and return at the next without knowing anything about the interval, least of all about how the expanding Hunnic presence affected the resident peoples. For thirty or forty years afterward, the history of the middle Danube was dominated by Huns: first, "kings" leading uncoordinated bands (425); then Attila's uncles until only Rugila (Rua) survived (432); next, the joint rule of Bleda and Attila, under whom the Roman annual gift to the Huns was doubled to seven hundred pounds of gold; finally, from 444 to 453, the sole rule of Attila, capped by his famous invasions of Gaul and Italy. Attila's sudden death in 453 and dissension among his sons led, in 454, to a revolt of the diverse peoples who, willy-nilly, had followed Attila's standards. The sons were defeated; Hunnish power broke up and withdrew to the east.[149]

The earliest evidence for the ethnic makeup of the "Hunnic Danube" comes in the 450s from two imperial panegyrics by Sidonius Apollinaris, a contemporary witness. The value of his evidence, however, is drastically limited by poetic convention. Sidonius, at suitable moments, summons up parades of foreign peoples, as poets had been doing for centuries. In the *Panegyric of Avitus* (January 456), Sidonius lists names in connection with Attila's campaign of 451:

barbaries totas in te transfuderat Arctos,
Gallia. pugnacem Rugum comitante Gelono
Gepida trux sequitur; Scirum Burgundio cogit;
Chunus, Bellonotus, Neurus, Bastarna, Toringus,
Bructerus,

In the *Panegyric of Majorian* (December 458), the context is the emperor's recruitment of troops from as far (poetically) as the Caucasus and the "Scythian Don" for a campaign againt Vandal North Africa. Little time elapsed between Sidonius's composition of the two poems:

Bastarna, Suebus,
Pannonius, Neurus, Chunus, Geta, Dacus, Halanus,
Bellonotus, Rugus, Burgundio, Vesus, Alites,
Bisalta, Ostrogothus, Procrustes, Sarmata, Moschus
post aquilas venere tuos; tibi militat omnis
Caucasus et Scythicae potor Tanaiticus undae.[150]

The trouble with these lists—not very different from Jerome's lineup of invaders of Gaul mentioned earlier—is that they weave together contemporary and antique names. Critics are able to discern some of the anachronisms. Neurus, Bastarna, Bellonotus in both lists are very likely to be padding. Others, such as Gelonus in list one and Procrustes in list two, are also good candidates for poetic license. But this process of critical elimination is far from scientific. Names and peoples have a way of lingering; the Bastarnae were certainly ancient, but their disappearance, though likely, cannot be taken for granted. The same holds mutatis mutandis in the other cases. We accept as contemporary the names that we guess to be so from later writings by Eugippius and Jordanes, a necessarily circular process. Sidonius is eloquent in what he does not say: Vandals, Marcomanni, and Quadi are wholly absent. Otherwise, we can value him only for foreshadowing sixth-century informants. From list one, (Burgundians, Huns,) Rugians, Gepids, Scirians, Thuringians, anticipate Eugippius. Add to these a few possible expansions from the second, even more padded list: Sueve, Pannonian, Alan, Vesus (a Gothic people), Ostrogoth, and Sarmatian. For Sidonius the Bellonoti are just as solid as the Rugi; we sift out those we guess are possible because we know of their existence from elsewhere. These lines of poetic eulogy contribute very little.[151]

The curtain over the middle Danube lifts in the sixth century, chiefly in the *Life of St. Severinus* by Eugippius, written in Italy towards 511, and Jordanes's *Gothic History*, written in Constantinople after March 551.[152] The one certainty they document is that, except for lingering Sueves and Sarmatians, the lineup of peoples on the middle Danube had changed completely from what it had been in 400.

The Vandals were gone and so were the arch-Suevic Marcomanni and Quadi; loosely attached by name to the expedition of 405, they vanished all the same. Sueves were too widespread and diffuse to fade away. Remnants made themselves sporadically visible into the next century; they even had a king. Also visible were the steppe-dwelling Sarmatians. Alans were not wholly absent, but only because some Alans were always around. The later Alans near the Danube were unconnected to the ones cut to pieces in Spain. Their washing up somewhere tended to be accidental.[153] It would be wrong to think that the conditions we discern thanks to Eugippius and Jordanes resulted directly or indirectly from the expedition of 405. The undocumented interval is too long; the effects of Hunnic predominance, though unknowable, have to be allowed for.

What our informants reveal, without explanation, is a totally transformed ethnic landscape. In order from west to east, down the Danube, we encounter Thuringians, Rugians, Sciri, Herules, Goths, and Gepids.[154] Only the Gepids (and perhaps the Thuringians) had been located in 400 in the vicinity of a people that invaded Gaul and Spain—the Gepids to the east of the Asding Vandals, the Thuringians to the north of the Silings. The Gepids, thanks to their ruler, Ardaric, had been very powerful at Attila's court. Ardaric led the revolt against Attila's sons and, victorious, remained in possession of the Hunnic heartland in the Tisza valley and points east (old Dacia), which Jordanes calls "Gepidia." Momentarily at least they saw themselves as successors to the Huns in other respects than territory. Byzantine historiography knows Attila as a Gepid, and a chronicle entry near 455 reports: "The Burgundians . . . [in] Gaul drove the Gepids away." This failed Gepid incursion may be recalled by the erroneous second Hunnic invasion of Gaul found in Jordanes and Procopius.[155]

Gepid movement in the Hunnic period seems to have been a westward extension of their fourth-century homes rather than a wholesale transmigration; the southward expansion of the Thuringians seems similar. The Rugians, Sciri, Herules, and Goths, however, had formerly resided in the lower Danube valley and points east. They could have attained the cantonments they had in the middle Danube in the 450s only by displacing themselves, in whole or in part, for a long distance upriver. It is assumed—there is no explicit evidence—that the Huns, who valued and used all of them as auxiliary troops, sponsored or forced their relocation to western parts of *barbaricum*. After Attila, we find them, reluctantly independent, in the lands once occupied by the Marcomanni, Quadi, and Vandals.[156]

These peoples do not lack pasts; Greek and Latin sources record quite a few of their earlier doings. The Scirian name, for example, is found in the pages of Pliny the Elder's *Natural History* in connection with the Vistula.[157] Enough of them survived into the post-Attilan period to send native sons to high positions in both halves of the Roman Empire.[158] Similar stories combining a past, a mid-Danubian phase, then a (sometimes short) future elsewhere might be told of the others. Several of them are examined in Chapter 7.

The movements of these barbarians from the east are embedded in the brief or core Migration Age (376–568), the narrative of movement directly associated with the end of the West Roman Empire. The "terminator" Odoacer sprang from the Sciri, and the army of Italy that helped him overturn the last Western emperor in 476 was mainly composed of Herules. If the narrative of a Migration Age were an ordinary argument subject to proof or disproof on the basis of evidence, the particular stories of the Rugians, Sciri, and Herules might bear on its validity. Were they simply roaming bands moving here and there capriciously (perhaps driven by want or overpopulation, as ancient Greek ethnographers would put it)[159] or was there sense and purpose in their existence?

The Rugians, Herules, and others did not just happen to "move" from one settlement to the other in a mindless Brownian motion. How they transposed themselves is unknowable, except for our having every reason to think that Huns (no more closely definable) had a large part in their relocation. The peoples in question may have voluntarily accepted Hunnic patronage and not been dragged along unwillingly from their ancestral homes to be hewers of wood and military auxiliaries to the Huns. Just so, earlier in the century, the Alans had played a decisive, undocumented part in the emigration of the Vandals and Sueves, and, later, the Avars would encourage the Slavs. The Roman frontier zone was attractive not just because it offered opportunities for preying parasitically upon the productive populations of the provinces but also because it allowed the foreign kings or other leaders to be in reach of Roman governments that were willing to reward soldiers and officers. The case of Aetius dipping repeatedly into the pool of Hunnic military manpower is well known. Hunnic leadership in the fifth century allowed peoples from the lower Danube to position themselves more advantageously in relation to potential Roman paymasters.

There were rewarding careers to be made in either empire. These were not "barbarians" engaged in a mysterious "wandering" but long-established neighbors of the Empire well aware of the advantages to be gained from proximity to the developed lands to the south.

The *Life of St. Severinus* offers a glimpse of the Rugians, one of the post-Attilan inhabitants of the middle Danube. Their proximity to a Roman population helped keep them alive but not content. They occupied a frontier made uncomfortable by the presence of many other armed consumers and of too few industrious producers to maintain them. The predators competed keenly over the spoils, with the result that few found the climate congenial for lasting residence. The Rugian king Flaccitheus, a confidant of the saint, intended to head south with his people and win more secure employment with the West Roman government. The Goths of Valamer were his neighbors, however; to Flaccitheus they seemed to be very numerous and not at all friendly. They lay athwart the road to Italy, and Flaccitheus did not expect them to allow free passage. So, for the time being at least, the Rugians stayed north of the Danube.[160] Eventually they annoyed the West Roman government—Odoacer's—to such a point as to bring a punitive expedition upon themselves (488). Enough Rugian refugees survived with a royal leader to maintain their autonomy downriver as dependents of Theoderic the Amal and his Goths, whom they accompanied to Italy. Decades later, when Belisarius and an East Roman army terminated the Amal kingdom in Italy (540), the Rugian remnant not only was still a discernible force but was momentarily prominent in the revolt against the East Roman conqueror—the same revolt that became formidable under the Goth Totila. That moment of leadership was the final Rugian gasp.[161] Regardless of what one may think of this not particularly glorious history, it followed a deliberate course and is not a mindless wandering. The hagiographer of Severinus does not think of the Rugians as nice people, but he brings them to life all the same and allows them to exist as a force to be reckoned with, not a disembodied migration or "seepage."

Small peoples like the Rugians and Sciri, or larger ones like the Gepids and Ostrogoths, had acquired habits of dependence on rich and forceful patrons. Their existence was overshadowed by the Roman Empire, on which for centuries they had directly or indirectly relied. When denied recruitment into its army or military aristocracy, they could attempt to emulate the Goth Alaric and force themselves on the Romans' attention, or they could place themselves at the service of the Huns, who had a tested formula for acquiring the Roman goods that were prized everywhere as symbols of high rank and esteem. The Huns demanded to be bought off by the Romans and, if they were not, inflicted rapid, devastating raids of surprising extent.

Unlike the rooted mid-Danubians who detached themselves from ancestral homes in order to invade the Empire across the Rhine in 405, the peoples whom the Huns brought to the middle Danube were transients.[162] The Rugians, Sciri, and Herules were stamped out, and their remnants moved along to other venues. The Ostrogoths left the edge of the Eastern Empire, moved south into the interior to take a direct part in imperial politics. With the backing of Constantinople, they eventually invaded Italy and took charge of a near-empire.[163] The Gepids, one-time neighbors of the Vandals and political heirs to Attila's Huns, kept on behaving for a long time as though the Danube valley were their home, as indeed it was for many centuries. Their pretensions to endurance continually affronted an Eastern Empire that could not bear to have a force on its borders without wishing to destroy it. With Constantinopolitan encouragement, the Gepids were stamped out by the enterprising Lombards momentarily leagued with a newly arrived steppe people, the Avars.[164] As usual, the Eastern Empire gained nothing from acquiring the Avars as neighbors in place of the Gepids and learned nothing from the experience. The stage was set somehow for an unhindered Slavic takeover of the backyard of Constantinople. Only the westernmost part of the middle Danube had a different destiny: it became the home of the Bavarians, whose emergence and prosperity under Frankish auspices remains a mystery of sixth-century history.[165]

Migration Is Incidental to What Is Going On

Human beings always move about. When, by our standards, the world was virtually unpeopled, certain persons found a reason for pushing their way out of Eurasia to the American continent. Most actions in recorded history call for changes of place. The vast dispersal of Chinese over land and sea is a case in point. Colonization and conquests by Persians, Phoenicians, Greeks, and Romans involved movement; so did the Atlantic slave trade and the European peopling of the Americas and Australia. Migration is not contestable. It happens all the time on small and large scales. The humble commuter sacrificing five or more hours out of twenty-four for the ride or drive to and from work, when multiplied by all his likes, is also part of a vast migratory tide. In this or other forms, migration is incidental to other things—a desirable or unavoidable bridge from home to workplace, imperial expansion, trade, domination, flight from adversity, recreation, land hunger, a search for greener pastures, adventure. The "other things" are what matter; migration is the means to ends having another name.

The varied goings and comings of peoples include those of the Alans,

Vandals, and Sueves between 400 and 420. The concept of a "Germanic" *Völker-wanderung*, short or long, in which the peoples interesting us ostensibly belong, is anchored by centuries of usage in historical and other literature. Maps purporting to chart its multicentury tracks stare at us out of hundreds of historical atlases, textbooks, and monographs.[166] The question raised by "Migration Age" as the name for a historical period is whether there are wanderings par excellence, aggregates of displacements amounting to a single collective multidecade phenomenon that is deservedly singled out from more scattered human movements.[167]

This special status is so far from being a fact of world history that a recent *Atlas of International Migration* (from the dawn of mankind to the present) as much as drums the traditional *Völkerwanderung* off the stage. "Other historic migrations [than the Mongols']," it says, "such as those of the Vandals and other Northern Tribes against the dying Roman Empire AD 400–650 were also bereft of [positive] migration effects." The legacy of the Mongols was "almost entirely of destruction," that of the "Northern Tribes" presumably just as negative.[168] The same atlas singles out the destiny of the Slavs for attention. Unlike the passed-over Northerners and Mongols, the Slavs are allotted—in a very traditional, question-begging way—a "major" three-pronged emigration out of a "homeland" bounded by the Elbe, the northern Carpathians, and the Vistula.[169] If this atlas had been compiled between the two World Wars rather than fifty years after World War II, it is doubtful that the destiny of the "Northern Tribes" would, as here, have been wholly overshadowed by that of the Slavs.

The *Atlas of International Migration* may well have sloughed off difficulties; even its idea of a "dying" Roman Empire is out of step with current scholarly opinion.[170] Nevertheless, one point is beyond question: this synthesis takes the Migration Age that, otherwise, is deeply embedded in historical literature and finds it possible to consider it insignificant. The (almost) complete omission of the *Völkerwanderung* may be unwarranted or a mistake but is nonetheless eloquent. If omission is possible, the decision of (many) others to single it out as the migration par excellence has to be an error too. Only one thing seems certain, namely, that the "Migration Age" is not an isolated phenomenon; it shares space in world history with dozens of other important migratory tides, voluntary and forced, in ancient, medieval, and modern times.[171]

The lack of reliable statistics in the distant past and the extreme imperfection of casual observations make it difficult to chart the waxing and waning of aggregate human migrations in any reliable way. Susan Reynolds sensibly observes, "we have very little evidence at all, outside stories that were told and elaborated after the sixth century, that a larger proportion of the population of Europe moved around during the 'Age of Migration' than at any other time."[172]

The lack of quantifiable evidence matters because radical misconceptions about human movements are possible even when abundant statistics exist. Marc Bloch, a great historian particularly mindful of the social sciences, could look about the Western Europe he lived in and speak of it as a land of stable population contrasting with the restless movements that, as he believed, had characterized the West until the eleventh century and no later.[173] His opinion clashes glaringly with the observation that "the total number of international refugees since 1900 probably exceeds the total of involuntary international migrants in all previous recorded human history."[174] If a scholar of Bloch's stature could so fully misapprehend his own twentieth-century world, there is little hope that anyone should be able to speak authoritatively about the fluctuations of uncounted human movements in the distant past.

To Ludwig Schmidt (a respected voice) migration was the phenomenon that gave unity and coherence to the expansion of the "Germanic peoples."[175] Such an idea is wonderfully convenient for ordering historical information. Typically, readers are told (in a work published only a decade ago) that the Bastarnae whom Greek observers attest at the Black Sea in the third century B.C. "can be regarded as early precursors of the migration-age East Germans" and that "the journey of the Cimbri is to some extent the precursor of the great Migration-movements of late Antiquity. . . . For a long time Roman victories cut off similar thrusts."[176] Romans are thus cast as warding off a relentless "Germanic" force continually pressing down from the north for many centuries. Past and future are meaningfully linked. Émilienne Demougeot held together a two-volume account of "barbarian invasions" by a relentless rhetoric of migration.[177] The latest stratagem, inspired by ethnogenesis theory, is to replace "Völker" in the migratory compound with "cores of tradition (*Traditionskerne*)" and let the movements carry on just as before: "The snakelike lines in our historical atlases suggest that the wanderers were closed groups (*Verbände*) of identical descent. In reality [sic] the lines basically indicate the course of small cores of tradition that bore the tribal name onward and, around them, a larger, changing gathering of adherents of diverse origins."[178] In this abstract way, a formula is devised for upgrading the old maps and having them illustrate exactly the same thing as always—the glorious, millennial migratory expansion of the "Germanic" peoples.

This literary and visual device, which countless historians have availed themselves of and still utilize, has the effect of radically distorting the past. In the hurly-burly of time, whatever movements "Germanic" peoples engaged in necessarily jostled with the no less assertive contemporary movements of Celts, Eurasian nomads, Dacians, Romans, and any other peoples who might be relevant and did not sit still. The "unity" attributed to Germanic movements is won by resolutely minimizing or simply disregarding the movements of everyone else. The providential direction of the collectively moving subject turns out to be a literary (and, too often, patriotic) fiction rather than a truth discerned outside the imagination. The appeal to "migration" as an actor in history masks our ignorance, bridges gaps in our knowledge, and imparts ostensibly scientific seriousness to empty guesses.

The mid-Danubian members of the expedition of 405 were not wanderers but deeply rooted residents of the lands they abandoned. Their tradition was to stand still. Roman historians allow us to know that, in the days of Caesar Augustus, Marcomanni had been in the forefront of the peoples led by the fearsome Maroboduus and that, in the days of Marcus Aurelius, they had been joined by Sueves and Vandals in fighting against the Roman Empire.[179] By A.D. 400, however, the Vandals could look back to a settled past of more than two centuries, and their Suevic neighbors had been fixed in place for half a millennium or more. The mid-Danubians had no link across the centuries with the prehistoric Jastorf culture or the Scandinavian Bronze Age. Under no circumstance may they be described as transients pausing on their way to somewhere else. The earlier and later eras were total strangers until writers from the sixteenth century onward chose to connect them and invent a comprehensive "Germanic" expansion, embracing the Bastarnae, the Cimbri and Teutons, the Suevi of Ariovistus, and everyone else, so that any migration at any time that might be deemed (by the application of modern criteria) in any way "Germanic" forms part of a comprehensive united "movement."

Three features of the Rhine crossing are arresting. (1) The Vandals and their associates gave up on their age-old homelands, uprooted themselves, took to the warpath in a southward direction, before coming under the influence of the Alans. (2) Some Alans, eventually many of them, took a hand in the mid-Danubians' destiny and directed the enlarged expedition toward crossing the Rhine and breaking into Gaul. From the moment near 403 when the Alans appeared among the mid-Danubians down to their destruction by the Goths in 418, they "lorded it" over their associates. (3) The four peoples in Spain, having won a moment's calm, tried to organize for themselves a provincial settlement foreshadowing what the patrician Constantius would do for the Goths in Aquitaine in 418. Their misfortune was to be rebuffed by Honorius's government. They were not sufficiently cowed or deserving of Roman consideration; a lawless gathering, they were marked for elimination. However that may be, they were never migrants. Rooted at the start and rooted again in Spain, their destructive six-year travels, painful as they must have been to their victims, were no more than a means to an end.

Some ancient historians today think that "what might have happened had there been no barbarian invasions is an interesting hypothetical question," and that "the barbarian migrations" were a "totally unforeseen factor." They labor under the misapprehension that there was a "continuous migration of northern people" whose reasons, alas, "remain obscure."[180] Such views are surprisingly naive. The Roman Empire could not help having edges that touched peoples living beyond them; it had always had edges. In the eyes of its neighbors, the Empire loomed much larger than the neighbors did in the Empire's.[181] The insouciance of ordinary Romans was of long standing, but the military leadership of the Empire had always had to be watchful. The expensive apparatus of imperial defense was mounted to maintain the peace against foreign troublemakers who were never expected to stop their troublemaking ways. They were not going to go away or "learn reason." If the Empire was to be safeguarded it would have to continue to pay the price. It also had to take care, within, to abstain from the imperial usurpations and civil wars that denuded frontiers of their guardians.[182] The experts knew that one way to deal with these foreigners was to give them what they wanted—a part in the Empire, outlets for their martial ardor and for the abilities of their leaders. The history of Rome had been one of continual absorption of strangers into its fabric. There was no reason to think that the present constellation of outsiders was different.

Peoples foreign to the Empire moved in late antiquity; their inclination, however, was not to expand but to remain where they and their forebears had lived. Starting from a quite normal inertia, they were shaken from their roots by multiple circumstances, some of their own devising, others external to themselves. Once dislodged, they set on their diverse ways to a future that proved to be more often tragic than prosperous. The Rhine crossing of the early 400s documents a critical chapter of these events.

Chapter 6
The "Techniques of Accommodation" Revisited

Barbarians and Romans and Its Critics

Twenty-five years ago, I published a book called *Barbarians and Romans: The Techniques of Accommodation*. It took up an old subject—the legal technicalities involved in settling Goths and Burgundians in the Roman provinces of Gaul, Italy, and Spain in the fifth and sixth centuries. I argued, contrary to earlier opinion, that the Roman tax machinery was central to these settlements and that tax proceeds rather than landed property were awarded to individual barbarians. Time has passed. The book has had a few adherents and many detractors.[1] I have had the opportunity to think over the subject, with and without the help of its critics. In particular, I have become convinced that military billeting, usually denoted in these discussions by the word *hospitalitas*, has nothing to do with barbarian settlement. I have also found it possible to improve every aspect of the fiscal interpretation of the settlements laid out in *Barbarians and Romans* and to eliminate its weaknesses. The goal of these pages is to report my second thoughts and to arrive at a revised conclusion.

Serious study of these "techniques of accommodation" was inaugurated in 1844 by Ernst Theodor Gaupp, of whose achievement it has recently been said, "Few historical works of the Biedermeier period have retained their validity for so long." This is high praise.[2] Gaupp's fundamental work is a sobering reminder that, in historical studies, up-to-dateness can be irrelevant to the unraveling of a problem.[3] Though I sometimes disagree with Gaupp, he has my sincere respect. In order to deal with this subject, I had to build on him rather than on his would-be improvers.

*   *   *

A simplified summary of Gaupp's argument and my revision may help to understand what follows. At various dates in the fifth century, Visigoths and Ostrogoths, as well as Burgundians, settled in Roman Gaul and Italy. The settlements apparently took place peacefully, without visibly disturbing the resident landowners and cultivators. This was no conquest and forcible peopling; the initial steps were taken under the auspices of Roman generals. Gaupp asked, How was this done? What was the legal basis for this lawful process? His answer was military billeting. Roman law provided that proprietors must take in traveling soldiers and allow them one-third of their house. On this precedent (generally called *hospitalitas* by modern authors), barbarian soldiers were assigned places, and landowners yielded to them one-third of their property. A partition of land came about, and each Goth or Burgundian settled on the third of his "host's" property that fell to him. Thus far Gaupp. My revision began by observing that his reading of the Roman law of billeting was flawed; a measure allowing a soldier temporary occupancy of one-third of a house could not turn into an authorization for a barbarian to take enduring possession of one-third of someone's landed property. There had to be some other way to achieve a transfer of property to the newcomers. The method used, I argued, was to mobilize the tax resources of the affected territories. In each of them, the total tax assessments were conveyed from the Roman government to the barbarian king, and he divided this total, by a simple fraction (one-half or one-third), between himself and the rank and file. Out of the fraction of tax assessments assigned to the troops, separate allotments of approximately equal size were apportioned and distributed. Individual Goths or Burgundians each received a "share" of tax assessment; he had the assessment and the revenue arising from it, whereas the Roman proprietor retained ownership and cultivation of the assessed land. The barbarian's allotment authorized him to collect and pocket an annual (tax) payment from the assessed Roman landowner. "An allotment of your own feeds you," the Gothic king of Italy said to his troops. This was the new shape of military pay, direct from the producer to the consumer.

I was not alone in attempting to improve Gaupp's scheme. Jean Durliat, of the University of Toulouse–Le Mirail, also did so in the context of wide-ranging, visionary, and often admirable studies of late Roman and early medieval public finance. His plan, which agrees with mine in many respects, has been published in a long article (cited in n. 10). The differences between Durliat and me are (I suggest) that my arguments cling closely to specific evidence, whereas his operate within a powerful general interpretation that sometimes accounts satisfactorily for the evidence and at other times does not. Because I do not subscribe to Durliat's general interpretation, his results and mine, though often similar, do not comfortably combine. Our views, independently worked out, are best kept apart.

*   *   *

Barbarians and Romans has come into many hands and was widely reviewed. Its subtitle heads the present chapter, since the contents of the book are more clearly indicated by the words after the colon than those before it. The tax-based mode of barbarian settlement that Durliat and I advocated occasioned a learned conference at Zwettl Abbey in Austria (May 1986), with published proceedings. The conference was organized by Herwig Wolfram of the University of Vienna to celebrate the reception of Durliat's and my teaching into his *Geschichte der Goten* and its translations; I am very grateful to Professor Wolfram for having given a high profile to Durliat's and my findings.[4] Since then, there have been additional studies of the Goths and, in the nineties, an outpouring of collected papers giving much attention to the barbarians in late antiquity and their "accommodation." Most critics have been intent on demolishing my tax-based scheme, and at least one is simply skeptical of any change. Both groups agree on the adequacy of Gaupp's results.[5]

Two of the earliest reviews of *Barbarians and Romans* merit special notice. Herwig Wolfram's "Zur Ansiedlung reichsangehöriger Föderaten: Erklärungsversuch und Forschungsziele" (1983), which expressed an initial opposition that he later withdrew, had the virtue of very clearly spelling out the difference between his approach to this problem and mine.[6] He wished to pile up the cases of settlement and the evidence for them, regardless of how eloquent any of these was about "the techniques of accommodation";[7] I, on the contrary, made it clear that my book was strictly confined to the few texts that bear narrowly on the settlements in Gaul and Italy, since these were—as far as I could (and still can) see—the only sources whose clarification would allow this discussion to progress. Wolfram's disagreement was a creditable question of method. No less reputable was the critique of Maria Cesa, whose virtue (to my mind) is that she was totally accurate and scrupulous in her grasp of my argument.[8] I cannot understand why, in the end, she preferred to stand with Ferdinand Lot rather than with me. Lot is one of my heroes, and I treat his views with affection; puzzling through "Du régime de l'hospitalité" tended to be everyone's initiation to serious study of this subject.[9] Yet it is hard to come away from Lot's article without a sense that he did not get beyond being baffled by the sources; he certainly falls far short of satisfactorily solving the puzzle. However that may be, Cesa is welcome to her preferences as long as she expresses, as she does, a high level of understanding of my book.

What is common to most of the criticism of *Barbarians and Romans* (with the exception of the interventions of Durliat and the articles just mentioned) is that it is content to test whether or not my revision is acceptable and to assume that, after rejection, nothing more needs to be done.[10] It goes unnoticed that, long before introducing a tax argument, *Barbarians and Romans* demolished the old position—Gaupp's—by a close examination of the Roman laws on which it is chiefly based. A study of these laws showed that the award of "allotments" (*sortes*) to barbarians could not be envisaged as a "simple" or even a complicated extension to Roman farms or "estates" of the rules for receiving soldiers temporarily under a roof (*hospitium*).[11] Jochen Martin, who appraised barbarian settlement incidentally to a general book on late antiquity, grasped what had happened; he pointed out that I had ruined the earlier explanation and that, as a result, "the 'settlement' of the Germans [is] again an open question."[12] What Martin perceived was almost unanimously overlooked by others. Gaupp had realized that there was a "great distinction" between shelter for a soldier and the award of landed property, but he rolled over this difference and drove on.[13] In recent literature even the "great distinction" detected by Gaupp has been missed. This confusion has to be overcome. A new explanation, mine or someone else's, is needed for the awards that, on the one hand, made barbarians content with their role in the Roman provinces and, on the other hand, did not overturn the proprietary and social stability of Gaul and Italy.[14]

Owing to the very limited agenda of reviewers—innovation has been on trial, not tradition—the discussion of barbarian "accommodation" has not made headway as a result of critical appraisals of my book, or by independent accounts of the Goths and Burgundians in the fifth century in which the same problems have been aired. Gaupp's version of *hospitalitas* is still central to discussions; there is no more clarity today—perhaps even somewhat less—than there was when *Barbarians and Romans* was published. Wolfram (after initial hesitation) has kindly endorsed what he calls the Durliat-Goffart teaching.[15] Many others have rejected it.

No critique of my book has won more credit than that of Sam Barnish, whose "Taxation, Land and Barbarian Settlement in the Western Empire" (1986) had the merit of being among the first extensive reviews to appear in English. Standard practice, especially in Britain, is now to cite my book with a cutting comment or two and then call on Barnish for the truth.[16] His refutation is deemed complete and his authority rarely questioned. Barnish shines by affirming that the former teaching on this subject is adequate. The innovator is refuted; nothing more stands in the way of awarding "land" to the Goths and Burgundians, a process that is always assumed to be simple and self-explanatory.

Barnish's key text is a letter of Cassiodorus on the distribution of allotments (*Variae* 2.16.5). Largely on its basis (though much else is cited), he concludes that the evidence about barbarian settlement leaves us nothing to explain; a division of land took place and that's that. "On face value, the documentary evidence gives ample support to the land division, at least."[17] Such, too, is Ian Wood's opinion in an appendix on "The Settlement of the Burgundians" to an article of his that appeared in 1990; this mainly addresses the decisive Burgundian evidence (led by LB54). Barnish and Wood agree in narrowing the argument over *Barbarians and Romans* to a contest between awards of land and awards of tax proceeds. They stand firm in espousing what seems to them to be a sound, well established "default position," according to which every barbarian to be settled was given a plot of real Roman "land," soil that he could cultivate, that satisfied his "land hunger" in a basically agrarian economy. Readers are to understand that, if my *Barbarians and Romans* produces nothing forcing scholars to reject the "face value" of the texts, then any other than the "default position" is a superfluous eccentricity (though Wood condescends to having been "immensely stimulated" by Durliat and me).[18] This tenacious faith in the adequacy of a "default position" explains why the many pages devoted to criticism of *Barbarians and Romans* have been sterile.

The "Default Position": Expropriation by Grace of *Hospitalitas*

The "default position" that Barnish and Wood (as well as most other critics) invite us to reinstate is basically derived from what everyone used to believe about the so-called "*hospitalitas* system," based on Gaupp's teaching and mainly documented by the title *de metatis* ("concerning billets") of the Theodosian Code.[19] As late as 2001, Walter Pohl expressed a sturdy continuing certitude "that the distribution of land was carried out 'in keeping with the principles of the Roman billeting system' "; regardless of what I [W. G.] might say, Pohl insists, it was not "a 'misapprehension' of Gaupp's model" to believe in the relevance of these rules.[20] What has gone unnoticed despite my clear warnings in *Barbarians and Romans* is that modern scholarship has crudely distorted Roman billeting.

For standard twentieth-century views of the principles of Roman billeting one may begin with J. B. Bury's normally excellent *History of the Later Roman Empire*: "The old Roman system of quartering soldiers on the owners of the land . . . bound [the owner] to give one-third of the produce of his property to the guests whom he reluctantly harboured. This principle was now applied to the land itself." Bury's explanation is absurd: a soldier in transit needed a roof over his head, not a large fraction of his host's "produce," let alone land. Besides, Roman law specified that no "produce" at all was to be given to the military "guest" or to his horse.[21] Pohl, who evokes "the provisioning of 'guests' on the traditional model (*der Versorgung von 'Gästen' nach traditionellen Muster*)," seems to have overlooked that no such tradition was in force, though it may have been in the earlier Empire.[22] Expressing the same idea as Bury more summarily, Katherine Fischer Drew shifted the burden from produce to real estate: "the old Roman precedent of quartering soldiers on the land, allowing them one-third of the property of the original owner," and Alvaro d'Ors took the same tack:

"According to [the Roman regime of military quartering], a military *hospes* [guest] received a *tertia* [third] of the country estate in which he took up residence."[23] Blind to the documented rules of Roman billeting, Bury, Drew, and d'Ors substituted rules unknown to the laws but admirably suited for barbarian settlement; they ask us to believe that traveling soldiers in need of shelter for the night were made part-owners of landed estates. No less an authority than Karl Ferdinand Werner forthrightly affirmed that "the regime of *hospitalitas* forced Roman landowners to yield to barbarians a part of their properties and their slaves." So conceived, the billeting system itself existed not to house soldiers on the march but to endow barbarians with agrarian property.[24]

One more example, by the respected legal historian Ernst Levy, illustrates the pitfalls of a leap from billets to landownership:

In all the three kingdoms the rulers adopted the general idea, though not the detail, of the quartering system (*hospitalitas*) which the emperors had been applying to their own soldiers. As a result, the estate of a Roman was divided between him and a member of the victorious people by a generally determined quota. A Visigoth, e.g., obtained two-thirds of that specific *fundus*, while the rest remained with the Roman, and the same held good among the Ostrogoths. . . . Each of the two *consortes* then acquired individual ownership of the quota allotted to him. It was left to them to carry through the corresponding spatial partition of the *fundus* as and when they pleased. Up to that time they continued to be co-owners *pro indiviso*. But they were also free to prefer a middle course by proceeding to the separation of the arable land (RB30.4), houses (LB38.7) and gardens, while keeping forests and pastures of the estate in common use (LV10.1.9; LB13 and 31; cf. LV8.5.2).[25]

All is muddle here. In what way the "general idea" of quartering might be transformed into a rule for dividing an estate and seizing its larger portion is left unexplained. *Fundi* (farms or estates) necessarily of different sizes (and rarely mentioned in the relevant sources) are assumed to be the framework of division, and the Goths of Italy are granted "two-thirds" contrary to the evidence. Levy conveniently interprets any text with the word *consors* (partner) as relating specifically to sharing by Romans and Goths, although it is doubtful that any clauses of the so-called *Lex Romana Burgundionum* or the *Leges Visigothorum* have that sense at all; partners or co-sharers are far too common in Roman practice for the word to be limited specifically to sharing by a barbarian and a Roman. The contention that, after the grant, each partner acquired individual ownership of his quota makes no allowance for the clearly differentiated degrees of ownership enjoyed by Burgundians in respect to plain *terrae* (land) as distinct from *agri cum mancipiis* (fields with dependents).[26] Gaupp's teaching is treated as though it were a solid foundation that leaves only "details" uncertain.[27] This is not the case: one cannot leap without intermediary steps from partition of a house for temporary occupancy to partition of "estates" or "land" for enduring ownership and cultivation. Gaupp himself, however admirable, needs correction. What is worse, his ideas were increasingly cheapened as they passed from historian to historian on the way into the twentieth century.[28]

Neither Barnish nor Wood talks about old Roman precedents; they endorse venerable tradition more guardedly—by simply turning a blind eye to the problems. They consider the awards written into the sources, most glaringly the Burgundian Laws, to be self-explanatory; only translate the words, preferably by cognates, and clarity is there without further need for interpretation. I was not the first to sense how hard it was to deal with the main Burgundian law at face value or to uncover its "natural meaning"; Delbrück and Lot sensed the problems, too.[29] None of these difficulties was an obstacle to Barnish and Wood; they just pushed on, disregarding all dissent: "At some point," Wood says, "there was also a division of Roman estates and slaves, perhaps based on a pre-existing arrangement of *hospitalitas*, with the Burgundians taking two thirds of the former and one third of the latter"; "all the Burgundians were billeted, but those who had received gifts from the king or his *parentes* were prevented from taking a third of the slaves and two thirds of the land, when these were later conceded."[30] To Wood the "taking" or "concession" of land and slaves is a perfectly ordinary process calling for no comment: a Burgundian had been hanging around a Roman "estate" for some time until, one fine day, a royal law was issued entitling him to go to the owner and say he was taking possession of one-third of his slaves and two-thirds of his land; this was easily carried out, and Burgundian and Roman lived happily side by side ever after. Wood invites us to accept this improbable scenario as though it were the most natural thing in the late Roman world. Moreover, the astonishing fact that lands and "slaves" are in a precise ratio of 1:2 escapes his attention. He even overlooks that the lands held by Burgundians "*iure sortis* [or] *hospitalitatis*" are glaringly different in quality from the gifts of "fields with slaves" in full ownership made by the Burgundian kings to individuals.[31] Wood has no time for oddities, however significant; his only goal is to affirm that nothing could have been given to Burgundians except agricultural assets.

Barnish is more circumspect. He prizes LB54 for what he believes it reveals about "the social details of settlement." The actual division is set out summarily: "[the allotments] included two thirds of the land and a third of the *mancipia* of the Roman estate, with equal rights in pasturage and woodland, and half the farm-buildings and orchards."[32] "*The* Roman estate," he says, leaving readers to ponder the mystery of how Roman properties of very diverse sizes, not concentrated in one place but scattered, were turned into uniform "estates" from which—to use Wood's language, also proper here—Burgundians might "take" two-thirds of the land and one-third of the *mancipia*. Unlike Wood, Barnish grants me that these *mancipia* were likely to be undifferentiated dependents, not slaves alone. Also unlike Wood, Barnish observes the "curious disproportion between land and work-force," and he pays attention to Lot's and my views on the subject. Brushing aside the alarmingly precise proportion of *mancipia* to *terra*, he happily espouses the opinion of P. D. King: "The divisions have not been sufficiently considered from the point of view of their possible economic benefit to Roman land-owners faced with a depleted labour force, and high taxes."[33]

The "default position" reaffirmed by Barnish and Wood has not been tenable ever since I indicated in *Barbarians and Romans* how hard it is without Bury's, Werner's, or someone else's distortion of *hospitalitas* to account for what we know took place, namely, the relatively smooth provision of lucrative allotments of some kind—*sortes*—to Goths and Burgundians in Gaul and Italy.[34] It does not help to say, as does Averil Cameron, "The traditional view is that the barbarians *hospites*, beginning with the Visigoths, were to be entitled to a share of the land on which they were settled, in the surprisingly high proportion of two-thirds to one-third."[35] Barbarians being "entitled" to a "surprisingly" large share of the "land" on which they were "settled" explains absolutely nothing about the legal basis for the award of allotments or about the process by which they were awarded. Military billeting (*hospitalitas*) does not supply this basis unless the relevant laws are laughably distorted. The issue never was land versus taxes, though grants of tax proceeds were the solution I offered to the problem. If I was wrong, it is still necessary to devise an alternative explanation of how the Roman authorities secured the resources by which Goths and Burgundians were fitted into Roman countrysides with a minimum of illegality and conflict. That is where the problem still stands.

While we are near Barnish's, Wood's, and Cameron's handling of "land," it seems appropriate to problematize this all-too-simple seeming commodity.[36] Roman cultivators farmed their lands; their work either for their owners (if they were slaves) or for their landlords (if they were tenants) or for themselves (if they were owners) was the foundation of economic life. Proprietors owned productive land and, if they had enough, could afford to live from the rents remitted by their tenants or managers. Public authorities—municipal, religious, imperial, or royal—were also rent-collecting proprietors, usually with special privileges. Not least, the government set valuations on arable fields (and perhaps other assets) and used this assessment as a basis for the imposition and collection of taxes.[37] Cultivation, rent roll, and assessment register all referred to the same patches of soil and to different shares of revenue arising from them.[38] A constant process of sale and lease, inheritance and dowry, confiscation by the state, distribution to state beneficiaries, and much else affected these various overlapping acres.[39] If "land" was given to barbarians it had to be taken away from its proprietors, by a lawful process or by force, with or without coercion. Outside Vandal North Africa, the scene of much violent dispossession, we have only one documented instance of collective seizure by force.[40] Modern commentators who speak of gifts or partitions of "land" should be ready to specify whether the award or division related to cultivation, to ownership, or to assessment. Similarly, if it is understood that land in its guise as tax assessment is in question, references to the award of "tax proceeds" can hardly be contrasted to awards of "land." Someone to whom a personal share of tax assessment and its revenues was given could correctly speak of "his land" and "the revenues of his 'estate' (*praedium*)," even though the sitting cultivators and the owner retained their respective roles and could each speak of "his (or her) land" without contradicting the other parties. "Land" was at least three dimensional. The Burgundian Code forces attention to this ambiguity when it distinguishes simple *terrae* from *agri cum mancipiis*. Reduce these words to commonplace "lands," "field," and "slaves"; disregard the levels of cultivation, ownership, and assessment; leave this interlocking complexity unexplained; and you are nowhere.[41]

Hospitalitas on Trial

In view of the severe tone that critics of *Barbarians and Romans* adopted toward some of my arguments (such as my reading of Cassiodorus's letter on the "assignment of 'thirds' " [*Variae* 2.16.5]), I am amazed at the number of delinquencies other historians have been forgiven when dealing with this subject. E. A. Thompson is a case in point. He evokes the beginning of barbarian settlement in the West in 418 and explains: "[The Roman Patrician] Constantius gave each Visigothic optimate a portion (*sors*) of a Roman senatorial estate—the smaller estates were not affected—and this *sors* was made up of two thirds of the arable and one half of the pasture and woodland of the estate, which now supported two *consortes*, 'partners,' one Roman and the other barbarian, instead of a single Roman owner. In 443 Aetius settled the Burgundians in Savoy, south of the Lake of Geneva, in similar conditions; and the system was transferred to Spain by the Visigoths when they finally settled there. This method of billeting the barbarians was known as *hospitalitas*."[42] These remarkable assertions merit a closer look. Because the details of the initial Visigothic settlement are wholly undocumented, Thompson had no specific knowledge that Constantius used this "method of billeting."[43] He spoke by analogy from the terms of King Gundobad's LB54, issued in a different part of Gaul and many decades later than

Constantius's dispositions.[44] Not content with this tacit liberty, Thompson decided that (1) among the Visigoths, only "optimates" received grants; (2) Roman "estates" were the basis for carving out grants; (3) smaller estates were exempted from division; (4) major Roman estate-owners were deprived of two-thirds of their arable and one-half of their pastures and woodlands without any legal process or justification; (5) the reference of LB54 to *mancipia* could be ignored; (6) deprived Romans could be set alongside enriched barbarians to live together thereafter as harmonious partners; and (7) in conclusion, the reference of LB54 to *hospitalitas* denoted a "method of billeting" derived from the laws *de metatis* in the Theodosian Code, none of which in fact documents such a system. Not all of these decisions are necessarily indefensible, but none was defended. These are astounding liberties—not surprising, perhaps, in the light of the ludicrous distortions built into the "normal" accounts of *hospitalitas* quoted a moment ago, but much more artfully concealed than my argumentation in *Barbarians and Romans* for a tax-based system. The difference is that Thompson, however willful in handling evidence, was faithful to a century of tradition, whereas I had the effrontery to suggest something that had not been tried before.

Gaupp's main achievements in explaining barbarian settlements were to insist that a peaceable and legal process took place and, saliently, to set *hospitalitas* at the heart of the argument. Yet it seems to me, on reflection, that the part of *Barbarians and Romans* in which I went farthest astray was the chapter entitled "*Hospitalitas* and the Fifth-Century Settlements."[45] Quite a few correct things are said in it. I pointed out that halves and thirds are common fractions that occur in many legal contexts and can on no account be regarded as signposts of laws on military billeting. I also observed that "hospitality" never lost its common meaning—the one that survives with positive connotations to our day.[46] Pohl mentions a letter in which Gregory the Great (590–604) says that someone's *domus* destined for the foundation of a nunnery is currently burdened "ab hospitibus et supervenientibus [by guests and passers by]." Pohl comments, "These *hospites* must have been billeted soldiers."[47] I doubt that very much; there is nothing inherently military about a *hospes*. In the absence of any explicit sign of a military presence, the *domus* in question was more probably encumbered by squatters and transients whom Christian charity allowed to overstay their leave.[48]

Hospitalitas in the guise of military billeting has appealed to modern scholars because, as a state institution distinct from common hospitality, it appeared to offer a framework for expanding the soldier's part of a house into a barbarian's part of an estate.[49] However much I tried in *Barbarians and Romans* to escape the notion of a technical term attached to an institution, I could not find a way to break completely free from it: "It cannot be doubted [I said] that 'hospitality' of some kind played a part in the transactions we have been discussing"; "Contrary to what Gaupp and many others believed, the Roman *metatorum praebendorum onus* [= military billeting] is not the key to the allotments in Gaul and Italy, but it was, demonstrably, a practice that the state resorted to in order to provide shelter for barbarians as well as native troops . . . [It was, besides, an original synthesis, consisting] of two things, an administrative process borrowed from military quartering and a definable social relationship between the affected parties based on the accepted roles of host and guest."[50] I regret these lines and withdraw them along with the accompanying amplifications.[51] A more correct interpretation of *hospitalitas* is needed and has to be sought along different lines.

Hospitalitas in relation to property is featured in no more than two texts, both in the Burgundian Laws. The decisive one is LB55.2; it prohibits Burgundians from interposing themselves in the lawsuits of Romans over the "boundaries of fields" that Burgundians possess "by right of hospitality" (*de agrorum finibus, qui hospitalitatis iure a barbaris possidentur*); Burgundians, it says, are to stand completely clear of such lawsuits but may vindicate their legitimate rights after each case is settled.[52] As documented here, the Roman litigants are the owners of the land, engaging in a boundary dispute with fellow Roman owners, whereas the Burgundians who must stand clear are persons having an interest (only) by right of hospitality (*iure hospitalitatis*) in the fields in dispute. Although LB55.2 severely restricts Burgundian prerogatives, it does bring before our eyes a Burgundian who somehow possessed "fields by right of *hospitalitas*." Complementary to this text is a passage of LB54 referring to "a place [or locality] in which *hospitalitas* was assigned (*delegata*)."[53] It allows us to believe that *hospitalitas* could be "given" or at least "assigned" in some definite locality. Two texts exist, therefore, in which *hospitalitas* looks as though it refers to an asset or an object of value.[54]

The arresting reference to fields or land that Burgundians possess "by right [or law] of hospitality" seems to direct us to a body of law, such as the Theodosian title *de metatis* or to something new developed out of these rules. The common opinion is that possession by right of *hospitalitas* was a lucrative entitlement, as though to say "by right of military billeting." We have seen, however, that the proprietary interpretation of Roman military billeting is an illusion, a lamentable distortion on the part of modern historians for which no Roman legislator bears responsibility. Billets were uncompensated shelter, not property. The terms laid down by LB55.2, by being negative, are open to an alternative reading; the context in which *ius hospitalitatis* is found suggests that the phrase refers not to a benefit but to limitations sharply restricting the Burgundians' rights. These constraints are further intensified by laws circumscribing the sale of allotments (LB84), curtailing their alienation (LB1.2), and restricting their inheritance to males (LB78.3). A tour through the Roman evidence leads to additional legal rules setting "guestship" in a context of limitation rather than lucrative right.

The Roman law of Justinian's *Digest* sheds a little light on "hospitality." It specifies that *hospitium* is temporary, clearly distinct from "living" somewhere (the terms for which are *habitatio* and *domicilium*). *Hospitium* also involves the right to reside without charge; in general, the guest envisaged by the *Digest* is fed as well as housed. Such hospitality is especially applicable to soldiers and government officials.[55] The most unequivocal feature of hospitality in the *Digest* is that it is temporary.

Legal sources supply another subject of interest. Someone to whom the "bare usage (*nudus usus*)" of a farm or a house, as distinct from its "usufruct," has been bequeathed or otherwise granted has more rights over property than a guest; nevertheless, this *ius utendi* usefully supplements the conditions we have seen: "He who has bare usage of a farm is understood to be able to avail himself of nothing other than vegetables, fruit, flowers, hay, straw, [and] wood for daily use; he is allowed to tarry in this farm on condition that he does not annoy the owner of the farm or those who carry out farm work; and he may not avail himself of any right to give something by sale, lease, or gratis. . . . He who has bare use of a dwelling is understood to have only the right to reside, and he may not transfer this use to anyone else; he is barely even allowed to receive a guest."[56] These lines evoke someone who has the personal right to live, with his family, alongside the owner of a farm and his laborers. He is obliged to keep out of their way and is entitled only to a limited subsistence. He is much further than a usufructuary from "owning" the property on which he resides. Where "guestship" is concerned, the interest of *nudus usus* is that it dramatizes a situation in which the "real" owner and a second party manage somehow to exist side by side and share the same property to a very limited extent. One might see in this an analogy to the relationship between host and guest.

The laws of the Theodosian Code are notable for tariffing the amount of space allowed to official guests and for repressing their abusive demands. Contrary to the modern distortions reported above, the Theodosian title *de metatis* contains nothing even faintly suggestive of the award of property to transiting soldiers and officials. Billeting took place primarily in towns, in the *domus* of someone. It entailed a temporary inconvenience to the owners of houses, but no transfer of produce, let alone of real estate: soldiers and officials in transit could not possibly have been weighted down with such encumbrances. When a proprietor was allowed to commute billeting in his house, he paid the government one-third of its rent; the rest of his property was unaffected.[57] The salient postclassical change in billeting was that the feeding of *hospites* was terminated. That former obligation was now replaced by a separate process, namely, the state's supply of rations (*annonae*), as still attested in the Burgundian Code and, several times, in Theoderic's Italy.[58]

In the light of these strictly Roman laws, the Burgundian Code appears at first glance to embody a dramatic change. A comparison of the *hospes* of the *Digest* to the beneficiary of *ius hospitalitatis* whom we have seen in LB55.2 suggests an increase of entitlement for the "guest" from a momentary stopover to a permanent grant of "fields." Such an inference, however, cannot be correct. It is barred by another Burgundian law, LB38, which in ten articles sets out rules obligating the entire population of the kingdom, Burgundian and Roman, to provide hospitality for ambassadors and other travelers. The same law also defines a secondary procedure, akin to a special tax, by which a community is charged for feeding distinguished transients and, in winter, their mounts. LB54 and 55 look as though they might imply awards of "land" (as seen above) whereas LB38 lacks any hint that real estate would change hands; yet the same word "hospitality" is found in all three.

LB 38 De hospitalitate legatis extranearum gentium et itinerantibus non negante [On not denying hospitality to ambassadors of foreign peoples and travelers.]

1. Quicumque hospiti venienti tectum aut focum negaverit, trium solidorum inlatio multetur. [Whoever denies a roof and fire to a guest passing by is fined by a payment of three shillings.]
2. Si conviva regis est, 6 solidos multae nomine solvat. [If (the denier) is a royal table-companion, let him pay six shillings by way of fine.]
3. De legatis vero extranearum gentium, ut dictum est, id volumus custodiri: ut ubicumque eos mansio contullerit, unum porcum aut unum vervecem praesumendi habeant facultatem. Et qui fieri prohibuerit, 6 solidos multae nomine cogatur exsolvere. Quodsi datum legatis fuerit, ei qui dedit ab his, qui intra terminum villae ipsius commanent, conpensetur. [Concerning the aforementioned ambassadors of foreign peoples, we wish this to be observed: wherever they take shelter, let them have the right to requisition one pig and (or?) one ewe. Whoever prevents this is forced to pay six shillings by way of fine. And whatever is given to the ambassadors, let it be offset to the one who gave it by those who live within the boundaries of the village in question.]
4. Hiemis autem tempore si quid legatus foeni aut ordei praesumpserit, similiter et a consistentibus intra terminum villae ipsius, tam Burgundionibus quam Romanis, sine contradictione aliqua conferatur. Quod tamen [i.e., autem] a maioribus personis praecipimus custodiri. [In winter time, if an ambassador requisitions any hay and barley, again let it be granted without any rebuff by those living within the boundaries of the village, both Burgundians and Romans. We command that this be also obeyed by persons of rank.]
5. Ceterum si talis persona est, quae ex munificentia nostra legatum possit excipere, ipse tantum sua expensa legatis una nocta praeparet mansionem. Quod si non fecerit, 12

solidos se multae nomine noverit inlaturum. [If the person is of (such eminence) that he can receive an ambassador from (the proceeds) of our generosity, let him provide hospitality to the ambassadors for one night only at his expense. If he does not do so, he should know that he must pay a fine of twelve shillings.]

6. Si in causa privata iter agens ad Burgundionis domum venerit, et hospitium petierit, et ille domum Romani ostenderit, et hoc potuerit adprobari, inferat illi, cuius domum ostenderit, solidos 3, multae nomine solidos 3. [If a traveler on private business comes to the house of a Burgundian and asks for shelter and (the Burgundian) points out to him the house of a Roman, and if this can be proved, let (the Burgundian) pay three shillings to him whose house he pointed out, and three shillings as fine.]

7. Si quis in agro regio vel colonica voluerit adplicare, et non permisus fuerit, colonus fustigetur. [If someone wishes to camp in a royal field or tenancy, and he is not allowed, let the tenant farmer be cudgeled. (cf. LV8.4.24)]

8. Si autem hospes ibidem aliquid insolenter everterit, in novigildo restituat. [If, on the other hand, the guest presumptuously damages anything, let him restore it ninefold.][59]

9. Si in villa conductor ingenuus est, et tectum aut focum non dederit, inferat multae nomine solidos 3; si servus est, fustigetur. [If the chief-tenant in the village is free, and he does not give shelter and fire, let him pay three shillings by way of fine; if he is a slave, he is cudgeled.]

10. Quod de Burgundionum et Romanorum omnium colonis et servis praecipimus custodiri. [We order this rule to apply to the tenants and slaves of everyone, Burgundians and Romans.][60]

This fascinating law deserves a long commentary and will be referred to again. At the outset, it is essential to observe that the legislator speaks at length about a *hospitium* limited to a temporary "roof and hearth"—that, nothing more, is the positive content of *hospitalitas*—and that he lays down separate rules for the feeding of ambassadors and their mounts. It is obvious that the legislator who speaks as firmly as this about temporary "hospitality" under a requisitioned roof cannot have simultaneously associated hospitality with the (permanent or temporary) award of agricultural assets, such as *agri cum mancipiis*. The Burgundian Laws are not alone; a similarly nonproprietary sense of *hospitium* is found in a Visigothic law, in connection with someone sheltering a person not known to himself for up to a week (LV9.1.6).[61] The Burgundian Code cannot call for a different meaning of *hospitalitas* every time it uses the term. A single gloss is needed fitting all cases, both Roman billeting and the Burgundian *ius hospitalitatis*.

Ernst Levy, who recognized that LB38, 54, and 55 embodied a contradiction, contrasted a Roman "hospitality" in LB54 and 55 to a nonproprietary "Germanic" hospitality in LB38; but this desperate remedy cannot save the distorted sense of "billeting" as an award of property.[62] Instead, the three laws demand a definition of *hospitalitas* applicable to both the settling of Burgundians and the housing of travelers. The meaning that I find persuasive is based on what traveling soldiers, ambassadors, pilgrims, and even certain kinds of agrarian settlers have in common in their resort to "hospitality": they are granted temporary *occupancy*; the guest enters the host's property as a stranger being sheltered temporarily and without payment.

The practice of hospitality in this limited sense was not confined to Burgundian territory. A set of Visigothic laws protects the rights of travelers to have space to camp and to graze their animals alongside public roads, not just on the road allowance but also in nearby unenclosed fields, provided they stay no longer than two days (longer if the owner agrees).[63] The similarity of these laws to LB38 is obvious. An imperial law of 413 about military billeting spells out the strict limits: "We grant only occupancy" with no food for man or beast and a timely departure. Additional laws on billeting (*de metatis*) are compatible with this gloss. A soldier is said to sojourn "by right of occupancy" or to enjoy "the convenience of occupancy" (*hospitalis commoditas*).[64] On this basis a specifically military hospitality is irrelevant; the *ius hospitalitatis* is the same for all in its denial of any prerogative for the guest except for just being there. "If the guest presumptuously damages anything [in the place sheltering him], let him make ninefold restitution": Burgundian law fines a troublemaking guest at a very severe level of punishment (theft entails only twofold restitution).[65] The resemblance of these rules to the personal right of "bare use" are apparent; *ius hospitalitatis* is just a shade less advantageous than *ius utendi.* Except for the Visigothic two-day tolerance, no laws provide for the eventual eviction of occupants, civilian, religious, or military, who overstay their leave.[66]

The letters of Sidonius Apollinaris mention a certain Seronatus, a Roman official who collaborated closely with the Visigoths. Sidonius tells us inter alia that Seronatus daily "fills villages with guests" (*implet . . . villas hospitibus*).[67] When taken together with LB38, the Sidonius passage suggests that the ordinary powers of the Roman government included that of imposing guests upon villages. Villagers could be required by state officials to make space among themselves for authorized strangers—strangers whose sojourn was subject to the very restricted rights of occupancy. To this limited extent, we can understand the phrase in LB54.2 about *hospitalitas* being assigned in some locality.

Hospitalitas as "occupancy" is more negative than positive; it is a "right (*ius*)," but one characterized by severe restrictions. If that is its sense, there is little point in referring to Roman military billeting for relevant rules. Besides, the salient difference of Gaul from Africa and Italy needs to be recalled: barbarian allotments (*sortes*) were distributed in Vandal North Africa and Gothic Italy, but there is no sign in the relevant sources that these settlements had anything to do with *hospitalitas* of any kind.[68] Like the barbarians in Africa and Italy, those in Gaul had to acquire their allotments pursuant to a measure wholly alien to military "hospitality." *Hospitalitas* was invoked in Gaul for only one reason, namely, to define the very limited "right" by which the barbarians possessed.

*   *   *

This concludes my demonstration that military billeting, wrongly called *hospitalitas,* could never have been the basis of barbarian settlement anywhere; the connection of military billeting with the award of "land" in Gaul and Spain lacks any basis. My critics have been almost unanimous in believing that billeting legitimized distributions of "land," tacitly defined as cultivable soil; even Cameron, without mentioning *hospitalitas,* embedded its (supposed) terms in her summary. *Barbarians and Romans* made it clear—perhaps too succinctly—that the "Gaupp model" of billeting as a basis for settlement was a mistake. The confident advocacy of the "default position" in response to my book mainly illustrates how hastily and inattentively scholarship is read. The irrelevance of the Gaupp model has now been shown again. Moreover, in place of the equally unanimous practice of leaving "land" undefined but very tangible, I have offered a breakdown of "land" into three coexisting components—cultivation, ownership, and state assessment—two of them considerably more abstract than cultivable soil. This tripartition goes far toward bridging the polarity that has been assumed to exist between "land" and "taxes."

The clarification of *hospitalitas* and "land" makes it superfluous to deal with the critics of *Barbarians and Romans* one by one and respond to objections that proceed from demonstrably mistaken premises.[69] Among them, only Dietrich Claude appears to have taken the trouble to devise a scheme of barbarian settlement detached from *hospitalitas.* I shall eventually return to it and show its frailty.

One postulate of *Barbarians and Romans* needs to be repeated, namely, that the establishment of the Goths and Burgundians was peaceful and lawful. This observation goes back to Gaupp in person and many others since then; I did not originate it. The orderliness of the process is one of the incentives for devising a form of barbarian settlement less disruptive than the law of conquest. Somehow, certain steps were taken in the fifth century that persuaded the Roman provincials, including prominent senatorial landowners in Italy, to remain placid and calm, and resulted in an undisturbed passage of the countryside from antiquity to the Middle Ages. Several critics of *Barbarians and Romans* managed to remain unmoved by this observation and even to try to undermine it.[70] I shall return to it several times.

The rest of Chapter 6 mainly retraces and carefully analyzes the evidence concerning the settlement of the Visigoths in southwestern Gaul, the Burgundians in southeastern Gaul, and the Goths of Theoderic in Italy. The discussion focuses on the same legal texts studied in *Barbarians and Romans*, but every aspect has been reconsidered and refined. The order of discussion, deliberately skewed in *Barbarians and Romans*, has been straightened to the ostensibly chronological sequence of Visigoths, Burgundians, and Ostrogoths.[71] My reexamination of the three Visigothic laws most relevant to this subject shows that they provide solid footings for a fiscal interpretation of the Visigothic settlement. The main Burgundian law (LB54) has been central to almost all serious discussion of this subject. I analyze it thoroughly; it contains many unique features, but documents an allotment scheme very similar to the Visigothic. For Italy, the crucial letter of Cassiodorus about Liberius's "assignment of 'thirds' " (*Variae* 2.16) can now be shown, too, to attest to awards of units of tax proceeds rather acres of soil. Moreover, I dissect the letter of Cassiodorus (*Variae* 2.17) that is, in effect, the sole surviving evidence from anywhere for the grant of anything to a barbarian. Special attention is drawn repeatedly to an aspect of the settlements emphasized in *Barbarians and Romans* but resolutely evaded by its critics: in all the lands of barbarian settlement the total Roman tax resources were partitioned between the barbarian kings and their rank and file. These partitions, and not Roman laws about billeting, are at the origin of thirds and halves in the relevant sources. In closing the chapter, I draw attention to the evidence for abuses by the barbarians after settlement in their relations with their Roman neighbors.

How Did Constantius Finance Gothic Settlement in Gaul?

Gregory of Tours reports an incident of the 570s that involved the sharing of land between two non-Roman peoples in a part of inner Germany. Saxons in large numbers had abandoned their lands so as to join King Alboin in the Lombard invasion of Italy (568). After a few years there and Alboin's assassination, they decided to detach themselves from the Lombards, leave Italy, and return to the lands they had left. Less than ten years had passed between their departure and their return. In the meantime, the Frankish king who oversaw these inner German territories had allowed Swabians (Alamanni?) to settle the lands that the Saxons had vacated. The returning Saxons were escorted through Gallo-Roman districts of Frankish Gaul, not without clashes with the inhabitants; Saxon manners were not improved by desperation.[72] Eventually, the king of Frankish Austrasia brought them to the land they had left. Gregory's account follows in paraphrase:

The returning Saxons were angered to find others in possession and resolved to expel them. The new settlers numbered 6,400, the returning Saxons 26,000. In an effort to make peace, the Swabians offered the Saxons one-third of the land, saying, "Surely we can live together without hostilities" (*tertiam partem terrae, dicentes: Simul vivere sine consilium ne possumus.*). But the Saxons would not hear of peace. The incumbents increased their offer to one-half, then two-thirds, keeping only one-third for themselves. The Saxons still refused. The incumbents then also offered them all their livestock as long as they refrained from war. The Saxons, rejecting all offers, prepared for war; they were already quarreling among themselves over the division of booty. Battle was joined, and the Saxons, though much more numerous, were badly beaten, losing the larger part of their numbers. The surviving Saxons swore to try again. They did so and were virtually wiped out.[73]

Gregory attributes the outcome to God's compassion, intervening on earth to cast down the proud and raise up the meek.[74] The edifying quality of the story detracts from its credibility, but verisimilitude matters more for our purposes than fidelity to fact. The Swabians, outnumbered four to one by the returned Saxons, could well afford to surrender a large part of the territory granted to them by the Frankish king provided the loss gained them cooperation and a tranquil modus vivendi with the Saxons. The prospect of living without livestock on one-third of the occupied territory still seemed preferable to violent expulsion with loss of life. In the event, God favored their cause and did away with the truculent aggressors. Two points deserve special notice: a division of land by simple fractions did not need the assistance of supposed Roman rules for military quartering; and the partition between the two parties, Swabians and Saxons, was distinct from any distribution to individuals, about which nothing is said.[75] Gregory suggests conditions applicable anywhere, without special reference to Rome.

   In the case of fifth-century settlement of barbarians, the terminology of "hosts" and "guests" occurs only in the Burgundian and Visigothic evidence, the latter of which is, except for two articles of Euric's Code (ca. 475), extremely late by comparison with the time when settlements took place. The laws in question were revised in the reign of King Leuvigild (569–86) almost two hundred years after the "original" arrangements that we assume took place between the patrician Constantius and King Wallia.[76] In spite of this chronological spread, the sources for settlement in the Gothic and Burgundian kingdoms in Gaul have so many points of tangency that their common origins are more than likely. Chronicles even claim that the Burgundians settled in Gaul at the invitation of the Goths and with their patronage.[77] The two kingdoms agree on their operative fractions—two-thirds for the barbarians, one-third for the taxpaying Romans, regardless of what the shares might refer to and of the nature of partition.[78] They have additional features in common, even though a precise resemblance cannot always be grasped.

Where southwestern Gaul is concerned, the fundamental problem of explaining barbarian settlement is this: in 418 the Roman government welcomed the Visigoths as permanent residents of a defined territory (we would say, the Garonne Valley); when this happened, what lucrative commodity could the patrician Constantius avail himself of to give to the Visigothic leadership and military rank and file? Contrary to what we are told, such as by Thompson above, we have no information about what Constantius did. Western chroniclers tell us that he called the Visigoths back from Spain and gave them *sedes*—a collective "seat"; geographical details are supplied, but nothing is said about transfers of property.[79] The Greek church historian Philostorgius, presumably basing himself on Olympiodorus, says that the Visigoths were given rations and land for tillage. This report is not self-explanatory and, even if it were taken at face value, it leaves us guessing about ways and means.[80] To overcome our lack of information, we make a "serious guess" that either Constantius or the Visigothic king gave individual awards to the Visigoths. Then we ask further, how did Constantius finance the settlement of the Visigoths? What objects of value, what resources, were there for Constantius to give either to King Wallia or to the Visigothic rank and file? That, I suggest, is the crucial question.

One avenue of interpretation is now closed: allotments were not supplied to Visigoths by virtue of the Roman laws *de metatis*; no laws about billets or hospitality authorized a government official to give the land or revenues of innocent Roman proprietors to soldiers, barbarians, or any other beneficiary. The halves and thirds mentioned in billeting laws refer to fractions of a residence; they were never meant to signify the house owner's total or partial property. Once and for all, military billeting was not a legal mechanism for dispossessing Roman hosts and handing over real estate to anyone. If the patrician Constantius needed to convey property to King Wallia or to individual Visigoths, the only method by which he could give away the lands of the resident provincials was to expropriate them, by substituting the rule of force for socioeconomic stability. We know that this did not happen. The collections of Visigothic and Burgundian law, whatever else they may mean, attest to the perpetuation in these lands of legality and the rule of law. We are driven back to the fundamental question: what lawful resources were there for Constantius to give?

In asking after the basis for Visigothic allotments, I am guiding the argument in the fiscal direction Durliat and I have both taken. It is, I maintain, the only way to go. Although Constantius could not seize the private properties of the provincials, he did not lack an alternative.[81] As the representative of the Roman government, he had at his disposal the economic resources of the state. One Visigothic law (as we shall see) comes as close as the texts permit to documenting precisely that: Roman taxes came into the possession of the Visigothic king; they were paid to his fisc.[82] This law is best approached in company with the two other Visigothic laws that relate most centrally to the barbarian settlement. The fractions they deploy—two-thirds and one-third—have invariably been read in the context of a misconstrued *hospitalitas* and so have been turned into fractions of individual Roman "estates." Detached from the discredited model of military billeting, as they must be, they lead elsewhere than is generally thought.

At first glance, the main Visigothic evidence for barbarian and Roman "shares" looks promising for the theory of land assignment—"simple" division and sharing out. What needs emphasis is that the fractions that occur in these laws hang in the air and have no stated or clearly defined reference point; we have to determine what they refer to. Commentators with billeting in mind have hastened to inject an imagined process of carving up of lands and have conjured up Roman *fundi* or "estates" as the substance being divided.[83] An artist has even depicted a scene in which a cowed Roman acquiesces to his dispossession to the profit of a magnificently armored Goth.[84] Such ideas have little or nothing to do with what the Visigothic texts actually contain.

CE277 Sortes Gothicas et tertias Romanorum, quae intra L annis non fuerint revocate, nullo modo repetantur. Similiter de fugitivis, qui intra L annis inventi non fuerint, non liceat eos ad servitium revocare. . . . Et alias omnes causas . . . quae intra XXX annis definitae non fuerint . . . nullo modo repetantur.

[Gothic allotments and the "thirds" (*tertiae*) of Romans that have not been recovered in fifty years are on no account to be reclaimed. The same holds for fugitive (bondpersons): if they have not been found in fifty years, it is not allowed to recall them to servitude. . . . And all other cases . . . that are not terminated in thirty years . . . shall on no account be reopened.][85]

This law concerns time limits for lawsuits; its Burgundian counterpart is LB79, "De praescriptione temporum." To illustrate the principle involved, one might say that, if an intruder has squatted upon some land without permission, the landowner has a set number of years, but no more, in which to vindicate his title and evict the intruder or force him to pay rent; unless the owner's claim is made good in this period of time, the intruder's ownership is beyond challenge. The thirty-year limit specified by CE277 is high by our standards, but well entrenched in late Roman law; the fifty-year limit laid down in the opening clauses of CE277—almost doubling the standard—is extravagant but definitely imposed there for certain kinds of lawsuits.[86]

The purpose of CE277—to affirm time limits—is more evident than the meaning of its main clauses. Fugitives are self-explanatory in a slave society, but the legislator forces us to ask whether he refers only to private law slaves or also includes categories like *coloni*, whose obligation to remain fixed on their tenancies was a matter of state law; in other words, do the fugitives of CE277 include persons whose "servitude" was "public"?[87] This unanswerable question is secondary to that of the *sortes* and *tertiae*. If it is assumed that all the landowners of the Visigothic kingdom were either Goths or Romans, and that the former had *sortes* whereas the latter had *tertiae*, it would seem to follow that the two categories of *sortes* and *tertiae*, added to each other, comprised all the landed property in the realm.[88] This reasoning leads to unacceptable results. The law would be saying that all landed property as well as all bondpersons were subject to a fifty-year time prescription; the reference to "sortes Gothicas et tertias Romanorum" would be decorative, lacking any significance in its own right. The naming of the two categories is too prominent, however, to be incidental. The alternative is that the legislator mentioned these categories because there was something specific about the *sortes* and *tertiae* to which this extravagant time limit applied: only property of that kind qualified. As explained earlier, agrarian property had at least three superimposed aspects: cultivation, ownership, and assessment for taxation. Which of these three applies here? All three at once do not have to be referred to; only one dimension may be in question. Another possibility is that *sortes* and *tertiae*, rather than being landed property itself, were obligations, burdens, or servitudes weighing upon property; CE277 would accordingly grant litigants fifty years in which to claim and vindicate the rights or profits given them by this obligation from a party failing to honor it. To sum up, *sortes* and *tertiae* were not the total property in the kingdom; they designated either special lands or a special dimension of land, distinct from other aspects of land, notably ownership and cultivation, to which the ordinary thirty-year limit applied.

The other law in which these special terms are featured provides more substance to ponder:

LV10.1.8 De divisione terrarum facta inter Gotum adque Romanum. Divisio inter Gotum et Romanum facta de portione terrarum sive silvarum nulla ratione turbetur, si tamen probatur celebrata divisio, ne de duabus partibus Goti aliquid sibi Romanus presumat aut vindicet, aut de tertia Romani Gotus sibi aliquid audeat usurpare aut vindicare, nisi quod a nostra forsitan ei fuerit largitate donatum. Sed quod a parentibus vel a vicinis divisum est, posteritas inmutare non temtet.

[About a division of lands made between a Goth and a Roman. A division made between a Goth and a Roman concerning a quantity of lands or woods shall on no account be contested, if it is proved that a division actually took place; provided (however) that no

Roman shall take or defend for himself any of the two parts of the Goth, or that a Goth shall dare to usurp or defend any of the "third" of the Roman, except if it has perchance been given to him by our (royal) generosity. Let not posterity venture to alter what was divided by (its) progenitors or by neighbors.][89]

This law does not dramatize the moment when (according to the old teaching) divisions of Roman "estates" conveyed a large share of Gallic farmland to Gothic possession. Much more routinely, the law provides for the divisions or partitions of property that are frequent among partners and neighbors in any countryside. The legislator states that, normally, all lawful divisions are unassailable; and he specifically confirms the validity of earlier divisions by relatives and neighbors (*parentes seu vicini*).

The special feature of LV10.1.8, necessitating a new law, is that some divisions are between a Goth and a Roman. The law spells out a decisive impediment to divisions between these persons: the division cannot result in the Roman's acquiring any of the *duas partes Gothi*, or in the Goth's acquiring any of the *tertia Romani* unless the *tertia* was given to him by the king. This impediment forces us to reflect. Our normal expectation, deduced from the discredited *hospitalitas* scheme and stated a moment ago in connection with CE277, is that the property of Goths consists of *duas partes*, alias *sortes*, and that of Romans consists of *tertia*. But if this interpretation were correct, divisions between them, however fair and equal, would unavoidably necessitate the exchange of forbidden *sortes* and *tertia*: there would be nothing else to divide. Yet, plainly, the law does not forbid all property adjustments between Goths and Romans; it is taken for granted that *terrae sive silvae* will be divided every now and then by mutual consent of the owners. The same dilemma confronts us here as in the law on time limits. To make sense of the text, we are forced to conclude that *sortes/duas partes Gothi* and *tertia Romani* are not identical with the concrete *terrae sive silvae* that may legitimately be partitioned and shared. They are a distinct aspect or dimension of property; perhaps, as just suggested, they are an obligation weighing on property rather property itself. The twice mentioned "Goth" and "Roman" are also not identical: those who do the dividing are individuals engaging in lawful processes, whereas those associated with the *duas partes* and *tertia* are there as definers of a type of property or obligation.

The fractions two-thirds and one-third in these laws have been taken by earlier commentators to refer to partitions of individual properties, large or small; the image of a Goth authorized—by the law on military billeting, to be sure—to seize a part of the "estate" of some designated Roman continues to come to mind.[90] This discredited model does not fit CE277 and LV10.1.8. Nowhere do we see a partition of individual properties; the means for it—compact "estates" neatly available for simple fractioning—did not exist, and no words to that effect occur in the law. The conclusion we are left with is that "*duas partes* of the Goth" refers not to a single Goth but, synecdochically, to all of them; and that the same holds for the *tertia Romani*, not, thus, of a particular Roman but of the collectivity of Romans. Both laws involve a global category: the total "two-thirds" share allocated to *sortes Gothicae*, and the Roman category of "one-third" subject to paying taxes to the royal government and available to the king for individual (supplementary) gifts to Goths. The Roman and Goth of LV10.1.8 who carry out a division were participants in a larger scheme of *sortes* and *tertia* that their otherwise lawful divisions were forbidden from affecting. *Sortes* and *tertia* were the entities worthy of being defended by an extravagant time prescription. If they were not land as patches for cultivation, or land as properties owned by private law, there was only one other thing for them to refer to, namely, land assessed by the state for purposes of taxation. The terms *sors* and *tertia* would refer not to the proprietary relations of individual Goths and Romans to each other, but to the total registered resources, or property assessments for tax purposes, of the (former) Roman state, now shared between the king, to whose fisc some *Romani* continued to pay taxes, and "the Goths," whose allotments (*sortes*) were distributed to individuals out of the balance of "two parts." *Tertia* and *sortes* were pools of assets, the former under direct royal control to keep or give away, the latter distributed to the Goths in individual shares.

A special glance at the *tertia Romani* confirms the direct relationship of this category of property to the tax system. The key text on this question is LV10.1.16; it shows that *tertia* was attached not only to those *Romani* of the kingdom who paid public taxes, but simultaneously to the Gothic king or royal government, which received the proceeds of taxation and might make individual gifts of *tertia* to Goths. Underscoring these aspects of *tertia*, LV10.1.16 specifies that, if ordinary Goths take away any bit of *tertia*, royal officials are to intervene spontaneously and restore the alienation without delay to "the Romans," the reason for this summary process being "that nothing might thereby be lost to the fisc."[91]

This law is important, first, because it disproves the billeting-inspired belief that *tertia* refers to the one-third of an "estate" presumed to have been left in an individual Roman proprietor's possession after two-thirds was given to a Goth as his *sors*. *Tertia* does not mean that at all; neither it nor the complementary two-thirds relate to individual properties or "estates."[92] *Tertia* refers to a global category of property whose distinctive feature was that it paid taxes to the royal fisc. An obvious conclusion (explained again in a moment) is that the *tertia Romani* was one-third of the total tax assessment that, in Roman days, before the distribution of *sortes*, had weighed upon the entire territory. The tight

control that LV10.1.16 shows the government exercising over the *tertia* also reveals what had happened to the other two-thirds of the assessment: these *duas
partes Gothi* were applied to providing "allotments," *sortes*, for individual Goths,
allotments considered so important that they could not be alienated to Romans
and were protected by the same fifty-year prescription defending the *tertia* on
whose returns the royal income depended. The feature of *tertia Romani* is clearly
that such property was obligated to tax payments to the royal fisc; this obligation was protected by a fifty-year prescription. A similar obligation, and time
prescription, weighed upon the *duas partes Gothi*—not on Goths but on the
(Roman) property underpinning Gothic allotments and obligated to Gothic
beneficiaries.[93]

These Visigothic texts—with the law on *tertia* in the lead—answer more
than just the one question of what resources were available to Constantius to finance Visigothic settlement (and to Aetius to finance that of the Burgundians).
They also document a primary sharing of these resources between the king and
the rank and file. They allow us, once and for all, to dismiss from our minds the
"one-third" of the law on billeting, and to focus instead on a totally different,
global division of Roman resources, of a kind found in Vandal North Africa and
fifth-century Italy as well as in the Visigothic and Burgundian kingdoms.[94] That
division operated at two simultaneous levels: first, a sharing of resources between the barbarian king (or government) and the Gothic rank and file; second,
a division of Roman assessed land into one category obligated to pay its taxes
to the royal government and another category obligated, piece by piece, to pay
to the holders of allotments.[95] The division of Roman assessed land between
barbarian king and followers entailed a simultaneous division of Roman
landowners-taxpayers, some obligated to the king, others to the *sors*-owners.[96]

Under the Empire, the area in which the Visigoths would receive their collective *sedes* had been full of agricultural properties owned by Roman proprietors, recorded in the assessment books of the state, and annually paying to the
government the taxes of their assessment. Most of these assets probably survived the period of disorder preceding the Gothic settlement of 418, and the
registers in which they were assessed were surrendered to the new regime. When
the transfer took place, both the sitting cultivators and the owners stayed in
place, undisturbed in their farming and proprietorship; their tax liability continued as before. Nothing so crude took place as an assignment of one Visigoth
to one Roman landowner for purposes of stripping the latter and enriching the
former; the texts we have seen invoke the generality of Romans and Goths.
There was a division of "land," but the land in question consisted only of the official assessment and the annual taxes arising from it. The division affected, not
only the "land," but also the persons concerned, both Roman proprietors and

Gothic newcomers. The total tax resources yielded by the Romans to the Goths were shared in proportions of one-third and two-thirds between the royal government and those members of the Gothic rank and file lofty enough to deserve an allotment—something lucrative to sustain them. Accordingly, one-third of Roman taxes and their payers were kept by the king as obliged to his fisc, and the other Romans were destined to be the taxpayers of individual Goths.

The process or mechanism by which allotments were awarded to individual Visigoths escapes us because undocumented, but may have been comparatively simple since written records were mainly involved. The recipient of a *sors* needed to be informed of three things: his tributaries, the assets giving rise to liability, and the amounts to be paid to him.[97] By grace of public records, the awards of *sortes* did not have to coincide with the map of ownership; no survey and partition of the tangible ground was necessary. Moreover, the recipient of a *sors*, like a Roman rent-collecting landowner, did not have to be resident on "his land" or engage in active farming.[98] Another advantage was that allotments like these, carved out of the tax registers, could be of roughly equal size. They were units of revenue, not of cultivation or of landownership. Just as the king collected the taxes from his *tertia*, so the qualified Goths, by proxy or in person, annually collected the taxes arising from the share of assessment individually awarded to them. The share in question came out of the *duas partes Gothi*, the pool of Roman taxpayers permanently attributed, *sors* by *sors*, to the Gothic rank and file. In this comparatively simple way, the countryside and its longtime occupiers were left largely undisturbed, and the Gothic regime, both king and troops, received ample endowments.

"Occupancy" and the *Sortes* of Burgundians

About two decades after penetrating imperial territory, the Burgundians suffered a severe defeat in northern Gaul in 436 and vanished for about seven years. But they made a comeback. A chronicle tells us, at 443, that their "remnants" were settled by the generalissimo Aetius in a part of southeastern Gaul called Sapaudia. They are said to have "divided" the territory with the "natives (*indigenae*)," and, by a later chronicler, with the Gallic "senators," probably meaning the major landowners.[99] The chronicle entries, as normally, are sparing in details; as with the Visigoths, they are silent about the mechanism and proportions of division and about what allowance was made for the Burgundian rank and file. This second Burgundian kingdom held its own for a little less than a century. It was conquered by the Franks in 534 and, although the place name "Burgundy" lived on (as we know), the original Burgundians quickly blended into the Frankish kingdom, in which nevertheless the ethnic name vigorously endured.

Many more measures concerning barbarian settlement occur in the Burgundian Laws than in the Visigothic ones. As seen above, it contains the law decisive for showing that *hospitalitas* did not mean "military billeting" (LB38). Surpassing any other relevant evidence in importance is LB54, often mentioned already, clearly the richest single text documenting the "techniques of accommodation." Many historians have cited it as though it were the fundamental law of barbarian settlement, which it cannot be. Its rules have been widely generalized, as by Thompson.[100] The thirds and halves that it prominently cites have been taken as directly mirroring the rules of Roman billeting and, accordingly, implying a face-to-face relationship of guest and host. LB54 allows us to think that *sortes*-receivers obtained a bundle of agrarian assets; commentators have transposed such bundles to the Goths of Gaul and Italy. On the basis of LB54, Wood devised a scenario of Burgundians loitering in Roman farms until the day when the king authorized them to help themselves to quotas of land and slaves, after which they presumably lived amicably alongside their unresentful Roman neighbors.[101] LB54 has been abused; it needs careful interpretation.[102] The law contains many unique features: it implies that a set of earlier enactments projected over a period of time led up to its issuance; it refers to types of agrarian property faintly attested in the Visigothic evidence and not at all in Italy; it documents a distribution of assets to the Burgundian rank and file additional to what they had first received; and it distinguishes at least two different types of landholding. As though this were not enough, another Burgundian law, concerned with land sales (LB84), gives some impression of what became of allotments to barbarians after they were awarded.

The Burgundian Code is first attested by a ninth-century manuscript. The abundant critical discussions that the Code, and this law in particular, have occasioned can be bypassed. The contents are our concern. It suffices for our purposes that LB54 was issued between 501 and 516 by Gundobad, perhaps the most noteworthy of the Burgundian kings.[103]

Partly because LB54 has been widely misunderstood, but also because of its inherent interest and importance to barbarian settlement, it must be very attentively examined. I begin by citing it in full.[104] Note that the words *terrae* and *mancipia* are left untranslated. What *terrae* means is not particularly mysterious, provided one pays attention to the aspect of *terra* that is in question rather than to undefined "land." But the sense of *mancipia*, "slaves," cannot be literal, as we shall see: there were no herds of slaves complementing the acres of *terrae*. The meaning of both will be clarified by the end of my discussion and in

Appendix 3. Meanwhile, the untranslated terms are reminders of their provisionally indefinite sense.

[Title] De his, qui tertiam mancipiorum et duas terrarum partes contra interdictum publicum praesumpserint. [About those who, contrary to public prohibition, illegally seized the one-third of *mancipia* and two parts of *terrae*.][105]

[1] Licet eodem tempore, quo populus noster mancipiorum tertiam et duas terrarum partes accepit, eiusmodi a nobis fuerit emissa praeceptio, ut quicumque agrum cum mancipiis seu parentum nostrorum sive nostra largitate perceperat, nec mancipiorum tertiam nec duas terrarum partes ex eo loco, in quo ei hospitalitas fuerat delegata requireret, tamen quia complures comperimus, inmemores periculi sui, ea quae praecepta fuerant excessisse, necesse est, ut praesens auctoritas, ad instar mansurae legis emissa, et praesumptores coerceat et hucusque contemptis remedium debitae securitatis adtribuat. [Although, at the time when our people received the one-third of *mancipia* and two parts of *terrae*, we issued an order to the effect that whoever had obtained an *ager cum mancipiis* by the gift of our parents or ourselves should not claim the one-third of *mancipia* or two parts of *terrae* from that place in which hospitality had been assigned to him: nevertheless, since several persons, as we see, disregarding their peril, transgressed these things that were ordered, it is necessary that the present order, issued as an enduring law, should coerce those who seize illegally and should offer a remedy of due security as regards whatever has been illegally seized until now.]

[2] Iubemus igitur: ut quidquid ab his, qui agris et mancipiis nostra munificentia potiuntur, de hospitum suorum terris contra interdictum publicum praesumpsisse docentur, sine dilatione restituant. [We therefore order that those who are in possession of *agri* and *mancipia* by our generosity should restore without delay whatever *terrae* of their hosts they are shown to have seized contrary to public prohibition.]

[3] De exartis quoque novam nunc et superfluam faramannorum conpetitionem et calumniam possessorum gravamine et inquietudine hac lege praecipimus submoveri: ut sicut de silvis, ita et de exartis, sive anteacto sive in praesenti tempore factis, habeant cum Burgundionibus rationem; quoniam, sicut iam dudum statutum est, medietatem silvarum ad Romanos generaliter praecipimus pertinere; [By this law we also order that the new and superfluous claim and allegation of the *faramanni* (= Burgundians) regarding clearings be now removed from the burden and disturbance of the landowners: let (the latter) hold an account with the Burgundians about clearings, both past and present, as (they do) about woods, since, as has already been laid down, we order in general that half the woods should pertain to the Romans.]

[4] simili de curte et pomariis circa faramannos conditione servata, id est: ut medietatem Romani estiment praesumendam. [The same stipulation is laid down to the *faramanni* regarding the enclosure and the fruit-gardens, namely, that the Romans may have possession of one-half.][106]

[5] Quod si quisque constitutum huiuscemodi praeceptionis excesserit et non a vobis fuerit cum districtione repulsus, non dubitetis commotionem iracundiae nostrae in vestrum periculum esse vertendam. [If anyone transgresses the letter of this command and is not repelled with severity by you (= royal officials, judges), do not doubt that the transports of our anger will be turned to your peril.]

Far from LB54 being accessible at "face value," one could spend a long time arguing about it, since the surface text conveys little self-evident meaning. Interpretations of LB54 hitherto have been poured through the grid of military billeting. This can no longer be done. A new grid is now available for LB54, namely, the Visigothic case just examined. One crucial point made in its connection was that the "land" referred to in these texts consisted not of the soil or the ownership (which stayed with the Romans) but of the registered tax assessments and the tax revenue arising from them (which was conveyed to the barbarians). *Terra* as used in LB54 and related laws is understood here to have that same qualified meaning: not the soil, not the ownership, but the tax assessment and resulting annual payments. A second important feature established by the Visigothic case is that the total tax assessments of the territory conveyed to the incoming barbarians were divided between the barbarian king and his soldiers. The division between king and people underlies the fractions of thirds and halves found in the sources. LB54 with its thirds of "*mancipia* and *terrae*" and its "place in which *hospitalitas* was assigned" used to be the promised land of the "Gaupp model." It remains to be seen what can be made of it without the sanction of military billeting. (Readers wishing to bypass the detailed argument may jump to the summary beginning on p. 153.)

The Nature of the Law

LB54 is not a general statute concerning settlement. It is a supplementary law whose object is to repress abuses arising from what I shall call the "recent measure." That measure was supplemented by a royal command (*praeceptio*) restricting its application. The existence of the "recent measure" and the *praeceptio* are reasonable inferences from the text that we can actually examine, namely, LB54, which represses violations of the *praeceptio*. The thrust of LB54 is to protect Roman proprietors from ostensibly legal harassment by Burgundians. LB54, therefore, stands at the end of a series of measures and actions reaching back over a period of years: the original allotments to the *faramanni*, which are faintly discernible (as we shall see); the "recent measure" somehow affecting the allotments; a *praeceptio* restricting the application of the "recent measure"; individual violations of the *praeceptio* over a period of time; and, finally, LB54, which seeks to protect the Romans by repressing abuses of the "recent measure" by Burgundians. These complexities suggest both the copiousness of LB54 and the delicacy of its interpretation.

The Cast of Characters

LB54 is a royal enactment in a series reaching into the past. The king alludes to past actions—the three or more measures leading up to LB54 as well as official gifts of property formerly made to individual Burgundians by himself and his relatives (*parentes*). Two categories of Burgundians are addressed in LB54: first, "our people," also called *faramanni*, definable as all Burgundians entitled to an individual allotment (I call them "ordinary Burgundians");[107] second, a smaller group of *faramanni* (here called "privileged Burgundians") who, over the years, had received from the king, besides their *sortes*, individual gifts of "agri cum mancipiis." The Burgundians enriched by royal gifts are also documented by LB1.3–4, 38.5, and 55.2 and 5 (discussed later); they were prominent in the kingdom. LB54 also mentions Romans, but discreetly. They appear without national label as *hospites*, "hosts," and as *possessores*, "landowners"; they are explicitly called Romans in connection with the fixed rule that one-half of "subsidiary assets" (to be defined shortly) is guaranteed to them.[108] In short, the law refers to the king, to "his people," namely ordinary and privileged *faramanni*, and to Romans.

The Objects at Issue

As a result of the king's "recent measure," the "ordinary Burgundians" received two-thirds of the *terrae* and one-third of the *mancipia*. This statement need not mean that they received the award in one piece and at one time. Clauses 1–2 of LB54 are concerned with the "main assets" dealt with by the law, namely, *terrae* and *mancipia*. These assets completely differ from the "subsidiary assets" addressed in clauses 3–4.[109] A 50 percent rule governing "subsidiary assets," both before and after the "recent measure," is recorded in LB54.3–4. This long-standing rule implies that "ordinary Burgundians" had not been propertyless prior to the laws under discussion; it seems likely that not only "subsidiary" but even some "main assets" were in their possession before the "recent measure" came into force. The long-standing rule governing subsidiary assets is the hint LB54 contains of an "original" Burgundian settlement. This, obviously, is very important.

In the Visigothic laws mentioning *tertia* and *duas partes* (CE277; LV10.1.8; 10.1.16), fractions refer to distinct pools or global allocations of assets. The same should be understood to hold true in LB54. The Burgundian allocations are possibly different in composition from the Visigothic ones, but they are expressed in the same abstract, collective sense as "the two parts of the Goth" in LV10.1.8. The reference to "one half" in LB54.3 is said explicitly to be a long-standing general principle; it would be consistent if the thirds of LB54.1 (and the title) were understood in the same general sense, and not as individual allotments.

LB54.3–4 concern "subsidiary assets." These are mentioned in more concrete terms than the *terrae* and *mancipia* constituting the "main assets." LB54.3

concerns "silvae et exarta," probably meaning, not only cleared land ("assarts"), but also wastes and pastures, as well as light woods suitable for clearing and development into cropland. LB54.3 suggests that subsidiary lands had long—that is, before the "recent measure"—occasioned abusive claims by Burgundians against Romans. The similar LB54.4, consisting of "houses and gardens," will concern us later.

"Subsidiary assets" were not fixed quantities of anything; they had not been surveyed and appraised; and they were not "given" but simply governed by an established rule antedating LB54 and specifying a quota. They were resources to be appropriated by both Burgundians and Romans within long-standing regulated limits fixing the Roman quota as one-half. The method of compensation by which these assets were shared half-and-half is detailed in several laws in the Burgundian and Visigothic collections. Burgundians might not take possession of "subsidiary assets" in excess of one half of the total pool of unappropriated land.[110]

The Occasion of the Law
The royal *praeceptio* had set limits on the application of the "recent measure." Despite that restriction, the change had incited both "privileged" and "ordinary Burgundians" to take abusive steps to increase their property. These abuses—a scramble by Burgundians for both kinds of assets—imply that the "recent measure" had lawfully enlarged the *sortes* of all the "ordinary Burgundians," but not of the "privileged" ones. Disregarding the *praeceptio*, "privileged Burgundians" had taken advantage of the enlargement to seize additional "agri cum mancipiis" in the "places (*loci*)" in which "occupancy (*hospitalitas*)" had been assigned to them (these words show that "privileged Burgundians," just like their "ordinary" fellow *faramanni*, had once been awarded allotments; the royal gifts were extras). The abuse engaged in by "ordinary Burgundians" was different. They had previously been annoying the Roman *possessores* over "subsidiary assets"; now they tried to increase the long-standing one-half quota of such assets awarded to them and, accordingly, to encroach on the quota guaranteed to Romans. The probable reason why the "ordinary Burgundians" now tried to break through the 50 percent limit was that the "recent measure" increased their quota of "main assets," that is, *terrae*.

An Additional Law Relating to Settlement
Another text from the Burgundian Laws, LBExtravagans 21.12, bears centrally on the issue of settlement. This is a later law than LB54, but it documents a "new" event, namely, the initial settlement of a group of refugee Burgundians, forced back into the kingdom from an area seized by the Italian Goths: "We lay down

the following about the Romans: let the Burgundians [who withdrew] not requisition any more from them than is needed at present, [namely] half the *terrae*.
Let the other half with the totality of *mancipia* be retained by the Romans."[111]
The phraseology is more abstract than it may seem. Contrary to the surface
sense, this division is not really between Burgundians and Romans. Roman proprietors and cultivators were everywhere and were not about to be dispossessed
and evicted; that is not the sense of "requisition." Moreover, it should not be inferred that the "half " allotted to the Burgundians was entirely empty of *mancipia*, in the broader sense of agrarian dependents; that would be absurd. What
the law shows is not a parceling out of concrete land and laborers, but allocations of abstract *terrae* and *mancipia* between Burgundian rank and file and
their king: out of the affected all-Roman territory, one half of the assessment
pool (*terrae*) would go to the rank and file, and the other half, with the totality of
mancipia—which also looks like a pool of assets—would stay with the king.[112]

An Arithmetical Puzzle

Much of the complexity of LB54 comes from its fractions. To understand what
is going on, one must decide what the figures are and what lies behind them.

   LB54 provides two figures: first, it expresses the "main assets" as "one-third
of the *mancipia* and two-thirds of the *terrae*"; next, "subsidiary assets" are subject to a fixed quota of one-half. LBExtravagans 21.12 adds two more figures. In
the division it details, the total of *terrae* is shared half and half. Half is given to
the Burgundians; the other half, kept by the king, is accompanied by the undivided total of *mancipia*.

   It may help to tabulate these four figures and give them arithmetic expression:

LB54, "main assets"	*mancipia* 0.33	*terrae* 0.66
LB54, "subsidiary assets"	Roman 0.50	Burgundian 0.50
LBExtravagans 21.12 assets "given"	*mancipia* 0.0	*terrae* 0.50
LBExtravagans 21.12 assets "kept"	*mancipia* 1.0	*terrae* 0.50

One Award of "Main Assets" or Two?

The main question arising from study of these figures is whether the amount of
"main assets" in LB54 represents a single award to the *faramanni* or two separate
ones. If one, it would be the sole grant made (long ago) to the *faramanni*; if two
awards, the figure would represent the sum of an initial grant made at one time,
and then a second, later grant enlarging the first.

   There are two reasons for preferring separate awards. First, the partition of
subsidiary assets in LB54.3–4 is said to be subject to a long-standing rule of

equal shares, which Burgundians had been trying to breach before as well as after the "recent measure." Next, LBExtravagans 21.12 tells us that the *terrae* allocated to the refugee Burgundians amounted to half the total. Both rules lead to the provisional assumption that an initial allocation was made to the Burgundians consisting of one-half the *terrae*, no *mancipia*, and half the "subsidiary assets."

The difference between the "main assets" of LB54 (0.33 + 0.66) and an initial grant of "one-half " (0 + 0.50) is 0.33 *mancipia* and 0.166 *terra*. This difference would represent the second award made to the "ordinary Burgundians," enlarging their initial allocation. If so, the figure with which LB54 begins (0.33 + 0.66) represents the sum of two awards, one of one-half *terrae* (and subsidiary assets), the second of one-third *mancipia* and one-sixth *terrae*. The sum of these awards corresponds precisely to the "*manciporum tertiam et duas terrarum partes*" which "our people received (*populus noster accepit*)" at the opening of LB54.1. In accord with this reasoning, the "recent measure" had laid down an increase in allotments on behalf of all "ordinary Burgundians": their core grants of 0.5 *terra* were enlarged to 0.66 *terra* and 0.33 *mancipia*.

"Agri cum mancipiis" Means Royal Land

The main unresolved question arising from this sum is the meaning of *terrae* (or *agri*) *cum mancipiis*. The evidence bearing on this point is the salient, and already observed, oddity of LBExtravagans: that all the *mancipia* went with half the *terrae*. This strange ratio is twice echoed in LB54 when its numbers are subjected to calculations. If the enlarged amount of "main assets" (0.33 + 0.66) is subtracted from the totality of assets (1.0 + 1.0), the difference is 0.66 *mancipia* and 0.33 *terrae*; again, twice the amount of *mancipia* goes with one unit of *terrae*. A third confirmation comes in the enlargement resulting from the "recent measure": an increase of one-sixth *terrae* carries with it one-third *mancipia*.

We have no reason to think that, in the territories in question, some fields were empty of laborers, whereas the balance was overpopulated, and that this inequality was measurable in a precise unchanging ratio of 2:1. The certainty to be inferred from the stark and unvarying ratio is that the *mancipia* in question cannot possibly be real human heads. This impossibility forces us to consider the alternative that these assets were administrators' abstractions.

The abstract nature of *terrae* does not need explanation; as already seen many times, we are dealing there, as elsewhere, with "fiscal land," the aspect of *terra* recorded in the assessment registers—abstract words and numbers but standing for real soil. This cannot be the case with *mancipia* as a reference to real people; the invariable ratio of 2:1 defeats the idea that *mancipia* stood for real bondspersons. However translated, the *mancipia* were not a standard animate commodity expressible in precise ratios vis-à-vis the land they lived on. A solution must be sought in the language of tax assessment rather than in the literal meaning of the word.[113]

The fact most relevant to the meaning of *mancipia* is that the word is never detached from *terrae*. As much is implied by the invariable ratio of 2:1, but there is more. The commodity given by the kings over many years to "privileged Burgundians" consisted of *agri cum mancipiis* (54.1, 55.5): the new award to the "ordinary Burgundians" consisted of *mancipia* and *terrae*; and half the *terrae* in LBExtravagans 21.12 were accompanied by the totality of *mancipia*. *Mancipia* attracted *terrae*, but not the other way around. There is a Burgundian law "on the sale of *terrae*" (LB84), but none on the sale of *mancipia*, which make no appearance, not even allusively, in the law on land sales.

Several things are known about *agri cum mancipiis*. Such *agri* by royal gift, owned *ex integro* (LB55.5), were clearly different from lands "by right of allotment (*iure sortis.* LB55.2)." and preferable to them. They entitled the owners to litigate by Roman law and to transmit such property however they wished (LB1.3-4). We know also that, in LB38.5, special obligations weighed upon persons who had received gifts from the Burgundian king.[114]

Two questions help us to sort out these facts: at whose disposal was the "the other half of *terrae* with the whole of the *mancipia*" evoked in LBExtravagans 21.12 and what or who was it who supplied the 0.33 *mancipia* and 0.166 *terrae* by which Burgundia *sortes* were augmented in the "recent measure"? Both questions lead to the same conclusion.

The Visigothic case suggests an answer. There, the king retained one-third of the total land assessment and taxes that the Roman government had made over to the Visigoths; this was the *tertia Romanorum*, and we know that, out of this fund called *tertia*, reserved to the royal fisc, the king made occasional gifts to his followers (LV10.1.8).[115] The resemblance to Burgundian practice is too close to be accidental. We do not know how the abstract Burgundian phrase *agri (terrae) cum mancipiis* was coined, or how it acquired its technical sense. Nevertheless, all the evidence suggests that the *agri cum mancipiis* of Burgundian law had the same meaning as the Visigothic *tertia Romanorum*. Like its Gothic analogue, the Burgundian phrase meant "land belonging to the king." The term *mancipia* did not refer to an aggregate of laborers separate from *terrae* or *agri*; nowhere does it have this role. Instead, for some reason we can only guess at, *mancipia* had become the distinguishing feature of "royal land." *Agri cum mancipiis* was the pool of government resources from which the king (besides nourishing his treasury) not only rewarded individuals, but also dipped into to make a collective gift whose effect was to enlarge the *sortes* of all the "ordinary Burgundians."[116]

Allotments Acquired and Lands Refunded

This section focuses on two passages: "[Seize] from that place in which occupancy had been assigned to them" (*[Requirere] ex eo loco, in quo ei hospitalitas fuerat delegata*) and "give back without delay whatever amount of the lands of their hosts . . . they are shown to have appropriated" (*quidquid ab his . . . de hospitum suorum terris . . . praesumpsisse docentur, sine dilatione restituant*). These phrases take us into a new level of documentation—not pools of total assets, but the actual acquisition of a *sors* in a definite place. LB54.1–2 address these lines to the "privileged Burgundians" who were now forced to refund what they had abusively seized; but the process of "requiring from the place of occupancy" must also have applied to the "ordinary Burgundians," who benefited from the "recent measure" and could presumably address themselves to "their hosts (*hospites*)" for the lawful enlargement (out of the royal land in the Romans' charge) of the *sortes* the Burgundians had long held. The Roman *hospites* were the trustees of the royal land from which the enlargement of allotments would take place.

LB54 evokes only the privileged Burgundians who violated the "recent measure," but it implies larger numbers of legitimate claimants ("ordinary Burgundians"). At the start of the settlement the tax registers of the entire territory were conveyed to the Burgundians (the transfer could be symbolic); as a result, both the lands kept by the king and those distributed as *sortes* must have been strewn about, side by side, all over the kingdom. The *agri cum mancipiis* obtained by "privileged Burgundians" as lawful gifts from the king were likely to adjoin other desirable land that the king retained, which the "privileged" would have been eager to appropriate for themselves. In the Visigothic kingdom, royal *tertia* were called "of the Romans"; a similar special connection of Romans to the Burgundian royal lands is likely. We see precisely that in LBExtravagans 21.12: the half of the *terrae* with the *integritas mancipiorum*, that is, *agri cum mancipiis*, were to continue to be held by "the Romans." Properly understood, this means that all royal or fiscal land continued in Roman hands, paying taxes to the king, just like the Visigothic *tertia Romanorum*.

The implication of LB54.1 is that, before the original distribution of *sortes* took place, all *faramanni* had been "assigned occupancy" in a locality (*locus*), presumably a public district (town, village, hamlet, and so on) and not someone's estate. The term used gives no compelling reason to identify *locus* with the property of some definite Roman. More likely is the sort of locality evoked in LB38.3, a "villa" with its responsible consortium of inhabitants.[117] The *loci* (localities spread over the territory transferred by Rome) had perhaps served the Burgundians as a way station in the short period between when an individual *faramannus* and his family were physically present at the *locus* and the time when a permanent *sors* was awarded to him. It was in that locality that the original *sors* consisting of *terrae* was distributed, but since this operation was carried out on the basis of the tax registers, the boundaries of *sortes* did not have to coincide with the boundaries of Roman ownership. Each *sors* awarded to a Burgundian was occupied by (Roman) taxpaying inhabitants; from them, the beneficiary obtained the revenue owed to him from the tax assessment (*terrae*) given to him as allotment.[118] The beneficiary had an interest is safeguarding the possessions and livelihood of his personal "tributary" or "tributaries," more graciously called "host."

Burgundians came face-to-face with Romans when royal land changed hands. (Royal land was no less abstract, detached from the soil, than the allotments given to individual barbarians.) The Roman *hospites* were the trustees or managers of royal lands, in charge, locality by locality, with safeguarding these lands or, when suitably ordered, with conveying them to whomever the king wished to reward. A Burgundian to whom the king had made a gift of *ager cum mancipiis* applied to the local (Roman) *hospes* for conveyance of his award. (These "hosts" had nothing to do with military billeting; the term was used to describe the collective position of Roman landowners vis-à-vis Burgundians and vice versa.) The same happened when "ordinary Burgundians" came around to have their *sortes* enlarged pursuant to the "recent measure." Finally, the *hospites* were in the front line for resisting the privileged Burgundians when they abusively demanded the same enlargement granted to lesser Burgundians.

The Apportionment of "Main Assets": A Summary

Before moving to the "Subsidiary Assets" in LB54.3-4, it may help to summarize the Burgundian settlement as far as it applied to the main asset in question, namely, *terrae*.

The process began at the time of settlement, by a "division" between the Roman "natives" and the newcomers. The division, so called, was initially horizontal; a slicing of the same land into separate rights, it left to the Romans the cultivation and ownership of the total of registered soil of the territory of settlement (that is, the private property of Roman landowners), and it conveyed to the Burgundians all the assessment registers of the territory and the annual tax payments arising from them (that is, the state's fiscal share of the territory). Settlement by Burgundians did not imply any tax relief for the Romans, nor was it meant to. All of one aspect of "land"—cultivation and ownership—was kept by the Romans, and all of the other aspect was obtained by the Burgundians. We might say that Roman *agri* (fields, soil) were overlaid by Burgundian *terrae* (assessed land). Here as elsewhere, the words *agri* and *terrae* are not meant as technical terms and may be interchanged.

The next step was a (vertical) division between the king and the Burgundian rank and file: the king, or government, retained half the land assessments but also "all the *mancipia*" (still undefined, but having the effect of tagging the *terrae* in question as a specially privileged "royal land"); the other half of land assessments and payments (*terrae*) was attributed to the rank and file. The latter half, like the first, was a pool; out of it, allotments were carved out of the assessment registers for individual *faramanni*. Thanks to the official records, the allotments could approximate a standard, equal size, not limited to or imposed by the size of individual Roman properties. The taxes of the *terrae* awarded to each *faramannus* as his allotment were periodically paid to him; they were his revenue, presumably compensating him for being a member of the standing Burgundian army. (It should be emphasized that *sortes* in the Burgundian kingdom as well as in the two Gothic ones were awarded in lieu of basic, continuing military pay; that was their justification. The receivers and their descendants were obligated to serve in the army when summoned by the king. Gothic Italy is the best source of information about this aspect of the settlement scheme.)

A unique feature of LB54 is that it affords a glimpse of the process of settlement: Burgundians were assigned to "places"—small public districts, not individual units of Roman ownership. The Burgundians' interval of occupancy (*hospitalitas*) among the inhabitants was terminated when the Burgundians obtained individual *sortes* carved out of the registers for the appropriate district.[119] Once this was done, the Burgundian *sortes*, collectively amounting to one-half of the assessment registers (or less), lay side by side with the other half of the registers, namely, the royal lands (*agri cum mancipiis*). Although any given allotment did not have to coincide with one Roman property, *sortes* inevitably consisted entirely of lands owned by Romans and would have a geography mainly corresponding to Roman properties. A "map" of Burgundian *terrae* (both royal and of the *faramanni*) would have overlaid the map of Roman ownership and cultivation. The two grids were linked by the Romans' annual payments: first, to the king of the taxes of the widely strewn *agri cum mancipiis*; and next, to the individual owners of *sortes* of the (tax) payment applicable to their *terrae*. There is no sign that Burgundians had any part in the cultivation of *terrae*; their connection to the soil was limited to the outlying lands discussed below under "subsidiary assets."

So much for the background, prior to the "recent measure." In the years since the original distribution of allotments, some Burgundians had been "privileged" by having their *sortes* augmented by gifts of royal *agri cum mancipiis* (perhaps adjoining what they already had); these gifts are attested by LB1.3-4, 38.5, 54.1, and 55.5. Such signs of royal generosity made them "privileged Burgundians"; besides being singled out from the other *faramanni* for enrichment, they shared in the privilege attaching to royal land.

Finally, there was Gundobad's "recent measure." It provided that the former pool of one-half out of which the original *sortes* had been awarded would be enlarged by one-sixth, and all the *faramanni* not individually enriched hitherto by the king would now have their *sortes* increased. The royal *agri cum mancipiis* were diminished to finance this general grant. Precisely how this expansion was administered cannot be known. All those who qualified were presumably authorized to claim royal land (*agri cum mancipiis*) near the location of their *sortes*. For purposes of administration, one way to determine the amount of the increase was to conceive of each original *sors* as "one-half " (that is, an individual portion of the original global allocation of "one-half ") and to calculate the increase as being *terra* to the amount of one-sixth the original size of the *sors*. The extra was appropriated from the local fund of royal land, and consisted of *agri cum mancipiis*—that is, *terrae* having the privilege of royal land. LB54 suggests that the allowed increase was a contentious matter, on whose basis both ordinary and privileged Burgundians tried to maximize their gains at the expense of Romans perhaps, but certainly at the king's.

(Readers wishing to bypass further intricacies of the Burgundian scheme may skip to the end of the discussion on p. 158.)

Subsidiary Assets

These are a unique aspect of LB54. Except for a few laws in the Visigothic Code, none of the other sources documents anything but "land" in the restricted sense we have seen. "Main assets," *terrae*, were registered in the official registers of tax assessment; thanks to the written records, they could be grasped in their entirety and be apportioned accordingly. "Subsidiary assets" were appropriated bit by bit. In the most general sense, they were commodities not registered for assessment and accordingly untaxed.

The key document for understanding what they involved is LRB17.5, "There is a common right to woods, mountain pastures, and grazing ground, as it is available to each person in proportion to his ownership (*Silvarum, montium, et pascui ius, ut unicuique pro rata possessionis subpetit, esse commune*)." This rule is filled out by LB67, which specifies a sharing of vacant resources proportional to holdings of *terra*.[120] From LB13 and 31 we learn that the half-and-half sharing of these resources was implemented at the moment when the "common" resources were individually appropriated, that is, ceased to be free. Each landowner in a district had a right to common (unowned) agricultural assets proportional to the size of his property. Burgundians were not owners of the soil, but they owned their *sortes*, and there probably was a general correspondence between the geography of *sortes* and that of Roman ownership. On these premises there was a way to fit Burgundian registered *terrae* into the concrete countryside of Roman-owned *agri,* namely, to decree that Burgundi-ans and Romans were each entitled potentially to half the common or unappro-priated assets of each district.

This even division did not entail a general survey or distribution. The ap-plicable rule came into force whenever an entitled individual, Roman or Bur-gundian, set apart and developed some amount of common assets. When this happened, the developer was obliged to delimit an equal amount of the type of asset he had appropriated and convey it to his opposite number—either the owner of the *sors* or the owner of the ground. Each appropriator would eventu-ally turn the common land he had developed (and the portion he had set apart and conveyed to the other party) into private property and separate his "half" from the other. The process—whose result would be to privatize the assets in question, detached from the scheme of *sortes*—is described in both Burgun-dian and Visigothic laws. There is no reference in this process to *ius hospitali-tatis* or *sortis.* Developed *exartae* (or other assets of this subsidiary kind), duly divided with a Roman proprietor, became the *possessio* of a Burgundian (or vice versa), to be owned on the same unconditional basis as land bought from Romans.

The Attempt to Enlarge Subsidiary Assets

The problem envisaged by LB54 is that many Burgundians were eager to manip-ulate the "recent measure" in forbidden ways. The privileged Burgundians, as we saw, sought to increase their *agri cum mancipiis.* The ordinary Burgundians had received a lawful enlargement of *terrae* from one-half to two-thirds; on this pretext, they were now trying to increase their quota of "subsidiary assets" by the same fraction (one-sixth) and thus turn their one-half into two-thirds. The king rebuffed them: the Roman quota of one-half was unalterable.

Barbarians and the Soil

The laws showing barbarians with direct interest in cultivable soil, such as by clearing light woods (assarts) or planting vines, concern subsidiary assets only. The fact that relevant laws show or imply barbarians taking part in cultivating the soil has been generalized by commentators, who invite us to think that *sors* owners personally farmed the "land" of their allotment.[121] Nothing encourages this inference; the soil and ownership were in Roman hands. Wherever found, *sors* owners were expected to adopt the social style of Roman absentees collect-ing the proceeds of their land, owned or allotted, without personally participat-ing in its exploitation. But they were not wholly excluded. The laws concerning subsidiary assets show in what direction barbarian initiative and enterprise were encouraged—as an extra, not the main source of revenue.

Houses and Gardens (LB54.4)

The claims of *sortes* receivers to a share of undeveloped common resources (such as woods, pastures, and wastelands) is comparatively simple to explain; the same is not true of the "houses and gardens (*de curte et pomariis*)" of LB54.4. These clauses are absolutely unique in all the sources about barbarian settlement. As with the other "subsidiary assets," the rights of all *faramanni* to them were limited to one-half and no more. The clear implication is that, for a long time, the *faramanni* had enjoyed the right to one-half of these assets. The only change at present was that, by virtue of the "recent measure" increasing their share of *terrae* by one-sixth, some "ordinary Burgundians" were trying to increase their share of "houses and gardens" from one-half to two-thirds.

No clause of LB54 is more concrete than this one. It suggests that, as far back as the original settlement, houses and gardens were apportioned evenly, *locus* by *locus*, between the Roman owner-residents and the Burgundian newcomers; and it further implies that, in this case and none other, a genuine confiscation and alienation of Roman property for the benefit of the Burgundians took place. Here would be a solitary case in which the rules of military billeting were imposed, at their preferential rate and, it seems, permanently, on the Roman population.[122] LB38 shows us Romans and Burgundians living side by side in villages and cooperating more or less harmoniously in the reception of traveling guests. One cannot help wondering whether this harmony is compatible with a situation in which the Romans who had been robbed of half their "houses and gardens" lived among the Burgundians on whose behalf they had been robbed. There is something odd and unbelievable about this scenario. I do not like to think that this draconian confiscation took place; it is out of keeping with everything else known about barbarian settlements in Roman territory. But I have not found a plausible way to circumvent a literal reading of LB54.4.[123]

Enforcement

Though long and complex in phraseology, LB54 seeks to accomplish surprisingly little. Its most severe rule affects the privileged Burgundians who violated the royal *praeceptio*. They would have to return to the government those *agri cum mancipiis* they had managed to seize by pretending that they, too, were entitled to the enlargement allowed to ordinary Burgundians. As regards subsidiary assets, the law only reaffirms the existing rule. The rule would presumably be enforced at the time when a legal division of developed and enclosed lands took place. That should have been easy to do; divisions between neighbors often took place. What we are not told but may legitimately infer is that the "recent measure" let loose a frenzy of Burgundian claims that, inevitably, weighed heavily on the Roman owners and cultivators who were the underpinning of both the *sortes* and the *agri cum mancipiis* and who, for the sake of all concerned, needed to be left undisturbed.

* * *

LB54, with its many intricacies, tells us almost more than we wish or need to know. The settlement it documents is much more complex than the one visible in the Visigothic texts, but that need not be a Burgundian peculiarity; Visigothic complexities may have left no traces in the records we have whereas Burgundian ones are all too evident in LB54. What matters more is the underlying pattern common to Gaul and instituted by Roman officialdom: conveyance to the barbarians of the total assessment of the affected territory; partition of the total between king and rank and file; award of allotments to individual barbarians; and, thereafter, receipt by the king of the taxes from his share and by the individual beneficed barbarians of the taxes (very similar to rents) owed by their allotments, that is, by their individual Roman tributaries. The resident Romans, secure in their continued ownership and cultivation of the soil, had no (immediate) reason to complain. LB54 involves many associated details, such as subsidiary assets and dwelling places. The law allows us to glimpse them, but they do not affect the structure of the system.

The Burgundian Law on Land Sales and the Future of Burgundian Allotments

After LB54 and LBExtravagans 21.12, the most interesting text on allotments in the Burgundian Laws spells out rules affecting their sale. LB54, as we have seen, documents complications involved in establishing the *sortes*. The law on the sale of allotments provides a glimpse at the efforts of the government to combat threats to the scheme.

(LB84) De venditione terrarum. [On the sale of "lands" (*terrae*)]

[1.] Quia agnovimus Burgundiones sortes suas nimia facilitate distrahere, hoc praesenti lege credidimus statuendum, ut nulli vendere terram suam liceat nisi illi, qui alio loco sortem aut possessionem habet [Because we recognize that the Burgundians sell their allotments too easily, we believe that it should be laid down in the present law that no one may sell his "land" except to someone who has an allotment or property in another place.]

[2.] Hoc etiam interdictum, ut quisque, habens alibi terram, vendendi necessitatem habet, in comparandum, quod Burgundio venale habet, nullus extraneus Romano hospiti praeponatur, nec extraneo per quodlibet argumentum terram liceat comparare.

[This, too, is forbidden: in case someone who has "land" elsewhere and needs to sell, no stranger is set ahead of the Roman host in buying what the Burgundian has for sale, nor is a stranger allowed on any pretext to buy the "land."]

[3.] Observandum tamen, ut de illo ipso hospes suus comparet, quem alibi terram habere constiterit. [Moreover, this is commanded: that someone's "host" should buy from that very person who is known to have an allotment elsewhere.]124

The situation occasioning the law is reasonably clear even though the legislator had trouble describing it (there is a paraphrase of LB84 in the note).125 Burgundians were cashing in their allotments, preferring present enjoyment to future security. Eager to find purchasers, they cared little for the niceties of a system of allotments in which "lands" consisted in an annual land-based revenue whereas the physical soil belonged to someone else (a Roman). Some Burgundians were even divesting themselves completely of their "lands," which they tried to sell to the highest bidder, even to complete strangers.

The law laid down severe remedies. If Burgundians wished or needed to sell their *sortes* or "lands," they had to have an allotment or property elsewhere in the kingdom; they could not sell themselves out of the allotment scheme. Burgundians buying "land" from other Burgundians also had to be in the scheme; both seller and buyer had to own "lands" or an allotment additional to that being sold or bought. Burgundians were not a threat to the system; that came from outside, from strangers (*extranei*). Presumably, these were mainly Romans alien to the district in which the sale was to take place. The way to exclude them was to institute a strict right of preemption on behalf of Roman hosts. The exclusion of "foreigners" abruptly and drastically narrowed the pool of potential buyers; Roman strangers need not apply. The only Romans allowed to acquire "lands" from Burgundians were the "hosts," that is, those proprietors on whose soil the allotment lay. "Hosts" were not a class of Romans, but individuals dealing person to person with a Burgundian "guest." These "hosts" were well aware that the value of Burgundian land was very different from the value of a Roman owner's land, since tax value, to which Burgundians were entitled, was much less than the rental value due to an owner. Burgundians would know how to bargain with fellow Burgundians inside the same scheme of allotments, but where Romans were involved, only the Roman host and the Burgundian seller were fully aware of what Burgundian "land" consisted of, were able to evaluate what it was worth, and so could establish a suitable price.126

The allotments of the Burgundians were not *agri cum mancipiis*; they had the restricted quality spelled out by LB1.2, 55.2, 78, and 84. The beneficiaries obtained regular payments and were presumably informed of the acreage giving rise to this revenue, but the soil belonged to Roman owners and cultivators, whom the Burgundians were well advised to leave alone. LB22 and 55.1 decree that Burgundians were to keep clear of Romans litigating among themselves, for example, over boundaries. LB84 evokes a potential Burgundian seller who has both a *sors* or a *possessio* elsewhere than the place where he sought to sell his *sors*. Enterprising Burgundians, enriched by war (and possibly rewarded with *agri cum mancipiis* by the king), presumably took the precaution of buying land and becoming full-fledged proprietors on the same basis as Romans.

The Roman proprietor buying the *sors* or *terrae* of his Burgundian "guest" pursuant to LB84 was not acquiring land so much as redeeming a debt; he was liberating his property "a sorte barbari," as we read in a Ravenna papyrus.[127] We know that he was releasing it from taxation; perhaps he realized that too, but whether it was called tax or rent did not matter. Under whatever name, an annual sum had to be paid without fail to the Burgundian beneficiary. From the Roman standpoint, *sors barbari* was a claim to annual payment, the sort of claim protected in Visigothic law by a fifty-year prescription. That debt, because originally a tax arising from the assessment register, and not a rent arising from private law ownership, had a fiscal and not a market relationship to the soil. The Roman "host" already possessed the ownership and cultivation of the soil; what he would be buying from his "guest" was that third aspect of his "land" that the Burgundian had been awarded as his *sors*. It took much more land assessment to yield a given sum as (tax) payment than to obtain the same sum as rent from one's property.[128] The purchase of a *sors* by the Roman host from its Burgundian recipient consisted in effect in the host's redemption of an annual debt weighing on (the assessment of) his land. The value of that debt had to be determined in a different way from the going price of land. The Burgundian "land" that a Roman host bought and liberated from *sors barbari* was in effect emancipated from taxation.

LB54 and 84 allow barbarian settlement to be envisaged as a dynamic relationship. *Sortes* (whatever their composition) were a not a very pleasing form of assets; they were destined to be gradually exchanged for more desirable and permanent ones. In the very first law of LB, a Burgundian was authorized to make gifts freely from family property and property acquired by him, but was cautioned that this right did not extend to property by grace of his allotment (*sortis titulo*, LB1.2); the estate he left was composed of several kinds of property. Restrictions on alienation made *sortes* useful for another purpose: daughters who became nuns could be maintained out of property *sortis titulo*, since their guaranteed childlessness assured that the shares assigned to them would, at death, revert to their families (LB14.5–6).[129] Rights to woods and wastes arising from the *sors* are shown in the laws as potentials that turned into better kinds of ownership once improved and exchanged (LB13, 31).[130] The *ius sortis* or *hospitalitatis* was more limited than full ownership.[131] Recipients of royal gifts of *agri cum mancipiis* were better off than beneficiaries of mere *sortes*; and the award of *agri cum mancipiis* to the holders of *sortes* not only enriched them but also improved their proprietary condition; the privilege of royal land rubbed off. The scattered references to Burgundians with *possessiones* suggests that individual barbarians invested the liquid resources they had or acquired in whatever (Roman) land was available for purchase. Ownership detached from the restrictions of *titulus sortis* would also include new developments, such as assarts and vineyards, separated from the land of the adjoining Roman proprietor in return for compensation.

An analogy points in the same direction of changing status. Procopius reports that, after Justinian's conquest of North Africa, the widows of Vandals tried to claim their late husbands' lands for their new Roman husbands.[132] Durliat has cogently argued that these possessions were not the heritable allotments that Geiseric had given to individual Vandals in the Proconsular province ninety years earlier, but rather the estates of varied size and composition that the original beneficiaries and their successors had developed out of their *sortes* in the intervening years.[133] Original awards did not remain frozen.

The main way for Goths and Burgundians to escape the limitations of their *sortes* would have been to redeem their right to revenue from their Roman hosts for a mutually agreeable share of private-law property—a formal cession of some soil and an exchange of "occupancy" for "property." A *sors* in this case was a redemption consisting of whatever amount of land (or money) a Roman host was willing to part with to a Burgundian, and the latter was willing to accept, in order to liberate his property (or a part of it) of the charge "by right of barbarian allotment (*sorte barbari*)" encumbering it.[134] Another result, as noted above, was to make the redeemed Roman land tax free.

Among the Burgundians, the weighty contrast between a limited tenure and unrestricted ownership (LB55.2, 5) hinged on the distinction between mere *sortes* (consisting of only *terrae*) and formerly royal land (*agri cum mancipiis*). Barbarian *sortes* were a heritable tenure no doubt and lucrative as well, but the rights they involved fell short of the ownership vested in Roman proprietors. The inferior standing of Burgundians in relation to property must have been unmistakable: the king observed that Burgundians sold *sortes* too thoughtlessly, and he required Romans buyers to control these sales (LB84). Barbarian allotments, however enduring, were a stepping stone to the full incorporation of Burgundians into the landscape of Roman proprietorship.

*   *   *

The adjective "unique" has occurred repeatedly in the exposition of LB54. The law documents much not found elsewhere, but these extras fit within a framework of barbarian settlement fundamentally similar to what we know about the Vandals and the Goths of Gaul and Italy. This is hardly surprising: these mechanisms were devised and at least initially implemented by officials steeped in Roman laws and administrative practices.

The Visigothic and Burgundian evidence fits closely together. The fractions involved applied to the total of Roman public resources handed over collectively to the barbarians being settled, and to their division between the king and his troops. The allotments were carved out of the share of the rank and file, not as fractions of anything, but as units (*sortes*) of revenue-yielding assessed "land" of approximately equal size. The geography of ownership and that of *sortes* cannot have precisely coincided. Barbarian allotments concerned only one aspect of "land." They left the ownership of the soil and its cultivation to the Romans, who were not to be disturbed. The Italian case, to which we now turn, though different in documentation, is also in keeping with the experience of barbarian settlement in Gaul.

"Accommodation" in Italy

In 476, as everyone knows, Romulus Augustulus was overthrown by Odoacer, a barbarian in the high command of the army of Italy. According to Procopius, the occasion for the coup d'état came when the emperor's father, the patrician Orestes, refused to grant the troops a land settlement. After the emperor's dismissal, Odoacer granted the wishes of the troops. Procopius's very memorable report is that the "third part of the land" of Italy was given to the troops in 476 (or thereabouts) at Odoacer's command. Procopius is the sole authority linking the troops' demand for land with the downfall of the young emperor (and Western emperorship); the several other sources give no hint of a mutiny or its reason. Years passed. The Goths enter the picture only after 488, when Theoderic, encouraged by the emperor of Constantinople, marched to Italy with his people, fought Odoacer to a standstill, and, in 493, personally killed him. The award of allotments to the Goths in Italy probably took place soon after this. We do not have an exact date but know from a letter of Cassiodorus (speaking for Theoderic) that the praetorian prefect of Italy Liberius was much applauded for his skill in carrying out this operation with a minimum of disturbance to all concerned.[135]

Although the reports of Procopius and Cassiodorus are generally regarded as complementing each other, they are incompatible in several respects. According to Procopius, Odoacer was the party responsible for dispossessing the Italians of one-third of their land; the historian also adds that, after the Gothic conquest, the awards to Odoacer's troops were transferred to Theoderic's. Cassiodorus contradicts this account. His letter (*Variae* 2.16.5), is about twenty-five years later than Odoacer's accession, and almost fifty years earlier than Procopius's report. It attributes the operation to Theoderic's official Liberius, who carried out what Cassiodorus calls "the distribution of 'thirds,'" meaning the award of allotments to the Goths. Cassiodorus's version makes it look as though the original settlement were ordered by Theoderic, without Odoacer's having had anything to do with it; there was no "transfer" from Odoacer's people to Theoderic's. Either Procopius sets the distribution of *sortes* one reign earlier than it took place, or Theoderic (via Cassiodorus) blots out an earlier operation and takes all the credit for himself. One way or the other, the reports do not mesh. For a study of the "techniques of accommodation," the discrepancy matters little, but it should not be overlooked.

The word *hospitalitas* does not occur in Gothic Italy; this is well known but sometimes forgotten. The Zwettl conferees argued for a long time over a letter of Cassiodorus in which *hospitium* is mentioned, but no conclusion was reached. I gave my account of it in the conference papers. The letter shows King Theodahad allowing the count of Pavia to retire to hot springs to nurse his gout. As often in the *Variae*, Cassiodorus includes a digression, predictably here on gout. The delicate word occurs in a context of barbarians and violence: "more gentium barbararum hospitium corporis occupatum suis indiciis violenta defendit."[136] Cassiodorus would have forestalled a long argument in 1986 if he had not brought *gentes barbarae* into proximity with this *hospitium*. As it is, we would be mistaken to suppose that these barbarians were taking shelter, let alone seizing lands. Cassiodorus simply says that once gout enters the body, its signs endure and keep debilitating the victim: "Departing, [the disease] leaves miserable symptoms and, in its violent way, it defends with its signs the lodgment in the body seized in the way barbarian peoples [seize]." The *mos* of the barbarians refers to *occupatum*, the abrupt, sneaky way of appropriating the lodgment, and not to its defense.[137] One hopes that this letter will not be heard of again in this context.

Quite a few texts that, like this one, have no business in discussions of the "techniques of accommodation" continue to be cited as though they did. One scholar sifted through the correspondence of Ennodius of Pavia for relevant passages and thought he had a considerable harvest. Not one, however, survives critical scrutiny.[138] Older favorites are the images of Sidonius with ten greasy-haired Burgundian soldiers quartered in his premises, and of Paulinus of Pella convincing an Alan chief to abandon the siege of Bazas, reporting the misfortunes of his sons among the Goths in Bordeaux, and being saved from ruin by a Goth who bought a property he wished to sell.[139] Sources have minds of their own; they testify to the preoccupations of their authors rather than to what modern users would like them to say, but the temptation of wrenching them into a form that will fit what is wanted is rarely resisted. For example, the undeserved prominence of Sidonius in accounts of the Burgundian settlement is almost impossible to chase from the specialist literature.[140]

The absence of "hospitality" is not the main difference between Gallic conditions and those of Italy. The salient contrast is that, in the Italy of Odoacer and the Gothic kings following him, Roman government continued virtually intact. The event of 476 involved the toppling of an intruded emperor and his replacement, first, by a viceregal Odoacer, and later by a Theoderic who came very near to being a substitute emperor. Aside from this change at the summit, the machinery of government was in very respectable running order, all the way down to the volunteer municipal level of city councils.[141] There was no interruption of government. Conditions and institutional continuity in "imperial" Italy were much more sedate and secure than in the more remote lands to the north of the Alps.[142]

My account in *Barbarians and Romans* of the settlement in Italy has been faulted for the violence I have been said to commit in interpreting two texts glanced at a few pages ago: the report of Procopius about a division of land and Cassiodorus's letter praising Liberius for his role in distributing allotments to the Goths. Reacting to my attack on Procopius, my critics felt obliged to defend the great historian of Justinian's reign.[143] Claude even managed to find Procopius giving "a clear report of the land assignments to the Ostrogoths," where others might be more tempted to discern the opposite of clarity. I recognize that my earlier handling of Procopius's report was flawed. I did not see then that he supports my interpretation without any need to impugn his competence or veracity.

The relevant lines of Procopius's *Gothic War* are as follows:

Under the fair name of alliance [the Romans of Italy] were more and more tyrannized over by the intruders [that is, Sciri, Alani, and other "Gothic" nations] and oppressed by them; so that the barbarians ruthlessly forced many other measures upon the Romans much against their will and finally demanded that they should divide with them the entire land of Italy. And indeed they commanded Orestes to give them the third part of this, and when he would by no means agree to do so, they killed him immediately. Now there was a certain man among the Romans named Odoacer, one of the bodyguards of the emperor, and he at that time agreed to carry out their commands . . . [B]y giving the third part of the land to the barbarians, and in this way gaining their allegiance most firmly, he held the supreme power securely for ten years. . . .
    [Theoderic, Odoacer's successor by conquest] himself committed scarcely a single act of injustice against his [Italian] subjects, nor would he brook such conduct on the part of anyone else who attempted it, except, indeed, that the Goths distributed among themselves the portion of the lands which Odoacer had given to his own partisans.[144]

Procopius firmly delineates the insolence of barbarian "intruders" in Roman employ (Gildas makes the same complaint in Britain).[145] The three separate accounts that he gives of land settlements in the introductory sections of the *Vandal* and *Gothic Wars*, including the one just quoted, stand out as not being casual or incidental facts but subjects with a special place in the historian's thinking about foreign peoples. He probably intended them to attract the (Constantinopolitan) readers' special attention and rouse their emotions. He was phlegmatic about the Vandals' migrating from an original home in the Maeotian swamp to Roman Gaul, though he was the first to report their doing so; but he cared very much about Vandal dealings with Romans over property in both Spain and North Africa. He mentions or devises a law of Honorius (†423) providing that the time of Vandal presence would be subtracted from thirty-year prescriptions affecting Roman properties. It is as though the Vandals were in transit and that legal time stopped while they were present.[146] The same special attention accorded to Vandal settlement is given to the "allies" from among the "Gothic nations" serving in Italy, their mounting arrogance, and their outrageous demand granted by Odoacer. This, Procopius suggests, was what happened when "the barbarian element among [the Romans] became strong." Procopius has much praise for Theoderic, but the start of his reign had one prominent blot: the "portion of the lands" awarded to Odoacer's troops was redistributed to the Goths. Procopius neither says nor clearly implies that a just ruler would have refunded the original award, only the outrage of 476 was not reversed.[147]

We saw a few pages ago that Procopius's account does not dovetail neatly with Cassiodorus's letter. They markedly disagree about the date of the original settlement and the person responsible for it. Another difference (not necessarily a discrepancy) is that Procopius focuses on the total award whereas Cassiodorus is concerned with grants to individuals. In 476, the outrageous demand of the barbarian army of Italy was for a "division" of Italy with "one-third of [the whole land]" going to the army; and Odoacer after his usurpation gave them "the third part of the land." Procopius pays little attention to individual awards; the main question is what he means by "the third part of the land." There are three ways to understand his words: 1. a political division of Italy, such that the army obtained rule of one third of the territory ("land"); 2. a division of the public resources of Italy (land assessed for taxation), such that, for example, the army was guaranteed one-third of the annual state revenue; 3. the allocation of "one-third" (of the land in some sense) as a fund for individual awards to Odoacer's "partisans." Nowhere does Procopius say or even suggest that private Roman estates were confiscated and divided with barbarian troops; Procopius's words have to be interpreted, since the "surface" or "natural" sense offers no guidance.

His goal was to shock the audience, not to provide a "clear report of the land assignments" (as Claude contends). If we focus on his last lines and infer individual awards, as I think we should, we are still at a considerable remove from his surface meaning, which implies a collective one-third/two-thirds "division" of the total land of Italy in some undefined sense. Even without reference to the Visigothic and Burgundian (and Vandal) precedents, the likelihood that Procopius's "division" was between the government and the troops does much more justice to his words than that it was between individual soldiers and all landowners of Italy.

The common inference from Procopius's account—espoused, for example, by Barnish, who appeals to "face value" but tacitly injects an alien billeting model—is that all, most, or some private Italian properties were partitioned and one-third of each one was conveyed to a barbarian (Odoacer's, then Theoderic's) as his property. This would mean that Odoacer inaugurated his rule by a massive expropriation from every kind of Roman proprietor and a redistribution of these confiscations in unrestricted ownership to the barbarians of the army of Italy.[148] Something more has to be accepted. This operation in a period of instability would, for lack of any outcry in contemporary sources—Procopius's indignation is expressed about seventy years later than Odoacer's advent—have been endured by its victims, rich and poor, without protests or complaints. To avoid some of these awkward consequences, most modern commentators, Barnish prominently among them, have made arbitrary revisions or curtailments unjustified by Procopius or anyone else.[149] The best reason for doubting that Procopius meant one-third of the private property of every Italian landowner is that he never comes near to saying anything of the kind. The "division" that he mentions has no explicit or implied relation to private properties, and there are no supplements tending to make such a reading believable.[150] No process of partition, no trace of expropriation, no protesting landlords, no agricultural dependents fleeing from their new masters, and so forth peer through Procopius's pages or those of any other source.

In earlier Roman history, after the great civil war victory of Philippi (41 B.C.), Octavian was charged with the "arduous and unpopular" task of settling the remains of twenty-eight legions, perhaps one hundred thousand men, in the eighteen wealthy Italian cities that had been designated two years before to satisfy the troops. This task entailed spoliations of innocent proprietors on a larger scale than Sulla's proscriptions (senatorial properties were eventually exempted) and led to the most critical moment of Octavian's rise to imperial power. The embarrassment of the organizer and the cries of the victims, who included several poets, have left clear traces in the records.[151] Four hundred years later the barbarian leaders and their Roman sponsors did not loom over

Gaul and Italy as implacable victors; their positions vis-à-vis the provincials among whom they settled did not allow them to cow an offended populace and endure the odium of confiscations. No murmurs of despair or other sign of discontent survive from among the many rich, eloquent, and influential persons who would, in theory, have been deprived of one-third of their property.[152]

We need to look for something less improbable and better attested than massive confiscations and distributions of private property. Procopius makes two complementary statements: "The Goths distributed among themselves the portion of the lands which Odoacer had given to his own partisans," that "portion" surely being the third part of the whole land of Italy mentioned a few lines earlier. This "third" cannot be equated with fractions of every Italian private estate; there is no warrant for such a reading. As already pointed out, the "land" encountered in the sixth-century countryside had at least three coexisting levels: cultivation, ownership, and state assessment. It may be taken for granted, I believe, that Odoacer's soldiers (and Theoderic's) were uninterested in establishing themselves upon *colonicae* and other peasant tenures and working the soil with their battle-roughened hands. Private property taken from Roman owners is just as improbable, for the reasons already given: its acquisition would have necessitated uncompensated expropriations and the impoverishment of the owners. Procopius gives us no encouragement for reading his text in this sense. What is left is tax assessment, that is, the "land" as registered by the government on its books and paying taxes. Out of the properties registered for taxation in the records of the Italian government, a division could be made, and allotments could be carved out for distribution perhaps to Odoacer's followers, certainly to the Goths.

Procopius wanted to shock his Constantinopolitan audience: theft was what happened when "intruders" were preferred to Roman soldiers and allowed to take too great a place in the state. To bring home the lesson, Procopius trotted out his "one-third of the land." What sort of land: peasant tenancies, private property, or tax assessments? We know from Cassiodorus's *Variae* that a tax called the *illatio tertiarum* was paid throughout Theoderic's Italy and that this *illatio* was not an additional tax; it was a share—probably a one-third share— of the normal tax paid to the state but administered as a separate account. Theoderic authorized one town to fold this *illatio* into the tax total (*tributaria summa*); he considered it unnecessary to maintain the distinction at least in this town and at this time. It appears as though a one-third share of tax assessments was segregated from the "ordinary" two-thirds, that is, the share that the government retained. Just as assignment to the troops had been only a paper operation, so its abolition and return to the *tributaria summa* was simply a matter of accounting having no effect on individual landowner-taxpayers.[153] The *illatio tertiarum* helps to sort out Procopius's "one-third." The *tertiae*, one-third of property assessments, was a fund or pool, present in all Italian tax districts, out of which the government could award allotments (*sortes*) in lieu of pay primarily to soldiers, but also to other deserving Goths (*Variae* 2.17). If Procopius had been prosaically precise and resorted to technical terminology, he would have specified one-third of the land *assessments* of Italy—outrageous enough in its way, but not disruptive of private ownership.[154]

The many scholars who have believed that Roman properties were seized and redistributed did not reflect enough on the implications of such actions. It is entirely possible that, decades later, in the days of Justinian's reconquest, many Goths owned land and that they even left distinctive traces on the ground (though I am not convinced of this). The *Variae* also attest to the existence of ownership by Goths of land on the same taxpaying terms as Romans. The Burgundian settlement enabled the enterprising and ambitious to outgrow *sortes* and become proprietors, and the same appears to have been true among the Vandals; the Goths of Italy would not have been exceptions.[155] But the starting point in Italy as in Gaul was more provisional than the seizure of private property from Roman owners and its tranfer to individual soldiers. The starting point had to be gentler if Roman society was not to be rocked to its foundations by massive, lawless expropriations.

However wrongly, Procopius is the main prop for the idea that a large quantity of private land was distributed to barbarian troops; he is thought to be amply confirmed by the letter of Cassiodorus (*Variae* 2.16.5), briefly discussed already. Cassiodorus's letter is the principal account of the distribution of "land" to the troops of Gothic Italy. It appears to undercut the fiscal interpretation just given of Procopius by closely associating the awards to Theoderic's Goths with the vocabulary of landownership and even of gritty soil: *possessiones, praedia, cespitis divisio, pars agri, termini constituti*. The letter puts us in mind of an award to Goths of "clods of earth" cut away by division from Roman clods. Nothing in it suggests a distribution of shares of tax assessment and payment.[156] But its wording loses much its concreteness when interpreted in the light of the three possible meanings of "land."

As already pointed out, Cassiodorus's letter disagrees with Procopius's narrative. The latter implies that Odoacer was Roman; he alone reports the army mutiny and appropriation of land by Odoacer; and he portrays the distribution ordered by Theoderic, after his victory, as a transfer from one set of soldiers to another. Both Ennodius of Pavia and Cassiodorus (who speak many decades before Procopius) disregard Odoacer and attribute the original operation to Theoderic, acting through the admirable praetorian prefect Liberius.[157] Neither one knows anything about an earlier award and its transfer. It is conceivable that Procopius, to safeguard Theoderic's reputation, attributed to Odoacer an appropriation of "the third part of the land" of Italy that took place only under Theoderic. There is no way to decide how to balance Cassiodorus's silence against Procopius's allegations. One may only observe that neither account is complete or understandable at its "face value."

Ennodius of Pavia praised Liberius in a letter to him: "You have enriched the countless hordes of Goths with generous grants of lands, and yet the Romans have hardly felt it. The victors desire nothing more, and the conquered have felt no loss." Ennodius's land grants are specifically called a *larga praediorum conlatione*—the terminology of ordinary landowning.[158] Casssiodorus's longer praise, also couched in this language, occurs in a letter recommending Liberius's young son Venantius to the Roman Senate as ordinary consul, an obvious compliment to his father: "It gives us pleasure to refer to the way in which in the assignment of the thirds (*tertiae*) [Liberius] united both the possessions and the hearts of Goths and Romans. For though men usually quarrel when they are neighbors, the sharing of estates seems in this case to have produced harmony. For the result has been that both peoples, by living together, have achieved concord, an unprecedented and altogether praiseworthy accomplishment. By the division of the soil the hearts of the owners have been united, the friendship of the people has grown by their losses, and at the cost of a part of the land a defender has been acquired so that the security of the estate is wholly preserved."[159] Liberius carried out an operation called "the assignment of *tertiae*." No hint is given of an original award and its transfer from Odoacer's men to Theoderic's; Cassiodorus's preoccupation is the management of relations between Goths and Romans. If his reference to the "assignment of *tertiae*" is combined with Procopius's statement that one-third of Italian land was given to the army of Italy, a sensible interpretation might be that a large fraction of the regular tax assessments was segregated as a fund or pool of resources earmarked for the troops, and that individual allotments were awarded out of this pool. The award process is illustrated in Cassiodorus's very next letter (*Variae* 2.17), as we shall see.

On its surface or "natural" meaning, *Variae* 2.16.5 may seem to concern divisions of physical land, but the surface meaning is only provisional; the letter lends itself to another explanation once it is understood that the cultivable soil or its ownership were not the only dimensions of land that could be divided. Cassiodorus tells us that Liberius's assignment joined the *possessiones* of Goths and Romans to each other. Goths did not have to own the soil for this to be the case; LB55.2 and 84 show how one could "possess by right of allotment" (*iure sortis*) without extinguishing the prerogatives of the Roman owner and vice versa. The assessment and tax payments of land could be divided from its ownership and cultivation; an award of the tax assessment and proceeds would have the same effect as a division of the soil in joining the *possessiones* of Goths and Romans to each other. The *possessio* of Romans was ownership, that of Goths tax assessment; they were inseparably joined by the soil common to both. Next, Cassiodorus refers to a *praediorum communio*, adding that, contrary to the normal quarreling of neighbors with each other, the association of Roman and Gothic *praedia* had linked the interests of the two peoples and fostered their concord. The condition of this *communio* did not have to be a partition and redistribution of concrete fields; a "community" of interests in the same land would also result if the Goths received the annual taxes of the *praedia* and the Romans retained ownership and cultivation. Cassiodorus then raises the emotional level. Something really unusual and praiseworthy has taken place: the soil is divided (*cespitis divisio*) but the hearts of the owners (*domini*) are joined. Not every division, even of "clods," required a surveyor's rod. Just as much "division" would take place if the tax payments of the "clod" were set to one side and assigned to Goths, while the crops were left to the Roman cultivators and the rentals to the owners. The text continues: someone has been damaged, but the outcome is an increase in the friendship between the peoples. More practically, by the cession of "a part of the field"—probably the same collective "part" as the one-third reported by Procopius—a defender (the Gothic army) has been acquired to guard the security of all Italian real estate. However concrete Cassiodorus may sound, his words are wholly compatible with the idea that the substance of the "division" was the government's share of the land in question, not the shares of the owners and cultivators.

We have a choice, in reading *Variae* 2.16.5, of emphasizing words smacking of private property, or of observing that Cassiodorus draws our attention to unusual conditions. Because Barnish emphasizes the concrete and the negative, he wishes us to dwell on damage: "*amicitiae . . . per damna creverunt*," which looks even worse if *amicitiae* is omitted. The letter does have Barnish's "face value." Provided inconvenient details are disregarded, Cassiodorus might be read as definitely describing a land division—Goths spread around Roman communities as *domini*, "landowners," living together with Roman neighbors and cultivating the "clods" divided from Roman "clods" in a "community of estates" acquired by damaging the former proprietors.[160] But, as has now been seen, this reading of Cassiodorus's letter may be subverted without resort to force and replaced by one in which tax assessment is set apart from both ownership and cultivation and is the asset being divided. We have to reflect that this letter was written to an assembly of landowners, presumably major victims of any raid on one-third of Italian lands and unlikely to join in a celebration of their dispossession. A. H. M. Jones provides the necessary corrective: "It would hardly have been tactful to use such language . . . if [those addressed] felt bitterly resentful at their losses."[161] Ennodius says that "the Romans have hardly felt it": the damage was minor.[162]

Cassiodorus was using concrete language for a reason; the technical administrative or fiscal devices available to the government for cushioning shocks may not have lent themselves to being expressed in decorous prose.[163] But the nature of the division he spoke about was bound to be clear to those who knew what was going on. It would be extremely imprudent to invoke this letter as prime evidence for a large scale carving up of "estates" and award of private law *praedia* to the Goths of Italy. At the least, anyone arguing along these lines would have to show that some of the predictable consequences of expropriation and dispossession could be detected in the Italian countryside. Without strain, Cassiodorus's language can be reconciled with a distribution of shares of tax assessment rather than an improbable theft and partition of gritty soil.

Although Procopius and Cassiodorus differ over the date and authorship of the Italian settlement, their accounts of its nature—neither of them very clear—complement each other. There are two conditions for understanding them: that the "distribution of 'the thirds' " caused no turmoil, and that the sense of "land" in both documents is neither the soil nor proprietorship but only tax value, that is, the official assessment of land and the taxes arising from it. Cassiodorus makes it clear that many allotments from the pool of available "land" were made to the Gothic troops. The process was basically the same as we detected among the Visigoths and Burgundians, with one salient difference: the division of state resources in Italy left two-thirds of the register of assessments in the hands of the government and assigned only one-third to the troops. Several possible explanations for this difference come to mind and need not be spelled out. As in Gaul, the *sortes* to the troops could be grouped wherever the leadership chose or thought it best to group them; and, thanks to the assessment registers as the basis for assignment, a rough measure of equality could be achieved for each *sors*. Distinguished Goths might be singled out by the award of *sortes* of exceptional size or simply be given land from the royal two-thirds in excess of the basic allotment.

If allotments were distributed to the Goths in Theoderic's Italy, it was not to satisfy their hunger for land or to encourage their agricultural vocation, but to pay them. In his *sors*, each qualified Goth obtained a permanent lucrative endowment that superseded the distribution of rations (*annonae*) that had formerly been their pay. Theoderic's successor told the troops, "allotments of your own feed you" (*cum vos et sortes alant propriae*) and money is given to you as supplementary pay: "our gifts, God helping, enrich you."[164] No source suggests that Goths were fed by their *sortes* only if each one applied to it the sweat of his brow and made it productive. This transformation of military pay (*annona et donativa*) into a secure income (*sors*) had been what, in Procopius's introduction to the *Gothic Wars*, the Italian army had "ruthlessly" asked for and killed the patrician Orestes so as to obtain. Odoacer, taking command, satisfied the soldiers' demand that they should no longer have their pay doled out bit by bit but, instead, obtain individual and permanent awards.[165] A Gothic *sors*-holder obtained his *annona*—his basic, enduring military pay—from his allotment, whatever its composition might have been; he was the beneficiary of an entitlement that descended to his heirs.

The Allotment Given by Theoderic to the Gothic Priest Butila

The letters of the *Variae* are sometimes grouped by topic, though never in a predictably systematic way. One cannot help noting that *Variae* 2.16, the letter about Liberius's assignment of the *tertiae*, is directly followed by a letter concerning a Gothic priest called Butila—the only document from anywhere in the late Roman world illustrating the award of an allotment to anyone. It is hard to read this letter as a grant of "clods" separated from Roman clods and destined to be Gothic property. The sense it does make is that Butila's *sors* is related to the "assignment of *tertiae*" and to the machinery of taxation associated with *tertiae*.

In *Barbarians and Romans*, I emphasized two Cassiodoran letters from which one might infer that the Goths with allotments were called *millenarii*. I proposed that this term did not refer to "commanders of one thousand" or "chiliarchs," since the context called for these *millenarii* to be equivalent to "all the Goths." What the term meant (I said) was "beneficiaries of *millenae*," *millenae* being a widely attested fiscal unit used here to express standardized awards of tax proceeds, rather than (as more commonly in legal texts) units of assessment; *millenae* here were a unit of payment rather than of liability. I laid the foundation of this argument in an article showing that Cassiodorus twice used such fiscal abstractions in the sense of units of payment rather than units of assessment, and that other instances of such usage could be found in Roman texts concerning taxation. It followed from these sources that the Goths called *millenarii* in Italy were given *sortes* consisting of awards of tax proceeds to the amount of a *millena*. These *millenae* issued out of tax revenues were how Goths "obtain[ed] each year the rewards of Our Mildness" and how "allotments of [their] own feed [them]," as the *Variae* attest.[166] The annual emoluments were distinct from the donatives that they received now and again from an openhanded king. The fuller discussion of *millenae* as awards of tax proceeds given in my earlier book need not be repeated here, especially since it has not fared badly with critics.[167]

Thanks to Durliat's discussions of the mechanisms of Roman taxation, my focus has tended to shift away from *Variae* 5.27–28 and toward *Variae* 2.17, a letter of Theodoric to the dignitaries of Trent (ca. 508).[168] As noted above, it is the one text from the late Roman period documenting an allotment to an individual Goth or to any other barbarian for that matter:

King Theodoric to the honorably-discharged-officials, proprietors, guardians, and city councillors of the city of Tridentum [modern Trent].

We do not wish our generosity to be damaging to anyone, lest what is granted to one person should result in losses to another. Know, therefore, that, by the present royal command, no one should pay any state payment ["tax"] on account of the allotment that we have granted by our generosity to the priest Butila. [Know, rather,] that whatever gold pieces are comprised in that [public] payment are excused to you from the payments of "the thirds." We definitely do not wish anyone to pay what, by our humanity, we have remitted to another, lest—awful to say—the gift made to a well-deserving person should chance to damage an uninvolved party.[169]

As often said before, a puzzling fact of the barbarian settlements if they consisted of seized land is the apparent lack of protest by injured landowners. Another serious problem is that of legal justification. Military billeting is irrelevant to Italy even if it were not otherwise discredited. Failing that sanction, what right did any government associated with Rome have to expropriate wide tracts of fertile land for distribution to its troops? Governments can always dispose of a certain amount of public land, perhaps even large tracts, but there is no sign whatever in the relevant evidence from Gaul or Italy (or North Africa for that matter) that such lands were awarded to barbarian troops or were the basis for such awards. The silence of the sources on this subject is weighty; any appeal to public lands in a context of barbarian allotments is frivolous and lacks any probable basis.[170] In Gothic Italy, the letters about the *millenarii* point in a different direction. The letter about Butila is even more useful in defining a mechanism for rewarding Goths that avoids the drastic step of despoiling Roman proprietors.

The letter only indirectly documents the award to Butila. It shows Theoderic compensating Trent for the consequences that the award to Butila will have for the local flow of taxation. We hear of Theoderic's gift as being "sortem quam Butilani presbitero nostra largitate contulimus." The delicate word is *sors*, allotment. No precise information is given about what Butila receives. *Sors* is an abstraction needing to be defined by context. Like our word "property," the word signifies an asset whose precise content is unstated.[171] The major clue to the nature of Butila's allotment is the statement *quam remisimus* (to Butila); the relative pronoun *quam* refers to payments to the state, mentioned earlier as *praestatio* or *functio fiscalis calculi*, both meaning "tax payments." Theoderic fears that, owing to this forgiveness (remission) to Butila of "tax payments," someone at Trent will be unjustly charged with payments to the state. This "fear" is a certainty, of course, not a contingency. The major problem arising from the letter is how something "remitted" (or "forgiven") to Butila might turn into a loss to some other person. This injustice, which Theoderic is bent on avoiding, is not attributed to malfeasance; the letter implies that the normal tax machinery permits this injustice to happen. Theoderic therefore orders that the obligation to payment of *illatio tertiarum* arising from Butila's *sors* should be blotted out, so that no uninvolved stranger will be penalized for royal generosity. The sense of the letter is that Butila has been excused from public *praestatio*; he has obtained a tax exemption. This grant to the beneficiary of the right not to pay the state the tax owed by the quantity of assessment composing his *sors* is, I suggest, itself the lucrative aspect of the king's gracious "allotment conferred upon the priest Butila"; Butila gets to collect the taxes of his allotted assessment and keep them; he is excused from passing them on.

Two sides are implied by the letter: Butila obtains a *sors* consisting of a forgiveness of taxation (the taxes are glossed as payments to the *illatio tertiarum*), but, unless the royal government gives relief, one or more Tridentines will have to continue paying amounts to the government that they may once have owed but, in justice, should not be paying any longer. Theoderic does not want them to be penalized; repeating a sentiment voiced in the preambles of other letters, he does not want persons to be charged for taxes they do not owe.[172] How has this problem come about? Durliat's account of tax management helps to provide an answer.

The letter is not addressed to Butila but to four categories of local dignitaries forming a group, a consortium—a body that might, in this context, be called the "tax commission" of Trent. Taxpaying did not involve the taxpayers and the government in a face-to-face relationship of tax debtors and tax collectors. In practice the local tax commission (composed of persons who were taxpayers themselves) served as the interface, assuming a dual role: first, collectors of taxes and, next, responsible trustees for the government of the public payments they collected. The commissioners gathered in payments from the local taxpayers, including themselves; and they forwarded or expended the proceeds as instructed by the government.[173]

The commission faced inward toward the local taxpayers (collection) and outward to the royal government (payment)—credit from collections and debit from outflows at state command. In relation to local taxpayers, the commission raked in the payments of the persons entered in the assessment registers, including themselves. Taxes were partly in commodities, partly in money; they

necessarily involved commutations according to official scales in a process managed by the commissioners.[174] Vis-à-vis the royal government, the tax commission resembled a treasury that the government could draw upon for making
state payments. In this outflow, the unit of account was the gold piece (*solidus*,
one seventy-second of a pound of gold). Careful reckonings of receipts and expenditures had to be rendered to the government, but the amounts collected
from taxpayers stayed close to where they were collected until the tax commission received orders from the central bureaus about how to disburse them. In
real life, matters would not be quite so neat; for example, some payers probably
were in arrears, and the government might be overdrawn. For the sake of clarity,
my explanation smooths over difficulties.

The two faces of the tax commission help to explain the possible injustice
Theoderic sought to avert. His remedy involved abolishing a certain number of
solidi of payment to the government from the tax account known as *illatio tertiarum* (as noted above, this was one-third of the *tributaria summa*, "tax total").
The way this relief is expressed clearly indicates that only the outgoing side of
the tax commission's activity is affected. The gold pieces lighten the debt of the
Trent tax commission to the royal government, but do not impinge on the collecting side of the equation.

The possibility that someone would be unjustly penalized for Butila's *sors*
presupposes a system in which the hand that collected from taxpayers was not
directly connected to the hand owing taxes to the government. If so, the tax relief allowed by Theoderic to Butila operated on the collecting or incoming side
of the tax process. That side of the tax commission's activity was short by the
amount Butila collected, which, because it was paid to him and, because he was
relieved of tax obligation, he was legitimately entitled to keep for himself. But
no corresponding relief was automatically allowed to the Trent tax commission; the total amount owed to the government on the outgoing side of the
ledger stayed the same. Only Theoderic's command could change this situation
and bring obligations to the government back into line with diminished collections. Because outgoing payments were not strictly related to collections
(and the assessments giving rise to them), a royal remedy was indispensable if
Theoderic was to avoid an injustice toward one or the other of the tax commissioners of Trent.

Variae 2.17 tells us that Butila was freed from taxation in respect to his *sors*,
and that the tax commission of Trent was graciously shielded by Theoderic
from the consequences of this remission. Can we probe more deeply into the
nature of Butila's *sors*? There seem to be three possibilities: that the allotment
was land of some sort, that it was a state salary, or that it was a grant of tax assessment and its proceeds, collectable from those obligated.

If land of some sort were in question, the letter would have to be under-stood to concern not the allotment proper, but an incidental aspect of it, namely, its tax exemption. The real award would have been "land," a productive estate not mentioned but implied by the existence of tax liability. Hypotheti-cally, Butila would have been awarded an estate and also would have been ex-empted from its tax debt. Theoderic's letter remedied a possible unfairness arising from this incidental tax exemption; it would concern a relatively minor aspect of an allotment consisting of tax-free productive land. This interpretation is less than ideal. The assumed "land" is totally hidden; its existence cannot be com-pletely ruled out, but there is no positive trace of it. Besides, we are left wonder-ing by what legal means Theoderic would have acquired the land he gave away. Theoderic states clearly that the gift or award made to Butila will damage someone on the tax commission. Since everything is possible, the "gift" (*munus*) referred to in *Variae* 2.17 may be incidental to another, larger, and never men-tioned gift (of land); but it seems more reasonable to conclude that the harm potentially affecting the Trent tax commission came directly from the one and only award given to Butila.

Butila's allotment might be a state salary. Some of the *Variae* award a mea-sured amount of tax proceeds to a public service (for example, the municipal baths of Spoleto), and a series of Cassiodorus's letters, especially among those issued when he was praetorian prefect, are called *delegatoria* and order that a government official be given a stated amount of provincial revenue as salary.[175] The equivalence of "allotment" (*sors*) and salary cannot apply to Butila, how-ever, because Theoderic's letter does not refer to or imply payment to him of a regular sum. Rather, Theoderic abolishes a certain amount of debt owed by Trent to the government. If Butila's "remission" justified relieving the Trent tax commission of equivalent future payments, the commission was surely not pay-ing Butila a salary.

The third possibility has the advantage of involving a commodity that the government was in a position to give. The situation in this case was that Butila's *sors*—all of it—consisted of a diversion to him of the taxes of a set quantity of assessed property in Trent (a quantity attributed in the tax records to the "pay-ment of 'the thirds' " [*illatio tertiarum*]) and a remission to him of the obliga-tion to pay these taxes to the state via the tax commission. This is the method I proposed twenty-five years ago.[176] A modern analogy is possible, at least in a set-ting of relatively unchanging assessments and taxes. In such a case, one might take the assessment books of, say, New Haven (Connecticut); select a group of houses whose property tax would yield an annual revenue of, say, $15,000 to the city or, if diverted from the tax system and awarded to an individual, would yield the same to John Doe.[177] The amount once set, Mr. Doe would be provided with a list of the houses whose taxes he was entitled to claim; and the rest was up to him. He was presumably armed with the authority to collect the assigned sum. The assessment (*professio*) of these houses, permanently removed from the tax registers and transferred to Mr. Doe, existed as the principal of an annual debt and might even be envisaged as a type of estate (the houses whose taxes Doe pocketed might justifiably be called "his houses"). Mr. Doe would see to it that he or his agents collected the proceeds of that debt, which the state allowed him to keep in perpetuity as his personal revenue. If we leave the New Haven analogy and return to Gothic Italy, we observe that the ownership and cultivation of the properties paying to Butila did not change hands but remain unimpaired in Roman hands. Butila was allowed to claim only the government's share of revenue arising from them and to exercise the remedies of a debt collector against those persons who failed to pay. Butila or his agents were in direct contact with the primary layer of taxpayers; his allotment would have been on the income side of the tax equation. As a final point, Butila did not have to turn farmer or get his hands dirty. The *sors* given him by Theoderic provided an income almost indistinguishable from that of a Roman landed gentleman living off agrarian rents.

The entire process of allotment (*deputatio tertiarum*) could be, and probably was, mainly a matter of bookkeeping, with little reference to the soil or even the assessment records. (The almost miraculous simplicity of the scheme helps to explain the tone of wonder adopted by Cassiodorus in *Variae* 2.16.5.) The attribution of "the third part of the land [of Italy] to the barbarians" was simply a rule of fiscal accounting, needing no corresponding delimitation of the "thirds" in the tax registers, let alone on the ground. Only when a *sors* was actually awarded to someone, such as Butila, was there a transfer out of the assessment books of a locality and a listing of the properties (or parts of properties) affected by the transfer. The applicable accounting principle was that up to one-third of the total assessment of a tax district, but no more, could be distributed as individual *sortes* to Goths, leaving at least two thirds to the government. An allotment like Butila's could comprise any appropriate and convenient part of a local assessment record, the official limit being that the award of individual *sortes* could not reduce the government's share of local tax proceeds by more than one-third; when all allotments in a given tax district were totted up, no more than one-third of local assessment could be deducted from the "tax total" (*tributaria summa*). The *illatio tertiarum* was not a tax but a special fiscal account that kept track both of the amounts given to individuals and of the balance left to the royal government. The *illatio* was composed of the total tax revenue paid to the state from one-third of the local assessment (never mind what third) minus the amounts awarded to beneficiaries of *sortes* (never mind where in the district they were located). In a given locality, an absolute minimum of two-thirds of the total assessment paid its taxes to the royal government (via the tax commission), and at the most one-third of the assessment could be alienated as *sortes* to individual beneficiaries, each of whom was authorized to collect the taxes of his "land" as his private revenue. The difference between the part of the *illatio* alienated as *sortes* to Goths and the part still paying taxes to the king was of course retained by the government.

Many of Cassiodorus's collected letters were meant to serve as model charters or to record legal precedents. On the basis of the letter about Butila, judges in Ostrogothic Italy were given clear instructions about the remedy available to local tax commissions that had been deprived of tax payments by the award of *sortes*. The legal principle laid down by *Variae* 2.17 was that local tax commissioners were entitled to have their tax debts to the government (expressed in gold pieces) scaled downward to the amount of each allotment (*sors*) awarded to a Goth (or other state beneficiary). The presupposition giving rise to this principle was that each award of an allotment consisted of a remission of tax liability to the government from the landed assessment in question and a transfer of this liability, that is, right to collect and keep annual tax payments, to the beneficiary of each *sors*.

*   *   *

In a practical sense, very little changed in the Italian countryside. Some tax payments formerly made to the local tax collector or his agent were, henceforth, diverted to the Goth entitled to them or to his agent. Matters looked rather different to the newly settled Goth. He obtained an "estate" consisting wholly of the payments formerly made in the guise of taxes; the payments came from proprietors with uncontested physical and economic control of the lands in question. The Goth had an income, even conceivably a large one; but he was excluded from the soil, which was wholly retained and occupied by the private law owners from whom he collected. Planting roots was a secondary matter, which the Goth could presumably look after out of his own resources (what used to be called the *peculium castrense*). There is no need, without specific evidence, to transpose to Italy the clause about "houses and gardens" in LB54.4. Neither houses nor courtyards in villages and towns would have been beyond the means of Theoderic's followers to acquire from their own resources. Around this homestead, a small-scale estate could be organized, keeping track of the annual inflow from the allotted payers, whose payments would almost immediately turn in appearance from "taxes" into "rents." It was a platform from which, by purchases of land and royal gifts, a Goth could gradually increase his presence in the countryside.

So conceived, the Italian system differed somewhat from the one instituted in Gaul, but not in its results. The idea everywhere was to cushion the shock of incorporating barbarians into the provincial countryside. The barbarians of higher rank than camp followers were not candidates for peasanthood but proud veterans enriched by booty and hoping for a life of martial leisure. The territories into which they were to be blended may have been past the best days of Roman prosperity; nevertheless, they were (on the eve of the awards to barbarian troops) fully operational in yielding a living to their cultivators, revenues to absentee or resident landowners, and taxes to the government.

From Occupancy to Ownership

Those forced to rely on evidence from law codes and other legal materials, such as Cassiodorus's *Variae*, understandably chafe at the inadequacy of the picture such sources present. Modern legal sources are not complete either. The Connecticut General Statutes run to dozens of volumes, with detailed indexes to guide inquirers through their intricacies. Nowhere in them, however, does one encounter any reference to "plea bargaining," the practice by which very many criminal cases are disposed of. To go by the official printed record this essential part of the criminal justice system simply does not exist.[178] If the materials of today, voluminous as they are, conceal crucial aspects of everyday practice, it is hardly surprising that the legal sources of the distant past leave us resentful at their grudging and ambiguous testimony. And whereas persons interested in the conditions of the state of Connecticut can resort to mountains of additional evidence of all kinds, that alternative is not open to inquirers into barbarian settlement. Other avenues have been explored with sterile results. If answers are wanted, the few ambiguous texts we have dealt with are the sum of what we are allowed.

Dietrich Claude, in closing an outspokenly hostile review of *Barbarians and Romans*, lifted a few ideas from its last pages and, with modifications, turned them into the trouble-free solution he envisioned for the settlement problem: "The barbarians obtained their landholdings not long after their admission to imperial territory by concluding private contracts with Roman landowners, who yielded a part of their holdings in return for the cancellation of the duty to pay taxes."[179] This sounds smooth and nice. The government gave what it could—in Claude's system, tax relief—to make up to Roman landowners for their loss of property. Presumably the quid pro quo was attractive enough to stifle any Roman complaints about being dispossessed at spearpoint. We are taken back to the artist's portrayal of a meek Roman handing over his duly signed charter to a magnificently armed barbarian.[180] Claude thinks my system raises new, unanswerable problems; his own substitute does a fair job of raising problems not perhaps new but certainly unanswerable. How were the two parties selected? Who brought them together? Who set the standards for the "part" of Roman property to be yielded? Were the barbarian kings pleased by the wholesale cessation of tax payments? Unlike other advocates of a "land" solution, Claude deserves credit for suggesting a comprehensive land-based alternative to my proposal, but the surviving sources are searched in vain for any trace of the private contracts that are the key to his scheme, or for any implication of their existence.

Simplicity, the utopia of a "land" scheme—segregating one body of owners and smoothly dividing their assets with a set of owners-to-be—is not an available option. It does not produce an intelligible interpretation of the omnibus LB54. It does not take account of the laws providing that common woodlands or wastes once developed were to be shared on a fifty-fifty basis. It forces *millenarii* in Gothic Italy to turn improbably into a minority of "commanders of one thousand" instead of a collectivity of "holders of a *millena*," whose income were determined by a standard unit of tax proceeds. By directly carving out individual allotments on the discredited basis of the billeting rule, it disregards the primary conveyance of assets by one government to another and is blind to the sharing between king and followers. The eighteenth-century idea of Germanic conquest and seizure of Roman provincial land (*Landnahme*) was a simple, straightforward, and wholly undocumented solution.[181] Once conquest and the law of the victor are left behind as contrary to what the evidence shows, it is difficult to get away from complexity—a complexity that is probably greater for us, unaccustomed to Roman administration, than to those who were inured to its intricacies.

Claude deserves to be heard in his vigorous protest that a tax-based scheme raises unanswerable problems:

Late Roman taxation presupposed a central, strictly organized administration for continual verification and revision of the cadaster. Attributions of taxes to individuals would have disrupted this system in a short time. If thousands of barbarians obtained the taxes of one or several provincials, and they themselves levied the payments, an extreme fragmentation was unavoidable. In particular, such attributions of taxes would soon be made worthless by property changes and deaths among those liable to taxes.

The system assumed by G[offart] presupposes stable taxes. In late antiquity as well as the Middle Ages, the level of the payments to be made by each tax unit was subject to notable variations. . . . In several Germanic kingdoms a central tax administration (admittedly slowly disintegrating) is demonstrable. This fact alone contradicts G.'s thesis.[182]

To take the last of these objections first, the continuity of royal taxation does not contradict a scheme of awards of tax-based allotments. In Italy, for example, the awards to individual Goths, soldiers, priests (like Butila), or others left at least two-thirds of all lands registered for taxation (the total that Claude calls "the cadaster") to continue paying its taxes to the royal government. Because awards of *sortes* almost certainly fell short of the one-third allocated to them, the fraction of the assessment retained by the government was bound to be larger than two-thirds. In the Burgundian and Visigothic kingdoms, the rulers also kept for themselves notable quantities of assessed land not distributed as *sortes*. It is true that the assessments awarded as *sortes barbarorum* were lost once and for all to the royal financial administration, but the loss was amply compensated: the drop in tax revenue was offset by the end of government payments of *annona* and *stipendia* to a standing army. Despite there being a serious shrinkage of assessed acreage, the comparatively small number of Goths and Burgundians to be settled in Gaul and Italy meant that the part of the assessment rolls paying taxes to central treasuries continued to be very large. As Cassiodorus's *Variae* amply document for Italy, the management of government revenue did not cease to preoccupy royal officials or to employ a numerous personnel, including curials (as Pohl has pointed out).[183]

Claude's vision of late Roman tax administration gives it too much credit for regularity and efficiency. The impression obtained from such evidence as the *Variae* is not of a systematic, continual aggiornamento of assessments, but rather of tax districts becoming dislocated over a period of years and having to be restored to order by special delegations. Revisions were not strict and timely but conducted when they became necessary.[184] What mainly happened as a result of barbarian settlement was a narrowing of the tax base. The award of personal taxpayers to a barbarian recipient was, in effect, the conversion of a public tax into a private rent. The case of Butila makes this perfectly clear: the *functio* remitted to Butila was wiped off the slate of the commissioners' tax obligations to the state. Butila acquired a rent roll, with the same advantages and problems accruing to him as to any other landowner with a rent roll: possible fragmentation; possible disruption by death and changes of ownership. Erosion of revenue could be resisted by Butila and his likes in the same way that these problems were dealt with by the innumerable Roman landlords dealing with their tenants. Public taxes administered by the government could be augmented by *superexactio* and other devices, and they could be temporarily lowered in case of enemy action or natural calamity. Nevertheless, they had a stable core: Cassiodorus could not write about them as he does unless they did.[185] A private rent roll may have been subject to fewer adjustments than a public tax roll, but was not drastically different. Tenants fell into arrears vis-à-vis their landlords; they needed relief in bad years, and so forth. The essential point in reply to Claude is that a *sors* composed of tax assets was privatized at the moment of award and was simply subtracted from the tax base. It did not continue, as he believed, to be a part of the tax machinery and have the potential to interfere with it. The main effect of barbarian settlement in both Gaul and Italy was to transform the military payroll from a centralized redistribution of resources managed by government officials into a charge on assessed land, with payments going directly (and permanently) from agricultural producers or managers to individual military families. State resources were used to bring into being a new breed of proprietors looking (in their relations to the laboring and paying population) very much like the old.[186] The new breed differed from the old chiefly in being obligated on account of their *sortes* to respond to a royal mobilization and perform military service.

Two things need to be primarily clarified in attempting to reconstruct the settlement of Goths and Burgundians in the western provinces: first, the practical difficulties of financing the settlement of barbarians without resorting to illegal expropriations and disrupting the social and economic order of the countryside, and, second, the absence of protests on the part of Roman landowners. The problems posed by these two considerations are solved if the resources mobilized and conveyed are understood to have stemmed from the tax machinery of the Roman state. Even if the acquiescence of resident landowners is an argument from silence, the undisturbed condition of the countryside is hard to overlook. Roman and ecclesiastical landlords march quietly into the Middle Ages alongside landlords bearing non-Roman names. One chronicler says, the Burgundians were given a district to divide with "the natives"; another, long after, has the Burgundians divide the land with the "senators."[187] What were the assets that the senators could divide with the Burgundians without jeopardizing their fortunes? In sixth-century Gaul "senators" were not lofty ex-officials attending to public business in the Senate house of Rome; they were the local dignitaries, such as the "tax commission" of Trent in the letter about Butila, dignitaries whose main charge was precisely to be responsible vis-à-vis the government for the tax payments of their district.[188] The main asset available to the imperial authorities for conveyance to the Goths and Burgundians about to become permanent residents was the state's share of land revenues, based on registers of property assessment. Roman landowners and cultivators were the human underpinning of these records. The barbarian kings kept some of these assets and distributed the balance in suitable allotments to their armies in lieu of pay for military readiness. The taxpaying Romans, lofty and humble, were shared out with their properties among the royal or the individual Gothic or Burgundian receivers of taxation, to whom the Romans would now answer more or less directly (the use of agents and other intermediaries was presumably widespread). It did no harm to the working countryside if the pressure of armed tax collectors weighed upon the producing population, or so it may have seemed to those Romans still obligated as subjects of the king to retain their places in the fiscal machinery, perhaps on the pretext of being "hosts."

Gaupp was much concerned with a misapprehension of earlier writers on barbarian settlements, namely, that the barbarians no sooner arrived in their district of settlement than they divided land with the Romans. He insisted that there had to be a pause between arrival and division, and he proposed to fill that pause, at least in part, with a period of military billeting.[189] Gaupp was on the right track. Unless one subscribes to a scenario of conquest and forcible imposition of a new order, there had to be an interval between a provisional arrangement supplying necessities to the newcomers and an ordered resolution fitting the old and new populations into the countryside without collision and ill-feeling. The end point had to be that Burgundians and Goths existed alongside Romans as full-fledged landowners enjoying the same rights over the land and its cultivators as the established owners of the countryside. The Burgundians and Goths could not continue indefinitely as possessors limited by a strictly qualified, inalienable *ius hospitalitatis*. But the desired result could not be attained except over a period of years. That is the sort of provisional solution that was somehow found and set up by the responsible authorities in Gaul and Italy. Tax proceeds, turning from state receipts into revenues directly collected from the creators of wealth, not only cushioned the transition, but did so slowly enough for traces of the scheme to survive in the law codes, in spite of the chronological distance of the applicable laws from the moments of settlement. Early medieval society was dominated by owners of wide acres—some royal, many ecclesiastical, still others laymen somehow obligated to serve their king. The appropriation of agricultural production by these landlords hinged on a combination of private and public rights, some derived from ownership, some from taxation. The "techniques of accommodation" facilitated the incorporation of Goths and Burgundians into this society.

Afterward: Barbarians as Oppressive Neighbors

Unlike the expropriations carried out by the Triumvirs near end of the Roman Republic, the mechanism of barbarian settlement in Gaul and Italy produced no complaints. The absence of such outcries is a serious reason for doubting that wholesale confiscations or other flagrant illegalities took place. The documented cases of the Alans in Gaul and the Vandals in North Africa suggest that, when dispossessions occur, they are likely to be noticed and find their way into the sources.[190]

The orderliness of the initial settlement does not mean, however, that the introduction of Goths and Burgundians among the landowners of Gaul and Italy had no adverse consequences for their neighbors. Texts of different origins suggest that, after the settlement took place and barbarians became participants in the ongoing life of the countryside, Goths and Burgundians abused their position to enrich themselves at the expense of their Roman neighbors. Individual incidents occasioned fervent complaints. In *Barbarians and Romans* I drew attention to a series of texts indicating that Romans were being damaged by their new neighbors, and I cited them *in extenso*.[191] I do not believe that any others can be found. Here is a list of these texts with a summary of the contents:

1. *Passio s. Vincentii Aginensis*, 6 (ed. Beaudouin de Gaiffier, in *Analecta Bollandiana* 70 [1952]: 180): one Gothic family had managed "sub hostilitatis sorte" to deprive all the old inhabitants of Agen of their property. (Quoted, *B&R*, p. 165 n. 7, trans. pp. 95–96; Courcelle, *Histoire littéraire*, pp. 339–47.)[192]
2. *Vita s. Bibiani episcopi Sanctonensis*, ed. B. Krusch, MG SRM 3:96: the Goths who had already deprived the *mediocres* of their riches devise a plan to extend their depredations to the *nobiles* and become the sole landowners of Saintes. (Trans. and comments, *B&R*, pp. 96–97.)
3. *Vita patrum Iurensium* 94, a Roman oppressor of the poor should beware lest "the new guest (*novus hospes*)," by an unexpected abuse of law, should seize [the Roman's] ill-gotten acres. (Text, *B&R*, p. 165 n. 7.)[193]
4. Pseudo-Fulgentius, *Sermo* 80: a Gothic and barbarian "guest," brandishing weapons and arrows, comes to torture, despoil, and injure Romans. (Text, *B&R*, p. 165 n. 7.)
5. Cassiodorus, *Variae* 8.28, two Romans accuse a Goth of seizing their *agellum* and threatening to reduce them to slavery. (Trans. and discussed, *B&R*, pp. 93–95.)
6. Boethius, *De consolatione philosophiae* 1.4.35: he often defended "poor wretches" harassed by the "unpunished covetousness" of barbarians. (Trans., *B&R*, p. 94.)

An additional, less definite passage is supplied by Procopius in his account of the Gothic counterattack in Italy during the 540s. Several times he shows the honest young king Totila pondering aloud why the Goths of Italy, with their superabundant resources of men and wealth, had quickly collapsed in the face of Belisarius. He adverts to the misdeeds of Theoderic's nephew, Theodahad, "who made less of justice than of his desire to become wealthy"; but Procopius once has Totila generalize this accusation: "The Goths in earlier times paid less heed

to justice than to any other thing, and treated each other and their Roman subjects as well in an unholy manner; wherefore God was then moved to take the
field against them on the side of their enemies."[194] Vague as these reproaches are
(by comparison with the texts from Gaul), they echo the complaints of Boethius,
with the difference that, in Procopius's version, the Goths were no less unjust to
each other than to the Romans. That comes as no surprise in the context of the
scramble for riches and power in the countryside.

The examples we have of such incidents are entirely plausible. They pre-
clude any temptation to surround the "techniques of accommodation" with a
pink glow of idealization. The texts disappoint us by being expressed in general
terms (the ironic reference to a "sors hostilitatis" is a precious exception). The
authors had a moral purpose and saw no need to supply technical details. At
best, situations are evoked in which the barbarians were in a position to oppress
Romans landowners by exploiting the terms of the allotments in such a way as
to put their Roman neighbors in proprietary jeopardy and even reduce them to
servitude. It is plausible that barbarian *sortes* of the kind I have presented
should have made it possible for the beneficiaries to abuse their position, especially if the Roman owners fell behind in their payments. Well-armed rent collectors are disquieting neighbors. Barbarian allotments were transitional; there
was an inbuilt incentive for barbarians who were so minded to push toward becoming men of full-fledged property. Roman *potentes* ran the risk of being superseded by barbarians eager to seat their own power as securely as possible in
landownership.

What must be loudly said about these and the unrecorded instances of
barbarian oppression is that, far from testifying to the advent of alien lawless-
ness, such behavior was in the finest tradition of the law-abiding Roman countryside. The system of settlement worked: it created rural tyrants picking up
where tyrannical Romans had left off and where some were surely still carrying
on.[195] The misdeeds of Goths in Agen and Saintes were as much a symptom of
the continuity of Roman ways as were the measures granting them the prerogatives they abused. Gothic conduct followed the paths blazed by the oppressive
Roman *potentes* of the fifth century and their ancestors in earlier Roman history.
Salvian is notorious for his eloquence in denouncing fifth-century misdeeds by
ostensibly Christian *potentes* vis-à-vis their poorer neighbors. St. Augustine, in a
sermon, dramatizes the ruses by which a covetous landowner maneuvers to an-
nex his neighbor's fields.[196] Well represented in the Roman past, greedy and
oppressive *potentes* are a continual presence in one guise or another in the
medieval or modern future. The impugned Goths, by abusing their legally acquired positions, showed themselves to be apt pupils of their predecessors. Our
documentation of greed regardless of ethnic coloring is appropriately capped

by Gregory of Tours's grimly comic account of Bishop Badegisel of Le Mans, a Frank and ex-official. Not a day or moment went by in which Badegisel "did not wallow in plundering his fellow citizens or in quarreling over something or the other"; "Just because I've been made clergy," he cried, "doesn't mean I can't be the avenger of wrongs done to me."[197]

Chapter 7
None of Them Were Germans:
Northern Barbarians in Late Antiquity

A second, and particularly prevalent problem is the term "Germanic" itself. . . . [I]t was suggested that the term "Germanic" be dropped completely in this volume, but to substitute it with "barbarians" would only mean adopting another (Roman) ideology which, in the final analysis, is as inadequate as "Germanic." The only neutral alternative, therefore, would be to simply speak of late antique and early medieval peoples and kingdoms, but, of course, this would merely be evading the problem.
—H.-W. Goetz, "Introduction" to Regna and Gentes.

The title of this chapter draws attention to the absence of "Germans," "the Germanic," and "Germany" from the Migration Age. None of the participants called themselves by such a name, and even late Roman observers, whose ancestors had placed the term into circulation, used it rarely. When they did, they almost invariably meant it in the narrow sense of western barbarian peoples, such as the Franks, who lived more or less near the one incontrovertibly Germanic thing, namely, the two Roman provinces of "Germania," on the middle and lower course of the Rhine river.[1] Whether or not, as Goetz suggests above, the term "Germanic" evokes a "Roman ideology" is a matter of opinion; the certainty is that modern uses of "German" or "Germanic" in the Migration Age, unless more meticulous than they normally are, introduce glaring anachronisms wherever they are deployed. It may or may not be true that "barbarian" evokes a Roman ideology, but it is certain that the term was in current use in late antiquity, and that it continued to be standard in the Middle Ages and beyond. Its meaning may be open to debate; its use may be politically incorrect; but there is no doubt at all that, in contexts calling for general terms, "barbarian" is appropriate to late antique usage whereas "Germanic" is grossly anachronistic.[2] There is also a third course, namely, to pay the actors the compliment of using their own names and to become conversant with minor ones as well as with stars. Only a few names of barbarian peoples—Goths, Franks, Vandals,

Saxons—are household words, but that is just a matter of training. With a little practice, "Sarmatian" and "Gepid" can also become familiar. The multiplicity of names for "barbarians" brings home the pivotal lesson that the Roman Empire faced many different peoples beyond its frontiers—not a collectivity whose packing into a single term has served for many centuries mainly to distort the past.[3]

This chapter is concerned with the barbarian peoples in late antiquity, both in general, as a collective phenomenon dealt with by Rome, and severally, in case studies of seven less prominent peoples of the Migration Age and of their respective destinies. A final part, centering on the last phase of Gothic rule in Italy, attempts to show that ethnicity was radically inadequate at that time as a basis for political cohesion.

Late Roman Conditions and Barbarian Penetration

The main difference in the relations between northern barbarians and the Roman Empire in the early and the later periods is that, whereas the barbarians were excluded from the earlier Empire except under due control, the authorities of the later Empire allowed them to have a continually expanding role in imperial society. The phrase "barbarization of the Empire" has long been used to describe late Roman conditions; the phenomenon is analogous to the contemporary "Christianization."[4] The Empire that disposed of its former religions wholesale, and exchanged them for a once-alien monotheistic creed, also underwent a social transformation in which foreigners (originally) from beyond the borders—rarely from remote distances—were both more needed and more accepted than they had ever been. From the third century, large and increasing numbers of foreigners were taken into the armed forces, and their leaders were given high military rank and honorific dignities; from the late fourth century and into the fifth, whole nations were allowed onto imperial soil as "treaty peoples" (*foederati*), from the fifth century as well, more or less independent (barbarian) kingdoms on Roman soil were authorized to exist and rule Roman provincials; and, in the sixth century, the emperor Justinian tried and in part succeeded in eliminating these "foreign" dominations over Romans, leaving only a few, but large, western ones to survive.

The barbarians in late antiquity did not materialize out of the blue on the Roman frontiers. They had always been there, face to face, more or less, with the imperial armies. The imperial government established the frontiers or frontier zones where it was thought advantageous and desirable to set a limit to its expansion. In most parts of the world, the often fuzzy line of demarcation set apart lands that were as fully inhabited on one side as on the other. At least initially, before development, the outer edges of imperial provinces could not have looked very different from *barbaricum*, the land of the foreigners.[5] It is incorrect to claim (as at least one distinguished historian has recently done) that "obscure" reasons brought "totally unforeseen" migrations of northerners to the frontiers—as though Rome had once looked out onto empty land and was subjected to unexpected, severe pressure by newly advancing foreigners.[6] The problem was not new or sudden; the Empire had always had large numbers of untamed foreigners on and beyond its borders.

Frontier defense, often of an active kind, was the raison d'être of the Roman army, the most expensive outlay in the imperial budget. One frontier or the other was always troublesome for the imperial government.[7] What was even more serious was that the presence of armed and potentially aggressive barbarians set strict limits on the freedom of politics among Romans. From the time the imperial regime began, the emperorship was the main issue of politics, and usurpations the most radical response. The first big crisis of this kind, in A.D. 68–69, showed how dangerous it was to external security to withdraw armies from the borders and unleash them at one another in civil war.[8] At no time was this danger more apparent than in the third century, when, for a fifty-year period, the imperial office was subject to fierce instability and competition. Encouraged by the denuding of the frontiers by civil war, the barbarians engaged in the business of invasion and contestation at many points and involving many peoples. Rome recovered with great effort from this prolonged crisis; the emperorship came into the hands of a line of military emperors culminating in Diocletian and his partners in the imperial college called the Tetrarchy. Little by little stability was restored both within and without, in part by greatly enlarging the armies and the apparatus needed to keep them supplied.[9]

The renewed Empire of late antiquity was well suited to giving barbarians a large part in its destiny. A prominent pattern in imperial history involved opening the emperorship to able men coming from farther and farther from the center. The Romans-of-Rome of the Julian-Claudian dynasty gave way to the Italian Flavians, in turn succeeded by the Spaniards Trajan and Hadrian, and later still by the North African Septimius Severus. A period of Syrians then yielded to the Thracian Maximinus, soon followed by an emperor from Arabia. The soldier emperors, just mentioned, came particularly from the Balkans. Diocletian was from Dalmatia, Galerius from Dacia, Constantine and his father from Moesia; later in the fourth century, Valentinian and Valens were from Pannonia, and the usurper Maximus from Britain. The eclipse of the imperial center and the advance of the periphery is unmistakable. When the highest office in the Empire could be occupied by Pannonians, Moesians, and Britons, it need not have been shocking or unendurable that outright foreigners in Roman service should attain positions of command and rule.[10]

Customs and practices of imperial government had changed in ways that facilitated such an evolution. In the early Empire, the typical provincial governor served both as the effective commander of its military garrison and as the chief magistrate and administrator of the province; he needed both military and civil training. The ruling classes pursued a career pattern such that someone specializing in civil magistracies nevertheless engaged in stints of serious military service, and a military specialist-in-training alternated periods in civilian offices with his longer appointments with troops. This versatility did not endure. In the third-century plague of usurpations, it seemed essential to promote strictly military specialists and (as a check on usurpations) to hold the more civilian, genteel, and aristocratic members of society away from military appointments. The eventual result was that the later Empire practiced a division of civilian and military careers, making it possible, among other things, for persons without a liberal education, and possibly without any letters at all, to assume military commands.[11] Practical training on the job mattered most for lofty generalships; military paperwork could be left to notaries and accountants. Under the circumstances, it made very little difference whether high commands went to persons born outside rather than inside the borders of the Empire; both were likely to be alien to civilian graces and accomplishments.

A parallel evolution affected the composition of the imperial army. This was a paid, long-service professional force in which noncitizen provincials in the auxiliary regiments had always complemented the legions of Roman citizens.[12] The tendency of recruiting sergeants had been, or at least was reputed to be, to seek out manpower from the country rather than from cities, and from the more remote, less favored parts of the countryside rather than from well-tilled farmsteads. The cruder the recruit's background, the more toughened and better suited he was likely to be for military life. The stories told of the backwoods Thracian who became the emperor Maximinus (235–38) suggests the strong-man ideal sought for in soldiers.[13] The farther from the Mediterranean, the closer to the northern frontier, the better the ground for recruit hunting. It marked a significant moment in the composition of the imperial forces when the Praetorian Guard, once composed of Italians and citizens of the most Romanized provinces, was exchanged for Danubians from the frontier legions (ca. 193).[14] A comparable stage in the evolution of recruitment was attained when, under Constantine, outright barbarians were mustered into the palatine and comitatensian regiments, the highest quality units of the army.[15] The penetration of barbarians into such units was soon accompanied by the emergence of barbarians in the Roman high command.

Although the traditional Roman nobility was roughly handled in the internal political turmoil of the third and early fourth century, the late Empire regained an influential senatorial aristocracy, some of whose members cultivated the refined pursuits, such as letters, that traditionally belonged to this class.[16] But, alongside the noble civilians, and closer than they to real power, the later Empire had something new, namely, a separate military aristocracy, with its own freemasonry, paths of advancement, and intermarriage.[17] Sons of generals were enrolled at an early age in the imperial guard, the nursery of field rank officers.[18] At moments when imperial dynasties died out, as that of Constantine in 363, new emperors were drawn from this military charmed circle. What is more, high-born barbarians, possibly offensive to civilian notables, were welcomed without hesitation into the ranks and marriage alliances of the Roman military aristocracy.

The emergence of barbarians at the highest levels of Roman leadership was not a casual or exceptional occurrence. The prominence of Frankish generals under the successors of Valentianian I (†375) was highlighted by the second ordinary consulate of Merobaudes in 383, a distinction normally reserved only for emperors. The name-giving consuls for 384 and 385 were also Franks.[19] The emperor Theodosius married his favorite niece Serena to Stilicho, Roman-born son of a Vandal officer in Roman service; Theodosius made the same Stilicho guardian of his minor son, Honorius, and thus regent for at least the West when Theodosius died. Theodosius's other son, Arcadius, married the daughter of a Frankish general and fathered the quarter-Frankish son who, in 408, became the emperor Theodosius II. The emperor Honorius's half sister married the Gothic leader Athaulf. Another imperial daughter married the son of the fearsome Geiseric, king of the Vandals, with the result that a grandson of Valentinian III eventually came to the Vandal throne. No less a barbarian than Attila took seriously the offer of marriage made to him by the wayward sister of Valentinian III. The Hun Edeco had been a trusted henchman of Attila; after the latter's death, one of Edeco's sons acquired high military rank in East Rome while the other, Odoacer, did even better in the West.[20] There was nothing "ideological" about these family relationships: leaders recognized one another for what they or their fathers were. These family solidarities and matrimonial maneuvers in the confraternity of fighting men show how far from repulsive barbarians were in the late Roman world. Christian bishops and civilian aristocrats, however refined, cultivated high-placed soldiers of whatever origin, well aware that they had power and were better courted than scorned.[21]

Instinctive Greco-Roman hostility to barbarians coexisted with a long and proud Roman tradition of openness to outsiders. Rome at its mythical birth in the 700s B.C. had been a melting pot, a conglomerate of renegades who had obtained wives by theft; so the legend went. One of the themes of Roman history, and historical writing, involved a struggle in which the plebeians demanded rights and acceptance from the patricians. Later, magistracies were gradually opened to New Men, and the Roman franchise was successively extended beyond the City to the Italian allies and, later still, to conquered provinces, such as Gaul (and, eventually, of course, to the entire Empire).[22] The views of Roman authors about barbarians can be strung together into a tapestry of insults and derogation. Hostility to barbarians was built into the language; almost by definition, barbarians stood for what imperial citizens shunned. But literature does not directly mirror everyday reality. Sheer aversion was not a practical attitude in an age of rapid social and cultural change. The admission of élite barbarians into the Roman military élite was an established fact in the third century and only increased as time went on.

The opening chapter of my *Barbarians and Romans* indicated how, in the usual modern narratives of the Migration Age, the account of how the northern barbarians became ostensibly superior to the Romans seemed out of balance with the actual results. An explosive tale of increasing barbarian power contrasted with the modest inroads they made in the Roman world; most barbarian peoples, in fact, were snuffed out and did not survive into the Middle Ages.[23] I ended with a capsule description of what, in contrast to onrushing barbarians, I thought was really going on: "The attractive power of the empire, typified by the government's welcome of foreign military élites, had a more certain role than any impulse from the barbarian side in establishing foreign dominations on provincial soil. When set in a fourth-century perspective, what we call the Fall of the Western Empire was an imaginative experiment that got a little out of hand."[24]

Brash lines of this sort attract unwelcome attention, and this one did. Is any part of my comment worth retaining? I am tempted to conclude, in retrospect, that I was not crazy enough: the attractive power of the Empire was not experimental (it was an irreversible step), and its results were controlled and positive, not a process that got out of hand. If, instead of looking ahead from the fourth century, one looks back from the late sixth century, it is hard to avoid concluding—regardless of the ambitions and successes of Justinian in claiming the total imperial inheritance for Constantinople—that the West experienced an effective *translatio imperii* (transfer of empire) to barbarian leadership, not a set of lamentable usurpations by greedy and destructive aliens.

Voicing such an idea is not the same thing as establishing that it fits the facts. Can one show that, at some point, western Romans rallied to their barbarian rulers, threw themselves (figuratively) into their arms, and were thoroughly reconciled to their existence? There are obtrusive signs in the age of Justinian suggesting that this was *not* the case. Even though the Vandals in North Africa had settled comfortably into the Roman way of life from 439 on, and even, on occasion, found a taste for Latin verse, they had not gained the love and allegiance of their subjects. When the army of Belisarius came in 533–34 the Afro-Romans greeted the imperial forces as liberators.[25] The case of Italy under the Goths is even more significant because the Goths governed Italy well or at least creditably; the peninsula enjoyed much greater security and tranquility under Odoacer and Theoderic than it had under its last Roman emperors. Even so— and this made Goths understandably bitter—Italians were happier with the newcomers from Constantinople (who maltreated them) than with the Gothic incumbents.[26] Procopius's testimony makes us draw these conclusions about North Africa and Italy, and he is persuasive enough to prevent our venturing to contradict him.

There were other western lands, though, places farther removed from the eastern Mediterranean and out of Procopius's sight. The contemporary voice of Gildas the Briton (ca. A.D. 540), as remote a spokesman as one might hope to have, is a valuable complement. Gildas no longer had any expectation that Britain would be rescued by Rome. So convinced was he of Britain's isolation that, in his account, he conjured up and identified himself with pre-Roman Britain (of which, after about five hundred years, he could have had no personal knowledge). The Romans are regarded as having been only an interlude, however distinguished, in British history.[27] But this vision of the past by no means reconciled Gildas to the barbarians who, at present, were occupying and preying upon his land; banish the thought that the mandate of heaven should have fallen upon these wild beasts! Procopius and Gildas, very different witnesses, force us to conclude that any thought of a wholesale rallying by western "Romans" to their "foreign" rulers is illusory. A rapprochement and *translatio imperii*, if there was one, did not take this form.

A less abstract and more promising approach to reconciliation and amalgamation is suggested by the illuminating research of Alexander Demandt into the military aristocracy of the later Roman Empire and the personal and family connections among the prominent personalities of the age. "In the genealogy of the ruling class," Demandt shows with the support of genealogical charts, "there was an abrupt break in the third century A.D., but no break in the Völkerwanderung, no break during the end of the Roman Empire, no break in the dark seventh century. From the time of Diocletian on we have continuity in the ruling families into the Middle Ages and further on."[28] In this uninterrupted military aristocracy whose power was made secure in Diocletian's Tetrarchy and in the ruling figures descending stemmatically from it, there was no barrier between Roman and barbarian, only a community or "family" of wielders of power. Nineteen family connections carry back from Charlemagne (†814) to Theodosius I

(†395). Another eight steps and we reach Diocletian, but no farther: the sharp transition from one set of leaders to another, professionally military and unrefined, took place in the Roman third century. From then onward "in the military and political upper class nearly everybody is related to everybody." This conglomerate of strong men and women, some imperial and royal, some not, passed legitimacy among themselves and, in a very personal and unsystematic way, controlled and moderated the advent of non-Romans and Romans alike as rulers of the Roman inheritance. "Political power in all centuries," Demandt comments, "was based to a great extent on the simple fact of renown, and if you belong to a famous family, you have some popular credit."[29]

Diocletian's Tetrarchy was an artistic institutional construction, an abstract system by which a succession of chosen, able men was meant to step up the ladder into each other's shoes as death or retirement claimed the seniors. The "system" was paralleled by a more personal set of dynastic interconnections, by which blood relationships reinforced (to the extent that they could) the abstract chain of succession. The architectural model blew away quickly in the face of human motives; where the "system" said there should be two Augusti, there soon were six and, not very long after that, only one, Constantine the Great.[30] Yet the family network endured, sheltered from the frailty of more sophisticated mechanisms. The Tetrarchy, though proved vain, was not immediately forgotten. Constantine, in designing his own succession, introduced the refinement of making room for cousins alongside his sons in sharing rule of the Empire. The army decided otherwise when he died: the collaterals were purged, and the Empire went to Constantine's sons exclusively (337).[31] Narrow dynasticism won out, and it won again when Valentinian, chosen on the strength of his late father's military renown, insisted on elevating his brother Valens to his side and dividing the empire with him (364). "[F]rom antiquity to the *medium aevum*," Demandt comments, "[there was] a shifting from institutional concepts to personal concepts of political thinking."[32]

A clear sign of the personalization of late Roman politics is the prominence of murders in the fifth century; these were the "ministerial crises" of the day. The overthrow and beheading of Stilicho (408) was still garbed in official niceties, but accompanied by the extralegal massacre of his satellites. The generals Boniface and Aetius fought it out man to man for supremacy in the Western Empire, with the latter prevailing over his rival (and gaining a wife) when Boniface died of his wounds (432). Aetius, at the height of his power, was slain "in the palace," a locale beyond investigation (454). His death was avenged by the killing of the emperor Valentinian III (455). A rival of the strongman Ricimer, Marcellinus, was assassinated in Sicily (468), in connection with a failed war that, in the East, sealed the fate of Aspar, the long-lived strongman of

Constantinople (471). To avoid bloodshed, the dethroned usurper Basiliscus and his family were thrown in a pit and left to the mercy of nature (476). Theoderic the Ostrogoth personally killed two rivals: Recitach, son of Theoderic Strabo (484), and Odoacer (493). The usurper Vitalian was a thorn in the side of the emperor Anastasius; honored at the accession of Justin I, he soon met his death "in the palace" (520).[33] These events and others like them were not unprecedented in Roman history, but were overshadowed then by decorous institutions; their persistence in the political life of late antiquity underscores the importance of individuals and alliances among them.

The results of "personal concepts" often defied reason, as when the incapable sons of Theodosius I proved amazingly secure on their thrones, while experienced, able men blazed briefly and were doomed. Fathers produced unworthy heirs, marriages disappointed, women assumed masculine roles: but such familial vicissitudes, for all their too-human shortcomings, were still more stable and reliable than abstract chains of command. If family connections did not succeed at first, perhaps they would the second and third times; natural causes, such as early death or sterility, intervened as often as human volition. In Demandt's words, "private connections and personal factors, such as weddings and relationship, gained importance." Descent from famous fathers or uncles and marriages into qualified families counted for more than the political, institutional, and ideological abstractions that today's historians (myself included) instinctively look for. "The internationality of the breaking [Roman] empire was upheld in the leading families."[34]

The military aristocracy proceeding from the third-century Roman army did not pay attention to ethnicity. Contrary to the recent allegation that, in the late fourth century, "ethnicity began to return to the power struggles within the Roman world," the practices of the political leadership ensured that, in a world full of problems, ethnicity was not one of them.[35] Membership in the aristocracy was just as open to Persians and Armenians, Goths and Huns, from outside the Empire as it was to backwoods Moesians, Britons, and Isaurians from within. Ethnic snobbery was relegated to the musings of senators and literati. The criterion for admission was not ethnic but established admissibility, determined by one's rank and connections in one's homeland. The credentials of lofty Franks and Huns, their credit among their countrymen, were accorded face value in the Empire. At one level or another, achievements might matter, too.

A salient example of the priority of family ties over official position involves the history of the Visigoths. When Alaric made the distinguished senator Attalus emperor as a rival to Honorius, he gained nothing but trouble for the Goths; but when Athaulf married Honorius's consenting half sister, Galla Placidia, he elevated the Visigothic leadership into the extended ruling "family" of the Empire.

The common purpose of the military aristocracy was practical, not ideological; the goal was to rule and wield power and retain these privileges for one's blood and in-law relatives. The "family" was hardly egalitarian, but it was indifferent to ethnicity and open to talent, especially martial valor. Upstarts, or imperial usurpers, were not repugnant in principle, since they had become part of the power structure, however briefly; their relatives became interesting persons, not marked for elimination.[36] Engagements that did not result in marriage could still have importance. Being qualified and being invited in, regardless of "nationality," mattered more than any particular course of conduct.

The military aristocracy was not an artificial system; the institutional foundations it rested on were private and common to all. These were its strength. It was a collection of persons, events, or happenings projected into an uncertain future. The Catholic daughter of the Frankish king Childebert I married "a gentleman of Kent," the pagan son and heir of King Eormanric. The outcome of this union was unusually positive: the bride's chaplain was soon joined by an entire delegation of Roman monks, sent by the pope. The marriage so unassumingly reported by Gregory of Tours was the first step in the religious conversion of the lost provinces of Britain and their recapture for the Mediterranean world.[37] A second example is less heartening. Some years after the Kentish marriage, another Catholic daughter of a Frankish king left home; herself half Visigothic, she went to Arian Spain and married one of the king's sons. Asked to convert to the local form of Christianity, she refused and was maltreated by her stepmother-in-law (who was also her maternal grandmother). The young couple was sent to cool off away from court, and the husband rebelled against his father, with fatal results. His widow and infant fell into Byzantine hands and were taken to Constantinople.[38] The intertwining of family connections with politics and religion was not a recipe for spontaneous harmony or for automatic success for one or another course of action. But it was a guarantee that relations existed, that the larger family—the international association of power wielders—carried on and sometimes grew and expanded at a human level.[39] "In the politico-military upper layer from late antiquity to the early Middle Ages there exists a social continuity."[40] Real pains were taken to guarantee at least that degree of endurance, and much hinged on it.

The development of the late Roman military aristocracy that took in men and women of all nationalities can be examined from the Tetrarchy onward, and it can also be glimpsed retrospectively from the Middle Ages. Matthew Innes has recently decried a widespread belief that "the new leaders of the post-Roman west brought with them a set of common ['Germanic'] cultural traits"; that belief, he adds, "effectively rests on the identification of a vast array of practices typical of the early medieval period with a postulated 'Germanic warrior culture' brought by the incomers."[41] Demandt's military aristocracy allows this "Germanic" postulate to be outgrown. The military aristocracy, with its culture, was neither specifically Roman nor specifically Gothic, Frankish, or "Germanic" but a compound of ruling élites connecting with each other; "in the west the superior officers, the imperial dynasty and the barbarian kings formed a politico-military leadership layer by means of the continual marriage relations of a small-meshed network."[42] The late antique political leadership, open without restriction (though not indiscriminately) to well-connected warriors of all peoples and all religions, supersedes the postulate of a "*Germanic* warrior culture." If Etzel the Hun, Dietrich the Goth, and Etzius the Roman (Attila, Theoderic, and Aetius) meet as brothers in medieval poetry, it is because they had already been "family" in the ethnically undifferentiated military aristocracy of the late Roman world.[43]

As noted earlier, Roman provincials did not rally to Vandals, Goths, or Saxons; no *translatio imperii* could be said to take that form in the lands in question and probably not elsewhere. Constitutional continuity is also out of the question. The integrity of Roman imperial rule did not pass on either in the fragmented West or in the drastically attenuated East. But in both East and West the common heritage of command and leadership was conveyed to and retained by interconnections within an extended "family" of ruling persons and dynasties embodying a certain kind of international order, a precarious successor to the *pax Romana*.

A Medley of Barbarian Peoples

Introduction

The barbarians in the age of Rome's fall were not Germans even though they have long been called so. None of them in late antiquity, either as individuals or as groups, ever appealed to this name as though it were theirs. They did not imagine that the words coming out of their mouths were variants of a common Germanic tongue or that the customs they practiced proceeded from a common Germanic civilization. Lombards, Franks, Goths, and all the others did not studiously pore over Tacitus's *Germania* and take care that their individual and collective behavior should conform to the package of mores described by the Roman ethnographer. German *Altertumskunde* and Tacitus's *Germania* are among the things we have to unlearn if we wish to come to terms with the encounter of Rome and Christianity with the barbarians of late antiquity. Instead of appealing to ethnosociological abstractions and ostensibly institutional connections, we would do well to pay attention to dynasties and family relationships among the leading elements of society, regardless of nationality, and most of all strive to maintain a tight relationship between what we say and the sources on which it is based.

There is no "prototypical" barbarian people. Neither the Huns nor the Goths nor any other is "representative." No special group of peoples, not even those whom we lump together as "Germanic," was singled out by divine providence as its special favorite in the course of events. The northern sector of the Roman frontier contained quite a few peoples that cannot be labeled "Germanic" and nevertheless attracted contemporary attention. The Romano-Britons, stripped of their Roman defenders, considered the Irish and Picts to be their major enemies and eventually imported Saxons from the Continent as military auxiliaries against them. The Picts were still a military menace on the eve of the age of Bede.[44] Elsewhere, ten Roman emperors fought so hard and often against the Sarmatians that they called themselves "Sarmaticus" in honor of their victories; the Sarmatians were a nomadic people classified by us as "Iranian."[45] Aurelian, the Tetrarchs, and Constantine battled the Carpi so strenuously that they called themselves "Carpicus" in honor of their victories; the Carpi were Dacians outside Dacia.[46] The Moors of North Africa had been a menace to the Roman province and were an even greater one to the Vandals. The modern German masters of Migration Age history have convinced themselves and us that whatever relations involved non-Germans were side shows, incidental to the main act.[47] Yet the ostensible "main acts" involving Goths, Vandals, and Lombards may be subsidiary to aggressive impulses proceeding from nomadic Alans, Huns, and Avars.[48] The scanty information available to us does not permit certainties.

Books about barbarians in late antiquity often examine individual peoples one by one. Tacitus included something of this sort in part two of the *Germania*; so did Beatus Rhenanus, more elaborately, in his 1531 treatise on the Germans. Karl Zeuss rejuvenated the exercise in a famous work called *Die Deutschen und die Nachbarstämme* (The Germans and the Neighboring Peoples).[49] Surveys of this sort are prevalent in accounts of the "Migration Age." The already mentioned standard works of Schmidt, Bury, Musset, and Demougeot all take this course, as does the recent *Die Völkerwanderung: Eroberung und Integration* by Walter Pohl.[50] These accounts trace each people in chronological order from an "original homeland" through its "migrations" down to an outcome—for some, stable settlement; for others (more numerous) annihilation.

Although my "medley" falls within this tradition, its purpose is not to provide comprehensive coverage of all possible peoples over as long as possible a span of time, but to offer a new model of "tribe-by-tribe" survey and to set an example for such presentations. I confine myself here to a selection of ostensibly minor—certainly less written about—peoples, and I deliberately avoid piling up conjectures about their histories. I scorn all attempts to spotlight homelands and trace ancient routes of "advance." The reasons for my reticence are simple: these exercises in probing the voiceless past have amply proved themselves to be irrelevant to what happened to the barbarians and Rome in late antiquity, and they have long deceived the curious with nonexistent shades of continuity, especially institutional continuity out of Tacitus into the Western Middle Ages.[51] These explorations of the unknown and the unknowable unknown involve even more futile hypotheses and arbitrary inventions than have to be resorted to, regrettably, in sorting out ill-documented parts of the core Migration Age.[52] Some of the seven peoples I deal with had occasion to move over short or long distances in historical time. If they did, it was for reasons known to themselves (rarely to us); they were not prompted by an inner urge to migrate. None of them was "migratory." If that name is applied to any of them, it is not by their doing but as a result of modern scholarly reconstructions and speculations dating to the sixteenth century and still actively engaged in today. These distortions about the prehistory of northern barbarians had their time and place; they are a chapter in Europeans' efforts to understand their past. A curtain needs now to be drawn over these fancies. My main concern is to foreground and make what I can of the evidence there is, here understood (without apologies) as written evidence. With the fourth century as base line, I try to determine how matters stood at the onset of the core Migration Age and what may be fairly said from then on.

Gepids

Burdened with a name that seems to echo the Latin word for "feet," *pedes*, the Gepids early fell into the clutches of etymologists and have not yet escaped from them. Isidore of Seville explained: "The Gepids go into battle on foot rather than mounted, and are named after this fact."[53] Jordanes tried a different approach: "One of the three ships [bringing the Goths from Scandza to the continent] proved to be slower than the others . . . and thus it is said to have given the tribe their name, for in their language . . . *gepanta* means something slow and stolid. . . . I do not believe this is very far wrong, for they are slow of thought and too sluggish for quick movements of their bodies."[54] In Greek, -*pedes* could be construed as -*paides*, turning the Gepids into the *Gétipaides*, or "children of the Goths."[55]

The last idea—that the Gepids were offshoots or close relatives of the Goths—is deeply rooted in current scholarship. None of the evidence is reliable. Once one ceases to nurse the illusion that Jordanes embodies "Gothic tradition," it turns out that all the witnesses to Gepid family relationships are Byzantines availing themselves of the learned ethnology of the day. Procopius announces, in the prologue to the *Vandal War*: "There were many Gothic nations in earlier times, just as also at the present, but the greatest and most important of all are the Goths, Vandals, Visigoths, and Gepaedes. . . . [I]t seems to me, they all came originally from one tribe. . . . This people used to dwell about the Ister [= Danube] from of old. Later on the Gepaedes got possession of the country about Singidunum and Sirmium, on both sides of the Ister River, where they have remained even down to my time."[56] Procopius was right about where the Gepids currently held sway; this was a weighty matter, also emphasized by Jordanes. The account of their ancestry was more fanciful. The Gepids were as Gothic as were the Vandals, which is to say not Gothic at all. Greek ethnographic science, which long ago had conceived of Celtic and Scythian peoples, now devised the generic concept of "many Gothic nations," sharing the same language, white bodies, blond hair, and Arian form of Christianity. Procopius's fusion of the Danubian peoples facing the Eastern Empire does not by itself authenticate ethnic filiations.[57]

Until the days of Attila in the mid-fifth century, the Gepids were minor players in late Roman history. Their settlement areas, wherever they were, were remote enough from the imperial frontier for them not to appear in the Verona List or in the histories of Ammianus or Orosius. Early references occur here and there, just enough to assure us that Gepids existed at least in the third century, sometimes linked with the Vandals, and hovered in the background of the encounters of barbarians and Romans on the lower Danube.[58]

Our main informants on the Gepids—Jordanes and Procopius—both wrote after 550, less than twenty years before the Gepids were overwhelmed and destroyed by a combined onslaught of Lombards and Avars, with the Romans quietly looking on. Only Jordanes was concerned with the Gepid past, including incidents from legendary times. To the migration story summarized above, he added an account of the Gepids' living somewhere on the Vistula under a king named Fastida, who led them to a great victory over the Burgundians. Fastida then provoked Ostrogotha, king of the not-yet-separated Ostrogoths and Visigoths; he threatened war unless the Gepids were given better land to live on than they had. A bloody battle took place between adversaries evenly matched owing to their kinship. The Goths prevailed, and Fastida retreated duly humbled.[59]

Jordanes is intent on impressing the common origin of the Gepids and Goths on his readers. The subject comes up twice again; in one case, the Visigoths spread the poison of Arianism to their kinsmen, the Ostrogoths and Gepids; in the other, Attila is confident that his Ostrogothic and Gepid auxiliaries will fight their kinsmen, the Visigoths.[60] There is an ominous quality to this emphasis on family ties. By 551, two of Procopius's "Gothic peoples" had been suppressed by Justinian and a third was teetering on the edge of extinction; the turn of the fourth, the Gepids, could not be far distant, and it wasn't.[61]

The Gepids, under a king named Ardaric, break into the light of history in the days of Attila and the Huns, first, as Attila's leading and very numerous auxiliaries and, after his death, as the people who led Attila's subjects in revolt against his sons' plan to share them among themselves as though they were slaves (ca. A.D. 453). Jordanes's account insinuates Valamer and his Goths as the equals of Ardaric and the Gepids in the trust Attila reposed in them and the weight they had in his counsels. Although this effort to even the ethnic scales can be only doubted and not discredited, scattered evidence bracketing the Gepids with the Huns (and even calling Attila a Gepid) suggests that Ardaric and his followers were at the forefront of the agrarian peoples assisting Attila in the exploits of the Huns.[62] The Gepids' prominence in Attila's kingdom and in the revolt against his sons was where, if anywhere, they made their martial reputation and acquired the capital of esteem that sustained their kingdom for more than a century.

Like Procopius, Jordanes is at pains to inform his readers where the Gepids lived in the mid-sixth century; as many as four paragraphs take an interest in their geographical localization, including the comment that old (Roman) Dacia beyond the Danube was now "Gepidia."[63] Other than their whereabouts we learn only that, after Ardaric's successful revolt and the victorious battle of the Gepids and their allies against the sons of Attila, the Gepids took possession of what had been Attila's heartland in the Hungarian plain and Tisza valley. They made a peace treaty with Constantinople and received annual good-will gifts, "customary offerings from the Roman emperor" that continued *usque nunc,* "until today," that is, the 550s.[64]

The possession of a territory in *barbaricum,* even with annual gifts from Constantinople, was a passport to insignificance.[65] After Ardaric's successful revolt (ca. 453), there is no trace of Gepid political development, and only a scattering of kings are known. Virtually nothing is heard of the Gepids until the "Valamer-Goths" evacuated Pannonia (473), soon after which the Gepids seized the strategic Roman city of Sirmium, athwart the land route from Constantinople to Rome. The seizure could not ingratiate them with the East Roman emperor, but the city with its Romanized surroundings became their capital and gave them political importance. Sirmium was where the Gepids were, with a resident king, in 488, when Theoderic led the Ostrogoths out of the Balkans on the way to contest Odoacer's rule of Italy. Probably in league with Odoacer, the Gepid king Thraustila opposed the Gothic advance and was beaten and killed in a hard-fought battle.[66]

The outcome shook the Gepids. Thraustila's son, Thrasaric, regained control of Sirmium but possibly under Ostrogothic overlordship, and the Tisza Gepids to the north acquired a king of their own. An attempt to unite these branches gave the now-great Theoderic a pretext for ousting Gepid rule (but not all Gepids) from Sirmium and adding this stronghold to his Italian kingdom, much to the displeasure of East Rome (504). The Gepids were by no means reconciled to the permanence of this loss, nor was Constantinople. Sirmium was a key position in the architecture of the Roman world.[67] An early Gepid attempt to exploit Gothic weakness to regain Sirmium failed (530), but the recapture succeeded as soon as the Goths of Italy were suitably distracted by Belisarius's campaign of 535. Justinian's Italian campaign even emboldened the Gepids into sending raids southward into Illyricum. They met a Roman army there in 539 and killed its general. The long friendship between Constantinople and the Gepids was strained.[68]

Several decades before these developments, the Gepids had acquired the Lombards as new western neighbors. Relations between them had been cordial as long as the Herules had stood between them as a common object of hostility; but ca. 508 the Lombards destroyed the Herules, sent them flying to various protectors, and acquired their territory. Nevertheless, a marked change in Lombard-Gepid relations came about only after Justinian decided to cultivate the Lombards, invited them into Noricum and Pannonia, and gave them annual gifts (546–47). In slowly evolving three-way dealings, the Lombards, who contributed many thousand troops to Justinian's decisive campaign against Totila, became firm allies of Constantinople and, in 552, won a major victory over the Gepids, including the killing of the king's son and a great loss of Gepid lives.[69]

The end of the Gepids occurred fifteen years later. How it came about is inadequately documented; our informants personalize the events by means of a fierce enmity between the Lombard king, Alboin, and the Gepid Cunimund, involving the latter's daughter.[70] They pay too little attention to new Danubian complications, notably the now prominent Slavs and especially the advent of the pony-riding, Hun-like, and very enterprising Avars. In 566 King Cunimund obtained East Roman support against a Lombard attack by promising to cede Sirmium—a promise not carried out.[71] The next year the Lombards consented to all the Avars' harsh conditions for an offensive alliance; Constantinople stood aside owing to the Gepids' retention of Sirmium; and the campaign that "terminated" the Gepids took place. Cunimund was killed, perhaps by Alboin in person; some defeated Gepids joined Alboin in going to Italy; most of the survivors became subjects of the Avars; a few, including the keeper of the Gepid treasure, were welcomed into East Roman territory; and Sirmium fell into Constantinopolitan hands for a few years until the Avars seized it.[72] As often in Byzantine experience, the devil one knew and scorned proved much less fearsome than his successor.

Long remote from the Roman border, the Gepids never held more than a bridgehead of Roman territory. It was a decisive handicap. For all the Gepids' being *foederati*, they rarely supplied contingents to Roman armies. As late as 551, only 400 joined Narses's great army for the final conquest of Italy, as compared to the thousands of troops furnished by the Herules and Lombards. They also appear to have failed to inject themselves into the military aristocracy of the age. The only Gepid woman we hear of is Cunimund's daughter, and she only acquired a name long after the incidents that made her famous. The Gepids' collective high point, never again equaled, was as auxiliaries to the Huns—or so at least it appears in the pages of our ill-disposed Byzantine informants. Merely to occupy the Carpathian basin as subsidized friends of the Roman people was not a formula for political development and endurance.

Sciri

The war of Theoderic the Ostrogoth for control of Roman Italy dragged on for four years (489–93). So as to end it, Theoderic entered into a power-sharing compromise with the incumbent ruler, Odoacer. Soon after, Theoderic personally murdered his partner and had all his followers put to death. Odoacer had headed the West Roman government without contestation for thirteen years; with him the last known Scirian was overthrown. At least he fell to his doom from an almost imperial perch.[73]

The exceptionally long trail leading the Sciri to this eye-catching extinction is narrow and studded with catastrophes.[74] I set out the evidence in point form to draw attention to the long time intervals between the individual items. Much more is heard about annihilations of the Sciri than about their existing anywhere. There is no way to shape these fragments into a "Sciri story."

1. An inscription at Olbia (a Greek colony situated east of present day Odessa and west of the Crimea) commemorates an attack by Sciri leagued with Galatians toward 220 B.C.[75]
2. For about five hundred years, the Sciri leave no trace in our sources except a vague mention in Pliny's *Natural History*.[76]
3. Toward A.D. 300, the Verona List of barbarian peoples adjoining the Roman Empire locates the Sciri between the Sarmatians to the west and the Carpi to the east. The placement suggests that the Sciri lived in the lower Danube valley.[77]

4. Zosimus, *Historia nova* 4.34.6 (probably citing Eunapius), reports an attack south of the Danube in 381 by the Sciri accompanied by the Carpodaces (that is, Carpi) and with a few Huns among them. The invaders were forced back north of the Danube by the troops of the emperor Theodosius.[78]

5. CTh 5.6.3 (409): "We [the emperors] have subjected to our rule the barbarian nation of the Scyri, having routed the very large forces of Huns to which they had joined themselves." The Sciri were part of the luckless invasion by the Hunnic leader, Uldin, who lost his life.[79] Captured by the Romans, they were to be turned into farmers (not enslaved) and kept away from the Balkans. These captured Sciri were evidently only a fraction of the Scirian people.

6. Sidonius, *Carmina* 7.322, lists the Sciri among the peoples accompanying the Huns of Attila in the great invasion of Gaul in 451.[80]

7. Jordanes, *Getica* 265, states that, when Attila's domination broke up, the East Roman government gave the Sciri and two other small peoples settlements in Scythia Minor and Lower Moesia—far downstream in the Danube valley.[81]

8. Jordanes, *Getica* 275–76, relates a crushing Scirian defeat. Incited by Hunimund, king of the Danube Sueves, the Sciri broke with the Goths of Valamer and attacked them. Valamer was killed but the Goths exacted a severe revenge: "The Goths fought in such wise that there remained of all the race of the Sciri only a few who bore the name, and they with disgrace. Thus were all destroyed."[82]

9. Priscus, fragment 45 (Blockley): The Scirian survivors and the Goths both appealed for help to the East Roman government. The military strongman, Aspar, urged neutrality, but the emperor Leo ordered his general of Illyricum to help the Sciri.[83]

10. Jordanes, *Getica* 277–79: the Sciri with their *primates* Edica and Hunuulf joined the Suevic king Hunimund in a coalition against the Goths; they fought a great battle in which the Goths prevailed with great slaughter (469).[84]

11. Priscus, fragment 64 (Blockley): In fighting with the emperor Anthemius in Rome (470), the patrician Ricimer was supported by "Odovacer, a man of the tribe called the Sciri, whose father was Edeco and whose brother was Onulf [= Hunuulf], the bodyguard and the murderer of Harmatius."[85]

12. Procopius, *Wars* 5.1.3, a short time before 476, the Romans "induced the Sciri and Alani and certain other Gothic nations" to enter into alliance with them. "Gothic" is Procopius's generic term for the barbarians bordering Roman territory along the lower Danube.[86]

13. Jordanes, *Romana* 344–46 and *Getica* 242; *Excerpta Valesiana*, pars posterior, 37–38: Odoacer took power in Italy with a (Roman) army composed of Sciri, Herules, and other peoples.[87]

* * *

In view of the early date of the Greek inscription and its reference to Galatians, the residents of Olbia are very likely to have classed the Sciri as "Celts." Five centuries later, when the Sciri are encountered not very far from where they had been when annoying Olbia, it hardly matters what ethnic conglomerate they had belonged to so long before. The most suitable way to describe them now is geographically, as lower Danubians. The Verona List flanks them with Sarmatians, an Iranian steppe people, and with Carpi (Carpodaces), the term used for Dacians outside Dacia (in our classification, a Thracian people). In a half millennium, much intermarriage is likely to have taken place. We have no idea how the name survived. There is no trace of a Scirian tradition.

We are so far from hearing of Scirian kings that the only "leading men" found mentioned by name in their connection are Edeco (Edica), a Hun married to a Scirian, and his sons Hunuulf and Odoacer. The hints that Odoacer led troops in Gaul before going to Italy are contestable.[88]

There is no evidence for the recruitment of Sciri into the Roman army until the days of Odoacer. The Sciri are conspicuous for their poor choice of allies or, alternatively, for being able to survive disaster in war. If they may be said to have a history at all, its most noticeable trait is that their final downfall as a people coincides with the prominence of two half-Scirians, sons of a famous father, in the military aristocracy of the Roman Empire.

Herules

The Herules exist for scholars as a nest of intractable, probably insoluble but fascinating problems. There was, for a time, at least one Herule principality on the Danube, with a possible other, unrelated, misty one on the lower Rhine or thereabouts; but neither was closely enough observed for anything to be known about its corporate life.[89] The Danubian one stands out most vividly at the moment when it was destroyed by the Lombards, its erstwhile clients (ca. A.D. 508). This prominent defeat notwithstanding, the Herules were mostly fighting men, hundreds upon hundreds of them, turning up in all theaters of war, the most reliable source of East Roman foreign recruits in the sixth century. According to Jordanes, they were the finest light infantry in the world.[90]

Procopius does not group the Herules among the "Gothic peoples," and the signs that they were "Germanic" rather than something else are equivocal.[91]

The main scholarly problem they pose is whether "Herule" refers to one people, possibly in two branches, or to two, possibly altogether distinct from each other. The evidence divides rather clearly into western and eastern clumps, the infantry just referred to being emphatically eastern. But this division, which the older literature took for granted, has now been disputed, though inconclusively. The hypothesis of unrelated western and eastern Herules would be easier to entertain if it were not for the long digression in which Procopius describes some defeated Herules traveling from the Danube to the north and eventually settling near the Gauti in Thule (his name for Scandinavia). Procopius's account continues: the Thule Herules were sought out by a delegation of their brethren from the south; the emissaries needed someone of royal blood to rule over the southerners and duly brought back a candidate, to whom they rallied. This arresting but unverifiable narrative is perplexing, especially if one mistrusts Procopius as an ethnographer. Does his account bear on the question of the eastern and (north)western Herules? Modern German teaching used to be firm that the Herules were one trunk with two branches, and that the Danubians who trekked north to Thule were simply "returning" to the common homeland. Good sense has prevailed, however, and yielded to the observation that Procopius says nothing of the kind: his Herules had "ancestral" mid-Danubian homelands, and (as far as we may tell) those who went north proceeded into terra incognita.[92]

A rather clearly circumscribed body of evidence testifies to the existence of Herules somewhere in reach of the North Sea coast. They attacked Gaul in the third century and, soon after, furnished the Roman army a regiment of "Eruli," usually paired with one of "Batavi" (from modern Holland); the two regiments are often mentioned by Ammianus as though they were crack troops.[93] The Herules who twice attacked the northern coast of Spain in the 450s presumably came from the westerners, and so did the one Herule present at the court of the Visigothic king Euric in about 475.[94] The two letters of Theoderic the Ostrogoth to an unnamed king of the Herules (early 500s) were also directed to the northwest; the first is a circular sent also to the Warni and Thuringians in the hope that all three kings would by their pressure discourage the Frank, Clovis, from attacking the Visigoths.[95] Jordanes's account of "Scandza," early in the *Getica*, reports that the Herules, who claimed to be the tallest people of the region, had been driven from their homes by the Dani.[96] These western Herules presumably disappeared by blending into another people, such as the Saxons. While the scraps of information fall short of bringing them to life, they are difficult to amalgamate with the somewhat more abundant information about the eastern ones.

Procopius mentions the (eastern) Herules often and, as already noted, devotes a very lively digression to them. Though appreciative of their military qualities, he goes out of his way to blacken their character—"they are the basest of all men and utterly abandoned rascals," "no men in the world are less bound by convention or more unstable." His low opinion may result from the "special relationship" the Herules appear to have had with Justinian's eunuch general, Narses, whom Procopius disliked.[97] Procopius was in a position to know Herules, but lacked any notion of their past. To him, they had, for all practical purposes, always lived in the Danubian principality that is the point of departure of his digression. The Herules had not in fact reached these lands until the mid-400s, about one century before Procopius's time of writing. He appears to have done no research in the Greek historians who could have enlightened him.

For us, the Herules burst onto the historical stage in southern Russia in the second half of the third century, as part of a coalition of northern barbarians, including the Goths, who conducted two vast and largely seaborne raids setting out from the eastern end of the Black Sea and falling on the exposed portions of the Roman Empire (A.D. 267, 269). Bloodied in these not wholly successful endeavors, the Herules are not heard of again until the mid-fourth century. Under a king named Alaric, they were attacked by the great Goth, Ermanaric, and subjected to his overlordship. They passed before long from his domination to that of the Huns.[98] As Hunnic subjects, the Herules kept a low profile; they are missing from Sidonius's catalogue of Hunnic auxiliaries. Nevertheless, it was in this period that their center of operation passed, voluntarily or under Hunnic duress, from southern Russia to the middle Danube valley. They reemerge in the lineup of peoples who revolted under Gepid leadership against Attila's sons and broke the power of the Huns (ca. 453). In the aftermath of this event, the Herules acquired what Procopius twice calls their "ancestral" lands.[99] Where on the middle Danube they were is not made clear by our informants; the assumption is that they were to the east of the Rugians and west (or northwest) of the Gepids.

Here, too, the Herules attracted little notice.[100] The clearest trace of them after the Hunnic downfall comes more than twenty years later: alongside a contingent of Sciri, Herules formed a large part of Odoacer's army of Italy (476). One source even specifies that Odoacer, after overthrowing Romulus Augustulus, was proclaimed *rex Herulorum*, meaning of those serving in Italy.[101] "Odoacer and his Herules" are featured as a major enemy of Theoderic the Ostrogoth in a seventh-century legendary narrative.[102] But the Herules on the Danube did not remain wholly inactive. They appear to have been made livelier when the forces of Odoacer out of Italy destroyed their Rugian neighbors in 487–88. The next we hear is that the Herules, under a king named Rudolf, were overlords of the Lombards who had taken over the old Rugian lands. According to Procopius's entertaining story, Rudolf's followers, impatient with the lack of lucrative war, forced the king to pick a fight with his Lombard protégés; in spite of all the latter's entreaties for peace, war broke out, and the maltreated Lombards won, killing Rudolf and many others (ca. 508): "Only a few succeeded in saving themselves." (A second version of the legend, by Paul the Deacon two hundred years later, gives the Herules a legitimate casus belli but turns poor Rudolf into a fool.)[103] Whatever the circumstances, the Herules' moment of dominating others was at an end; they lost their territory, wherever it was, and turned more or less willingly into the dependents of others.[104]

A new page in Herule history opened in 512, when they were allowed by the emperor Anastasius to settle in Roman territory, in a district that eventually included the vicinity of Singidunum, the modern Belgrade.[105] The refugees had first fled to the Gepids, but that had not worked out. Their transplanting onto imperial soil was not popular among the imperials, and it did not work out either—they lawlessly manhandled the Romans—until Anastasius sent an army to force them into relative submission. Procopius emphasizes the shrinkage of their numbers from successive humblings by Lombards, Gepids, and Romans.[106] A turn for the better came with the advent of Justinian (527), who, it seems, gave them an improved deal and brought about their conversion to Christianity. In 528, he stood godfather to their king Grepes, who was baptized at Constantinople "with his senators and twelve of his relations."[107]

The pool of Herule manpower lay open to fill Justinian's armies. Procopius reports the presence of Herules under their own leaders in Persia, Africa, Italy, Thrace, and Lazica. A detachment even participated in the butchery of civilians at Constantinople that ended the Nika riots. Herule infantry receives a special description. A detachment of Herules under Pharas, whom Procopius personally praises, brought about the surrender of the Vandal king, Gelimer (534).[108] As Roman troops, Herules suffered casualties in Italy at the hands of the Gothic "rebellion" of 541, and, at the great final battle of Narses against Totila, dismounted Herules stood alongside dismounted Lombards in the Roman center (552).[109] No other barbarian people compares with the Herules in contributing troops to Justinian's wars.

For all that, Procopius was not mollified. The Herules were part of his panorama of an entire "West" that, owing to Justinian's neglect, had come into the possession of the barbarians by the late 540s. As Roman provinces had been ceded to the Lombards and now served as bases for plundering to the south, so had lands been granted to the Herules, who used them in the same way, "overrunning and plundering Illyricum and the Thracian towns very generally."[110] The crowning irony, in the historian's view, was that, because some Herules served as Roman foederati, they both plundered Roman subjects and collected pay from the Roman emperor.[111]

What became of the Herules is not easily deciphered from Procopius's account. Twenty years after baptism, King Grepes and his twelve relatives had vanished, possibly as victims of the great plague of 541–42. The Herules on imperial territory "display[ed] their beastly and fanatical character" by overthrowing their king Ochus and promptly ran out of royalty. They then remembered that there was much royal blood among their brethren who had trekked north early in the century and so sent an embassy to them. While the envoys were on their long mission, the fickle Herules asked Justinian for a king and were given Suartuas, a reliable man, long in imperial service. The envoys returning from Thule drew near with their candidate ruler, Datius, accompanied by his brother, Aordus, and two hundred youths. The new Herule king ordered his people to go to meet the challenger and eliminate him, but they promptly defected, and Suartuas fled back to Constantinople: "Thereupon the emperor earnestly undertook with all his power to restore [Suartuas] to his office, and the Eruli, fearing the power of the Romans, decided to submit themselves to the Gepaedes."[112] So Procopius closes his narrative, leaving us with open mouths: does the story of the Herules really end so abruptly?

There is a follow-up in the next book. Apparently the Herules split apart; only two-thirds went to join the Gepids, and the rest stayed loyal to Constantinople.[113] While King Datius's brother Aordus was serving with the Gepids against the Lombards (547), he came upon a Roman detachment and was killed in the ensuing skirmish. Later than this, Narses must have performed some magic of Herule relations and somehow extracted a mounted force of three thousand for the climactic Italian campaign (551–52).[114] The next we hear is that Justinian was negotiating with the Avars, newly arrived on the Roman Danubian frontier (ca. 561): he offered them the lands that the Herules had vacated. The Herules, it seems, had indeed gone away.[115]

The very last Herule news is reminiscent of Odoacer and the end of the Sciri. A subordinate of Narses's in Italy, Sinduald, fought supremely well, leading the Herules in the battle that destroyed Frankish invaders in 554. As a reward, he and his troops were deployed as defenders of a key sector of the northern Italian frontier. Eventually, Sinduald defected and made himself king, but not for long: Narses suppressed the rebel and put him to death (566).[116]

The prognosis for a Herule future in the Balkans was bleak regardless of whether they stayed in the Empire or joined the Gepids. Within the next century, not only "Gepidia" but also Roman Thrace and Illyricum were overrun by Slavs with and without Avar encouragement, as the Empire proved helpless to defend its European backyard. The problems the Herules leave us with are matters of modern scholarship. How probable is it that there were two unconnected Herule peoples? Procopius's digression, remarkable enough by itself, is interrupted by a long ethnographic description of Thule, to which the author says he wishes he could go.[117] What are we to make of these remarks, and what sort of information lies behind them? Intriguing though these and related questions are, they are more relevant to Procopius than to the Herules. Our information on the latter has enough substance to provide at least the whisper of a history.

Sueves in Spain

In a relaxed moment, the able French historian Lucien Musset said, "In historical terms nothing very important would have been changed had the Sueves of Spain never existed."[118] Historians, at least of this period, are well advised to refrain from such judgments. Musset almost wholly disregards the Gepids, Sciri, and Herules; were their claims to existence even less than the Sueves'? Once a note of dismissal is struck, it may be hard to stop.

Hydatius, the Hispano-Roman bishop of Chavès in remote Gallaecia (from 427), is the only reason why the Sueves of Spain exist for us in any sort of detail. Hydatius had a copy of the world chronicle of Jerome, whom, in the early fifth century, his father had taken him to visit in Bethlehem; and he carried out an edition and continuation of Jerome's chronicle for as long as he could, which turns out to be 468. Hydatius spent his adult life cheek-by-jowl with the Sueves; he found nothing good to say about their activities, but he filled his chronicle with their doings, and so they live for us down to 468 and no longer. For moderns, Hydatius opens the window on the abiding theme of "The End of Roman Spain," with the Sueves as resident scoundrels.[119] The rest of the Sueves' years as an independent force—almost twice longer than the span covered by Hydatius— is packed into a few skeletal lines appended to Isidore of Seville's history of Spain under the Goths. Our diet is very unbalanced. One personage sets off the Sueves' post-Hydatian kingdom; he is a Catholic monk from the Eastern Empire named Martin, who became bishop of Braga—the most enduring center of Suevic Gallaecia—and has a tidy set of writings to his credit (†579).[120]

The coming of the Sueves to Spain and their early years have been discussed in Chapter 5. After the Asding Vandals withdrew precipitately to Baetica in 419, the Sueves under their king, Hermeric, were the sole military force left in formerly shared Gallaecia; and, after the same Vandals left Baetica for North Africa in 429, the Sueves were the only barbarians left in Spain. They were not numerous; they were pagans; and they were isolated, decisively cut off from their Danubian homelands and probably without any formal link to the imperial government.[121] Roman Spain, a vast land, had been fought over, plundered, and damaged since 409 (and even some years earlier, thanks to Roman usurpers); yet it remained a heavily populated and urbanized, agriculturally very rich, and Catholic land, with its northeast (the province of Tarraconensis) still fully attached to the Roman Empire. Hermeric and the Sueves, by no means strong in this context, had little to bargain with except armed force. It is little wonder that they looked ugly.

It took the Sueves about eight years, many recriminations, and several interventions by emissaries from the West Roman strongman, Aetius, to hammer out a modus vivendi with the Gallaecians. The rapprochement probably included the marriage of Hermeric's son, Rechila, with a local Hispano-Roman: their son Rechiar was raised as a Catholic, a sign of the probable religious orientation of the Sueves as a whole.[122] The agreement of 438 coincided with Hermeric's being incapacitated by disease and having to share his throne with Rechila. The Roman government took the occasion of this succession to launch a major attack, which Rechila decisively defeated. Secure in Gallaecia, Rechila seized as much of Spain as he could: Merida in 439, Seville, Baetica, and Carthaginensis in 441, the year of Hermeric's death. In 446, a Roman army with Gothic auxiliaries contested Rechila's conquests and was again beaten. Carthaginensis and Baetica were thoroughly plundered by both the invaders and the defenders. Two years later, Rechila died in Merida and was succeeded (with some internal opposition) by his Catholic son, Rechiar.[123]

Rechiar reminds one of a "failed Clovis," not in the details of his reign, but in his political potential if he had been luckier, abler, or better advised.[124] His reign opened in splendor, with marriage to the daughter of the long-lived Visigoth Theoderic I (who died in the great battle with Attila, 451). But Rechiar, in the footsteps of his father (who had been cautious), bent every effort to conquer the Roman province of Tarraconensis and so win the whole peninsula for the Sueves. His ambition coincided with the Visigoths' drawing near the Roman government and believing they would get Tarraconensis for themselves. Rechiar was faced in 456 with a large Visigothic invasion force reinforced with Burgundians and led by King Theoderic II in person. Defeated with great slaughter, Rechiar was captured in flight and put to death (456).[125] It was a grave setback for the Gallaecians as well as the Sueves; Hydatius wrote, "the Kingdom of the Sueves was destroyed and terminated" (*regnum destructum et finitum est Suevorum*).[126] The epitaph was not at all applicable to the Suevic survivors, who set about finding a new leader, but it held good for the almost Catholic *regnum* that Hydatius himself, King Hermeric, Aetius's envoys, and others had helped to create in 438.

The ten very confused years that followed might be seen as featuring the efforts of Sueves to rise above Rechiar's defeat and recover a monarchy; many lines in Hydatius confirm this impression. The Sueves were not cowed by the downfall of their royal family (the sixth-century Goths of Italy and Spain would not be either). But the Visigoths had entered Spain in 456 with the intention to stay. The real issue turned out to be not the revival of Suevic power, but the right of some Sueve leader to be the manager of western Spain for the Goths of Toulouse. As the years passed, various Sueves were made kings and fought each other. The one who eventually stuck, Remismund, did so with Visigothic support.[127] The clearest sign of Gothic influence was the arrival of the *senior Arrianus* Ajax, by whose doing, to the desolation of Bishop Hydatius, the Sueves were introduced to Arianism, the Gothic branch of Christianity (465–66).[128] Since Arianism was no more "barbaric" than Catholicism, the future of the Sueves (and Gallaecians) was being determined by nothing more exotic than a choice between two Roman imperial creeds.

Isidore of Seville (†636), who was as keen a reader of Hydatius as we are, grandly skipped seventy years as soon as the Sueves became Arians: "Then after many kings of the Suevi had persevered in the Arian heresy, at last Theudemir took up the authority of the kingship . . . [and] at once destroyed the error of the Arian impiety."[129] Our knowledge does not exceed Isidore's; uninformed after Hydatius falls silent, we are left to guess what might have happened in the interval. What did it mean to be a Sueve by 466, fifty-five years and four generations of kings after reaching Gallaecia? What did it mean by 561, 150 years later? Did a taint of the invasion of 409 still linger? In a land of Catholics whose episcopacy was not dismantled, the advent among the Sueves of Gothic-style Arian Christianity at least introduced one definite element of distinctiveness between adherents to the ruling people and their Hispano-Roman subjects.[130]

As known to us, the balance of Suevic history—down to conquest by the Visigothic king in 585—circles almost entirely around religion. The Suevic leadership passed flexibly from paganism to Catholicism to Arianism, back to Catholicism (ca. 550); then, after the 585 conquest to be described presently, the Sueves returned to Arianism, and, after less than five years, went back durably to Catholicism when the Visigoths themselves converted. These peaceable religious vacillations are a sign of how the relations of barbarians and Romans in the Western provinces contrast with those in the East.

To return for a moment to King Remismund and Visigothic tutelage, the main influence on Suevic events perceptible in the century after the late 460s is the sharp decline of Visigothic power after 507 and the fragmentary control of the Goths over Spain. Instability among the Goths was bound, sooner or later, to increase the independence of the kings of the Sueves. The low point for the Visigoths falls probably near 550 when Justinian sent the aged patrician Liberius with a small army that was supposed to do in Spain what small forces had already done in Africa and Italy.[131] About then (as earlier mentioned), a Catholic Pannonian named Martin, who had spent many years in desert asceticism in the East, arrived in Gallaecia and established a model center of Christian life at Dumio near Braga.[132] He had a particular veneration for the fourth-century St. Martin, his namesake and compatriot, whose tomb in Tours—accessible by boat from the north shores of Gallaecia—sparkled with miraculous cures. The reconversion of the Sueves to Catholicism is said to have taken place when King Chararic (rather than Isidore's Theudemir) obtained a cure for his sick son from St. Martin of Tours with Martin of Dumio to help the transition.[133] In 561 and again in 572 Catholic bishops (with Martin among them) met at Braga in assemblies wholly in keeping with the episcopal councils of the Roman Christian world.[134]

These expressions of Suevic or Gallaecian maturity and independence had no future. The Visigoths of Spain, with their backs to the wall, made a comeback and produced an able unifying king, Leovigild (568–86), who checked the Byzantine incursion and beat down the forces of disintegration. In Suevic Gallaecia, King Chararic was followed by a Catholic son, Mir. When Mir helped a Gothic usurper, Leovigild surrounded his army and forced him and, soon after, his young son to swear fidelity to the Goths. Other Sueves rebelled, overthrowing the compliant king; it did not matter. John of Biclar reports under 585: "King Leovigild devastated Gallaecia, seized King Audeca and deprived him of kingship. He reduced the people, treasure, and homeland of the Sueves to his power and made it a province of the Goths."[135] A last rebel rose and was suppressed by Leovigild's generals. The Sueves did not easily renounce their independence. However that may be, the conversion of the Visigoths soon took place and, after a two-century detour, Gallaecia—its frontiers somewhat changed—returned to being a province of a Catholic Spain.[136]

The most intriguing aspect of the history of the Sueves in Spain concerns their largely hidden relations with the Gallaecians and other nearby Hispano-Romans. The Gallaecian experience is reminiscent of the little we know of the relations of the Saxons with the Romano-Britons. Difficult as it was for the two parties to find and reach an accommodation, that is what had to be done if the future was to contain more than sterile and destructive conflict. It seems that in Gallaecia the rapprochement was attained by 438; the Sueves secured their base of operations and could move cautiously forward. But either the leadership or the circumstances cut short that promising start. After 468 the long Suevic silence results from our lack of information, not from their character flaws. When information briefly returns, the centrality of religion in the course of events is illuminating in itself. That, too, brings to mind the experience of ex-Roman Britain.

Frisians

The northwest coast of Europe, from the mouths of the Scheldt all the way to Jutland, is a long, flat zone of combat between land and water, and between men in search of living space and a furious northern sea intent on defeating human efforts. The collective name for this coastline, broken up by many islands, tidal flats, and river months, is Friesland—the land of the Frisians.[137] Ever since the eleventh and especially the thirteenth century, campaigns of dike building have contained the ocean (not without grave setbacks) and raised bulwarks against the invasion of tides and storm surges. But the medieval dikes were simply a new strategy in a much older battle to give humans a livelihood in this desolate and sometimes beautiful zone of conflict. Along all these shores modern research has located hundreds upon hundreds of mounds called *terpen* in Dutch, *wierden* in the dialect of Groningen, *Wurten* in German.[138] *Terpen* are artificial piles of whatever materials came to hand, sometimes quite small, sometimes village-sized, that elevated men, animals, and their dwellings over water levels, creating the conditions for holding the waters at bay just enough to permit the continual exploitation of once barren land. In an uninterrupted application of human effort, the culture of the *terpen* took hold before the current era and continued through Roman and medieval times, extending in breadth and ambition, and eventually giving way to the even more ambitious culture of dikes and large-scale land reclamation that still prevails in that part of the world.[139]

The Frisians (not always under that name) occupied this land when *terpen* began to be piled up, and, after more than two millennia, they occupy it still. A Frisian language, distinct from both Dutch and German, struggles to survive to this day. The Romans came north to these lands in the last century B.C. to round out their Gallic annexation, and the Frisians made friends with them for a time, revolted against them, were subdued, provided troops, and were generally unnoticed.[140] Yet the *terpen* were remarkable enough to come to the attention of Pliny the Elder, who allotted a paragraph to them in his *Natural History*:

A number of races are in this necessitous condition [of living without any trees or any shrubs]; but so also are the races of people called the Greater and the Lesser Chauci, whom we have seen in the north. There twice in each period of a day and a night the ocean with its vast tide sweeps in a flood over a measureless expanse, covering up Nature's age-long controversy and the region disputed as belonging whether to the land or to the sea. There this miserable race occupy elevated patches of ground or platforms built up by hand above the level of the highest tide experienced, living in huts erected on the sites so chosen, and resembling sailors in ships when the water covers the surrounding land, but shipwrecked people when the tide has retired, and round these huts they catch the fish escaping with the receding tide. . . . Their only drink is supplied by storing rain-water in tanks in the forecourts of their homes. And these are the races that if they are nowadays vanquished by the Roman nation say that they are reduced to slavery![141]

Pliny had a capacity for wonder at the spectacle of men against the sea. He was especially amazed that any people could bear to live in conditions quite so wretched as these and yet rejoice at being free of a Rome that assured its subjects a much more desirable livelihood.

In the late Roman period, the attackers and eventual invaders of Britain came through these lands, and some Frisians undoubtedly joined them. The conquest and settlement of lowland Britain was a North Sea affair, involving many peoples within reach of these waters and extending over many decades.[142] Britain, much developed in its centuries of Roman rule, was a prey that any agrarian population might lust after; Gildas and Bede both present images of a land eminently preferable to the equivocal marshes and mud flats of the Frisian shores.[143] But no wholesale abandonment of the *terpen* took place; opportunity in Britain appealed only to a few. The Frisians—most of them—stayed put, sometimes forced to pay tribute to the Frankish kings, at other times regaining degrees of independence. They had had kings as long ago as the reign of Nero (†A.D. 68); the most famous of them, long afterward, would be Radbod, in the days of Charles Martel (716–41). Frisians branched out into seafaring and acquired a reputation for interregional trade. Their main fame in the seventh and eighth centuries came from their resistance to Christian evangelization evidenced by their slaying the ecclesiastical organizer and missionary, St. Boniface. The Franks under the Carolingians were too powerful to allow such conduct to last very long. The various districts of Frisia were gradually incorporated into the Carolingian empire and its descendants.[144] Its medieval adventures do not concern us. What merits attention is the direct continuity out of the Roman past of the *terpen* culture, whether called Frisian or something else.

Dwellers in a land that no one would dream of migrating to, the Frisians came from nowhere and went nowhere; they were in place for as far into the past as anyone need look and remained so, confidently, into the Middle Ages. The physical evidence of their presence impresses us still in the majesty with which it traverses the centuries, proof of a single-mindedness not to be shaken by so flimsy a historian's fancy as the *Völkerwanderung*.

Thuringians

"The core problem of Thuringian tribe formation (*Stammesbildung*)." Wenskus begins by saying, "is the question of the relationship of the Thuringian name to that of the Hermunduri," and he spends the better part of his discussion squarely on this.[145] It is a strange point of departure, but not in *germanische Altertumskunde*. What we are asked to ponder is whether the initial *Thur-* of Thuringian stems from the final *-dur* of Hermunduri. If yes, then the link is secure and the tribal baton may be taken as passed on; the Thuringians carry forward from the comfortingly ancient Hermunduri, recorded in Tacitus's *Germania* and also, more remarkably, in the Verona List.[146]

From a less philologico-etymological standpoint, the salient feature of the Thuringians is their persistent association with horses. Never mind a tribal tradition: the tribal occupation, for which they were famed inside Roman territory, was horse raising. The first mention of the name occurs precisely in this connection. The *Toringi* and *Burgundiones*—breeds of horses, not people— were known to be the finest chargers for war. This piece of information dates perhaps from the last quarter of the fourth century, perhaps from the fifth; and it is not isolated in content.[147] Cassiodorus at the court of Theoderic in Italy was well aware of splendid Thuringian horses; and so was Jordanes in Constantinople in the 550s.[148] Our sources record no creditable exploits by Thuringians other than that they reared these prized cavalry remounts of the Migration Age.

Thuringia is in inner Germany, far to the east of the Rhine and outside the limits of the Roman Empire. In the Middle Ages, it long was a frontier zone, standing on the edge of territory inhabited by Slavs. Thuringian space was remote from the pages of ancient history: whatever contact it had with Roman arms in the first century subsided and ceased as soon as the Roman frontiers were stabilized far to the west. By the late fourth century Thuringia had a reputation, as we have just seen; perhaps its famed export product reached Roman markets to the south through Augusta Vindelicorum (modern Augsburg), capital of the Roman province of Raëtia.[149] The Thuringians did not escape the power of Attila's Huns; without having to be relocated they participated alongside Gepids, Goths, and Rugians in the great invasion of Gaul in 451; but that passed quickly. After Hunnic power receded, the reach of Thuringians extended as far as the Danube valley: the *Vita s. Severini* features some of them as plunderers.[150] The noteworthy Thuringian development in late antiquity was a kingship—one hesitates to say "monarchy"—that, in the short time that we hear of its existence, succeeded in establishing personal links at long distances and in giving birth to both a Constantinopolitan general and a Merovingian saint.

The passage of the Thuringians on the historical stage was brief but prominent. Clovis, the founder of Frankish power, was the son of a Thuringian mother. His father, Childeric, had been driven from his throne and had taken refuge with Bysinus, the first recorded Thuringian king. After regaining the Frankish throne, Childeric was—it is said—joined by Bysinus's wife, Basina, Clovis's mother. Clovis himself expended some of his energy in attacking Thuringia, but without permanent results.[151] The decisive action took place in the days of Clovis's eldest son, Theuderic (511–33), whose eastern border marched with Thuringia.

Thuringian kingship at the time was shared by three brothers, Herminifred, Baderic, and Berthachar, in a divided royalty well known from Merovingian practice and with comparably lethal rivalries. Herminifred appears to have been senior and to have promptly disposed of Berthachar.[152] Theoderic the Ostrogoth, the great king of Italy, as part of an effort to associate himself with all the kings of the West, sent his niece, Amalaberga, to marry Herminifred (ca. A.D. 500).[153] When Theoderic tried to encircle Clovis diplomatically to keep him from attacking the Visigoths, he called on the Thuringian king along with other northern royalty to hold the Frank in check. The alliance had little practical effect; Theoderic eventually had to send his own troops to arrest the southward extension of Frankish power.[154] At least the Thuringian tie was fruitful: Amalaberga presented King Herminifred with a son, Amalafrid, and a daughter. The children of the late Berthachar grew up with them.

The contest between the Franks and Herminifred of Thuringia comes to us in two heavily colored accounts, one by Gregory of Tours, about forty-five years after the events, the other by Widukind of Corvey, almost three hundred years later.[155] Neither one takes notice of what Procopius reports, namely, that Ostrogothic power ceased to restrain Frankish expansionism after the death of Theoderic, ruler of Italy (526). As Gregory tells the story, the tragedy began with Herminifred's being incited by his Gothic wife to eliminate his surviving brother, Baderic. Enlisting the help of his Frankish neighbor Theuderic, Herminifred disposed of Baderic, but once he was sole king of Thuringia he forgot his helper. At this point Procopius injects the paralysis of the Goths of Italy as encouraging the Merovingians to act (ca. 532). In Gregory's account, Theuderic incited his people against the Thuringians and won the support of his brother, Chlothar, and son, Theudebert. In a major campaign the Thuringians were routed and subjected to Frankish rule. Herminifred, who survived the battles, was lured to Theuderic's presence and killed by treachery. Thuringia was added to the Frankish kingdom; Theuderic's son, Theudebert, announced the conquest to Justinian as a proud achievement.[156] But Thuringia was always an outlying possession whose degree of obedience varied from time to time. What mattered was that the eastern border of Frankish hegemony, and of security for Gaul, was set very far to the east of where the old Roman frontier had run. Never again independent, Thuringia acquired many configurations in the centuries to come and persists as a geographical entity to this day.

The fall of Thuringia has two epilogues. Herminifred's children fled with their mother, Amalaberga, to the Amal court in Italy. They were taken to Constantinople when Belisarius overcame the Goths of Italy in 540. Ten years later, Herminifred's son, Amalafrid (whom Procopius calls a Goth), was a general of Roman troops with a major role in the Lombard victory over the Gepids in 552.

Appropriately, Amalafrid's sister, grandniece of Theoderic the Ostrogoth, was engaged to the Lombard king, Audoin.[157] Through these two half-Thuringian descendants of Theoderic, some shadow of the Gothic title to Italy passed to the Lombards before the invasion of 568.

The other epilogue concerns the children of the long deceased Berthachar. When Thuringia fell to the Franks, these children were allotted to Theuderic's royal half brother Chlothar, who had helped in the campaign. The son of Berthachar, whose name we never learn, was raised at his captor's court; his sister, named Radegund, was chosen by Chlothar to be his wife, but was not yet marriageable. Sent to a royal country estate to be reared, Radegund, pagan born, learned not only to read and write but also to be a pious Catholic. She took to the practice of charitable asceticism and retained it even after becoming Chlothar's wife. Her brother, meanwhile, decided to travel to Constantinople and seek out his cousin, Amalafrid, of whom no news had come to Frankish Gaul in all these years. For some reason, Chlothar had him killed on his journey.[158] Radegund took the occasion of her brother's killing to separate permanently from Chlothar and enter upon full-time religious life in a nunnery she established for herself in Poitiers. After Chlothar's death, her stepson Sigibert, Merovingian ruler of Poitiers, helped her obtain relics for her nunnery from Constantinople. The empress Sophia, wife of Justin II (Justinian's successor), sent her fragments of the True Cross. An Italian poet and priest, Venantius Fortunatus, became her lifelong friend; in her name he wrote a poem on "The Ruin of Thuringia (*De excidio Thoringiae*)." She died in 587.[159] At two ends of the Christian world, the fall of the ephemeral Thuringian kingdom had an enduring resonance.

Bavarians

The prominence of Bavaria in medieval and modern Germany hardly needs to be pointed out. In 788, after Charlemagne deposed the autonomous duke Tassilo III, Bavaria became a Carolingian subkingdom in the charge of Charles's brother-in-law, Gerold, and formed the core inheritance of Charles's grandson Louis "the German" in 840.[160] Whether as a duchy or a kingdom or a modern "Land," Bavaria has never ceased to have a major place in German life. But its name does not occur earlier than the sixth century, and the circumstances of its origin are a mystery that no one expects to solve.[161]

There are two early references to the Bavarians. The more securely dated of them is in Jordanes (after 551): Thiudemir, king of the Goths, crossed the frozen Danube and fell suddenly on the Swabians; "that region of the Swabians has the 'Baibari' to the east, the Franks to the west, the Burgundians to the south, and the Thuringians to the north."[162] The other reference, of no certain date, is similar in its starkness. The document in question is the so-called "Frankish Table of Nations," perhaps East Roman or Ostrogothic in origin. Its first line of "nations" corresponds almost precisely with Procopius's four "Gothic peoples"; its third line groups the largely Catholic "western" peoples, such as the Franks and Bretons; and its second line ("middle peoples"), very similar to Procopius's quartet, groups the Bavarians ("Baioarii") with the Thuringians, Burgundians, and Lombards.[163] Both Jordanes and the anonymous tabulator take the existence of Bavarians for granted. After this skeletal introduction, evidence comes more easily. An Italian poet observed the Bavarians when journeying to the Frankish kingdom ca. 565; and about ten years earlier, a duke Garibald of Bavaria obliged a Frankish king (in fine Merovingian style) by marrying the widow of the king's royal grandnephew, whom bishops would not allow the king to marry; the bride in question was the daughter of a Lombard king and a Gepid mother.[164]

Where did the Bavarians come from? The formerly consecrated answer is worth recalling because, among other things, it allows us to glimpse the (modern German) ideal type of a *Völkerwanderung:* "Down to our days, a fixed component of the Old Bavarian-Bavarian *Stamm-*and state ideology, as well as a requirement of the historical conception of the beginnings of state and people suggested by Herder's 'Volksmythos,' was that the 'Bavarians' were a *Stamm* of the Migration Age that immigrated from the east into the Danube valley under the leadership of an army-king [called] herizogo (duke) and, in a conscious or planned settlement ('Landnahme'), took possession of the territory in several stages. . . . This hypothesis is a legend because not a single proof for it can be brought, not even an archaeological one."[165] The author of these lines, Karl Bosl, assures us that the wrong question was asked. No immigration and settlement in the future Bavaria is known to have taken place during the available time span. The one written source concerned with this part of the world is the *Vita s. Severini,* often mentioned above, composed in Gothic Italy by a monk named Eugippius ca. 511. What it describes is the life of the middle Danube valley between about 454 and the time, toward 488, when Odoacer ordered the withdrawal to Italy of the remaining population. Bavarians are never mentioned in Eugippius's narrative. Between the time of this evacuation and the first decades of the sixth century, in the vacuum ensuing from the abandonment of the Roman provinces of Noricum and Raëtia, there materialized the collectivity that Germanic-speaking neighbors, such as the Swabians, Franks, or Lombards, almost immediately called "Bavarians."[166]

The appropriate answer to the question of origins is not what new people arrived, but what peoples and underpinnings were already there. The land between the Lech and Enns rivers, the Alps and the Danube, had been well populated since prehistoric times. Long a center of what we call "Celtic (or La Tène)" civilization, it came into Roman possession under the emperor Augustus and was gradually planted with towns—Augsburg (a trading point for *barbaricum*), Regensburg (a legionary fortress), Passau, Lorch, Salzburg; it was crisscrossed by major military roads, further developed agriculturally, and ambitiously garrisoned. There were Roman villas and estate management calling for written records.[167] Late antiquity brought the Christian church, martyrs' cults, and ecclesiastical organization. Besides being equipped with most of what could be found in contemporary Gaul, the future Bavaria was particularly well situated to communicate with Italy. The territory was far from intact; it had been periodically plundered and had surely lost population. From the fifth century, the remnants of the old residents had also seen "new" faces: Alamanni (Swabians), Rugians, Sciri, Herules, Thuringians, to say nothing of Huns. Many passed through; some stayed.

Bavaria is likely to have begun as a political or militarily defensive creation by the expanding kingdom of the Franks. In his lifetime, Theoderic the Ostrogoth (†526) extended the rule of his Italian kingdom at least loosely to the Danube and touched on the sphere dominated by the Thuringians, with whom he had marriage ties. His "empire" began to be tested and shaken first by the lapse of his realm into the hands of a regency, then from 535 by the invasion of Belisarius at the head of Justinian's troops. The Franks broke the power of the Thuringians in the early 530s and extended their hegemony down the Danube to the edges of the lands occupied by the Lombards. The boastful letter of the Frankish king Theudebert to the emperor Justinian (ca. 540) advertises his control of the lands from Pannonia to the North Sea. Over the large frontier district soon called Bavaria—we do not know why—Theudebert (†548) appointed as duke a magnate from the probably Frankish Agilolfing family. He was the Garibald encountered above receiving a "surplus" Lombard bride ca. 555. This frontier defender proceeded to organize and manage the human and material assets in his charge. Bavaria was set in motion as a part of Merovingian and Lombard political history.[168]

The one link of Bavarian origins with the wider history of barbarians in late antiquity is Garibald's marriage to a Lombard princess given to him by a Merovingian king. Other marital links would follow, notably of Theudelinda, Garibald's daughter, to several Lombard kings in succession. There may have been no Bavarian past, but the Agilulfingians were admitted to the club of international military aristocrats. Otherwise, the arresting trait of Bavarian beginnings is what they lack. The Bavarians are not in Tacitus's *Germania* or associated with the "Germanic institutions" he described.[169] They have no record of combats with Rome; they were not recruited into the Roman army or entered into *foederati* relationships. No Bavarian was appointed to a Roman generalship. There is no Bavarian migratory trail, or period of subjection to the Huns, or participation in the revolt against Attila's sons. No moment may be seized upon as that of a Bavarian *Landnahme*; they were simply there, possessors of what the Celtic and Roman past equipped them with, and only just overlapping in time the Gothic prolongation of West Roman government. Bereft of all the customary signposts of "Germanic antiquity," they were, very simply, an early medieval people, composed of whatever populations and ethnicities happened to be there trying to eke out a livelihood. If any "Bavarian tradition" had come into being by the eighth century it could reach no farther back than to the remnants of Roman provinces in a land that more powerful neighbors had not cared to bring under their direct control.[170] Yet what the Bavarians had was enough; no contact with earlier layers of the past was needed for them to be a cornerstone of the German future.

Reflections

One conclusion to be drawn from the evidence gathered above is that it was more blessed to be a western barbarian people than an eastern one. Western ones lived on. Although their political independence tended to be brief, their name, territory, and fame had an excellent chance of enduring through the ages, and of even having recurrent political expressions. Eastern barbarians were smashed on the Constantinopolitan anvil, with Jordanes and Procopius standing by to sing their requiems.

Another lesson is the irrelevance of the distant past of these peoples. The entire exercise of setting out in search of "primitive homelands" and tracing routes of migration proves to be what it is gradually being recognized as—a modern way of annexing to the northern "Germanic" lands peoples who had no demonstrable relations to them. The half-Hunnish, half-Scirian Odoacer may well have been culturally Gothic; there is no denying the impact of the Goths on the culture of *barbaricum* in late antiquity, not least as the mediators of a Roman product, Arian Christianity, to their fellow peoples. But that culture, which affected Alans and Huns as well as Sciri and Herules, had much to do with present conditions and circumstances, and little or nothing with the distant past.

Superfluous, too, is the unthinking modern transposition into history of a common "Germanic" language family—a concept borrowed from comparative philology. The history of a language as known to philologists has nothing to do with that of human beings. Under Attila's approving gaze, Ardaric-Gepids and Valamer-Goths spilled their blood in central Gaul to defeat Visigoths, Franks, and Burgundians; Herules tried to oppress Lombards; Lombards organized the destruction of the Gepids; Sciri and Danube Sueves combined against the

Valamer-Goths; Alaric-Goths stamped out the Siling Vandals; Franks defeated Visigoths and forced Burgundians and Thuringians to be their subjects; Herules ably assisted in the destruction of the Vandals in Africa and the Goths of Italy. There were few if any "Germanic" solidarities; the idea itself is an anachronism. Historians reared on the interminable combats of Christian Europeans among themselves should have no trouble in recognizing that, in late antiquity, immediate advantage took priority over linguistic brotherhood. No discernible benefit comes from our being reminded again and again in modern writings that many of these barbarians at each other's throats probably spoke dialects of the same language. The G-word can be dispensed with.

How migratory was the Migration Age? The record just given of seven peoples is mixed. Frisians, Thuringians, and Bavarians stood in place. The Gepids did not move far enough for it to count. Nor were the Herules and Sciri wandering in search of land or a sunnier climate; they were caught up by the Huns in the early fifth century and transposed from the lower to the middle Danube; their moves were deliberate, regardless of whether the motive force was their own or imposed on them. As for the Sueves of 405, their change of place took place in a single journey, under admittedly mysterious circumstances. By comparison with other phases of European history, such as the eastward movement of peasant colonizers in the high Middle Ages, the "wanderings" of the seven barbarian peoples considered here hardly seem prominent enough to substantiate the aquatic imagery—waves, tides, floods—of our depictions of the Migration Age. The Christianizing and militarizing (or "barbarizing") energies of the Roman Empire, not a "wave" from outside, were the motive force of the Migration Age.

To challenge the maneuvers of *deutsche Altertumskunde* and *germanische Frühgeschichte* does not have to mean losing interest in the peoples who lived on and even beyond the edges of the Roman world. I hope that these seven case studies have both shed light on individual circumstances and illustrated new ways of narrating "tribal" histories. The past of these peoples may be virtually nonexistent, or a terrain for unending and sterile speculations, but their present was real enough to find a place in contemporary records. There is room for narratives that spurn the vagaries of traditional modern accounts and strive to remain in close contact with the sources, critically appraised.

Gothic Italy and the Ethnic Bastion That Never Was

Between 535 and 552, control of Italy was wrested from the Goths in a two-stage campaign by the armed forces of the emperor Justinian. At first, Justinian's commander Belisarius outgeneraled his Gothic opponents and, in less than four years, with meager resources, brought about the surrender of the Gothic king and army. A second stage immediately began: those Goths not yet disarmed found a new leader, Totila, who enjoyed initial successes against divided Roman garrisons but, after ten indecisive and destructive years, was crushed by a large Roman relief army led by Narses, another of Justinian's generals. Gothic control of Italy was blotted out and replaced by rule from Constantinople; the Italian branch of the Goths effectively vanished.[171]

A disconcerting aspect of these events to modern observers is that, to our eyes, they conspicuously lack an abstract "Gothic cause." The negotiations that accompanied this protracted crisis feature flagrant treason by many of the foremost Goths; and, in the long second stage, the Goths under Totila had no other aim than to reverse Justinian's conquest and win back a firm hold over the Italians. Absent from these events is a transpersonal Gothic symbol, a focus of loyalty that would have shamed turncoats and rallied defenders to a common ethnic cause. The Roman side had abstractions that were appealed to and held sacred—the *nomen Romanum*, the emperor as a magistrate in a government of magistrates, even the iconic SPQR. The Goths had nothing, and that absence astonishes us. Much as modern observers may sympathize with the Gothic defenders of Italy against the imperial bully from Constantinople, they are forced to conclude that the defenders and attackers fought as two gangs struggling for control of the same territory and population, but with the difference that one gang had the *nomen Romanum* on its side and never had to contend with a Gothic alternative.[172]

A famous story told by the Christian historian Orosius about a much earlier Goth, Athaulf (relative and successor of Alaric), bears on this issue: "[Athaulf], at first, was ardently eager to blot out the Roman name and to make the entire Roman Empire that of the Goths alone, and to call it and to make it, to use the common expression, *Gothia* instead of *Romania*. . . . But having discovered from long experience both that the Goths . . . could not by any means obey laws, and that the state should not be denied the laws without which a state is not a state, he chose to seek for himself the glory of completely restoring and increasing the Roman name by the forces of the Goths."[173] Three times, Orosius evokes a transpersonal *respublica*, "state"; Athaulf endorsed the need for such a thing and wanted to have it, but his Gothic followers lacked its merest presupposition, the ability to be law-abiding. And so, the necessary cement for Goths as well as Romans was for everyone concerned to sustain the *nomen Romanum* by laws and force of arms. Subordination to that symbol was the condition of any kind of public order. The alternative (at least to Orosius) was *effrenata barbaries*, the unbridled savagery of those unable to submit to laws.

The Goths of Italy, thanks to their first leader, Theoderic, were much more strongly entrenched than the Goths of Athaulf had been. But, for all the plenty and security in which they lived (for a time), they had not found another raison d'être than Athaulf's. They were in Italy to "restore and increase" the *nomen Romanum*, and not to replace *Romania* with *Gothia*.

The story of the "betrayal" of the Goths of Italy by their highest leaders is quickly summarized. Theodoric's daughter, Amalasuintha, was regent for her underage son; whenever she was backed into political corners, she turned covertly to Constantinople for support. She once, as a precaution, had the royal treasure packed onto ships ready for transport across the Adriatic if she had to flee to imperial territory. J. B. Bury commented, "If Amalasuntha seriously contemplated [resigning her power into the hands of the Emperor], it was, though defensible theoretically on constitutional grounds, an act of gross treachery toward her own people."[174] Meanwhile, Amalasuintha's nearest of kin, Theodahad, who had made himself the largest landed potentate in Tuscany, secretly negotiated with Constantinople to exchange his Tuscan "principality" for a lavish retreat in the security of the Empire. When Belisarius crossed from Sicily to the Italian mainland, Theodahad's son-in-law spontaneously surrendered himself and his forces to him.[175] Next, Theoderic's granddaughter, Matasuintha, unhappy with her forced marriage to Wittigis (a general of no pedigree), "opened secret negotiations [with a high-born Byzantine general] concerning marriage and the betrayal of [Ravenna, the chief Gothic stronghold]."[176] And in 540–41, one of the "rebels" made king in opposition to Belisarius's conquest used his position for no other purpose than to negotiate a golden parachute for himself.[177] Although our emotional response to these actions resembles Bury's, and although some sort of betrayal of the Goths by these leaders was unquestionably involved, it is clear that the "traitors" did not think of themselves as repudiating "the Gothic people" and turning to a "foreign" power; there was no Gothia to be betrayed. The modern model of exclusive sovereignties does not apply; that of medieval overlordship is more pertinent. As Athaulf subordinated himself and his Goths to the *nomen Romanum*, so had Theoderic and his descendants done the same thing. It was no betrayal to turn to the sole Roman emperor in Constantinople and convey Roman Italy to him.

Perhaps Athaulf (a participant in the sack of Rome in 410) had nursed the subversive thought of eliminating the Roman *respublica* and giving it an ethnic successor, but such an idea appears to have never occurred to the youthful king Totila about 130 years later. Yet, the opportunity for a Gothia to be called into existence was not wholly lacking. Just when Belisarius was rolling up the main Gothic forces, Justinian in Constantinople faced a deteriorating situation on his border with Persia and sought to bring the Italian war to a hasty close. He sent an embassy to the West with terms of peace to be made with the Gothic king, Wittigis. Belisarius's campaign was to be ended by a compromise—the partition of Italy at the Po river: all the land to the south would be Justinian's and every-thing to the north, the center of gravity of Gothic settlement, was to form a Gothic kingdom.[178]

Belisarius short-circuited this negotiation. He was convinced, rightly, that a complete victory over the Goths was in his grasp, and he prevented the em-peror's diplomacy from snatching this prize from him.[179] Justinian's compro-mise was never formally proposed to King Wittigis. Instead, Belisarius lured Wittigis and the Goths into believing that he would accept their offer to make him their new ruler; he secretly undertook to assume the kingship over the Goths and Italians as soon as Wittigis and his army surrendered Ravenna. The surrender duly took place, but Belisarius did not carry out his part of the bar-gain. The Goths living south of the Po were dismissed to their homes; the Gothic king and the best elements of his army were packed off to the East; and Belisarius himself, officially recalled, sailed in the same direction.[180]

The situation Belisarius left behind was by no means stable. Scattered over northern Italy were many armed Goths along with several leading figures (in-cluding Wittigis's capable nephew) and several major fortified cities, such as Verona and Pavia; none of these had surrendered to Roman control. The Ro-man generals and troops remaining in Italy were expected to deal with all these now headless Goths in mopping up operations.[181]

Justinian's proposal of a Gothic Italy north of the Po was still in the air. The Goths left out of Wittigis's surrender were not disposed to submit sponta-neously, but they took some time to acquire a leader worthy of their confidence. The obvious candidate refused; the dignitary he designated in his place was soon assassinated; the choice of the leading Goths then fell on a certain Eraric, the leader of the Rugian people long incorporated in the Gothic kingdom. Er-aric did nothing constructive and was killed after a few months. His sole initia-tive was to send an embassy to Justinian with two sets of instructions: the secret one offered Eraric's surrender in return for money and a high Byzantine rank; the official one asked that the partition of Italy at the Po be made the basis for a new peace. In view of the secret instructions, the offer of a partition was not taken seriously in Constantinople and, in any case, Eraric was killed before the embassy returned to Italy.[182] The interest of the episode is that the plan of a cur-tailed Gothic kingdom north of the Po was well known in the leading circles of the Goths at the time when the old Amal dynasty was being replaced by impro-vised kings in search of stability.

Herwig Wolfram comments, "From our point of view the solution would have been almost ideal for all parties. Italy would have been spared the really de-structive phase of the Gothic war and a small but compact transpadane Gothic kingdom would have been the best protection for the peninsula. The *regnum* of the Goths and imperial Italy would have adjusted to each other peacefully."[183] For the authentic conditions of Gothic Italy at this critical moment, Wolfram's "solution ideal for all parties" tells us much less than the tacit but emphatic rejection of this compromise by all parties. No partition at the Po is ever heard of again after Eraric's embassy; no one entertained the possibility of a "compact transpadane Gothic" bastion in the North; no spokesman ever advocated bringing a defensible Gothic "homeland" into existence.

Instead, Gothic leaders even before the advent of Totila were unanimous about the goal of the renewed war against Justinian's forces: the still numerous Gothic remnants would undo Belisarius's victory, overcome the Roman troops, and regain the lost cities; they would "recover the kingdom and sovereignty of Italy for the Goths." The prize was dominion over the Italians; Totila never wavered in that war aim.[184] After defeating the mobile Roman forces in the north and Tuscany, Totila took his victorious army into the center and south, where it largely remained for years on end. Much of the Gothic royal treasure was secreted in Cumae, between Rome and Naples.[185] The many peace envoys Totila vainly sent to Justinian invariably asked for what the earlier Gothic kings had had—the rule of all Italy—sometimes sweetened by the offer of alliance with Constantinople against all enemies, tribute for the peninsula, and the cession of Dalmatia and Sicily.[186] The decade-long exertions of Totila's forces were not for the freedom of the Gothic people in a secure territory but for the right of the Goths to be Justinian's subcontractors in upholding the *nomen Romanum* in Italy.

The Goths of Italy may hardly be blamed for failing to meet our expectations or being backward in their thinking. However alien Jordanes would later have them look, Totila's Gothic followers were not foreigners to the land they fought over. They must all have been Italian-born, perhaps of Italian-born parents; Gothicness, to them, could not be something hatched even as far away as Theoderic's Pannonian birthplace. The ethnic tradition that these Goths had, whatever it was and however real, could not be transmuted into an effective polity detached from Roman roots. The kingdom of the Goths in Italy rested on Roman foundations and collapsed when these foundations were sufficiently undermined. Totila was justifiably angry that the Italians so poorly repaid the Goths for their good government; but once the Constantinopolitan "head office" contested the control of the local "branch manager," the latter would have had to be superlatively skilled to restore its credit in the face of the depositors. The Italians of whatever social and ethnic background would very probably have done better under the Goths than they did as a colony of Constantinople; Gothic defenders would have coped better with the destructive future invasions by Franks and Lombards. But such speculations are otiose. The Goths of 541 faced a crisis of survival; they had an appealing, honest leader and were still well supplied with men and resources; yet they were unable to devise an effective strategy against usually inadequate Roman forces. Their adversary, Justinian, proceeded as though he realized that, even with too few troops in Italy, he held the upper hand. For him, the subjection of the Goths called for no more than patient persistence; and he was right.

In retracing the melancholy story of the end of the Goths in Italy, I have had in mind the arresting affirmation of Reinhard Wenskus that the "land-seizing" peoples of late antiquity were politically momentous: "The '*Gentilismus*' [ethnic consciousness] of the conquering (*landnehmenden*) peoples was a politically stronger conception (*Denkform*) than the Roman imperial consciousness (*Reichsbewußtsein*) of the provincials."[187] As a test of Wenskus's idea, no phase of the Migration Age can equal that of the Goths in Italy, admirably documented by a contemporary observer. What Gothic Italy after 540 shows is the inadequacy of *Gentilismus* to make any difference in the face of the Roman *Reichsbewußtsein*. Personal connections, not *Gentilismus*, were the legal tender of the day. Totila was unmarried and, though linked through his late uncle to an insecure king of Gothic Spain, he did not otherwise belong to the international ruling families. In 549 or 550 he tried to win a royal wife from one of the Frankish courts, but his advances were repelled with derision: he had bungled the seizure of Rome.[188] This failed quest for a Frankish bride foreshadowed the tragic end of his effort at a Gothic restoration.

Conclusion

In a 1972 review, I observed, "The history of the migratory tribes is a sturdily German province of historical study, and profoundly affected by modern German nationalism"; and, after praising the qualities of the book under review, I concluded, "One would give a great deal for a work by someone . . . who seriously questioned or even broke with the form and presuppositions of the *Geschichte der deutschen Stämme*."[189] Nothing has happened since then to fill this desideratum. On the contrary, the front of the stage has been occupied by talk of "ethnogenesis" and of the importance of ethnicity in late antiquity. Philology, archaeology, comparative religion, etymology, and whatever else have been exploited in the tried and true fashion of *deutsche Altertumskunde* in efforts to render the "tribes" more tribal than ever. As little thought as possible has been given to making them less resolutely German. It is as though dire consequences for Germany and Europe would ensue if "German" descent from the Bronze Age ceased to be an article of faith.[190]

In the three parts of this chapter, I have tried to show that a history of the barbarians in late antiquity free of *deutsche Altertumskunde* not only is possible but also holds more promise as a comprehensive and sympathetic account of the course of events than alternative versions. The "barbarization," or social militarization, of the later Empire needs to be looked upon as a process no less deliberate and accident-prone than its concurrent Christianization. Gibbon's comment about recounting "the triumph of barbarism and religion" does not refer to developments that happened against the wishes or better judgment of the participants, as a departure from preferable conditions.[191] Barbarism and religion were desired outcomes, creative responses to the urgent needs of the day, deliberately brought about by the leaders of society to the limited degree that human beings then as now are able to meet their responsibilities and guide the destinies of those placed in their charge.

To the extent that these processes happened, they did so within the Roman world and only then extended outward from it. The mechanism is well enough known where Christianity is concerned. No one doubts that it was from within the Empire that Christianity made its way to Ireland, Ethiopia, Bavaria, Lazica, and so forth. The extension of Christianity is not a neat or necessarily a visible process; to take a very small example, it is not clear how the Vandals became Arian Christians. But the Mediterranean roots of Christianity are not in question. In the case of "barbarism," however, the idea of something coming from outside—as redemption or as ruin—rears its head and has dominated the terrain for a long time. One need only evoke the eighteenth-century conception of a threefold "Germanic" *Wanderung, Landnahme,* and *Reichsgründung*: tribes march in, settle, and establish kingdoms; modern history begins at the further end of the transformatory *Völkerwanderung*. This model was accepted by the Göttingen historian Johan Christoff Gatterer (†1799), detached from any shade of *germanische Altertumskunde*.[192] Never replaced, it may be found regaining strength after World War II in the Göttingen historian Reinhard Wenskus, in the Cambridge classicist A. H. M. Jones, and in hundreds of scholars outside as well as inside Germany, all agreed in seeing an existing "Germanic world" getting the better of a "Roman world." That vision of outsiders intruding successfully where they were not wanted is an illusion fostered however innocently and festering ever since the sixteenth century.

When the admirable Beatus Rhenanus said (1531), "Ours [= modern Germans'] are the triumphs of the Goths, Vandals, and Franks. Ours are their kingdoms (*imperia*) established in the finest provinces of the Romans and even in Italy and Rome itself," he voiced a conviction that others would soon have articulated if he had not.[193] The question is not how so distorted an identification of present with past was born, but what efforts we, today, are ready to make to overcome it. The "barbarization" of the Roman world came from within. The term is our shorthand for the ineluctable militarization of imperial society set in motion by Diocletian (if not before) and continually elaborated by the efforts of successive governments to meet the military and religious obligations of the Roman state in the face of competing priorities and scarce resources. Social militarization ("barbarization") meant a leadership of backwoods generals from inside and outside the imperial borders. It involved faith in dynastic succession and the acceptance of foreign royalty, the practice of *connubium* among power-wielding families, the conveyance of mechanisms of rule, the apportionment of state resources, the sharing of the burdens of empire and the shouldering of its responsibilities. Its eighth-century culmination in both East and West is visible in armed forces and their leaders sustained directly by agricultural producers—what is called "feudalism" in Marxist history. Even the Byzantium of Procopius, in the sixth century, was hardly less "barbarous" than the Gaul of Gregory of Tours. Clothing itself momentarily in the trappings of a more differentiated and obsolete past, it soon paid the price by proving unable to defend any but a small fraction of its territory from hungry Slavs and Muslims.[194] The more obstinately military West made the considerable sacrifice of dispensing with civilian culture outside the church; its leaders devoted enough resources to warfare to hold old and new rivals at bay. In whatever part of the once-Roman world, the vicissitudes marking the dawn of the Middle Ages had nothing to do with the present or future of "Germans."

Chapter 8
Conclusion: The Long Simplification
of Late Antiquity

In 734, a year before his death, the monk Bede wrote a letter of admonition and advice to Egbert, bishop of York, a cousin of Ceolwulf, the reigning king of Northumbria. Bede paid special attention to an abuse that he regarded as a clear threat to Northumbrian society:

> There are innumerable places, as we all know, allowed the name of monasteries by a most foolish manner of speaking, but having nothing at all of a monastic way of life. . . .
> And because there are many and large places of this kind, which, as is commonly said, are useful neither to God nor man, in that neither is there kept there a regular life according to God's will, nor are they owned by [soldiers or officers] of the secular power, who defend our people from the barbarians; if anyone should establish an episcopal see in those same places . . . , he will be proved . . . to be doing an act of virtue. . . . [I]t . . . behoves your Holiness, with the religious king of our people, to annul the irreligious and unjust acts and writings of our predecessors, and to provide for those things which may be useful to our province, whether in matters of Church or State; lest in our times by the ceasing of religion, love and fear of [H]im who sees into the heart be abandoned, or else, by the dwindling of the supply of secular troops, there arise a lack of men to defend our territories from barbarian invasion. For . . . those who are totally ignorant of the monastic life have received under their control so many places in the name of monasteries . . . that there is a complete lack of places where the sons of nobles or of veteran [soldiers] can receive an estate . . . and on this account they either leave the country for which they ought to fight and go across the sea, or else . . . devote themselves to loose living and fornication.[1]

In these lines of social commentary, Bede took for granted the existence in Northumbria of a cultivated countryside populated by a laboring population sustaining itself and producing a flow of revenue from the soil. This substrate went without saying. His concern was with how the Northumbrian social level supported by this revenue should share or apportion it among themselves. He allows us to see that some Northumbrians had found a way of reviving what, in classical antiquity, had been one of the earthly blessings most worth striving for—*otium cum dignitate* or, as we might say, "noble leisure." These ingenious Northumbrians, sanctioned by charters ("acts and writings") from kings and synods creating ostensible "monasteries," were diverting revenues to something other than soldiering or praying, namely, a dignified, peaceable, and pleasurable existence.[2] In Bede's understanding of eighth-century conduct, this rediscovery of civilian ease was a scandalous outrage, an ugly departure from divine and human order. It was self-evident to him (and, in his view, to everyone) that men who received revenue without labor had only two choices: to engage in a continuously religious life according to a strict, God-approved rule, or to train as soldiers and maintain themselves in readiness for mobilization to fight "the barbarians," that is, the armed enemies of their country. Any revival of *otium cum dignitate* implied starving one or the other pillar of social life. No more succinct proof exists of Gibbon's observation that "barbarism and religion" had completely superseded the way of life of classical antiquity. A medieval society without room for leisured civilians had well and truly taken form.

* * *

On the morrow of World War II (1946), the French ancient historian André Piganiol published a major account of the fourth-century Roman Empire; he ended it with the dramatic statement that "Roman civilization did not die a natural death. It was murdered."[3] Piganiol meant by this that the internal conditions of the later Empire were viable and that its death came from outside, at the hands of the invading "Germanic" barbarians. Not surprisingly at that date, war-nourished resentment was thought to have warped his judgment. Two decades later (1964), another eminent ancient historian, A. H. M. Jones, echoed Piganiol's opinion in a much less provocative form. On the understanding that "the internal weaknesses of the empire" were not responsible for its decline, Jones lent his authority to "the simple but rather unfashionable view that the barbarians played a considerable part in the decline and fall of the empire."[4] After still another twenty years (1984), the bias that seemed to detract from Piganiol's judgment completely evaporated. A German ancient historian, Alexander Demandt, in an exhaustive survey of all opinions about "the fall of Rome," personally endorsed a conclusion framed much like Piganiol's and Jones's. The survival of Byzantium, he said, undercuts the notion that the totality of the ills of the Empire explain its fall; and this "gives weight to the idea that external pressure is an indispensable factor in understanding the late Roman situation. . . . [T]he collapse [of Rome] was hastened, or even brought about, by the pressure of Germans since the Marcomannic War."[5] What in 1946 had seemed to be an imprecation against modern Germans turned after forty years into calm orthodox history. The verdict was in and continues to be widely espoused today: what occasioned the "decline and fall" of the basically sound later Roman Empire was an "external pressure" weighing more heavily on the West than on the East.

The proposition set forth by three esteemed ancient historians helps to explain why barbarians in general and certain peoples in particular, which were always prominent in discussions of this subject, have lately attracted attention. Barbarians are the subject of the present book, but need to be framed by the premise shared by Piganiol, Jones, and Demandt, namely, that the Roman Empire was internally sound and not in the grips of terminal disease. The thesis of internal Roman "rot" was prevalent before World War II; Gibbon himself had ventured that the Empire was doomed even if all barbarians suddenly dropped dead.[6] Piganiol, Jones, and Demandt exemplify a sharp turn of interpretation in a much more positive direction. In their wake or independently, the admiring study of late antiquity, especially its religious and artistic aspects, blossomed in the later twentieth century; the name of Peter Brown is symbolic of these efforts.[7] Even the massive late Roman state regime, ominously called the "Dominate," has, after our experiences with swollen but beneficent welfare states, shed its formerly negative cast and been deemed necessary and bearable (Jones was central to this revision). It has now become very difficult to look upon the later Roman Empire as an exemplification of "decadence." The Christian Roman Empire of Constantine, Theodosius, and Justinian was different from the Romes of the past, but it, too—so it is held—was viable.

What, then, of the barbarians or "external pressure" that are claimed by Piganiol, Jones, and Demandt to have choked off what retained great vitality? In a historiographic perspective that was well established as early as the eighteenth century and since then has altered only in details, there seems to be a clear explanation for what took place. Europe had northern peoples, "Germans," who for centuries had expanded and migrated out of the north to such effect that, by the late Roman period, their expansionary drive had reached the edge of the Empire. This was the *Völkerwanderung*, a concept filled out and amplified by practitioners of *germanische Altertumskunde* and *germanische Frühgeschichte*. It was understood that, from the late 300s on, the Germans pushed their way onto imperial soil in a course of conquest, land seizure, and kingdom foundation. The major peoples engaged in this movement gave rise in outline to the future west European states—France, England, Spain, Portugal, and Italy—and initiated the medieval and modern worlds. However Christian and vigorous the late Romans may have been, they met the greater vigor of the migrating Germans and gave way. Out of the north and onto once imperial territory the "Germans" imported their energy, embryonic institutions, and "ethnic identities" and founded the European Middle Ages.[8] This well-worn scenario still faces us today, enlivened by such new words as ethnogenesis and ethnosociology; it is the "ethnic" complement to the invitation of the ancient historians for an external force to terminate classical antiquity.

A grand narrative of this kind, long rooted in historical literature, concerns not only the peoples often called "early Germans" but also the belief that these foreigners ruined the later Roman Empire. It is not easily disloged. My four historiographical chapters have chipped away at the main pillars of this edifice:

1. The familiar notion of a "Migration Age" acknowledges that, in a two-century period (370–568), various sedentary peoples, settled to the north and east of the Roman borders, moved noticeably from one stable position to other stable positions. These were not "wandering peoples." Their moves, though sometimes extending over a period of years, were from one point to another, almost invariably for deliberate reasons. Migrations were no more salient an aspect of these centuries, or involved more people, than in other ages.[9]

2. The claim that "the Germans overthrew the Roman Empire" has never been substantiated. Even Alexander Demandt, an eminent and skilled advocate, cannot muster adequate evidence to justify such a conclusion. Most of the northern peoples involved in late Roman history were destroyed in its course; they vanish from recorded history. The survivors settled on formerly Roman soil as adherents to the Roman religion, defenders of Roman populations and laws, and preservers of the Roman language.[10]

3. There were no Germans until a Germany materialized little by little in the European Middle Ages. Rome faced outward toward multiple and mutually antagonistic peoples. The existence of an ancient common Germanic civilization reaching deep into the B.C. period is a learned invention of sixteenth-century Germans, based on classical sources well known to us. The invention was and continues to be refined and exuberantly developed by generations of writers inside and outside Germany; it is no less mythical for that. The associated idea that the Vandals, Goths, Gepids, and Herules were distant foreign peoples who had migrated into Roman space from a remote "womb of nations" is a tendentious fiction born in Justinian's Byzantium.

4. The etiology of a "Germanic people" held in greatest reverence by modern scholars has been the tale of Gothic migration from Scandinavia first found in the *Getica* of Jordanes. Long believed to embody an authentic "folk memory," this story was devised in Justinian's Constantinople at the moment when the Goths of Italy were being stamped out by Justinian's armies. Jordanes's Byzantine deformation of the past of

the Goths suitably complemented the crushing of their present by armed force.

In sum, the Roman Empire did not face a "barbarian world" in the grips of a migratory tide that swept over the frontiers and exerted "pressures" to which the western provinces succumbed. There was no "Germanic civilization" long ripening north and east of the imperial frontiers to be transplanted onto ex-Roman soil. The traces we have of ethnic migration legends proceed initially from Constantinople where they were crafted to give an alien look to faces that had been familiar presences within the Empire for two centuries.

What happened instead is that northern barbarians participated with Romans in the larger stirrings of late antiquity, and notably in the long-range simplification or militarization that affected the underpinnings of late Roman society. The lines by Bede quoted at the start of this chapter evoke a mature society ordered very differently from that of even the later Roman Empire. It appears from Bede's comment that (at least as an ideal) the clergy and soldiery had appropriated the whole of the available economic "surplus" and divided it among themselves. This is the process—extending over a long time, and occasioning severe readjustments of social priorities—that Gibbon outlined when he referred to "the triumph of barbarism and religion." Bede's upper social ranks of armed protectors and praying clergy were by no means confined in the 700s to remote Northumbria; they were paralleled at the far end of the Mediterranean by a Byzantium whose army, settled in "themes," was directly sustained by the cultivators of the soil, and whose clergy and monks were almost all that was left (outside Constantinople) of a "civilian" element in the lands that still called themselves "the Roman Empire."[11] It had taken time and effort to bring about this result from end to end of the former ecumene.

The Roman Empire of the fourth century, in which generals held the reins of power alongside a large civilian government, and in which the Christian church was only beginning to carve out a place, had looked very different from Bede's world and, most of all, had manifested a much greater division and specialization of labor and occupations. It had been much more complex than Bede's Northumbria or the contemporary Byzantium of the "themes."[12]

The fourth-century Roman Empire had vast frontiers holding back more than fifty diverse kinds of "outsiders"; it had a recently expanded army to carry out this task, and an elaborate machinery of civil government extending from imperial palaces through prefectures, dioceses, provinces, and municipalities all organized to appropriate adequate quantities of the production of the laboring population and to recirculate these proceeds in multiple ways for the upkeep mainly of the army, but also of imperial metropolises and the other, varied expenses of the state. The image is one of a multiplicity of callings and duties, supported by a sophisticated governmental apparatus, with an economic life capable of sustaining not only state services but also a leisured landowning class in both the cities and the capitals of the Empire. The members of this "civilian" class, some grossly rich but most mediocre in wealth, carried out periodic stints of public service, and coexisted with a paid, professional class of officials and soldiers occupied full time in maintaining the smooth working and safety of the Empire. One simplification was conspicuously taking place throughout the Empire by the 330s (the date is arguable); it was the dismantling of the multifarious religious cults that had been built into everyday life since time immemorial, and the parallel development of a new, single religion staffed by a full-time clergy.

A striking image in late antiquity is that of Diocletian, the great reforming emperor, laying down power in 305 and retiring to what he hoped would be a peaceful private life in the enjoyment of his Dalmatian gardens. He was confident of having set the Empire so completely back on its tracks that, after him, an experienced team would step into place and keep the machinery moving smoothly and steadily, allowing its master-builder a tranquil and comfortable retirement. So confident was Diocletian in his achievement that he even forced his reluctant fellow Augustus into abdication. By stepping aside, Diocletian dramatized what he hoped would be the fruit of his lifework for the entire Empire: a return to normality, in which civil repose and ease would reward the population for the sacrifices it endured to support a large army keeping continuous watch at the widespread frontiers. Diocletian was overoptimistic. He had built well enough to assure his personal repose, but the edifice of imperial concord was shaky: the second Tetrarchy lasted only a year and a half. The members of the imperial college experienced twenty more years of ambition and instability, during which the Christian church (which Diocletian had tried to suppress) was legalized. To overcome the troubles that drove the Empire off its Diocletianic tracks called for the simplifications of dynastic emperorship and monotheistic religion, both symbolized by Constantine.[13]

One of the most precious commodities that the Roman Empire had created and diffused over its far-flung territories was private or civilian life—the possibility for landowners to secure the rents of their far-flung agricultural property and enjoy them in an urban setting in the company of their peers, engaged in the diversions of their class, with moderate responsibility for occasional unpaid service to their fellow citizens.[14] No one wished to eliminate this gracious civic existence. For everyone lucky in the pursuit of economic gain or involved in the strenuous forms of civil or military state service, withdrawal to private life was the light at the end of the perilous tunnel of worldly striving, as it had been for Diocletian. Much later, in the crisis of Gothic Italy, the clearest sighted (and most privileged) Goths wished for nothing better than a comfortable retirement in a safe backwater of Byzantium.[15] Private life was a blessing whose elimination was not deliberately sought by anyone. Yet over a period of three or four centuries, nothing proved harder to protect against the dual inroads of military exigency and religious fervor; *otium cum dignitate* was simplified out of existence. Byzantium retained an autocratic Roman emperor, but was almost as completely deprived as the West of what had been the finest flower of the Roman way of life. At that crucial level, the two *partes imperii* experienced the same fate.

The process of simplification undergone by the later Roman Empire is a vast subject whose exploration has been initiated in one way or another by hundreds of scholars.[16] The detailed contribution to its elaboration made in this book (and in *Barbarians and Romans*) is the demonstration of how Goths and Burgundians were settled in Gaul and Italy. A hasty glance at this operation might yield a peremptory verdict: a Roman state that gave barbarians the provincial lands they coveted instead of defending them with its own troops sloughed off its responsibilities and took the easy course. But Constantius and Aetius did more than impose a quick and dirty solution; streamlining was involved, but not a facile sacrifice of the interests of the sitting population. The texts at our disposal show how the Western imperial authorities abandoned a complex military system based on the collection of taxes and their redistribution to soldiers as rations and pay, and exchanged it for a scheme in which taxpayers and their assessed properties were directly assigned to individual (barbarian) soldiers as the permanent, hereditary source of their sustenance. These awards, which left private property intact, did not completely dismantle the tax system in the lands in question. At least one-third of the assessed taxpayers in southern Gaul and two-thirds in Italy continued to make their payments to a government; Gothic and Burgundian kings had resources far exceeding their subjects'. Clear traces of Roman complexity are documented by the financial items in Cassiodorus's *Variae*; unmistakable signs of Roman fiscality are discernible in Frankish Gaul; even Bede in remote Northumbria presupposed that its armed defenders should, by rights, receive "estates" (*possessiones*). What took place in fifth-century Gaul and Italy was a retreat, but a retreat in good order, leaving intact notable remnants of the systems that were discarded. The assessment records of the late Roman state begat the estate records of the early medieval countryside.[17]

In detailing the events of 476 in Italy, Procopius, a voice of Roman conservatism, fully sympathized with the patrician Orestes, father of Romulus Augustulus, when he turned away the demand of the army of Italy that its compensation should be changed from regular pay and rations to something wholly inelastic, namely, the permanent assignment to the army of one-third of Italian landed assessments and the award of individual endowments out of this pool. Orestes lost his life in defense of the existing system; the insecure government of an imperial usurper could hardly deny its army the same terms of employment as the patricians Constantius and Aetius had granted decades ago to the Goths and Burgundians of Gaul.[18] It became almost an established principle throughout the West that "soldiers" were each entitled to have a quota of dependent "taxpayers" of their own, and that, conversely, all landowners having tributaries answerable to them were obligated to service as "soldiers"—unless, to be sure, these tributaries answered to a church and its clergy. The claims of the Christian church to support for its activities, and (less absolutely) to freedom from armed service, were as insistent and irresistible as the claims of soldiers to the price of their protection.[19]

The historical chapters of this book have shown the barbarians of whatever name taking part in the continual efforts of the late Roman state to carry out its responsibilities within the means available.

The Alans, Vandals, and Sueves of Chapter 5 were not remote newcomers suddenly materializing out of nowhere and taking an innocent Empire unaware. They were established parts of the landscape. The Alans, newer than the other three, made up for their comparative strangeness by the intensity of their involvement since the 370s with the Roman army. What decided the Danubians to combine with the Alans and launch a one-way invasion across the Rhine is beyond our powers to determine. We can only be certain that, in these years, their behavior was hardly anomalous. Although the Empire left itself open to attack, it mattered more that *barbaricum* seemed worthy of being abandoned for a better if more perilous life. The odds favoring success in this quest for improvement turned out, in fact, to be poor.

A salient fact of later imperial history is that the military or diplomatic encounters of the barbarians with Rome produced a long line of vanished names. Imperial retreats were measured and did not exclude counterattacks; hostility to barbarians was unwavering, built into the language. Orosius, a good Christian ready to recognize barbarians as, on occasion, rightful instruments of God's wrath upon sinful Romans, and as candidates for evangelization, also invited readers to relish the spectacle of alien kings and their followers voluntarily killing each other off for the greater glory of the Empire.[20] The Alans and Siling Vandals who easily crossed the Rhine and rampaged through Gaul ultimately met with near extinction in Spain; the successful acquisition by the Burgundians of a territory west of the Rhine ended, after less than a generation, in annihilation; Attila's "empire" dissolved soon after its most spectacular campaigns; three out of four of Procopius's "Gothic peoples" were put down in a span of

thirty years in the sixth century. Those barbarians foolhardy enough to penetrate Roman frontiers were curbed and broken by barriers of determination at
least as often as they had enduring effects.

Though sometimes treated with the utmost harshness, barbarians belonged to Rome's world, as a resource that lent itself to being wisely exploited by
imperial governments unendingly trying to economize and balance competing
priorities. Except for the demands of a growing Christian church, the later Roman empire offers a face of almost continual contraction. Typically, a city council that in the early fourth century might have had a hundred members to share
its burdens would have shrunk by A.D. 600 to an anxious committee composed
of a bishop and two or three elders. An expansive Justinian could achieve astonishing things, but was powerless to alter the pattern of loss and retrenchment
for longer than his lifetime. The conquest of the Vandal and Gothic kingdoms
added no strength to his empire, and neither did the construction (and reconstruction) of Haghia Sophia.[21] After Justinian, East Roman armies became ever
smaller and harder to finance until, ultimately, their units had to be withdrawn
from areas of operation and regrouped (in good order) on the lands in Asia Minor that they would garrison in return for being fed. In this panorama of relentless shrinkage, barbarians as recruits or suppliants for peace could consistently
be perceived as the desirable lower-cost alternative. Valens and his advisers saw
this very clearly when the Goths in 376 presented their request for a large-scale
admission south of the Danube. The cost-benefit equation of their request offered an opportunity not to be missed.[22]

For all their promise of lower costs, barbarians can hardly be expected to
have been any less self-seeking and less greedy than their Roman counterparts.
Although some of them, such as Theoderic the Amal, gave exemplary accounts
of themselves as statesmen, Vandals and Goths did not, as Salvian hoped, replace Roman vices with a new moral severity. Why should they have? What
mattered more was that they introduced no alternative to the *nomen Romanum*;
they were not rivals, proposing a different way of life or competing for loyalties.
That was one point of Orosius's story about Athaulf and of my story, in Chapter
7, of the sad fate of Totila's Gothic rebellion.[23] The barbarians could be recruited
into the imperial enterprise because they asked for nothing more than to carry
it forward and share its blessings. They also shared its retrenchments.

Surprisingly or not, the third-century Empire reshaped itself extraordinarily well to permit the rise to high places not only of military professionals from
backward Roman provinces, but also of barbarians from beyond the Rhine
and Danube. The part of Chapter 7 in which this story is told with reference to
the emergence of a multiethnic military aristocracy retraces circumstances
whose exploration by earlier scholarship deserves to be newly emphasized. The

"barbarization" or militarization or simplification of the Roman world—to use Gibbon-tinged language for developments over a long period—was as much a socioeconomic as a cultural process. It was set in motion domestically in the third century to remedy the problems of an Empire challenged by internal instability and external attack, and to bring its strained finances back to solvency; but the readiness of this process to admit talents of whatever social origin to positions of leadership contributed almost at once to opening the door of imperial service to immigrants from beyond the frontiers. Little by little, in spite of efforts to preserve traditional niceties, barbarization crowded out both the paganism and the civilian life of classical antiquity and allocated whatever resources there were either to the military elements of society or to the various branches of the Christian church. It was a story that, at least in the West, enriched the once-Roman world with new leadership and renewed purpose.

Alexander Demandt on the Role of the Germans in the End of the Roman Empire

Alexander Demandt, Der Fall Roms: Die Auflösung des römischen Reiches im Urteil der Nachwelt (Munich, 1984), pp. 587–97; my translation. My use of Demandt's pages has been graciously authorized by the publisher, Beck Verlag, Munich, Germany. This is the full text corresponding to the material set out in point form and condensed in Chapter 2 (above). Demandt's references to his authorities are in the German original and are not reproduced here. My translation is more literal and less readable than it would be if designed for frequent use. Its function here is to serve as a check on my condensation. Its goal therefore is to be as faithful as possible to the original, even if the result lacks elegance.

That the fall of the Empire cannot be explained by the totality of its ills is proved by imperial continuity in the East: Byzantium survived. This is an old argument—already used by Panvinius (1558), Krause (1789), Mommsen (1893), Baynes (1943), and Jones (1964)—and it gives weight to the idea that external pressure is an indispensable factor in understanding the late Roman situation. The argument is convincing. Owing to the disadvantageously long river frontiers, the attack of the northern peoples on the European provinces could not be resisted, whereas Asia Minor was comparatively shielded by geography. The Persians were not in search of land and had inner problems; the Isaurians could be integrated; and the Germans did not cross over the Bosphorus.

So as to allow internal decadence to retain its comprehensive explanatory force in the face of [the facts just mentioned], it is occasionally claimed that the Eastern half was always healthier in its internal structure than the West. This claim does not work. The farther-reaching urbanization of the East is no criterion for affirming a capacity for resistance; just think of the defenselessness of city-rich North Africa vis-à-vis the Vandals. Conversely, large landownership by senators in the West should not be regarded categorically as a sign of weakness. Whoever takes feudalism to be progressive has to consider large landownership as an element of superiority; whoever considers it reactionary has to take into account that both the Germans and the Byzantines, notably in Egypt, built up a landowning structure of this kind.

Montesquieu believed that European troops were normally superior to Asiatic ones; so did Mommsen. In the second and first century (B.C.) the Hellenistic East collapsed without a sound in the face of the legions; at Pharsalia, Philippi, and Actium generals of the West triumphed over generals of the East. The postulated progressiveness of the East must have taken form in the imperial period: did it therefore benefit from the imperial system that made the West backward? Until the civil war between Constantine and Licinius no sign can be found that the Eastern half had greater capability for military defense. Later civil wars, Magnentius and then Julian against Constantius, Maximus and then Arbogast against Theodosius, are poorly suited to be test cases for the relations of force because, in the meanwhile, the strength of the emperors came to depend entirely on the barbarian auxiliaries they happened to have at their disposal. By then, Germanic bands were already dominant in both halves of the Empire, regardless of whether they fought for the East or for the West, for or against Rome. The Danubian provinces, formerly so rich in soldiers, were the part of the ostensibly healthier Byzantine Empire that the Germans and Huns attacked; they were just as defenseless as the West.

The role of Germanic attacks in the collapse is normally devalued by the objection that the Romans had had to do with the Germans ever since the Cimbri and Teutons and had always been able to hold them at bay: why should that no longer have been possible after 376? Does the inferiority of Rome thereafter not prove its inner collapse? Of course! It would foolish to dispute it. Nevertheless, the collapse was hastened, or even brought about, by the pressure of Germans since the Marcomannic War. The pressure became more intense.

The idea that conditions in Germanic space remained essentially the same from Ariovistus to Alaric, and the ignorance of developments that occurred there, are discipline-conditioned defects of the explanations that ancient historians attempt. Even the work of A. H. M. Jones suffers from cyclopian one-eyedness in this respect. The situation at the frontiers cannot be grasped unless the developments in *barbaricum* [are taken into account] (*Barbaricum* is a Latin word for the "land of the barbarians, beyond the imperial frontiers"). The so-called *Völkerwanderung* [migration of nations] was no abrupt event set loose only by the attack of the Huns. Rather, it is the turbulent last stage of a Germanic expansion that is visible ever since early in the first millennium B.C. Proceeding from south Scandinavian/north German space, the Germans expanded in all directions. The Bastarnae already reached the Black Sea in the third century B.C. The Roman military frontier set a bar in the face of the southward migration, a bar backing up the pressure of Germanic population.

The condition for this development was the love of warfare that ancient authors repeatedly attest among the Germans, warfare both against each other and against Rome. Caesar reports it: "all life consists in hunting and military training (*vita omnis in venationibus atque in studiis rei militaris consistit*)." Pomponius Mela and Seneca provide confirmation. Precious testimony about the warlike self-confidence of the Germans is given by Tacitus in the anecdote about the two Frisian kings who came to Rome as envoys and, unbidden, took the places of honor at the theater, declaring: "no mortals exceed the Germans in fighting ability and fidelity (*nullos mortalium armis aut fide ante Germanos esse*)." The ideal attributed to the Germans is not prosperity but freedom. Uncomprehendingly, the elder Pliny notes at the close of his description of the simplicity of German living conditions: "these people, if conquered today by the Roman people, say they are subject to servitude; . . . fortune spares many for a penal existence (that is, what they call 'freedom') (*et hae gentes, si vincantur hodie a populo Romano, servire se dicunt! ita est profecto: multis fortuna parcit in poenam*)." That Fortuna spared the Germans from the blessing of Roman rule so as to punish them was scarcely the view that those spared had of themselves. How they valued their way of life by comparison with that of antiquity is something we only rarely learn; perhaps [an idea turns up] in the command of the Gothic king in 269 not to burn the books of the Athenians since, by studying them, they were kept from military exercises, or from the fact that Germans shunned life in cities.

At all times the warrior ideal ruled Germanic society. Unlike the [Roman] municipal and senatorial upper class dishabituated to arms, the Germanic élite was and remained a nobility of the sword. The adult man was a warrior. Hardly anything better characterizes the difference between the two peoples than the contrasting ways in which they used prisoners of war. The Romans mainly enrolled captured barbarians in their own army in order to spare the peasantry [from being recruited and taken away from their fields], whereas the Germans utilized many thousands of Roman captives in production, so as to gain their own people for war. This contrast in attitude to war explains why the always huge numerical superiority of the total population of the Empire vis-à-vis the barbarians had no effect. Our modern democratic-egalitarian image of humanity blinds us to how interests and the means applied to them can differ. The further aversion to weapons spread, the fewer weapons were needed to terrorize the [minority that continued to bear arms]. The political history of antiquity was always determined by well-armed and well-led minorities.

Besides a bellicose spirit and hunger for freedom, another constant factor and dynamic element [in the equation] was the population increase of the Germans. Antique observers always regarded it as a threat. Tacitus noted that Germans did not limit their number of children in artificial ways. In late antiquity the profusion of new blood of the Germanic tribes is attested for the Franks and

Burgundians. Jordanes calls Scandinavia "a workshop of peoples or womb of nations (*quasi officina gentium aut certe velut vagina nationum*)." Germanic population increase can be established archaeologically by the increase of grave finds and an enlargement of the area of settlement by inland colonization.

The reason for this manifest increase may be sought in social conditions, understandable, if one wishes, as the expression of a certain biological strength of the people. Besides, when the homeland was too narrow, the Germans equipped their children and sent them to foreign parts, just as the Greeks and Romans had also done in their beginnings. In late Greek and late Roman society one finds on the contrary a control of births by abortion, exposure, and contraception. Among the rich the reasons for this were the limitation of heirs and the enjoyment of the flattery of those soliciting inheritances; among the poor, need played a part. Yet we know that the living standard of poor Romans on the whole surpassed the German average; there was no physical impossibility to feed children in Rome. The Empire had enough land. The emperors took extraordinary pains to make the *agri deserti* fruitful again. Again and again since the days of Augustus large groups of Germans were settled in the Empire in order to augment the numbers of soldiers and peasants: "Roman provinces were filled with barbarian slaves and Scythian cultivators; a barbarian was turned into a soldier, a Goth into a farmer (*impletae barbaris servis Scythicisque cultoribus Romanae provinciae, factus miles e barbaro, colonus e Gotho*)." The fact that the native Roman population would not let itself increase—a somewhat trivial fact in any case in view of absolute relations—may have been conditioned by a certain hopelessnes. The fear was that any increase would be eaten up by the tax collector.

For Romans, war against the Germans meant at best a maintenance of things as they were; for the Germans war against Romans promised improvement of their own circumstances. Men's conduct normally depends less on conditions than on expectations.

Developments within Germania were marked not only by population increase but also by a civilizing process, influenced by Rome. By employment as mercenaries and by trade the Germans since Caesar learned from the Romans. This is proved by the reports of ancient authors, by archaeological finds, and by the early layers of borrowing of civilized concepts by Germanic languages. About six hundred borrowed words for technical, legal, economic, and military things were taken over before the second (Old High German) sound shift; they prove how strong the Roman cultural influence was during the imperial period. To a special degree the Germans assimilated Roman military techniques. An emphatically confirmed pragmatic rule in the development of civilizations is that the military sector leads in being modernized. Weapons are brought to the most modern level before anything else. In the army of Arminius only the first line of battle owned iron weapons, the followers fought at least in part with wooden spears hardened by fire. In Tacitus's time the Chatti, who were neighbors of the Romans, had adopted the Roman way of war. In the course of the second century iron weapons increased, step by step to be sure with Roman imports.

Whereas the Germans of the early imperial period fought with their upper bodies bare, they later had a protective suit and a chain shirt though not the Roman plate armor. About A.D. 200 bow and arrow are encountered, and with the introduction of distance weapons the Germans could dare open battle. Needle-pointed arrows were instituted against chain armor, wide lance heads and rapiers against plate armor, battle axes against bronze helmets. Along with simple imitation and adoption of Roman weapons, elaborated native forms made their appearance.

Ever since the third century the equipment of officers, from the fourth that of the rank and file, attained equality among the Romans and Germans. The so-called *laeti*-armament is found on both sides of the *limes*. In the third century Germanic cavalry increased in importance, and the Romans were forced to adopt the military method of the opponent. Gallienus created a heavy cavalry. The teachability of the Germans in matters of military technique was known to the Romans. They tried to prevent the Germans from assimilating the achievements of Roman warfare. This is shown by Dexippus in the third century; the *Anonymus de rebus bellicis* in the fourth; and *Codex Theodosianus* 9.40.24 in the fifth. A notable part of the weapons with which Germans fought against the Romans was of Roman manufacture; the imperial embargo on weapons had little success. Since the middle of the fourth century city walls offered Romans little real protection any longer. The Franks first took Cologne in 355, the Alamanni Mainz in 368. The Germans were so good at sieges that numerous cities fell into their hands in Gaul and on the Danube. Their fall was the first step to the taking of Rome in 410.

A third factor of development besides population increase and advancing military technique was the Germans' political consolidation into large war-alliances against Rome. The successes of Arminius and Marbod show how much could already be achieved by individual Roman-trained princes from the age of small tribes. In the third century the political landscape changed, the west Germanic small tribes brought themselves into the so-called tribe-associations of Franks, Alamanni, and Saxons. Large task forces took form aimed at the Empire. The success of this new policy is shown by the disasters of the third century, when the Franks drove through Gaul and Spain as far as North Africa, the Alamanni overran the *limes*, and the Saxons plundered the coasts. The attacks of the Sasanids on the Euphrates frontier facilitated these German successes.

Individual observers on the Roman side had foreseen this development. Besides Tacitus, Seneca anticipated it. He wrote: "In view of their physical and mental constitution, which avoids any kind of civilized blemish, the Germans need only be given reflection (*ratio*) and training (*disciplina*), and the Romans for their part will have to return to their ancestral customs, or . . ." Seneca did not spell out the frightening alternative.

The demographic, technical, and political strengthening of the Germans did not have only negative effects on Rome. The saying of Scipio Nasica that Rome needed a whetstone applied to the German threat as it had to the Carthaginian. The army that was always necessary on its account was an essential instrument of Romanization, civilization, and integration of the population into the Empire. In time, however, the Germanic whetstone proved harder than the legionary's sword. Ever since the first century the emperor sought to buy the good conduct of the Germans, paying them money to keep still. Tacitus doubted their "vincibility" and hoped for inner German divisions as the finest gift of the gods averting Rome's end. To finance defense against the Marcomanni, Marcus Aurelius had to auction off the crown jewels and to arm slaves. The Marcomanni could be pushed back, and the Alamanni were also thrust back at first. But when the Neo-Persian Sasanian Empire made its appearance as an additional enemy, the Empire was overstrained. Because an emperor had to be present at every major front, the plague of emperor-making characteristic of the epoch of soldier-emperors broke out. Its result was that external wars were joined by a continual civil war.

The beginnings of dissolution of the Roman state were prepared by the constraints of war on many fronts, and these exigencies were never wholly overcome. The beginning came with the first real double emperorship, by Marcus Aurelius and Lucius Verus, as the Danube and the Euphrates frontiers were simultaneously threatened. The so-called separate empires of the third century are understandable as defense measures for the whole Empire against Germans and Persians. Even the plural emperorship of late antiquity, with its transposition of the capitals to the vicinity of the frontiers, does not in any sense mirror internal particularism, but served to master problems coming from the outside.

The Diocletian-Constantinian reforms at first surmounted the crisis. A glance at the army teaches at what price. Twice as many soldiers served in the army of the late Roman state as in the army of Augustus. And they had to be nourished by provinces that had been plundered many times. An apparatus of officials, formerly unnecessary, collected the taxes. The economic wretchedness of the Dominate related primarily to costs of defense. To this extent the Germanic attacks were the essential cause for the inner difficulties of the late Roman Empire.

No one will dispute that a blamelessly operating administration, a social order bringing satisfaction, and capable emperors at the head of the available resources would have been able to pull their weight more effectively than was actually the case. Men like Julian and Valentinian I show what was possible. But one may hardly argue on the basis of human deficiencies since these customarily occur on both sides. We are best informed about the afflictions of the imperial population; on the Germanic side, we are entirely in the dark and imagine, for this reason, that conditions were healthy. Was there no misery, no violence, no discord in that quarter? The few indications of the sources allow us to suspect that, in contrast to the sporadic civil wars in the Empire, the state of war was normal among the Germanic tribes. As we carefully tally what weakened Roman defense, we should also take account of what diminished Germanic offensive capabilities. Let us imagine that the Cimbri and Teutons had not split up, that Arminius and Marbod had acted together against Rome, that during the Marcomannic War the Rhine Germans had also attacked: in these eventualities Rome's end might have taken place centuries before it did. Tacitus once mentions sixty thousand dead in wars of Germans against Germans, and there always were inner-German wars. Whereas decay in the Empire weakened the defense, privation in *barbaricum* strengthened the attack, showing how irrelevant inner factors are when taken in isolation.

What drew the Germans into the Empire was the quest for land and booty. Through trade and mercenary employment, they knew what was to be sought there. In one way or another Rome had to yield to the external pressure. Was the dissolution of the unity of the state the only possibility? Two alternatives are conceivable. The first was stated by Ennodius to Theoderic: Rome rejuvenates itself in that the parts that have become old and slack, namely the distant provinces, are amputated. Could not the Empire have shrunk healthily in this way centuries earlier? Yes and no. Yes to the extent that the upsurge of Constantinople may, in a certain way, be called a salubrious shrinking of this kind. The East never put more means at the disposal of sustaining the West than it could spare, and left it to its own devices as soon as it could no longer be held militarily. [And thus the East saved its health.] No [to healthy shrinking]: to the extent that Italy in the imperial period increasingly lost its role as core of the Empire. The reservoir for military manpower was Illyricum, the economic centers lay in the Levant, in Africa, and in Gaul. Romanitas was a sociocultural varnish over the entire imperial territory. To be sure, a certain return flow toward Italy could be observed from the threatened frontier territories, from Britain, the Rhine and Danube frontiers, but that was not enough to hold back the advancing German army. It would have contradicted the Roman idea of empire to build Italy as a military and economic fortress at the cost of the provinces, a fortress that one could have defended over a spacious glacis. The Roman state-idea extended beyond the borders of peoples. In times of expansion this was its strength, in times of decline its weakness.

An alternative would have been an intensified admission of barbarians into the Empire. They were not hereditary enemies of Rome and had always deferred to the emperors. Since the fourth century they had been not only enemies but also buttresses of the Empire. To what extent their incorporation would have succeeded remains disputed. Since the defeat of Adrianople (378) Roman policy toward the Germans had experienced a fateful antinomie: the greater the losses that were endured at the hands of the barbarians, the greater the efforts that had to be undertaken to win the [barbarians] as warriors and settlers, so that the gaps made by Germans might be filled by Germans. The emperor's courtiers recommended this homeopathic procedure, but critical contemporaries like Ammianus and Synesius rightly disapproved. Even Christian authors like Ambrose and Prudentius occasionally adopted very hostile tones toward the Germans. But the emperors had no choice. The hostility of senatorial and Christian circles toward the barbarians provided no foundation for successful policy. The foreigners had long been indispensable as slaves and mercenaries. No one saw this better than Theodosius, the "friend of peace and of the Goths," and Stilicho, his Germanic testament-executor. The last time Roman national troops made an appearance was in the revolt of Pavia (408) which led to the downfall of Stilicho. The sequel showed that Hunnic mercenaries were the sole alternative to a Germanic army in the West. The Romans (*Romane*) no longer fought; for centuries they had been accustomed to having others fight for them. When Geiseric (429) appeared in Africa with eighty thousand persons—not warriors—and subjected this province rich in cities and inhabitants, the provincials, though twenty or thirty times greater in numbers, did not feel competent for defense. They closed the city gates and waited for the emperor to send an army or to name Geiseric master of the soldiers and so solve the problem in a legalistic way. With Alaric this had been possible.

The readiness of the Germans to fit into the Roman system allows us to suppose that they could have grown more into the Empire than they did. If a successful large scale settlement of land-hungry groups on the waste fields of Greece, Italy, and Africa had succeeded, the collision harmful for the Empire might have been avoided at the time when it took place [that is, put off till later]. Just as the Roman emperors of the third and fourth centuries were predominantly Illyrian, so could Romanized Germans have been emperors. Magnentius and Silvanus were Germanic usurpers; Eucherius, Patricius, and Thela, sons of Germanic generals, were in the line of imperial succession. Graf Stauffenberg's vision of a *translatio imperii* (or a continuing *imperium Romanum*) taking place not just in 800 but three or four centuries earlier is not so far off the track. The Isaurians of Asia Minor succeeded in being integrated. They won a bad name in the fourth and fifth century as barbarian plunderers, but ever since their prince Tarasicodissa became Byzantine emperor as Zeno, they took to fighting for the Empire, no longer against it. The irreconcilable Isaurians were resettled.

To this extent, the dissolution of the Empire can be conceived of not only as a failed defense, but equally as a failed incorporation of the Germans. It is hard to decide whether the Romans deserve blame on this account, for a system that was so superior in civilization and still so liberal in politics had to have some sort of boundary to its capacity for integration. The differentiated ways of life and thinking of autonomous groups always secrete a basis for conflict. The capacities of each decided the outcome. Taken in themselves, the conduct of both sides is understandable: on the Roman side, the desire to endure (the conservative principle), and on the Germanic side the desire to improve one's position (the progressive principle). From this perspective the end of the Empire is the result of a failed compromise of these principles—failures in the sense that the Romans ultimately lost what they had, but the Germans did not gain what they sought. They proved unable to carry forward the Roman culture that seemed worthy of enthusiasm and did not learn how to retain for themselves the land they had conquered. With the exception of the Frankish kingdom the Germanic states on imperial soil vanished.

The idea of an ingrained decadence as a result of which any blow must lead to collapse is unconvincing. The Germanic threat was not an interchangeable accident. Those of the other barbarians were. Berbers and Blemmyes, Saracens, Sarmatians, and Picts cannot be compared to the Germans even in numbers. Not even the Persians were a danger of the same order. To be sure they were culturally superior to the Germans, but they did not have the same reserves of men and did not seek room for settlement.

The Huns were significant as a triggering factor. Their appearance at the Black Sea was the occasion for the Westgoths (376) to seek and find admission to the Empire. To this extent the Huns determined the moment when the Danube frontier fell. In the framework of the Gernans' "persistent hammering," which placed the Emperor in an enduring "state of siege," one may attribute to the Huns only a momentarily intensifying effect. The Germans further weaken [the Huns' significance] in that they cushioned the first Hunnic shock (ca. 370), which would otherwise have affected the Empire, and they supplied the most important troops that, with Aetius, warded off the invasion of Attila into Gaul

(451). If the Huns were removed from the play of forces, a delay of the political dissolution might have to be reckoned with. That is the lesson of the German attacks of the third century. On the other hand, if the role of the Germans were taken away, hardly anyone can be seen who, in their place, would have brought about the dissolution of the Empire. Since no Roman group worth naming had an interest in doing so, the dissolving force could only come from the outside. Possibly a substitute agent might be found in the Arabs of the seventh century or in the Turks of the eleventh; but it is doubtful that they could have broken up the undivided, unweakened Empire. If a factor shows its importance by having a delaying effect, then the prime role must be attributed to the northern peoples.

The dissolution of Roman domination by Germanic domination is a process with many parallels in the preindustrial age. The civilized zones of the Mediterranean were always threatened from the barbarian regions. Out of the Arabian wastes Semitic nomads overran the Mesopotamian and Mediterranean city cultures: this began with the Akkadians and Amorites in the early second millennium and ended with the Arabs. Since the early first millennium Egypt fell under the domination of Libyan and Nubian mercenary leaders. Out of the woods of northern Europe land-seeking Indogermanics often broke into the Mediterranean lands: the Mycenaeans into the Minoan world, the Dorian into the Mycenean culture, Macedonians and Epirotes into classical Greece. At various times Celts, Germans, and Slavs advanced into the richer and warmer south. Out of the Asiatic steppes rider nomads fell time and again upon the southern civilized lands: the Huns upon the Sasanian and Roman empires, the Avars, Bulgars, and Turks upon the Byzantine Empire. Customarily the contest of force was preceded by a peaceful immigration and followed by a cultural adaptation. The inheritance of a culture falls upon its stepchildren.

The question raised for late antiquity poses itself in the same way for all the cases mentioned. Against the barbarian exterior the civilized states always manifest a tendency toward encapsulation but never prevent the barbarians from elevating themselves to the height of the civilized people in military technique. And because the longing of the barbarians for the wealth of the civilized lands increases the more they experience it and [the more] the civilized lands lose defensive force, [and] the longer a life of peaceful prosperity lasts, the invasion comes about at some time. This experience stood behind the classical model of decadence that was the basis of the political philosophy of antiquity. Daniel (5:20) pronounced it before Belshazar, and Ibn Khaldun explained with it the superiority of desert dwellers over city humanity.

In each case the question arises whether, without the attack from outside, inner decadence would ever have somehow led to the downfall of the system in question. What would have become of the Achaemenid Empire without the invasion of the Macedonians, of Babylonia without the invasion of the Medes? The seizure from outside always came about before the inner development was completed, but what does "completed" mean? Cultural history knows only interrupted experiments.

Appendix 2
Chronicle Evidence for the Burgundian Settlement

Four passages from chronicles address the circumstances that are described in the Burgundian Laws (Chapter 6, above). They extend from a near-contemporary chronicler in the mid-fifth century to a Frankish historian in the later seventh. In every case, the information supplied is sparse and ambiguous.

1. *Chronicle of 452*, a. 443, "Sapaudia Burgundionum reliquiis datur cum indigenis dividenda" (Sapaudia is given to the surviving Burgundians to be divided with the native [Romans])

The *Chronicle of 452* is a continuation of the Eusebius-Jerome world chronicle by an author, probably writing in Marseilles, who took a dim view of what was going on in the world about him. His line about the Burgundian settlement is set out as one of several events illustrating the low estate of the Roman Empire in these years.[1]

The Burgundians had had a kingdom in northeast Gaul for about twenty years after 413. Eventually, their king's ambition to widen his territory aroused the ire of Aetius, who called on Hunnic auxiliaries to teach the Burgundians a lesson they would not forget. In 436, their kingdom was totally destroyed by this Hunnic attack. The *reliquia* of the quotation are the survivors of the Burgundian disaster.

We have no idea where the survivors spent the intervening seven years (possibly east of the Rhine in company with Burgundians who had not moved to Gaul). It was this cowed "remnant" to which "Sapaudia," was given by the Roman government, still controlled by Aetius. Sapaudia is assumed but not firmly known to be Savoy; Geneva was an early center of Burgundian rule. The *indigenae* referred to are presumably the leaders or dignitaries of the district, appropriately glossed as *senatores* by Marius of Avenches (no. 2).[2] "To divide" could be in any proportion; when unqualified, it might be understood to mean equal shares. The object of division was Sapaudia itself, a territory or public district. If the private property of the *indigenae* had been what the Roman government granted, its cession would have been nothing less than a wholesale authorization to the Burgundians to seize whatever they wished without legal restraint. There is no sign that this took place. What the *indigenae* could be ordered to share were the resources of the state in the territory of settlement.

The chronicler's few words omit much that is found in the relevant Burgundian laws. We could hardly guess that the Burgundians had a king or that Aetius, in the name of Rome, dealt with him as government to government.

2. Marius of Avenches, a. 456, no. 2, "Eo anno Burgundiones partem Galliae occupaverunt terrasque cum Galliis senatoribus diviserunt"[3] (In this year, the Burgundians seized a part of Gaul and divided the lands with the Gallic dignitaries.)

Marius, bishop of Avenches (in western Switzerland), resided in the Frankish kingdom of Burgundy in the late sixth century. His chronicle ends in 581, and he died in 593. He refers to the same circumstances more fully described in no. 3 that resulted in an expansion of Burgundian settlement. His main value is in the use of the term *senatores*, probably meant here to signify local dignitaries—not senators of Rome, but local city councilors and electors of bishops.[4]

The wider circumstances are spelled out in no. 3. Even though, in this case, the Burgundian leadership took the initiative, rather than the Roman government as in no. 1, an arrangement with the local authorities was involved; the leaders of Roman Gaul, incensed at the overthrow of "their" emperor, Avitus, cooperated with the barbarian leadership. "Dividing lands" has the same indefinite sense as in no. 1. Once again, the text gives us no reason to think that the senators were offering up their own private property for division. The image conveyed is rather of two authorities, the Burgundians and the senators, dividing a bundle of public assets for their mutual advantage. The emperor Majorian came to terms with the Burgundians (and the Gallo-Romans) in 458.[5]

3. *Copenhagen Continuator of Prosper*, a. 456, "Post cuius [i.e., Reciarii regis Suevorum] caedem Gundiocus rex Burgundionum cum gente et omni praesidio annuente sibi Theudorico ac Gothis intra Galliam ad habitandum ingressus societate et amicitia Gothorum functus."[6] (After the killing of [Rechiar, king of the Sueves in Spain], Gundioc, king of the Burgundians, with the assent of Theoderic and the Goths, entered Gaul

for permanent residence with his people and all their belongings. He enjoyed the alliance and friendship of the Goths.)

The *Copenhagen Continuator of Prosper* is a distinctive continuation of the *Chronicle* of Prosper of Aquitaine apparently carried out in Italy in the first quarter of the seventh century on the basis of a variety of sources (it survives in a Copenhagen manuscript). Its last entry dates from 625. The early material, concerning the years 455 to 493 and constituting perhaps the fullest source for this period, is generally ascribed to a near contemporary (used by the compiler of 625). The Burgundian entry falls within this early block.[7] (The report might be taken as earlier in date than that of Marius of Avenches.)

The Continuator of Prosper refers to the same incident as no. 2. In 456, the Visigothic king Theoderic II was allowed by Avitus, emperor with Gothic support, to make a major effort to bring order to Spain and extend his control in that direction at the expense of the Sueves. The Gothic expeditionary force included Burgundians and other troops. Theoderic's plan was disturbed by the overthrow of Avitus. In order to bottle up the next emperor, Majorian, in Italy, Theoderic in 457 invited the Burgundians to extend their settlement into Gaul, notably into the province of Lyons (Lugdunensis Prima). Additional details are given in no. 2.

The information that Gundioc acted with Gothic support may help to explain why the Burgundian and Visigothic legal evidence on settlement is complementary.

4. Fredegar, *Chronicon* 2. 46, "Et cum ibidem [i.e., ad Rhenum] duobus annis [Burgundiones] resedissent, per legatis invitati a Romanis vel Gallis, qui Lugdunensum provinciam et Gallea comata, Gallea domata et Gallea Cisalpina manebant, ut tributa rei publice potuissent renuere, ibi cum uxoris et liberes visi sunt consedisse."[8] (And while [the Burgundians] paused [at the Rhine] for two years, they were invited by envoys from the Romans or Gauls who lived in the province of Lyons and Gallia comata, Gallia domata, and Gallia cisalpina, so that [the Romans or Gauls] might refuse tribute to the [Roman] empire. So [the Burgundians] transmigrated there with their wives and children.)

The anonymous historian normally called Fredegar worked in the vicinity of A.D. 660 using a large variety of source material. Although we lack his name, he is anything but a "nameless" chronicler; the chances are that, like Marius (no. 2), he worked in the Frankish kingdom of Burgundy. The more one studies his pages, the more he emerges as an author with a personality and causes to advocate. His presence in the lines about the Burgundians is readily betrayed by stylistic signposts, such as the phrase "visi sunt consedisse" and hostility to taxation. Fredegar does not passively transmit what he has read somewhere. He conveys a personal message.

The chronological setting of this passage differs from nos. 1-3; it is not the mid-fifth century but the reign of Valentinian I (364–75). The text directly follows a well known line from the Eusebius-Jerome-Hydatius chronicle about the coming to the Rhine of eighty thousand Burgundians. Ian Wood (among others) asks us to believe that these lines were "misplaced"; but Fredegar was not a bungler who just happened to drop this event in the wrong place. Though guided by information about the fifth-century Burgundian settlement, he deliberately collapsed time here because a late date did not suit his purposes. He was not interested at all in "the techniques of accommodation." The refusal of taxes is a piece of self-evident motivation that comes easily to his pen. The detail that mattered to him, as shown by the loving list of places, was the area of settlement. Here was the territorial birth certificate of the Burgundian kingdom, deliberately transposed to as early a moment in the chronicle as possible.

Appendix 3

The Meaning of agri cum mancipiis *in the Burgundian Kingdom*

In analyzing LB54 in Chapter 6, I showed that the repeated references to *agri cum mancipiis* in Burgundian laws referred to royal or fiscal assets, but I could not explain why royal property had that name. The definition of *terra* (or *ager*) as "assessed land" or "land registered for taxation" is not far-fetched; the cases examined in Chapter 6 repeatedly show that the aspect of land "divided" between the Romans and the barbarians was not its cultivation and ownership, which remained Roman and unchanged by barbarian settlement, but the state's portion—the assessments for purposes of taxation—which, in all the barbarian kingdoms, was shared by the king with his followers. In the initial Burgundian division, I argued, half the *terrae* were kept by the king as the basis for his finances (the fisc), and the other half went to the Burgundians as the pool out of which individual allotments were distributed. *Mancipia*, however, which in this context occur only in the Burgundian evidence, were a different matter, whose definition I left open and am concerned with here.[1] It is a delicate subject.

One certainty about *mancipia* is that, regardless of dictionaries (whose basic definition of *mancipium* is "slave"), the term in a context of Burgundian settlement does not denote only human beings.[2] LB54 might be read as documenting the existence of herds of *mancipia* out of which "one-third" were collected by Burgundians from Roman "hosts" and taken away as laborers to the allotments of *terrae* granted to them. The words of the law permit this reading. It is tempting, too, to look at the compound *agri cum mancipiis* and accept its surface sense as "fields with slaves"; with Wood and Barnish as guides, nothing looks more natural than that the king should dip into his fisc and reward selected Burgundians with arable land and slaves to cultivate them.[3] These literal interpretations have proved tempting, but the scenarios they imply are impossible. As shown in Chapter 6, *mancipia* have the awkward peculiarity of occurring everywhere in a ratio of two units to one unit of *terra*. The crucial evidence is LBExtravagans 21.12. In the partition laid down there, the Burgundians were awarded half the *terrae* whereas the king kept the other half of the *terrae* and the totality (*integritas*) of *mancipia*.[4] In real life, resident laborers, slave and free, must have been distributed more or less evenly over the cultivable land of the Burgundian kingdom, and no one could have gained from moving them around. That one half the land should be empty of laborers while the other half was overburdened with a double ration defies good sense. *Mancipia* in LBExtravagans 21.12 cannot denote only human beings, slave or free; and if that is true, the other occurrences of *mancipia*, in which the ratio 2:1 is also found, cannot be merely human either.

The 2:1 ratio is not mysterious; it stares us in the face in LBExtravagans 21.12. If *mancipia* are provisionally labeled as an "unidentified commodity," the law shows that the king and the ordinary, allotment-receiving Burgundians each had 50 percent of the assessed *terrae* but that the king kept 100 percent of the unidentified commodity. Each unit of royal *terra* had two units of royal *mancipia* associated with it; the fisc, after the initial division of Roman tax assets with the *faramanni*, was twice as rich in *mancipia* as in *terrae*. In the course of time, the kings gave away some *agri cum mancipiis* to selected individuals, and eventually the royal issuer of LB54 made a major award to the ordinary *faramanni*, ceding to them one-sixth unit of *terra* and a one-third unit, twice as much, of *mancipia*. This alienation left the royal fisc with one-third of the assessments of "land" and two-thirds—the double ratio again—of the assessments of *mancipia*, whatever they might be. What commodity did the royal fisc have twice as much of as land assessments, *terrae*?

If *mancipia* cannot be simply human beings, the alternative is that, like *terra*, the term belongs to the language of tax assessment and reflects what was in the Roman records given to the Burgundian government. The term *mancipia*, I suggest, does not signify only agrarian dependents (typically, slaves and coloni) but an assessment unit consisting of both persons and the resources at their command. In other words, *mancipia* in this context means "dependent tenancies."

In an article investigating the term *condoma* and its variants in late Roman and early medieval evidence, I showed that one of its meanings was "a human unit of agrarian lease," and that it resembled the terms *familia* (in Bede), *cassati* and *manentes* (in the English land books), *casati* (in Carolingian texts), and *massarii* (in Italy), all of which comprised both persons and their possessions. The same name formation would result in the term *mancipium* being a reference not only to one (slave) person but also to his family and possessions, again a "human unit of agrarian lease." Seventh-century Visigothic evidence explicitly attests to *mancipia* in this sense.[5] The term contrasts with *terra*, tentatively translated as "owner's lands." ("Home farm" is another possibility, but too specific.) *Agri cum mancipiis* did not mean fields with slaves to cultivate them; instead, the phrase referred to two different types of tax assessment added to each other—owner's lands (*agri* or *terra*) and, complementing them, the associated tenancies (*mancipia*).

Both *terrae* and *mancipia* were resources recorded for purposes of taxation in the *censuales paginae*, the state's registry of taxable property. In this context, *terra* was equivalent to what Frankish estate documents call *indominicatum*, the land and other assets in the direct charge of a *dominus* or landowner (*possessor*). Different from this *terra*, separable from it, but basically complementary were the *mancipia*—cultivators, free and slave, with their families and the lands they lived on and worked—corresponding to the dependent *mansi* of the Frankish sources. These terms allow us to infer that, at least in the area of the Burgundian settlement, the *censuales paginae* of the Roman state registered owner's lands, *terra*, apart from dependent tenancies, *mancipia*, and that this distinction was embedded in the tax records obtained by the Burgundians at the beginning of their settlement.[6]

In proposing this definition of *mancipia*, I am very conscious of following in the footsteps of Ferdinand Lot, whose main contribution to the literature of the "régime de l'hospitalité" consisted in filtering LB54 through the grid of the "grand domaine" as documented by the famous early ninth-century polyptyque of St. Germain des Prés and other estate records of the same period: "Puis on a pensé, et justement," Lot wrote, "que l'explication de l'anomalie [that is, the award of two-thirds the *terra* and only one-third the *mancipia*] devait être cher-chée dans la constitution même de la propriété foncière de l'époque. [New parag.] On sait que le grand domaine—c'est sur lui qu'est installé le Barbare—est divisé en deux parties."[7] The two parts Lot refers to were those of the "clas-sic" bipartite medieval seigneurie or domain, in which the *mansus indominicatus* of a proprietor is carefully distinguished from the *mansi ingenuiles et serviles* of the dependent peasantry. As a test, Lot conjured up a typical village (of the St. Germain type), composed of *indominicatum* and *mansi*. and tried to apply the Burgundian evidence to this bipartite model. After doing the necessary arith-metic, partitioning the estate, and attributing shares of *terra* and *mancipia* to the Burgundian and the Roman, he abandoned the test as too complicated and unwieldy.[8] The indecisiveness of Lot's study stemmed mainly from his not being able to filter the evidence satisfactorily through the grid.

Lot left himself open to an obvious objection. In referring to "la constitu-tion même de la propriété foncière de l'époque," he asked for a prodigious sus-pension of disbelief: he presupposed that the structure of fifth-century large private properties in the Burgundian kingdom was basically identical to that of the Paris countryside in the age of Charlemagne, a leap of three centuries. Lot implied that both structures, Burgundian and Parisian, stemmed from an invis-ible, Roman-age creation of the "grand domaine" by large landowners (whom he would probably have called latifundiaries). This scheme focusing on private landowners is virtually undocumented and does not work.[9] It is precisely because of the lack of evidence for a "private" origin of the "grand domaine" that Durliat and I have sought connections between the late Roman tax system and ninth-century "estates," or, as Durliat cogently maintains, assessment subdivisions, "assiètes fiscales." Although it continues to be imprudent to read the St. Germain polyptyque back into fifth-century conditions (as Lot did), there is a sound basis for supposing that the evidence of Burgundian settlement, rooted in late Roman taxation, foreshadows the medieval environment.[10]

To explain how the bipartite scheme applies to the Burgundian case, one starts, as shown in Chapter 6, by the Roman authorities' divesting themselves of the assessment records, *censuales paginae,* of the entire territory of settlement. This tax register, I suggest, distinguished *terrae,* owner's lands, from *mancipia,* dependent tenancies. The ratio of *terra* to *mancipia* was bound to be irregular, but the complementarity of *mancipia* to *terra* was not. One probable task of the *terra* proprietor (singular or plural)—a task of economic importance, to be taken seriously—was to collect the taxes of the dependent tenants (with a fee to the collector), to be responsible for shortfalls, and to manage the proceeds as instructed by the government.[11] The area of assessment was not a private property, let alone a large, centrally managed estate, but, in Durliat's words, an "assiètte fiscale," in English a "tax subdivision" or sphere of assessment, such as a village or township. The Roman *censuales paginae* of the Burgundian kingdom were subdivided into villages or other public units whose taxable resources were itemized and coupled with the annual tax charge arising from the assessment. Initially, at least in theory or as a paper operation, the entire assessment of the territory, all the *terrae* and *mancipia,* were conveyed from the Roman government to the king and his financial administration or fisc, inherited from Rome. The royal fisc may have included state lands in a narrower sense, that is, lands of which the state was the proprietor as well as the tax collector; but these were exceptions, of no concern here. The main fiscal resource was the assessed owners' lands (*terrae*) and dependent tenancies (*mancipia*), and the regular payment of taxes arising from them.

The relationship in question here is one of tax administration, not of cultivation or ownership. Within a given tax subdivision, not all owner's lands had to have a single proprietor, and the dependent tenancies did not have to be rent-paying or obligated to the working of the owner's lands. Many possibilities are conceivable; i's should be left undotted in the absence of evidence. What seems probable is that the owner's lands were the collecting point for the taxes of the dependent tenancies. It was to the advantage of the fisc as receiver of tax revenues to stand clear of the dealings of the *dominus* with the *mancipia* of the tax subdivision. The proper task of the fisc was to control the process by auditing the accounts of the owner in his guise as tax collector.

The passage of the tax system to the Burgundian king was accompanied, perhaps immediately, by an agreement that these resources would be shared between the king and those barbarians qualified to obtain individual allotments (*faramanni*). The division allocated to the rank and file one-half of the assessment of the owners' lands (*terrae*) as the pool for the distribution of individual allotments. The royal fisc was left with the other half of the registered *terrae* and the totality of registered *mancipia*.

The royal monopoly of dependent tenancies, which may have lasted many years but not for the entire life of the kingdom, merits attention. The share of the kingdom-wide assessment assigned to the *faramanni* consisted of only half of one of the two forms of assessed property, conceivably, therefore, as little as one-quarter of the total tax base. Royal need or covetousness may have been the cause, but practical considerations are more likely. For the sake of tax receipts, it mattered that the link between the property of landowners and the tenancies answering to the *domini* for tax payments (in some cases also for rents) should not be disrupted by a fractioning of tenancy assessments among many claimants. The guideline seems to have been that dependents should answer only to their immediate, customary *domini*. The half-and-half division of *terrae* assessments between the royal fisc and Burgundian allotment holders did not disturb the countryside. Under the royal aegis, the Roman owners of the *terra* were in complete charge of management; their obligation to the Burgundian allotment owners meant only that, at tax payment time, the Roman proprietors dealt with two sets of collectors, fiscal and individual, and gave to each one-half the taxes owed by the owner's land, *terra*. Dependent tenancies were another matter; presumably, all Burgundians, royal or lowly, kept clear of them. There was good reason, especially at the start of settlement, to leave all the *mancipia* in the sole charge of the proprietors, *domini*, under the distant oversight of the king, and safeguarded from possible interference by Burgundian *faramanni*.

The royal fisc gradually lost its monopoly of dependent tenancies; both individual and collective alienations took place, transferring much of the assessment of *mancipia* from the king to individual Burgundians. It is not hard to imagine how a royal gift of *agri cum mancipiis* might work. If, in a given village or other tax subdivision, one *faramannus* had an allotment consisting of one-half the assessment of owner's land (*terra*), it follows that the balance of the subdivision—that is, the other half of the owner's land and all the dependent tenancies—answered to the royal fisc. Our hypothetical *faramannus*, if deserving, might petition the king to give him the still royal parts of the tax subdivision; LB55.2 refers suitably to the end point as *agri ex integro cum mancipiis publica largitione percepti* (*ex integro cum mancipiis* echoes the *integritas manci-piorum* of LBExtravagans 21.12). If the petition was granted, the "privileged" Burgundian would gain not only in income but also, conceivably, in social status; from being the beneficiary of a mere share of a tax revenue, he would substitute himself for the king in the entire subdivision as superior of its lands and dependents. LB55.5 explicitly tells us that, as the owner of *agri cum mancipiis*, he could sue and be sued by Roman law. He would be on a par with the Roman *domini* of *terrae*.

The other royal alienation of *mancipia* is the one documented by LB54. It looks very much like a political act—a major concession by the king to all the "ordinary Burgundians." Its most noteworthy feature is that, once the *fara-manni* obtained their total allocation of two-thirds the *terra* and one-third the *mancipia*, their share in the total tax assets of the kingdom grew from possibly one-quarter to fully one-half. The royal fisc, already diminished by gifts of *agri cum mancipiis* to individuals, emerged much poorer from its collective grant to the *faramanni*. Between the "privileged Burgundians" and the newly enriched, the number of *domini* in the kingdom had increased significantly, diluting the supremacy of the king and of Roman landowners. These are possibilities suggested by LB54; the evidence to confirm them does not exist.

The interpretation of *mancipia* in the Burgundian texts as "dependent tenancies" adequately accounts for the situations encountered in the laws. What this interpretation implies—an ostensible stepping-stone from fourth-century fiscal evidence to Carolingian estate records—is astonishing and not wholly predictable. It remains to be seen what will happen to the *mancipia* as "dependent tenancies" when subjected to critical scrutiny.

Abbreviations

For additional sources, see the Bibliography, below.

Ammianus	Ammianus Marcellinus. *Rerum gestarum libri.* Ed. and trans. J. C. Rolfe. 3 vols. LCL. London, 1956–58.
CE	*Codex Eurici.* Ed. K. Zeumer. MG LNG, vol. 1. Ed. by A. d'Ors, *Estudios Visigoticos.* Vol. 2., *El Codigo di Eurico.* Instituto Juridico Español. Cuadernos 12. Rome, 1960.
CSEL	*Corpus scriptorum ecclesiasticorum Latinorum.* Vienna, 1867–.
CTh	*Codex Theodosianus.* Ed. T. Mommsen and P. M. Meyer. 2 vols. 2nd ed. Berlin, 1954.
Demougeot, *Formation de l'Europe*	Demougeot, Émilienne. *La formation de l'Europe et les invasions barbares.* 2 vols. in 3. Paris, 1969–79.
Dig.	Justinian *Digesta.* Ed. T. Mommsen and P. Krueger. 10th ed. Berlin, 1954.
FIRA 2	*Fontes iuris Romani antejustiniani.* Vol. 2, *Auctores.* Ed. J. Baviera and J. Furlani. Florence, 1968.
Gaupp, *Ansiedlungen*	Gaupp, Ernst Theodor. *Die germanischen Ansiedlungen und Landtheilungen in den Provinzen des römischen Weltreiches.* Wroclaw [Breslau], 1844.
Goffart, *B&R*	Goffart, Walter. *Barbarians and Romans* A.D. *418–584: The Techniques of Accommodation.* Princeton, N.J., 1980.

Goffart, *Rome's Fall and After*	Goffart, Walter. *Rome's Fall and After* (collected studies). London, 1989.
Gregory of Tours, *Historiae*	Gregory of Tours. *Historiarum libri X.* Ed. B. Krusch and W. Levison. MG SRM, vol. 1, 2nd ed.
Gregory of Tours, *Miracula s. Martini*	Gregory of Tours, *Miracula et opera minora.* Ed. W. Arndt and B. Krusch. MG SRM, vol. 1, pt. 2.
Hoops Reallexikon	*Hoops Reallexikon der germanischen Altertumskunde.* 2nd ed., 1–. Berlin, 1973–.
Inst.	Justinian. *Institutiones.* Edited by P. Krueger. In Dig., pp. xix–56.
Jordanes, *Getica*	Jordanes. *De origine actibusque Getarum.* Ed. T. Mommsen. MG AA 5 part 1; ed. Francesco Giunta and Antonino Grillone, Fonti per la storia d'Italia. Rome, 1991; trans. C. C. Mierow. Princeton, N.J., 1915; trans. Olivier Devillers, *Histoire des Goths.* Paris, 1995.
Jordanes, *Romana*	Jordanes. *De summa temporum vel origine actibusque gentis Romanorum.* Ed. T. Mommsen. MG AA 5 part 1.
LB	*Leges Burgundionum.* Ed. L. R. de Salis. MG LNG, vol. 2, pt. 1; ed. F. Bluhme, MG *Leges* (in folio), 3:407–630. Trans. K. F. Drew, *The Burgundian Code.* 1949. Reprinted, Philadelphia, 1972.
LBExtravagans	*Leges Burgundionum extravagantes,* in LB.
LCL	Loeb Classical Library.
LRB	*Lex Romana Burgundionum,* in FIRA 2, pp. 714–50.
LV	*Leges Visigothorum.* Ed. K. Zeumer. MG LNG, vol. 1. Trans. S. P. Scott, *The Visigothic Code.* Reprinted, New York, 1982.

MG	Monumenta Germaniae historica.
	AA *Auctores antiquissimi.*
	Formulae *Legum section V: Formulae.* Ed. K. Zeumer.
	LNG *Legum sectio 1: Leges nationum Germanicarum.*
	SRL *Scriptores rerum Langobardicarum et Italicarum saec. IX–XI.*
	SRM *Scriptores rerum Merovingicarum.*
NTheod II	*Leges novellae Theodosii II.* In *Leges novellae ad Theodosianum pertinentes.* Ed. P. M. Meyer. CTh vol. 2.
NValent III	*Leges novellae Valentiniani III.* In *Leges novellae.* CTh vol. 2.
Marini	Gaetano Marini. *I papiri diplomatici.* Rome, 1805.
Patrologia Latina	*Patrologiae cursus completus, Series Latina.* Ed. J. P. Migne.
Pauly-Wissowa	Pauly, A., G. Wissowa, and W. Kroll. *Real-Encyclopädie der klassischen Altertumswissenschaft.* Stuttgart, 1893–.
PLRE	*Prosopography of the Later Roman Empire.* Ed. J. R. Martindale et al. 3 vols. Cambridge, 1980–92.
Procopius, ed. Dewing	*Procopius.* Ed. and trans. H. B. Dewing, LCL. Vol. 1 (Persian War), vol. 2 (Vandalic War), vols. 3–5 (Gothic War), vol. 6 (Anecdota). London, 1953–54.
Schmidt, *Ostgermanen*	Schmidt, Ludwig. *Geschichte der deutschen Stämme bis zum Ausgang der Völkerwanderung, Die Ostgermanen.* 2nd ed. Munich, 1941.
Schmidt, *Westgermanen*	Schmidt, Ludwig. *Geschichte der deutschen Stämme bis zum Ausgang der*

Völkerwanderung, Die Westgermanen.
2nd ed., pt. 1. Munich, 1938.

Stein, *Histoire du Bas-Empire* — Stein, Ernst. *Histoire du Bas-Empire,* ed. J. R. Palanque, 2 vols. Paris, 1949–59.

Variae, ed. Mommsen — Cassiodorus. *Variae epistolae.* Ed. T. Mommsen. MG AA vol. 12. Trans. S. J. B. Barnish, *Cassiodorus's* Variae (selections). Translated Texts for Historians, 12. Liverpool, 1992; trans. Thomas Hodgkin, *The Letters of Cassiodorus.* London, 1886.

Wenskus, *Stammesbildung und Verfassung* — Wenskus, Reinhard. *Stammesbildung und Verfassung: Das Werden der frühmittelalterlichen gentes.* Cologne, 1961.

Notes

Introduction

1. My discussion is limited to this definite context. Anyone tracing "ethnogenesis" through Internet search engines realizes that it has a rich life in more contexts than anyone might imagine. Only rather recently has it been applied to the northern barbarians. For a brief, sober account of its breadth, see Alexander Callander Murray, "Reinhard Wenskus on 'Ethnogenesis,' Ethnicity, and the Origin of the Franks," in *On Barbarian Identity: Critical Approaches to Ethnicity in the Early Middle Ages*, ed. Andrew Gillett (Turnhout, 2002), p. 41 with nn. 10–11. See further Susan Reynolds, "Our Forefathers? Tribes, Peoples, and Nations in the Historiography of the Age of Migrations," in *After Rome's Fall: Narrators and Sources of Early Medieval History: Essays Presented to Walter Goffart*, ed. Alexander Callander Murray (Toronto, 1999), pp. 35–36; she suggests that ethnogenesis is an attempt "to save something from old historiographic traditions that we have now formally discarded."

2. Walter Pohl, "Introduction: Strategies of Distinction," in *Strategies of Distinction: The Construction of Ethnic Communities, 300–800*, ed. Walter Pohl and Helmut Reimitz (Leiden, 1998), p. 1. On ethnicity in recent studies of late antiquity, see Patrick Amory, *People and Identity in Ostrogothic Italy, 489–554* (Cambridge, 1997), pp. 1–42; in an early medieval context, see Florin Curta, *The Making of the Slavs: History and Archaeology of the Lower Danube Region, c. 300–700* (Cambridge, 2001), ch. 1 (a very theoretical discussion). On this "wave" in social studies, see M. E. Burgess, "The Resurgence of Ethnicity: Myth or Reality?" *Ethnic and Racial Studies* 1 (1978): 265–85; her scope is the current world, not the past; so is Eugeen Roosens, *Creating Ethnicity: The Process of Ethnogenesis* (Newbury Park, Calif., 1989), an absorbing and learned illustration of how these terms apply to present-day conditions.

3. A. H. M. Jones, *The Later Roman Empire, 284–602: A Social, Economic and Administrative Survey*, 3 vols. (Oxford, 1964); 2 vols. (Norman, Okla., 1964). Jones comes closest to this theme when considering whether doctrinal differences among early Christians were a mask for "national" sensitivities (pp. 965–67).

4. F. Lot, *The End of the Ancient World and the Beginning of the Middle Ages*, trans. P. and M. Leon (London, 1931; reprinted, New York, 1961); Henri Pirenne, *Mohammed and Charlemagne*, trans. Bernard Miall (London, 1939), ch. 1; J. M. Wallace-Hadrill, *The Barbarian West 400–1000*, 3rd ed. (London, 1967; first published 1952).

5. Herwig Wolfram, *Geschichte der Goten* (Munich, 1979); I cite the revised 2nd edition of 1980 (which I reviewed in *Speculum* 57 [1982]: 444–47). The 3rd German edition (1990) is renamed *Die Goten*. H. Wolfram, *History of the Goths*, trans. T. J. Dunlap (Berkeley, 1988). German 2nd ed., p. 1, "Der Verfasser ist Mediävist historischer Observanz." The "Schluss" (pp. 448–60) is entitled "Entwurf einer historischen Ethnographie am Beispiel der Goten." This appears mutatis mutandis as the Introduction to the American edition, p. 1, "Gothic History as Historical Ethnography." Wolfram is well aware of his predecessors

and appreciative of them. A particularly clear account of "ethnogenesis theory" is given in the perceptive review of Wolfram's Gothic history by A. C. Murray in *International History Review* 11 (1989): 529–31. See also Reynolds, "Our Forefathers?" pp. 35–36. As is well known, Wolfram's concern with ethnogenesis was inspired by Reinhard Wenskus, *Stammesbildung und Verfassung: Das Werden der frühmittelalterlichen gentes* (Cologne, 1961); see Murray, "Wenskus on 'Ethnogenesis.' "

6. J. B. Bury, *The Invasions of Europe by the Barbarians*, ed. F. J. C. Hearnshaw (London, 1928; Norton paperback, New York, 1967); Lucien Musset, *Les Invasions*, vol. 1, *Les vagues germaniques*, Nouvelle Clio 12 (Paris, 1965), trans. E. and C. James, *The Germanic Invasions: The Making of Europe AD 400–600* (University Park, Pa., 1975).

7. Abbreviated here as Schmidt, *Ostgermanen* and *Westgermanen*; see the Abbreviations. Wolfram's Gothic history (n. 5, above) began as part of a collective rewriting of Schmidt's work. It was detached from this undertaking on the grounds that it was a "historical ethnography." Wolfram does not explain what this means. Émilienne Demougeot, *Formation de l'Europe* (see List of Abbreviations).

8. E. von Wietersheim, *Geschichte der Völkerwanderung*, 2 vols., 2nd ed. (Leipzig, 1888). Parts of Dahn's works have been recently reprinted: Felix Dahn, *Die Germanen: Westgermanen* (Essen, 1999); also his *Die Könige der Germanen* (reprinted, Hildesheim, 1973).

9. For titles of Wolfram's detailed studies, see Wolfram, *History of the Goths*, pp. 572–73. The quotation is from Murray, "Wenskus on 'Ethnogenesis,' " p. 57. In one example of his modus operandi, Wolfram, pp. 228–31, presents at length the "tribal" findings of Ernst Gamillscheg, *Romania Germanica* (Berlin, 1934–36), without hinting at the deep interwar political taint clinging to this work; contemporary French dissent is mentioned (p. 473 n. 467) but disregarded. On the tainted scholarship, see Hubert Fehr, "*Volkstum* as Paradigm: Germanic People and Gallo-Romans in Early Medieval Archaeology since the 1930s," in *On Barbarian Identity*, ed. Gillett, pp. 177–200.

10. Some definitions of "ethnogenesis": Patrick Geary, "tribal transformation"; Ian Wood, "written tales of origins"; Guy Halsall, "the process of the formation of peoples after the end of the Roman Empire"; Matthew Innes, "the processes by which ethnic identity is shaped." On the basis of a wider sampling, Charles E. Bowlus points out, "[ethnogenesis] can be employed so vaguely that it is totally devoid of meaning." See Geary, *Before France and Germany: The Creation and Transformation of the Merovingian World* (New York, 1988), p. 53; Wood, "*Gentes*, Kings and Kingdoms—The Emergence of States: The Kingdom of the Gibichungs," in *Regna and Gentes: The Relationship between Late Antique and Early Medieval Peoples and Kingdoms in the Transformation of the Roman World*, ed. H. W. Goetz, J. Jarnut, and W. Pohl (Leiden, 2003), pp. 243, 245; Halsall, review in *English Historical Review* 118 (2003): 1349; Innes, "Danelaw Identities: Ethnicity, Regionalism, and Political Allegiance," in *Cultures in Contact: Scandinavian Settlement in England in the Ninth and Tenth Century*, ed. D. M. Hadley and J. D. Richards (Turnhout, 2000), p. 66; Bowlus, "Ethnogenesis: The Tyranny of a Concept," in *On Barbarian Identity*, ed. Gillett, p. 242.

11. Geary, *Before France and Germany*, p. 53. Geary is the major channel of transmission for Wolfram's ideas to the English-speaking public.

12. Barbara H. Rosenwein, *A Short History of the Middle Ages* (Peterborough, Ontario, 2002), pp. 25–26.

13. For Bury, Schmidt, and Musset, see nn. 6–7, above.

14. Sometimes the sources fail to cooperate, as observed by Hans-Werner Goetz, "*Gens* Terminology and Perception of the 'Germanic' Peoples from Late Antiquity to the

Early Middle Ages," in *The Construction of Communities in the Early Middle Ages: Texts, Resources and Artefacts*, ed. Richard Corradini, Max Diesenberger, Helmut Reimitz (Leiden, 2003), p. 59: "It is difficult to investigate the structure of early medieval ethnogenesis . . . because contemporary authors of that time did *not* perceive such a process." The modern historian is therefore in search of what is unattested.

15. There are comprehensive collections of this material, e.g., Joachim Herrmann, ed., *Griechische und lateinische Quellen zur frühgeschichte Mitteleuropas bis zur Mitte des 1. Jahrtausends u. Z.*, 4 vols. (Berlin, 1988–92). For the meaning of "German" in Latin texts, see the works cited in Chapter 7, n. 1, below. For an explicit assertion that Germanic learned research is the counterweight to Greek and Roman sources, see the statement of Edward Schwarz (1967) cited in Goffart, *B&R*, p. 23.

16. E.g., Johann Jakob Mascov, *The History of the Ancient Germans . . . who overthrew the Roman Empire*, trans. Thomas Lediard (London, 1738); Ferdinand Lot, *Les invasions germaniques: La pénétration mutuelle du monde barbare et du monde romain* (Paris, 1935; reprint, 1945); Musset, *Germanic Invasions*; Pierre Courcelle, *Histoire littéraire des grandes invasions germaniques*, 3rd ed. (Paris, 1964); Karl Friedrich Stroheker, *Germanentum und Spätantike* (Zurich, 1965); Herwig Wolfram, *Das Reich und die Germanen* (Berlin, 1990); and many more. The Library of Congress subject catalogue includes "Germanic invasions of Rome, 3rd–6th centuries."

17. For a detailed discussion of this subject, see Alexander Demandt, ed., *Deutschlands Grenzen in der Geschichte* (Munich, 1990).

18. Demandt, *Deutschlands Grenzen*, p. 18, points out that the usage of "deutsch" to qualify the ancient Germans is already in medieval authors, but he exaggerates the anticipation (Germanic continuity is agreeable to him; see his "Die westgermanischen Stammesbünde," *Klio* 75 [1993]: 387–406). Primitive Germans do occur before the sixteenth century in medieval imaginative literature, which does not shy from anachronisms.

19. A casual recent example of this uninhibited usage in titles to scholarly works is Bruno Luiselli, *Storia culturale dei rapporti tra mondo romano e mondo germanico* (Rome, 1992). Equally uninhibited is Herwig Wolfram's title "*Origo gentis*: The Literature of German Origins," in *Early Germanic Literature and Culture*, ed. Brian Murdoch and Malcolm Read (Rochester, N.Y., 2004), p. 39; the literature Wolfram evokes consists of Latin writings on Gothic, Lombard, Saxon, and other barbarian origins, none of them "German" except in unreflective modern usage.

20. As is implied by the title of Geary's book, *Before France and Germany*, and by that of K. F. Werner's, *Vom Frankenreich zur Entfaltung Deutchlands and Frankreichs* (Sigmaringen, 1984).

21. Vegetius, *Mulomedicina* 3.6, ed. E. Lommatzsch (Leipzig, 1903), p. 249. The Bavarians are casually mentioned as being to the east of the Swabians: Jordanes, *Getica* 280, ed. T. Mommsen, MG AA 5, p. 130. The date of Jordanes's work is after March 551 (see Chapter 4, nn. 54–56, below). The Frisians, Thuringians, and Bavarians are discussed at length in Chapter 7, section "A Medley of Barbarian Peoples," below.

22. Murray, "Wenskus on 'Ethnogenesis,'" pp. 59–60, carefully retraces Frankish origins with reference to Wenskus's account of the same subject. See also Timothy D. Barnes, "The Franci before Diocletian," in *Historiae Augustae Colloquium Genevense 1991*, ed. Giorgio Bonamente and François Paschoud (Bari, 1994), pp. 11–18.

23. The (heretical) Arian brand of Christianity, which most barbarians espoused, was as imperial in its origins as the (orthodox) Nicene variety.

24. Geary, *Before France and Germany*, p. 43. His views are by no means isolated. According to Walter Pohl, *Die Germanen*, Enzyklopädie deutscher Geschichte 57 (Munich, 2000), p. 10, "This population [of the Jastorf culture] cannot be unhesitatingly defined archaeologically as 'Germanic.'" Arnulf Krause, *Die Geschichte der Germanen* (Frankfurt, 2002), pp. 18–19, unreservedly extracts the early Germans from the Jastorf culture.

25. Hans Frede Nielsen, *The Early Runic Language of Scandinavia: Studies in Germanic Dialect Geography* (Heidelberg, 2000), pp. 299–300; H. Steuer "Germanen, Germania, germanische Altertumskunde. Wirtschafts- und Sozialgeschichte," in *Hoops Reallexikon* (Berlin, 1998), 11:352.

26. See the major methodological discussion of Michael Kulikowski, "Nation Versus Army: A Necessary Contrast?" in *On Barbarian Identity*, ed. Gillett, pp. 73–74 n. 14, indicating inter alia how major spokesmen in the ethnogenesis debate are committed to outdated archaeological interpretations, notably the "ethnic ascription approach."

27. This was shown by Edward James and has not ceased to startle: *The Merovingian Archaeology of South-West Gaul*, 2 vols., British Archaeological Reports, International Series 22 (Oxford, 1977).

28. Reinhold Kaiser, *Die Burgunder*, Kohlhammer Urban-Taschenbücher 586 (Stuttgart, 2004), pp. 87–88, 92 (summarizing the conclusions of a conference on this subject). Kaiser says much more about archaeology as it affects the (presumed) adventures of the earlier Burgundians in eastern Europe (pp. 88–92). The discrepancy is likely to exist because critical methods have been applied to the material remains in France and lag in application in eastern Europe.

29. For maps, see, e.g., Musset, *Germanic Invasions*, p. 44. For a critique of received opinion, see Michael Kulikowski, *Late Roman Spain and Its Cities* (Baltimore, 2004), pp. 266–71.

30. Guy Halsall, "The Origin of the *Reihengräberzivilisation* Forty Years On," in *Fifth-Century Gaul: A Crisis of Identity*, ed. J. Drinkwater and H. Elton (Cambridge, 1992), pp. 196–207; see also Hubert Fehr, "*Volkstum* as Paradigm," pp. 193–98.

31. Subtitled *Urban Public Building in Northern and Central Italy*, AD 300–850 (Oxford, 1984).

32. Kulikowski, *Late Roman Spain*.

33. Peter S. Wells, *The Barbarians Speak: How the Conquered Peoples Shaped Roman Europe* (Princeton, N.J., 1999), pp. 187–88. See also my comments about archaeology in *B&R*, pp. 28–30, based mainly on the very sensible and well-informed teaching of Malcolm Todd, *The Northern Barbarians 100 B.C.–A.D. 300* (London, 1975).

34. Quoted at Chapter 5, n. 172, below.

Chapter 1

1. Films for the Humanities and Sciences, P.O. Box 2053, Princeton, N.J. 08543.

2. The interweaving of "invasions" and "movement" as complementary ideas is well illustrated by Carlton Huntley Hayes, *An Introduction to the Sources Relating to the Germanic Invasions* (New York, 1909), pp. 5–6. (It is a curious fact that, in this once influential work, Hayes never refers to "migrations" or uses the term "*Völkerwanderung*".)

3. Konrad Peutinger, "De gentium quarundam emigrationibus brevis epitome," in *Procopii Caesariensis de rebus Gothorum, Persarum ac Vandalorum libri VI una cum aliis mediorum temporum historicis*, ed. Beatus Rhenanus (Basel, 1531), pp. 687–88. The title "de inclinatione Romani imperii, & exterarum gentium, praecipue Germanorum, con-migrationibus, epitome," heads Peutinger's brief account. The same "epitome" is situated at the end of Jordanes's *Getica* in Peutinger's (unpaged) 1515 first edition of Jordanes and Paul the Deacon. Its scope is from Alaric (395) through the great Hunnic battle of 451, a much shorter span than we have come to expect. Cf. Jacques Ridé, *L'Image du Germain dans la pensée et la littérature allemandes de la redécouverte de Tacite à la fin du XVIème siècle*, Diss, Paris IV, 3 vols. (Lille-Paris, 1977), p. 357.

4. For a recent affirmation of this definition, see Jochen Martin, *Spätantike und Völkerwanderung*, Oldenbourg Grundriß der Geschichte, ed. J. Bleicken et al. (Munich, 1987), p. 35, "den Ereignissen [of the 370s], die gemeinhin als Beginn der Völkerwan-derung angesehen werden." He also recognizes a broader sense (121). For confirmation, see Capelle (n. 8, below), who presupposes the existence of a core Migration Age.

5. Georgio Bombi, *Atlas of World History*, trans. T. Tonioli and C. Title (London, 1987), p. 87. The same subject, with a very developed caption, in *Atlas historique Larousse*, ed. G. Duby (Paris, 1978), p. 180. For a variant, see J. F. Horrabin, *Atlas of European History* (London, 1935), p. 17 (about his map 3).

6. One of the rare recent historians who worked with both the Asian and the European versions was Louis Halphen, who concluded in "La place de l'Asie dans l'histoire du monde," in *À travers l'histoire du Moyen Âge* (Paris, 1950), pp. 6–7, that the Huns were at the Danube and the Elbe fifty years after having left the banks of the Yellow River. This opinion is not widely shared. Lot, *End of the Ancient World*, pp. 191–93, uncritically es-poused some of the Asian version mainly as decoration.

7. See Appendix 1, below, p. 242. The author is Alexander Demandt (1984).

8. For an earlier statement than Demandt's of how the expanded concept of Migra-tion Age relates to the core meaning, see *Das Alte Germanien: Die Nachrichten der griechischen und römischen Schriftsteller*, ed. and trans. Wilhelm Capelle (Jena, 1929), p. 4 (my translation), "What is commonly called the *Völkerwanderung* is basically no more than the last act of the great world-historical drama signified by the Germanic *Völker-wanderung* [which was already in motion long before the invasions of Roman territory by the Cimbri and Teutons]." Capelle, like Demandt (and a host of others), wishes us to equate the prehistoric expansion of the Germanic peoples with a Migration Age.

9. On Gatterer and d'Anville, see Walter Goffart, *Historical Atlases: The First 300 Years* (Chicago, 2003), pp. 272–73, 237–38.

10. Peter Heather, "The Huns and the End of the Roman Empire in Western Eu-rope," *English Historical Review* 110 (1995): 4–41.

11. Heather took his cue from the impressive final sentence of Jones, *Later Roman Empire*, p. 1068: "The internal weaknesses of the empire cannot have been a major factor in its decline."

12. Theodor Mommsen, *Die Weltreich der Caesaren*, quoted in Alfons Dopsch, *Eco-nomic and Social Foundations of European Civilization*, condensed trans. M. G. Beard and N. Marshall (London, 1937), p. 49.

13. The notion of grants to barbarian troops pursuant to law was persuasively ar-gued by Ernst Theodor Gaupp, *Die germanischen Ansiedlungen und Landtheilungen* (Breslau, 1844), which retains credit today (and is discussed in Chapter 6, below).

14. "Progressive fusion" comes from Ferdinand Lot, *Invasions germaniques*, p. 165.

15. Goffart, *Historical Atlases*, pp. 193–94; Bellin's map is lost.

16. Edward Gibbon, *History of the Decline and Fall of the Roman Empire*, ed. J. B. Bury, 7 vols. (London, 1896–1900), 3: 281, with Bury's demurring note, 3: 493–94. On Gatterer, Goffart, *Historical Atlases*, pp. 168–73, 272–73, and "The Scenario of Gatterer's 'Charten zur Geschichte der Völkerwanderung,' " in *Geschichtsdeutung auf alten Karten. Archäologie und Geschichte*, ed. Dagmar Unverhau, Wolfenbütteler Forschungen 101 (Wiesbaden, 2003), pp. 213–20.

17. Thomas Hodgkin, *Italy and Her Invaders*, 8 vols. (London, 1885–99), 2 [2nd ed.]: 1–36, quotations, pp. 27, 5. Almost convinced that the theory was false, Hodgkin was loath to omit the excellent summary of de Guignes's argument given in his first edition. Another interesting summary of de Guignes is Laszlo Torday, *Mounted Archers: The Beginning of Central Asian History* (Edinburgh and Durham, 1997), pp. 168–69. See also the judicious and well-documented appraisal in Andrew Bell-Fialkoff, ed., *The Role of Migration in the History of the Eurasian Steppe: Sedentary Civilization vs. "Barbarian" and Nomad* (New York, 2000), pp. 215–16.

18. L. S. Stavrianos, *A Global History: From Prehistory to the Present*, 6th ed. (Englewood Cliffs, N.J., 1971), p. 143, "The period from the third to the sixth century was one of Eurasia-wide invasions comparable to the bronze and iron invasions of the second millennium B.C."; *The Columbia History of the World*, ed. J. A. Garraty and P. Gay (New York, 1972), p. 429; Jean Favier, "The Scourge of God 451," in *Milestones of History: 100 Decisive Events in the History of Mankind* (New York, 1970), p. 183, "The various peoples of Hunnic stock . . . left their native steppes of central Asia to invade India and Persia on the one hand, and central and eastern Europe on the other." In a similarly muted form, *(Brockhaus) Die Weltgeschichte*, vol. 2, *Antike Welten* (Leipzig, 1997), p. 508. See also Richard N. Frye, *The Heritage of Central Asia: From Antiquity to the Turkish Expansion* (Princeton, 1996), pp. 167–82, "Return of the Nomads." Suggesting a new tendency, the Huns are virtually absent from Claude Mossé, ed., *(Larousse) Histoire du Monde: Antiquité* (Paris, 1993); Jerry H. Bentley and Herbert F. Ziegler, *Traditions and Encounters: A Global Perspective on the Past* (Boston, 2000); Richard W. Bulliet, et al., *The Earth and Its Peoples: A Global History* (Boston, 2001).

19. Ammianus Marcellinus 31.2.1, ed. Rolfe, 3:381, "dwelling beyond the Maeotic Sea near the ice-bound ocean." He says nothing more about where the Huns came from. After reviewing de Guignes's theory and its development, Denis Sinor, "The Hun Period," in *The Cambridge History of Early Inner Asia*, ed. D. Sinor (Cambridge, 1990), pp. 177–79, returns to Ammianus as the only authoritative voice.

20. On Ambrose and Gog, see Wolfram, *History of the Goths*, p. 28; on Isidore, Chapter 3 at n. 27, below. But see now Kulikowsky, *Late Roman Spain*, pp. 403–6 n. 81: some of these texts are not Isidorian. For casual references to peoples coming from Scandinavia or the Elbe, see Chapter 3, nn. 34 and n. 35, below. The Lombards were at the Elbe in the days of Tacitus, but they lived near the Danube for many centuries before invading Italy.

21. On Procopius and the Vandals, see Chapter 5 at n. 48, below; Jordanes and Scandinavia, see Chapter 4, below; the Trojan and Macedonian legends, see Chapter 3, at nn. 21, 28, below.

22. Murray, "Reinhard Wenskus on 'Ethnogenesis,' " p. 52, points out the surprising fact that Wenskus's influential book "begins with the palaeolithic," far outdoing the merely postdiluvian outlook of medieval authors.

23. Beatus Rhenanus, *Rerum Germanorum libri tres* (Basel, 1531), p. 28. Book 1 of this treatise foreshadows the many future accounts of Germanic "emigrations." For current views of the ethnicity of the Cimbri, see Chapter 3, n. 46 (not Germanic).

24. Donald Kelley, "*Tacitus noster*: The *Germania* in the Renaissance and Reformation," in *Tacitus and the Tacitean Tradition*, ed. T. J. Luce and A. Woodman (Princeton, N.J., 1993), p. 162.

25. Gustaf Kossinna, *Die deutsche Vorgeschichte: Eine hervorragend nationale Wissenschaft* (Würzburg, 1912; often reprinted); id., *Ursprung und Verbreitung der Germanen in vor- und frühgeschichtlicher Zeit*, Mannus-Bibl. 6 (Leipzig, 1928), p. v.

26. Ridé, *Image du Germain*, p. 1196, has good lines about this.

27. On ethnogenesis and Germanic continuity, see Gillett, "Introduction: Ethnogenesis, History, and Methodology," in *On Barbarian Identity*, ed. Gillett, pp. 14–18.

28. Walter Pohl, "A Non-Roman Empire in Central Europe: The Avars," in *Regna and Gentes*, 572 n. 5; by stiffly insisting that "there was a considerable migration by barbarian warriors in the decades after 375," Pohl shows how far he is from problematizing "migration." His book, *Die Völkerwanderung: Eroberung und Integration* (Stuttgart, 2002), earnestly traces one people after the other to its "homeland" and "migrating" from there. He perpetuates a long-standing tradition (see Chapter 3, n. 22).

29. For further reflections on migrations, see Chapter 5, below, notably pp. 114–18.

Chapter 2

1. About Polybius, see Santo Mazzarino, *The End of the Ancient World*, trans. G. Holmes (London, 1966), p. 23. Latin poets and the north, Suzanne Teillet, *Des Goths à la nation gothique: Les origines de l'idée de nation en Occident du Vè au VIIè siècle* (Paris, 1984), pp. 18–21. Sallust, *Jugurtha* 114.2, ed. Alfred Ernout (Paris, 1958), p. 267.

2. For historians supporting external causation, see Walter Goffart, *Rome's Fall and After* (London, 1989), pp. 1 n. 2 (Piganiol, Jones), 7 n. 21 (Finley), 112 n. 4 (Momigliano. But Momigliano was critical of Jones's position on causation; see his *Quarto contributo alla storia degli studi classici*, Storia e letteratura 115 [Rome, 1969], p. 646). The notes cited list additional spokesmen for the views in question. About internal problems, see Jones, *Later Roman Empire*, p. 1068. Heather, "Huns and the End," about which see Chapter 1, at nn. 10–11, above.

3. Alexander Demandt, *Der Fall Roms: Die Auflösung des römischen Reiches im Urteil der Nachwelt* (Munich, 1984), pp. 587–97; quotation, Appendix 1, p. 250. Demandt's argument is anticipated in earlier twentieth-century German writings by accounts of a long contest between *Germanen* and Romans, written forthrightly as a continuing two-sided campaign that the Germans ultimately won. In *Neue Propyläen Weltgeschichte* (Berlin, 1940), 2:52, Hermann Aubin sets the theme: except for Arminius (leader of an uprising that destroyed three Roman legions) there would be "no point of departure for German (*deutsche*) history." The heroization of Arminius in Germany goes back to the sixteenth century, when the link between ancient and modern Germans was forged. That this outlook was not a Nazi-period aberration is shown, e.g., by the standard *Gebhardts Handbuch der deutschen Geschichte*, 7th ed. (Stuttgart, 1930), 1:64, with typical statements such as "The assault of the youthfully fresh Germans now directed itself upon this internally

calcifying Empire (*Auf dieses innerhalb verkalkenden Reich richtet sich nun der Ansturm der jugendfrischen Germanen*)."

4. For more on the contrast between East and West, see Goffart, *Rome's Fall and After*, pp. 17–18. Demandt espouses a minority position (with which I agree). It is more normal to detect special virtues in the East that allowed it to survive.

5. One advantage of having an event or process called *Völkerwanderung* is that it brings disparate peoples under the same umbrella. The idea that migration unifies the early Germans is propounded by Ludwig Schmidt as cited in Chapter 5, n. 175, below.

6. On "pressure," Goffart, *Rome's Fall and After*, p. 1 n. 2.

7. Demandt's phrase "The Roman Empire and the Germans were military rivals" is unobjectionable if it simply means "Germans fought Romans" (and vice versa). Its literal meaning is inadmissible, since (except in an anachronistic modern perspective) there was no Germanic collectivity to "rival" the Romans.

8. The splintering of Rome's northern neighbors is easily seen in a document such as the Verona List (which never mentions either the ancient or the modern sort of "Germans"); see Chapter 3, n. 5, below.

9. On fears about northern peoples, see n. 1, above.

10. An old and widespread view, set out in Chapter 1 at nn. 7–8, above, differentiates the core meaning of "Migration Age" and the chronologically and spatially expanded "Germanic" meaning that is widely preferred. See Felix Dahn, introduction to Wietersheim, *Geschichte der Völkerwanderung*, 1:3, "The so-called *Völkerwanderung* is only the last wave-blow of a centuries-long movement . . . the termination of an age-old development."

11. Recent works on the theme are cited in Chapter 3, n. 22. A current sample of this literature is Walter Pohl, *Die Germanen*, Enzyklopädie deutscher Geschichte 57 (Munich, 2000); ostensibly bent on revision, it shows extreme reluctance to sever ties with older scholarship. Pohl is, of course, committed to the existence of his subject, a coherent "Germanic" people foreshadowing the "Deutsche" of today. That is the presupposition that badly needs testing.

12. About Kossinna, see Chapter 1, n. 25; Chapter 3, nn. 11–12. About the learned reconstructions of the "early Germans" enthusiastically carried out since the sixteenth century (*deutsche Altertumskunde*, the "science" of German antiquities), see Chapter 3.

13. Demandt prudently goes out of his way to base his reading of "Germanic" traits out of other sources than Tacitus's *Germania*. Pohl, *Die Germanen*, asserts that one may not speak of "the wars of 'the Germans' against Rome" (p. 87) but combines this denial with a long survey of "Elements of Germanic Society" (pp. 65–85), on the premise that Germanic society was a unit. See Allan A. Lund, *Germanenideologie im Nationalsozialismus: Zur Rezeption der 'Germania' des Tacitus im 'Dritten Reich'* (Heidelberg, 1995), ch. 2.

14. As shown by Wells, *The Barbarians Speak*, pp. 187–88.

15. See the comment of Kelley in Chapter 1 at n. 24, about the prevalence in this research of a mystic search for forefathers. The absence of living actors and the consequent dominance of impersonal forces are pointed out on the same page.

16. For Florus, see Chapter 3, n. 5, below. Though Florus takes special note of "Germany" as a trouble spot, his list of rebellious peoples is heavily weighted with middle and lower Danubian peoples (Noricans, Moesians, Thracians) who had nothing "Germanic" about them.

17. Tacitus, *Germania* 37.2–5, ed. Allan A. Lund (Heidelberg, 1988), p. 98, affirmed that the Germans had resisted Rome longer than any other people and were still unsubdued. His historical comparisons are at least contestable in the light of, e.g., the very prolonged Roman conquest of Spain. See also Chapter 3, n. 6, below.

18. Arthur Ferrill, *The Fall of the Roman Empire: The Military Explanation* (London, 1986), pp. 161–69, summarizes the problems; enervation is not one of them. Some authors believe in an inner collapse of the Roman army, which is not easily proved.

19. When Belisarius invaded southern Italy at the start of his imperial conquest of Ostrogothic Italy, Cassiodorus, as praetorian prefect, wrote urging civilians to continue cultivating their fields and not to interfere with military activity. *Variae* 12.5.4–5, ed. Mommsen, p. 364; the division of labor is pithily summed up: "defensorum maxima laus est, si, cum illi videantur praedictas regiones protegere, isti non desinent patrioticas possessiones excolere."

20. Alexander Demandt, *Die Spätantike: Römische Geschichte von Diocletian bis Justinian, 284–565 n. Chr.*, Müller's Handbuch, 3te Abt., 6ter Teil (Munich, 1989), p. 39.

21. Hildegard Gräfin Schwerin von Krosigk, *Gustaf Kossinna: Der Nachlass: Versuch einer Analyse* (Neumünster, 1982), p. 80: "Der von Kossinna stets angenommene Bevölkerungsüberschuss als Ursache für die Abwanderung . . ." This is very suspect company for Demandt to keep. In the previous century, Felix Dahn had been a major proponent of surplus population as the element of change. One discerns Malthus in the background rather than historical evidence; see Bury, *Invasions of Europe by the Barbarians*, pp. 5–9. As we see in Paul the Deacon's *Historia Langobardorum* 1.1–2 (*De Germania, quod plures nutriat populos*: "concerning Germania, which nourishes many peoples"), MG SRL pp. 45, 47–49, ancient and medieval science was as favorable as modern to this all-purpose demographic explanation. Paul's history was written ca. 790.

22. This is well documented by Curt Weibull, *Die Auswanderung der Goten aus Schweden* (Göteborg, 1958), pp. 18–20.

23. For the view that the barbarians over the centuries did not increase in military effectiveness, see Hugh Elton, *Warfare in Roman Europe, A.D. 350–425* (Oxford, 1996), pp. 45–88. Along similar lines, E. A. Thompson, "Early Germanic Warfare," *Past and Present* 14 (1958): 2–29. Wells, *The Barbarians Speak*, is more welcoming to such ideas than his evidence allows; he equates the return to *barbaricum* of veterans of Roman service with improvements, but this by no means follows. It takes more than drill instructors to create effective armies.

24. Even late Rome was in a position to learn from foreigners. See, on mounted archers, Procopius 5.27.26–29, ed. Dewing, 3:259–61; they were considered by Belisarius to be the decisive means of Roman superiority over the Goths in Italy.

25. H. Jänichen, "Alemannen: Geschichtliches," in *Hoops Reallexikon*, 1:138, proposes that the Franks, Alamanni, and Juthungi (an Alamannic subgroup) originated "durch die ständige Beziehung gewisser Heerhaufen zu bestimmten römischen Provinzen." In war and peace the Franks related mainly to Cologne, the Alamanni to Mainz, the Juthungi to Augsburg. "Häufige Treffen bestimmter germanischer Häuptlinge in Köln bzw. Mainz oder Augsburg mögen zu gemeinsamem Vorgehen und Schließlich zum Bund geführt haben." This conception deeply undermines the idea of an inner "constitutional" development within the peoples in question.

26. For a recent account of the third century that departs sharply from Demandt's one-dimensional vision of a "Germanic offensive," see Thomas S. Burns, *Rome and the Barbarians, 100 B.C.–A.D. 400* (Baltimore, 2003), pp. 248–308.

27. Barbara Yorke, "Anglo-Saxon *gentes* and *regna*," in Regna *and* Gentes, pp. 385–90, 401–5. On the Continental Saxons, Musset, *Germanic Invasions*, p. 233; Roger Collins, *Early Medieval Europe, 300–1000*, 2nd ed. (New York, 1999), p. 281.

28. The most eloquent evidence of Goths fighting for Rome is related to a defeat commemorated in the trilingual inscription of the Persian ruler, Shapur (A.D. 262): Wolfram, *History of the Goths*, pp. 20, 44.

29. See Chapter 1 at n. 9, above.

30. Fergus Millar, *The Roman Empire and Its Neighbours* (London, 1967), p. 319, "All these incursions . . . were only made possible by the continual withdrawing of frontier troops to fight the Sassanid Persians on the eastern frontier of the Empire, as well as rival claimants to the Imperial throne."

31. The spectacle of armies fighting on several, widely separated fronts was not extraordinary during the centuries of Roman expansion. In the Second Punic War alone, Rome sent major forces to Greece, Sicily, and Spain while struggling with Hannibal in Italy; and, to cite another case at random, Crassus could launch an unnecessary war against Parthia while Caesar was fully engaged in conquering Gaul (Max Cary, *History of Rome*, 2nd ed. [London, 1954], pp. 164–71, 359–60). It will not do to pretend that war on two fronts began for Rome in the reign of Marcus Aurelius.

32. J. C. Mann, "The Frontiers of the Principate," in *Aufstieg und Niedergang der römischen Welt*, part 2, *Principat*, ed. Hildegard Temporini (Berlin, 1974), 1:520–21.

33. Although Demandt's comments in no. 4 make good sense, they are as little grounded in evidence as those in nos. 2–3.

34. Goffart, *B&R*, pp. 4–5.

35. On the stabilization of the northern frontier, see Stephen Williams, *Diocletian and the Roman Recovery* (London, 1985), pp. 45–77.

36. Ammianus Marcellinus 22.7.8, ed. Rolfe, 2:210.

37. This saying is quoted in Chapter 7, at n. 173.

38. Appendix 1, p. 248, below.

39. Demandt's writings on the incorporation of barbarians are prominently featured in Chapter 7, section "Late Roman Conditions and Barbarian Penetration," below. For Toynbee's phrase and its context, Goffart, *Rome's Fall and After*, p. 1 with n. 1.

40. The phrase is picked out as noteworthy by Walter Pohl, "The Politics of Change: Reflections on the Transformation of the Roman World," in *Integration und Herrschaft*, ed. Walter Pohl and Max Diesenberger, Forschungen zur Geschichte des Mittelalters 3 (Vienna, 2002), p. 284. Demandt repeats this same judgment in his *Die Spätantike*, p. 491.

41. See Chapter 3, nn. 7, 9, below, where these circumstances are more accurately sketched than here.

42. For dependents of the Huns, see Chapter 7, section "A Medley of Barbarian Peoples," below.

43. The barbarity referred to here concerns parentage only. Aspar was a courtly grand seigneur who like a public spirited citizen gave Constantinople an enormous cistern; Zeno had the endearing feature of shrinking from bloodshed.

44. J. B. Bury, *History of the Later Roman Empire from the Death of Theodosius I to the Death of Justinian*, 2 vols. (London, 1923), 1:314–23, 389–402, 429–36, 447–52; Stein,

Histoire du Bas-Empire, 1:351–64; 2:7–106, 177–85, 219–23. See also Chapter 3 at n. 60, and 7, section "Late Roman Conditions and Barbarian Penetration," below.

Chapter 3

1. J. R. Palanque, "La vie et l'œuvre d'Ernest Stein," in Stein, *Histoire du Bas-Empire*, 2:vii–xvii.

2. Stein, *Histoire du Bas-Empire*, 1:5–6, 194, 290, 309–10, 326, 237, 340; 2:49, 151, 567. Stein's acceptance of a collective Germanic civilization, though not prominent in his book, peers through here and there as something taken for granted.

3. On a one-to-one confrontation won by foreigners, see Chapter 2, above. On the "Germanic world," see Geary, *Before France and Germany*, p. vi. Geary's sentence has been very widely echoed, but what it precisely means has never been explained.

4. These subjects are dealt with in Chapters 1 and 2, above.

5. *Laterculus Veronensis* 1–12 (empire), 13–14 (*gentes barbarae*), in *Notitia dignitatum utriusque imperii*, ed. Otto Seeck (1876, reprinted, Frankfurt, 1962), pp. 247–53. On its date, late 314, see Timothy D. Barnes, "Emperors, Panegyrics, Prefects, Provinces and Palaces (284–317)," *Journal of Roman Archaeology* 9 (1996): 549–50. For a second-century snapshot of the northern barbarians, see Florus, *Epitoma* 4.12.1–39, ed. Paul Jal (Paris, 1967), 2:63–70. He pictures them as unruly and disinclined to bow their heads, but not migratory or a special danger to the Empire.

6. Tacitus, *Germania* 37.2–5, ed. Lund, p. 98, complains that the Romans have been "vanquishing" Germans for more than two centuries without subduing them, and adds that German "liberty" is a greater threat to the empire than even Parthia. This has been music to the ears of modern historians of the early Germans, but Tacitus's ominous note was not echoed in later imperial literature: it cannot be considered representative of enduring Roman attitudes toward its northern neighbors. For very levelheaded comments on the difficulty of extracting "renseignements exacts" from the *Germania* and on how Tacitus's contemporaries would have discounted a "Germanic threat," see Claude Nicolet, *La fabrique d'une nation: La France entre Rome et les Germains* (Paris, 2003), pp. 47–48. For "wild nations," see E. A. Thompson, *A Roman Reformer and Inventor* (Oxford, 1952), 97 (anon., *De rebus bellicis* 6.1), "imperium Romanum circumlatrantium ubique nationum perstringat insania et omne latus limitum . . . appetat dolosa barbaries."

7. Matthew Innes, "Teutons or Trojans? The Carolingians and the Germanic Past," in *The Uses of the Past in the Early Middle Ages*, ed. Y. Hen and M. Innes (Cambridge, 2000), p. 234. See also Heinz Thomas, "*frenkisk*: Zur Geschichte von *theodiscus* und *teutonicus* im Frankenreich des 9. Jahrhunderts," in *Beiträge zur Geschichte des Regnum Francorum*, ed. Rudolf Schieffer, Beiheft der *Francia* 22 (Sigmaringen, 1990), pp. 67–95. The step from awareness of a common language to awareness of a common history *as Germans* took much longer than Innes may seem to suggest; a common past could exist in the absence of a single ethnic umbrella. The Carolingian scholars were concerned with Gothic names, not with a Gothic language, which no one had been speaking for a long time.

8. Erich Zöllner, *Die politische Stellung der Völker im Frankenreich*, Veröffentlichungen des Instituts für österreichische Geschichtsforschung 13 (Vienna, 1950), pp. 43–45;

see also, along somewhat different lines, Innes, "Teutons or Trojans?" p. 232. Innes, p. 234: the famous Saxon monk Gottschalk referred to the *gens theodisca*, simply meaning those people who spoke the vernacular—not "the Germans." (Modern English, inconveniently, does not distinguish the *Germanen* of antiquity from the *Deutschen* of medieval and modern times.)

A nest of ninth-century Fulda-centered scholars mentioned the *lingua Germanica*, meaning the same thing elsewhere called *theudiscus sermo*; see Hennig Brinkmann, "Theodiscus, ein Beitrag zur Frühgeschichte des Namens 'Deutsch' " (1941), in *Der Volksname Deutsch*, ed. Hans Eggers, Wege der Forschung 156 (Darmstadt, 1970), pp. 191–92. The noteworthy fact is that *Germania* was recognized not as something belonging to the natives, but as a classical, "learned" term, especially featured, in a geographical sense, at the opening of Paul the Deacon's *Historia Langobaralorum*, as Chapter 2, n. 21, above.

9. See Heinz Thomas, "Die Deutschen und die Rezeption ihres Volksnamens," in *Nord und Süd in der deutschen Geschichte des Mittelalters*, ed. W. Paravicini (Sigmaringen, 1990), pp. 19–50. The "people" name is derived from the (earlier established) "language" name and begins to be attested ca. A.D. 1000; it was used in an Italian context before acquiring currency in the north. For a bibliographically oriented discussion of the subject, see Johannes Fried, *Die Formierung Europas 840–1046*, Oldenbourg Grundriss der Geschichte, ed. Jochen Bleicken et al., 6 (Munich, 1991), pp. 119–22. Louis's surname "the German" was applied to him many centuries later and is irrelevant to the argument.

10. For a compact introduction to this story (whose actors included many non-Germans), see Léon Poliakov, *The Aryan Myth: A History of Racist and Nationalist Ideas in Europe*, trans. E. Howard (New York, 1974); German myths of origin are summarized, pp. 71–105.

11. Kossinna's disciple Hans Reinerth credited him with personally adding two millennia to German history, not without having to struggle to obtain vindication: "Die Urgermanen," in *Vorgeschichte der deutschen Stämme: Germanische Tat und Kultur auf deutschen Boden*, ed. Hans Reinerth, 3 vols. (Leipzig, 1940, reprinted, Struckum, 1986–87), 1:2. This Nazi-sponsored collective work embodies the apotheosis of Kossinna's theories; note its recent reprinting. For an incidental endorsement by a prominent historian of the idea of a "first" *Völkerwanderung*, see Hermann Aubin, "Zur Frage der historischen Kontinuität im Allgemeinen," *Historische Zeitschrift* 168 (1943): 254–55.

12. One of Kossinna's ultranationalistic books, *Die Herkunft der Germanen* (Würzburg, 1911), was reprinted in 1978. It is clear (e.g., in the light of Poliakov, n. 10, above) that Kossinna's racism and his exaltation of the Germans as central to the European civilization then dominating the globe were ideas widely shared in and outside Germany; he was not a crank in his context. Also, in this sense, Bruce G. Trigger, *A History of Archaeological Thought* (Cambridge, 1989), p. 164. But, on the eve of World War I, Kossinna was already a byword for German racialism; see Nicolet, *Fabrique d'une nation*, pp. 238, 241.

13. As, for example, in England, the historians William Stubbs (1825–1901) and Edward Freeman (1823–92); see J. W. Burrow, *A Liberal Descent: Victorian Historians and the English Past* (Cambridge, 1981), pp. 108–25, 188–92 (Freeman's racialism), 205–15. English society before the Normans was understood to descend from a "primitive Teutonic polity," based on Tacitus; see n. 45, below. It is not certain that this idea has been outgrown.

14. Frank L. Borchardt, *Germanic Antiquity in Renaissance Myth* (Baltimore, 1971), pp. 327–28 (Joachimsen). Borchardt's book admirably documents the profusion of early traditions.

15. E. G. Stanley, *The Search for Anglo-Saxon Paganism* (Cambridge, 1975), p. 91. As Stanley well knows, Grimm's outlook is by no means universally repudiated. One influential survival is sketched by Innes, "Teutons or Trojans?" p. 229, "The assumption that the new leaders of the post-Roman west brought with them a set of common cultural traits ['Germanic warrior culture'] remains almost pervasive to this day."

16. For this idea and its sources, see Heinz Thomas, "Julius Caesar und die Deutschen: Zu Ursprung und Gehalt eines deutschen Geschichtsbewußtseins in der Zeit Gregors VII. und Heinrichs IV.," in *Die Salier und das Reich*, ed. Stefan Weinfurter, 3 vols. (Sigmaringen, 1991), 3:245–77. Thomas, p. 254 with n. 46, shows the legend becoming unpalatable centuries before Wilhelmine times.

17. On the crucial philological or linguistic dimension (associated with the eighteenth-century discovery of the Indo-European family of languages), see, in brief, Poliakov, *Aryan Myth*, pp. 188–214, 255–61. The widely adopted substitution of "Indo-Germanic" for Indo-European first took place in 1823.

18. Bury, *Invasions of Europe by the Barbarians*.

19. Patrick J. Geary, ed., *Readings in Medieval History*, 2nd ed. (Peterborough, Ontario, 1997), p. viii. A section on "Late Antiquity" fills in the premedieval background. The inclusion of *Hildebrandslied* nods in the direction of a line of argument not discussed here, according to which medieval heroic poetry "stands for" chains of tradition reaching back continuously to, and documenting, a pan-Germanic heroic age in late antiquity. For a brief, critical account of this (still lively) belief, see Innes, "Teutons or Trojans?" pp. 236–37, 246–47; in the same critical vein, Amory, *People and Identity*, Appendix 2. See also Walter Goffart, "Conspicuously Absent: Martial Heroism in the *Histories* of Gregory of Tours and Its Likes," in *The World of Gregory of Tours*, ed. K. Mitchell and I. Wood (Leiden, 2002), pp. 365–93; my postscript (pp. 387–93) directly addresses the question of heroic legend. There is no sign that the impulse to find early history in this medieval literature is weakening; see, e.g., Reinhard Schmoeckel, *Deutsche Sagenhelden und die historische Wirklichkeit: Zwei Jahrhunderte deutscher Frühgeschichte neu gesehen* (Hildesheim, 1995).

20. Tacitus *Germania* 2.1, ed. Lund, p. 70 (aborigines). Jordanes on Germans, *Getica* 10, 11, 24, 30, 58, 67, 120, 191, 257, ed. Mommsen, pp. 56, 60, 61, 70, 73, 89, 108, 124; on emigration, see Chapter 4, below.

21. Fredegar, *Chronicon* 2.4–6, 8, 3.2 (Franks), 2.46 (Burgundians), 3.65 (Lombards), 3.9 (Frankish dynasty), ed. Krusch, pp. 45–47, 93; 68, 110; 95. It seems to me that the point of the Trojan legend was not that the Franks were "equal" to the Romans but that they came from the same cradle, i.e., were one. It is notable that Fredegar's three other stories are all built on etymologies.

22. (Vienna, 2001); the subtitle means "conquest and integration." I note in passing another recent example of the type, Magdalena Mączyńka, *Die Völkerwanderung: Geschichte einer ruhelosen Epoche im 4. und 5. Jahrhundert* (Zurich, 1993). The author, though well read in specialist literature, is basically uncritical and very fond of the migration motif. I have not examined Klaus Rosen, *Die Völkerwanderung* (Munich, 2002). For earlier works, see the selection cited by Demougeot at n. 37, below.

23. *Getica* 4, 9, 10, 12, 13, 16, 19, 25, 29, ed. Mommsen, pp. 54–58, 60–61. Modern authors relying on Jordanes's emigration story arbitrarily discard his date for this event and substitute a date they consider more probable.

24. Jordanes, *Getica* 26 (Vandals), 94–95 (Gepids), ed. Mommsen, pp. 60, 82. See also Chapter 4. The Goths, Vandals, and Gepids featured by Jordanes in their remote, foreign origins were regarded in his Constantinople as *the* Gothic peoples (see Chapter 7, n. 56, below). Their total suppression in the near future was anticipated (see Chapter 7, n. 61).

25. John Malalas, *Chronicle* 2.9–10, 4.13, 7.1–14, and passim, trans. Elisabeth Jeffreys et al., Byzantina Australiensia 4 (Melbourne, 1986), pp. 15–16, 38, 91–99. Malalas is full of weird and wonderful lore about the origins of Rome and Byzantium. John Lydus, *De magistratibus*, trans. Anastasius C. Bandy (Philadelphia, 1983); Roman history in an account of the origin and descent of current magistracies. Evagrius Scholasticus, *Ecclesiastical History*, trans. Michael Whitby, Translated Texts for Historians 33 (Liverpool, 2000). Evagrius wrote near the end of the century; his commemoration of emperors (3.41) completely ignores westerners. Michael Maas, "Roman History and Christian Ideology in Justinianic Reform Legislation," *Dumbarton Oaks Papers* 40 (1986): 18, "Never before in Roman law has historical data, often fanciful and inaccurate, . . . been so systematically tailored." On the carrying over of Scandinavian origins, see Innes, "Teutons or Trojans?" p. 233.

26. Beatus Rhenanus, *Rerum Germanorum libri tres* (Basel, 1531), 21, 29 (*emigrationes*); Konrad Peutinger, "de inclinatione Romani imperii, & exterarum gentium, praecipue Germanorum, conmigrationibus, epitome." See Chapter 1, n. 3, above.

27. Isidore of Seville, *Historia Gothorum*, ed. T. Mommsen, MG AA 11: 267, 268, 304 (Dedicatio ad Sisenandum). But, as regards the attribution to Isidore, see now Kulikowski, *Late Roman Spain*, pp. 402–6 n. 81.

28. Widukind, *Res gestae Saxonicae* 1.2, ed. A. Bauer and R. Rau, 2nd ed., in Ausgewählte Quellen zur deutschen Geschichte des Mittelalters 8 (Darmstadt, 1977), pp. 20–22. Widukind mentions the Macedonians as an alternative to an origin from the "Danes and Northmen."

29. Frechulf of Lisieux, *Historiae* 1.2.26, lines 160–74 (as a postcript to the Trojan War), ed. Michael Allen, Corpus Christianorum continuatio medievalis 169A (Turnhout, 2002), pp. 147–48. Frechulf's dependence on Jordanes about Scandinavia is plain, but he adds an argument from a common language: "quod et idioma linguae eorum testatur." For the context of Frechulf's comment, see Thomas, "*frenkisk*," p. 77.

30. Zöllner, *Politische Stellung*, pp. 46–47. Zöllner, pp. 47–48, amplifies his charge by alleging that "The Franks did not accept without resistance the darkening of their early history by the Trojan myth." We are to understand that they were victimized by aliens. Innes, "Teutons or Trojans?" p. 233, entertains the belief that all references to Scandinavian origins derive ultimately from Jordanes—a more probable hypothesis than that espoused by Zöllner of independent "correct" oral traditions. Innes's opinion is sustained by the very full account of Hachmann, *Die Goten und Skandinavien* (Berlin, 1970), pp. 16–34. On origins in Jordanes, see Gillett, "Introduction," pp. 16–17.

31. One starting point for circular modern arguments is stated as an obiter dictum by Schmidt, *Ostgermanen*, p. 549, "In der Erinnerung der germanischen Völker sind oft weit zurückliegende Ereignisse mit großer Treue festgehalten worden."

32. Few authoritative memories, or scholarly principles, restrained medieval imaginations. Typically, the Saxons are identified as immigrants from Britain in Rudolf of

Fulda, *Translatio S. Alexandri* (in Ausgewählte Quellen, 8:12); Hrabanus Maurus derived the "Northmen" (Vikings or Danes) from the (Danubian) Marcomanni (Thomas, "*frenkisk*," 77); and Frechulf (*Historiae* 1.2.26) completed his northern derivation of the Franks by saying: "Est enim in eadem insula [i.e., Scandinavia] regio quae, ut ferunt, adhuc Francia nuncupatur." No one claims Frechulf's "ut ferunt" here as an authentic oral tradition.

33. On Annius and Trithemius, see Borchardt, *German Antiquity*, pp. 89–91, 127–35. On Lazius, see Goffart, *Historical Atlases*, pp. 61–64. For an enlightening study of the effects produced in Great Britain by Jordanes's tale of emigration from Scandza, see Samuel Kliger, *The Goths in England: A Study of Seventeenth and Eighteenth-Century Thought* (New York, 1972).

34. Hans-Joachim Diesner, *The Great Migration*, trans. C. S. V. Salt (London, 1978), p. 90. Pohl, *Völkerwanderung*, shows that this habit is as respectable as ever today: e.g., pp. 44–49 (Goths), 71–73 (Vandals), 103–6 (Huns), 165–68 (Franks and Alamanni), 188–91 (Lombards). So also Bruno Krüger, *Die Germanen: Mythos—Geschichte—Kultur—Archäologie* (Langenweissbach, 2003), pp. 115–31, 197–211, and passim. The practice is by no means confined to German authors; e.g., about the Vandals, see Courcelle, *Histoire littéraire*, pp. 80–81, "Issues de Scandinavie . . ." Distant origins are an obligatory theme; the appropriateness of the quest is never questioned.

35. Quotation from Arnulf Krause, *Die Geschichte der Germanen* (Frankfurt, 2002), p. 179. For the historical traces of the Lombards, see Musset, *Germanic Invasions*, p. 86 (with reference to Roman historians only).

36. Pohl, *Völkerwanderung*, is original in being ostensibly focused on six major leaders of the Migration Age; but this facade is applied to a wholly traditional people-by-people exposition, with obligatory emphasis of distant origins (as n. 34).

37. Demougeot, *Formation de l'Europe*, 1:9: "à [la connaissance] de l'Europe romaine, correspondent les premières synthèses de K. Müllenhoff, de F. Kauffmann et d'A. Meitzen jusqu'à la *Vorgeschichte der deutschen Stämme* publiée sous la direction d'H. Reinerth, reprise ou résumée par divers *Germanische Stammeskunde*, et jusqu'à la *Geschichte der deutschen Stämme* de L. Schmidt, études générales qu'approfondissent encore les monographies consacrées aux différents peuples et États barbares."

38. After forcefully criticizing Kossinna-style accounts of the early Vandals, Christian Courtois reversed his field: "Mais ainsi définies les limites et la mesure de notre savoir, il ne me semble pas qu'il soit interdit à l'historien d'imaginer." His next paragraph leaps to the beginning of the Bronze Age (ca. 1800 b.c.). *Les Vandales et l'Afrique* (Paris, 1955), p. 18. It is hard to imagine what gods Courtois was sacrificing to in launching into what he himself recognized to be speculation.

39. Demandt, *Der Fall Roms*, pp. 104–5. For a less indulgent view, see Poliakov, *Aryan Myth*, p. 80: "The witness of Tacitus, being above suspicion as coming from a Roman, was the main 'fragment of reality' around which the megalomaniac delirium of the Germans organized itself in modern times."

40. A recent work on the early Germans attains unprecedented patriotic extravagance by asserting the unity and collective determination of the Germanic peoples throughout their *Frühgeschichte*: Konrad Hoefinger, *Germanen gegen Rom: Ein europäischer Schicksalskampf* (Tübingen, 1986). The much more respectable Gerhard Dobesch, *Vom äusseren Proletariat zum Kulturträger: Ein Aspekt zur Rolle der Germanen in der Spätantike*, Geographica historica 6 (Amsterdam, 1994), does not hesitate to discourse about

282 Notes to Pages 49–50

a nonexistent collectivity and to extoll its great deeds. Note also Kurt Pastenaci, *Die beiden Weltmächte: Der 500jährige Kampf der Germanen mit Rom* (1938, reprinted, Viöl, 1995).

41. Martin Schanz, *Geschichte der römischen Literatur*, 2/2, 3rd ed. (Munich, 1913), pp. 328–29, 332–33; the brief revival of interest in Tacitus ca. A.D. 400 did not extend to the *Germania*; Francis Haverfield, "Tacitus during the Late Roman Period and the Middle Ages," *Journal of Roman Studies* 6 (1916): 195–200. The ninth-century user, Rudolf of Fulda, copied extracts from *Germania* 4, 9, 10, and 11 (without credit), to describe the early (sixth-century) Saxons; see Tacitus, *The* Germania *of Tacitus: A Critical Edition*, ed. R. P. Robinson (Middletown, Conn., 1935), pp. 278, 285–87. The fate of the *Germania* between its writing and its rediscovery fourteen centuries later is omitted from a recent comprehensive stocktaking: Herbert Jankuhn and Dieter Timpe, eds., *Beiträge zum Verständnis der* Germania *des Tacitus*, 2 parts (Göttingen, 1989).

42. Eduard Norden, *Die germanische Urgeschichte in Tacitus* Germania (Leipzig, 1920), p. 5, "[das Werk habe] eine gütige Fee unserm Volke als Patengeschenk in die Wiege seiner vaterlaendischen Geschichte gelegt." Norden, a supremely talented Latinist, was dismissed from his German professorship as a Jew and died in Switzerland. The excellence of his Tacitus scholarship is not in question.

43. Cassiodorus, *Variae* 5.2 (based on Tacitus, *Germania* 45, ed. Lund, 104–6), ed. Mommsen, pp. 143–44.

44. Abraham Ortelius, *Aurei saeculi imago, sive Germanorum veterum vita, mores, ritus, et religio iconibus delineati et commentariis ex utrumque linguae auctoribus descriptae* (Antwerp, 1596); and Philipp Clüver, *Germania antiqua* (Leiden, 1616; 2nd ed., 1631). Full-page depictions of ancient Germans are a notable adjunct of Clüver's work (*imagines, priscum Germanorum cultum moresque referentes*).

45. On this enterprise, see the perceptive comment of Donald Kelley in Chapter 1 at n. 24. Hayes, *Introduction to the Sources*, pp. 51–52, points to the construction by nineteenth-century commentators of a highly influential concept of a "primitive Teutonic polity"; "The *Germania* created the 'primitive Teutonic polity'; the devotees of the 'primitive Teutonic polity' adored and magnified the *Germania*."

46. The Cimbri are no longer classed as Germanic; see Allan A. Lund, *Die ersten Germanen: Ethnizität und Ethnogenese* (Heidelberg, 1998), pp. 70–71. See also Leandro Polverini, "Germani in Italia prima dei Cimbri?" in *Germani in Italia*, ed. B. and P. Scardigli (Rome, 1994), pp. 1–10; and Dieter Timpe, "Kimberntradition und Kimbermythos," in ibid., pp. 23–60.

47. For these well-known incidents, see, in summary, Cary, *History of Rome*, pp. 501–2, 655–56, 723–30.

48. The sketchy *Forschungsbericht* of Evangelos Chrysos, "Conclusion: De foederatis iterum," in *Kingdoms of the Empire: The Integration of Barbarians in Late Antiquity*, ed. Walter Pohl (Leiden, 1997), pp. 185–87, seems to celebrate the continuity of the subject across the divide of World War II. Chrysos detects no fundamental reconsideration (only the Third Reich, he suggests, injected a virus into the subject, now safely purged).

49. Wolfram, *Geschichte der Goten*, 2nd ed., p. 3, announces that Wenskus's *Stammesbildung und Verfassung* (1961), rescued German *Altertumskunde* from its postwar discredit. His comment stems from the belief that "the science of Germanic antiquity" stood narrowly on a racial conception of tribes; once deprived of a racial core, the "science" was discredited, but Wenskus—so runs the reasoning—by detaching *gentes*

from a racial basis, restored the whole "science" to respectability. Wolfram has much too limited an idea of what is wrong with German *Altertumskunde.*

50. I borrow this summary from my article "Does the Distant Past Impinge on the Invasion Age Germans?" in *On Barbarian Identity*, ed. Gillett, p. 21.

51. Zöllner, *Politische Stellung*, p. 43.

52. A compact expression of Wolfram's beliefs is found in his "*Origo et religio*: Ethnic Traditions and Literature in Early Medieval Texts," *Early Medieval Europe* 3 (1994): 19–38. The Latin words of the title, Wolfram's own coinage, illustrate his authenticating devices. For a critical appraisal of Wolfram's argumentation, see Walter Goffart, "Two Notes on Germanic Antiquity Today," *Traditio* 50 (1995): 9–30, and "Does the Distant Past Impinge," pp. 31–37. For articulations of Wolfram's theses about *origines gentium*, see the contributions of Hans Hubert Anton and Johann Weißensteiner in *Historiographie im frühen Mittelalter*, ed. Anton Scharer and G. Scheibelreiter, Veröffentlichungen des Instituts für österreichische Geschichtsforschung 32 (Vienna-Munich, 1994).

53. Kossinna invoked the Bornholm origin of the Burgundians as an unquestionable fact; see Hachmann, *Goten und Skandinavien*, pp. 150–51. Pohl, *Völkerwanderung*, p. 154, does not fail to announce that the Burgundian name, like the Gothic, is attested in Scandinavia, by Bornholm (he does not add how late this name is first attested). Readers are free to draw the conclusion that, where there was a name, there must have been if not a people at least a "core of tradition" to wander southward. For a judicious account of the Bornholm myth and the "Skandinavienthese," see Kaiser, *Die Burgunder*, pp. 22–24.

54. For characteristic claims by Wolfram to being rejected and misunderstood see his *Treasures on the Danube: Barbarian Invaders and Their Roman Inheritance*, ed. G. Langthaler (Vienna, 1985), p. 54 (there is also a German edition); Wolfram, *History of the Goths*, p. 1 (opening sentence); Wolfram, "*Origo et religio*," pp. 19, 26 n. 28. Walter Pohl pretends that a factual comment about a deceased Germanist (and confirmed Nazi) is a personal slur on himself: "Ethnicity, Theory, and Tradition: A Response" in *On Barbarian Identity*, ed. Gillett, pp. 222–24. These allegations of victimhood are appeals for audience sympathy.

55. Aubin, "Zur Frage der historischen Kontinuität," p. 259. Another "triumph" of German revision of the past concerned prehistory: Kossinna (and others) replaced the idea that "light" came from the Near East with the notion of civilization coming from the Indogermanic *Urvolk*, spreading southward out of southern Scandinavia and northern Germany. The Putzger *Historischer Schul-Atlas*, ubiquitous in schools, opens its 1937 edition with maps illustrating the old and new "concept of history" (*Geschichtsbild*).

56. On this subject, see Chapter 7, section "Gothic Italy and the Ethnic Bastion That Never Was," below.

57. For the consulship of Nevitta, see Ammianus Marcellinus 21.10.8, 12.25, 22.7.1, ed. Rolfe, 2:138, 154, 206. Ammianus chided the emperor Julian for hypocrisy in denouncing his relative, Constantine the Great, for having given high honors to barbarians and then himself bestowing the ordinary consulship on Nevitta (a general of the highest rank), whom Ammianus considered wholly unworthy. Ammianus's feelings notwithstanding, Nevitta was the first of a series of ordinary consuls of Frankish origin—a clear sign that *novi homines* had arrived. See also Chapter 7, section "Late Roman Conditions and Barbarian Penetration," below.

58. The maps with their contrasting colors give the "Romano-Germanic" kingdoms an exaggerated appearance of cohesion and independence. Typically, Lot, *End*

of the Ancient World, pp. 209–15, launches after 476 into an account of "lost" Roman lands; those ruled as though they still were the Roman Empire come into focus only at pp. 237–42. On religious policies, see Goffart, *Rome's Fall and After,* pp. 25–27.

59. For the lady-in-waiting, see PLRE 2:63, s.v. "Amalafrida." On marriages, see Chapter 7, section "Late Roman Conditions and Barbarian Penetration," below.

60. The intertwining of families documents the unity of the period from the advent of Marcian to the death of Anastasius (451–518). These long-standing links were broken by the near-revolutionary, pro-Chalcedonian election of Justin I. See Stemma 5, 7, 9, in PLRE 2:1311, 1312, 1314.

61. Brian Croke, "AD 476: The Manufacture of a Turning Point," *Chiron* 13 (1983): 81–119, is a superb demonstration of what is announced by its title. See also *The Chronicle of Marcellinus,* ed. Brian Croke, Byzantina Australiensia 7 (Sydney, 1995), pp. 26–27, 101–2. An enormous capital of modern scholarship is invested in the proposition that the West Roman Empire "fell" in 476 (anyone involved in teaching can understand the attractions of a firm hitching post, but that is only part of the reason). It has proved easy to accept Croke's demonstration and to continue nevertheless to maintain the validity of the "turning point."

62. Procopius's words to this effect are quoted in Chapter 6 at n. 141, below.

Chapter 4

1. "Eine Nation, die nicht den lebendigen Zusammenhang mit ihrem Ursprung bewahrt, ist dem Verdorren nahe, so sicher wie ein Baum, den man von seinen Wurzeln getrennt hat. Wir sind heute noch, was wir gestern waren." My translation. A slightly different version of this chapter was published under the same title in *Speculum* 80 (2005): 379–98.

2. Walter Goffart, *Historical Atlases,* pp. 240, 271.

3. Jordanes, *Histoire des Goths,* trans. Olivier Devillers (Paris, 1995), p. 131 n. 36, "information d'autant plus précieuse qu'on la fait remonter à la tradition orale des Goths." One quirk of this able and learned translation is that the extensive notes never acknowledge sources.

4. Borchardt, *German Antiquity,* p. 18, "Only the last two origins given by our Renaissance authors—for Goths and Langobards—seem to reflect a real state of affairs"; pp. 23, 302–3, espousing the common illusion of Germanic philologists that historical events "lay behind" various legends. Borchardt's excellent book suffers little from this illusion. Another believer is Giuseppe Zecchini, *Ricerche di storiografia Latina tardoantica* (Rome, 1993), pp. 200–201. For the widely implemented practice of omitting a reference to Jordanes and substituting the phrase "gotische Stammsage" in its place, see n. 15, below.

5. Zöllner, *Politische Stellung,* pp. 46–47. Flawed thinking similar to Zöllner's is found in Lotte Hedeager, "The Creation of Germanic Identity: A European Origin-Myth," in *Frontières d'Empire: Nature et signification des frontières romaines,* Mémoires du Musée de Préhistoire d'Ile de France 5 (Nemours, 1993), p. 124. She reasons that, by comparison with Trojan and biblical origin myths, the Scandinavian version is "oldest" and therefore more authentic. To the contrary, see the important article by Hermann

Bollnow, "Die Herkunftssagen der germanischen Stämme als Geschichtsquelle," *Baltische Studien* N.F. 54 (1965): 14–25 at 25: "Noah-, Troja- und Skandinavienfabel stehen gleichwertig nebeneinander. Sie wurzeln alle drei in antiken Fragestellungen, sind von Römern aufgebracht worden."

6. Jordanes, *De origine actibusque Getarum* 9, 25, 94–95, 313, ed. Mommsen, pp. 55–56, 60, 82, 138. This is still the standard edition (see my review of the recent Giunta-Grillone edition, in *Gnomon* 67/3 [1995]: 227–29). Mommsen has accustomed us to call Jordanes's work *Getica* for short. "Getae," the Greek name for Dacian peoples, was understood in antiquity to be an "old" or literary name for Goths (many of whom were settled in "Getic" territory). It has long been customary in scholarship to alter the date of emigration arbitrarily and without comment to something more probable sounding, such as the first century A.D. I have written at length about Jordanes, including his Roman history as well as the Gothic one, in *The Narrators of Barbarian History (A.D. 550–800): Jordanes, Gregory of Tours, Bede, and Paul the Deacon* (Princeton, N.J., 1988; reprinted Notre Dame, Ind., 2005), pp. 20–111. Although the present chapter allows me to refine my views, I stand by my earlier discussion. I have not been able to examine C. E. P. Vermeulen, *Op zoek naar de Gotische Traditie: Een onderzoek in Casssiodorus' Variae en Jordanes' Getica* (Rotterdam, 1999). Jordanes encounters Michel Foucault in Edward H. Jacobs, *Accidental Migrations: An Archaeology of Gothic Discourse* (Lewisburg, Pa., 2000), pp. 33–57 ("Jordanes's *Getica* and the Rhapsody of Migration; or, How the Goths Came to Kent"). Nothing of value may be gleaned from Luigi Maria Buonomo, "Introduzione alla lettura delle opere di Giordane," in *Mutatio rerum: letteratura, filosofia, scienza tra tardo antico e altomedioevo*, Atti del convegno di studi (Napoli, 1996), ed. Maria Luisa Silvestre and Marisa Squillante (Naples, 1997), pp. 115–46.

7. Peter Heather, *The Goths*, The Peoples of Europe (Oxford, 1996), p. 26; Arne Søby Christensen, *Cassiodorus, Jordanes, and the History of the Goths: Studies in a Migration Myth* (Copenhagen, 2002), p. 276. I am much indebted to Professor Niels Lund (Copenhagen) for sending me Christensen's work. See also Herwig Wolfram, "Einige Überlegungen zur gotischen *origo gentis*," in *Studia linguistica Alexandro Vasilii filio Issatschenko a collegis amicisque oblato*, ed. Henrik Birnbaum et al. (Lisse, The Netherlands, 1978), pp. 487–99, at 496, "Die Herkunft der Goten aus 'Übersee' steht und fällt derzeit allein mit der Möglichkeit, die Getica historisch zu rechtfertigen."

8. Herwig Wolfram, "Die Aufnahme germanischer Völker ins Römerreich: Aspekte und Konsequenzen," *Centro Italiano di studi sull'alto medioevo: Settimane di studio* 29/1 (1983): 122 (discussion). My translation. Similar statements by Wolfram are quoted in n. 28, below.

9. On Cassiodorus, including his history of the Goths, see PLRE 2:265–69, s.v. Cassiodorus 4.

10. Cassiodorus, *Variae* 9.25.5, ed. Mommsen, p. 292. For the context, with a slightly different wording, see Goffart, *Narrators*, p. 35; more literally (p. 37), "he made Gothic history to be Roman history." Thomas Hodgkin translated the words in four ways: "he made 'the Origin of the Goths' a part of Roman History" (*Italy and Her Invaders*, 8 vols. [London, 1885–99], 1:27); "Thus did he assign a Roman origin to Gothic history" (ibid., 3:293); "he 'made the Gothic origin Roman'" (ibid., 3:294); and, in paraphrase, "[he] proved that the origin of the Gothic people belonged to Roman history" (Hodgkin, *The Letters of Cassiodorus* [London, 1886], p. 412). Christensen, *Cassiodorus, Jordanes*, p. 72 n. 62, "From Gothic origins he made a Roman history"—endorsing the version of S. J. B.

Barnish, *Cassiodorus's* Variae, Translated Texts for Historians 12 (Liverpool, 1992), p. 128. Another reading is proposed with explanations, by Lars Boje Mortensen, "Stylistic Choice in a Reborn Genre: The National Histories of Widukind of Corvey and Dudo of St. Quentin," in *Dudone di San Quintino*, ed. Paolo Gatti and Antonella Degl'Innocenti (Trento, 1995), p. 84: "he turned stories of Gothic origin into a history composed in Latin." Cf. Christensen, pp. 73–74 n. 65.

11. Wolfram, *History of the Goths*, p. 4. The English introduction includes much from the conclusion of the second German edition. In explaining his activity—"Eine Geschichte der Goten ist bloß dann aus der allgemeinen Geschichte des Altertums und des Frühmittelalters zu lösen, wenn sie als historische Ethnographie dargestellt wird"— Wolfram never spells out how his "historical ethnography" differs in structure and content from the many other modern narratives that also detach Gothic history from a wider whole. As far as I know, his questionable proposition that Roman history is the goal of tribal histories has nowhere been demonstrated.

12. Wolfram, *Geschichte der Goten*, 2nd ed., p. 1.

13. Ibid., p. 3.

14. Wolfram, "Einige Überlegungen," comes closest to the problem of Cassiodorus/Jordanes. The article often illustrates Wolfram's practice of inserting personal conclusions as premises of his discussion. Typically, the title assumes the (unproved) existence of a Gothic *origo gentis* in Wolfram's private definition of this term (see n. 28, below).

15. Walter Pohl, "Die Gepiden und die Gentes an der mittleren Donau," in *Die Völker an der mittleren und unteren Donau im 5. und 6. Jahrhundert*, ed. H. Wolfram and F. Daim (Vienna, 1980), pp. 241, 264; frequent references in Volker Bierbrauer, "Archäologie und Geschichte der Goten vom 1.–7. Jahrhundert," *Frühmittelalterliche Studien* 28 (1994): 51–171. Wolfram's *Origo Gothica* has a progenitor. For a long time, German scholarship has based a variety of hypotheses on the ostensibly solid ground of what is called the "gotische Stammessage"—a glorified reference to Jordanes; see, e.g., Bruno Krüger, *Die Germanen*, p. 129.

16. E.g., Franz Brunhölzl, *Geschichte der lateinischen Literatur des Mittelalters* (Munich, 1975), 1:29–31; Goffart, *Narrators*, pp. 21–22. See also the characterization of the *Getica* by Erik Lönnroth in n. 59, below. Many commentators have used the form "Cassiodorus-Jordanes" to indicate the proximity or marriage of the two authors.

17. Wolfram, *Geschichte der Goten*, 2nd ed., p. 1: "In der Praxis bleibt der Interpret einer antiken oder frühmittelalterlichen Origo gentis . . . , auf eine traditionelle . . . Literaturgattung angewiesen, . . . Schließlich geht es um die Selbstbehauptung des Historikers."

18. Goffart, *Narrators*, pp. 24–26, 70–73, in which the relevant literature is cited. I particularly recommend Brian Croke, "Cassiodorus and the *Getica* of Jordanes," *Classical Philology* 82 (1987): 117–34. Peter Heather, *Goths and Romans, 332–489* (Oxford, 1991), pp. 38–52, aims his artillery jointly at Momigliano and me. See also Zecchini, *Ricerche di storiografia* pp. 193–97.

19. Jordanes's Eastern perspective is strongly affirmed by Devillers, in Jordanes, *Histoire des Goths*, p. xvii. See also Jordanes, *Getica* 266, 316, ed. Mommsen, pp. 126–27, 138; Goffart, *Narrators*, pp. 42–44. Zecchini, *Ricerche di storiografia*, p. 80, does not help matters by having Jordanes standing on a "ridge" between Eastern and Western historiography. Italian commentators tend to be speculative about Jordanes's biography (see

n. 25, below). Helmut de Boor, *Das Attilabild in Geschichte, Legende und heroischer Dichtung* (Bern, 1932), p. 44, comments, "Jordanes gibt sich schon durch die Art, wie er Attila sieht, als Germanen und Erben germanischer Tradition zu erkennen." This comment illustrates the ability of reputable scholars to transmute what was Byzantine into what they wish us to believe was "German." Jordanes's loud applause for Belisarius in 540 draws attention away from his deliberate omission of Italian developments after that date (see also n. 52, below).

20. Goffart, *Narrators*, p. 60. The meaning of *generatio* may be "leading family."

21. Ibid., pp. 32–34 (date of Cassiodorus's history). On his exile, see PLRE 2:265–69. Consultation of Cassiodorus's history, see Jordanes, *Getica* 2, ed. Mommsen, p. 54.

22. Goffart, *Narrators*, pp. 61–62. Throughout the present study I treat Jordanes as a real person. It is safer, no doubt, to assume that he was. In *Narrators*, pp. 104–5, I suggest that Jordanes is a pseudonym for an author who only pretends to be a Goth. I do not insist on this conjecture but do not withdraw it either.

23. Fredegar, *Chronicon*, book 3, ed. Krusch, pp. 89–118. The third book condenses Gregory, but also interpolates new stories. Krusch helps us by typography to distinguish the Gregorian substrate from Fredegar's additions. In a strange reversal of the logic of comparison, Dennis R. Bradley asks the lost text to control the surviving one: "In the absence of the 'Gothic history' [of Cassiodorus], however, it is impossible to arrive at any view of the 'independence' of Jordanes": "*In altum laxare vela compulsus*: The 'Getica' of Jordanes," *Hermes* 121 (1993): 221.

24. Eligius Dekkers, *Clavis patrum Latinorum*, 2nd ed. (Brugge, 1961), nos. 896–911, gives the full list of Cassiodorus's writings (including disputed attributions) and the places where they may be found.

25. Carl Schirren, *De ratione quae inter Iordanem et Cassiodorum intercedat commentatio* (Dorpat [Tartu], 1858); Rolf Hachmann, *Goten und Skandinavien*, pp. 474–98; Johann Weißensteiner, "Cassiodor/Jordanes als Geschichtsschreiber," in *Historiographie im frühen Mittelalter*, pp. 308–25. I came late upon Angela Amici, *Jordanes e la storia gotica*, Quaderni della Rivista di Byzantinistica, ed. Antonio Carile, 6 (Spoleto, 2002), whose first chapter is, "Il *De origine actibusque Getarum* di Iordanes e la sua dipendenze dalle opere di Cassiodoro" (pp. 3–48). As shown by the allegation (p. 1) that Jordanes is "un vescovo goto," she is unable to break free from the speculations (e.g., Jordanes at Vivarium) piled up by the Italian school of Jordanes criticism and embedded in the Giunta-Grillone edition (n. 6, above).

26. Goffart, *Narrators*, p. 66. Pohl, *Völkerwanderung*, p. 134, concurs.

27. Walter Goffart, "From *Historiae* to *Historia Francorum* and Back Again: Aspects of the Textual History of Gregory of Tours," in *Religion, Culture, and Society in the Early Middle Ages*, ed. T. F. X. Noble and J. Contreni (Kalamazoo, 1987), pp. 64–66. The early abridgments of Gregory are the subject of an important article by Helmut Reimitz, "Social Networks and Identities in Frankish Historiography: New Aspects of the Textual History of Gregory of Tours' *Historiae*," in *Construction of Communities*, pp. 229–68.

28. Wolfram does not defend the historicity of the migration legend: he presupposes it. See, e.g., Herwig Wolfram, "Theogonie, Ethnogenese und ein kompromittierter Großvater im Stammbaum Theoderichs des Großen," in *Festschrift für Helmut Beumann*, ed. K.-U. Jäschke and R. Wenskus (Sigmarigen, 1977), p. 80: it was a notorious Amal tradition that their *origo* was rooted in Scandinavia; "Einige Überlegungen," p. 495, "Was die Goten des sagenhaften Berig mit den Amalern des sechsten Jahrhunderts

verbindet, was die gemeinsame gentile Tradition und das Bekenntnis zu ihr." See also the passage cited at n. 8, above, and *History of the Goths*, pp. 36–37, "certain Gothic clans came from the north across the Baltic Sea to the Continent"; they came bearing the core of "gentile" tradition and passed it on.

29. Wenskus, *Stammesbildung und Verfassung*, p. 464 (my translation), "Bei der Suche nach den Gründen, die einen Chronisten des 6. Jahrhunderts dazu veranlassen könnten, entgegen den historischen Tatsachen die Abkunft seines Stammes aus Skandinavien zu behaupten, kommt man zu dem Ergebnis, daß es schlechterdings keine gibt. Im Gegenteil, es lag den Geschichtsschreibern dieser Zeit wesentlich näher, eine Anknüpfung an die berühmten Völker des Altertums herzustellen, wie viele Beispiele zeigen. Die Behauptung des Jordanes ist für seine Zeit ganz untypisch und beruht daher mit recht großer Sicherheit auf Überlieferungen, die einen hohen Grad von Wahrscheinlichkeit besitzen." Christensen, *Cassiodorus, Jordanes*, p. 251, has the merit of drawing attention to this key passage. Wenskus, unlike Anselm, immediately stacks the deck by introducing two unargued and undefended qualifications—Jordanes as an obscure "chronicler" and his contradicting "factual history." Murray, "Reinhard Wenskus on 'Ethnogenesis,'" in *On Barbarian Identity*, ed. Gillett pp. 39–68, is a profound analysis of Wenskus's work.

30. On Procopius, see Averil Cameron, *Procopius and the Sixth Century* (London, 1985). Other historians included Count Marcellinus, John the Lydian, John Malalas (an Antiochene).

31. I follow in the tracks of Curt Weibull, *Die Auswanderung der Goten aus Schweden* (Göteborg, 1958), pp. 18–20, which contains additional arguments, notably about climate theory.

32. Walter Pohl, "Ethnicity, Theory, and Tradition: A Response," in *On Barbarian Identity*, ed. Gillett, pp. 228–29.

33. The identification occurs in *Getica* 58.

34. Walter Pohl, "Introduction: Strategies of Distinction," in *Strategies of Distinction*, pp. 12–13, 7. For one return of this argument, see Walter Pohl, "Memory, Identity and Power in Lombard Italy," in *Uses of the Past*, p. 24, "None of these authors [about the ancient Lombard past] could write without taking a limited but qualified public into account." This "public" is a postulate that has never been argued or defended. In the Lombard case, Pohl would have us believe that three authors well separated in place and time all recoiled independently in horror at "embarrassing pagan aspects" of what they were writing.

35. *Variae* 9.25.4, ed. Mommsen, p. 291 lines 32–34; trans. Barnish, p. 128, edited: my "old men" replaces Barnish's "our elders." There is no "our," though it might be implied. Wolfram, *History of the Goths*, p. 30, expands to "white-haired elders."

36. *Variae* 9.25.6, ed. Mommsen, p. 292, lines 4–7; trans. Barnish, p. 128, edited: I have changed Barnish's "prince" into "ruler" and made the final verb present rather than future. Pohl, "Introduction: Strategies of Distinction," p. 7, supplies a translation full of mistakes.

37. Heather, *Goths*, p. 27; after further considerations of oral material, Heather reaches his conclusion (p. 30), "Some obscure Gothic material has been given a secure Scandinavian location, not for any genuinely Gothic reason, but because classical geographical traditions seemed to suggest that this was the most likely locale." The "obscure Gothic material" is a guess.

38. D. M. Metcalf, "Viking-Age Numismatics. 1. Late Roman and Byzantine Gold in the Northern Lands," (President's Address), *Numismatic Chronicle* 155 (1995): 413–41; the peak moment for gold coin imports was the third quarter of the fifth century (p. 417).

39. Procopius 3.1.4–13, ed. Dewing, 2:2–7, traces and tallies up the boundaries of the Roman Empire.

40. Goffart, *Narrators*, p. 88 n. 327, summarizing *Getica* 4–28, 38. I have added the bracketed words to the text of the note. On the "silly legend," see Heinz Löwe, "Vermeintliche gotische Überlieferungsreste bei Cassiodorus und Jordanes," in *Ex ipsis rerum documentis: Beiträge zur Mediävistik: Festschrift für Harald Zimmermann*, ed. K. Herbers et al. (Sigmaringen, 1991), pp. 26–30, who relates it to the Unnuguri. Löwe deserves a hearing, but I agree with the many commentators who take "quorum" to refer to the Goths.

41. *Getica* 4, 9, 10, 12, 13, 14, 16, 19, 28, 29, ed. Mommsen, pp. 54–58, 60–61; Goffart, *Narrators*, p. 90 n. 334.

42. On songs as an ethnographic cliché, Goffart, *Narrators*, p. 30 n. 49.

43. The point about the cultural specificity of place names is made in Goffart, *Narrators*, p. 89. For the date of Berig's migration according to Jordanes, see *Getica* 313. According to Wolfram, "Einige Überlegungen," p. 495, Cassiodorus and Jordanes supplied the tribal names "zur Rechtfertigung ihrer Theorie . . ." There is no sign that a theory was being presented.

44. Christensen, *Cassiodorus, Jordanes*, pp. 346–47. See also Erik Lönnroth, "Die Goten in der modernen kritischen Geschichtsauffassung," in Studia Gotica: *Die eisenzeitlichen Verbindungen zwischen Schweden und Südosteuropa*, ed. U. E. Hagberg (Stockholm, 1972), pp. 57–62. Lönnroth repudiates the tale of migration from Scandinavia in keeping with the radical change in scholarship brought about by the findings of Hachmann (next note).

45. Hachmann, *Goten und Skandinavien*, pp. 152–53: the "big three" of nineteenth-century Germanic studies—Kaspar Zeuss, Jacob Grimm, and Karl Müllenhoff—all rejected the historicity of the migration story. So had the Enlightenment; see Joseph Svennung, *Zur Geschichte des Goticismus* (Uppsala, 1967), p. 61. Hachmann highlights the crucial importance of Gustaf Kossinna (between 1895 and World War I) in winning acceptance of a "Skandinavientopos" on the basis of programmatic propositions that he never got around to proving (pp. 145–82). Even Hachmann's powerful demonstration has not succeeded in shaking Kossinna's influence from existing scholarship.

46. Wenskus, *Stammesbildung und Verfassung*, pp. 1–2 (my translation). His idea echoes the proposal of the historian and publicist, Alfred Dove (1844–1916), that the end of antiquity witnessed the "reentry of the national principle into world history (*Wiedereintritt des nationalen Princips in die Weltgeschichte*)"; see Heinz Thomas, "Der Ursprung des Wortes Theodiscus," *Historische Zeitschrift* 247 (1988): 300. For an interesting (and contestable) reconsideration of Wenskus's statement, see Fried, *Formierung Europas*, p. 16.

47. Amory, *People and Identity*, pp. 33–34, "For Wolfram, the ultimate myth of royal prestige and tribal origins survives in the *Getica* of Jordanes. . . . Overreliance on the *Getica* is the main weakness of the ethnogenesis school." With Pohl, the focus of attention for ultimate myths has shifted some two hundred years, to Charlemagne's contemporary, Paul the Deacon.

48. A tripartite periodization (including a "middle age") was already in circulation, but the bipartite scheme remained basic even in the nineteenth century, when the English universities instituted schools of "modern" history, equivalent to our "medieval and modern."

49. Particularism itself need not have been exclusively imported by the *gentes*. The divisions of the Roman Empire since the third century, such incidents as the distribution of the Empire among the sons of Constantine the Great, and the occurrences of civil war in late antiquity all suggest that imperial unity was threatened domestically as well as by barbarians.

50. Goffart, *Narrators*, pp. 32–42.

51. Ibid., p. 46 with n. 119. Cf. Wolfram, "Einige Überlegungen," p. 489: "Cassiodor und sein Epitomator Jordanes unterscheiden sich in ihrer Tendenz kaum voneinander . . ." This is one of the grand illusions of early medieval history.

52. Jordanes, *Romana* 377–82, ed. Mommsen, pp. 50–51, takes very seriously and tragically the Gothic revolt that he calls *clades Italiae*; he lacks any trace of sympathy for the Gothic side, in sharp contrast to Procopius's appealing image of Totila. Readers of the *Getica* were not expected to have read the *Romana* and kept its information in mind. Few enough modern readers of the *Getica* have paid any attention to the *Romana*.

53. The Fredegar chronicle is a good example of an inadvertent ending. Also suggestive, but not beyond argument, is the ending of Paul the Deacon's *Historia Langobardorum*.

54. Goffart, *Narrators*, pp. 183–86 (Gregory). On Bede's ending, see Walter Goffart, "The *Historia ecclesiastica*: Bede's Agenda and Ours," *Haskins Society Journal: Studies in Medieval History* 2 (1990): 41–44. Historians are not reprehensible for crafting their dates of completion.

55. Goffart, *Narrators*, p. 100.

56. In work after work, readers are guided elatedly through the steps leading to the date March 551, as though this date, already mentioned in *Getica* 81, truly marked the moment when Jordanes laid down his pen. See Goffart, *Narrators*, p. 97 with n. 357. The ultracredulous handling of the date by Heather, *Goths and Romans*, pp. 47–49, goes hand in hand with his compulsion "to take Jordanes at face value." The energetic and clearsighted discussion of Jordanes by Amory, *People and Identity*, pp. 291–307, would have benefitted from a tighter date for the *Getica* than "550 or 551."

57. What matters in respect to Spain is not so much Jordanes's reference to Liberius's expedition (*Getica* 303) as the intimation in *Getica* 245 that Alaric II (†507) was the last Visigothic king—an unfulfilled East Roman wish. For Justinian's animosity toward the Goths in 551, see Procopius 8.24.5, ed. Dewing, 5:305.

58. There are numerous *testimonia* to its existence.

59. This puts a completely different slant on the widely accepted, moderate image of the *Getica* as "eine kurze und unselbständige Bearbeitung der Gotengeschichte Cassiodors" (Lönnroth, "Goten," p. 58). Short, yes; derivative, yes; but transformed by the scissors of an abridger who had a clear directive about what to do with the original. In a bizarre effort to explain the *Getica*, Walter Pohl, "The Politics of Change: Reflections on the Transformation of the Roman World," in *Integration und Herrschaft*, p. 278, proposes that "the Byzantine side," as one of its "propaganda moves," commissioned a "laudatory History of the Goths . . . cast directly after Theoderic's dynastic propaganda." Even Pohl's footnote offers nothing tending to support this last-ditch effort to make us believe that the *Getica* directly mirrors Amal thinking.

60. Justinian's Roman Empire as portrayed by Procopius in the *Anecdota or Secret History*, ed. Dewing, LCL, vol. 6, is not perceptibly less "barbarous" than the Merovingian Gaul portrayed by Gregory of Tours.

61. H.-H. Kortüm, "Geschichtsschreibung," in *Hoops Reallexikon* (Berlin, 1998), 11:485, illustrates a tenacious misconception: "Aber auch nachdem Cassiodor längst aus der aktiven Politik ausgeschieden war, besaß das in der Cassiodor-Jordanes-Chronik [*sic*] vorgeschlagene Programm einer ethnischen Verschmelzung von Goten und Römern große Aktualität." Such an interpretation is completely incompatible with the date of the *Getica* and the declared sympathies of the author.

62. About Jordanes as a real person, see also n. 22, above. In a recent, commendable summary, Brian Croke, "Latin Historiography and the Barbarian Kingdoms," in *Greek and Roman Historiography in Late Antiquity, Fourth to Sixth Century A.D.*, ed. Gabriele Marasco (Leiden, 2003), pp. 358–75, states, "The emerging consensus is that Jordanes is best taken at his word. This means that the *Getica* is a conscientious [history]" (p. 373). Plainly put, Croke agrees with Heather (n. 56, above). I emphatically dissent from this "consensus." Anyone who ponders the mendacious dating of the *Getica* and *Romana*, and the *suppressio veri* involved in the closing paragraphs of the *Getica*, should think twice about taking Jordanes at his word about anything, including his identity. In another misstep (pp. 363, 367), Croke draws on common knowledge of 551 and, in this way, deforms the finality of Jordanes's ending into an "anticipation" of things not even hinted at.

63. As already said in Goffart, *Narrators*, pp. 110, 432. The contrary is still asserted as though it were uncontested; see Patrick J. Geary, *The Myth of Nations: The Medieval Origins of Europe* (Princeton, N.J., 2002), p. 61. On the question of genre, see Goffart, *Narrators*, pp. 3–6, 8, 14; and Walter Goffart, "Two Notes on Germanic Antiquity Today," *Traditio* 50 (1995): 22–23. For a somewhat different view, see now Mortensen, "Stylistic Choice," pp. 79–86.

64. Hachmann, *Goten und Skandinavien*, pp. 16–34, is an excellent account of the early influence of Jordanes.

Chapter 5

1. (Mascov) "Under Honorius the dams that had protected the frontiers completely broke, and so began the so-called great migration of the peoples. The West-Goths went into Italy and Alaric conquered. The Rhine could no longer hold back the German neighbor; the Vandals and Sueves established kingdoms of their own in Spain, and the former finally went to Africa."

(Lot) "The consequences of the Rhine crossing by these hordes were infinitely more serious, more lasting, than the passage of the Danube by the Goths thirty years before. In truth, this was the event whose consequences would disorganize, bleed, and finally slay the Western Empire."

2. For the improbable idea that "responsible" historians no longer speak of the fall of Rome, see Glen Bowersock, "The Vanishing Paradigm of the Fall of Rome" (1996), in *Selected Papers on Late Antiquity* (Bari, 2000), p. 196.

3. For the redating of the Rhine crossing to 405, see Michael Kulikowski, "Barbarians in Gaul, Usurpers in Britain," *Britannia* 31 (2000): 325–31. Note that only one day of

405 is involved, namely December 31. One does not go far wrong by referring to 406, provided it is understood to begin on January 1.

4. On the "Migration Age," see Chapter 1, above. According to Demougeot, *Formation de l'Europe*, 2:19, the "Migration Age" in the West starts with the invasion of the Alans, Vandals, and Sueves. This is not a new or individual opinion. Guillaume Delisle, the celebrated early eighteenth-century cartographer, thought exactly the same when producing his famous *Theatrum historicum ad* A.D. *400* (Paris, 1705). It is the western alternative to a 370s beginning date in eastern Europe.

5. Gibbon, *Decline and Fall*, ed. Bury, 3:262–63; Heather, "Huns and the End," pp. 4–41.

6. E. A. Thompson, *A History of Attila and the Huns* (Oxford, 1948), p. 28. A revised edition of this work, with an afterword, has been issued by Peter Heather under the title *The Huns* (Oxford, 1996). The revision usefully relates Thompson's views to those of later writers on the Huns, such as Maenchen-Helfen (n. 8, below) and Fritz Altheim.

7. Heather, *Goths and Romans*, p. 228 n. 4.

8. Heather, "Huns and the End," pp. 16–18; Otto Maenchen-Helfen, *The World of the Huns* (Berkeley, 1973), pp. 45–67. Maenchen-Helfen goes astray in arguing that the Huns were dominant in the Danubian plain as early as 384.

9. Uldin, who ended the adventure of the Goth Gaïnas (400), was the first noteworthy Hun established in the lower Danube valley, along the Roman frontier. See Heather, "Huns and the End," pp. 8–10; PLRE 2:1180.

10. Demougeot, *Formation de l'Europe*, 2:171; she has no authority for the circumstantial details that she deploys; modern geographical names color her narrative. Cf. Lot, *Invasions germaniques*, p. 79: "Il ne paraît pas douteux qu'ils fuient les Huns, qui s'installent dans la Hongrie actuelle. La conquête hunnique, après avoir marqué un temps d'arrêt, après la destruction de l'Empire des Alains et de celui des Goths en 376, reprennait sa marche." Likewise, S. I. Oost, *Galla Placidia Augusta* (Chicago, 1968), p. 75 n. 122, referring to Orosius, *Historia adversum paganos*, 7.37.3, ed. Zangemeister, pp. 537–38 (inapplicable to these circumstances).

11. Maenchen-Helfen, *World of the Huns*, p. 61 (Radagaisus, not mentioned before, will be introduced in a moment. The Alans etc. might be substituted for him in this quotation.) Heather, "Huns and the End," p. 16, recalls identifiable authorities whose testimony we lack because their work is lost. If Ammianus were lost, we would still know about the sudden Hun assault from Ambrose, Orosius, and Jordanes. In the early 400s, however, there is no redundancy; no hint of Hunnic sweeps can be detected. Maenchen-Helfen was thinking about a billiard-ball argument reaching into Asia; his repudiation of the foremost push is what matters for us.

12. Heather, "Huns and the End," pp. 20, 19.

13. Ibid., pp. 7–8, 14–15.

14. In the passage quoted at n. 148, below, Ernst Stein emphasizes our sheer ignorance of what went on. J. H. W. G. Liebeschuetz, "*Gens* into *regnum*: the Vandals," in *Regna and Gentes*, p. 63, does not advert to the Huns but asserts "In the late 390s the Vandals began to move." There is no evidence for this. What he cites concerns the incursion of 401 into Raëtia discussed below.

15. For Stilicho's agreement with Alaric, see John Matthews, *Western Aristocracies and Imperial Court* A.D. *364–425* (Oxford, 1975), pp. 274–75; Alan Cameron, *Claudian: Poetry and Propaganda at the Court of Honorius* (Oxford, 1970), p. 156. At the time, Alaric

and his people were in the diocese of Illyricum, more or less patiently awaiting Stilicho's pleasure. ("Diocese" in late Roman terminology is a grouping of several provinces. Its head, the vicar, represented the praetorian prefect. Ecclesiastical dioceses [= bishoprics] are different and smaller units.)

16. The sources call Radagaisus simply a "Goth." Among recent scholars, François Paschoud (Zosimus, *Histoire nouvelle* [Paris, 1986], 3 part 1:200) affirms that Radagaisus was certainly an Ostrogoth. His followers were Ostrogoths according to Herwig Wolfram, *History of the Goths*, pp. 443 n. 332; Radagaisus a Greutung, p. 169. Émilienne Demougeot, *De l'unité à la division de l'Empire romain* (Paris, 1954), p. 354 with n. 8, explains that Ludwig Schmidt formulated the currently orthodox argument according to which Radagaisus and his followers were Greutungs (alias Ostrogoths), as follows: Orosius states that Radagaisus and followers were pagan; but the western Goths (alias Visigoths) were Christian converts; therefore, the pagan Radagaisus had to be Ostrogothic. Wholly lacking evidence, Schmidt's syllogism contrasting pagan Ostrogoths to Christian Visigoths seems hollow. Obviously, not all western Goths, especially when still north of the Danube, had become Christians; the argument cannot stand. Current practice is to reserve "Ostrogoth" for the followers of Theoderic the Amal; Heather, *Goths and Romans*, pp. 8–10, 231–32, 311, 321–22, and passim, showed the way.

17. For Goths as a generic name, see Chapter 7, n. 56. There is little information about Goths left behind, and that little has not been worked over; e.g., Wolfram, *History of the Goths*, pp. 168–70.

18. Blood lust of the invaders: Orosius, *Historia* 7.37.5, "as is the custom of barbarian peoples of this kind." The two halves of the report of Radagaisus's invasion in the *Gallic Chronicle of 452* (a not very contemporary source: MG AA 9:652) are separated by a statement to the effect that these events revived and propped up the almost vanished Arians of the Roman Empire. On this basis, some modern commentators have managed to present the army of Radagaisus as favorable simultaneously to paganism and to Arianism. The association of Radagaisus with Arianism is a mistake. The chronicler transposes responsibility from the certifiably Arian Visigoth, Alaric, to the later-coming pagan, as explained by Steven Muhlberger, *The Fifth-Century Chroniclers: Prosper, Hydatius, and the Gallic Chronicler of 452*, Arca, Classical and Medieval Texts, Papers and Monographs, ed. Francis Cairns et al., 27 (Leeds, 1990), p. 181.

19. Zosimus 5.26.4, trans. Ridley, p. 113: Stilicho tried to recruit auxiliaries against Radagaisus among the Alans as well as the Huns. No Alan detachment is seen in Stilicho's service on that occasion.

20. Wolfram, *History of the Goths*, p. 254; Heather, "Huns and the End," p. 16 n. 1 (earlier authorities agreeing on Huns); Courcelle, *Histoire littéraire*, pp. 39, 81. Wolfram, as cited: "It appears that Radagaisus was trying to avoid the Huns rather than break out of Scythia." No source or argument supports this opinion.

21. Stein, *Histoire du Bas-Empire*, 1:231, 249; Wolfram, *History of the Goths*, pp. 142–43, 153; PLRE 2:44–46.

22. Stein, *Histoire du Bas-Empire*, 1:140–41, 142–44; Glen W. Bowersock, *Julian the Apostate* (London, 1978), pp. 56–57.

23. András Mócsy, *Pannonia and Upper Moesia: A History of the Middle Danube Provinces of the Roman Empire* (London, 1974), pp. 342–43. About Stilicho, see Orosius, *Historia* 7.38.1–3, ed. Zangemeister, pp. 542–43. Allegedly, he meant to make his son emperor (Orosius is not alone in uttering this slander).

24. Courtois, *Vandales et l'Afrique*, p. 38; Otto Seeck, *Geschichte des Untergangs der antiken Welt*, 6 vols. (Stuttgart, 1910–25), 5:303–5.

25. Eutropius, *Breviarium* 8.13.1, MG AA 2:144, "bellum Marcomannicum confecit, quod cum his Quadi, Vandali, Sarmatae, Suebi atque omnis barbaria commoverat, multa hominum milia interfecit, ac Pannoniis servitio liberatis." The date of Eutropius's very popular *Breviarium* is 369. The *Historia Augusta* (Marcus Aurelius) also places Vandals in the Marcomannic War; it is not necessarily additional to Eutropius.

26. *Cambridge Ancient History*, 12 vols. (Cambridge, 1923–39), 11:95; Demougeot, *Formation de l'Europe*, 2:319. See also the next note.

27. Sarmatians continued to be active in the fourth century (and later). They and the Quadi fought as allies. Otherwise, the Sarmatians experienced internal dissensions and may have been much weakened: Demougeot, *Formation de l'Europe*, 2:68–78, 94–97, 112–15, 124, 135, 301–3, 319–22, 780, 800. The last two entries concern the late fifth century. For Courtois's conjecture that the "Alans" of the Rhine crossing were a Sarmatian people, see n. 70, below. Sarmatians and Alans are mixed together by Reinhard Wenskus, "Alanen," in *Hoops Reallexikon*, 1:122–23. It would not be surprising if Sarmatians crossed the Rhine with the Alans; see Jerome, n. 29, below. Courcelle, *Histoire littéraire*, p. 87, cites Paulinus of Béziers, mentioning depredations by Sarmatians, Vandals, and Alans. Sarmatians, a very broad term, may have included the Alans, but the two peoples were not interchangeable. It follows from Eutropius (n. 25, above) that the invaders of 405 included peoples long rooted in the Danube Valley, but these did not include the Alans. The Sarmatians had centuries of residence near the Danube, the Alans did not.

28. R. W. Burgess, ed. and trans., *The* Chronicle *of Hydatius and the* Consularia Constantinopolitana: *Two Contemporary Accounts of the Final Years of the Roman Empire* (Oxford, 1993), pp. 81, 82; my translation: "The Alans and Vandals and Sueves entered the Spains [= the civil diocese of Spain] in [date] . . . The Vandals and Sueves occupied Gallaecia. . . . The Alans obtained Lusitania and Carthaginensis, and the Vandals surnamed Siling received Baetica." (There is a fuller discussion of this passage below at nn. 125–27.) See also Hydatius, *Chronique*, ed. and trans. Alain Tranoy, 2 vols., Sources chrétiennes 218–19 (Paris, 1974).

29. Jerome, *Epistolae* 123.15, ed. Jérôme Labourt, 8 vols. (Paris, 1949–63), 7:91–92, "Quadus, Vandalus, Sarmata, Halani, Gepides, Heruli, Saxones, Burgundiones, Alemanni, et, o lugenda respublica! hostes Pannonii." Courcelle, *Histoire littéraire*, pp. 84–85.

30. Literary device, Suzanne Teillet, *Des Goths à la nation gothique* (Paris, 1984), pp. 18, 20. Kulikowski, "Barbarians in Gaul," p. 325 n. 5, speaks of Jerome's making "a display of ethnic virtuosity." Clearly a long list, rather than a meticulous one, was the author's goal.

31. Orosius, *Historia* 7.40.3, ed. Zangemeister, p. 543, "excitatae . . . gentes Alanorum, ut dixi, Sueborum Vandalorum multaeque cum his aliae . . . Rhenum transeunt."

32. Ludwig Schmidt, *Histoire des Vandales*, trans. H. E. Del Medico (Paris, 1953), p. 18: Tervingi and Taifals fought Vandals and Gepids ca. A.D. 290 (in the lower Danube region)—a conflict lying long enough in the past to have been remembered only in written records.

33. Orosius, *Historia* 7.38.3, ed. Zangemeister, p. 543; Musset, *Germanic Invasions*, p. 62. Kaiser, *Die Burgunder*, p. 27, has them cross with the Alans, Vandals, and Sueves on

Jerome's authority. I believe that, though the Burgundians shared the chaos of these years with the Alans, Vandals, and Sueves, their crossing had its particular circumstances (the usurpation of Jovinus) unconnected to theirs. The Burgundians, though traditionally classed as "East Germanic," had been neighbors of the "western" Alamanni for a century and a half at least.

34. J. F. Drinkwater, "The Usurpers Constantine III (407–411) and Jovinus (411–413)," *Britannia* 29 (1998): 272, also denies that Alamanni and Burgundians took part.

35. *Laterculus Veronensis*, 13–15, ed. Seeck, pp. 251–53; the list of barbarian peoples, arrayed in geographical order, complements the list of dioceses and provinces. Even Roman memories were short. Modern scholars know that the Herules moved from the east to the middle Danube ca. 440, but the historian Procopius, ca. 550, treats the middle Danube as the Herules' ancestral home; see Chapter 7, section "A Medley of Barbarian Peoples," below. See also the comment of Salvian about the Vandals' point of origin, in n. 46, below.

36. Courtois, *Vandales et l'Afrique*, p. 30.

37. Tacitus, *Germania* 38, trans. Herbert W. Benario, *Tacitus' Agricola, Germania* (Norman, Okla., 1991), p. 82. The Lombards, settled on the lower Elbe in Tacitus's time, were Suevic; Caesar defeated the Sueve Ariovistus. Tacitus did not exaggerate the ubiquity of this people. Schmidt, *Westgermanen*, bears this out. The first part of his account of the Sueves is in four sections: early history, Marcomanni and Quadi, Bavarians, and the Suevic kingdom in Spain. The never published second part would presumably have dealt with the Alamanni and still other branches. Heather, "Huns and the End," p. 13 with n. 1, is overimpressed by the lack of explicitly named Sueves in the middle Danube in the fourth century.

38. In connection with this expedition, see Gregory of Tours, *Historiae* 2.2, ed. Krusch-Levison, 1:39. Almost two centuries separate Gregory from the events. Seeck, *Untergang*, 5:378.

39. The traditional practice has been to equate the two (Jerome mentions Quadi, but no Sueves): e.g., Stein, *Histoire du Bas-Empire*, 1:250; Friedrich Lotter, "Zur Rolle der Donausueben in der Völkerwanderungszeit," *Mitteilungen des Instituts für österreichische Geschichtsforschung* 76 (1968): 275–98 at 280; and many others. Sueves on the middle Danube after 453 have attracted recent attention: Lotter, as cited, and Pohl, "Die Gepiden und die gentes an der mittleren Donau," pp. 274–76.

40. Demougeot, *Formation de l'Europe*, 2:296–97. The Marcomanni, open to Christian conversion, were slipping into Roman service and territory. Mócsy, *Pannonia and Upper Moesia*, p. 345; Wenskus, *Stammesbildung und Verfassung*, p. 67, with reservations, endorses the disappearance of the Marcomanni in the fifth century. See also Schmidt, *Westgermanen*, pp. 184–87.

41. Lynn F. Pitts, "Relations between Rome and the German 'Kings' on the Middle Danube," *Journal of Roman Studies* 79 (1989): 52; John Matthews, *The Roman Empire of Ammianus* (Baltimore, 1989), pp. 267–68. In retelling this dramatic incident, the church historian Socrates (*Historia ecclesiastica* 4.31) substitutes Sarmatians for Quadi.

42. Jordanes, *Getica* 274–77 (ca. 467–69), ed. Mommsen, pp. 129–30. Lotter, "Zur Rolle," p. 280, exaggerates the importance of the Sueves in the Rhine crossing. To judge from the partition of Spain in Hydatius, they and the Asding Vandals were the weakest

contingent (see n. 126, below). Lotter emphasizes that Jerome's list of attackers begins "Quadus." About later Danube Sueves, see n. 39, above. I have deliberately taken no account of the many misconceptions in Hans J. Hummer, "The Fluidity of Barbarian Identity: The Ethnogenesis of Alemanni and Suebi, A.D. 200–500," *Early Medieval Europe* 7/1 (1998): 1–27.

43. Brief account in Musset, *Germanic Invasions*, pp. 56–60; more recently, Liebeschuetz, "*Gens* into *regnum*," pp. 55–83.

44. *Additamentum ad Prosperum Havniensis*, in MG AA 9:299, "Arcadio et Probo coss. Wandali rege Gunderico transito Reno totam Galliam crudeli persecutione vastant, collocatis secum in comitatu Alanis gente moribus et ferocitate aequali." The quotation shows its age—long after the events—by anticipating the rallying in Spain of the defeated Alans to the Asdings (n. 136, below). Prosper, in MG AA 9:465. "Wandali et Halani Gallias traiecto Rheno ingressi." Prosper also wrote after the Vandal invasion of Africa.

45. Procopius, 3.3.2, ed. Dewing, 2:22, Vandals joined forces with the Sueves and Alans. For Olympiodorus, see Andrew Gillett, "The Date and Circumstances of Olympiodorus of Thebes," *Traditio* 48 (1993): 25. Gillett corrects the misconception that Olympiodorus ended his work as early as 425. The myopia of fifth-century historians has not been allowed for in modern works: Demougeot, *Formation de l'Europe*, 2:448, on the eve of 411, "Le peuple vandale unissant Hasdings et Silings était le plus puissant" (contrary to her claim the Asdings and Silings show no sign of having been united); Thomas S. Burns, *Barbarians within the Gates of Rome* (Bloomington, Ind., 1994), p. 203, Vandals and others; Courcelle, *Histoire littéraire*, pp. 80–81: Vandals were the most terrible attackers. Typically, Courcelle introduces them with a reference to (supposed) Scandinavian origins, followed by a quote from Tacitus about a particularly ferocious people deemed Vandal. Everything is mentioned except Vandals as they were in A.D. 400. But see Liebeschuetz, "*Gens* into *regnum*," p. 63: they had been quiet for two centuries.

46. Sidonius Apollinaris, *Carmina* 2:358–70, ed. W. B. Anderson, 2 vols., LCL (Cambridge, Mass., 1963–85), 1:40, calls Vandals cowardly (when facing Wallia). Orosius deprecates Vandals in connection with Stilicho (*Historia* 7.38.1). The same adjective is in Salvian, *De gubernatione Dei* 7:27–28, 50, ed. George Lagarrigue, Sources chrétiennes 220 (Paris, 1975), pp. 450, 464; *ignavissimi hostes, infirmissimi hostes, ignavissima gens*. This may be Roman badmouthing of barbarians; but the concentration of comments about Vandals suggests that, for a while, the contempt they inspired had a factual basis. Along the same lines, Stein, *Histoire du Bas-Empire*, 1:320. Salvian 7.50, extracts them *a solo patrio*; banish the thought that they might come from far away.

47. Courtois, *Vandales et l'Afrique*, pp. 15–31; Wenskus, *Stammesbildung und Verfassung*, p. 73 (Vandals widespread in East Germany and Poland ca. A.D. 1); p. 464, also called Lugii in the first century; p. 230, the geographer Ptolemy refers to Silings, distinct from Lugians; pp. 503–5, Asdings were distinguished from Lugians in the second century. Pohl, *Die Germanen*, p. 53, adds the Lakringi to the Silings and Asdings as another subgroup. Jes Martens, "The Vandals: Myths and Facts about a Germanic Tribe of the First Half of the 1st Millennium AD," in *Archaeological Approaches to Cultural Identity*, ed. Stephen Shennan One World Archaeology, ed. P. J. Oeko, 10 (London, 1989), pp. 57–65.

48. Procopius, 3.3.1–2, ed. Dewing, 2:23; Jordanes, *Getica* 26 (a very modest report), ed. Mommsen, p. 60.

49. Tim Cornell and John Matthews, *Atlas of the Roman World* (New York, 1982), p. 209 (tacitly after Procopius). Mócsy, *Pannonia and Upper Moesia*, p. 279; Bernard

Bachrach, *A History of the Alans in the West* (Minneapolis, 1973), p. 51. Demougeot, *Formation de l'Europe*, 2:311, seems to endorse the report in very attenuated form. The salient "fact" continually distilled by moderns from Procopius's obviously fictional account of migration from the Sea of Azov is its imputed cause: material want or famine. See, for example, Pohl, *Völkerwanderung*, p. 73, alleging that Procopius gives "hunger" as the reason for the movement of the Alans, Vandals, and Sueves into Gaul. Maenchen-Helfen, *World of the Huns*, p. 72, "According to Procopius, the Vandals left Hungary because 'they were pressed by hunger.'" Along the same lines, Maria Cesa, *Impero tardoantico e barbari: La crisi militare da Adrianopoli al 418* (Como, 1984), p. 125; Liebeschuetz, "*Gens* into *regnum*," p. 63. Procopius knows nothing of Vandals in Hungary or starving at the Rhine. The hunger is no more factual than the Maeotian homeland and must not be detached from its context. Procopius supplies hunger as the cause for the Vandals' fictional westward movement from the Maeotian swamp—in no other circumstances.

50. Jordanes, *Getica* 114–15, ed. Mommsen, pp. 87–88. The report is accepted, e.g., by Franz Miltner, "Vandalen," in Pauly-Wissowa, 8A:303; rejected by Wolfram, *History of the Goths*, pp. 34–35, 62–63 with n. 151; Courtois, *Vandales et l'Afrique*, pp. 34–35, explains why scholars generally dismiss this (late) report.

51. For this layering of the evidence, see Martens, "The Vandals: Myths and Facts," pp. 57–65.

52. Martens, p. 63, goes astray about Christianity among the Vandals. The Vandals are a prime example of the continuing impact of ethnic identifications in archaeology; see the comments of Kulikowski cited in Introduction, n. 26, above.

53. The Asdings are thought to have been situated between Goths to the east (in Dacia) and Sarmatian Iazyges to the west (bordering on Roman territory).

54. Isidore of Seville, *Historia Gothorum Wandalorum Sueborum*: MG AA 11:276 line 17, emphasizes that the Vandals in Gallaecia (i.e., the Asdings) were the ones with a future. This was more certain when Isidore wrote than in 411.

55. Famous princely graves in Silesia are attributed to Asdings by Schmidt, *Ostgermanen*, p. 107; by others to the Silings. Musset, *Germanic Invasions*, p. 55, locates the Silings on the upper Main from 278 on (see the next note). He favors motion over rest. "About 401 [the allied Asdings and Silings] were just across the Danube from Raëtia"; ca. 405 they were at the Rhine "in the midst of the peoples who were trying to break through the *limes*." Such imaginative migrations are endorsed inter alios by Courtois, *Vandales et l'Afrique*, p. 40, who interprets a raid into Pannonia in 392 as documenting "les premières manifestations de la grande migration en marche vers les Gaules," it being taken for granted that the invasion of 405 had to be the culmination of "migration." It is true that Vandals invaded Roman Raëtia in 401 (n. 62, below).

56. Zosimus 1.67.1–3, trans. Ridley, p. 21 (the battle of 278 with the emperor Probus). Courtois, *Vandales et l'Afrique*, pp. 37, 40, explains the localization shown by his sketch map. There is no sign of Vandals living at the Main or acting with Burgundians after 278.

57. Courtois, *Vandales et l'Afrique*, p. 27.

58. Ibid., pp. 35–36; Martin Jahn, "Die Wandalen," in *Vorgeschichte der deutschen Stämme*, 3:1001–19, is more voluble. Also forthright is Demougeot, *Formation de l'Europe*, 2:311–12. For more of these mists, see Chapter 7, section "A Medley of Barbarian Peoples," below. Modern critics insist that archaeology cannot establish ethnic identity (see Introduction, p. 10, above).

59. Pitts, "Relations between Rome and the Middle Danube," pp. 46, 52; Andreas Alföldi, in *Cambridge Ancient History*, 12:139.

60. Mócsy, *Pannonia and Upper Moesia*, p. 34.

61. Provincials like Jerome's renegade Pannonians (n. 29, above).

62. Claudian, *De bello Gothico* lines 278–81, 363–65, 400–404, 414–29, ed. M. Platnauer, 2 vols., LCL (Cambridge, Mass., 1963), 1:146, 152, 154, 156. See also Demougeot, *Formation de l'Europe*, 2:171–72, and Cameron, *Claudian*, pp. 375–76.

63. Demougeot, *Formation de l'Europe*, 2:171–72, claims that the barbarians were met by Roman *limitanei*, i.e., garrison troops at the frontier. Claudian's poem makes it clear, however, that all or much of Stilicho's field army was sent against the invaders (that is why Alaric's entry into Italy could not be stopped in its tracks).

64. Claudian, *De bello Gothico*, lines 400–404, ed. Platnauer, 1:154. The Vandals had been ineffective, sustaining the poor reputation they long had; see n. 46, above.

65. Demougeot, *De l'unité*, p. 355 n. 9, Vandals and Alans; Demougeot, *Formation de l'Europe*, 2:171, the other lineup; Cameron, *Claudian*, pp. 375–76. Claudian, ed. T. Birt, in MG AA 10:xlix. Courtois, *Vandales et l'Afrique*, p. 40: columns pushed back from Raëtia turn toward the Rhine. References to Alans presuppose that they could be found in quantities on the mid-Danube. The only available ones, however, were the (now discredited) tri-people group referred to in n. 80, below.

66. "Multis ante vastatis urbibus Radagaisus occubuit: cuius in tres partes per diversos principes divisus exercitus aliquam repugnandi Romanis aperuit facultatem. Insigni triumpho exercitum tertiae partis hostium circumactis Chunorum auxiliaribus Stilico usque ad internicionem delevit": MG AA 9:652. The division in three helped Roman defense. The main column alone may have deserved notice, without implying that the two others escaped.

67. Stein, *Histoire du Bas-Empire*, 1:250, eliminates the three-part division almost as soon as he mentions it; p. 552 n. 161, connecting Rhine crossers with the Radagaisus invasion "n'est qu'une hypothèse fondée sur des bases très fragiles." Others are less sensible. Demougeot, *De l'unité*, p. 355 n. 9. She changed her mind in *Formation de l'Europe*, 2:305. Cf. Patrick Périn and Laure-Charlotte Feffer, *Les Francs*, vol. 1, *À la conquête de la Gaule* (Paris, 1987), p. 76; amid verbs of seizing, scattering, and dragging, they have the Vandals go south under the leadership of Radagaisus; after Fiesole, the debris of their army is led by a new king, Godegisel, and joins the Alans of Respendial. Much ingenuity has gone into adapting the three-part division to wider history but the solutions offered are unconvincing. Seeck, *Untergang*, 5:376–77, is as elaborate as Demougeot; escapees from Radagaisus's army form most of the expedition across the Rhine. Another hypothesis proceeding from three columns is developed by Paschoud in Zosimus, *Histoire nouvelle*, 3 part 2:22–23 n. 115. John Michael O'Flynn, *Generalissimos of the Western Roman Empire* (Edmonton, 1983), p. 41, combines Orosius's tale of Stilicho's betrayal (*Historia* 7.38.1–5, ed. Zangemeister, pp. 542–44) with the imagined fate of two columns.

68. The *Chronicle of 452* was written fifty years after the events and deserves cautious handling; see Muhlberger, *Fifth-Century Chroniclers*, pp. 136–92, especially 146–47. For another possibility see Paschoud, in Zosimus, *Histoire nouvelle*, 3 part 2:22–23 n. 15. Zosimus speaks quite vaguely of invaders into Gaul through the Alps. Paschoud takes these seriously and identifies them with at least one of the three columns of the Gallic chronicle. Cesa, *Impero tardoantico*, p. 124, adheres to Paschoud's system, but I cannot

make sense of it. The sources are so scarce and contradictory that anyone's guess must be treated kindly.

69. See nn. 95 and 118, below. Hydatius, a. 418, ed. Tranoy, p. 122: "Alani, qui Vandalis et Suevis potentabantur" See also n. 127, below.

70. Documentation for these events will be given shortly. Courtois, *Vandales et l'Afrique*, pp. 40–41, who concedes that steppe nomads "originated [the Vandals'] migration," denies that they were Alans from South Russia: they were Sarmatians with "Alan" in their name ("Roxalani"). Along the same lines, Wenskus, "Alanen," in *Hoops Reallexikon*, 1:122–23, affirming that the Alans were the most important of the Sarmatian tribes and that those who crossed the Rhine had already moved into the Danube basin in the third century or before. It is hard to see how Courtois and Wenskus arrived at their respective hypotheses. Sarmatians had been European neighbors of the Empire from the time its conquests reached the lower Danube. The Alans, first encountered by Rome on the eastern frontier of Asia Minor, had no presence west of the Don before the 370s.

71. For an account of Alan-Roman relations in the High Empire, see Demougeot, *Formation de l'Europe*, 1:206–11; Bachrach, *Alans in the West*, pp. 3–25. The Alans were "a Gothic people" to Procopius (*Wars* 3.3.1, ed. Dewing, 2:23). The Alan strong men in Constantinople (next note) had close ties to Goths encamped in Thrace. Ammianus Marcellinus 31.2.12–23, ed. Rolfe, 3:386–94, takes pains to distinguish Alans from Huns, but admits similarity in way of life; they were less savage. See also Jordanes, *Getica* 126–27, ed. Mommsen, pp. 90–91 (similar to Ammianus): Alans equalled the Huns as fighters.

72. Modern scholars who like to think that, after the misadventures of Gaïnas, the East Roman government did without "barbarian" generals forget the long dominance of the Aspars (e.g., Averil Cameron, *The Later Roman Empire* [London, 1993], p. 139). The Western chief generals, Castinus, Felix, Boniface, and Aetius, were more "Roman" than their Eastern counterparts. See Bachrach, *Alans in the West*, pp. 26–28, 33, 42–51. Ardaburius Aspar, PLRE 2:164–69. His homonymous father was consul (= cos.) in 427; himself cos. 434; his homonymous son, cos. 447. I am unaware of any source that associates the Aspars with Alan troops. See also Heather, *Goths and Romans*, pp. 254–55.

73. Jordanes, *Getica* 194–95, 197, 236; ed. Mommsen, 108, 109, 118; Bachrach, *Alans in the West*, pp. 65–67, 33.

74. Omelian Pritzak, "Alans," in *Oxford Dictionary of Byzantium*, 3 vols. (New York, 1991), 1:31–32 (particularly useful for after A.D. 600). Byzantines also applied the name "Alan" to other Caucasian peoples. The empress Mary of Alania was Georgian (ibid. 2:1298). Nevertheless, Alans lived on. A fourteenth-century emperor is credited with settling ten thousand of them in Asia Minor. For earlier Alans, see also, but cautiously, George Vernadsky, "The Eurasian Nomads and Their Impact on Medieval Europe (A Reconsideration of the Problem)," *Studi medievali*, 3rd Ser., 4/2 (1963): 401–34, esp. 421–25. T. Sulimirski, *The Sarmatians* (New York, 1970), wholly integrates the Alans among the Sarmatians; his broad chronological scope and familiarity with archaeology do not wholly compensate for a naive historical outlook.

75. Interpretation of Alan history: Musset, *Germanic Invasions*, p. 33; Ammianus 31.2.17, ed. Rolfe, 3:390.

76. Ammianus 31.9.1, ed. Rolfe, 3:394–96. Ambrose, *De Expositio evangeli secundum Lucam* 10.10, CSEL 32 (Vienna, 1902), p. 458: "Hunni in Alanos, Alani in Gothos, Gothi in Taiphalos et Sarmatos insurrexerunt. Nos quoque in Illyrico exules patriae Gothorum exsilia fecerunt, et nondum est finis." The turn of phrase is somewhat misleading,

especially in giving the events a billiard ball appearance. The Huns attacked the Alans so that they might together attack the Goths. In Ammianus the Huns have first place in damaging the Goths. The equivalent of our billiard-ball theories appealed to Ambrose (for their rhetorical effectiveness) as it has appealed to many modern commentators, who present them as fact. The Alans were no better liked than other aliens. *Epitome de Caesaribus* 47.3, ed. F. Pichlmayr, in *Aurelius Victor*, Teubner Classics (Leipzig, 1911), p. 173: after Adrianople, Thrace and Dacia swarmed with (among others) "omni pernicie atrocioribus Hunnis et Alanis."

77. Alans delay Gratian, see Ammianus 31.11.6, ed. Rolfe, 3:460. The quotation, *Epitome de Caesaribus*, 47.3, ed. Pichlmayr, p. 173. Much the same is in Zosimus 4.35.2, trans. Ridley, p. 86. The Alans in question are generally identified with the "Comites Alani" in *Notitia dignitatum, Occ.* 7:163, ed. Otto Seeck, p. 140. The portrayal of Gratian as an "Alan-lover" may be Theodosian propaganda, but Gratian also needed a counterweight to the predominance of Franks in his army; K. F. Stroheker, "Heermeister fränkischer Abstammung," pp. 12–13.

78. Heather, "Huns and the End," p. 9; Ambrose, *Epistolae* 30.4, 8, CSEL 88 (Vienna, 1978), pp. 208–12.

79. See n. 70, above.

80. Émilienne Demougeot, "Modalités d'établissement des fédérés barbares de Gratien à Théodose," *Mélanges d'histoire ancienne offerts à William Seston* (Paris, 1974), pp. 150–53, is a representative illustration of the view, refuted by Heather, *Goths and Romans*, pp. 145, 153, 334–44.

81. Orosius, *Historia* 7.37.3, ed. Zangemeister, pp. 537–8: "taceo de ipsorum inter se barbarorum crebris dilacertationibus, cum se invicem Gothorum cunei duo, deinde Alani atque Huni variis caedibus populabantur."

82. Orosius, *Historia* 7.37.2–4, ed. Zangemeister, pp. 537–38: "[1] taceo de Alarico rege cum Gothis suis saepe victo, saepe concluso semperque dimisso. [2] taceo de infelicibus illis apud Pollentiam gestis, cum barbaro et pagano duci, hoc est Sauli, belli summa commissa est, cuius inprobitate reverentissimi dies et sanctum pascha violatum est cedentique hosti propter religione, ut pugnaret, extortum est: cum quidem, ostendente in brevi iudicio Dei et quod favor eius possit et quid ultio exigeret, pugnantes vicimus, victores victi sumus. [3] [previous note][4] [Radagaisus]." Orosius distinguishes the three conflicts between Romans and barbarians from the one instance of barbarians fighting among themselves. His apparent meaning is that the latter involved barbarians of no special distinction, simply regiments in imperial service (*cuneus*, "wedge," is the technical term for a category of cavalry unit in the late Roman army; see Jones, *Later Roman Empire*, pp. 99–100). It seems improbable that he referred to barbarians outside the Empire, as Thompson and some others have believed. Outsiders would be incongruous in Orosius's set of four.

83. All four incidents are presumably "Western." Something like the troubles in the East involving Gaïnas are not in question. Orosius was not in principle opposed to mutual slaughters among barbarians; he applauded later ones; see n. 130, below. Slaughters, and the quarrels that occasioned them, are deplored here as signs that something was gravely wrong with the leadership of the Empire. See Maenchen-Helfen, *World of the Huns*, p. 72, who reads the passage as I do.

84. For the Alan-Hun contingent, see n. 78, above. Concerning Orosius's set of four, Wolfram, *History of the Goths*, p. 115 with n. 295 (on p. 441), thinks "there are two

possible ways of interpreting the tribal conflicts in the sense of Orosius without having to invent anything." He identifies the Gothic *cunei* with the peoples of Radagaisus and Alaric and the others with the troops of Uldin and Sarus (all in Orosius). Wolfram finds pairs; but because (inter alia) his pairs did not engage in the mutual slaughter that Orosius deplores, neither one fits.

85. Bachrach, *Alans in the West*, p. 34.

86. J. F. Haldon, *Byzantium in the Seventh Century*, rev. ed. (Cambridge, 1990), p. 41; P. B. Magocsi, *Historical Atlas of East Central Europe* (Toronto, 1993), p. 7: "The Antes were organized into a powerful travel league by Alanic military leaders (from whom the name Antes derives)." I have not verified whether this etymology is compelling.

87. Thompson, *Attila*, pp. 136–37, 153–58.

88. Demougeot, *Formation de l'Europe*, 2:68–78, 94–97, 112–15, 124, 135, 301–3, 319–22, 780, 800; Sulimirski, *Sarmatians*, pp. 178–82. Paul the Deacon lists Sarmatians among the invaders of Italy under Alboin (568); Wenskus, *Stammesbildung und Verfassung*, p. 492. They are impressively tenacious.

89. PLRE 2:940.

90. About Goar, see PLRE 2:514–15: king of (the) Alans a. 410–42. In 411, Goar and the Burgundian Guntiarius backed the usurpation of Jovinus in Germania II. In 442 Aetius allowed Goar and his Alans to settle in Armorica. Goar was pagan and considered very truculent. Bishop Germanus of Auxerre talked him out of ravaging Armorica. Goar is probably not the unnamed and apparently Christian Alan king who besieged Bazas in 414.

91. My comments have much in common with those of Walter Pohl, "Ethnicity in Early Medieval Studies," *Archaeologia Polona* 29 (1991): 42–43.

92. Cameron, *Claudian*, p. 375 (who cites the relevant lines of poetry): Stilicho spent 396 building up his army with barbarian recruits before facing Alaric.

93. Claudian, *De bell. Gothic.* 421–22, ed. Platnauer, 1:156: "remotis excubiis Rhenum solo terrore relinquunt." *De consulatu Stilichonis* 1, 232–45, ed. Platnauer, 1:380: Franks, devoted to the emperor, offer their arms for his defence. They often renewed the offer and were not offended when refused; aid refused but loyalty praised.

94. Kulikowski, "Barbarians in Gaul," p. 326, referring to a "depleted frontier," is more believable than the contradictory assessments of Britain and the Rhine given by Drinkwater, "The Usurper Constantine III," pp. 273, 275.

95. Lost history of Renatus Profuturus Frigeridus, cited by Gregory of Tours, *Historiae* 2.9, ed. Krusch-Levison, pp. 55–56: "Interea Respendial rex Alanorum, Goare ad Romanos transgresso, de Rheno agmen suorum convertit, Wandalis Francorum bello laborantibus, Godigyselo rege absumpto, aciae viginti ferme milibus ferro peremptis, cunctis Wandalorum ad internitionem delendis, nisi Alanorum vis in tempore subvenisset." Orosius, *Historia* 7.40.3, ed. Zangemeister, pp. 549–50, locates the fighting with the Franks before the Rhine crossing. The chronicler cited n. 44, above, has the Vandals cross under Gunderic, Godegisel's son. Although "twenty thousand" looks exaggerated, it undermines the contention of Drinkwater, "The Usurper Constantine III," pp. 272, 273, 274, that the invaders were few in numbers. Phillip Wynn, "Frigeridus, the British Tyrants, and the Early Fifth Century Barbarian Invasions of Gaul and Spain," *Athenaeum: Studi di letteratura e storia dell' Antichità* 85 (1997): 69–117, at 69, 77, 80, 92–94, and passim, strictly interprets Gregory's introductory words: "when [Frigeridus] comes to tell us how Rome was captured and destroyed by the Goths," i.e., in 410. Wynn reinterprets

Frigeridus on this basis, so that the Franks and Vandals fight each other in 410 and therefore in Spain. His radical revision hinges on a literal reading of Gregory's dating clause. The argument develops a genuine possibility, and merits praise for this reason; but it is not compelling in view of the treatment of chronology in other sources. Orosius (a contemporary) shuffles the events out of order: the Rhine crossing in connection with Stilicho (*Historia* 7.38.1–4, ed. Zangemeister, p. 542–43), then more fully, in retrospect, after the taking of Rome (7.38.7, 39.1–18 [taking of Rome], 7.40.3 [Rhine crossing], ed. Zangemeister, pp. 544–50). The same looseness of chronology is found in Olympiodorus: Zosimus, *Histoire nouvelle*, ed. Paschoud, 3 part 1:205–7 n. 59, 3 part 2:17–23 nn. 114–15; also, R. C. Blockley, *The Fragmentary Classicising Historians of the Later Roman Empire* (Liverpool, 1983), 2:157–95. The events of these years made it difficult for historians, including Frigeridus, to hold strictly to chronological order. An argument similar to Wynn's, on the same basis, is made by Werner Lütkenhaus, *Constantius III: Studien zu seiner Tätigkeit und Stellung im Westreich 411–421* (Bonn, 1998), pp. 41–42. It fails for the same reason.

96. For the passage of Orosius, see n. 31, above.

97. For a firm and confident account of 405–22, see now Kulikowski, *Late Roman Spain*, pp. 156–75, based partly on the fuller discussions in his "Barbarians in Gaul." My own goal is to forge a workmanlike link between the invaders' crossing of the Rhine and their crossing of the Pyrenees; I believe that certainties are unattainable.

98. A few extracts derive from the church historian Philostorgius; see Blockley, *Fragmentary Classicising Historians*, 2:157, 167, 169, 185, 191, 199, 203, 207.

99. To judge from Zosimus's summary (5.43, 6.1. 2, 2.1, 3.1, trans. Ridley, pp. 122, 127–28), Olympiodorus switches from Alaric in 409 back to the British usurpations, then further back to the invasion of the Vandals and Alans. Dramatic incidents: Olympiodorus, ed. Blockley, fragm. 17 (Gerontius), 18–19 (end of Sarus and Athaulf); also 14 (death of Eusebius, mutilation of Attalus), 15 (end of Allobich).

100. Émilienne Demougeot, "Constantin III, l'empereur d'Arles" (1974), reprinted in É. Demougeot, *L'Empire romain et les barbares d'Occident (IVè–VIIè siècles): Scripta varia* (Paris, 1988), pp. 171–213, is a useful collection of material rather than a synthesis; the successively cited sources illustrate inextricable problems of reconciliation.

101. The sole source for the invaders' activities after the Rhine crossing is Jerome, *Epistolae* 123.15–16, ed. Labourt, 7:91–92. Orosius, *Historia* 7.40.3 (ed. Zangemeister, pp. 549–50) gives the impression that the barbarians, having ravaged the north, headed straight south in a continuous movement. But the evidence is not clear-cut; neither Jerome nor Orosius was committed to a step-by-step retracing of the events.

102. The British usurpations down to Constantine in Gaul 407: Orosius, *Historia* 7.40.4, ed. Zangemeister, p. 550; Olympiodorus, Blockley fragm. 13. The historians directly relate the Rhine crossing to the British usurpation (the British troops were afraid of being cut off). For other sources, see PLRE 2:316.

103. Zosimus 6.3.1–2, trans. Ridley, p. 128; ed. Paschoud, 3 part 2:7–8. Zosimus 6.2.6, speaks of Constantine setting guards in the Alps in 407–8; then explicitly switches to an earlier time (6.3.1) when the Vandals, Sueves, and Alans "après . . . avoir franchit ces passages," ravaged the transalpine provinces. It looks as though the "passages" refer to the Alps *later* garrisoned by Constantine, but I see no serious obstacle to reinterpreting these lines to refer to the Rhine crossing. Zosimus 6.3.3, specifies that Constantine also restored the Rhine frontier. See n. 67, above, in which the conjectured link of Zosimus 6.3.1

to the Radagaisus invasion is discussed. Drinkwater, "The Usurper Constantine III," pp. 277–78, seems to identify the invaders over the Alps with the attack of Sarus and his Goths against the usurper (late 407). Sarus certainly had to come across the Alps, but the unfolding of his attack is known and very different from the outcome reported by Zosimus.

104. Orosius, *Historia* 7.40.4, ed. Zangemeister, p. 550. Which barbarians tricked Constantine is not stated. Besides the Alans, Vandals, and Sueves, other peoples, such as the Franks and Alamanni, might be meant. They were established auxiliaries of the army of Gaul, and Constantine definitely dealt with them. Drinkwater, "The Usurper Constantine III," pp. 282–84, 285, develops the line of Orosius into a theory that Constantine saved the invaders as a pool of manpower and even quartered them in the cities of Gaul. These are ambitious hypotheses without evidence. No Alan, Vandal, or Suevic forces ever turn up under these names in Constantine's employ or, later, in that of the general Gerontius (the latter's faithful Alan *slave*, prominent in Olympiodorus, cannot be turned into regiments of troops) or of the usurper Maximus.

105. Zosimus, 6.2.3–6, ed. Paschoud, 3 part 2:6; Olympiodorus, Blockley fragm. 13. See also PLRE 2:316.

106. Kulikowski, "Barbarians in Gaul," pp. 334–36; Drinkwater, "The Usurper Constantine III," pp. 279–81; PLRE 2:310, s.v. "Constans 1"; 2:316–71, s.v. "Constantinus 21"; 2:508, s.v. "Gerontius 5."

107. Orosius, *Historia* 7.40.1, ed. Zangemeister, p. 550, has the invaders head directly for the Pyrenees, be stopped there, and turn back to plunder the "circumiacentes provincias." Owing to Orosius's preoccupation with Spain, this account can be challenged, but is not necessarily wrong.

108. Orosius, *Historia* 7.40.7–8, ed. Zangemeister, p. 551; Olympiodorus, Blockley fragm. 13.2, 15.2, 17.1. See also PLRE 2:508; and Drinkwater, "The Usurper Constantine III," pp. 283–84, who emphasizes the hopeless source situation, but believes that Gerontius stirred up the barbarians in Gaul, unintentionally bringing about their invasion of Spain.

109. See, in brief, Drinkwater, "The Usurper Constantine III," p. 285.

110. Kulikowski, "Barbarians in Gaul," pp. 331–32, uses the details of Jerome (references to specific cities) to depreciate his bold strokes (references to all Gaul and provinces). This procedure is not foolproof. The evidence of Orosius (*Historia* 7.40.1, ed. Zangemeister, p. 550) is also discounted. Kulikowski, *Late Roman Spain*, p. 362 n. 19, rightly minimizes modern attempts to weave heterogenous sources into a reconstruction of the barbarians' itinerary across Gaul.

111. Both users of Olympiodorus—Sozomen and Zosimus (6.3.2)—refer to the barbarians' regaining strength after setbacks in Gaul; see Blockley, 2:176–77 (Olympiodorus, fragm. 15.2).

112. Kulikowski, *Late Roman Spain*, pp. 161–67, gives Maximus a feature role. It is not self-evident that the unqualified "barbarians" mentioned in this connection are necessarily the four invaders of Spain (see n. 104, above). No specific evidence connects either Gerontius or Maximus with them.

113. Courcelle, *Histoire littéraire*, pp. 84–85 (Jerome), 87–88 (Paulinus of Béziers). There are somber, somewhat later commentators, whose observations combine experiences of the passage of the mid-Danubians with the Gothic entrance into Gaul in 412; e.g., "All Gaul smoked in a great funeral pile." See Courcelle, pp. 85–86, 92–102. These

observations, embedded in theological and spiritual exhortations, are impressive but should not be mistaken for historical or sociological appraisals. See also Kulikowski, "Barbarians in Gaul," p. 338.

114. On Orosius and Rutilius, see Courcelle, *Histoire littéraire,* pp. 102–13 (the section is called "Les espoirs de l'an 417"). For Sidonius's birth, see PLRE 2:115, s.v. Apollinaris 6. Gregory of Tours, *Historiae* 2.2, ed. Krusch-Levison, p. 39. Gregory's incident is loosely modeled on the attack of the Vandals on the Sueves on the eve of their crossing to Africa (Hydatius 90, ed. Tranoy, pp. 128–30). In an error-prone manner somewhat reminiscent of Procopius (3.3.3, ed. Dewing, 2:22), Gregory gets the Vandal king Gunderic right but has him succeeded by Transamund rather than Geiseric. The switch in rulers telescopes time: 428 turns into 496 (Gregory also blends one group of Sueves with another, calling them "Alamanni," i.e., Swabians). This leads directly into tales of persecution of Catholic Christians by Arian Vandals—Gregory's real interest. On Roman reactions to barbarians, Samuel Dill, *Roman Society in the Last Century of the Western Empire,* 2nd ed. (London, 1899), pp. 303–45, wears very well.

115. On Hydatius, see Burgess, Chronicle *of Hydatius,* pp. 3–10, and Tranoy, *Chronique d'Hydace,* pp. 9–70; Muhlberger, *Fifth-Century Chroniclers,* pp. 192–204; and now Kulikowski, *Late Roman Spain,* pp. 153–56. Hydatius's work is among the most copious of the late Roman chronicles.

116. For Hydatius, the first of the inset quotations below; Orosius, *Histora* 7.40.3–10, ed. Zangemeister, pp. 553–55.

117. This passage is discussed by Kulikowski, *Late Roman Spain,* pp. 161–62.

118. The diocese of Spain was a subdivision of the Gallic prefecture; see n. 15, above. My translations differ from Burgess, p. 83: "apportioned to themselves by lot areas of the provinces for settlement" (mistakenly implies that grants went to individuals); "the Vandals took possession of Gallaecia and the Sueves that part of Gallaecia which is situated on the very western edge of the Ocean" (as though the "extremitas" went with the Sueves only, instead of with Gallaecia as a whole). Burgess's readings have a long past, see, e.g., Demougeot, who gives Gallaecia to the Asdings and pushes the Sueves to the edge of the ocean. Rightly understood, Hydatius wants us to know that the whole of Gallaecia was shared by the Asdings and Sueves. Demandt, *Die Spätantike,* p. 147, "Die spanischen Städte 'unterwarfen sich der Sklaverei' " is an improbable interpretation. As life within the lawful Empire was deemed to be "liberty," so the same existence under illegitimate *dominantes* passed as "servitude"; literal slavery was not in question. The same qualified sense of *servitus* occurs, e.g., in Jordanes, *Getica* 291, ed. Mommsen, p. 133, and in Eutropius, n. 25, above.

119. E. A. Thompson, "Hydatius and the Invasions of Spain," in *Romans and Barbarians: The Decline of the Western Empire* (Madison, Wis., 1982), p. 155. He was convinced that the Alan share was too generous (see n. 126, below). The Latin phrase is derived from the church father Tertullian. Demougeot, *Formation de l'Europe,* 2:448, underscores that there was no *foedus* and emphasizes *sorte:* "Ce furent les chefs barbares qui procédèrent à la distribution des parts, tirées au sort entre leurs peuples." Demandt, *Die Spätantike,* p. 147: "Spanien teilten sich die Germanen im Losverfahren." Similarly, Schmidt, *Histoire des Vandales,* pp. 30–31; Stein, *Histoire du Bas-Empire,* 1:263. Kulikowski, *Late Roman Spain,* p. 166, assumes that *sors* has only one meaning.

120. Pacatus, *Panegyricus Theodosio dictus* 10.3, "excubias sorte agere"; in the trans. of Edouard Galletier: "prendre la garde à son tour." *Panégyriques latins* (Paris, 1953), 3:77.

About Attila's sons: Jordanes, *Getica* 259, ed. Mommsen, p. 125: "gentes sibi dividi aequa sorte poscebant, ut ad instar familiae bellicosi reges cum populis mitterentur in sortem." The sons demanded "equal shares," as though warlike kings and their peoples should be "put up for division" like domestic dependents (in the partition of a private inheritance). Jordanes's sentence usefully illustrates how distant *sors* normally is from gambling, Pohl to the contrary notwithstanding (*Völkerwanderung*, p. 118, "durch das Los"). On the division of the Ostrogoths, see Jordanes, *Getica* 283, ed. Mommsen, p. 131, "qui [Theodemir, father of Theoderic the Amal] accito germano missaque sorte hortatus est, ut ille in parte Italiae, ubi tunc Glycerius regnabat imperator, ipse vero sicut fortior ad fortiorem regnum accederet Orientalem: quod et factum est." Thiudemir went east not because of lot-casting but because his Goths were the stronger force. Demandt, *Die Spätantike*, p. 186, likens the incident to the lot casting in Spain. *Missa sorte* in Jordanes (taken with his *mittere in sortem*, above) implies an idiom "to share out a capital (or) distribute an inheritance." Commentators are overinclined to cling to the magic roots of *sors*. Consciously or unconsciously, their fondness for the drawing of lots by barbarians echoes Tacitus, *Germania* 10.1, ed. Lund, p. 76: "Auspicia sortesque ut qui maxime observant." There seems to be a compulsion to color barbarians primitive or childlike, as n. 123, below.

121. *Oxford Latin Dictionary*, ed. P. G. Glare (Oxford, 1982) ss.vv. sors 4 and 5; sortior 3 and 4. The verb Hydatius uses in connection with the Alans and Silings has the sense of something "falling to" someone in a division. It is just as remote from gambling as *sors*. In a society very familiar with property transactions partitions were commonplace occurrences designated by ordinary words (they still are). Modern English dictionaries list "lot" as a reference to property, but devote more space to meanings involving chance. This distribution is based on lexicographic considerations rather than a scale of social importance. *Sors* is discussed again in Chapter 6 at n. 34, below.

122. Orosius, *Historia* 7.40.9–10, ed. Zangemeister, p. 552. The passage quoted above opens: "prodita Pyrenaei custodia claustrisque patefactis cunctas gentes, quae per Gallias vagabantur, Hispaniarum provinciis inmittunt isdemque ipsi adiunguntur: ubi actis aliquamdiu magnis cruentisque discursibus" (continuation in my text).

123. Javier Arce, "The Enigmatic Fifth Century in Hispania," in *Regna* and Gentes, pp. 137, 139–42, 146–48, 156, chooses wrong on all issues concerning the invasion of the Alans, Vandals, and Sueves: they make a treaty with Gerontius, choose by lot, divide Gallaecia, and have official participation in the sharing out. Typically, Arce explicitly invokes the barbarians' reputed fondness for appealing to chance (n. 120, above)!

124. Prosper, MG AA 9:409, 474. Lewis and Short, *Latin Dictionary*, s.v. *habito*, "to have possession of, to live [in]." Recognition of the repeated occurrences of this phrase by Schmidt, *Geschichte der Wandalen*, 2nd ed. (Munich, 1942), p. 22.

125. The relation of the Spanish apportionment to the strength of the four invaders has already been mentioned and exploited. See pp. 80, 83, 86, 89, above.

126. Thompson, *Romans and Barbarians*, pp. 155–56, considered the Asding share miserably small in view of the eighty thousand Vandals who crossed to North Africa in 429. The eighteen-year interval mattered, however; their numbers did not need to increase only biologically. About the eighty thousand, see Goffart, *B&R*, Appendix A. Presumably, the Sueves were few in numbers; they may also have lacked cohesion, because originating from a diversity of mid-Danubian Suevic peoples (see n. 42, above). Liebeschuetz, "*Gens* into *regnum*," p. 66, acknowledges the Asdings as weakest; he pays no attention to the Sueves.

127. The extravagant share of the Alans has been observed: Hydatius, *Chronique*, ed. Tranoy, 2:52 ("une certaine suprématie des Alains"); Heather, "Huns and the End," p. 13; Pohl, *Völkerwanderung*, p. 75. For a complete misapprehension of the situation, see Wenskus, *Stammesbilding und Verfassung*, p. 497, "The tribes of the Spanish invasion had to be of approximately the same size, so that one tribe's claim to hegemony could not win out (*durchdringen*), as we find as a rule elsewhere"—a case of system overriding evidence.

128. Lütkenhaus, *Constantius III*, p. 45; Drinkwater, "The Usurper Constantine III," pp. 283–84, and Arce, "The Enigmatic Fifth Century," p. 137, infer from the vague reference of Olympiodorus, fragm. 17.1, of dealings by Gerontius and Maximus with "barbarians" that there were formal treaties between these parties and the Alans, Vandals, and Sueves. These claims cannot be disproved, but they are frail. See also n. 112, above.

129. Procopius 3.3.3, ed. Dewing, 2:22. Averil Cameron, *Procopius and the Sixth Century* (London, 1985), pp. 207–9, urges caution in approaching these passages. Godegisel died in 406, Honorius in 423.

130. Orosius, *Historia* 7.43.13–16, ed. Zangemeister, pp. 562–63: "[Vallia] Romanae securitati periculum suum obtulit, ut adversus ceteras gentes, quae per Hispanias consedissent, sibi pugnaret et Romanis vinceret. quamvis et ceteri Alanorum Vandalorum Sueborumque reges eodem nobiscum placito depecti forent mandantes imperatori Honorio: 'tu cum omnibus pacem habe omniumque obsides accipe: nos nobis confligimus, nobis perimus, tibi vincimus, immortali vero quaestu reipublicae tuae, si utrique pereamus.' quis haec crederet, nisi res doceret? itaque nunc cottidie apud Hispanias geri bella gentium et agi strages ex alterutro barbarorum crebris certisque nuntiis discimus, praecipue Valliam Gothorum regem insistere patrandae paci ferunt." Wallia and the Visigoths were operating mainly out of Barcelona, in the province of Tarraconensis. Peace with hostages (as referred to by Orosius's kings) resembled the arrangement Rome had with the tribes facing its frontiers, as documented by Claudian narrating Stilicho's tour of the Rhine border (n. 93, above). A *foedus* is simply a treaty; being a party to some treaty or other does not automatically create a "federate," i.e., a barbarian leader engaging to provide Rome with troops (Demougeot and others tend to equate *foedus* with federate).

131. The text might be taken to describe a competition among barbarians soliciting Honorius, a competition that Wallia "won." It lends itself better to a more metaphorical reading. Without expecting literal interpretation of the offer of the kings ("let us kill one another"), Orosius suggests that the *outcome* implies that a miraculous competition took place. His factual core, presumably, was the report telling of furious war among the barbarians, including Wallia's Goths. Their mutual slaughter inspired Orosius's vivid (but fanciful) account of the kings' proposal to the emperor. Orosius and others (such as the church historian Socrates) liked to celebrate the unique "felicity" of the pious Honorius. Along the same lines, the speech of Theoderic to Zeno in Jordanes, *Getica* 291, ed. Mommsen, p. 133.

132. Bury, *Invasions of Europe by the Barbarians*, p. 105. Schmidt, *Ostgermanen*, p. 109 (by a treaty with the emperor the barbarians were awarded shares of Spain as *foederati*); Stein, *Histoire du Bas-Empire*, 1:263 (they tried to obtain treaties); Seeck, *Untergang*, 6:61–62 (decision was left not to the emperor, but to chance [*sors*]); Hydatius, ed. Tranoy, 1:35–38; Courcelle, *Histoire littéraire*, p. 103; Wenskus, *Stammesbildung und Verfassung*, p. 123; Demougeot, *Formation de l'Europe*, 2:2:448–49; Liebeschuetz, "*Gens* into *regnum*," pp. 64–66; Thompson, *Romans and Barbarians*, pp. 151–54. Cf. Muhlberger,

Fifth-Century Chroniclers, p. 248 n. 120. Bachrach, *Alans in the West*, p. 56, conjectures a treaty between Honorius and the Asdings. Lütkenhaus, *Constantius III*, p. 45 with n. 115, argues for Maximus making a treaty with the barbarians on the basis of Olympiodorus's statement that Maximus eventually fled "to the *allied* barbarians." Since we do not know whom Maximus fled to, the one word is a frail basis for contradicting the silence of Hydatius and Orosius. For a well worked out case against federates, see R. Gibert, "Il reino visigodo e il particularismo español," *Centro Italiano di studi sull'alto medioevo: Settimane di studio* 3 (1956): 557–59.

133. The best evidence for cooperation comes when Prosper, *Chronicon* 1329, MG AA 9:475–6, shows that four Romans from Spain were with Geiseric in North Africa, assisting in his government.

134. The priority of domestic challengers is explicitly spelled out by Orosius, *Historia* 7.42.1–3, ed. Zangemeister, p. 555.

135. Hydatius, ed. Burgess, pp. 84, 86: "Cui succedens Valliam in regno cum patritio Constantio pace mox facta Alanis et Vandalis Silingis in Lusitania et Betica sedentibus adversatur. . . . [(Hydatius, ed. Tranoy, 1:122, omitted by Burgess) Fredbalum regem gentis Vandalorum sine ullo certamine ingeniose captum ad imperatorem Honorium destinat.] . . . Vallia rex Gothorum Romani nominis causa intra Hispania caedes magnos efficit barbarorum. Alani, qui Vandalis et Suevis potentabantur, adeo cesi sunt a Gothi ut extincto Addace rege ipsorum pauci qui superfuerant oblito regni nomine Gunderici regis Vandalorum qui in Gallicia resederat, se patrocinio subiugarent." The much discussed recall of the Visigoths is irrelevant to my theme. Burgess, p. 86, "Gothi intermisso certamine quod agebant per Constantium ad Gallias revocati sedes in Aquitanica a Tolosa usque ad Oceanum acceperunt."

136. Ed. Burgess, p. 86: "Inter Gundericum Vandalorum et Hermericum Suevorum reges certamine orto Suevi in Erbasis montibus obsidentur ab Vandalis. . . . Vandali Suevorum obsidione dimissa instante Asterio Hispaniarum comite et sub vicario Maurocello aliquantis Bracara in exitu suo occisis relicta Gallicia ad Beticam transierunt." Note the anomalous translation of Burgess, p. 87, "after a number of men under the *vicarius* Maurocellus had been killed while escaping from Bracara, the Vandals quit Gallaecia and crossed into Baetica." The victims were not Romans.

137. About the mountains, see Schmidt, *Geschichte der Wandalen*, p. 26 n. 1; Thompson, *Barbarians and Romans*, p. 157; Kulikowski, *Late Roman Spain*, p. 370 n. 106. I expect them to be north of Braga. The flight of the Alan survivors to the Asdings is recorded, but no search for refuge is attributed to the Siling Vandals, who vanish from history. Wenskus, *Stammesbildung und Verfassung*, p. 67, asserts without evidence that the Silings survived; he is echoed by Wolfram, *History of the Goths*, p. 171; also Alexander Demandt, "Die Anfänge der Staatenbildung bei den Germanen," *Historische Zeitschrift* 230 (1980): 265–91, here 282; and F. M. Clover, *The Late Roman West and the Vandals*, ch. 6, p. 3. There must be a reason why historians wish the Silings to persist despite the absence of any evidence that they did.

138. Courcelle, *Histoire littéraire*, p. 104, speculates that the Sueves made a deal with the Romans and, on this basis, pushed out the Vandals. This possibility is less interesting than the alternative that the impetus for conflict came from the Vandals reinforced by Alans.

139. Schmidt, *Histoire des Vandales*, p. 35 n. 2, claimed that Maurocellus could not order an armed attack, since the vicariate was a civil office. In a somewhat disorganized

diocese of Spain all the niceties of the chain of command may not have been observed. Hydatius does not say that Maurocellus commanded troops. Vegetius, *De re militari* 3:21: (chapter title) "Viam abscedendi hostibus dandam, ut deleant facilius fugientes," ed. Alf Önnerfors, Teubner (Stuttgart, 1995), p. 99.

140. For an account of the Sueves of Spain, see Chapter 7, section "A Medley of Barbarian Peoples," below.

141. Musset, *Germanic Invasions*, pp. 60–62, 56–60. Neither Hydatius, who often dealt with the Sueves of Spain, nor Jordanes, whose knowledge was indirect, speaks well of them. Liebeschuetz, "*Gens* into *regnum*," p. 66, gives few reasons for setting the Vandal turning point in 422; he claims they were "expelled" from Gallaecia.

142. Procopius 3.22.1–15, ed. Dewing, 2:185–89. Procopius positions the story not as news but as a commentary on the just related downfall of the Vandal kingdom (he also dwells on the impossibility for the Vandals after their fall to return where they had come from). Among the many authors citing this story as factual, e.g., Zöllner, *Politische Stellung der Völker*, p. 47; he affirms that the story (which he reports with arbitrary embellishments) has a "historical core."

143. Procopius (n. 49, above) did not know of Vandals as mid-Danubians. For him they lived near the Sea of Azov, then marched straight to their Rhine crossing.

144. The other instances involve Herules (Procopius 6.15.1–29, ed. Dewing, 4:415–23) and Italian Goths (8.35.33–36, ed. Dewing, 5:417–19). It is possible that all three are fictional (the Italian account is contradicted by Agathias, the continuator of Procopius). The stories are meant by Procopius to underscore the foreignness of the barbarians in question, and the impropriety of their living on Roman soil.

145. Another believer is Wenskus, *Stammesbildung und Verfassung*, pp. 41, 42, 45, 67, who affirms that Procopius is extraordinarily reliable in such matters (i.e., ethnography). That opinion has detractors; see n. 129, above; Gibbon, *Decline and Fall*, ed. Bury, 3:262 n. 67: "His views of ancient history are strangely darkened by ignorance and error." The main issue of Procopius's anecdote is whether the African Vandals should retain a refuge; the embassy from an unspecified Vandal homeland is incidental to a scene staged by Procopius to encapsulate the (just related) demise of the Vandal kingdom. Wenskus, like other modern users, disregards Procopius's intention and seizes upon the existence of stay-at-home Vandals—in the middle Danube, of course—and the maintenance of relations between the homeland and the conquered territory. One should not extract these details out of Procopius as though they were kernels of historical fact rather than stage decoration (for another instance of this modern abuse, see n. 49 above). Gregory of Tours, *Historiae* 4.42, 5.15, ed. Krusch-Levison, pp. 175–77, 213–14, relates that Saxons who went to Italy with Alboin returned to the land from which they had set out (they were wiped out by the new occupants); see Chapter 6, n. 72, below.

146. The view of Drinkwater is reported, n. 95, above. Pat Southern and Karen R. Dixon, *The Late Roman Army* (New Haven, Conn., 1996), pp. 85–86, says too little about Roman soldiers' families, as, for example, whether dependents accompanied soldiers ordered to travel (a documented subject). On the Roman as on the barbarian side, military movements may have routinely involved convoys of families. The prominent example occurs in Theoderic the Amal's campaigning in the Balkans. Malchus fragm. 20, lines 226–56, Blockley 2: 447–49.

147. Maenchen-Helfen, *World of the Huns*, p. 73. On the emissaries, see Heather, "Huns and the End," p. 11, citing Olympiodorus, fragm. 19 (Blockley 2:183), in which it is clear that the Huns in question were led by multiple "kings," among whom one was

"first." Heather, ibid., pp. 17–18, infers from Zosimus 5.50.1 that, in 409, when Honorius recruited a force of Huns, the latter were already where Olympiodorus would find them. That inference seems imprudent. Stilicho's recruitment of Huns did not presuppose their having moved west; the methods available to him were presumably available to Honorius.

148. *Histoire du Bas-Empire*, 1:289. Stein speaks judiciously (1:290) about the relations of the Huns to their "subjects."

149. See n. 147, above. Joint rule by Bleda and Attila, Priscus fragm. 2, ed. Blockley, 2:225–27; Attila eliminates Bleda, Prosper, *Chronicon* 1353, MG AA 9:480; on the heyday of Attila and the downfall of his sons, see Jordanes, *Getica* 178–227, 254–64 (180, Attila's father and uncles), ed. Mommsen, pp. 104–16, 123–26.

150. Sidonius Apollinaris, *Poems and Letters*, ed. Anderson, pp. 146–47 lines 321–24, 102 lines 474–77. For the dates of composition, see André Loyen, *Recherches historiques sur les Panégyriques de Sidoine Apollinaire* (Paris, 1943), pp. 35, 59; discussion of the names, 52 n. 4, 78 n. 3. "Alites" is apparently a hapax legomenon; Gelonus is out of Horace. Loyen is a minimalist in interpretation; e.g., he takes Pannonians, Getae, and Dacians in list two to be based on Lucan. He may be right.

151. Sidonius's reference to "Ostrogoths"—probably meaning the Goths of Valamer in Pannonia—is interesting as an early attestation of this name.

152. On the date of Jordanes's histories, see Chapter 4, n. 56, above.

153. See the works of Lotter and Pohl cited n. 39, above. Sulimirski, *Sarmatians*, pp. 142–82, dwells on the Sarmatians in (the future) Hungary.

154. Wolfram, *History of the Goths*, pp. 258–59.

155. Chapter 7, section "A Medley of Barbarian Peoples," below. Attila as a Gepid, John Malalas 14.10, trans. Jeffreys, p. 195. Gepids repulsed from Gaul: *Consularia Italica* 574, MGH AA 9.304. On the disputed interpretation of this passage, see Favrod, *Histoire politique du royaume burgonde*, pp. 226–27. Contrary to him, I agree with the reading of Ralph W. Mathisen, "Resistance and Reconciliation," *Francia* 7 (1979): 605, that the Burgundians did the repelling. There is a curious precedent for the Burgundian defense against the Gepids. The church historian Socrates reports that the Burgundians defeated a force of ten thousand Huns in the days of Attila's uncle, Octar (430): *Historia ecclesiastica* 7.30.1–6; see Thompson, *Attila and the Huns*, p. 66. Attila's second invasion of Gaul: Jordanes, *Getica* 225–28, ed. Mommsen, pp. 115–16; Procopius, *Wars* 3.4.29, ed. Dewing, 2:43 (plundering Europe after Aetius's death); there are also two battles in Fredegar's account of the incident: *Chronicon* 2.53, ed. Krusch, pp. 73–75.

156. On the Sciri and Herules, see Chapter 7, section "A Medley of Barbarian Peoples," below.

157. Pliny, *Historia naturalis* 4.97, in *Griechische und lateinische Quellen*, ed. J. Hermann 1:328.

158. Jordanes, *Getica* 275–77, ed. Mommsen, pp. 129–30. See PLRE 2: 791(Odoacer) and 806 (Hunulf, Onoulphus).

159. See the discussion of hunger and the Vandals, n. 49, above.

160. Eugippius, *Vita s. Severini* 5, ed. Philippe Régerat, Sources chrétiennes 374 (Paris, 1991), pp. 190–94. See also PLRE 2:473, s.v. Flaccitheus. I have commented on this hagiography in "Does the *Vita s. Severini* Have an Underside?" in *Eugippius und Severin: Der Autor, der Text und der Heilige*, ed. Walter Pohl and Max Diesenberger, Forschungen zur Geschichte des Mittelalters 2 (Vienna, 2001), pp. 33–39.

161. See Chapter 7, n. 182, below.

162. On Procopius and the "ancestral home" of the Herules on the middle Danube, see n. 35, above, and Chapter 7, section "A Medley of Barbarian Peoples," below.

163. Wolfram, *History of the Goths*, pp. 268–78; Heather, *Goths and Romans*, pp. 227–308; John Moorhead, *Theoderic in Italy* (Oxford, 1992), pp. 6–31. Theoderic's non-Roman dimension tends to be overemphasized by comparison with his extraordinarily honored standing in the Empire.

164. See Chapter 7, section "A Medley of Barbarian Peoples," below.

165. Ibid.

166. See Chapter 1. About maps, Walter Goffart, "The Map of the Barbarian Invasions: A Longer Look," in *The Culture of Christendom: Essays in Medieval History*, ed. Marc A. Meyer (London, 1993), pp. 1–27. The proliferation of attractively produced maps in current textbooks is noteworthy (barbarian migrations are a favorite subject). The famous F. M. Putzger, *Historicher Schul-Atlas* (Bielefeld and Leipzig, 1877–)—a standard setter outside as well as inside Germany—added to its 1923 edition a map called "Die neue Völkerwanderung. 16–20. Jahrhundert." It provides statistics and uses ribbons in contrasting colors to illustrate the global movements of Europeans, Africans, Indians, Chinese, and Japanese. The same map appears under the heading "European, African and Asiatic Migration," in William Shepherd, *Historical Atlas*, 7th ed. (New York, 1929), p. 177 (also in later editions). For its value as a comparative yardstick, see n. 174, below.

167. Musset, *Germanic Invasions*, p. 3, tries to express the distinctiveness of this age of migration in words.

168. Aaron Segal, *An Atlas of International Migration* (London, 1993), p. 8. The unidiomatic usage "migration . . . against" looks like a compromise between "*Wanderung*" and "invasion." Segal's omission is not unique. Anthony Pagden, *Peoples and Empires: A Short History of European Migration, Exploration, and Conquest from Greece to the Present* (New York, 2001), p. 37, wholly bypasses the "Migration Age" with an allusion to the Western Roman Empire being "overrun by waves of Germanic tribes." He despises all migrations prior to "the great [European] flotillas that would cross and recross the Atlantic and the Pacific" (p. 58). The same cut-off date is used by Robin Cohen, ed., *The Cambridge Survey of World Migration* (Cambridge, 1995), an extensive work. Clearly, the Migration Age ostensibly par excellence is not an obligatory theme in the history of world migrations. About the Mongols, see Christopher Kaplonski, "The Mongolian Impact on Eurasia: A Reassessment," in Bell-Fialkoff, ed., *The Role of Migration*, pp. 251–74.

169. Segal, *Atlas of International Migration*, p. 10, no. 14. The procedure transposes to the Slavs what used to be done for the "Germans"; it is just as mischievous for either group of peoples.

170. For representative samples of current opinion, see Heather's affirmation of the primacy of external causation (Chapter 1, nn. 10–11, above), and the assertion of Bowersock that "responsible" historians no longer speak of the fall of the Roman Empire (n. 2, above).

171. As illustrated, e.g., by Bell-Fialkoff, ed., *The Role of Migration*; Jean-Baptiste Duroselle, "*L'Invasion*": *Les migrations humaines, chance ou fatalité* (Paris, 1992); Guy Richard, ed., *Ailleurs, l'herbe est plus verte: Histoire des migrations dans le monde* (Paris, 1996).

172. "Medieval *Origines gentium* and the Community of the Realm," *History* 68 (1983): 379. The word has not yet gone out to journalists, e.g., Jane Kramer, "Taking the Veil," *New Yorker* (November 22, 2004), p. 60, "Muslims today are part of the biggest labor migration in Europe since the great migrations of the Roman Empire."

173. Marc Bloch, *Feudal Society* (1939), trans. L. A. Manyon (Chicago, 1961), p. 56: "Till [the eleventh century] these great movements of peoples have in truth formed the main fabric of history in the West as in the rest of the world. Thenceforward the West would almost alone be free of them."

174. Segal, *Atlas of International Migration*, p. 56. Almost certainly Bloch was acquainted with the Putzger historical atlas—a standard reference work (n. 166, above). The merest glance at its 1923 map of "Die neue Völkerwanderung" would have subverted his belief in a modern "West" uniquely free of great migrations.

175. Ludwig Schmidt, "Die Ursachen der Völkerwanderung," *Neue Jahrbücher für das klassiche Altertum, Geschichte und deutsche Literatur* 11 (1903): 340. The appeal of this organizing principle has not dwindled; see Krause, *Geschichte der Germanen* (2002), p. 18: "Die Geschichte der Germanen ist deshalb eine Geschichte ihrer Stämme und eines Entwicklungsprozesses, bei dem Bewegung eine entscheidende Rolle spielte." The unity is of modern historians' making, connecting up specks of evidence; it is not inherent in the sources.

176. Hans-Werner Goetz and Karl-Wilhelm Welwei, eds., *Altes Germanien*, Ausgewählte Quellen zur deutschen Geschichte, 1a; 2 vols. (Darmstadt, 1995), 1:16. Pohl, *Die Germanen*, p. 24, indicates that the philological idea of East German is no longer admitted into historical discourse.

177. For a good illustration of this rhetoric, see Richard, ed., *Ailleurs, l'herbe est plus verte*, in which a typical chapter opens in the following terms (p. 33): "Les 'grandes invasions' (IIIè–VIè siècles) représentent le deuxième volet de la ruée des Indo-européens sur la pointe occidentale et méridionale de l'Europe." Historical sociology of this sort, rich in metaphors, evokes peoples (the "Indo-Europeans") whose only factual basis is as a concept in linguistics. It has no common ground with intelligible history.

178. Demandt, "Anfänge der Staatenbildung," p. 269.

179. Cary, *History of Rome*, pp. 501, 549, 655–66.

180. Averil Cameron, *Later Roman Empire*, p. 191; Averil Cameron, *The Mediterranean World in Late Antiquity* AD 395–600 (London, 1993), pp. 55–56; Demougeot, *De l'unité à la division*, pp. 566–70: "[Les barbares] ne sont qu'un facteur insolite de l'histoire générale, fonçants inexplicablement sur la scène politique, à la manière d'un *deus ex machina*." Where ancient historians such as Cameron see continual inexplicable migrations from the north, Germanists allege the triumphant expansion of the glorious Germanic peoples; one illusion feeds on the other.

181. Residents of Canada know how remote Canada is to its main trading partner—the empire on its southern border.

182. On the relationship of civil war and barbarians, see Goffart, *Rome's Fall and After*, pp. 8–9, 19–20.

Chapter 6

1. My articles on closely related subjects, notably tax law, are relevant to this chapter and to *B&R*. Few critics have examined them. They are: "From Roman Taxation to Mediaeval Seigneurie: Three Notes," *Speculum* 47 (1972): 165–87, 373–94; "Old and New in Merovingian Taxation," *Past and Present* 96 (August 1982): 3–21; "Merovingian Polyptychs: Reflections on Two Recent Publications," *Francia* 9 (1982): 57–77. All three are

reprinted in *Rome's Fall and After*, pp. 167–253. Also relevant is my "After the Zwettl Conference: Comments on the Techniques of Accommodation," in the conference proceedings cited in n. 5, below.

2. Ernst Theodor Gaupp, *Die germanischen Ansiedlungen und Landtheilungen in den Provinzen des römischen Westreiches* (Wroclaw [Breslau], 1844). (The year 1844 saw the publication of an even more enduring monument, Benjamin Guérard's edition of the Polyptyque of St. Germain des Prés.) Gaupp is praised by Walter Pohl, "*Per hospites divisi*: Wirtschaftliche Grundlagen der langobardischen Ansiedlung in Italien," *Römische historische Mitteilungen* 43 (2001): 180. (The Biedermeier period, mainly a central European phenomenon, is dated 1815 to 1849.) I am grateful to Walter Pohl for sending me a copy of his article, which is far and away the furthest-reaching recent effort to come to terms with barbarian settlement. Pohl's article centers on the case of Lombard Italy, which I discuss at length in *B&R*, pp. 175–205, but do not return to in the present book. The Lombard evidence is so thin and so late that I have nothing more to say about Italian conditions than I have already said.

3. Rommel Krieger, *Untersuchungen und Hypothesen zur Ansiedlung der Westgoten, Burgunden, und Ostgoten* (Bern, 1991), pp. 51, 179, takes me particularly to task for departing from Gaupp. Krieger is not at home in English and has only a limited grasp of my work. He harbors illusions about *hospitium* being a personal prerogative of Roman soldiers and about Goths creating a new *hospitium* of their own (pp. 38–42); he knows of a *wahre Hospitalitas*.

4. Wolfram's statement on this subject is in *History of the Goths*, pp. 223, 295–96, 504 n. 243 (about the Zwettl conference).

5. For a selection of titles, see n. 14, below. The review of this literature in Pohl, "Wirtschaftliche Grundlagen," pp. 180–89, is very comprehensive and useful. Pohl, p. 185, says that the "new model" was intensively discussed at Zwettl. I very much enjoyed the conference but not as a venue for the exchange of ideas on barbarian settlement, since most participants were unfamiliar with my book (they seemed no better versed in Durliat's work). There is value in the published proceedings: *Anerkennung und Integration: Zu den wirtschaftlichen Grundlagen der Völkerwanderungszeit, 400–600*, ed. H. Wolfram and A. Schwarcz, Denkschriften der österreichischen Akademie der Wissenschaften, phil.-hist. Klasse 193 (Vienna, 1988).

6. Herwig Wolfram, "Zur Ansiedlung reichsangehöriger Föderaten: Erklärungsversuch und Forschungsziele," *Mitteilungen des Instituts für österreichische Geschichtsforschung* 91 (1983): 5–35. Along the same lines of inclusiveness, see also Herwig Wolfram, "Neglected Evidence on the Accommodation of Barbarians in Gaul," in *Kingdoms of the Empire*, pp. 181–83. The individual case of Sidimund, mentioned there, though interesting, sheds no light visible to me on the collective fate of Goths and Burgundians.

7. Dietrich Claude, review of *B&R* in *Francia* 10 (1982): 753–54, reproached me for not having taken account of *laeti* settlements or archaeology or toponymy; Émilienne Demougeot, review of *B&R* in *Byzantinische Zeitschrift* 76 (1983): 55–59, also underscored my neglect. The *laeti* and associated subjects have been solicited before in this connection, but, I am afraid, have never had anything useful squeezed out of them. Although reaching out to them has a semblance of virtue—Claude despises my "few written sources (*wenigen Schriftquellen*)"—that does not compensate for the lack of results.

8. Maria Cesa, "Hospitalità o altro techniques of accomodation [*sic*]? A proposito di un libro recente," *Archivio storico italiano* 140 (1982): 539–52.

9. Ferdinand Lot, "Du régime de l'hospitalité," *Revue belge de philologie et d'histoire* 7 (1928): 975–1011. For the earlier literature on this subject (other than Gaupp), see *B&R*.

10. Many of Jean Durliat's relevant publications are listed in his *Les Finances publiques de Dioclétien aux Carolingiens (284–889)*, Beiheft der *Francia* 21 (Sigmaringen, 1991), pp. 343–44. In the present context I single out his weighty contribution to the Zwettl proceedings (n. 5, above): "Le salaire de la paix sociale dans les royaumes barbares," in *Anerkennung und Integration*, pp. 21–72. On the relations between his work and mine, see the brief comments on p. 120, above. We differ on the reading of key texts, but it is beyond doubt that our respective schemes, independently arrived at, have much in common. His *Finances publiques* is a major contribution to early medieval studies.

11. See Goffart, *B&R*, p. 104 n. 2, about Philostorgius (whose testimony has been given undue weight, see n. 80, below).

12. Jochen Martin, *Spätantike und Völkerwanderung*, Oldenbourg Grundriß der Geschichte (Munich, 1987), p. 165, "die 'Ansiedlung' der Germanen [ist] wieder ein offenes Problem." See also André Chastagnol, review of Goffart, *B&R*, *Revue historique* 269 (1983): 166.

13. Gaupp, *Ansiedlungen*, pp. 198–202. But see also n. 24, below.

14. For the reason stated here, almost all critics agree on the same, faulty point of departure; I respond to them collectively below, with special attention to Barnish and Wood. See the comprehensive survey of recent writings by Pohl, "Wirtschaftliche Grundlagen," pp. 180–89. I have already cited Krieger, Pohl, Wolfram, Cesa, Claude, and Demougeot (nn. 3, 5–8). In addition, see (in order of publication) S. J. B. Barnish, "Taxation, Land and Barbarian Settlement in the Western Empire," *Papers of the British School at Rome* 54 (1986): 170–95; Ian Wood, "Appendix: The Settlement of the Burgundians," to his "Ethnicity and the Ethnogenesis of the Burgundians," in *Typen der Ethnogenese unter besonderer Berücksichtigung der Bayern*, ed. H. Wolfram and W. Pohl, part 1 (Vienna, 1990), pp. 65–69; J. H. W. G. Liebeschuetz, *Barbarians and Bishops: Army, Church and State in the Age of Arcadius and Chrysostom* (Oxford, 1990); Evangelos Chrysos, "Conclusion: De foederatis iterum," in *Kingdoms of the Empire*, p. 191; Wolf Liebeschuetz, "Cities, Taxes and the Accommodation of the Barbarians: The Theories of Durliat and Goffart," in *Kingdoms of the Empire*, pp. 135–51; R. W. Mathisen and H. Sivan, "Forging a New Identity: The Kingdom of Toulouse and the Frontiers of Visigothic Aquitania (418–507)," in *The Visigoths. Studies in Culture and Society*, ed. A. Ferreiro (Leiden, 1999), pp. 12–15; Peter Heather, "*Gens* and *regnum* among the Ostrogoths," in *Regna and Gentes*, pp. 88–133; Kaiser, *Die Burgunder*, pp. 82–87. Add to these the works cited below: Behrends, n. 24 (does not cite *B&R*); Favrod, n. 51; Garcia Moreno, n. 34; Garnica, n. 79; Heather, nn. 70, 92.

15. Wolfram, as cited n. 6, above. Other valued endorsements come from Michael Hendy, "From Public to Private: The Western Barbarian Coinages as a Mirror of the Disintegration of Late Roman State Structures," *Viator* 19 (1988): 42–43 n. 42, who believes I should have observed the similarity of the late Roman scheme to the Islamic *iqta'* and Byzantine *pronoia*; and from Edward James, review of *B&R*, *Speculum* 57 (1982): 886–87.

16. A choice example is Penny MacGeorge, *Late Roman Warlords* (Oxford, 2002), p. 282 n. 58, complete with an obtuse handling of "land" (see also n. 46, below). Liebeschuetz, *Barbarians and Bishops*, p. 74 n. 218, adverts to Barnish's "excellent discussion of Goffart's theories"; content with a few superficialities, he endorses the "default" opinion of sharing land. Perceptively, Hendy, "From Public to Private," is not swept away by Barnish.

17. Barnish, "Taxation, Land," p. 170; Liebeschuetz, *Barbarians and Bishops*, pp. 74–75, prefers to speak of "natural" interpretation and "natural meaning," but limits his demonstration of "natural" exegesis to a pair of laws whose relevance to the subject he fails to establish; and he steers clear of attempting a "natural" interpretation of LB54. Several important arguments of mine are endorsed here and there in Barnish, "Taxation, Land," pp. 177 n. 67 (inapplicability of the Roman billeting law to land), 177–78 (definition of the *illatio tertiarum*), 182 n. 116 (verb form), 183 (*millenarii*), 184 (interpretation of *Variae* 2. 17), 184 (shares of tax proceeds).

18. Wood, "Settlement of the Burgundians," p. 67 n. 15.

19. CTh 7.8; the next title is also relevant.

20. Pohl, "Wirtschaftliche Grundlagen," p. 181 n. 7. The Gaupp system is presented as the default position in Pohl, *Völkerwanderung*, p. 138.

21. Bury, *History of the Later Roman Empire*, 1:206. The law stating limitations: CTh 7.8.10 (a western law, 413). Gaupp was well aware of this law. An earlier law, CTh 7.4.12 (364), also insists that soldiers must be content with their rations.

22. Pohl, "Wirtschaftliche Grundlagen," p. 201.

23. Katherine Fischer Drew, *The Burgundian Code* (1949; reprinted, Philadelphia, 1979), p. 62 n. 1; Alvaro d'Ors, *Estudios Visigoticos*, vol. 2, *Il Codigo di Eurico* (Rome-Madrid, 1960), p. 173. The Roman state was so far from turning a rule for houses into a rule for land that, when individuals were excused from billeting, they were required to pay one-third of the rent (*pensio*) of the exempted house to the government: *NTheod II* 25.2 (444). The rental of a house is trivial by comparison with a full third of a proprietor's landed property.

24. K. F. Werner, *Vom Frankenreich zur Entfaltung Deutschlands und Frankreichs* (Sigmaringen, 1984), p. 3. The authorities I have mentioned are chosen out of a longer list of respected names that might be cited making the same mistake. More are cited in *B&R*, pp. 40–41. According to O. Behrends, "Einquartierungssystem," in *Hoops Reallexikon* (Berlin,1989), 7: 27, there was a "simple" and an "expanded" billeting; the latter kind was devised by Constantius and Aetius specifically for barbarian settlement (p. 29), and it involved the appropriation of the provincials' properties (*Landgüter*) (p. 27). Besides inventing these initiatives (for which there is no evidence), Behrends alleges that *hospitalitas* (of his expanded kind) was exacted in North Africa and Italy (p. 28), which the evidence explicitly contradicts. Behrends's bibliography contains items to 1983, but not *B&R*.

25. Ernst Levy, *West Roman Vulgar Law: The Law of Property* (Philadelphia, 1951), pp. 84–85. Claude, review in *Francia* 10 (1982): 753, also limits obscurities in this problem to "Einzelheiten."

26. This is a literal translation of *agri cum mancipiis*; what the phrase actually means is discussed at nn. 114–15 and especially Appendix 3, below.

27. Pohl, "Wirtschaftliche Grundlagen," p. 215 with n. 121, goes so far as to suggest (without evidence) that a billeted soldier could sell to a third party, i.e., alienate, the share of a house that he was allowed to occupy. I hope this is only a slip of the pen.

28. Goffart, *B&R*, pp. 40–41 with n. 6, 49 with n. 27

29. LB54, the text is quoted in full, p. 145, below; it is also in Goffart, *B&R*, pp. 127–29. Lot, "Régime de l'hospitalité," pp. 979–84, and Hans Delbrück, *The Barbarian Invasions: History of the Art of War*, trans. Walter J. Renfroe, Jr., 4 vols (Lincoln, Nebr.,

1980), 2:322–23. The bibliography of *B&R* includes many other efforts to grapple with this difficult text. A comprehensive discussion of LB54 is given below in connection with the Burgundian evidence.

30. Wood, "Settlement of the Burgundians," pp. 68, 66. Wood's casual invocation of *hospitalitas* gives readers no idea of what it might mean. The comprehensive account of the barbarian settlements by Ian Wood in *Cambridge Ancient History*, ed. A. Cameron and P. Garnsey (Cambridge, 1997), 13:522–25, lacks clarity and coherence.

31. The contrast between possession *iure hospitalitatis* and individual royal gifts of *agri cum mancipiis* leaps to the eye in LB55.2 and 5 (cited at nn. 52, 114, below); see also for gifts LB54.1–2, p. 145, below. The texts are quoted in the section on the Burgundian settlement.

32. Barnish, "Taxation, Land," pp. 188–89.

33. Barnish, "Taxation, Land," p. 189. P. D. King, *Law and Society in the Visigothic Kingdom* (Cambridge, 1972), p. 206 n. 5.

34. Goffart, *B&R*, pp. 49–50. An earlier discussion of *sors*, in a context of distributing whole Roman provinces, occurs in Chapter 5, nn. 119–21, above. *Sors*, plural *sortes*, basically meaning "lot," is often treated in writings on "techniques of accommodation" as though it were a fixed *terminus technicus*, which it is not. The term has a wide range of definitions—the "principal" of a debt (D. T. Lewis and C. Short, *A Latin Dictionary* [Oxford, 1879], pp. 1732–33, s.v. *sors* II D 2), the "kingdom" of a barbarian king (Sidonius, *Epist.* 7.6.10, 8.3.3; LB6.1, 20.2), the undefined award made to Butila, a Gothic priest (Cassiodorus *Variae* 2.17 [see n. 169, below]), or even "destiny" in a poem featuring Alans (Goffart, "After the Zwettl Conference," in *Anerkennung und Integration*, pp. 83–84 with n. 37). The word is an abstraction defined by its context. One's "lot in life" is different from the "lot" on which a house is built. The term cannot be directly turned into something concrete and strictly limited, such as a "land grant." Durliat, "Salaire de la paix," p. 56, says, "En effet *sors* ou *consors* possède dans [le royaume des Wisigoths] comme chez les Burgondes et comme dans la législation romaine, le sens de propriété privée." This is like saying that the English word "property" specifically means "private" property, which is obviously not true. Durliat bases his opinion on L. A. Garcia Moreno, "El termino 'sors' y relacionados en el 'Liber Judicum,'" *Annuario de historia del derecho español*, 53 (1983): 137–75, an early response to *B&R*. Attempts to make *sors* inherently concrete rather than an abstraction are bound to fail.

35. Averil Cameron, *The Mediterranean World in Late Antiquity*, p. 48; "the land on which they were settled" is code for a *hospitalitas* envisaged not as shelter but as settling on land.

36. See also my complaint about "simple" land in Goffart, "After the Zwettl Conference," p. 78. The threefold analysis of land engaged in here is one of the main differences between my account in *B&R* and the one of this chapter.

37. This process is not peculiar to the Roman tax system; it is still basic to ours. Property tax in municipalities is a simple analogy: houses are assessed (i.e., their value is estimated), and taxes are levied on the assessment (as a percentage of the valuation).

38. They still do. E.g., a house today can be separated into the three categories of occupancy (by a renter or the owner), ownership (as proprietor and, if applicable, as occupant), and public tax assessment and payment (weighing on the owner but possibly paid by a tenant). Just as occupancy can be leased to a tenant, so it is possible (though

avoided by modern governments) for the taxes of a house to be renounced by the public power and transferred to an individual or organization. Tenant, owner, and government can all speak of the house in question justifiably as being theirs ("my house").

39. Delbrück, *Barbarian Invasions*, 2:321–22, has his own way of filling in this background.

40. About the Vandals, see n. 68, below. The instance in Gaul: *Chronicle of 452*, a. 440, 442, MGH AA 9:660; "Deserta Valentinae urbis rura Alanis, quibus Sambiba praeerat, partienda traduntur"; "Alani, quibus terrae Galliae ulterioris cum incolis dividendae a patricio Aetio traditae fuerant, resistentes armis subigunt et expulsis dominis terrae possessionem vi adipiscuntur." (There appears to be a discrepancy between the deserted condition of the fields assigned to the Alans and the expulsion of Roman landlords.) The main lesson of the violence is that the Romans were not supposed to resist or the Alans to dislodge the owners and seize their property. According to the rules for "partition" that Aetius imposed, the Romans were to remain resident, retain *possessio*, and not resist an (otherwise undefined) partition with the Alans. These reports suggest that outright expropriation makes noise. See also *B&R*, pp. 112–13; and n. 151, below.

41. Goffart, *B&R*, p. 117.

42. Thompson, *Romans and Barbarians*, pp. 50–51. The properly Gothic LV10.1.8 refers to the "two parts of the Goth" (whatever that means; see the discussion, pp. 139–41, below) but Thompson's basis, as stated (with shares of other assets), has to be LB54.

43. Prosper, *Chronicon* 1271, MG AA 9:469; Hydatius, *Chronicle* a. 581, MG AA 11:19; Stein, *Histoire du Bas-Empire*, 1:267. The sources specify the territorial limits of settlement and indicate that a permanent arrangement was involved; they say nothing about individual allotments.

44. Thompson was hardly alone in taking this liberty. One of the most common abuses in writings on this subject consists in describing the Visigothic (and Italian) settlements in terms lifted out of Gundobad's LB54. See, e.g., Martin, *Spätantike und Völkerwanderung*, pp. 42, 50.

45. Goffart, *B&R*, chapter 6, pp. 162–75.

46. Goffart, *B&R*, pp. 163 with n. 5 (the instances of common fractions in other laws could be multiplied almost indefinitely; they are numerous in the Burgundian Code), 167–70. Pohl, "Wirtschaftliche Grundlagen," p. 199 with n. 72, reluctantly admits that a one-third fraction does not necessarily point to *hospitalitas*. According to MacGeorge, *Late Roman Warlords*, p. 282, there was an "older" time when "third" had a "precise and technical sense (from the old *hospitalitas* system)." Whether "third" has a technical sense depends on context. On hospitality in general, Ladislaus J. Bolchazy, *Hospitality in Early Rome: Livy's Concept of Its Humanizing Force* (Chicago, 1977), especially pp. 12–15. Bolchazy suggests that hospitality becomes commonplace (i.e., ceases to be a delicate matter) in developed societies accustomed to having continual contacts with strangers and foreigners.

47. Pohl, "Wirtschaftliche Grundlagen," p. 196, "Es muß sich bei diesen *hospites* also um einquartierte Soldaten gehandelt haben"; Gregorius Magnus, *Registrum epistolarum* 4.8, ed. Paul Ewald, MG. Epistolae 1:240.

48. Goffart, *B&R*, p. 164 n. 6, draws attention to Ennodius *Vita s. Antonii Lerinensis*, in which the saint, as a way of divesting himself of his possessions, filled his lands with *hospites*—squatters, strangers to the owner and owing no rent.

49. See the "expanded" billeting of Behrends, n. 24, above.

50. Goffart, *B&R*, pp. 162, 171; also withdrawn is a similar comment on p. 124.

51. A special reason for regret is the errors to which these lines have given rise. Thus, Justin Favrod, *Histoire politique du royaume burgonde (443–534)* (Lausanne, 1997), p. 190, believes that I advocate two kinds of *hospitalitas*, one for billeting, another for barbarian settlement. This is not true, but I bear some responsibility for Favrod's false impression. Krieger, n. 3, above, and Behrends, n. 24, above, are much more explicit sources for theories of a dual *hospitalitas*.

52. LB55.2, ed. de Salis, p. 90, "Quotiens de agrorum finibus, qui hospitalitatis iure a barbaris possidentur, inter duos Romanos fuerit mota contentio, hospites eorum non socientur litigio, sed Romani in iudicio contendentes expectentur, ut, cuius barbari hospes evicerit, cum ipso postmodum de re obtenta habeat rationem." This supplements LB22, which forbids Burgundians from interfering in lawsuits between Romans. It may have a Gothic counterpart in CE276, which, among other things, prescribes what barbarians are to do when the boundaries between properties are defined. See n. 83, below. Texts about *hospitalitas* have to be specific; the various laws in which *hospites* (or the singular, *hospes*), "hosts" or "guests," occur cannot be relevant for that reason alone, since the word is not technical; it has no specific association with military billeting. LV9.1.6. is an important illustration of this point.

53. "Ex eo loco, in quo ei hospitalitas fuerat delegata" (ed. de Salis, p. 88).

54. Wood in *Cambridge Ancient History*, new ed., 13:125, observes correctly that "*ius hospitalitatis* and *ius sortis* are synonymous."

55. Dig. 9.3.1.9, 50.4.3.13–14. *Vocabularium iurisprudentiae Romanae*, 5 vols. (Berlin, 1903–39), 3:272–73: *hospes*, "Generaliter = is, qui per aliquod tempus in domo recipitur et cui victus et habitatio praebetur"; "Specialiter = miles, cui cubite et cibaria praebenda sunt." I accept the idea that the guest was fed, but do not see an explicit text to that effect among those cited. These texts are a useful corrective to the idea often expressed in the literature that military billeting was a late Roman innovation.

56. Inst. 2.5.1–2, "is, qui fundi nudum usum habet, nihil ulterius habere intellegitur, quam ut oleribus pomis floribus feno stramentis lignis ad usum cottidianum utatur: in eoque fundo hactenus ei morari licet, ut neque domino fundi molestus sit neque his, per quos opera rustica fiunt, impedimento sit: nec ulli alii ius quod habet aut vendere aut locare aut gratis concedere potest. . . . Item is, qui aedium usum habet, hactenus iuris habere intellegitur, ut ipse tantum habitet, nec hoc ius ad alium transferre potest: et vix receptum videtur, ut hospitem ei recipere liceat." He has the right to reside with wife, children, and freedmen, provided the shelter is suitable for female habitation. He can avail himself of the service and work of slaves on the premises, but by no means transfer these services to someone else. See also Dig. 7.8, *De usu et habitatione*. 7.8.11, which agrees with the above; but 7.8.10, seems more indulgent to the "user." There is a certain lack of agreement regarding the limitations on the "user." See Adolf Berger, *Encyclopedic Dictionary of Roman Law*, Transactions of the American Philosophical Society, new ser., 43/2 (Philadelphia, 1953), p. 755.

57. See, in general, CTh 7.8 and 9. Although the legislator's assumption of billeting in towns is important, nothing prevents the same rules from being applied to villages or detached country dwellings. On commutation, see *NTheod II* 25.2 (see n. 23, above). This law would have been a good point of departure for a regular tax on urban house property. Behrends, "Einquartierungssystem," pp. 25–26, bears out my interpretation of the material in the Theodosian Code.

58. CTh 7.9.4 (taxpayers are subject only to the regular *indictio*; soldiers are to be content with imperial largesse); CTh 7.7.4 (415), on the same grounds, soldiers are not to demand anything on account of pastures. LB38.3–4, quoted below. Cassiodorus, *Variae* 3.42 reverses 3.40, with the royal government sparing the Gallic provincials the cost of *exercituales expensae* (glossed as *alimonia nostris Gothis*); ed. Mommsen, pp. 100, 99. *Variae* 5.13, 6.22, 10.10, ed. Mommsen, pp. 150, 194–95, 304, document issues of rations without reference to housing. *Variae* 10.18, ed. Mommsen, p. 309, lucidly differentiates shelter and rations. See also Goffart, *B&R*, p. 43 n. 11. Gaupp very clearly distinguished the feeding of soldiers by the *annona* from their billeting: *Ansiedlungen*, pp. 75–92.

59. I assume that *ibidem* does not refer specifically to the aforesaid *agro regio* but has the general sense of "in whatever place where he takes shelter."

60. LB38, ed. de Salis, pp. 69–70 (ed. Bluhme, p. 547). My translation. I believe that none of the critics of *B&R* has brought this crucial law into the discussion. *Solidus*, translated "shillings," is the name of the standard Roman gold coin, amounting to one seventy-second of a pound of gold.

61. LV8.2.3, 8.4.24–27, ed. Zeumer, pp. 320, 340–43, have obvious similarities to LB38 and will be discussed presently.

62. Levy, *West Roman Vulgar Law*, p. 126. The origin of LB38 in late Roman law is clearly indicated by its careful distinction of housing a guest from feeding him (n. 58, above).

63. See the laws cited in n. 61, above.

64. CTh 7.8.10 (413), 7.8.1 (361, *hospitale iure*), NTheod II, 25.2 (444). Also *hospitalitatis gratia*, as n. 58, above. For an early sixth-century occurrence of the term, see *Epistolae imperatorum [et] pontificum (Collectio Avellana)*, ed. O. Guenther, CSEL 35 (Vienna, 1895), no. 158.2, p. 605, (a letter of instruction to papal ambassadors to Constantinople) "neque ab his [= occurrentes episcopi] vel victualia praesumatis accipere nisi tantum subvectionem, si causa poposcerit, et hospitalitatem." The envoys may accept "transport and shelter," presumably because these are state allowances without religious overtones.

65. LB38.8, above.

66. The tolerance, LV8.4.27, ed. Zeumer, p. 343.

67. Sidonius, *Epistolae* 2.1.3, ed. Anderson, 1:414, dated about 470. Cf. Goffart, *B&R*, pp. 245–48 (I no longer subscribe to all my comments on this text). Sidonius's observation implies that Seronatus, in imposing these "guests" on villages, was acting pursuant to Roman legality; he was not giving away anyone's lands.

68. The basic texts on the Vandal settlement are Procopius 3.5.11–17, ed. Dewing, 2:51 ("he robbed the rest of the Libyans of their estates . . . and distributed them among the nation of the Vandals, and as a result of this these lands have been called 'Vandals' [allotments, *kléroi*]' up to the present time") and Victor of Vita, *Historia persecutionis Africanae provinciae*, 14.13, ed. C. Halm, MG AA 3 part 1 (Berlin, 1979), 4–5. Victor's key sentence about the settlement is, "Disponens quoque singulas quasque provincias, sibi Byzacenam, Abaritanam atque Getuliam et partem Numidiae reservavit, exercitui vero Zeugitanam vel proconsularem funiculo hereditatis divisit." The reference to a "surveyor's rope" at the end is a biblical reminiscence (1 Chron. 16:18) that I consider to be meant metaphorically; Geiseric apportioned these provinces to the troops in hereditary lots (it is superfluous to imagine that surveys took place in this connection). Both authors assert that Roman owners were arbitrarily dispossessed and are outraged, but they

are far from precise in describing what was involved. There are commentaries by Courtois, *Vandales et l'Afrique*, pp. 275–83, and Durliat, "Salaire de la paix," pp. 40–45.

69. See n. 14, above.

70. I spell out the absence of protests and resistance in: Goffart, *B&R*, p. 58. Prominent earlier adherents to this point: Thompson, *Romans and Barbarians*, p. 27; Delbrück, *Barbarian Invasions*, 2:326. Liebeschuetz, "Cities, Taxes," p. 141 n. 13, bravely refuses to see a problem. So does Peter Heather, "*Gens* and *regnum* among the Ostrogoths," in *Regna and Gentes*, p. 113. According to Wood, the absence of Roman protests is only an argument from silence, something so feeble that it can be bypassed: "Settlement of the Burgundians," p. 69. Barnish, "Taxation, Land," pp. 175–76, admits that there is problem.

71. *B&R*, pp. 36–39.

72. Gregory of Tours, *Historiae* 4.42, ed. Krusch-Levison, pp. 176–77 (down to the point when they were escorted to their old homes). I find it difficult to tell whether Alamanni are "Suebi" or differ from them.

73. Ibid., 5.15, ed. Krusch-Levison, pp. 213–14. I have rearranged Gregory's account for clarity. The most disquieting aspect of the passage is that it is, in effect, the doublet of an incident in which Gregory shows the stay-at-home Saxons being confronted by angry Franks, and in this case earning God's help by being the peacemaking party (4.14, pp. 145–47).

74. There is a similar story in Socrates, *Historia ecclesiastica* 7.30: three thousand Burgundian converts to Catholicism defeat the attack of ten thousand Huns. See also the hostilities between the Herules and the Lombards as told by Procopius 6.14.13–22, ed. Dewing, 3:406–9.

75. We hear only about the offers made by the Swabians. Gregory obviously says nothing about the methods by which individual transfers of "land" would have been made.

76. My discussion of the Visigothic evidence should imply that the method of settlement, whatever it is, also applied to Spain. This may be the case, and I believe it did. But the case of Spain, which the Visigoths began to penetrate in the 450s (but did not control until long after), presents special problems that have no bearing at all on the mechanisms of settlement that are my central concern. Clearly, the laws relating to Gothic allotments still interested sixth-century Visigothic codifiers in Spain. I leave Spain at that, without further comment. See now the authoritative monograph of Kulikowski, *Late Roman Spain*.

77. See Appendix 2, nos. 2–3. This was an extension of settlement, not the initial one in 443.

78. For a "taxpaying Roman," see LV10.1.16, ed. Zeumer, p. 389. The Burgundian Laws contain no explicit evidence that Romans paid taxes; but the subject was not forgotten; see Appendix 2, no. 4, below. These divisions will be more closely analyzed; the idea of a split between Goths and Romans is an oversimplification. See below.

79. Contrary to what Behrends, "Einquartierungssystem," p. 27, implies, there is no whisper in the chronicles of a distribution of property to individual Goths. *Sedes* in this context cannot mean anything other than the entire district assigned to the Visigoths; it definitely does not refer to an aggregate of grants to individual Goths. Lütkenhaus, *Constantius III*, p. 92, conjectures plausibly that the promise of settlement in southern Gaul was part of Athaulf's treaty with Constantius in 416; the recall of the Goths from Spain

implemented the treaty. There is nothing to be drawn from Ana Maria Jiménez Garnica, "Settlement of the Visigoths in the Fifth Century," in *The Visigoths from the Migration Period to the Seventh Century: An Ethnographic Perspective*, ed. Peter Heather (San Marino, 1999), pp. 93–115.

80. Cited in Goffart, *B&R*, p. 104 n. 2. Olympiodorus is not strictly contemporary; he wrote in the 440s; see Chapter 5, n. 45, above. The few words in question are in a tenth-century epitome of Philostorgius. They have been turned into a non-negotiable rampart of English belief in the handing over of "actual land" to the Goths; e.g., Heather, *The Goths*, p. 182. This assumes that the Visigoths were keen to farm the soil, for which there is little evidence. There are at least two other possibilities for interpreting Philostorgius's "land for tillage" than the literal one (which poses problems anyway): (1) It was flattering to the Empire that barbarians should appear to be settled as mere laborers scratching the soil. Jean-Michel Carrié, underscores the linking of soldiers and cultivation as a literary theme for civilian consumption; "L'État à la recherche de nouveaux modes de financement des armées," in *The Byzantine and Early Islamic Near East*, vol. 3, *States, Resources, Armies*, ed. Averil Cameron (Princeton, N.J., 1995), p. 46. (2) The phrase is metaphorical, a way of saying "fertile soil," i.e., "land" without specification of which of the three possible senses is meant.

81. An obvious objection might be that the Roman state was an owner in its own right, and capable of alienating various assets, including deserted and state lands (e.g., *agri deserti, res privata, fundi rei publicae*, etc.). This objection is now widely heard from commentators searching for plausible escapes from fiscal explanations (e.g., Heather, at n. 154, below; Kaiser, *Die Burgunder*, pp. 86–87). It is an empty speculation. There is no evidence at all in Gaul, Italy, or North Africa for the distribution of state lands to barbarians (unless the *deserta rura* attributed to the Alans, n. 40, above, are taken to belong to the state, which is by no means certain). It is pointless to bring hypothetical assets into the argument about barbarian settlement when there is nothing anywhere pointing in their direction.

82. LV10.1.16, ed. Zeumer, p. 389.

83. I omit any comment about CE276 because it contributes nothing to the argument; it certainly does not substantiate a theory of land division between Romans and Goths. See my extensive discussion in *B&R*, Appendix B, pp. 235–40.

84. A student of mine at the University of Toronto downloaded this image for me from the World Wide Web many years ago; I do not know the URL. The artist was Angus McBride, an eminent illustrator.

85. Alvaro d'Ors, *Codigo di Eurico*, p. 21; Goffart, *B&R*, p. 118. On the misinterpretation of this law by Lot and d'Ors, see ibid., p. 119 n. 26; they unjustifiably claim that it was about the "division" of *sortes* from *tertia*. In the revised LV, the contents of this law appear under the title "de quinquagenarii et tricennalis temporis intentione" (10.2, ed, Zeumer, p. 391)." In a translation widely available in the Internet Medieval Sourcebook, S. P. Scott, *The Visigothic Code* (reprinted, New York, 1982), p. 343, renders "sortes Goticae et tertiam Romanorum" as "Lands apportioned between Goths and Romans." This wrong translation—"apportioned between" is interpolated without a textual basis—is how Scott justifies his premise that a general "division" had taken place (see nn. 88–89, 91, below).

86. Zeumer, the editor of LV, considers the prescription "longissima [extremely long]" (p. 398 n. 1).

87. CE277.4, ed. Zeumer, p. 5–6, specifies that suits over status (i.e., whether one is a *mancipium* or not) fall under the thirty-year prescription; this sheds no light on the sense of *mancipia*. I do not believe that the text allows the sense of *mancipium* to be determined.

88. Unintentionally confirming the merit of this deduction, Scott, *Visigothic Code*, p. 343, translates "sortes Gotice et Romane" in the title to LV10.2.1 as "property," without qualification.

89. Ed. Zeumer, pp. 385–86. Scott, *Visigothic Code*, p. 337, adds many words to the Latin text so as to turn this law into one edicting a general division of lands between Romans and Goths. The additions are indefensible.

90. Liebeschütz, *Barbarians and Bishops*, p. 75, assures us that "[The] natural meaning [of the Visigothic laws] is that the Goths received a share of the land itself." Unfortunately, he does not explain what this "natural meaning" is and how, if at all, it relates to the texts in question. The law on billeting is very likely to lurk behind the allegedly "natural" interpretation.

91. LV10.1.16, ed. Zeumer, p. 389, "Ut, si Goti de Romanorum tertiam quippiam tulerint, iudice insistente Romanis cuncta reforment. Iudices singularum civitatum, vilici adque prepositi tertias Romanorum ab illis, qui occupatas tenent, auferant et Romanis sua exactione sine aliqua dilatione restituant, ut nihil fisco debeat deperire; si tamen eos quinquaginta annorum numerus aut tempus non excluserit." Scott, *Visigothic Code*, pp. 339–40, expands in the usual way (e.g., *tertiam Romanorum* = "third part of land belonging to Romans").

92. Like Scott, Heather, *Goths*, p. 284, presupposes an "original land partition" in which Goths had obtained "a two-thirds share" of some tacitly interpolated individual Roman property.

93. It may be useful to emphasize that, just as the ownership and cultivation of *tertia Romani* were in Roman hands, while its taxes went to the king, so the ownership and cultivation of *sortes Gothicae* were also in Roman hands, while its tax proceeds were distributed in individual packets to the Goths. A *sors* would have been regarded as property from the Gothic standpoint; but, from the standpoint of the Roman owners, it might have been more accurately deemed to be an obligation or burden weighing on land, comparable to a rent. As for *tertia Romani*, this is the name LV uses for king's or fiscal land, the king's share of the total assessment of the kingdom, which by its taxes fed his treasury or was available for royal gifts to individuals.

94. For Vandals, see n. 68, above; Burgundians, p. 154, below; Italy, p. 171. The Italian arrangement, as told, e.g., by Procopius (n. 144, below), involved a division of one-third to the troops and two-thirds kept by the king (and government); the *illatio tertiarum* marked out the troops' share of total tax assessments. The Vandal and Italian cases have special importance since (almost) everyone agrees that military billeting had no part in their settlements.

95. See the index to Goffart, *B&R*, under "division between king and people." Eager to affirm the priority of land grants over awards of tax proceeds, critics of *B&R* have paid virtually no attention to this aspect of my scheme (plainly documented in the Vandal and Italian evidence).

96. One might speculate that the division took account of the solvency or social status of taxpayers, but there is little evidence to sustain considerations of this kind.

97. The one document illuminating the process of allotment is the Italian letter concerning the priest Butila, discussed below pp. 172–78. The methods in Gaul need not have been identical.

98. The Visigothic laws contain a few texts indicating that Visigoths were not wholly uninterested in the soil. These laws are so similar to those (more abundant) of the Burgundian Laws that they are best discussed together. See nn. 110, 120, below.

99. See Appendix 2, where the chronicle entries are examined in detail. A slightly fuller account of the Burgundians before 436 is given in the Appendix.

100. See the quotation at n. 42, above.

101. See at nn. 30–31, above. The Burgundian Code itself illustrates the ubiquity of fractions in other laws than those concerned with barbarian allotments.

102. In a *mise au point* appropriately centering on this law, Favrod, *Royaume burgonde*, pp. 189–205, tacitly combines some of my ideas with some of Durliat's and blends both with his own misunderstandings of tax practices. This eclectic mixture is confusing. Typically, Favrod pays no more attention to LB38 (n. 60, above) than anyone else. For earlier opinions about the nature of LB54, see *B&R*, p. 130 with nn.

103. For a recent account of scholarship about the Burgundian Code, see Kaiser, *Die Burgunder*, pp. 126–33; Kaiser cites ca. 480 as the date for LB54 (p. 82). This estimated date and other details concerning LB54 and the other laws do not impinge on my discussion. I leave them to Kaiser and the works he cites. Ian Wood, review of Goffart, *B&R*, *History* 220 (1982): 306, suggests that the date of LB54 is very important; this may be true in some contexts, not in mine.

104. Ed. de Salis, pp. 88–89. I follow the five paragraph-division of an older edition (by Bluhme, MG Leges [in folio]), in preference to the three paragraphs of de Salis. My translation in *B&R*, pp. 127–29, is slightly different. I have completely avoided the translation of Drew, *Burgundian Code*.

105. Here and later, one might translate "a third of the bondsmen and two parts of the lands" (without a definite article). My translation presupposes that the legislator refers to a global allocation; the phrase (I maintain) is an abstract technical expression, a restricted usage, not layman's language, which makes no sense, as seen at nn. 17–18, 29–32, above.

106. Favrod, *Royaume burgonde*, p. 177, translates "maisons et jardins"—a possible alternative that merits attention and is not overlooked in my comments.

107. *Faramanni* has occasioned much controversy. I define it here by context, as meaning (in the singular) "any Burgundian entitled to an allotment." Its etymology and strict sense, which seem to hinge on *fara*, I leave for others to decide. My account in *B&R*, pp. 131–32 n. 6, is less restrained than I am now inclined to be.

108. Like "halves" and "thirds," the term *hospes* (host or guest, here the former) is a common term, not a signpost of Roman military billeting (cf. the passage of Ennodius of Pavia in n. 48, above, and Seronatus filling "villages with *hospites*," in n. 67, above). Host and guest are appropriate terms for describing the relationship of Romans and Burgundians to each other. *Hospes* in the sense of "Burgundian guest" occurs in LB55.2, 4.

109. Against Favrod, *Royaume burgonde*, p. 199, I disclaim any connection between these fractions and "land and capitation taxes." Favrod, like many other commentators, is unaware that levied taxes are distinct from tax assessment.

110. Burgundian and Visigothic laws concerning subsidiary assets: LB67 (ed. de Salis, p. 95). "De silvis hoc observandum est. Quicumque agrum aut colonicas tenent,

secundum terrarum modum vel possessionis suae ratam sic silvam inter se noverint dividendam; Romano tamen de silvis medietate in exartis servata." LB13 (ed. de Salis, p. 52), "De exartis. Si quis, tam Burgundio quam Romanus, in silva communi exartum fecerit, aliud tantum spatii de silva hospiti suo consignet et exartum, quem fecit, remota hospitis commotione [= communione], possideat." Cf. LV10.1.9, ed. Zeumer, p. 389. LB31.1–2 (ed. de Salis, pp. 66–67), "De plantandis vineis. Inter Burgundiones et Romanos id censuimus observandum: ut quicumque in communi campo nullo contradicente vineam fortasse plantaverit, similem campum illi restituat, in cuius campo vineam posuit. Si vero post interdictum quicumque in campo alterius vineam plantare praesumpserit, laborem suum perdat et vineam cuius est campus accipiat." Cf. LV10.1.6–7, ed. Zeumer, pp. 384–85.

111. LBExtravagans 21.12, ed. de Salis, p. 121, "De Romanis vero hoc ordinamus, ut non amplius a Burgundionibus, qui infra venerunt, requiratur, quam ad praesens necessitas fuerit: medietas terrae. Alia vero medietas cum integritate mancipiorum a Romanis teneatur, nec exinde ullam violentiam patiantur." See further, Goffart, *B&R*, pp. 132–33, 138.

112. Cf. LV10.1.16 (n. 91, above), where "tertia Romani" really means "the king's land"—the land whose taxes are paid by Romans to the royal fisc (rather than to individual *sors* holders). Durliat, "Salaire de la paix," p. 52, interprets *terra* as "terre" and *mancipia* as its inhabitants; in *Finances publiques*, p. 108, he understands the same terms as references to land and head taxes. Both are awkward solutions.

113. Or in the assessment registers, as I attempted to do in *B&R*, pp. 132–40 (completely superseded by the account given here).

114. LB55.5, ed. de Salis, p. 90, "Sane si quis eiusdem agri finibus, quem barbarus ex integro cum mancipiis publica largitione perceperit, fuerit contentio cepta, licebit ei, seu pulsatus fuerit, seu ipse pulsaverit, Romano iure contendere [If a dispute should arise concerning the limits of the same field which a barbarians obtained by public (i.e., royal) generosity, in its entirety with dependents, the same (barbarian) is allowed to contend by Roman law, regardless of whether he is sued or himself sues]." A comparison with LB55.2 (n. 52, above) illustrates the sharp distinction of "agri iure hospitalitatis" from "agri ex integro cum mancipiis publica largitione percepti."

115. See above at nn. 91, 112.

116. The difficult problem of *mancipia* is worked out in Appendix 3, The Meaning of *agri cum mancipiis* in the Burgundian Kingdom.

117. St. Jerome speaks, ca. 400, of *villa* as the correct translation for "oppidulum," "viculum," or "civitatulum": Jerome, *In Esaiam* 9. 1, *Patrologia Latina* 24:328C–D.

118. In the fifth-century documents from Vandal North Africa known as *Tablettes Albertini*, a hierarchy of terminology divides land broadly into *fundi* bearing a name (noted as administrative centers), then at the next level down into *loci* or *agri*, with a further step down to units of ownership divided among *cultores*. *Tablettes Albertini: Actes privés de l'époque vandale (fin du Vè siècle)*, ed. Christian Courtois et al. (Paris, 1952), p. 198. Dig. 50.16.60.2, states that a *fundus* had established boundaries (*fines*), whereas "locus vero latere potest quatenus determinetur et definietur." This sheds light on why a *fundus* is the subject of CE276 (n. 83, above). Much the same hierarchy of terms is visible in parts of Gaul documented by model charters (*formulae*): "illa viniola, plus menus iuctus tantus, et residit in terraturium sancti illius, in fundo illa villa." A sale; *Formulae Andegavenses* 4, ed. K. Zeumer, MG *Formulae* p. 6. The vineyard lies within a *fundus* bearing a name typically formed by a proper name (*ille*) followed by *villa*. Many

form charters illustrate that the unit of ownership lies within "places," "fundi," "villae," of merely administrative (not proprietary) significance; e.g., *Cartae Senonicae* 41, ed. Zeumer, p. 203 line 35: "in ipso pago in agro illo portione mea . . . quicquid in ipsa loca portio mea est."; *Formulae Arvernenses* 6, ed. Zeumer, p. 31: "manso nostro in pago Arvernico, in vico illo, in villa illa que de alode vel de atracto visi sum habere." These early medieval model charters repeatedly list properties as being *in loco nuncupante illo*, suggesting that *locus* refers to a hamlet or a comparable village-like locality—like *fundus* in being an administrative rather than a proprietary term. Longnon rightly observes that, in sixth-century evidence, *locus* is "the vaguest of the words used to designate an inhabited place." Auguste Longnon, *Géographie de la Gaule au VIè siècle* (Paris, 1878), p. 23. *Locus*, "place," is of course a very flexible term, with a broad spectrum of meanings. It cannot be pinned down as a fixed technical usage. See J. G. Niermeyer, *Mediae Latinitatis lexicon minus*, ss.vv. *locus, fundus*. To bear out how difficult it is to attain consistent usage, the word occurs in *Form. Visigothicae* nos. 36–37, ed. Zeumer. p. 591, as someone's possession ("in loco iuris vestri"). Niermeyer defines *fundus* as "finage, township"; French *finage* (i.e., the outer edge of a village or other territorial unit) can also be construed as "administrative district."

119. This interval can be imagined along the lines suggested by *nudus usus* discussed at n. 56, above.

120. LRB 17.5, ed. Johannes Baviera, FIRA 2 (Florence, 1968), p. 730. The additional laws have been cited at n. 110, above.

121. Barnish, "Taxation, Land," pp. 184–86.

122. In the main billeting law (CTh7.8.5) one-half is the preferential rate, reserved for persons of the highest rank.

123. For my earlier views on this subject, see *B&R*, pp. 143–45, and Appendix C, pp. 241–44.

124. LB84, ed. de Salis, pp. 106–7.

125. The sense of the law is better conveyed by a paraphrase than by my literal translation. 1. Anyone selling his "land" or allotment has to have "land" or an allotment elsewhere. 2. A *sors* may not be sold except to someone also in the allotment scheme (such as by a *faramannus* to another *faramannus*). 3. A Burgundian having "land" elsewhere and needing to sell, may sell what he has for sale to no other Roman than his "host" (i.e., the Roman in whose property the *sors* lies). No exception for (Roman) strangers is allowed. 4. A Roman host who buys from his Burgundian guest may do so only if he knows that the seller has "land" elsewhere.

126. LV10.1.8 (text at n. 89, above) suggests that "the Gothic two parts" could not be exchanged out of existence, but it does not forbid their redemption by sale to the owner (as in LB84).

127. See Jan-Olof Tjäder, ed., *Die nichtliterarischen lateinischen Papyri Italiens aus der Zeit 445–700*, vol. 2 (Stockholm, 1982): 68 lines 6–8 (no. 31 = Marini 115): parts of two *fundi* sold in 540 are warranted to be "Liberas autem inlibatas . . . ab omni nexu fisci, deviti populi pribative et ab here alieno, litibus, causis controversihisque omnibus necnon et a sorte barbari et a ratione [tutelaria sed et cure] et ab obligatione citerisque aliis titulis vel honeribus." For the same formulary without a reference to barbarian *sors*, see 2:108 lines 38–40 (no. 35 = Marini 120), "Liberas autem inlivatas ab omni nexu fiscali, debeti populi pribative ceterisque honeribus." For an effort to make constructive use of the Ravenna papyri, see Pohl, "Wirtschaftliche Grundlagen," pp. 202–17.

128. Normally, the assessed property (*professio*) yielding a tax value of, say, $3,000 has to be much larger than a leased property yielding a rental of the same amount.

129. LB1.1, ed. de Salis, p. 41, "decrevimus, ut patri etiam antequam dividat de communi facultate et de labore suo cuilibet donare liceat, absque terra sortis titulo adquisita, de qua prioris legis ordo servabitur." I take the *prioris legis ordo* to refer to LB78 ("De hereditatum successione"), which provides for the devolution of *sortes* and restricts their succession to males. The *sors* was expected to descend to male members of the family only, but an exception was made in favor of daughters in religion (whose childlessness ensured that the fraction given to her would revert to the family): LB14.5–7.

130. For the texts, see n. 110, above.

131. On the equivalence of *ius hospitalitatis* and *ius sortis*, see n. 54, above.

132. Procopius 4.14.8–10, ed. Dewing, 2:329–31.

133. Durliat, "Salaire de la paix," pp. 44–45.

134. For a Visigothic parallel, see n. 93, above.

135. Procopius is quoted at n. 144, below; for Cassiodorus, see n. 159, below.

136. *Variae* 10.29.4, ed. Mommsen, p. 316; see Goffart, "After the Zwettl Conference," pp. 84–85.

137. Goffart, "After the Zwettl Conference," p. 84.

138. Thomas A. Burns, "Ennodius and the Ostrogothic Settlement," *Classical Folia* 32 (1978): 153–58; none of the passages adduced, when correctly read, has anything to do with the Italian settlement. See Goffart, "After the Zwettl Conference," p. 83 n. 31.

139. For the passages of Paulinus, see my discussion in "After the Zwettl Conference," pp. 82–84. The reference to a Goth as buyer of property documents merely that he behaved like a Roman and invested in land. Nothing Paulinus says implies that the Gothic buyer had a prior association with the property he was buying.

140. Goffart, *B&R*, p. 245. The shelter Sidonius was giving to this "tentful" of (transient) Burgundian soldiers had no demonstrable or implicit consequences for Sidonius's extensive landed property; it cannot even be inferred that he was supplying their food.

141. The continuity of the West Roman government to 540 goes unmentioned by the authors who insist on identifying the end of West Rome with the overturn of a boy-usurper in 476. About this continuity, see Heather, "*Gens* and *Regnum* among the Ostrogoths," pp. 114–15.

142. On the Visigothic and Burgundian kingdoms, see Stein, *Histoire du Bas-Empire*, 1:382–86.

143. E.g., Cameron, *Procopius and the Sixth Century*, 205, "Goffart needs, for his own argument, to discredit the evidence of Procopius, but this is not the way to do it." I now realize that there is no need to discredit Procopius; the problem is to understand him correctly.

144. Procopius 5.1.3, 28, ed. Dewing, 3:3–5, 11–13. Note how Procopius telescopes the past, blotting out the earlier fifth century. It is also remarkable that his Odoacer is never said to be of barbarian origin. He is alone in this pointed omission.

145. Gildas, *The Ruin of Britain*, 23.5, ed. Michael Winterbottom (London, 1978), p. 97. Only generalities can be extracted from these lines (the Saxons will endure dangers on behalf of their hosts and receive "rations" in recompense; they are soon dissatisfied with their pay, want more, and help themselves). Exaggerated claims for this information are made by Herwig Wolfram, "Typen der Ethnogenese: Ein Versuch," in *Die Franken und die Alemannen bis zur "Schlacht bei Zülpich,"* ed. Dieter Geuenich,

Ergänzungsbänder zum Reallexikon der germanischen Altertumskunde 19 (Berlin, 1998), pp. 620.

146. Procopius 3.3.3, ed. Dewing, p. 2:13. His description puts one in mind of the rules of "occupancy" or "guestship." Schmidt, *Geschichte der Wandalen*, 23, calls Procopius "für jene Zeit sehr unzuverlässigen," and suggests that he transposed to Honorius with other alterations part of a law of Valentinian III (*NValent III* 35.12, a. 452). Needless to say, the Vandals did not have an "original home" at the Maeotian swamp or migrate from there; see Chapter 5 at n. 49. For the Vandal seizure of Roman property in North Africa, see n. 68, above. On what legal time limits involve, see at n. 86, above.

147. Procopius could find injustices aplenty in the Vandal seizure of lands in North Africa; his account of the "ruthless" property settlement in Italy may have been meant to suggest an otherwise improbable parallelism of Italy with Geiseric's kingdom. Procopius maintains that Theoderic committed only one injustice, namely, the execution of Symmachus and Boethius: Procopius 5.1.32–39, ed. Dewing, pp. 13–15. He may have needed to absolve him of responsibility for assigning one-third of Italy to the troops.

148. The *Copenhagen Continuator of Prosper*, an excellent Italian source for the period of Odoacer, says nothing about a cession of "land" (MG AA 9:309–13). Ennodius, *Vita s. Epiphanii*, 95–100, MG AA 7:96, has the downfall of Orestes accompanied by mutinous soldiers plundering houses, but no generalized award of "land." The discrepancy merits notice; Procopius's testimony is not above suspicion. Taking the opposite tack, Barnish, "Taxation, Land," p. 180, claims that the "propagandists" Ennodius and Cassiodorus suppressed any reference to Odoacer's part in the settlement. Either way, there is an oddity.

149. E.g., Barnish, "Taxation, Land," p. 174, "At best, Procopius can mean [*sic*] that they got a third only of such properties as were located in those areas [i.e., limited districts of the north and north-center]." Nothing justifies this high-handed emendation except Barnish's desire to bring Procopius into line with the verisimilitude he happens to favor.

150. It looks as though modern commentators, such as Barnish, have been influenced by the (now discredited) model of confiscatory billeting, which makes expropriation and division by one-third seem simple and deeply entrenched in law.

151. T. Rice Holmes, *The Architect of the Roman Empire* (Oxford, 1928), pp. 70, 81 (two of the eighteen cities were removed from the list), pp. 93–94; the settlements after Actium were less tumultuous, but by no means painless, 159–60. See also Ronald Syme, *The Roman Revolution* (Oxford, 1939), pp. 196, 207; Max Cary, *History of Rome*, p. 435; F. A. Rehrmann, *Kaiser Augustus* (Hildesheim, 1937), p. 265; Delbrück, *Barbarian Invasions*, 2:327.

152. An unintentionally humorous passage about Italy occurs when Barnish tries to show with much erudition why senatorial landowners in Italy, made wretched by their responsibilities, "acquiesced not too unhappily in a barbarian land-taking": Barnish, "Taxation, Land," pp. 175–76. The idea was foreshadowed in Delbrück, *Barbarian Invasions*, 2:324.

153. Cassiodorus, *Variae* 1.14; note also 2.17 (ed. Mommsen, pp. 22, 56). Commentary, Goffart, *B&R*, pp. 73–77.

154. Heather, "*Gens* and *Regnum* among the Ostrogoths," pp. 108, 113, claims to subscribe to my interpretation of *tertiae*. In fact, he distorts my views, confuses *tertiae* with the *illatio* arising from them, then tacitly blends in his own invention about annual

donatives. He also conjures up "the substantial imperial and other public lands" as a basis for land grants to Goths. Absolutely nothing supports this proposal (see n. 81, above), and *Variae* 2.17 (the award of a *sors* to Butila) contradicts it.

155. *Variae* 1.19, 4.14, and 5.14, ed. Mommsen, pp. 24–25, 120–21, 151–52.

156. Barnish, "Taxation, Land," p. 184, believes that *Variae* 2.16 "tells very strongly" against my interpretation.

157. See the possibility outlined in n. 148, above. PLRE, 2:676–81, indicates Liberius's astonishingly long period of public survice (from Odoacer's reign to the last decade of Justinian's).

158. Ennodius, *Epistolae* 9.23.5, MG AA 7.307.

159. *Variae* 2.16.5, ed. Mommsen, pp. 55–56 (trans. Jones, *Later Roman Empire*, p. 251): "Iuvat nos referre quemadmodum in tertiarum deputatione Gothorum Romanorumque et possessiones [Liberius PP] iunxit et animos. Nam cum se homines soleant de vicinitate collidere, istis praediorum communio causam videtur praestitisse concordiae: sic enim contigit, ut utraque natio, dum communiter vivit, ad unum velle convenerit. En factum novum et omnino laudabile: gratia dominorum de cespitis divisione coniuncta est; amicitiae populis per damna creverunt et parte agri defensor adquisitus est, ut substantiae securitas integra servaretur. Una lex illos et aequabilis disciplina complectitur. Necesse est enim, ut inter eos suavis crescat affectus, qui servant iugiter terminos constitutos." I do not subscribe to the translation of Durliat, "Cité, impôt et intégration des barbares," in *Kingdoms of the Empire*, p. 164. The comments of Cassiodorus about Liberius's praiseworthy management of state finances, "censum non addendo, sed conservandum" (2.16.4) comes before the account of the "tertiarum deputatio" and has nothing to do with it, though various authors have claimed otherwise.

160. Barnish, "Taxation, Land," pp. 180–81.

161. Jones, *Later Roman Empire*, p. 251.

162. MG AA 7:307, "illas innumeras Gothorum catervas *vix scientibus Romanis . . .* ditasti. nihil amplius victores cupiunt et *nulla senserunt damna superati*" (my emphasis). If the greater Roman landowners had a part in collecting taxes from the smaller, and in being able to pocket the fees allowed to tax collectors, the institution of Gothic *sortes* would have eliminated (or taken away) the "collectors' crumbs." This minor loss may be what is referred to by Cassiodorus and Ennodius.

163. See also Goffart, *B&R*, pp. 72–73.

164. *Variae* 8.26.4.

165. See at n. 144, above. The lack of independent confirmation for Procopius's account of the mutiny and Odoacer does not detract from the basic situation of troops demanding to exchange "pay and rations" for an enduring entitlement, detached from the pleasure of the government. If the mutineers had known the vocabulary of the future, they might have said that they wished to stop being paid soldiers and become beneficed knights.

166. *Variae* 5.27.1, ed. Mommsen, p. 159: "eos qui annis singulis nostrae mansuetudinis praemia consequuntur," and 8.26.4, p. 257, "vos et sortes alant propriae"

167. Goffart, *B&R*, pp. 80–88; also, at some length, "After the Zwettl Conference," pp. 79–81. For the use of tax units to signify proceeds and not just assessments, see Goffart, "From Roman Taxation to Mediaeval Seigneurie," in *Rome's Fall and After*, pp. 167–77. Favorable reception, Barnish, "Taxation, Land," p. 183; John Moorhead, *Theoderic in Italy*, p. 34.

168. My discussion of this text in "After the Zwettl Conference," pp. 81–83, is superseded by my comments here.

169. *Variae* 2.17, ed. Mommsen, p. 56: "Honoratis possessoribus defensoribus et curialibus Tridentinae civitatis Theodericus rex. Munificentiam nostram nulli volumus extare damnosam, ne quod alteri tribuitur, alterius dispendiis applicetur. Et ideo praesenti auctoritate cognoscite, pro sorte quam Butilani presbytero nostra largitate contulimus, nullum debere persolvere fiscalis calculi functionem, sed in praestatione quanti se solidi comprehendunt, de tertiarum illationibus vobis noveritis esse relevandos. Nec inferri a quoquam volumus, quod alteri nostra humanitate remisimus, ne, quod dictu nefas est, bene meriti munus innocentis contigat esse dispendium." A word of caution to close readers: *damnosam* in 2.17 and *damna* in 2.16 do not signify the same thing, nor do they have to do so. "Damage" is a common concept; there is no call for making it restrictive here. In 2.17, Theoderic simply says, I do not wish the award to Butila to cause you (the tax commissioners) loss (*dispendium*) and, accordingly, give you compensation. The uncompensated *damna* of 2.16, however, are expected to be enduring.

170. See also above, at n. 81. The case of the Alans receiving *deserta rura* (n. 40, above) does not help unless interpreted in a biased way.

171. See at n. 34, above.

172. *Variae* 1.19; 2.26, 38; 5.16; 9.11, ed. Mommsen, pp. 24–25, 61, 67, 152–53, 276–77.

173. Durliat, "Salaire de la paix," pp. 30–31. Nevertheless, I differ very much from Durliat's interpretation of the Butila letter; see "Salaire de la paix," pp. 63–64.

174. Typically, Cassiodorus's appointment formula for a *defensor civitatis* emphasizes conversion scales of goods to money: *Variae* 7.11.2, ed. Mommsen, p. 209.

175. *Variae* 2.37, 11.35.3, 36.4, 37.4, 38.6, cf. 33, ed. Mommsen, pp. 67, 348–52.

176. *B&R*, p. 87; I point out there that the beneficiary (i.e., Goth) received "the tax contribution of the land, in whatever form it had customarily been paid," and I add (p. 88) that the sources leave us guessing about "precisely what kind of revenue [the beneficiary] derived from" his allotment. Both comments still apply; but I have tried here to be more specific. In "After the Zwettl Conference," p. 74, I modified my model in the light of Durliat's teaching; I accepted his belief that, even after barbarian allotments, the local authorities continued to act as intermediaries between taxpayers and beneficiaries. I now withdraw this concession and return to my earlier opinion: Goths and Burgundians obtained personal taxpayers, as in the "New Haven model" that I shall outline.

177. The analogy also helps to show that the three Roman categories of cultivation (physical possession of the soil or house), ownership, and assessment have clear-cut equivalents today, as spelled out in n. 38, above.

178. I am very grateful to Josh Chafetz (DPhil., Oxon.), degree candidate at Yale Law School and graduate affiliate of Berkeley College, for expert help with these lines.

179. Claude, review in *Francia* 10 (1982): 754.

180. See n. 84, above.

181. The highly regarded historian J. C. Gatterer († 1799; see Chapter 1, nn. 9, 16) illustrates a naive vision of the Great Migration as a German conquest: *Handbuch der Universalhistorie* (Göttingen, 1765), p. 68; *Einleitung in die synchronistische Universalhistorie zur Erläuterung seiner synchronistischere Tabellen* (Göttingen, 1771), pp. 463, 629; *Versuch einer allgemeinen Weltgeschichte bis zur Entdeckung Amerikens* (Göttingen, 1792), p. 428. The matter is clearly put by F. C. Savigny, *Geschichte der römischen Rechts im Mittelalter* (Heidelberg, 1815), 1:254, "Gleich bey der Eroberung war das Land zwischen den Burgundern und Römern getheilt worden" (trans. E. Cathcard [Edinburgh, 1829], 1:279).

182. *Francia* 10 (1982): 754; my translation.

183. Pohl, "Wirtschaftliche Grundlagen," pp. 216–17. The letters of Cassiodorus as praetorian prefect (*Variae* 10–12) are particularly revealing of the central management of tax revenues.

184. The most eloquent texts are two extensive reform "capitularies" of Theoderic: *Variae* 5.14, 39, ed. Mommsen, pp. 150–51, 164–66; see also *Variae* 9.10–11, 15.

185. *Variae* 9.10.3, 12.2; 11.7, 8; 12.2, ed. Mommsen, pp. 276, 277, 336–39, 360–61. There is much else in this letter collection implying the expectation of a fixed tax rate.

186. The new breed, unlike the old, had a personal military obligation to the government.

187. Appendix 2, nos. 2, 3.

188. On the senators, see Appendix 2, n. 4.

189. Gaupp, *Ansiedlungen*, pp. 197–201.

190. See nn. 40 and 68, above.

191. Goffart, *B&R*, pp. 93–99, 164–65.

192. The passage is particularly striking for the heavy irony of "hostilitatis," an evident transformation of "hospitalitatis." The passage tells us that, by judicious applications of force, the Goths had been able to parlay their heavily restricted "agri iure hospitalitatis" into a large increase in their power over the properties in the locality.

193. Wolfram, "Neglected Evidence," p. 182, unaware that this text was by no means "neglected" as far back as 1980, also misses the point that the *iura et iugera* of a Roman are going to be lost "inexpectata iuris dispectione," not to a lawful award. The barbarian's "guestship," which he lawfully has, is his springboard to an abuse.

194. On Theodahad's greed, see Procopius 7.8.21, ed. Dewing 4:219; on Gothic injustice, 7.21.6, ed. Dewing, 4:337. Procopius adverts to the Goths' "[eagerness] to wrong their subjects" and as a result their wishing to be ruled "more after the barbarian fashion" (during Amalasuintha's reign): 5.2.8, ed. Dewing, 3:17. For Theodahad being called to account by Theoderic, see *Variae* 4.39, 5.12, ed. Mommsen, pp. 131–32, 149–50.

195. As samples of continuing "oppression" by Romans in Ostrogothic Italy, see *Variae* 2.25, 3.20, 4.9, 5.14, ed. Mommsen, pp. 60, 89–90, 118, 150–51.

196. Salvian, *De gubernatione Dei*, 5.38–46, ed. Lagarrigue, 1:340–47; this is just a sample, especially oriented to taxation as a means for *potentes* to oppress the poor. Augustine of Hippo, *Sermo* 75.2, *Patrologia Latina* 38:1890. The hagiographer of the Jura fathers is no less eloquent about another example (*B&R*, p. 98 with n. 78).

197. *Historiae* 8.39, ed. Krusch-Levison, p. 405. In context, Badegisel's reference to "vengeance" should probably be understood to mean legal proceedings and not self help.

Chapter 7

1. The *locus classicus* for the meaning of "German" in late antiquity occurs in St. Jerome's *Vita s. Hilarionis* 22, *Patrologia Latina*, 23:39: "[provincia] inter Saxones quippe et Alemanos . . . apud historicos Germania, nunc Francia vocatur." For a fuller account, see André Chastagnol, "La signification géographique et ethnique des mots *Germani* et *Germania* dans les sources latines," *Ktèma: Civilisations de l'Orient, de la Grèce et de Rome antique* 9 (1984): 97–101. He confirms (p. 101) that *barbari*, often in a neutral sense,

was the standard collective term in late Roman use. Another useful account of "German" (down to Tacitus) is Henry H. Howorth, "The Germans of Caesar," *English Historical Review* 23 (1908): 417–26. Walter Pohl attests that, since late antiquity, "German" was a little used archaism: "Paolo Diacono e la costruzione dell'identità longobarda," in *Paolo Diacono: Uno scrittore fra tradizione longobarda e rinovamento carolingio,* ed. Paolo Chiesa (Udine, 2000), p. 419.

2. Goffart, *Rome's Fall and After*, pp. 4–5 and the works cited there. It is characteristic of the carelessness of current usage that Chastagnol, "Signification géographique," p. 101, casually injects the French word "Germains" in its anachronistic modern meaning of "all Germanic peoples as now defined."

3. On diversity, see Chapter 3, n. 5.

4. For the use of this expression by Mommsen, see Chapter 1, at n. 12, above. This convenient term is too often used synonymously with "Germanization," which injects not only an anachronism but also a false solidarity into the process. As said below, I speak of a "social militarization" of late antiquity rather than the inappropriate "Germanization." Many more native Romans than barbarians were involved in "social militarization."

5. C. R. Whittaker, *Frontiers of the Roman Empire: A Social and Economic Study* (Baltimore, 1994), has shed much light on this subject.

6. See the quotations by Averil Cameron, in Chapter 5, at n. 180, above.

7. Goffart, *Rome's Fall and After*, pp. 7–8, 111–12.

8. Ibid., pp. 8–9; Cary, *History of Rome*, pp. 614–16.

9. On this well-known crisis and recovery, see, e.g., *Cambridge Ancient History*, 12: chs. 2, 5, 6, 9, 11. Also the works cited in Chapter 2, nn. 26, 30, above. Current scholars minimize or at least limit the extent of this crisis; see Kulikowski, *Late Roman Spain*, pp. 16, 66–69 with nn. 10–11, p. 335.

10. For a strangely exaggerated view of this subject, see Glen W. Bowersock, "The Dissolution of the Roman Empire," in *Selected Papers on Late Antiquity* (Bari, 2000), p. 181.

11. For this entire development, see Alexander Demandt, "Spätrömische Militäradel," pp. 610–11. Vetranio (emperor, 350) is the extreme case of an illiterate general, elevated to the emperorship in an emergency; see PLRE 1:954.

12. Mann, "Frontiers of the Principate," p. 515, reports the little known fact that, for reasons of climatic adaptation, the eastern legions (of the Principate) were recruited in the East from non-Romans, mainly Galatians. Historians have long made a habit of calling barbarians in Roman service "mercenaries," as though being paid differentiated them from home recruited troops. For as long as anyone could remember, however, Roman soldiers had been paid, long-service professionals, no less "mercenary" than barbarians.

13. The directive about recruitment is spelled out in Vegetius, *Epitoma rei militari* 1.2–3, ed. A. Önnerfors, pp. 9–13. About Maximinus, *Historia Augusta, Maximini duo* 2–3, ed. Ernest Hohl, 2:3–5; Jordanes, *Getica* 83–86, ed. Mommsen, pp. 78–80.

14. *Cambridge Ancient History*, 12:4, 24.

15. Carrié, "L'État à la recherche de nouveaux modes de financement," p. 50. Carrié speaks of Rome engaging in "une barbarisation à outrance de son instrument de guerre" (p. 59). For details, see Dietrich Hoffmann, *Das spätrömische Bewegungsheer und die Notitia Dignitatum.* Epigraphische Studien 7 (Düsseldorf, 1969), pp. 135–45.

16. For an introduction, see Patrick Wormald, "The Decline of the Western Empire and the Survival of Its Aristocracy," *Journal of Roman Studies* 66 (1976): 217–26 (note particularly pp. 224–26, on the limits of survival); and S. J. B. Barnish. "Transformation and

Survival in the Western Senatorial Aristocracy, *c.* A.D. 400–700," *Papers of the British School at Rome* 56 (1988): 120–55. Neither of these estimable studies takes note of the existence of a distinct military aristocracy.

17. Demandt, "Spätrömische Militäradel."

18. Early enrollment also for young members of barbarian royal houses: ibid., p. 619; PLRE 1:408.

19. Stroheker, "Heermeister fränkischer Abstammung," pp. 11–12. In Roman practice, the two "ordinary" consuls gave their names to the year in which they served; the name-giving consulate was considered to be the loftiest distinction a Roman might receive. The first Frank so honored was Nevitta, by the emperor Julian, in 362 (Chapter 3, n. 57, above).

20. See at nn. 33, 73, below.

21. On Symmachus and Libanius courting Frankish generals, see Stroheker, "Heermeister fränkischer Abstammung," p. 27. Clovis, while still a pagan, was greeted in flattering terms by Bishop Remigius of Reims: *Epistolae Austrasicae* 2, ed. W. Gundlach, in Corpus Christianorum Series Latina 117:408–9.

22. This tradition of openness is nicely summarized in Alexander Demandt, "The Osmosis of Late Roman and Germanic Aristocracies," in *Das Reich und die Barbaren*, pp. 75–76. See also Aurelius Victor, *Caesares* 11.13, ed. Pichlmayr, p. 90, "Ac mihi quidem audienti multa legentique plane compertum urbem Roman externorum virtute atque insitivis artibus praecipue crevisse."

23. Goffart, *B&R*, pp. 4–12. For the allegation of growing barbarian power, see Chapter 2, pp. 26–32, above.

24. Goffart, *B&R*, p. 35. As a casual example of the ample attention paid to this comment, see *The Spectator* (London, August 27, 2005), p. 30.

25. F. M. Clover. "Carthage and the Vandals," and "The Symbiosis of Romans and Vandals in Africa," in his *The Late Roman West and the Vandals* (Aldershot, 1993), chapters 6 and 10. Procopius 3.16.3 (Belisarius counts on defections from the Vandals), 17.6, 20.1, 18–20 (but note also 23.4), 25.3–5, ed. Dewing, pp. 143, 151, 169–71, 175–77.

26. Procopius 7.1.28–33, 4.16–17, 7.6–14, 16.17–21, 18.20–23, 21.12–24, ed. Dewing, 4:159–61, 185–87, 223–25, 287–89, 309, 337–41. It is hard to improve on his testimony.

27. Gildas, *De excidio Britonum* 4 (Britons before Rome), 5–7, 14 (Roman conquest and withdrawal), 18 (final Roman disengagement), ed. and trans. Michael Winterbottom (London, 1978), pp. 90–91, 93, 94. On Gildas's date, see the literature cited in Goffart, *Narrators*, p. 169 n. 252. By contrast, Gregory of Tours disregards pre-Roman Gaul and touches on Roman Gaul perfunctorily (almost wholly in its Christian dimension).

28. Demandt, "Osmosis of Aristocracies," p. 80. See also Alexander Demandt, art., "Magister militum," in Pauly-Wissowa, Supplement 12: 553–790, and "Spätrömische Militäradel," above. These are the fundamental works on this subject.

29. Demandt, "Osmosis of Aristocracies," pp. 80, 84 (the two quotations).

30. For the details, see Timothy D. Barnes, *The New Empire of Diocletian and Constantine* (Cambridge, Mass., 1982), pp. 4, 6, 8, 12–13; the six include Maxentius and Maximian, classed as usurpers.

31. Stein, *Histoire du Bas-Empire*, 1:131–32; PLRE 1:241 (Dalmatius 7), 407 (Hannibalianus 2). The troops massacred the many collateral heirs (only two excepted) before the succession was finalized. Within three years, the killing of Constantine II narrowed the emperors to the sole sons of Constantine by Fausta.

32. Demandt, "Osmosis of Aristocracies," p. 84.

33. Stein, *Histoire du Bas-Empire*, 1:253–54 (Stilicho), 321–22 (Boniface), 348 (Aetius), 349 (Valentinian III), 391 (Marcellinus), 361 (Aspar), 363 (Basiliscus); Recitach, PLRE 2:936; Odoacer, PLRE 2:793; Vitalian, PLRE 2:1176.

34. Demandt, "Osmosis of Aristocracies," p. 84 (both quotations).

35. For the quotation, see Introduction, n. 2, above.

36. The marriage of Valentinian I to Judith, widow of the usurper Magnentius, is a case in point; see PLRE 1:934, 488–89 (Iustina). The fiction of Socrates, *Historia ecclesiastica* 4.31, is thought-provoking.

37. Gregory of Tours, *Historiae* 4.25, 9.26, ed. Krusch-Levison, pp. 156–57, 445. On "mixed" marriages by Merovingian princesses (to pagans or Arians), see Goffart, *Narrators*, p. 214 with n. 443.

38. Goffart, *Narrators*, p. 184 with n. 306.

39. The Frankish king, Chilperic, reputedly responsible for the murder of his Visigothic wife, was able nevertheless to arrange a Visigothic marriage for one of his daughters: Gregory of Tours, *Historiae* 6.18, 34, 45, 7.9, ed. Krusch-Levison, pp. 287–88, 304–5, 317–19, 331.

40. Demandt, "Spätrömische Militäradel," p. 627.

41. See Chapter 3, n. 15 above.

42. Demandt, "Spätrömische Militäradel," p. 622: "im Westen die hohen Offiziere, das Kaiserhaus und die Germanenkönige durch fortgesetzte Verschwägerung ein engmaschiges Geflecht einer militärisch-politischen Führungsschicht bilden."

43. These three personages are in the twelfth-century vernacular *Kaiserchronik: Der keiser und die kunige buoch oder der sogenannte Kaiserchronik*, lines 13843–14212, ed. Hans F. Massman, 3 vols. (Quedlinburg and Leipzig, 1849–54), 2:311–35.

44. On the British situation, see Gildas, *De excidio* 14 (Picts and Irish), 23.1–3 (Saxons), ed. Winterbottom, pp. 93, 97. The disaster of Nechtansmere (685) was a milestone in Northumbrian history (on its reverberations, see Goffart, *Narrators*, pp. 262, 269, 288, 320–21); it dramatizes a conflict in which the (Anglo-Saxon) Northumbrians were carrying on the Roman role of defending northern Britain.

45. Hermann Dessau, *Inscriptiones Latinae selectae*, 3 vols. in 5 (reprinted, Chicago, 1979), 3/1:281, 284, 294, 303, 304, 305, 307, 308, 310, 311; "Sarmaticus," in Pauly-Wissowa, Supplement 2, 2/1 (Stuttgart, 1921): 15–23.

46. Galerius alone (among the Tetrarchs) took credit for six victories over the Carpi: Barnes, *New Empire*, p. 256. On victory titles, Barnes, p. 27.

47. The comment of Demandt, cited Chapter 2, n. 3, above, is typical.

48. Heather, "Huns and the End," is a worthy effort to emphasize the role of the Huns.

49. Beatus Rhenanus, *Rerum Germanicarum libri tres*, pp. 21–77; Zeuss, *Die Deutschen* (Munich, 1837).

50. See Introduction, nn. 6–8 and Chapter 3, n. 37, above; for Pohl, Chapter 3, at n. 22.

51. See Introduction, at nn. 24–33.

52. For the "core Migration Age," see Chapter 1. For a good example of an unavoidably conjecture-rich span of Migration Age history, see Chapter 5, pp. 96–100, above.

53. Isidore, *Etymologiae* 9.2.92, ed. W. M. Lindsay, 2 vols. (Oxford, 1911), 1.unpaged: "Gipedes pedestri proelio magis quam equestre sunt usi, ex hac causa vocati."

54. Jordanes, *Getica* 94–95, trans. C. C. Mierow (Princeton, 1915), p. 78. The great Karl Müllenhoff indignantly denied than any German word cognate to *gepanta* meant what Jordanes claimed it did; cited in Jordanes, ed. Mommsen, p. 160, s.v. "Gepidae."

55. *Etymologicum magnum* 230, cited by Walter Pohl, "Gepiden, Historisches" in *Hoops Reallexikon* (Berlin, 1998), 11:131. The fullest recent account of the Gepids (and many others besides) is Walter Pohl, "Die Gepiden und die Gentes an der mittleren Donau," in *Die Völker an der mittleren und unteren Donau im 5. und 6. Jahrhundert*, ed. H. Wolfram and F. Daim (Vienna, 1980), pp. 240–72.

56. Procopius 3.2.2–5, ed. Dewing, 2:9–11. This classification was not Procopius's invention. It is found in whole or in part in contemporary Byzantine writings; see Walter Goffart, "The Supposedly 'Frankish' Table of Nations: An Edition and Study," [*Frühmittelalterliche Studien* 17 (1983): 98–130] in *Rome's Fall and After*, pp. 155–57.

57. Pohl, "Gepiden, Historisches," p. 131, finds proof of the family relationship in the incident involving Totila's death at the hands of a Gepid (in Roman service) told by Procopius 8.32.22–24, ed. Dewing, 5:383. But the context is social, not ethnic. Totila's words simply mean "You vile slave, how dare you kill a king?" (Totila was dressed as a private soldier.)

58. I do not subscribe to the idenfication of the Gepids with the Gifðas or Gefþas of the Old English *Beowulf* (line 2495) and *Widsith* (line 60). See *Widsith*, ed. Kemp Malone, Anglistica 13 (Copenhagen, 1962), p. 153; Rudolf Much, "Gepiden," in Johannes Hoops, ed., *Reallexikon der germanischen Altertumskunde*, 1st ed. (Strasbourg, 1913–15), 2:157–58; K. Malone, "The Suffix of Appurtenance in *Widsith*," *Modern Language Review* 28 (1933): 315–19 (presupposes the identification). No serious arguments substantiating the identification seem to me to have been set out.

59. Jordanes, *Getica* 94–100, ed. Mommsen, pp. 82–83 (Jordanes makes certain that we notice the unseparated condition of the Goths). Although the resemblance is not completely obvious, the story of the ships and Fastida is basically a doublet of the Gothic migration legend, with the victory over the Burgundians standing in for the Gothic victory over the Vandals. Rudolf Much, "Gepiden," realized what chronological difficulties Jordanes was in when invoking Fastida; so, without notice, he altered Jordanes, so as to make his account more plausible.

60. Jordanes, *Getica* 133 (Arianism), 200 (fighting kinsmen), ed. Mommsen, pp. 92, 110.

61. The Vandals and Italian Goths were destroyed; on the expected demise of the Visigoths, see Chapter 4, n. 57. Jordanes, *Romana* 386, ed. Mommsen, p. 52, records a major victory by the Lombard allies of "the Roman realm" over the Gepid "enemies"; the victory is normally dated 552. A Gepid-free future beckoned. An alternative title for the *Getica* might well be "De mortibus Gothorum."

62. Salvian, *De gubernatione Dei* 4.68, ed. Lagarrigue, 1:290 (Hun and Gepid linked); Attila as a "Gepid Hun" in the *Chronicon Paschale*, trans. M. and M. Whitby, Translated Texts for Historians 7 (Liverpool, 1989), p. 77, and as a Gepid in John Malalas, *Chronicle* 14.10, trans. E. Jeffreys, p. 195. Along the same lines, Pohl, "Gepiden, Historisches," p. 134. On Ardaric and the Huns, see Thompson, *History of Attila*, p. 166. Note also the Gepid incursion into Gaul, Chapter 5, n. 155, above. Jesse L. Byock, trans., *The Saga of the Volsungs* (Harmondsworth, 1990), p. 12, points out that "the Icelandic saga audience" in the thirteenth century disregarded "the ethnic difference between the Huns

and the Germanic tribesmen." Long, long before, the Byzantines did so too. The real question is who *started* to notice the differences.

63. Gepidia: Jordanes, *Getica* 74, ed. Mommsen, p. 75; other localizations, *Getica* 33, 113, 264, pp. 62, 87, 126.

64. Jordanes, *Getica* 264, ed. Mommsen, p. 126.

65. Frank E. Wozniak, "Byzantine Diplomacy and the Lombard-Gepidic Wars," *Balkan Studies* 20 (1978): 139–58, is an excellent account of this period of Gepid history. His decision to regard the Byzantines as moral superiors to their barbarian helpers seems unjustified.

66. The "Valamer" Goths, named after their paramount leader, are the former Gothic auxiliaries of Attila, the branch that spawned Theoderic, the future ruler of Italy. Jordanes's battle between Fastida the Gepid and Ostrogotha the Goth (n. 55, above) is reminiscent of Theoderic's victory over Thraustila.

67. The importance of Sirmium and related matters are ably discussed by Frank E. Wozniak, "East Rome, Ravenna and Western Illyricum: 454–536 A.D.," *Historia: Zeitschrift für alte Geschichte* 30 (1981): 351–82.

68. Marcellinus Comes, a. 539 no. 6, ed. Brian Croke, Byzantina Australiensia 7 (Sydney, 1995), p. 48; the fame of this battle is echoed by Jordanes, *Romana* 387, ed. Mommsen, p. 52.

69. Stein, *Histoire du Bas-Empire*, 2:530–35.

70. There is an irreconcilable discrepancy between the familiar story according to which Rosimund became Alboin's wife after the climactic battle, as war booty, and the (earlier) Byzantine version of Theophylact Simocatta, according to which "Albuis" fell in love with Cunimund's unnamed daughter and "in a surprise attack snatched the maiden. From this the war took its origins" (6.10.8–9, trans. M. and M. Whitby [Oxford, 1996], p. 174).

71. On Cunimund, see PLRE 3:364; Theophylact Simocatta, trans. Whitby, pp. 174–75.

72. Theophylact Simocatta, trans. Whitby, p. 23, n. 18.

73. *Excerpta Valesiana, pars posterior*, 55–56, ed. J. Moreau, p. 16; Procopius 5.1.24–25, ed. Dewing, 3:11; PLRE 2:791–93.

74. Faithful to German informants, Demougeot, *Formation de l'Europe*, 1:349, 377, extracts the Sciri together with the Bastarnae out of the north and calls them "les premiers émigrants germaniques." These widely shared fantasies of ancient migration out of the north have no basis in evidence.

75. Herrmann, ed., *Quellen zur Frühgeschichte*, 4:410–11.

76. Ibid., 1:328, 567 (commentary). The Sciri are listed in company with the Sarmatians and Venedi as being to the east of the Vistula.

77. *Laterculus Veronensis* 13.32, ed. Seeck (cited Chapter 3, n. 5, above), p. 252. For the date of the list, ibid.

78. Trans. Ridley, p. 86.

79. CTh 5.6.3 (*Codex Theodosianus*, ed. Mommsen, pp. 221–22). For the circumstances, Heather, "Huns and the End," pp. 14–15.

80. Ed. Anderson, 1:146.

81. Ed. Mommsen, p. 126.

82. Ed. Mommsen, p. 129; quotation, trans. Mierow, p. 131.

83. Blockley, *Fragmentary Classicising Historians*, 2: 353.

84. Ed. Mommsen, pp. 129–30.

85. Blockley, *Fragmentary Classicising Historians*, 2: 373.

86. Ed. Dewing, 3:3. For the generic sense of "Goth" in Procopius, see at n. 56, above.

87. Jordanes, ed. Mommsen, pp. 44 (Odoacer called a Rugian), 170. *Excerpta Valesiana*, ed. Moreau, p. 11, "superveniens autem Odoacer cum gente Scirorum."

88. On Odoacer, see PLRE 2:791–93. Odoacer's presence in Gaul is probably a case of mistaken identity. Demandt, "Osmosis of the Aristocracies," pp. 81–82, subscribes to the idea that there was a third brother, Armatus. This, too, is controversial, and I stand clear of the argument. Conceivably, Edeco was a Scirian with a Hunnic name (Sciri were cooperating with Huns as early as 408).

89. M. Taylor, "Heruler," in *Hoops Reallexikon* (Berlin, 1999), 14:470–73, summarizes scholarly problems and emphasizes contrary opinions (e.g., about there being two peoples).

90. Jordanes, *Getica* 118, ed. Mommsen, p. 88, "Gens quantum velox, eo amplius superbissima [a people swift of foot, and on that account more swollen with pride]. nulla siquidem erat tunc gens, quae non levem armaturam in acie sua ex ipsis elegeret." Procopius confirms this characterization (2.25.27–28, ed. Dewing, 1:487), but also specifies that the three thousand who accompanied Narses against Totila were mounted (8.26.13, ed. Dewing, 5:331).

91. The unusually numerous proper names of Herules reported by Procopius include: Aluith, Aordus, Arufus, Datius, Grepes, Fulcaris, Ochus, Phaniteus, Pharas, Philemuth, Sinduald, Suartas, Uligagus, Visandus. Note also Audonoballus and Naulobatus: Schmidt, *Ostgermanen*, p. 215; and Alaric in Procopius (not *the* Alaric). Some of them are definitely Germanic (e.g., Alaric, Aluith, Fulcaris, Sinduald).

92. Taylor, "Heruler," p. 472, makes this admirably clear. For the traditional view, e.g., Schmidt, *Ostgermanen*, p. 553, "die nordische Heimat."

93. Schmidt, *Ostgermanen*, pp. 558–59; Williams, *Diocletian and the Roman Recovery*, pp. 25, 46. These would be the same Herules who appear alongside the Saxons in the Verona List 13.6–7 (not Müllenhoff's reshuffling); ed. Seeck, p. 251. The earliest barbarian known to have been awarded Roman consular insignias was a Herule, presumably from the same people that supplied the troops: Demandt, "Spätrömische Militäradel," p. 610. Ennodius, *Vita s. Antonii* 13, MG AA 7:187, in a late fifth-century setting, groups Franks, Herules, and Saxons together as engaging in human sacrifice; the incident makes the Herules northwesterners by association.

94. Hydatius, *Chronicle* 171 (allegedly 400 strong), 194, ed. Tranoy, pp. 152, 162; in both cases they struck at the northern coast, as though they had been blown off course rather than were carrying out a planned raid. Sidonius, *Epistolae* 8.9.31–32, ed. Anderson, 2:446; Sidonius describes him as "haunt[ing] the uttermost retreats of Ocean"—not suitable for the Danube.

95. Cassiodorus, *Variae* 3.3, 4.2, ed. Mommsen, pp. 79–80, 114–15; *Variae* 4.45, about Herule suppliants, presumably relates to northwesterners too. Taylor, "Heruler," p. 471, is right that Theoderic's letter might have been sent to the Danube Herules; but since the latter had been prominent among Odoacer's troops, cordial relations with Theoderic cannot be taken for granted. Jordanes's report (*Getica* 24, ed. Mommsen, p. 60) of a Scandinavian king Rodulf fleeing to Theoderic has to be heavily interpreted before it means anything. Stein, *Histoire du Bas-Empire* 2:150, like Schmidt, *Ostgermanen*, p. 552

(and other German scholarship without hesitation), asserts that Theoderic made the Danubian Herule Rudolf his son-in-arms, but *Variae* 4.2 is anonymous ("regi Herulorum"); the addressee could be just as western as that of *Variae* 3.3. The unhesitating identification of *Variae* 4.2 with Rudolf should stop. There is no unequivocal evidence for relations between Theoderic and the Danubian Herules. Adoption by arms was probably a second-best to marriage (which these Herules were too minor to warrant). The evidence about western Herules does not contain a single named person (unless Jordanes's Rodulf fits there).

96. Jordanes, *Getica* 23, ed. Mommsen, p. 59.

97. Unstable rascals, Procopius 6.14.36, 41, ed. Dewing, 3:413. The special relationship, 6.18.6, 22.5, 7.13.21–22, 8.26.16–17, ed. Dewing, 4:21, 57–59, 261, 333. Procopius's Herule digression begins immediately after a report that two thousand of them had joined Narses's first Italian expeditionary force, as though as a comment on this report (6.13.18, ed. Dewing, 3:403). Cameron, *Procopius,* p. 201, Narses, "a man whose ability he is forced to admit but who would for him always be the wrong choice [to conquer Italy]."

98. Schmidt, *Ostgermanen,* pp. 549–50.

99. The catalogues: Sidonius, *Carmina* 7.320–25, ed. Anderson, 1:146. Revolt and settlement, Jordanes, *Getica* 261, Mommsen, p. 125. Procopius 6.14.23, 15.1, ed. Dewing, 3:409, 415.

100. *Vita s. Severini* 24.3, ed. Saupe, p. 20. Herules carry out a raid on a town about twenty miles from Passau, hanging the local priest from a cross. Passau is far west from the presumed Herule stamping ground. The implied chronology of the *Vita Severini* suggests pre-476.

101. *Auctarium Havniensis ordo prior,* a. 476 no. 2, "Eruli, qui Romano iuri suberant": MG AA 9:309, also 313; Ennodius, *Panegyricus dictus Theoderico* 53, MG AA 7:209.

102. Fredegar, *Chronicon* 2.57, ed. Krusch, MG SRM 2:79. Earlier reports of this desperate attack are in MG AA 9:318, 319, 11:159.

103. Procopius 6.14.10–22, ed. Dewing, 3:405–9 (this prolonged account has nothing in common with factual reporting). It may not be an exaggeration to say that any account of the Herules is mainly a study of Procopius's engagement with them. Paul the Deacon, *Historia Langobardorum* 1.20, MG SRL pp. 57–59, includes a remark on the Herules' vaunted military valor.

104. Procopius 6.14.24–25, ed. Dewing, 3:409–11. Contrary to what is sometimes said (e.g., Schmidt, *Ostgermanen,* p. 503), the land of the Rugians to which Procopius has them momentarily withdraw is not the Rugian territory known from the *Vita S. Severini,* but the lands downstream (in Moesia or Dacia?) to which fled the survivors from the Rugian defeat of 488.

105. Marcellinus Comes, a. 512, ed. Croke, p. 37. Croke (p. 117) infers from the text that Marcellinus disapproved of this settlement; he may be right. Stein, *Histoire du Bas-Empire,* 2:156, 305. Anastasius acquired Bassiana from the Ostrogoths ca. 510 and probably settled the Herules there.

106. Procopius 6.14.20–22, 27–28, 30–32, ed. Dewing, 3:409, 411.

107. Malalas, *Chronicle* 18.6, trans. Jeffreys, p. 247; Stein, *Histoire du Bas-Empire,* 2:305. This hint of a stately monarchical regime is the fleeting high point of Herule domestic history. Procopius 6.14.34, ed. Dewing, 3:411–13, intimates that Justinian brought about the conversion of all the Herules for the first time (necessarily to Orthodox Christianity); he also reports, 4.14.12, ed. Dewing, 2:331, that the Herules in the army

of Africa were Arian Christians (ca. 534). Arian Herules implies the presence of "Gothic" (i.e., culturally Gothic) clergy. There are various, speculative ways of reconciling this discrepancy. Nothing is easy where the Herules are concerned.

108. Persia (Procopius 1.24.41, 2.21.4, 24.12, 14, 18, 25.20–26, ed. Dewing, 1:233, 441, 477, 479, 485–87), Africa (3.11.11, 14.12, ed. Dewing 2:105, 129, also below), Italy (6.4.8, 13.18, 18.6, 22.5–8, 7.1.34–35, 34.42–43, ed. Dewing 3:321, 403, 4:21, 56–59, 163, 457), Thrace (7.13.25, ed. Dewing 4: 261–63); other theaters and at the Nika rebellion, see Schmidt, *Ostgermanen*, p. 556. Herule infantry: 2.25.27–28, ed. Dewing 1:487. Capture of Gelimer and praise of Pharas: 4.4.29–31, ed. Dewing 2:243.

109. Casualties, Procopius 7.1.34–5, ed. Dewing, 4:163. Final battle, 8.31.5, ed. Dewing, 5:371.

110. Panorama of fallen "West": Procopius 7.33.1–14, ed. Dewing, 4: 437–43 (this is much farther east than what we would call "West"). Jordanes, *Romana* 363, ed. Mommsen, p. 47, "Illyricumque saepe ab Herulis Gipidisque et Bulgaris devastantibus per suos iudices frequenter obstitit viriliterque cecidit." The subject is Justinian; the undated comment applies in general for the reign.

111. Crowning irony, Procopius 7.33.13–14, ed. Dewing, 4:441–43.

112. Procopius 6.14.38–42, 15.27–36, ed. Dewing, 3:413, 421–25.

113. Wozniak, "East Rome, Ravenna," p. 379, attributes the division among the Herules to religion: the Arian Herules went to join the Arian Gepids; he wholly disregards the issue of royalty. He may be right.

114. Skirmish, Procopius 7.34.42–45, ed. Dewing, 4:457. Narses levies recruits, 7.13.21, ed. Dewing, 4:261.

115. Stein, *Histoire du Bas-Empire*, 2:529, a good account of the end of the Herules; 2:543, offer to the Gepids, ca. 561.

116. Schmidt, *Ostgermanen*, pp. 557–58.

117. Procopius 6.15.4–26, ed. Dewing, 3:415–21, and Jordanes, *Getica* 16–24, ed. Mommsen, pp. 57–60. Some Herules migrate to Thule, Procopius 6.15.1–4, ed. Dewing, 3:415; the Goths emigrate from Scandza, Jordanes, *Getica* 25, p. 60. Procopius's Herules pass by the Danes without incident; Jordanes's Dani "Herulos propriis sedibus expulerunt" (p. 59). See also Goffart, *Narrators*, pp. 94–96.

118. Musset, *Barbarian Invasions*, trans. James, p. 62. Quite a few historians have, in fact, paid attention to the Sueves. The fascinating testimony of Hydatius attracts them, even if they are not Hispanic and so drawn to the Sueves, as to the Visigoths, as a chapter of national history.

119. E.g., E. A. Thompson, *Romans and Barbarians*, chs. 8–11. See now Kulikowski, *Late Roman Spain*, pp. 197–209, which provides an authoritative, detailed account of the fifth-century Sueves.

120. For his works, see *Clavis patrum Latinorum*, ed. Eligius Dekkers et al., 2nd ed. (Steenbrugge, 1961), nos. 1079–90. He is singled out for his interest in the classical (Hispanic) author Seneca: Pierre Riché, *Éducation et culture dans l'Occident barbare, 6è–8è siècle* (Paris, 1962), p. 344. See also n. 132, below.

121. Andrew Gillett, *Envoys and Political Communications in the Late Antique West* (Cambridge, 2003), p. 64, frames an interesting contrary hypothesis. Its basis is no stronger than mine. See also Andrew Gillett, "The Birth of Ricimer," *Historia: Zeitschrift für alte Geschichte* 44 (1995): 383; the marriage of Wallia's daughter to an unidentified prominent Sueve (ca. 418) does not require the Sueves' being imperial federates.

122. Reaching an agreement, Hydatius 91, 96–98, 100–101, 111, 113–14, ed. Tranoy, 1:130, 132, 134, 136. Hydatius 137, ed. Tranoy, 1:142, reports Rechiar's Catholicism only in connection with his accession; he is much too silent about the (good) relations of the Gallaecians with the Sueves after the conclusion of an agreement. The strength of Rechila and Rechiar came from their being able to rely on the Gallaecians in the same way as the Merovingians relied on the Gallo-Romans.

123. Hydatius 137, ed. Tranoy, 1:142, notes that he died a pagan (*gentilis*).

124. The Frank Clovis (486–511) is the model of a barbarian leader whose conversion to Catholicism (the faith of the Romans, Gallo- or otherwise) had a decisively positive affect on the fortunes of his people.

125. Reign of Rechiar, Hydatius 137, 139, 140, 142, 155, 158–59, 168, 170–75, 178, ed. Tranoy, 1:142, 148, 152, 154, 156.

126. Hydatius 175, ed. Tranoy, 1:156.

127. Jordanes, *Getica* 231–34, ed. Mommsen, pp. 116–18, provides a slick, problem-free account of these events. Hydatius 178–82, 186–90, 192–99, 201–8, 219–20, 223, 226, 229–32, ed. Tranoy, 1:156, 158, 160, 162, 164, 168, 170, 172, gets there the hard way. Tranoy, 2:119–20, argues strongly against the received opinion that the king whom Hydatius calls Recimund is identical to Remismund. Without deciding the issue, I think it is clear that the advent of Remismund (Hydatius 219, 220, 223; Jordanes, *Getica* 234) documents a decisive turn toward deference to the Visigoths, which is what basically matters. Isidore, *Historia Gothorum Vandalorum Suevorum* 89–90, MG AA 11:302, distinguishes the two men, but clearly encountered the same puzzling feature of Hydatius's text that occasions our difference of opinion. Wolfram, *History of the Goths*, p. 186: Remismund "probably became the 'son in arms' of Theoderic [II]." This goes much farther than Hydatius 226 allows. I would adduce CE310–11 and see the weapons sent by Theoderic II to Remismund as a (nonethnic) symbol of subordination.

128. Hydatius 232, ed. Tranoy, p. 172, calls Ajax "natione Galata." I take this to be a fancy or poetic form of "Gaul," i.e., Gallo-Roman; Hydatius adds that Arianism came "a Gallicana Gothorum habitatione." Others infer that Ajax was Galatian, i.e., from Asia Minor. This is improbable rather than impossible.

129. Isidore, *Historia* 89–90, MG AA 11:302. The name Theudemir given by Isidore conflicts with that of Chararic, given by the more contemporary Gregory of Tours; see n. 133, below. On this and other aspects of the subject, see E. A. Thompson, "The Conversion of the Spanish Suebi to Catholicism," in *Visigothic Spain: New Approaches*, ed. Edward James (Oxford, 1980), pp. 77–92; he emphasizes how little we know.

130. The stability of Catholic Gallaecia is inferred from a papal letter of 538: Schmidt, *Westgermanen*, p. 219.

131. Roger Collins, *Early Medieval Spain: Unity in Diversity, 400–1000* (London, 1983), pp. 36–39. On the Goths in sixth-century Spain, see now Kulikowski, *Late Roman Spain*, pp. 256–86, who minimizes the extent of Gothic control before Leovigild's campaign-filled reign.

132. Riché, *Éducation et culture*, pp. 321–22, 335. Martin's role as an organizer of monasticism deserves special emphasis; he translated two collections of Eastern monastic writings from the Greek (Riché, p. 349). A careful account of Martin's life is given by Claude W. Barlow, *Martini episcopi Bracarensis opera omnia* (New Haven, Conn., 1950), pp. 2–8, including a redating of his death. Dumio is now a suburb of Braga.

133. Gregory of Tours, *Miracula s. Martini* 1.11, 4.7, ed. W. Arndt, MG SRM 1:594–96, 651; Isidore, *Historia* 90–91, MG AA 11:302, mentions no miracle. Collins, *Early Medieval*

Spain, p. 44. Gregory calls the Suevic king Chararicus (as n. 129); the council of 561 calls him [Ch]ariaricus; the sources are discordant. It is a noteworthy fact that Gregory of Tours mentions a kingship of Gallaecia rather than of the Sueves. Geography serves as a unifier, in the same way that Spain does in Isidore, *Historia*, MG AA 11:267.

134. *Concilios Visigoticos e Hispano-Romanos*, ed. José Vives et al. (Barcelona, 1963), pp. 65–106; the signatories, pp. 77 and 85, include several bishops with non-Roman names. Martin was first bishop of Dumio itself (was it a regular diocese?), then metropolitan bishop of Braga (on the geography of these localities, see n. 132, above).

135. Gregory of Tours, *Historiae* 6.43, ed. Krusch-Levison, pp. 314–16 (fidelity); John of Biclar a. 585, no. 2: "Leovegildus rex Gallaecias vastat, Audecanem regem comprehensum regno privat, Suevorum gentem, thesaurum et patriam in suam redigit potestatem et Gothorum provincian facit"; MG AA 11:217. We do not know that Mir's father was Chararic; the family situation might have been more complex.

136. E. A. Thompson, *The Goths in Spain* (Oxford, 1969), pp. 87–91, has a thorough account of the conquest of Gallaecia and its religious implications. A large part of what is now Portugal was incorporated into Suevic Gallaecia.

137. For a fuller description, see Goffart, *Historical Atlases*, pp. 74, 92–93.

138. C. T. Smith, *A Historical Geography of Western Europe before 1800* (London, 1967), p. 513, with fig. 5.9, p. 285 (map). Schmidt, *Westgermanen*, p. 64, gives two more variant spellings; he has little use for *terpen*. Reinerth, ed., *Vorgeschichte des deutschen Stämme*, 1:77, 78, 84, provides partial maps of identified *terpen* in the Netherlands and north Germany, along with a cross-section of a mound.

139. B. H. Slicher van Bath, *The Agrarian History of Western Europe, A.D. 500–1850*, trans. O. Ordish (New York, 1963), pp. 151–53. There is an interesting account of a site at the German end of Friesland at www.pcl-eu.de.

140. Schmidt, *Westgermanen*, pp. 71–77.

141. Trans. H. Rackham in Pliny, the Elder, *Natural History*, 16.2, LCL 4 (Cambridge, Mass., 1945), pp. 387–89; Pliny spoke as an eyewitness. The Chauci were neighbors of the Frisians and eventually subsumed in the wider category (unless they turned into Saxons), see Tacitus, *Germania*, 34–35, ed. Lund, p. 96 (who does not speak about *terpen*).

142. James Campbell, ed., *The Anglo-Saxons* (Ithaca, N.Y., 1982), pp. 30–31.

143. Gildas, *Ruin of Britain* 3, ed. M. Winterbottom, pp. 89–90; Bede, *Historia ecclesiastica gentis Anglorum* 1.1, ed. C. Plummer, pp. 9–10. There is also a description of Britain in Jordanes, *Getica* 10–15, ed. Mommsen, pp. 56–57.

144. Schmidt, *Westgermanen*, pp. 77–80; Rosamond McKitterick, *The Frankish Kingdoms under the Carolingians* (London, 1983), pp. 30, 228–29.

145. Wenskus, *Stammesbildung und Verfassung*, p. 551.

146. Ludwig Schmidt, *Allgemeine Geschichte der germanischen Völker bis zur Mitte des sechsten Jahrhunderts* (Munich, 1909), p. 184, illustrates the connection at a time when the link seemed more assured than in Wenskus's. Early references: Tacitus, *Germania* 41–42, ed. Lund, pp. 100–102; *Laterculus Veronensis* 13.27, ed. Seeck, p. 252. It seems geographically possible that the Thuringians superseded the Hermunduri; but saying this tells us hardly anything at all.

147. Vegetius, *Mulomedicina* 3.6, ed. Lommatzsch, p. 249; Goffart, *Rome's Fall and After*, pp. 69–70 at n. 113. In early citations, an "o" in the first syllable is more normal than "u."

148. Cassiodorus, *Variae* 3.3, ed. Mommsen, pp. 79–80; Jordanes, *Getica* 21, ed. Mommsen, p. 59. It deserves notice that the sources continually link the Thuringians

with the Burgundians: Vegetius, as above; the Frankish Table of Nations, as below n. 163; Jordanes, *Getica* 280, ed. Mommsen, p. 130; Procopius 5.12.10–11, 13, 6.28.17, ed. Dewing, 3:119–21, 4:119. Procopius gives the Thuringians a skeletal origin story similar to that of the Burgundians in Ammianus.

149. Tacitus, *Germania* 41, ed. Lund, 100–102 (about the Hermunduri); I should probably resist the temptation to make this rapprochement.

150. Subjects of Attila: Sidonius, *Carmina* 7.323, ed. Anderson, 1:146. After Attila, *Vita s. Severini*, 27.3, 31.4, ed. Saupe, pp. 21, 23.

151. See PLRE 2:244, 285–86; the time is ca. 460. On Gregory of Tours's account of Childeric and Basina, see Goffart, *Narrators*, pp. 209–10. There is no guarantee that Basina was of the same people as her first husband. The Merovingian king Chilperic († 580) named one of his daughters after her. Schmidt, *Allgemeine Geschichte*, p. 185: Bisinus married a daughter of his to the Lombard king Wacho, and fathered the three sons whom we hear of next as kings. Clovis attacks Thuringia, Gregory of Tours, *Historiae* 2.27, ed. Krush-Levison, p. 73 (forces acknowledgment of Frankish overlordship).

152. Possibly Berthachar died of natural causes; we have only Gregory's word that Herminifrid killed him "vi opprimens" (*Historiae* 3.4, ed. Krusch-Levison, pp. 99–100).

153. On Herminifred, PLRE 2:549–50. Deservedly, Theoderic's marriage alliances are widely reported: e.g., Procopius 5.12.22, ed. Dewing, 3:123–25; Jordanes, *Getica* 299, ed. Mommsen, p. 135; *Excerpta Valesiana*, 2.63, ed. Moreau, p. 19.

154. On Theoderic's Frankish policy, see Stein, *Histoire du Bas-Empire*, 2:149–51; Wolfram, *History of the Goths*, pp. 313–15.

155. Widukind of Corvey, *Res gestae Saxoniae* 1.9–13, ed. A. Bauer and R. Rau, Ausgewählte Quellen 8, 2nd ed. (Darmstadt, 1977), pp. 28–40. Unlike Schmidt, *Allgemeine Geschichte*, p. 186 with n. 2, I take no account of Widukind's version of the story, not wishing to venture to extract history from this thoroughly fictional context. M. Springer, "Sachsen. Historisches," in *Hoops Reallexikon* (Berlin, 2004), 26:39, also refrains from any use of Widukind to document sixth-century events. Gregory's suspect element is the allegation that Amalaberga incited her husband to attack his brother; Gregory casts other wives in such roles.

156. Gregory, *Historiae* 3.4, 7, 8, ed. Krusch-Levison, pp. 99–100, 103–6; Procopius 5.12. 21–23, 13.1–2, ed. Dewing, 3:123–25, 133. Theudebert's letter to Justinian, *Epistolae Austrasicae* 20, Corpus Christianorum Series Latina 117:438–39.

157. This betrothal, which may not have resulted in a marriage (owing to either party's death), was almost certainly a second marriage for Audoin; see PLRE 3:152–53. On Amalafrid, see Procopius 8.25.11–14, ed. Dewing, 5:319–21; and PLRE 3:50–51. I find it difficult to believe on the strength of a single verb in a poem by Fortunatus that Amalafrid visited his cousin Radegund in Poitiers.

158. Persons of royal blood going to Constantinople need not have been harmless tourists. The Merovingian pretender Gundovald took shelter there and was recalled; see Bernard Bachrach, *The Anatomy of a Little War: A Diplomatic and Military History of the Gundovald Affair (568–586)* (Boulder, Colo., 1994), pp. 1–62. Radegund was more obliged to blame Chlothar than we are (even so, she remained on amiable terms with him).

159. Radegund, PLRE 3:1072–74; Fortunatus, PLRE 3:491–92. For a brilliant characterization of the latter's poetry in its Frankish context, see Peter Godman, *Poets and Emperors: Frankish Politics and Carolingian Poetry* (Oxford, 1987), pp. 1–37. On Radegund's quest for relics from Constantinople, see Bachrach, *Anatomy of a Little War*, pp. 20–24.

160. Gerold was the brother of Hildegard, and so the uncle of Charles's destined successors (like Gerold himself, all but one of them predeceased Charles). On Louis's sobriquet "the German," see Chapter 3, n. 9, above.

161. S. Hammann, "Bajuwaren," in *Hoops Reallexikon* (Berlin, 1973), 1:606, observes that no argument about Bavarian origins can be proved or disproved. For an important summary of recent debates over Bavarian origins, see Charles E. Bowlus, "Ethnogenesis: The Tyranny of a Concept," in *On Barbarian Identity*, ed. Gillett, pp. 249–56.

162. Jordanes, *Getica* 280, ed. Mommsen, p. 130. Jordanes often localizes peoples and places by listing neighbors in four directions, as here.

163. Goffart, "Table of Nations," in *Rome's Fall and After*, pp. 111–65.

164. Fortunatus (n. 159, above), *Carmina*, ed. F. Leo, MG AA 4:2, 318 line 644. Garibald: Gregory of Tours, *Historiae* 4.9; cf. 3.27, ed. Krusch-Levison, pp. 141, 124. Gregory makes it clear that King Chlothar bedded the widow before passing her on. The unnamed Gepid mother (and Lombard queen) doubles the number of recorded Gepid women (p. 203, above).

165. Karl Bosl, *Bayerische Geschichte* (n.p., 1990), pp. 35–36. It is characteristic of Wenskus, *Stammesbildung und Verfassung*, pp. 560–69, that he devotes the entire Bavarian section to a hunt for ethnic immigrants. Pohl, *Völkerwanderung*, p. 184, affirms the immigration of (Germanic) northerners and the establishment of a duchy "auf ethnischer Grundlage." There is no evidence for this.

166. The invention of the name by outsiders is suggested by Hamman, "Bajuwaren," p. 607.

167. Friedrich Prinz, *Die Geschichte Bayerns* (Munich, 1997), pp. 38–39, documents the survival of local Romans long into the Middle Ages.

168. Bosl, *Bayerische Geschichte*, pp. 36–38; Prinz, *Geschichte Bayerns*, pp. 40–42.

169. It is symptomatic that Andreas Kraus, *Grundzüge der Geschichte Bayerns*, 2nd ed. (Darmstadt, 1992), p. 2, manages to find a Tacitean connection.

170. There was no Bavarian origin myth until the twelfth century. Wenskus, *Stammesbildung und Verfasssung*, p. 562, tries to make something of it; Prinz, *Geschichte Bayerns*, p. 41, sensibly lets it rest. Bosl, *Geschichte Bayerns*, p. 38, offers an explanation for the name.

171. Comprehensive accounts: Bury, *Later Roman Empire*, 2:168–281; John Moorhead, *Justinian* (London, 1994), pp. 76–86, 101–8.

172. For a thorough retracing of these events with a different conclusion from mine, see Heather, *The Goths*, pp. 264–76, 305. Heather is impressed by the attachment to "Gothicness" shown through a twenty-year struggle by the Italian Goths. I possibly agree, but am far from certain about what "Gothicness" might be; the Goths in question must all have been Italian born and bred. To my mind, the main issue is different.

173. Orosius, *Historia* 7.43.3–6, ed. Zangemeister, pp. 559–60; my trans. is based on R. J. Deferrari, Fathers of the Church (Washington, D.C., 1964), pp. 361–62. The unabbreviated original:

Is, ut saepe auditum atque ultimo exitu eius probatum est, satis studiose sectator pacis militare fideliter Honorio imperatori ac pro defendenda Romana republica inpendere vires Gothorum praeoptavit. Nam ego quoque ipse virum quendam Narbonensem inlustris sub Theodosio militiae, etiam religiosum prudentemque et gravem, apud Bethleem oppidum Palastinae beatissimo Hieronymo presbytero referentem audivi, se familiarissimum Athaulfo apud Narbonam fuisse ac de eo saepe sub testificatione didicisse, quod ille, cum esset animo viribus ingenioque nimius, referre solitus esset: se inprimis ardenter inhiasse, ut oblitterato Romano nomine Romanum omne solum Gothorum imperium et faceret et uocaret essetque, ut vulgariter loquar, Gothia quod Romania fuisset et fieret nunc Athaulfus quod quondam Caesar Augustus, at ubi multa experientia probavisset neque Gothos ullo modo parere legibus posse propter effrenatam barbariem neque reipublicae interdici leges oportere, sine quibus respublica non est respublica, elegisse saltim, ut gloriam sibi de restituendo in integrum augendoque Romano nomine Gothorum viribus quaereret habereturque apud posteros Romanae restitutionis auctor, postquam esse non potuerat immutator.

174. Bury, *Later Roman Empire*, 2:163 n. 1; for Amalasuintha's doings, see Bury 2:159–67.

175. Theodahad, Procopius 5.3.3–5, 6.1–27, ed. Dewing, 3:23–25, 49–57; his son-in-law, 5.8.3, 3:69; Jordanes, *Getica* 308, ed. Mommsen, p. 137.

176. Procopius 6.10.11, ed. Dewing, 3:375. The general was John, nephew of Vitalian, about whom see PLRE 3:652–61 (Ioannes 46). This particular piece of treachery failed, but Matasuintha eventually got her wish for a distinguished Byzantine marriage. Heather, *Goths*, p. 276, adds the case of the prominent Gothic general Pitzias.

177. See n. 182, below.

178. Procopius 6.29.1–2, ed. Dewing, 4:125. The terms were made known to Wittigis and his court, who were delighted.

179. Wolfram, *History of the Goths*, pp. 348–49, comments that "generals [like Belisarius] prefer to fight until they have forced the enemy's unconditional surrender." This is not a universal truth. The demand for unconditional surrender in World War II was made by the allied political leadership, not imposed by the military. In 540 and before, Belisarius, the general-in-chief, was willing to offer conditions to the Goths provided they did not include a continuing Gothic domination.

180. Procopius 6.29.17–40, 30.25–30, ed. Dewing, 4:129–37, 145–47.

181. Bury, *Later Roman Empire*, 2:226–29.

182. Procopius, 6.30.3–26, 7.1.25–27, 34–49, 2.1–18, ed. Dewing, 4:139–45, 159, 163–73.

183. *History of the Goths*, p. 348.

184. Procopius 7.1.26, 2.5, ed. Dewing, 4:159, 169. Wolfram, *History of the Goths*, p. 153, opines that Totila was committed to this course "unless he wanted to share the fate of his predecessors." But the predecessors were not killed for having wavered in their commitment, and Totila soon acquired enough power, prestige, and durability to change direction if he had wanted to.

185. Procopius 8.34.19, ed. Dewing, 5:405; a smaller amount was in Pavia.

186. Procopius 7.21.18–25, 7.37.6–7, 8.24.3–5, ed. Dewing, 4:341–43, 5:15, 303–5.

187. Quoted in context, Chapter 4 at n. 46, above.

188. Procopius 7.37.12, ed. Dewing, 5:13.

189. W. Goffart, review of Eric Zöllner, *Geschichte der Franken*, *Speculum* 47 (1972): 578–79.

190. On the Jastorf culture, see Introduction, nn. 24–25, above.

191. Gibbon, *Decline and Fall*, ch. 71, ed. Bury, 7:308, "In the preceding volumes of this History, I have described the triumph of barbarism and religion."

192. I cite Gatterer only as an example of a view commonly held; see Chapter 1 at nn. 9 and 16.

193. Cited by Ridé, *Image du Germain*, p. 335. Beatus published these lines at the head of a Latin translation of Procopius. The reverse of Beatus's formulation was the assertion (e.g., by Italian authors) that the barbarians destroyed and laid waste the Roman Empire.

194. On the applicability of "barbarous" to Justinian's Byzantium, see Chapter 4 at n. 60, above.

Chapter 8

1. Bede's Letter to Egbert, trans. Dorothy Whitelock, *English Historical Documents c. 500–1042* (London, 1968), pp. 740–41; ed. Charles Plummer, *Bedae Opera Historica* (Oxford, 1896), 1:413–15:

sunt loca innumera, ut novimus omnes, stilo stultissimo in monasteriorum ascripta vocabulum, sed nichil prorsus monasticae conversationis habentia . . .

11. Et quia huiusmodi maxima et plurima sunt loca quae, ut vulgo dici solet, neque Deo neque hominibus utilia sunt, quia videlicet neque regularis secundum Deum ibidem vita servatur, neque illa milites sive comites secularium potestatum, qui gentem nostram a barbaris defendant, possident; si quis in eisdem ipsis locis pro necessitate temporum sedem episcopatus constituat . . . opus virtutis . . . agere probabitur. . . . [T]uam quoque sanctitatem decet cum religioso rege nostrae gentis irreligiosa et iniqua priorum gesta atque scripta convellere, et ea quae provinciae nostrae, sive secundum Deum, sive secundum seculum sint utilia, prospicere; ne nostris temporibus vel religione cessante, amor timorque interni deseratur inspectoris, vel rarescente copia militiae secularis, absint qui fines nostros a barbarica incursione tueantur. Quod enim turpe est dicere, tot sub nomine monasteriorum loca hii, qui monachicae vitae prorsus sunt expertes, in suam dicionem acceperunt, sicut ipsi melius nostis, ut omnino desit locus, ubi filii nobilium aut emeritorum militum possessionem accipere possint; . . . atque hanc ob rem vel patriam suam, pro qua militare debuerant, trans mare abeuntes relinquant; vel maiore scelere . . . luxuriae ac fornicationi deserviant.

2. Bede, *Historia ecclesiastica gentis Anglorum* 5.23 ("Qua adridente pace"), ed. Plummer, 1:351, refers naively to these abusive monasteries, as though they might be a good thing. A comparison with the Letter to Egbert shows that his naiveté is irony; see Goffart, *Narrators*, p. 255 with n. 103. This attempt to revive private, civilian life had to masquerade as monasticism; there was no other pigeonhole for it. In Judith McClure and Roger Collins, eds., *Bede, The Ecclesiastical History of the English People*, Oxford World Classics (Oxford, 1999), p. xxxi, the editors are dismayed by the thought that Bede's proposal "would have undermined the whole principle of security of tenure based on documentary proof of ownership." The comments of Patrick Wormald, *Bede and the Conversion of England: The Charter Evidence*, Jarrow Lecture 1984 (Jarrow, n.d.), pp. 19–23, are more concerned with "bookland" than with what Bede was saying. D. P. Kirby, *Bede's* Historia ecclesiastica gentis Anglorum: *Its Contemporary Setting*, Jarrow Lecture 1992 (Jarrow, 1993), p. 13, continues the practice of missing Bede's point. Better readings are found in Eric John, *Land Tenure in Early England* (Leicester, 1964), pp. 44–47, and *Orbis Britanniae* (Leicester, 1966), pp. 80–83.

3. Trans. Donald Kagan, in D. Kagan, ed., *Decline and Fall of the Roman Empire: Why Did It Collapse?* Problems in European Civilization (Boston, 1962), p. 91. Piganiol borrowed the phrase from the *Histoire de César* (1856) of Lamartine, who applied it to the Roman Republic; see Nicolet, *Fabrique d'une nation*, pp. 171–72. In its context, Piganiol's judgment is less impressive than it sounds; not many lines earlier he claims that Rome "chiefly" perished because it "relinquished compulsory military service for citizens"— something that, in fact, had happened well within the B.C. period of Roman history.

4. Jones, *Later Roman Empire*, pp. 1068, 1027.

5. Demandt, *Der Fall Roms*, pp. 587, 588 (see Appendix 1, below).

6. For an influential (and still interesting) exemplification of this tendency, see Lot, *End of the Ancient World*, pp. 5–186; e.g., p. 186, "Thus, under a still majestic appearance, the Roman Empire, at the end of the fourth century, was no longer anything but a hollow husk"; p. 236, "The Empire died of an internal malady." Gibbon, *Decline and Fall*, 3:480. A very influential advocate of an inner crisis of the Empire from the third century on was Michael Rostovtzeff (1926); see Kulikowski, *Late Roman Spain*, p. 335 n. 10.

7. In a brief survey of the literature, Heather, "Huns and the End," pp. 38–40, shows that recent partisans of internal causes for decline have been less resourceful and persuasive than persons confirming the socioeconomic viability of the later Empire (in the wake of A. H. M. Jones) and exploring the "cultural dynamism" of Christianity.

8. Heather, "Huns and the End," p. 40, would have us believe that archaeology has documented a process of startling development among the peoples to the east and north of the Roman frontiers during the first A.D. centuries. To the contrary, see Wells, *The Barbarians Speak*, p. 187–88.

9. This sentence echoes the words of Susan Reynolds, "Medieval *Origenes Gentium*," p. 379.

10. The case of Britain differs somewhat from Spain, Gaul, and Italy.

11. On the withdrawal of the Byzantine army to its sources of supply, see Michael F. Hendy, *Studies in the Byzantine Monetary Economy c. 300–1450* (Cambridge, 1985), pp. 619–26, 634–45; J. F. Haldon, *Byzantium in the Seventh Century*, rev. ed. (Cambridge, 1997), pp. 208–51. For an explicit parallel between East and West, see Hendy, pp. 644–45; and on Byzantine Italy, Haldon, pp. 249–50. Haldon's model for "settling on the land" is crude by comparison with the cases of fifth-century Gaul and Italy. See also for the military upper class in both Byzantine and Lombard Italy the good summary of Chris Wickham, *Early Medieval Italy: Central Power and Local Society 400–1000* (London, 1981), pp. 71–72, 74–76.

12. The provinces of the later Roman Empire were superseded in seventh-century Byzantium by military districts called "themes."

13. On Diocletian's retirement, see Lactantius, *De mortibus persecutorum* 18, 29, 42, ed. J. Moreau, Sources chrétiennes 39 (Paris, n.d.), pp. 307–16, 366–67, 418–23, with Moreau's commentary. Diocletian could not stay completely clear of politics (notably in 308); failing an established process of resignation, he retained imperial rank; but he resolutely safeguarded his retirement. On his abdication and retirement, see Williams, *Diocletian and the Roman Recovery*, pp. 186–200.

14. How ancient civilian life came into being does not need to be discussed here. Suffice it to say that the *pax Romana* offered greater scope and completeness to this way of life than any earlier epoch in antiquity.

15. See Chapter 7, nn. 174–76, above.

16. Peter Brown, "The Later Roman Empire," in *Religion and Society in the Age of Saint Augustine* (London, 1972), pp. 47–48, succinctly surveys older arguments about the decline of Roman society. Along the same lines, see also my comments in *Rome's Fall and After*, pp. 82–85.

17. I have written on this transmission; see *Rome's Fall and After*, pp. 167–211, 233–53. One might tentatively suggest that the fifth-century barbarian *sors* was the ancestor of the early medieval benefice.

18. See Chapter 6 at n. 144 for the text in Procopius. I assume here that Procopius's account is factual. Chapter 6 points out that it does not mesh with the premises of Cassiodorus, *Variae* 2.16.5.

19. In the passage quoted above, Bede inveighs against pretend monks. A system of the kind he envisages also runs the risk of creating pretend-soldiers.

20. See Chapter 5, at n. 130, above.

21. Evagrius Scholasticus, *Ecclesiastical History* 4.30, trans. Michael Whitby, Translated Texts for Historians 33 (Liverpool, 2000), p. 233, comments that Justinian "did a myriad other things which are pious and pleasing to God, provided that those who accomplish these should carry them out from their own resources" (written about thirty years after Justinian's death).

22. Jones, *Later Roman Empire*, p. 152.

23. See Chapter 7, section "Gothic Italy and the Ethnic Bastion that Never Was," above, with special reference to n. 173 (Athaulf).

Appendix 2

1. Muhlberger, *Fifth-Century Chroniclers*, pp. 136–37, 191–92.

2. Musset, *Germanic Invasions*, pp. 62–63.

3. Justin Favrod, ed., *La Chronique de Marius d'Avenches (455–581): Texte, traduction et commentaire* (Lausanne, 1991), p. 64; cf. ed. Mommsen, MG AA 9.232.

4. On the source for this entry, see J. Favrod, "Les sources et la chronologie de Marius d'Avenches," *Francia* 17/1 (1990): 6, 15. On local dignitaries and senators in the usage of Gregory of Tours, see Margerete Weidemann, *Kulturgeschichte der Merowingerzeit nach den Werken Gregors von Tours*, 2 vols. (Mainz, 1982), 2:307–19, 324–27. Also Durliat, "Salaire de la paix," p. 51 at n. 155. The question of "senators" has been discussed, not wholly conclusively, by F. Gilliard, "The Senators of Sixth-Century Gaul," *Speculum* 54 (1979): 685–97, and Brian Brennan, "Senators and Social Mobility in Sixth-Century Gaul," *Journal of Medieval History* 11 (1985): 145–61. My concern here is not to settle the question for Gregory of Tours or Gaul in general, but only for the chroniclers addressing Burgundian affairs.

5. Stein, *Histoire du Bas-Empire*, 1:378; Demougeot, *Formation de l'Europe*, 2:583 n. 53.

6. Ed. Mommsen, MG AA 9.305.

7. Steven Muhlberger, "Heroic Kings and Unruly Generals: The 'Copenhagen' Continuator of Prosper Reconsidered," *Florilegium* 6 (1985): 50–70, here 52.

8. Ed. Krusch, MG SRM 2.68.

Appendix 3

1. A situation similar to that of the Burgundian kingdom may or may not be implied by CE277, when it extends the fifty-year time limit to *fugitivi*. Owners of dependents (slaves) who were involved in the scheme of Gothic allotments and Roman *tertia* had fifty years in which to reclaim "fugitives" who had somehow managed to escape the

master's control (see Chapter 6 at n. 85, above). Where *mancipia* are concerned, there are many relevant passages in LV, but (except for the one just cited) not in a context of barbarian settlement. Inter alia, see CE291-2 and Fragmenta Gaudenziana 16, 18, 20, in MG LNG 1:469–72.

2. There are provisions in the Burgundian Laws in which *mancipium* does refer only to a human being; e.g. LB4.1. Context defines the meaning.

3. See Chapter 6 at nn. 30–33, above.

4. LBExtravagans 21.12 refers to "Romans" yielding *terra* and "Romans" keeping the other half; but these are legal niceties. Roman persons and properties occupied the entire kingdom; Roman "hosts" were taxpayers and had a part in the administration of the royal fisc. The figure masked by these Romans is the king, who yielded assets to the *faramanni* and kept for his fisc what was not given away.

5. Goffart, "From Roman Taxation to Mediaeval Seigneurie," in *Rome's Fall and After*, pp. 177–89, and more particularly, p. 191 n. 108. About Visigothic evidence, see also n. 1, above.

6. The same distinction in types of assessment is perfectly documented by Gregory of Tours in 579 (*Historiae* 5. 28, ed. Krusch-Levison, p. 234): tax increases are imposed on each *possessor* "de propria terra" and besides "de reliquis terris quam de mancipiis." Gregory distinguished the *mancipia* as persons from the *terrae* they cultivate.

7. Lot, "Régime de l'hospitalité," p. 979.

8. Ibid. pp. 984–86.

9. Current orthodoxy concerning the "grand domaine classique" is affirmed by Adriaan Verhulst, "Economic Organisation," in *The New Cambridge Mediaeval History*, vol. 2, *ca. 700–ca. 900*, ed. Rosamond McKitterick (Cambridge, 1995), pp. 488–90. This is unchanged from the doctrine Verhulst propounded thirty years earlier: "La genèse du régime domanial classique en France au début du moyen âge," *Centro Italiano di studi sull'alto medioevo: Settimane di studio* 13 (1966): 135–60, according to which the structures illustrated by the ninth-century polyptyques originated in the Frankish kingdom of the seventh century. Jean Durliat (*Finances publiques*) and I advocate a very different, fiscal interpretation. About mine, see *Le grand domaine aux époques mérovingienne et carolingienne*, ed. A. Verhulst (Ghent, 1985), pp. 12–14, including regrets about my nonattendance at a colloquium on the "grand domaine" to which I was not asked. See also Jean Pierre Devroey, *Études sur le grand domaine carolingien* (Aldershot, 1993).

10. I find myself having said that "the anachronistic use of the polyptychs has confused the study of late Roman social history" ("From Roman Taxation to Mediaeval Seigneurie," p. 193 n. 118). I am no longer so severe as that, provided polyptychs are understood to be tax records, not domainial ones. Another relevant work of mine on this subject is "Merovingian Polyptychs: Reflections on Two Recent Publications," in *Rome's Fall and After*, pp. 233–53.

11. The underlying idea is that the main landowner should carry out in the countryside the same tasks carried out in cities by a tax commission of some sort, such as the *curiales*. Durliat, *Finances publiques*, discusses this subject at length.

12. How Burgundians should petition the king for royal *munificentia* is spelled out in detail in LBExtravagans 21.14.

Bibliography

See also the List of Abbreviations, above.

After Rome's Fall: Narrators and Sources of Early Medieval History: Essays Presented to Walter Goffart. Ed. Alexander Callander Murray. Toronto, 1999.

Ambrose, Saint, bishop of Milan. *Epistolae.* CSEL 88. Vienna, 1978.

———. *De Expositio evangeli secundum Lucam.* CSEL 32. Vienna, 1902.

Amici, Angela. *Jordanes e la storia gotica.* Quaderni della Rivista di Byzantinistica, ed. Antonio Carile, 6. Spoleto, 2002.

Ammianus Marcellinus. See Abbreviations.

Amory, Patrick. *People and Identity in Ostrogothic Italy, 489–554.* Cambridge, 1997.

Anerkennung und Integration: Zu den wirtschaftlichen Grundlagen der Völkerwanderungszeit, 400–600. Ed. H. Wolfram and A. Schwarcz. Denkschriften der österreichischen Akademie der Wissenschaften, phil.-hist. Klasse 193. Vienna, 1988.

Anonymous. *De rebus bellicis.* See Thompson, *Roman Reformer.*

Anonymous. See also Valesian, below.

Anton, Hans Hubert. "Origo gentis—Volksgeschichte: Zur Auseinandersetzung mit Walter Goffarts Werk 'The Narrators of Barbarian History.'" In *Historiographie im frühen Mittelalter,* pp. 262–307.

Arce, Javier. "The Enigmatic Fifth Century in Hispania: Some Historical Problems." In *Regna and Gentes,* pp. 135–57.

Atlas historique Larousse, ed. G. Duby. Paris, 1978.

Aubin, Hermann. "Zur Frage der historischen Kontinuität im Allgemeinen." *Historische Zeitschrift* 168 (1943): 229–62.

———. "Die Umwandlung des Abendlandes durch die Germanen bis zum Ausgang der Karolingerzeit." In *Neue Propyläen Weltgeschichte.* Berlin, 1940, 2:45–172.

Aurelius Victor. *Liber de Caesaribus.* Ed. Franz Pichlmayr. Teubner. Leipzig, 1911.

Bachrach, Bernard. *The Anatomy of a Little War: A Diplomatic and Military History of the Gundovald Affair (568–586).* Boulder, Colo., 1994.

———. *A History of the Alans in the West.* Minneapolis, 1973.

Barlow, Claude W. *Martini episcopi Bracarensis opera omnia.* New Haven, 1950.

Barnes, Timothy D. "Emperors, Panegyrics, Prefects, Provinces and Palaces (284–317)." *Journal of Roman Archaeology* 9 (1996): 532–52.

———. "The Franci before Diocletian." In *Historiae Augustae Colloquium Genevense 1991,* ed. Giorgio Bonamente and François Paschoud. Bari, 1994, pp. 11–18.

———. *The New Empire of Diocletian and Constantine.* Cambridge, Mass., 1982.

Barnish, S. J. B., "Taxation, Land and Barbarian Settlement in the Western Empire." *Papers of the British School at Rome* 54 (1986): 170–95.

———. "Transformation and Survival in the Western Senatorial Aristocracy, c. A.D. 400–700." *Papers of the British School at Rome* 56 (1988): 120–55.

Bath, B. H. Slicher van, *The Agrarian History of Western Europe*, A.D. *500–1850*. Trans. O. Ordish. New York, 1963.

Beatus Rhenanus. *Rerum Germanicarum libri tres*. Basel, 1531.

Bede. *Bedae Opera Historica*. Ed. Charles Plummer. 2 vols. Oxford, 1896.

———. *Ecclesiastical History of the English People*. Ed. Judith McClure and Roger Collins. Oxford World Classics. Oxford, 1999.

———. *Letter to Egbert of York*. Trans. Dorothy Whitelock. *English Historical Documents c. 500–1042*. London, 1968.

Behrends, O. "Einquartierungssystem." In *Hoops Reallexikon*. Berlin, 1989, 7:24–33.

Bell-Fialkoff, Andrew, ed. *The Role of Migration in the History of the Eurasian Steppe: Sedentary Civilization vs. "Barbarian" and Nomad*. New York, 2000.

Berger, Adolf. *Encyclopedic Dictionary of Roman Law*. Transactions of the American Philosophical Society, new ser., 43/2. Philadelphia, 1953.

Bierbrauer, Volker. "Archäologie und Geschichte der Goten vom 1.-7. Jahrhundert." *Frühmittelalterliche Studien* 28 (1994): 51–171.

Bloch, Marc. *Feudal Society*. 1939. Trans. L. A. Manyon. Chicago, 1961.

Blockley, R. C., ed. and trans. *The Fragmentary Classicising Historians of the Later Roman Empire: Eunapius, Olympiodorus, Priscus and Malchus*. 2 vols. Arca, Classical and Medieval Texts, Papers and Monographs 6 and 10. Liverpool, 1981, 1983.

Bolchazy, Ladislaus J. *Hospitality in Early Rome: Livy's Concept of Its Humanizing Force*. Chicago, 1977.

Bollnow, Hermann. "Die Herkunftssagen der germanischen Stämme als Geschichtsquelle." *Baltische Studien* N.F. 54 (1965): 14–25.

Bombi, Georgio. *Atlas of World History*. Trans. T. Tonioli and C. Title. London, 1987.

Borchardt, Frank L. *Germanic Antiquity in Renaissance Myth*. Baltimore, 1971.

Bosl, Karl. *Bayerische Geschichte*. N.p., 1990.

Bowersock, Glen W. "The Dissolution of the Roman Empire." In *Selected Papers on Late Antiquity*. Bari, 2000, pp. 175–85.

———. *Julian the Apostate*. London, 1978.

———. "The Vanishing Paradigm of the Fall of Rome." 1996. In *Selected Papers on Late Antiquity*. Bari, 2000, pp. 187–97.

Bowlus, Charles E. "Ethnogenesis: The Tyranny of a Concept." In Gillett, ed., *On Barbarian Identity*, pp. 242–56.

Bradley, Dennis R. "*In altum laxare vela compulsus*: The 'Getica' of Jordanes." *Hermes* 121 (1993): 211–36.

Brennan, Brian. "Senators and Social Mobility in Sixth-Century Gaul." *Journal of Medieval History* 11 (1985): 145–61.

Brinkmann, Hennig. "Theodiscus, ein Beitrag zur Frühgeschichte des Namens 'Deutsch' (1941)." In *Der Volksname Deutsch*, ed. Hans Eggers. Wege der Forschung 156. Darmstadt, 1970, pp. 183–208.

Brown, Peter. "The Later Roman Empire." In *Religion and Society in the Age of Saint Augustine*. London, 1972, pp. 46–73.

Brunhölzl, Franz. *Geschichte der lateinischen Literatur des Mittelalters*. Vol. 1. Munich, 1975.

Buonomo, Luigi Maria. "Introduzione alla lettura delle opere di Giordane." In *Mutatio rerum: letteratura, filosofia, scienza tra tardo antico e altomedioevo*, Atti del convegno di studi (Napoli 1996), ed. Maria Luisa Silvestre and Marisa Squillante. Naples, 1997, pp. 115–46.

Burgess, M. E. "The Resurgence of Ethnicity: Myth or Reality?" *Ethnic and Racial Studies* 1 (1978): 265–85.

Burns, Thomas S. *Barbarians within the Gates of Rome.* Bloomington, Ind., 1994.

———. "Ennodius and the Ostrogothic Settlement." *Classical Folia* 32 (1978): 153–58.

———. *Rome and the Barbarians, 100 B.C.–A.D. 400.* Baltimore, 2003.

Burrow, J. W. *A Liberal Descent: Victorian Historians and the English Past.* Cambridge, 1981.

Bury, J. B. *History of the Later Roman Empire from the Death of Theodosius I to the Death of Justinian.* 2 vols. London, 1923.

———. *The Invasions of Europe by the Barbarians.* Ed. F. J. C. Hearnshaw. London, 1928; Norton paperback, New York, 1967.

Cambridge Ancient History. 1st ed. 12 vols. Cambridge, 1923–39.

Cameron, Alan. *Claudian: Poetry and Propaganda at the Court of Honorius.* Oxford, 1970.

Cameron, Averil. *The Later Roman Empire.* London, 1993.

———. *The Mediterranean World in Late Antiquity AD 395–600.* London, 1993.

———. *Procopius and the Sixth Century.* London, 1985.

———. See also Carrié.

Campbell, James, ed. *The Anglo-Saxons.* Ithaca, N.Y., 1982.

Capelle. See Germanic Antiquity.

Carrié, Jean-Michel. "L'État à la recherche de nouveaux modes de financement des armées (Rome et Byzance, IVè–VIIIè siècles)." In *The Byzantine and Early Islamic Near East.* Vol. 3, *States, Resources, Armies,* ed. Averil Cameron. Princeton, N.J., 1995, pp. 27–60.

Cary, Max. *History of Rome.* 2nd ed. London, 1954.

Cassiodorus. See *Variae* in the Abbreviations.

CE. See Abbreviations.

Cesa, Maria. "Hospitalità o altro techniques of accomodation [*sic*]? A proposito di un libro recente." *Archivio storico italiano* 140 (1982): 539–52.

———. *Impero tardoantico e barbari: La crisi militare da Adrianopoli al 418.* Como, 1984.

Chastagnol, André. Review of Goffart, *B&R. Revue historique* 269 (1983): 166.

———. "La signification géographique et ethnique des mots *Germani* et *Germania* dans les sources latines." *Ktèma: Civilisations de l'Orient, de la Grèce et de Rome antique* 9 (1984): 97–101.

Christensen, Arne Søby. *Cassiodorus, Jordanes, and the History of the Goths: Studies in a Migration Myth.* Copenhagen, 2002.

Chronicle of 452. MGH AA 9.

Chronicon Paschale. Trans. M. and M. Whitby. Translated Texts for Historians 7. Liverpool, 1989.

Chrysos, Evangelos. "Conclusion: De foederatis iterum." In *Kingdoms of the Empire,* pp. 185–206.

Claude, Dietrich. Review of *B&R. Francia* 10 (1982): 753–54.

Claudian. [Works]. Ed. and trans. Maurice Platnauer. LCL. 2 vols. London, 1963.

Clavis patrum Latinorum. Ed. Eligius Dekkers et al. 2nd ed. Steenbrugge, 1961.

Clover, F. M. "Carthage and the Vandals," and "The Symbiosis of Romans and Vandals in Africa." In *The Late Roman West and the Vandals.* Aldershot, 1993, chapters 6 and 10.

Clüver, Philipp. *Germania antiqua.* Leiden, 1616; 2nd ed., 1631.

Cohen, Robin, ed. *The Cambridge Survey of World Migration*. Cambridge, 1995.

Collins, Roger. *Early Medieval Europe, 300–1000*. 2nd ed. New York, 1999.

———. *Early Medieval Spain: Unity in Diversity, 400–1000*. London, 1983.

Concilios Visigoticos e Hispano-Romanos. Ed. José Vives et al. Barcelona, 1963.

The Construction of Communities in the Early Middle Ages: Texts, Resources and Artefacts. Ed. Richard Corradini, Max Diesenberger, Helmut Reimitz. Leiden, 2003.

Consularia Italica. MGH AA 9.

Copenhagen Continuator of Prosper. *Auctarium Havniensis ordo prior*, and *Additamentum ad Prosperum Havniensis*. MG AA 9.

Cornell, Tim, and John Matthews. *Atlas of the Roman World*. New York, 1982.

Courcelle, Pierre. *Histoire littéraire des grandes invasions germaniques*. 3rd ed. Paris, 1964.

Courtois, Christian. *Les Vandales et l'Afrique*. Paris, 1955.

Croke, Brian. "AD 476: The Manufacture of a Turning Point." *Chiron* 13 (1983): 81–119.

———. "Cassiodorus and the *Getica* of Jordanes." *Classical Philology* 82 (1987): 117–34.

———. "Latin Historiography and the Barbarian Kingdoms." In *Greek and Roman Historiography in Late Antiquity, Fourth to Sixth Century A.D.*, ed. Gabriele Marasco. Leiden, 2003, pp. 358–75.

CTh. See Abbreviations.

Curta, Florin. *The Making of the Slavs: History and Archaeology of the Lower Danube Region, c. 300–700*. Cambridge, 2001.

Dahn, Felix. *Die Germanen: Westgermanen*. Essen, 1999.

———. *Die Könige der Germanen*. Reprinted, Hildesheim, 1973.

de Boor, Helmut. *Das Attilabild in Geschichte, Legende und heroischer Dichtung*. Bern, 1932.

Delbrück, Hans. *The Barbarian Invasions*. Vol. 2 of *History of the Art of War*. Trans. Walter J. Renfroe, Jr. 4 vols. Lincoln, Nebr., 1980.

Delisle, Guillaume. *Theatrum historicum ad a. 400* [two maps with explanatory text]. Paris, 1705.

Demandt, Alexander. "Die Anfänge der Staatenbildung bei den Germanen." *Historische Zeitschrift* 230 (1980): 265–91.

———, ed. *Deutschlands Grenzen in der Geschichte*. Munich, 1990.

———. *Der Fall Roms: Die Auflösung des römischen Reiches im Urteil der Nachwelt*. Munich, 1984.

———, art. "Magister militum." In Pauly-Wissowa, Supplement 12. pp. 553–790.

———. "The Osmosis of Late Roman and Germanic Aristocracies." In *Das Reich und die Barbaren*, pp. 75–86.

———. *Die Spätantike: Römische Geschichte von Diocletian bis Justinian, 284–565 n. Chr.* Müller's Handbuch, 3te Abt., 6ter Teil. Munich, 1989.

———. "Die spätrömische Militäradel." *Chiron* 10 (1980): 609–36.

———. "Die westgermanischen Stammesbünde." *Klio* 75 (1993): 387–406.

Demougeot, Émilienne. "Constantin III, l'empereur d'Arles." 1974. Reprinted in *L'Empire romain et les barbares d'Occident (IVè–VIIè siècles). Scripta varia*. Paris, 1988, pp. 171–213.

———. *De l'unité à la division de l'Empire romain*. Paris, 1954.

———. *La formation de l'Europe et les invasions barbares*. 2 vols. in 3. Paris, 1969–79.

———. "Modalités d'établissement des fédérés barbares de Gratien à Théodose." In *Mélanges d'histoire ancienne offerts à William Seston*. Paris, 1974, pp. 143–60.

———. Review of Goffart, *B&R*. *Byzantinische Zeitschrift* 76 (1983): 55–59.

Dessau, Hermann. *Inscriptiones Latinae selectae.* 3 vols. in 5. Reprinted, Chicago, 1979.
Devroey, Jean-Pierre. *Études sur le grand domaine carolingien.* Aldershot, 1993.
Diesner, Hans-Joachim. *The Great Migration.* Trans. C. S. V. Salt. London, 1978.
Dig. See Abbreviations.
Dill, Samuel. *Roman Society in the Last Century of the Western Empire.* 2nd ed. London, 1899.
Dobesch, Gerhard. *Vom äusseren Proletariat zum Kulturträger. Ein Aspekt zur Rolle der Germanen in der Spätantike.* Geographica historica 6. Amsterdam, 1994.
Dopsch, Alfons. *Economic and Social Foundations of European Civilization.* Condensed trans. M. G. Beard and N. Marshall. London, 1937.
Drinkwater, J. F. "The Usurpers Constantine III (407–411) and Jovinus (411–413)." *Britannia* 29 (1998): 269–98.
Durliat, Jean. "Cité, impôt et intégration des barbares." In *Kingdoms of the Empire,* pp. 153–83.
———. *Les Finances publiques de Dioclétien aux Carolingiens (284–889).* Beiheft der *Francia* 21. Sigmaringen, 1991.
———. "Le salaire de la paix sociale dans les royaumes barbares." In *Anerkennung und Integration,* pp. 21–72.
Duroselle, Jean-Baptiste. *"L'Invasion": Les migrations humaines, chance ou fatalité.* Paris, 1992.
Elton, Hugh. *Warfare in Roman Europe, A.D. 350–425.* Oxford, 1996.
Ennodius, bishop of Pavia. *Panegyricus dictus Theoderico.* Ed. Frederick Vogel. MG AA 7:203–14.
———. *Vita s. Antonii.* Ed. Vogel, pp. 186–90.
———. *Vita s. Epiphanii.* Ed. Vogel, pp. 84–109.
Epistolae Austrasicae. Ed. W. Gundlach. Corpus Christianorum Series Latina 117. Turnhout, 1957.
Epistolae imperatorum [et] pontificum (Collectio Avellana). Ed. O. Guenther. CSEL 35. Vienna, 1895.
Epitome de Caesaribus. Ed. Franz Pichlmayr. See Aurelius Victor, above.
Eugippius. *Vita s. Severini.* Ed. and trans. Philippe Régerat. Sources chrétiennes 374. Paris, 1991; ed. Hermann Saupe. MG AA 1 part 2. Berlin, 1861.
Eutropius. *Breviarium ab urbe condita.* Ed. H. Droysen. MG AA 2.
Evagrius Scholasticus. *Ecclesiastical History.* Trans. Michael Whitby. Translated Texts for Historians 33. Liverpool, 2000.
Favrod, Justin. *Histoire politique du royaume burgonde (443–534).* Lausanne, 1997.
———. "Les sources et la chronologie de Marius d'Avenches." *Francia* 17/1 (1990): 1–21.
Fehr, Hubert. "*Volkstum* as Paradigm: Germanic People and Gallo-Romans in Early Medieval Archaeology since the 1930s." In Gillett, ed., *On Barbarian Identity,* pp. 177–200.
Ferrill, Arthur. *The Fall of the Roman Empire: The Military Explanation.* London, 1986.
Florus. *Epitoma.* Ed. Paul Jal. Collection des universités de France. Paris, 1967.
Formulae. *Cartae Senonicae; Formulae Andegavenses; Formulae Arvernenses; Formulae Visigothicae.* Ed. Karl Zeumer. MG Formulae.
Fortunatus, Venantius. *Carmina.* Ed. F. Leo. MG AA 4:2.
Frechulf, bishop of Lisieux. *Historiae.* Ed. Michael I. Allen. Corpus Christianorum continuatio medievalis 169A. Turnhout, 2002.

Fredegar. *Chronicon.* Ed. B. Krusch. MG SRM 2.

Fried, Johannes. *Die Formierung Europas 840–1046.* Oldenbourg Grundriss der Geschichte, ed. Jochen Bleicken et al., 6. Munich, 1991.

Garcia Moreno, L. A., "El termino 'sors' y relacionados en el 'Liber Judicum.' " *Annuario de historia del derecho español* 53 (1983): 137–75.

Gatterer, J. C. *Einleitung in die synchronistische Universalhistorie zur Erläuterung seiner synchronistischere Tabellen.* Göttingen, 1771.

———. *Handbuch der Universalhistorie.* Göttingen, 1765.

———. *Versuch einer allgemeinen Welgeschichte bis zur Entdeckung Amerikens.* Göttingen, 1792.

Gaupp, Theodor. See List of Abbreviations.

Geary, Patrick J. *Before France and Germany: The Creation and Transformation of the Merovingian World.* New York, 1988.

———. *The Myth of Nations. The Medieval Origins of Europe.* Princeton, N.J., 2002.

———, ed. *Readings in Medieval History.* 2nd ed. Peterborough, Ontario, 1997.

Gebhart, Bruno. See Schultze, Walther.

Germanic Antiquity. Capelle, Wilhelm, ed. and trans. *Das Alte Germanien: Die Nachrichten der griechischen und römischen Schriftsteller.* Jena, 1929.

———. Goetz, Hans-Werner, and Karl-Wilhelm Welwei, eds. *Altes Germanien. Ausgewählte Quellen zur deutschen Geschichte,* 1a. 2 vols. Darmstadt, 1995.

———. Herrmann, Joachim, ed. *Griechische und lateinische Quellen zur frühgeschichte Mitteleuropas bis zur Mitte des 1. Jahrtausends u. Z.* 4 vols. Berlin, 1988–92.

Gibbon, Edward. *History of the Decline and Fall of the Roman Empire.* Ed. J. B. Bury. 7 vols. London, 1896–1900.

Gibert, R. "Il reino visigodo e il particularismo español." *Centro Italiano di studi sull'alto medioevo: Settimane di studio* 3 (1956): 537–83.

Gildas. *The Ruin of Britain* (*De excidio Britonum*). Ed. Michael Winterbottom. London, 1978.

Gillett, Andrew. "The Birth of Ricimer." *Historia: Zeitschrift für alte Geschichte* 44 (1995): 380–84.

———. "The Date and Circumstances of Olympiodorus of Thebes." *Traditio* 48 (1993): 1–29.

———. *Envoys and Political Communications in the Late Antique West.* Cambridge, 2003.

———. "Introduction: Ethnogenesis, History, and Methodology." In Gillett, ed., *On Barbarian Identity,* pp. 1–18.

———, ed. *On Barbarian Identity: Critical Approaches to Ethnicity in the Early Middle Ages.* Turnhout, 2002.

Gilliard, F. "The Senators of Sixth-Century Gaul." *Speculum* 54 (1979): 685–97.

Godman, Peter. *Poets and Emperors: Frankish Politics and Carolingian Poetry.* Oxford, 1987.

Goetz, Hans-Werner. "*Gens* Terminology and Perception of the 'Germanic' Peoples from Late Antiquity to the Early Middle Ages." In *Construction of Communities,* pp. 351–96.

———. "Introduction" to Regna *and* Gentes, pp. 1–11.

———. See also Germanic Antiquity.

Gregory of Tours. See Abbreviations.

Goffart, Walter. "After the Zwettl Conference: Comments on the Techniques of Accommodation." In *Anerkennung und Integration,* pp. 73–85.

————. *Barbarians and Romans* A.D. *418–584: The Techniques of Accommodation.* Princeton, N.J., 1980.

————. "Conspicuously Absent: Martial Heroism in the *Histories* of Gregory of Tours and Its Likes." In *The World of Gregory of Tours*, ed. K. Mitchell and I. Wood. Leiden, 2002, pp. 365–93.

————. "Does the Distant Past Impinge on the Invasion Age Germans?" In Gillett, ed., *On Barbarian Identity*, pp. 21–37.

————. "Does the *Vita s. Severini* Have an Underside?" In *Eugippius und Severin: Der Autor, der Text und der Heilige*, ed. Walter Pohl and Max Diesenberger. Forschungen zur Geschichte des Mittelalters 2. Vienna, 2001, pp. 33–39.

————. "From *Historiae* to *Historia Francorum* and Back Again: Aspects of the Textual History of Gregory of Tours." In *Religion, Culture, and Society in the Early Middle Ages*, ed. T. F. X. Noble and J. Contreni. Kalamazoo, 1987, pp. 55–76; *Rome's Fall and After*, pp. 255–74.

————. "From Roman Taxation to Mediaeval Seigneurie: Three Notes." *Speculum* 47 (1972): 165–87, 373–94; *Rome's Fall and After*, pp. 167–211.

————. "The *Historia ecclesiastica*: Bede's Agenda and Ours." *Haskins Society Journal: Studies in Medieval History* 2 (1990): 29–45.

————. *Historical Atlases: The First 300 Years.* Chicago, 2003.

————. "The Map of the Barbarian Invasions: A Longer Look." In *The Culture of Christendom: Essays in Medieval History*, ed. Marc A. Meyer. London, 1993, pp. 1–27.

————. "Merovingian Polyptychs: Reflections on Two Recent Publications." *Francia* 9 (1982): 57–77; *Rome's Fall and After*, pp. 233–53.

————. *The Narrators of Barbarian History* (A.D. *550–800): Jordanes, Gregory of Tours, Bede, and Paul the Deacon.* Princeton, N.J., 1988; reprinted, Notre Dame, Ind., 2005.

————. "Old and New in Merovingian Taxation." *Past and Present* 96 (August 1982): 3–21; *Rome's Fall and After*, pp. 213–31.

————. Review of Durliat, *Finances publiques. English Historical Review* 107 (1992): 675–76.

————. Review of Jordanes, *Getica*, ed. F. Giunta and Grillone. *Gnomon* 67/3 (1995): 227–29.

————. Review of Wolfram, *Geschichte der Goten* (Munich, 1980). *Speculum* 57 (1982): 444–47.

————. Review of Eric Zöllner, *Geschichte der Franken* (Munich, 1970). *Speculum* 47 (1972): 578–79.

————. "Rome, Constantinople, and the Barbarians." *American Historical Review* 86 (1981): 275–306; *Rome's Fall and After*, pp.1–44.

————. *Rome's Fall and After* (collected studies). London, 1989.

————. "The Scenario of Gatterer's 'Charten zur Geschichte der Völkerwanderung.'" In *Geschichtsdeutung auf alten Karten. Archäologie und Geschichte*, ed. Dagmar Unverhau. Wolfenbütteler Forschungen 101. Wiesbaden, 2003, pp. 213–20.

————. "The Supposedly 'Frankish' Table of Nations: An Edition and Study." *Frühmittelalterliche Studien* 17 (1983): 98–130; *Rome's Fall and After*, pp. 133–65.

————. "The Theme of '*The* Barbarian Invasions' in Late Antique and Modern Historiography." In *Das Reich und die Barbaren*, pp. 87–107; *Rome's Fall and After*, pp. 111–32.

————. "Two Notes on Germanic Antiquity Today." *Traditio* 50 (1995): 9–30.

————. "What's Wrong with the Map of the Barbarian Invasions?" In *Minorities and Barbarians in Medieval Life and Thought*, ed. Susan J. Ridyard and Robert G. Benson. Sewanee Medieval Studies 7. Sewanee, Tenn., 1996, pp. 159–77.

Le grand domaine aux époques mérovingienne et carolingienne, ed. Adriaan Verhulst (Ghent, 1985).

Hachmann, Rolf. *Die Goten und Skandinavien*. Berlin, 1970.

Haldon, J. F. *Byzantium in the Seventh Century*. Rev. ed. Cambridge, 1990, 1997.

Halphen, Louis. "La place de l'Asie dans l'histoire du monde." In *À travers l'histoire du Moyen Âge*. Paris, 1950, pp. 3–14.

Halsall, Guy. "The Origin of the *Reihengräberzivilisation* Forty Years On." In *Fifth-Century Gaul: A Crisis of Identity*, ed. J. Drinkwater and H. Elton. Cambridge, 1992, pp. 196–207.

————. Review. *English Historical Review* 118 (2003): 1349.

Hammann, S. "Bajuwaren." In *Hoops Reallexikon*. Berlin, 1973, 1:606–10.

Haverfield, Francis. "Tacitus during the Late Roman Period and the Middle Ages." *Journal of Roman Studies* 6 (1916): 195–200.

Hayes, Carlton Huntley. *An Introduction to the Sources Relating to the Germanic Invasions*. New York, 1909.

Heather, Peter. "*Gens* and *regnum* among the Ostrogoths." In *Regna and Gentes*, pp. 88–133.

————. *The Goths*. The Peoples of Europe. Oxford, 1996.

————. *Goths and Romans, 332–489*. Oxford, 1991.

————. "The Huns and the End of the Roman Empire in Western Europe." *English Historical Review* 110 (1995): 4–41.

Hedeager, Lotte. "The Creation of Germanic Identity: A European Origin-Myth." In *Frontières d'Empire: Nature et signification des frontières romaines*. Mémoires du Musée de Préhistoire d'Ile de France 5 (Nemours, 1993), pp. 121–31.

Hendy, Michael. "From Public to Private: The Western Barbarian Coinages as a Mirror of the Disintegration of Late Roman State Structures." *Viator* 19 (1988): 29–78.

————. *Studies in the Byzantine Monetary Economy c. 300–1450*. Cambridge, 1985.

Hermann. See Germanic Antiquity.

Historia Augusta. Ed. Ernest Hohl. Teubner. Leipzig, 1965.

Historiographie im frühen Mittelalter. Ed. Anton Scharer and G. Scheibelreiter. Veröffentlichungen des Instituts für österreichische Geschichtsforschung 32. Vienna-Munich, 1994.

Hodgkin, Thomas. *Italy and Her Invaders*. 8 vols. London, 1885–99.

Hoefinger, Konrad. *Germanen gegen Rom: Ein europäischer Schicksalskampf*. Tübingen, 1986.

Hoffmann, Dietrich. *Das spätrömische Bewegungsheer und die Notitia Dignitatum*. Epigraphische Studien 7. Düsseldorf, 1969, pp. 135–45.

Holmes, T. Rice. *The Architect of the Roman Empire*. Oxford, 1928.

Hoops Reallexikon. See Abbreviations.

Horrabin, J. F. *Atlas of European History*. London, 1935.

Howorth, Henry H. "The Germans of Caesar." *English Historical Review* 23 (1908): 417–26.

Hummer, Hans J. "The Fluidity of Barbarian Identity: The Ethnogenesis of Alemanni and Suebi, A.D. 200–500." *Early Medieval Europe* 7/1 (1998): 1–27.

Hydatius. *The* Chronicle *of Hydatius and the* Consularia Constantinopolitana: *Two Contemporary Accounts of the Final Years of the Roman Empire.* Ed. and trans. R. W. Burgess. Oxford, 1993.

———. *Chronique.* Ed. and trans. Alain Tranoy. 2 vols. Sources chrétiennes 218–19. Paris, 1974.

Innes, Matthew. "Danelaw Identities: Ethnicity, Regionalism, and Political Allegiance." In *Cultures in Contact: Scandinavian Settlement in England in the Ninth and Tenth Century,* ed. D. M. Hadley and J. D. Richards. Turnhout, 2000, pp. 65–88.

———. "Teutons or Trojans? The Carolingians and the Germanic Past." In *The Uses of the Past in the Early Middle Ages,* ed. Y. Hen and M. Innes. Cambridge, 2000, pp. 227–49.

Inst. See Abbreviations.

Integration und Herrschaft. Ed. Walter Pohl and Max Diesenberger. Forschungen zur Geschichte des Mittelalters 3. Vienna, 2002.

Isidore, Saint, bishop of Seville. *Etymologiae.* Ed. W. M. Lindsay. 2 vols. Oxford, 1911.

———. *Historia Gothorum Vandalorum Suevorum.* MG AA 11.

Jacobs, Edward H. *Accidental Migrations: An Archaeology of Gothic Discourse.* Lewisburg, Pa., 2000.

Jahn, Martin. "Die Wandalen." In *Vorgeschichte der deutschen Stämme,* 3:1001–19.

James, Edward. *The Merovingian Archaeology of South-West Gaul.* 2 vols. British Archaeological Reports, International Series 22. Oxford, 1977.

———. Review of Goffart, *B&R. Speculum* 57 (1982): 886–87.

Jänichen, H. "Alemannen. Geschichtliches." In *Hoops Reallexikon.* Berlin, 1973, 1:138–42.

Jankuhn, Herbert, and Dieter Timpe, eds. *Beiträge zum Verständnis der* Germania *des Tacitus.* 2 parts. Abh. Akad. Göttingen, philol.-hist. Klasse, 3. Folge, 175. Göttingen, 1989.

Jerome, Saint. *Epistolae.* Ed. Jérôme Labourt. *Lettres.* Collection des universités de France. 8 vols. Paris, 1949–63.

———. *In Esaiam.* In *Patrologia Latina* 24:9–678.

———. *Vita S. Hilarionis.* In *Patrologia Latina* 23:29–54.

Jiménez Garnica, Ana Maria. "Settlement of the Visigoths in the Fifth Century." In *The Visigoths from the Migration Period to the Seventh Century: An Ethnographic Perspective,* ed. Peter Heather. San Marino, 1999, pp. 93–115.

John, Eric. *Land Tenure in Early England.* Leicester, 1964.

———. *Orbis Britanniae.* Leicester, 1966.

John Lydus. *De magistratibus.* Trans. Anastasius C. Bandy. Philadelphia, 1983.

Jones, A. H. M. *The Later Roman Empire, 284–602: A Social, Economic and Administrative Survey.* 3 vols. Oxford, 1964; 2 vols. Norman, Okla., 1964.

Jordanes. See Abbreviations.

Kagan, D., ed. *Decline and Fall of the Roman Empire: Why Did It Collapse?* Problems in European Civilization. Boston, 1962.

Kaiser, Reinhold. *Die Burgunder.* Kohlhammer Urban-Taschenbücher 586. Stuttgart, 2004.

Kaiserchronik: Der keiser und die kunige buoch oder der sogenannte Kaiserchronik. Ed. Hans F. Massman. 3 vols. Quedlinburg and Leipzig, 1849–54.

Kaplonski, Christopher. "The Mongolian Impact on Eurasia: A Reassessment." In Bell-Fialkoff, ed., *Role of Migration,* pp. 251–74.

Kelley, Donald. "*Tacitus noster*: The *Germania* in the Renaissance and Reformation." In *Tacitus and the Tacitean Tradition,* ed. T. J. Luce and A. Woodman. Princeton, N.J., 1993, pp. 152–67.

King, P. D. *Law and Society in the Visigothic Kingdom*. Cambridge, 1972.

Kingdoms of the Empire: The Integration of Barbarians in Late Antiquity. Ed. Walter Pohl. Leiden, 1997.

Kirby, D. P. *Bede's* Historia ecclesiastica gentis Anglorum: *Its Contemporary Setting*. Jarrow Lecture 1992. Jarrow, 1993.

Kliger, Samuel. *The Goths in England: A Study of Seventeenth and Eighteenth-Century Thought*. New York, 1972.

Kortüm, H.-H. "Geschichtsschreibung." In *Hoops Reallexikon*. Berlin, 1998, 11:477–88.

Kossinna, Gustaf. *Die deutsche Vorgeschichte: Eine hervorragend nationale Wissenschaft*. Würzburg, 1912. Reprinted at least four times before World War II.

———. *Die Herkunft die Germanen*. Würzburg, 1911; reprinted, 1978.

———. *Ursprung und Verbreitung der Germanen in vor- und frühgeschichtlicher Zeit*. Mannus-Bibliothek 6. Leipzig, 1928.

Kraus, Andreas. *Grundzüge der Geschichte Bayerns*. 2nd ed. Darmstadt, 1992.

Krause, Arnulf. *Die Geschichte der Germanen*. Frankfurt, 2002.

Krieger, Rommel. *Untersuchungen und Hypothesen zur Ansiedlung der Westgoten, Burgunden, und Ostgoten*. Bern, 1991.

Krüger, Bruno. *Die Germanen: Mythos—Geschichte—Kultur—Archäologie*. Langenweissbach, 2003.

Kulikowski, Michael. "Barbarians in Gaul, Usurpers in Britain." *Britannia* 31 (2000): 325–31.

———. *Late Roman Spain and Its Cities*. Baltimore, 2004.

———. "Nation Versus Army: A Necessary Contrast?" In Gillett, ed., *On Barbarian Identity*, pp. 69–84.

Lactantius. *De mortibus persecutorum*. Ed. Jacques Moreau. Sources chrétiennes 39. Paris, n.d.

Lewis, D. T., and C. Short. *A Latin Dictionary*. Oxford, 1879.

Levy, Ernst. *West Roman Vulgar Law: The Law of Property*. Philadelphia, 1951.

LB. See Abbreviations.

LBExtravagans. See Abbreviations.

Liebeschuetz, J. H. W. G. *Barbarians and Bishops: Army, Church and State in the Age of Arcadius and Chrysostom*. Oxford, 1990.

———. "Cities, Taxes and the Accommodation of the Barbarians: The Theories of Durliat and Goffart." In *Kingdoms of the Empire*, pp. 135–51.

———. "*Gens* into *regnum*: The Vandals." In Regna *and* Gentes, pp. 55–83.

Longnon, Auguste. *Géographie de la Gaule au VIè siècle*. Paris, 1878.

Lönnroth, Erik. "Die Goten in der modernen kritischen Geschichtsauffassung." In *Studia Gotica: Die eisenzeitlichen Verbindungen zwischen Schweden und Südosteuropa*, ed. U. E. Hagberg. Stockholm, 1972, pp. 57–62.

Lot, Ferdinand. "Du régime de l'hospitalité." *Revue belge de philologie et d'histoire* 7 (1928): 975–1011.

———. *The End of the Ancient World and the Beginning of the Middles Ages*. Trans. P. and M. Leon. London, 1931; reprinted, New York, 1961.

———. *Les invasions germaniques: La pénétration mutuelle du monde barbare et du monde romain*. Paris, 1935; reprinted, 1945.

Lotter, Friedrich. "Zur Rolle der Donausueben in der Völkerwanderungszeit." *Mitteilungen des Instituts für österreichische Geschichtsforschung* 76 (1968): 275–98.

Löwe, Heinz. "Vermeintliche gotische Überlieferungsreste bei Cassiodorus und Jordanes." In *Ex ipsis rerum documentis: Beiträge zur Mediävistik: Festschrift für Harald Zimmermann*, ed. K. Herbers et al. Sigmaringen, 1991, pp. 17–30.

Loyen, André. *Recherches historiques sur les Panégyriques de Sidoine Apollinaire*. Paris, 1943.

LRB. See Abbreviations.

Luiselli, Bruno. *Storia culturale dei rapporti tra mondo romano e mondo germanico*. Rome, 1992.

Lund, Allan A. *Die ersten Germanen: Ethnizität und Ethnogenese*. Heidelberg, 1998.

———. *Germanenideologie im Nationalsozialismus: Zur Rezeption der 'Germania' des Tacitus im 'Dritten Reich.'* Heidelberg, 1995.

———. See also Tacitus.

Lütkenhaus, Werner. *Constantius III: Studien zu seiner Tätigkeit und Stellung im Westreich 411–421*. Bonn, 1998.

LV. See Abbreviations.

Maas, Michael. "Roman History and Christian Ideology in Justinianic Reform Legislation." *Dumbarton Oaks Papers* 40 (1986): 17–31.

MacGeorge, Penny. *Late Roman Warlords*. Oxford, 2002.

Mączyńka, Magdalena. *Die Völkerwanderung: Geschichte einer ruhelosen Epoche im 4. und 5. Jahrhundert*. Zurich, 1993.

Maenchen-Helfen, Otto. *The World of the Huns*. Berkeley, 1973.

Magocsi, P. B. *Historical Atlas of East Central Europe*. Toronto, 1993.

Malalas, John. *Chronicle*. Trans. Elisabeth Jeffreys et al. Byzantina Australiensia 4. Melbourne, 1986.

Malchus of Philadelphia, fragments. See Blockley.

Malone, K. "The Suffix of Appurtenance in *Widsith.*" *Modern Language Review* 28 (1933): 315–19.

Mann, J. C. "The Frontiers of the Principate." In *Aufstieg und Niedergang der römischen Welt*, part 2, *Principat*, ed. Hildegard Temporini. Berlin, 1974, 1:508–33.

Marcellinus Comes. *The Chronicle of Marcellinus*. Ed. and trans. Brian Croke. Byzantina Australiensia 7. Sydney, 1995.

———. *Chronicon*. MG AA 11: 60–108.

Marius, bishop of Avenches. *Chronicle*. Ed. Justin Favrod. *La Chronique de Marius d'Avenches (455–581): Texte, traduction et commentaire*. Lausanne, 1991.

———. *Chronicle*. Ed. T. Mommsen. MG AA 11:227–239.

Martens, Jes. "The Vandals: Myths and Facts about a Germanic Tribe of the First Half of the 1st Millennium AD." In *Archaeological Approaches to Cultural Identity*, ed. Stephen Shennan. One World Archaeology, ed. P. J. Oeko, 10. London, 1989, pp. 57–65.

Martin, Jochen. *Spätantike und Völkerwanderung*. Oldenbourg Grundriß der Geschichte, ed. J. Bleicken et al. Munich, 1987.

Martin of Braga. See Barlow.

Mascov, Johann Jakob. *Geschichte der Teutschen bis zur Anfang der Fränkische Monarchie*. Leipzig, 1726.

———. *The History of the Ancient Germans . . . who overthrew the Roman Empire*. Trans. Thomas Lediard. London, 1738.

Mathisen, R. W., and H. Sivan. "Forging a New Identity: The Kingdom of Toulouse and the Frontiers of Visigothic Aquitania (418–507)." In *The Visigoths. Studies in Culture and Society*, ed. A. Ferreiro. Leiden, 1999, pp. 1–6.

Mathisen, Ralph W. "Resistance and Reconciliation: Majorian and the Gallic Aristocracy after the Fall of Avitus." *Francia* 7 (1979): 597–627.

Matthews, John. *The Roman Empire of Ammianus.* Baltimore, 1989.

———. *Western Aristocracies and Imperial Court* A.D. *364–425.* Oxford, 1975.

Mazzarino, Santo. *The End of the Ancient World.* Trans. G. Holmes. London, 1966.

McKitterick, Rosamond. *The Frankish Kingdoms under the Carolingians.* London, 1983.

Metcalf, D. M. "Viking-Age Numismatics. 1. Late Roman and Byzantine Gold in the Northern Lands" (President's Address). *Numismatic Chronicle* 155 (1995): 413–41.

Millar, Fergus. *The Roman Empire and Its Neighbours.* London, 1967.

Miltner, Franz. "Vandalen." In Pauly-Wissowa. 8A:298–338.

Mócsy, András. *Pannonia and Upper Moesia: A History of the Middle Danube Provinces of the Roman Empire.* London, 1974.

Momigliano, Arnaldo. Review of Jones, *The Later Roman Empire.* In *Quarto contributo alla storia degli studi classici.* Storia e letteratura 115. Rome, 1969, pp. 645–47.

Moorhead, John. *Justinian.* London, 1994.

———. *Theoderic in Italy.* Oxford, 1992.

Mortensen, Lars Boje. "Stylistic Choice in a Reborn Genre: The National Histories of Widukind of Corvey and Dudo of St. Quentin." In *Dudone di San Quintino,* ed. Paolo Gatti and Antonella Degl'Innocenti. Trento, 1995, pp. 77–102.

Much, Rudolf. "Gepiden." In *Reallexikon der germanische Altertumskunde,* 1st ed., ed. Johannes Hoops. Strasbourg, 1913–15, 2:157–58.

Muhlberger, Steven. *The Fifth-Century Chroniclers: Prosper, Hydatius, and the Gallic Chronicler of 452.* Arca, Classical and Medieval Texts, Papers and Monographs, ed. Francis Cairns, et al., 27. Leeds, 1990.

———. "Heroic Kings and Unruly Generals: The 'Copenhagen' Continuator of Prosper Reconsidered." *Florilegium* 6 (1985): 50–70.

Murray, Alexander Callander. "Reinhard Wenskus on 'Ethnogenesis,' Ethnicity, and the Origin of the Franks." In Gillett, ed., *On Barbarian Identity,* pp. 39–68.

———. Review of Wolfram, *History of the Goths. International History Review* 11 (1989): 529–31.

———. See also *After Rome's Fall.*

Musset, Lucien. *The Germanic Invasions: The Making of Europe* AD *400–600.* Trans. E. and C. James. University Park, Pa., 1975.

———. *Les Invasions.* Vol. 1, *Les vagues germaniques.* Nouvelle Clio 12. Paris, 1965.

Nicolet, Claude. *La fabrique d'une nation: La France entre Rome et les Germains.* Paris, 2003.

Nielsen, Hans Frede. *The Early Runic Language of Scandinavia: Studies in Germanic Dialect Geography.* Heidelberg, 2000.

Niermeyer, J. G. *Mediae Latinitatis lexicon minus.* 2 vols. Leiden, 1976.

Norden, Eduard. *Die germanische Urgeschichte in Tacitus Germania.* Leipzig, 1920.

Notitia dignitatum utriusque imperii. Ed. Otto Seeck. 1876. Reprinted, Frankfurt, 1962.

O'Flynn, John Michael. *Generalissimos of the Western Roman Empire.* Edmonton, 1983.

Olympiodorus of Thebes, fragments. See Blockley.

Oost, S. I. *Galla Placidia Augusta.* Chicago, 1968.

Orosius. *Historia adversum paganos.* Ed. K. Zangemeister. CSEL 5. Vienna, 1882. Trans. Roy J. Defarri. Fathers of the Church 50. Washington, D.C., 1964.

Ors, Alvaro d'. *Estudios Visigoticos.* Vol. 2, *Il Codigo di Eurico.* Rome-Madrid, 1960.

Ortelius, Abraham. *Aurei saeculi imago, sive Germanorum veterum vita, mores, ritus, et religio iconibus delineati et commentariis ex utrumque linguae auctoribus descriptae.* Antwerp, 1596.

Oxford Latin Dictionary. Ed. P. G. Glare. Oxford, 1982.

Pacatus. *Panegyricus Theodosio dictus.* Ed. and trans. Edouard Galletier. *Panégyriques latins.* Collection des universités de France. 3 vols. Paris, 1949–53, 3:68–114.

Pagden, Anthony. *Peoples and Empires: A Short History of European Migration, Exploration, and Conquest from Greece to the Present.* New York, 2001.

Palanque, J. R. "La vie et l'œuvre d'Ernest Stein." In Stein, *Histoire du Bas-Empire,* 2:vii–xvii.

Papyri. *Die nichtliterarischen lateinischen Papyri Italiens aus der Zeit 445–700.* Ed. Jan-Olof Tjäder. Vol. 2. Stockholm, 1982.

Paschoud, François. See Zosimus.

Pastenaci, Kurt. *Die beiden Weltmächte: Der 500jährige Kampf der Germanen mit Rom.* 1938. Reprinted, Viöl, 1995.

Paul the Deacon. *Historia Langobardorum.* MG SRL.

Périn, Patrick, and Laure-Charlotte Feffer. *Les Francs.* Vol. 1, *À la conquête de la Gaule.* Paris, 1987.

Peutinger, Konrad. "De gentium quarundam emigrationibus brevis epitome." In *Procopii Caesariensis de rebus Gothorum, Persarum ac Vandalorum libri VI una cum aliis mediorum temporum historicis,* ed. Beatus Rhenanus. Basel, 1531, p. 687–88.

Pirenne, Henri. *Mohammed and Charlemagne.* Trans. Bernard Miall. London, 1939.

Pitts, Lynn F. "Relations between Rome and the German 'Kings' on the Middle Danube." *Journal of Roman Studies* 79 (1989): 45–58.

Pliny, the Elder. *Natural History.* Ed. and trans H. Rackham. LCL, vol. 4. Cambridge, Mass., 1945.

Pohl, Walter. *Die Awaren: Ein Steppenvolk im Mitteleuropa, 567–822 n. Chr.* Munich, 1988.

———. "Ethnicity in Early Medieval Studies." *Archaeologia Polona* 29 (1991): 39–49.

———. "Ethnicity, Theory, and Tradition: A Response." In Gillett, ed., *On Barbarian Identity,* pp. 221–39.

———. "Gepiden, Historisches." In *Hoops Reallexikon.* Berlin, 1998, 11:131–40.

———. "Die Gepiden und die gentes an der mittleren Donau nach dem Zerfall des Attilareiches." In *Die Völker an der mittleren und unteren Donau im 5. und 6. Jahrhundert,* ed. H. Wolfram and F. Daim. Österreichische Akademie der Wissenschaften, Phil.-hist. Klasse. *Denkschriften* 145. Vienna, 1980, pp. 240–72.

———. *Die Germanen.* Enzyklopädie deutscher Geschichte 57. Munich, 2000.

———. "Introduction: Strategies of Distinction." In *Strategies of Distinction,* pp. 1–15.

———. "Memory, Identity and Power in Lombard Italy." In *The Uses of the Past in the Early Middle Ages,* ed. Yitzhak Hen and Matthew Innes. Cambridge, 2000, pp. 9–28.

———. "A Non-Roman Empire in Central Europe: The Avars." In *Regna and Gentes,* pp. 571–95.

———. "Paolo Diacono e la costruzione dell'identità longobarda." In *Paolo Diacono: Uno scrittore fra tradizione longobarda e rinovamento carolingio,* ed. Paolo Chiesa. Udine, 2000, pp. 413–26.

———. "*Per hospites divisi:* Wirtschaftliche Grundlagen der langobardischen Ansiedlung in Italien." *Römische historische Mitteilungen* 43 (2001): 179–226.

————. "The Politics of Change: Reflections on the Transformation of the Roman World." In *Integration und Herrschaft*, pp. 275–88.

————. *Die Völkerwanderung. Eroberung und Integration.* Stuttgart, 2002.

————. See also *Integration und Herrschaft; Kingdoms of the Empire; Regna and Gentes; Strategies of Distinction; Typen der Ethnogenese.*

Poliakov, Léon. *The Aryan Myth: A History of Racist and Nationalist Ideas in Europe.* Trans. E. Howard. New York, 1974.

Polverini, Leandro. "Germani in Italia prima dei Cimbri?" In *Germani in Italia*, ed. B. and P. Scardigli. Rome, 1994, pp. 1–10.

Prinz, Friedrich. *Die Geschichte Bayerns.* Munich, 1997.

Priscus of Panium, fragments. See Blockley.

Pritzak, Omelian. "Alans." In *Oxford Dictionary of Byzantium.* 3 vols. New York, 1991, 1:31–32.

Procopius. See Abbreviations.

Prosopography of the Later Roman Empire. Ed. J. R. Martindale et al. 3 vols. Cambridge, 1980–92.

Prosper of Aquitaine. *Chronicon.* MG AA 9.

Putzger, F. W. *Historischer Schul-Atlas.* Bielefeld and Leipzig, 1877–.

Regna *and Gentes: The Relationship between Late Antique and Early Medieval Peoples and Kingdoms in the Transformation of the Roman World.* Ed. H. W. Goetz, J. Jarnut, and W. Pohl. Leiden, 2003.

Rehrmann, F. A., *Kaiser Augustus.* Hildesheim, 1937.

Das Reich und die Barbaren. Ed. Evangelos Chrysos and Andreas Schwarcz. Veröffentlichungen des Instituts für österreichische Geschichtsforschung 29. Vienna, 1989.

Reimitz, Helmut, "Social Networks and Identities in Frankish Historiography: New Aspects of the Textual History of Gregory of Tours' Historiae." In *Construction of Communities*, pp. 229–68.

Reinerth, Hans. "Die Urgermanen." In *Vorgeschichte der deutschen Stämme*, 1:1–64.

Reynolds, Susan. "Medieval *Origines gentium* and the Community of the Realm." *History* 68 (1983): 375–90.

————. "Our Forefathers? Tribes, Peoples, and Nations in the Historiography of the Age of Migrations." In *After Rome's Fall*, pp. 17–36.

Richard, Guy, ed. *Ailleurs, l'herbe est plus verte: Histoire des migrations dans le monde.* Paris, 1996.

Riché, Pierre. *Éducation et culture dans l'Occident barbare, 6è-8è siècles.* Paris, 1962.

Ridé, Jacques. *L'Image du Germain dans la pensée et la littérature allemandes de la redécouverte de Tacite à la fin du XVIème siècle.* Diss. Paris IV. 3 vols. Lille-Paris, 1977.

Roosens, Eugeen. *Creating Ethnicity: The Process of Ethnogenesis.* Newbury Park, Calif., 1989.

Rosen, Klaus. *Die Völkerwanderung.* Munich, 2002.

Rosenwein, Barbara H. *A Short History of the Middle Ages.* Peterborough, Ontario, 2002.

Rudolf of Fulda. *Translatio s. Alexandri* (excerpt). Ed. A. Bauer and R. Rau. Ausgewählte Quellen zur deutschen Geschichte des Mittelalters 8. 2nd ed. Darmstadt, 1977, pp. 12–15.

Sallust. *Jugurtha.* Ed. Alfred Ernout. Collection des universités de France. Paris, 1958.

Savigny, F. C. *Geschichte der römischen Rechts im Mittelatler.* Heidelberg, 1815; Trans. E. Cathcard. Edinburgh, 1829.

Schanz, Martin. *Geschichte der römischen Literatur*. 2/2. 3rd ed. Munich, 1913.

Schirren, Carl. *De ratione quae inter Iordanem et Cassiodorum intercedat commentatio*. Dorpat [Tartu], 1858.

Schmidt, Ludwig. *Allgemeine Geschichte der germanischen Völker bis zur Mitte des sechsten Jahrhunderts*. Munich, 1909.

———. *Geschichte der Wandalen*. 2nd ed. Munich, 1942.

———. *Histoire des Vandales*. Trans. H. E. Del Medico. Paris, 1953.

———. "Die Ursachen der Völkerwanderung." *Neue Jahrbücher für das klassiche Altertum, Geschichte und deutsche Literatur* 11 (1903): 340–50.

———. See also Abbreviations.

Schmoeckel, Reinhard. *Deutsche Sagenhelden und die historische Wirklichkeit: Zwei Jahrhunderte deutscher Frühgeschichte neu gesehen*. Hildesheim, 1995.

Schultze, Walther. "Die Völkerwanderung und das germanische Mittelmeersystem." In *Gebhardts Handbuch der deutschen Geschichte*, 7th ed., ed. Robert Holtzmann. 2 vols. Stuttgart, 1930, 1: 64–114.

Schwerin von Krosigk, Hildegard Gräfin. *Gustaf Kossinna: Der Nachlass: Versuch einer Analyse*. Neumünster, 1982.

Seeck, Otto. *Geschichte des Untergangs der antiken Welt*. 6 vols. Stuttgart, 1910–25.

Segal, Aaron. *An Atlas of International Migration*. London, 1993.

Shepherd, William. *Historical Atlas*. 7th ed. New York, 1929.

Sidonius Apollinaris. *Poems and Letters*. Ed. W. B. Anderson. 2 vols. LCL. Cambridge, Mass., 1963–85.

Sinor, Denis. "The Hun Period." In *The Cambridge History of Early Inner Asia*, ed. D. Sinor. Cambridge, 1990, pp. 177–205.

Slicher van Bath. See Bath.

Smith, C. T. *A Historical Geography of Western Europe before 1800*. London, 1967.

Socrates. *Historia ecclesiastica*. Trans. A. C. Zenos. A Select Library of Nicene and Post-Nicene Fathers, ed. Philip Schaff and Henry Wace. Reprinted, Ann Arbor, 1976.

Southern, Pat, and Karen R. Dixon. *The Late Roman Army*. New Haven, 1996.

Springer, M. "Sachsen: Historisches." In *Hoops Reallexikon*. Berlin, 2004, 26:31–46.

Stanley, E. G. *The Search for Anglo-Saxon Paganism*. Cambridge, 1975.

Stein. "Sarmaticus." In *Pauly-Wissowa*, Supplement 2, 2/1.

Stein, Ernst. *Histoire du Bas-Empire*. Ed. J. R. Palanque. 2 vols. Paris, 1949–59.

Steuer, H. "Germanen, Germania, germanische Altertumskunde. Wirtschafts- und Sozialgeschichte." In *Hoops Reallexikon*. Berlin, 1998, 11:318–56.

Strategies of Distinction: The Construction of Ethnic Communities, 300–800. Ed. Walter Pohl and Helmut Reimitz. Leiden, 1998.

Stroheker, Karl Friedrich. "Zur Rolle der Heermeister fränkischer Abstammung im späten vierten Jahrhundert." In *Germanentum und Spätantike*. Zurich, 1965, pp. 9–29.

Sulimirski, T. *The Sarmatians*. New York, 1970.

Svennung, Joseph. *Zur Geschichte des Goticismus*. Uppsala, 1967.

Syme, Ronald. *The Roman Revolution*. Oxford, 1939.

Tablettes Albertini: Actes privés de l' époque vandale (fin du Vè siècle). Ed. Christian Courtois et al. Paris, 1952.

Tacitus. *Germania*. Ed. Allan A. Lund. Heidelberg, 1988.

———. *The* Germania *of Tacitus: A Critical Edition*. Ed. R. P. Robinson. Middletown, Conn., 1935.

————. *Tacitus' Agricola, Germania.* Trans. Herbert W. Benario. Norman, Okla., 1991.

Taylor, M. "Heruler." In *Hoops Reallexikon.* Berlin, 1999, 14:460–74.

Teillet, Suzanne. *Des Goths à la nation gothique: Les origines de l'idée de nation en Occident du Vè au VIIè siècle.* Paris, 1984.

Theophylact Simocatta. *History.* Trans. M. and M. Whitby. Oxford, 1996.

Thomas, Heinz. "Die Deutschen und die Rezeption ihres Volksnamens." In *Nord und Süd in der deutschen Geschichte des Mittelalters,* ed. W. Paravicini. Sigmaringen, 1990, pp. 19–50.

————. "*frenkisk*: Zur Geschichte von *theodiscus* und *teutonicus* im Frankenreich des 9. Jahrhunderts." In *Beiträge zur Geschichte des Regnum Francorum,* ed. Rudolf Schieffer. Beiheft der *Francia* 22. Sigmaringen, 1990, pp. 67–95.

————. "Julius Caesar und die Deutschen: Zu Ursprung und Gehalt eines deutschen Geschichtsbewußtseins in der Zeit Gregors VII. und Heinrichs IV." In *Die Salier und das Reich,* ed. Stefan Weinfurter. 3 vols. Sigmaringen, 1991, 3:245–77.

————. "Der Ursprung des Wortes Theodiscus." *Historische Zeitschrift* 247 (1988): 295–331.

Thompson, E. A. "The Conversion of the Spanish Suebi to Catholicism." In *Visigothic Spain: New Approaches,* ed. Edward James. Oxford, 1980, pp. 77–92.

————. "Early Germanic Warfare," *Past and Present* 14 (1958): 2–29.

————. *The Goths in Spain.* Oxford, 1969.

————. *A History of Attila and the Huns.* Oxford, 1948; New ed. Peter Heather under the title *The Huns.* Oxford, 1996.

————. *A Roman Reformer and Inventor.* Oxford, 1952.

————. *Romans and Barbarians: The Decline of the Western Empire.* Madison, Wis., 1982.

Timpe, Dieter. "Kimberntradition und Kimbermythos." In *Germani in Italia,* ed. B. and P. Scardigli. Rome, 1994, pp. 23–60.

Todd, Malcolm, *The Northern Barbarians 100 B.C.–A.D. 300* (London, 1975).

Torday, Laszlo. *Mounted Archers: The Beginning of Central Asian History.* Edinburgh and Durham, 1997.

Trigger, Bruce G. *A History of Archaeological Thought.* Cambridge, 1989.

Typen der Ethnogenese unter besonderer Berücksichtigung der Bayern. Part 1. Ed. Herwig Wolfram and Walter Pohl. Vienna, 1990.

Valesian Anonymous. *Excerpta Valesiana.* Ed. Jacques Moreau. Teubner. Leipzig, 1960.

Vegetius. *Epitoma rei militaris* (de re militari). Ed. A. Önnerfors. Teubner. Leipzig, 1995.

————. *Mulomedicina.* Ed. E. Lommatzsch. Teubner. Leipzig, 1903.

Verhulst, Adriaan, "Economic Organisation," in *The New Cambridge Mediaeval History,* vol. 2, *ca. 700–ca. 900,* ed. Rosamond McKitterick (Cambridge, 1995), pp. 448–90.

————. "La genèse du régime domanial classique en France au début du moyen âge," *Centro Italiano di studi sull'alto medioevo: Settimane di studio* 13 (1966): 135–60.

Vernadsky, George. "The Eurasian Nomads and Their Impact on Medieval Europe (A Reconsideration of the Problem)." *Studi medievali* 3rd Ser., 4/2 (1963): 401–34.

Verona List. *Laterculus Veronensis.* In *Notitia Dignitatum,* ed. Otto Seeck. 1876. Reprinted, Frankfurt, 1962, pp. 247–53.

Victor of Vita. *Historia persecutionis Africanae provinciae.* Ed. C. Halm. MG AA 3 part 1.

Vocabularium iurisprudentiae Romanae. 5 vols. Berlin, 1903–39.

Vorgeschichte der deutschen Stämme: Germanische Tat und Kultur auf deutschen Boden. Ed. Hans Reinerth. 3 vols. Leipzig, 1940, reprinted, 1986–87.

Wallace-Hadrill, J. M. *The Barbarian West 400–1000.* 3rd ed. London, 1967; 1st ed., 1952.

Ward-Perkins, Bryan. *From Classical Antiquity to the Middle Ages: Urban Public Building in Northern and Central Italy, A D 300–850.* Oxford, 1984.

Weibull, Curt. *Die Auswanderung der Goten aus Schweden.* Göteborg, 1958.

Weidemann, Margerete. *Kulturgeschichte der Merowingerzeit nach den Werken Gregors von Tours.* 2 vols. Mainz, 1982.

Wells, Peter S. *The Barbarians Speak: How the Conquered Peoples Shaped Roman Europe.* Princeton, N. J., 1999.

Weißensteiner, Johann. "Cassiodor/Jordanes als Geschichtsschreiber." In *Historiographie im frühen Mittelalter,* pp. 308–35.

Wenskus, Reinhard. "Alanen." In *Hoops Reallexikon.* Berlin, 1973, 1:122–23.

———. See Abbreviations.

Werner, K. F. *Vom Frankenreich zur Entfaltung Deutschlands und Frankreichs.* Sigmaringen, 1984.

Whittaker, C. R. *Frontiers of the Roman Empire: A Social and Economic Study.* Baltimore, 1994.

Wickham, Chris. *Early Medieval Italy: Central Power and Local Society 400–1000.* London, 1981.

Widsith. Ed. Kemp Malone. Anglistica 13. Copenhagen, 1962.

Widukind. *Res gestae Saxonicae.* Ed. A. Bauer and R. Rau. Ausgewählte Quellen zur deutschen Geschichte des Mittelalters 8. 2nd ed. Darmstadt, 1977.

Wietersheim, E. von. *Geschichte der Völkerwanderung.* 2 vols. 2nd ed. Leipzig, 1888.

Williams, Stephen. *Diocletian and the Roman Recovery.* London, 1985.

Wolfram, Herwig, "Zur Ansiedlung reichsangehöriger Föderaten: Erklärungsversuch und Forschungsziele." *Mitteilungen des Instituts für österreichische Geschichtsforschung* 91 (1983): 5–35.

———. "Die Aufnahme germanischer Völker ins Römerreich: Aspekte und Konsequenzen." *Centro Italiano di studi sull'alto medioevo: Settimane di studio* 29/1 (1983): 87–117, 119–30.

———. "Einige Überlegungen zur gotischen *origo gentis.*" In *Studia linguistica Alexandro Vasilii filio Issatschenko a collegis amicisque oblato,* ed. Henrik Birnbaum et al. Lisse, The Netherlands, 1978, pp. 487–99.

———. *Geschichte der Goten: Von den Anfängen bis zur Mitte des sechsten Jahrhunderts: Entwurf einer historischen Ethnographie.* Munich, 1979; revised 2nd edition, 1980; revised 3rd edition, under the main title *Die Goten,* 1990.

———. *History of the Goths.* Trans. T. J. Dunlap. Berkeley, 1988.

———. "Neglected Evidence on the Accommodation of Barbarians in Gaul." In *Kingdoms of the Empire,* pp. 181–83.

———. "*Origo et religio:* Ethnic Traditions and Literature in Early Medieval Texts." *Early Medieval Europe* 3 (1994): 19–38.

———. "*Origo gentis:* The Literature of German Origins." In *Early Germanic Literature and Culture,* ed. Brian Murdoch and Malcolm Read. Rochester, N.Y., 2004, pp. 39–54.

———. *Das Reich und die Germanen.* Berlin, 1990.

———. "Theogonie, Ethnogenese und ein kompromittierter Großvater im Stammbaum Theoderichs des Großen." In *Festschrift für Helmut Beumann,* ed. K.-U. Jäschke and R. Wenskus. Sigmarigen, 1977, pp. 80–97.

———. *Treasures on the Danube: Barbarian Invaders and Their Roman Inheritance*. Ed. G. Langthaler. Vienna, 1985.

———. "Typen der Ethnogenese: Ein Versuch." In *Die Franken und die Alemannen bis zur "Schlacht bei Zülpich*," ed. Dieter Geuenich. Ergänzungsbänder zum Reallexikon der germanischen Altertumskunde 19. Berlin, 1998, pp. 608–27.

Wood, Ian. "Appendix: The Settlement of the Burgundians." Appendix to "Ethnicity and the Ethnogenesis of the Burgundians," in *Typen der Ethnogenese*, pp. 65–69.

———. "The Barbarian Invasions and First Settlements." In *Cambridge Ancient History*, new ed. Averil Cameron and Peter Garnsey. Cambridge, 1997, 13:516–37.

———. "*Gentes*, Kings and Kingdoms—The Emergence of States: The Kingdom of the Gibichungs." In Regna *and* Gentes, pp. 243–69.

———. Review of Goffart, *B&R. History* 220 (1982): 306–7.

Wormald, Patrick. *Bede and the Conversion of England: The Charter Evidence*. Jarrow Lecture 1984. Jarrow, n.d.

———. "The Decline of the Western Empire and the Survival of Its Aristocracy." *Journal of Roman Studies* 66 (1976): 217–26.

Wozniak, Frank E., "Byzantine Diplomacy and the Lombard-Gepidic Wars." *Balkan Studies* 20 (1978): 139–58.

———. "East Rome, Ravenna and Western Illyricum: 454–536 A.D." *Historia: Zeitschrift für alte Geschichte* 30 (1981): 351–82.

Wynn, Phillip. "Frigeridus, the British Tyrants, and the Early Fifth Century Barbarian Invasions of Gaul and Spain." *Athenaeum: Studi di letteratura e storia dell' Antichità* 85 (1997): 69–117.

Yorke, Barbara. "Anglo-Saxon *gentes* and *regna*." In Regna *and* Gentes, pp. 381–407.

Zecchini, Giuseppe. *Ricerche di storiografia Latina tardoantica*. Rome, 1993, especially pp. 193–209.

Zöllner, Erich. *Die politische Stellung der Völker im Frankenreich*. Veröffentlichungen des Instituts für österreichische Geschichtsforschung 13. Vienna, 1950.

Zosimus. *New History*. Trans. Ronald Ridley. Byzantina Australiensia 2. Canberra, 1982.

———. *Zosime, Histoire nouvelle*. Ed. and trans. François Paschoud. Collection des universités de France. 3 vols. in 5. Paris, 1971–89. Includes an extensive commentary.

Index

Addax (Alan king), 89, 106

Adrianople, battle of, 30, 34, 87, 90, 91

Aetius (Roman generalissimo), 112, 127, 142–43, 194, 197, 211, 236–37, 253–54

Africa. *See* Vandals

Agilolfing (Bavarian dynasty), 220

agri cum mancipiis, 124, 127, 132, 147–48, 156, 158–59; defined, 257–62; as royal land, 150–55, 157, 160–61. *See also* Burgundian settlement

Alamanni: in 405–6, 81–82, 95, 220; in the fourth century, 31, 37, 53, 79, 91; as Suebi, 82, 88, 135, 319 n.72; in the third century, 26–27, 31, 33, 36, 50

Alans: history of, 20, 74, 77, 80–81, 90–94; join the Vandals and Sueves, 93–96, 108, 117, 227; preeminence of, 80–81, 89–90, 93, 96, 101–2, 104, 106, 112. *See also* Alans, Vandals, and Sueves; invasion of, 405–20

Alans, Vandals, and Sueves (the invaders of 405–20), 8, 73–76, 78, 80, 94, 97–100, 104–5, 109, 237

Alaric (Herule king), 207

Alaric, king of the Visigoths, 16, 26, 30, 32, 34, 74, 105, 108, 113, 195, 222–23; and Stilicho, 78–80, 87–89, 92, 94–98; takes Rome, 49, 73, 96–97

Alboin, king of the Lombards, 135, 202, 334 n.70

allotment (*sors*): Burgundian, 143–44, 151–62; enlargement of, 148–49, 155, 162; to individual barbarians, 122, 125–27, 136, 141–44, 147–48, 150, 152, 158, 162, 165, 167, 169, 171–74, 181, 185; and meanings of *sors*, 101–3, 173, 304–5 nn.119–21, 315 n.34, 321 n.93, 324 n.127; and military pay, 120, 154, 171–72, 182, 344 n.17; Ostrogothic, 163, 168; to the priest Butila, 171–78, 181; sale of, 151, 158–62; in Vandal Africa, 133, 138, 161–62; Visigothic, 138–43. *See also* taxation; *tertia*

Altertumskunde. See German antiquities

Amalaberga (Thuringian queen), 217

Amalafrid (Thuringian prince), 217–18

Amalasuintha, queen of the Ostrogoths, 224

Amals (Ostrogothic dynasty), 58, 63, 66, 68–69, 113, 217, 225. *See also* Theoderic

Ambrose, St., bishop of Milan, 18, 45, 62, 77, 90

Ammianus Marcellinus (historian), 18, 76–77, 90, 200, 206

Anastasius, emperor, 38, 195, 208

annona. See pay

Anthemius, emperor, 204

Aquitaine, 53, 84, 97–98, 103, 117, 255

Arcadius, emperor, 96, 98, 191

archaeology: abused, 15, 20, 27, 29, 42, 50, 227; and Vandal origins, 85–86; as source, 5, 10–12, 26, 219. See also *terpen*

Ardaric (Gepid king), 111, 201, 221

Arianism, Arians (Christian sect), 68, 83, 100, 196, 200, 212, 221, 228, 269 n.23, 293 n.18

Ariovistus (Suevic king), 19, 26, 29, 36, 117

aristocracy: military, 17, 39, 113, 191, 193, 195–97, 203, 205, 238; senatorial, 134, 166, 191

Arminius (Cheruscan chief), 19, 26, 30, 36, 50

army, Roman: barbarian recruitment of, 30–31, 34, 74, 90–91, 93, 113, 190, 205–6, 220, 237; of Belisarius, 113, 192, 222; of Italy (Odoacer's), 112, 162–69, 172, 205, 207, 236–37; of Narses, 203, 225. *See also* pay

Asdings (branch of the Vandals). *See* Vandals

Aspar (East Roman generalissimo), 38, 90, 194, 204, 299 n.72

assessment. *See* taxation

Athanaric (Gothic king), 78

Athaulf, king of the Visigoths, 34, 105, 191, 195, 223–24, 238

Attila, king of the Huns, 74, 78, 102, 109, 174, 191, 197, 201, 237; invasion of Gaul by, 21, 90, 93, 108–10, 204, 211; subjects of, 110–11, 114, 191, 200–201, 216, 221. *See also* Huns

Audeca, king of the Sueves, 213

Audoin, king of the Lombards, 218

Augsburg, 216, 220

Augustus, emperor, 27–28, 37, 50, 117, 220, 235; as Octavian, 166

Aurelian, emperor, 198

Ausonius (poet), 82
Avars, 3, 15, 20, 37, 198, 203, 209; and the Gepids, 114, 200, 202; and the Slavs, 93, 112, 202, 209
Avitus, emperor, 254–55
Azov, Sea of (Maeotian swamp), 18, 39, 54, 84, 165

Baetica (Spanish province), 74, 101, 104–7, 210–11
Balkans, 38, 60, 76, 93, 189, 201, 204, 209
barbarians: as farmers, 123, 143, 154–56, 167, 171–72, 177, 320 n.80; fitting into Rome, 6–9, 17, 26, 34–35, 188–97, 233–34, 237–38; homelands of, 21, 47, 56–57, 80, 107, 117, 195, 198–99, 206, 210, 221, 226, 233; hostility to, 191–93, 195, 237; medley of, 192–222; multiplicity of, 3–7, 19, 25–26, 32, 37, 41, 44, 48, 50, 72, 187–88, 233–34; oppression by, 135, 146–47, 155, 157, 183–86; origin stories about, 18, 82, 281 n.34; recruitment by Rome, 30–31, 35–38, 89, 188, 190, 203, 205–8, 220; resettlements of by Huns, 112–14, 201, 204, 207, 216, 221–22; at rest, 7, 14, 21, 47, 54, 74, 82–83, 86–87, 108, 114, 117; and Roman élites, 17, 35, 39, 53, 191–92; snuffed out, 192, 198, 233, 237–38. *See also* army; barbarian settlement; *barbaricum*; conquest; demography; invasion of 405–20; Migration Age; *names of individual peoples*
Barbarians and Romans (1980), 8, 71, 126, 135, 172, 184, 236; criticism of, 119–23, 127, 134, 164, 179–81; quoted, 33, 192; retraction of, 128–29
barbarian settlement: "default" explanation of, 123–27; peaceful, 122, 126, 128, 134, 137, 171, 173, 182–83, 319 n.70; system of, 153–55. *See also* Burgundian settlement; Goths; *hospitalitas*; Ostrogothic settlement; Procopius; Spain; Theoderic; Visigothic settlement
barbaricum (lands outside the Roman Empire), 26, 29–30, 33–34, 82, 87, 89, 94–95, 112, 189, 201, 220–21, 237
barbarization. *See* Roman Empire
Barnish, S. J. B., 122–26, 166, 170, 257
Bastarnae, 110, 116–17
Bavaria, Bavarians, 6, 36, 42, 114, 218–22, 228
Beatus Rhenanus (German humanist), 4, 19, 46, 52, 198, 228
Bede, the Venerable, 68, 71, 198, 215, 230–31, 234, 236, 258, 343 n.1
Belisarius (East Roman general): and Gothic Italy, 60, 70, 113, 184, 202, 217, 220, 222, 224–26; and the Vandals, 29, 83, 193
Berig (legendary Gothic king), 45, 64, 66

billeting. *See hospitalitas*
Boniface (Roman general), 194, 215
Bornholm (Baltic island), 51, 283 n.53
Braga (capital of the Suevic kingdom), 106–7, 210, 212–13
Britain, Britons, 65, 122; pre-Roman, 25, 28, 37, 66; Roman, 37, 74, 86, 88, 95–99, 189, 195, 198, 213, 215; Saxons in, 14, 31, 63, 196, 213, 215, 325 n.145; usurper from, 74, 96–98, 189. *See also* Gildas
Burgundian Laws (Code), 125, 127, 129, 131–32, 136, 144, 148, 158, 253–54, 257; LB38, 131–33 (text), 144, 151–52, 157; LB55, 129, 131, 151, 161, 169, 261–62, 317 n.52 (text), 323 n.114 (text); LB84, 130, 144, 151, 158–61, 324 n.125; LBExtravagans 21.12, 149–52 (text), 158, 257–58, 261–62, 323 n.111 (text); LRB, 123–24, 155 (text). *See also* LB54
Burgundians, 6, 8, 10, 14, 16, and passim; in northern Gaul, 81, 94, 143, 237, 253, 294–95 nn. 33–34
Burgundian settlement, 134, 143–62, 168, 171, 181, 253–62; chronicle evidence for, 183, 251–57; main assets in the, 147–49, 153–55; subsidiary assets in the, 147–49, 154–57, 160–61, 322–23 n.110 (texts). See also *agri cum mancipiis*
Burgundy, 144, 254–55
Bury, John Bagnell, 1, 3, 44, 73, 105, 123–24, 126, 198, 224
Butila (Arian priest), 172–78, 181–82
Byzantium, Byzantine. *See* Constantinople

Caesar (imperial heir apparent), 99
Caesar, Julius, 26, 43, 52
Cameron, Averil, 126, 134, 189
Carolingian epoch, 4, 37, 41–43, 46, 55, 215, 218, 258, 262
Carpathian mountains, basin, 21, 76–78, 115, 203
Carpi, 3, 37, 41, 198, 203–5
Carthage, 84, 107
Carthaginensis (Spanish province), 101, 104, 211
Cassiodorus (Italian dignitary): and fiscality, 176, 181, 236; and Gothic history, 58–61, 63–69, 71, 84, 285 n.10; on Ostrogothic allotments, 122, 127, 135, 162–65, 167–72, 177–79; *Variae* 2.16, 122, 135, 163, 168–70 (text), 172, 177; *Variae* 2.17, 135, 168–69, 173 (text), 175–76, 178
Catholic, Catholicism, 1, 7, 67–68, 196, 210–13, 218–19